A Guidance Approach for the Encouraging Classroom

THIRD EDITION

DEDICATION

In Memory of Three Education Professors
Ben Thompson of Antioch College, Yellow Springs, Ohio
Maurice Lucas of the University of North Dakota, Grand Forks and
Bill "Doc" McDowall of Bemidji State University Bemidji, Minnesota

A Guidance Approach for the Encouraging Classroom

THIRD EDITION

Dan Gartrell, Ed.D.
BEMIDJI STATE UNIVERSITY

THOMSON

DELMAR LEARNING

Australia Canada Mexico Singapore Spain United Kingdom United States

A Guidance Approach for the Encouraging Classroom, 3e
Dan Gartrell

Business Unit Executive Director:
Susan L. Simpfenderfer

Acquisitions Editor:
Erin O'Connor

Executive Production Manager:
Wendy A. Troeger

Production Editor:
Joy Kocsis

Technology Project Manager:
Joseph Saba

Executive Marketing Manager:
Donna J. Lewis

Channel Manager:
Nigar Hale

Cover Design:
Joy Kocsis

Composition:
Carlisle Communications, Ltd.

For permission to use material from this text or product, contact us by
Tel   (800) 730-2214
Fax   (800) 730-2215
www.thomsonrights.com

Library of Congress Cataloging-in-Publication Data

Gartrell, Daniel.
    A guidance approach for the encouraging classroom / Dan Gartrell.–3rd ed.
       p. cm.
Includes bibliographical references and index.
ISBN 0-7668-3015-2
    1.School discipline–United States. 2. Child psychology—United States. 3. Problem solving in children. 5. Interpersonal relations in children–United States. I. Title.

LB3012.2 .G37 2002
371.4'0973–dc21   2002020645

NOTICE TO THE READER

CONTENTS

APPENDICES

PREFACE

This third edition of *A Guidance Approach for the Encouraging Classroom* keeps features important to users of the text. Part One presents the historical and theoretical foundations of guidance, which together give direction to a paradigm shift from conventional discipline to guidance. Part Two details the dynamics in building an encouraging classroom, the physical and psychological "place" in which teaching and learning are imbued with guidance. Part Three explains intervention techniques with classroom conflicts that teach children to solve their problems rather than punish children for having problems they cannot solve.

Key terms and concepts originating in my writings continue to form a basis for the text, including *mistaken behavior, levels of mistaken behavior, democratic life skills, the encouraging classroom,* and *liberation teaching.* Although these terms may be new to some readers, my six articles in *Young Children* (along with other publications along with my workshops) are making the concepts widely known. These terms supplement important but more established concepts such as *developmentally appropriate practice, conflict management, class meetings, parent-teacher partnerships,* and *peace education.* Together, the newer and more established terms form the theoretical context for the book.

Much of my approach is to encourage the reader to look again at traditional terms and practices and to go beyond the cultural baggage that these terms carry with them into the early childhood classroom. The works of over 200 other authors are referenced in the text to demonstrate the depth and breadth of the guidance approach. Some 60 classroom anecdotes continue to provide a window into the use of guidance to build and maintain the encouraging classroom. (New anecdotes have been added for edition three.)

As with the earlier editions, the text is intended for capstone courses of two-year postsecondary programs, upper division baccalaureate programs, and some graduate classes. It is comprehensive enough to stand as a primary text in courses that integrate group management, learning environment, child guidance, and parent-teacher partnership topics. The text also can be used with more general textbooks in foundations of early childhood education classes.

Age Range of Three to Eight

A few readers have requested that infants and toddlers be more directly addressed in the book. Others have commented that more content should be directed to the elementary grades. The developmental scope of the text remains the early childhood period of from three to eight years old. In Piaget's classic terms, this is the period between when most children have progressed from the sensorimotor into the preoperational stage and most children have progressed from the preoperational stage into concrete operations.

During the preoperational period, children are learning to accommodate social experiences in ways unlike any other time in their lives. They enter the stage just beginning to understand the viewpoints and feelings of others. If successful at meeting the challenges of the stage, they progress into concrete operations with a foundation for balancing one's own needs with the needs of others that they will build upon for the rest of their lives. Complementing the challenges of social/emotional development, cognitive development during this stage is unequivocally physical in its orientation. By acting on the environment, with materials and in the company of others, children build the cognitive structures—through physiological development of the brain itself—that can make future learning more intriguing than stressful. For instance, at age four, learning that one can tell stories through art, personal script writing, and the spoken word can only assist a child with more advanced artistic, written and spoken expression later on.

Before preoperational thought begins, infants and toddlers are defining life experiences largely through attachments with a small number of family members and outside care providers. As children leave the preoperational stage (by about age eight), the game has completely changed. Children use increasingly abstract thought and increasingly complex social understandings to define themselves and the course of their interactions in home school, and community. For this author, the differences in learning and social behavior between children before age three and after age eight, from children in the targeted age range, are clear enough to provide practical delimitations for the text. (To put this idea in context, remember that five years also spans the age range separating seventh graders from high school seniors.) The role of the teacher in responding to the general learning dynamic of this the early childhood group, and to the unique dynamics shown by each child, makes the period of three through eight years one of great promise for the individual and the society.

Parent-Teacher Partnerships

As in the previous two editions, the concluding section in each chapter addresses the importance of building and maintaining parent-teacher partnerships. Topics include:

- scanning parent-involvement in early childhood education; an historical perspective
- explaining mistaken behavior to parents
- building relations with parents at the beginning of the year
- helping parents feel welcome in the classroom
- working with parent volunteers
- using notes, phone calls, e-mails, and conferences with parents
- planning and conducting conferences and parent meetings
- problem-solving with parents when there are disagreements
- empowering parents to progress in their level of involvement

The importance of initiating partnerships with parents right from the beginning of the program year is revealed by a situation posed in one of the chapters. You are outside with your children in January. A child on the other side of the playground slips, falls off a slide, and breaks an arm. Would you rather have this be your first contact with the parent, or would you rather have had a positive relationship with this family dating back to the previous September? To avoid discord over mishaps is not the main reason the book explores parent-teacher partnerships, of course. When parents work with teachers to help their children to learn and grow, the results of the education program, for all concerned, are likely to be satisfactory and successful.

Appendices

The emphasis on parent-teacher partnerships is carried over into the appendices of the book. Appendix A is the NAEYC Code of Ethical Conduct, which includes a section on teacher responsibilities to the family. Appendices B and C include sample materials for use with parents: sample greeting letters and surveys; a sample brochure explaining "The Education Program in Our Class," including "Suggestions for Parent Involvement." Appendix D is an updated version of the position statement by the Minnesota Association for the Education of Young Children on "Developmentally Appropriate Guidance" (suitable for use both with staff and parents). Appendix E is a sample Individual Guidance Plan Worksheet to use when teachers and staff need to take a comprehensive approach to children's serious mistaken behavior.

Aim and Purpose

While maintaining the scholarship required of postsecondary materials, I have tried to make the writing style informal and have used illustrative anecdotes and photos to make the text accessible for a variety of audiences. In this effort, I accept criticisms about the occasionally informal use of phrases and idioms. The challenge of the text has been to introduce new terms and concepts necessary for a paradigm shift away from traditional classroom discipline, while at the same time keeping the material readable and (dare I say it in regards to a textbook) interesting. This text is from my heart as well as my mind, and I believe no apologies are needed for instances of humor or passion that come through in theories illustrated and ideas expressed.

NEW FEATURES

New features in the text are in four categories: (a) a textwide emphasis on the goal of guidance—teaching democratic life skills; (b) numerous text revisions; (c) end-of-chapter application material; and (d) the addition of an Online Resource to accompany the text.

Textwide Emphasis on Democratic Life Skills

The widespread emphasis on educational accountability necessitates a response by those making guidance central to the teaching effort. Building from educators and psychologists ranging from Dewey to Gardner, the text proposes *Democratic Life Skills* as the standards by which the practice of guidance teaching can be assessed. Introduced in Chapter One, reference is made to teaching and modeling democratic life skills in each chapter. Liberation teaching, another key term in the text, can be viewed as the teaching of democratic life skills to those children whose many conflicts in the classroom might cause them particular difficulty in learning the skills.

Text Revisions

Part One includes a new Chapter Two, "Child Development and Guidance." Material pertaining to the classic theorists of child development contributing to the guidance approach—Piaget, Erikson, and Elkind—have been reorganized in this chapter. Added is new material on Vygotsky, brain development, multiple intelligences, and emotional development. Chapter Two now brings this foundation material into the new century and adds valuable perspective on the practice of guidance in the classroom.

Chapter Nine again focuses on conflict management and is a key chapter in the text. Rewritten for the third edition, Chapter Nine has been made more practical for the student reader. Rather than survey and discuss different models of conflict management Chapter Nine gives emphasis to two fundamentals in using conflict management with children. First, the chapter provides a five-step model for conflict management, which is illustrated and explained. Second, the chapter offers a strategy for applying, modeling, and teaching conflict management. Teachers are often given conflict management models, but are not often provided with strategies for teaching conflict management skills to children. Chapter Nine goes the extra step of showing how to model and teach conflict management in the early childhood classroom.

Chapter Twelve again serves as the capstone for the text, discussing the professional goal in the use of guidance of *liberation teaching*. The chapter has been revised to highlight the effects of societal violence on children's behavior in the classroom. From this perspective, the "hot topic" of *bullying* is given special attention. In these complex times, liberation teaching is reaching and including as positive group members those children who might be stigmatized (negatively separated from the group) as a result of physical or behavioral factors. Vulnerable for stigma are both children who bully and children victimized by bullying. Liberation teaching is about helping children to kindle resilience within them, overcome pain and suffering, and make clear progress as a group member in learning democratic life skills.

In the guidance approach, teachers discard such labels as "difficult child," "defiant child," and "challenging child." The liberating teacher focuses instead on assisting children to resolve the problems that cause them to show behaviors that teachers may regard as challenging. A comprehensive approach, which often includes working with parents and other professionals, is essential in this effort. Discussion of the use of comprehensive guidance is the subject of Chapter Eleven.

End-of-Chapter Application Material

The emphasis regarding end-of-chapter material has always been that activities be usable and reflective rather than academic.

Chapter summaries retain the "guiding question" format, for continuity across the chapter, but are shorter and more concise.

Key Concepts are now listed in the chapter end matter. In the second edition some terms are presented in boldface under each chapter. This practice is in line with the author's view that guidance, as the progressive alternative to traditional classroom discipline, needs and deserves its own distinct concepts and terms. While these terms continue to be listed in boldface and included in the glossary at the end of the text, they also appear as key concepts listed after each chapter summary. This change should aid review of each chapter for study and assessment purposes.

A single **discussion activity,** at the end of each chapter can be addressed either by the whole class, or by small groups with share-back to the class. This activity can be completed by individuals as well, though group discussion of individual experiences is the activity's main intent.

The **application activities** remain the same, each providing the student with an option of an observation with analysis or a teacher interview with analysis. In each case, comparison of empirical results with text material is encouraged. The priority for the application activities is to give students the opportunity to compare reading theory with everyday realities in early childhood education. My experience is that the construction of meaning resulting from this interaction enables learning of real significance.

Finally, a new **what you can do** section offers concrete follow-up guidance projects for use with children and parents. This new section will use as a springboard the major topics of each chapter.

Online Resources™

This third edition of *A Guidance Approach for the Encouraging Classroom* includes a new electronic interconnect for students and instructors an Online Resources™. The feature allows readers to link directly with the guidance ideas developed in the text. The Online Resources™ includes the following:

> **Guidance Web sites.** For each chapter, Web sites are listed with additional information, perspectives, and suggestions related to the chapter content.

Graphic schematics. For each chapter, key ideas are presented in chart, table, or figure form, to crystallize the narrative and provide usable key points for students and instructors. Supplemental visuals are included at the end of the Online Resources™.

Follow-up forum. For each chapter, the "discussion questions," "application questions," and the "what you can do" projects are provided. The chapter end matter, included in this electronic format will facilitate student and faculty access to this material.

Additional resources. For each chapter, supplemental materials, mainly in the form of videos, complement the list of recommended materials at the conclusion of each chapter of the text.

Information for applying individual guidance plans. Enhancing the usefulness of Appendix E, a practical explanation for using the Individual Guidance Plan is given. The explanation includes a **case study to show** suggestions for conducting the Individual Guidance Plan meeting.

For additional information on using the guidance approach in the classroom, visit our Web site at http://www.earlychilded.delmar.com

ACKNOWLEDGMENTS

Many persons have helped to make the third edition possible. First, deep appreciation goes to my mother, Beth Goff, who raised me this way, and to my wife Julie Jochum Gartrell, for unending assistance and support. Thanks are due to the many teachers I have worked with over the years, who practice guidance every day. I wish I could recognize them all, but a few who have contributed anecdotes and case studies are Susan Bailey, Nellie Cameron, Lynn Hart, Terry Leinbach, Diane Lerberg, John Ostby, Ina Rambo, Sharon Hoverson, Karen Palubicki, Pat Sanford, Marta Underthun, and Vicki Wangberg. In addition I would like to thank staff members of Bi-County Head Start (Bemidji and Blackduck), Campus Child Care, Early Childhood Family Education Program, and (the late) Paul Bunyan School of Bemidji, Minnesota. Their cooperation and positive practices with Bemidji State early childhood students have contributed much to guidance in northern Minnesota.

Special acknowledgment is continued to Dr. Steven Harlow for his important concept of *levels of social relations*. His concept has imbued my concept of mistaken behavior, a featured concept in the text. Lynn Gerhke of Concordia University, St. Paul, contributed significant material for the new Chapter Two and is listed as a co-writer of that chapter. For assistance with the Chapter Nine case study, appreciation is expressed to the staff, children, and families of St. Philip's School in Bemidji. Especially, gratitude is expressed to principal Carol Rettinger and the parent instrumental in their peace education program, Sue Liedl.

Thanks go to many locally for production assistance, including: Monte Draper and *The Bemidji Pioneer* for use of key photos in the book; Julie Jochum Gartrell and Lynn Gerhke for website research and compilation; Leah Pigatti for assistance with final reading; and Darla Finnegan and the Education Department student workers for much copying and collating.

My appreciation is extended to the reviewers enlisted through Delmar Learning for their constructive criticism and helpful suggestions. They include:

Richard Ambrose, Ph.D.
Kent State University
Kent, OH

Sylvia Brooks, Ed.D.
University of Deleware
Newark, DE

Martha Dever
Utah State University
Logan, UT

Teresa Frazier
Thomas Nelson Community College
Suffolk, VA

Jeffrey Gelfer, Ph.D.
University of Nevada
Las Vegas, NV

Robin Hasslen, Ph.D.
St. Cloud State University
St. Cloud, MN

Kathy Head
Lorain County Community College
Elyria, OH

Judith Lindman
Rochester Community and Technical College
Rochester, MN

Jennifer Rhinehart
San Jacinto College North
Houston, TX

Elaine Wilson
Oklahoma State University
Stillwater, OK

The entire editorial staff at Delmar Learning, headed by Erin O'Connor, have been supportive, professional, and efficient. They made the task easier. Special thanks go to Erin for her leadership with the third edition and to Amy Simcik Williams of Inkwell Studios.

ABOUT THE AUTHOR

During the 1960s, Dan Gartrell was a teacher at an inner city elementary school in Ohio and the Head Start Program of the Red Lake Band of Ojibwe in Minnesota. In the early 1970s Dan earned a Masters Degree at Bemidji State University in northern Minnesota. At Bemidji State, Dan became a field advisor, CDA trainer, and then director for the Child Development Training Program. Dan completed his doctorate at the University of North Dakota's Center for Teaching and Learning in 1977. He is currently Professor of Early Childhood and Elementary Education and Director of the Child Development Training Program at Bemidji State University. As a teacher, CDA trainer, and student teaching supervisor, Dan has been working with students in early childhood classrooms for more than 30 years.

Dan has led over 100 presentations on guidance in several states; Frankfurt, Germany; and Merida, Mexico. Additionally, he has written articles on this subject, including six for *Young Children.* Dan is an amateur photographer who enjoyed taking some of the photos that appear in the text. He is a member of a blended family that includes his wife, Dr. Julie Jochum Gartrell, five children in their twenties and thirties—Jesse, Kateri, Adam, Sara, Angie—and eight grandchildren. Dan comments that his family has added much to his understanding of guidance.

PART ONE

Foundations of a Guidance Approach

PREVIEWS

One **The Guidance Tradition**

Chapter One provides historical overview of the guidance tradition. Direct quotes by pioneers in the field are included to document their own thoughts about education and the role of guidance. Mid-20th century influences of the developmental and self psychologists are traced. The trend away from punishment and toward guidance in the 1980s and 1990s is presented. The tradition of parent-teacher partnerships within the guidance approach is explored.

Two **Child Development and Guidance**

Chapter Two explores child development theories of the last 70 years and discusses the relation of each to guidance principles. The developmental theories are those of Piaget, Vygotsky, Erikson, Gardner, and Goleman. An overview of important findings from brain research and attachment theory, and the implications for guidance of each is provided. The conclusion that guidance is the approach to children's behavior that comes closest to the essence of our growing understanding about child development is presented.

Three **Mistaken Behavior**

Chapter Three presents a concept in line with the work of the self psychologists for understanding young children's behavior: that behavior traditionally considered as misbehavior is more constructively viewed as mistaken behavior. Three levels of mistaken behavior are analyzed. Considerations for acquainting parents with the concept of mistaken behavior are discussed.

Four   **Guidance: The Bottom Line**

Chapter Four develops four principles of a guidance approach: that it means teachers are professionals, not technicians; builds from positive teacher-child relations; reduces the need for mistaken behavior; takes a solution-orientation; includes liberation teaching; and involves parent-teacher partnerships.

CHAPTER ONE

THE GUIDANCE TRADITION

GUIDING QUESTIONS

- Who were the pioneers of the guidance tradition?
- Who were mid-20th century influences in the guidance tradition?
- What was the significance of discipline trends in the 1980s?
- What is the state of the guidance tradition today?
- What is the role of parents in the guidance tradition?

Now in the 21st century, we want citizens to be able to think intelligently and ethically and to solve problems by the use of civil words. Through a comprehensive examination of the areas traditionally called discipline and classroom management, *A Guidance Approach for the Encouraging Classroom* explores the teaching and learning of these democratic life skills in early childhood education.

The guidance approach has its roots in the history of Western education and is tied to the thoughts of progressive educators over the last two centuries. The basis of guidance, the empowering of productive human activity, lies in the view that human nature, in the embodiment of the child, has the potential for good. In this view, the role of the adult is not to "discipline the child away from evil" but to guide the child to develop the personal strength and understanding necessary to make ethical, intelligent decisions. This capacity, which Piaget (1932/1960) termed **autonomy,** is a primary goal in the guidance approach. A companion goal, related and no less important, is to guide children in the use of **conflict management,** the ability in the everyday business of life to prevent and, if necessary, peaceably resolve conflicts. These two goals serve as themes that are interwoven throughout the text, sometimes directly addressed and sometimes implicit in the discussion, but always there.

In recent years a growing number of educators have come to believe that the term *discipline* is controversial. For these educators discipline implies punishment, a practice precluded in the use of guidance (Gartrell, 1997). In the guidance tradition, the goal is clear: to teach children the **democratic life skills** of getting along with others, expressing strong feelings in non-hurtful ways, and managing conflicts peaceably. For this reason, guidance transcends the function of conventional discipline, the use of rewards and punishments to keep children under the teacher's control (Gartrell, 1995; Greenberg, 1988; Kohn, 1999). Guidance is education for democracy, and a guidance approach is a teaching approach—the teaching of democratic life skills through all classroom situations.

The classroom environment through which children are empowered to learn democratic life skills is the **encouraging classroom.** In the encouraging classroom, all students feel that they are able learners and worthy members of the class. The teacher builds the encouraging classroom through active leadership with the children, their families, and the community. In the encouraging classroom, positive discipline practices merge with developmentally appropriate practices and become part of the everyday curriculum. For the teacher in the encouraging classroom, human differences—differing abilities, cultural backgrounds, appearances, and behavioral styles—become sources of mutual affirmation and respect. With both the individual and the group, the teaching approach for the encouraging classroom is guidance.

Part One provides the foundations of the guidance approach. This first chapter documents that over the years progressive educators consistently have called for an integrated education model, one that links the positive potential of the child, the interactive nature of an appropriate curriculum, and the guiding role of the teacher as democratic leader. Chapter One traces the guidance tradition in Western educational thought.

PIONEERS OF THE GUIDANCE TRADITION

A principle in the guidance tradition is that the management of behavior cannot be separated from the curriculum used, and that both are tied to views of human nature (Gartrell, 1997). This three-way relationship is no recent occurrence and can be seen in the 17th century in the writings of the educators of the time—the clergy. Osborn's informative chronology, *Early Childhood Education in Historical Perspective*, frames a fundamental disagreement about the nature of childhood that still impacts education and management practice today (1980). Osborn documents that within the clergy two contrasting reasons were given for the importance of education. The 1621 treatise, *A Godly Form of Household Government*, states:

> The young child which lieth in the cradle is both wayward and full of affection; and though his* body be small, yet he hath a wrongdoing heart and is inclined to evil. . . . If this spark be suffered to increase, it will rage over and

Guidance is based on the view that human nature has the potential for good.

---

* For purposes of accuracy, masculine pronouns are retained in quotes. Otherwise, the author has sought to reduce and balance gender-specific pronoun use.

Believing that children tended toward evil, schoolmasters of previous times "beat the devil" out of children—corporal punishment that would be considered child abuse today. (Courtesy, Corbis-Bettmann, *The developing person through childhood and adolescence,* New York: Worth Publishers, Inc.)

burn down the whole house. For we are changed and become good, not by birth, but by education. (p. 24)

An opposing point of view portrayed the child as a *tabulae rasae* (blank slate). This point of view can be seen in Earle's *Microcosmography* (1628):

The child is a small letter, yet the best copy of Adam. . . . His soul is yet a white paper unscribbled with observations . . . and he knows no evil. (p. 24)

Among Western cultures, the prevalence of the first view meant that strict discipline based on obedience and corporal punishment has been widely practiced into the 20th century (Berger, 1991; deMause, 1974). Corporal punishment as an issue is still unresolved in the nation's schools. Progress toward humane educational practice has been made, however, and some teachers of the attitude expressed by Earle probably always have used the tenets of guidance.

During the 19th century such European educators as Herbart, Pestalozzi, and Froebel fundamentally reformed educational practice, in no small part as a result of their views about human nature. Herbart and Pestalozzi recognized that children learned best through real experiences rather than through the rote recitation of facts. Pestalozzi put into practice schools for the "less well-to-do" and so modeled the beginning of universal education. He also co-wrote *Manual for Mothers,* which provided guidance for mothers of very young children and inspired Friedrich Froebel's interest in early childhood education (Lilley, 1967). Herbart wrote effectively about the importance of motivating students to take an interest in learning, a fundamental preventive guidance strategy (Osborn, 1980).

Friedrich Froebel

Froebel was the originator of the kindergarten, intended to serve children aged three to six. The purpose of the kindergarten was to provide an extension of the family life that Froebel thought all children should have. Education for Froebel was guidance so that the "innate impulses of the child" could be harmoniously developed through creative activity. In line with his views about the role of development in education, Froebel believed that the nature of the child was essentially good and that "faults" were the product of particular experiences. In *Friedrich Froebel: A Selection From His Writings* (1967), Lilley quotes the educator:

> There are many faults . . . which arise simply through carelessness. When children act on an impulse which in itself may be harmless or even praiseworthy, they can become so entirely absorbed that they have no thought for the consequences, and indeed from their own limited experience can have no knowledge of them. . . .
>
> Moreover, it is certainly true that as a rule the child is first made bad by some other person, often by the educator himself. This can happen when everything which the child does out of ignorance or thoughtlessness or even from a keen sense of right and wrong is attributed to an intention to do evil. Unhappily there are among teachers those who always see children as mischievous, spiteful . . . whereas others see at most an overexuberant sense of life or a situation which has got out of hand. (Lilley, p. 135)

In these views about children and their behavior, Froebel showed clear understanding of the need for a guidance approach to discipline.

Maria Montessori

As a transition figure between a pedagogy dominated by the religious philosophy of the 19th century and the psychology of the 20th, Maria Montessori was the first woman psychiatrist in modern Italy as well as the leading authority in early childhood education. Similar to Froebel, Montessori maintained that a fundamental principle in "scientific pedagogy" was that "the child is in a continual state of growth and metamorphosis, whereas the adult has reached the norm of the species" (Standing, 1962).

Montessori—as well as her American contemporary, John Dewey—abhorred traditional instructional practices, with children planted behind desks and expected to recite lessons of little meaning in their lives. Both criticized approaches to discipline based on this pervasive schooling practice. In her comprehensive, *The Montessori Method* (1912/1964), the educator asserted:

> We know only too well the sorry spectacle of the teacher who, in the ordinary schoolroom, must pour certain cut and dried facts into the heads of the scholars. In order to succeed in this barren task, she finds it necessary to discipline her pupils into immobility and to force their attention. Prizes and

punishments are ever-ready and efficient aids to the master who must force into a given attitude of mind and body those who are condemned to be his listeners. (1964, p. 21)

Montessori went on to devote an entire chapter of her text to an alternative discipline methodology that was more respectful of the child's development. For Montessori the purpose of education and discipline is the same: to encourage the development of responsible decision-making (1964).

John Dewey

John Dewey is considered the architect of progressive education in the United States. Over a 60-year period, Dewey raised the nation's consciousness about the kind of education needed in an industrial society. Like Montessori, Dewey viewed discipline as differing in method depending on the curriculum followed. In the 1900 monograph, *The School and Society*, Dewey commented:

If you have the end in view of forty or fifty children learning certain set lessons, to be recited to the teacher, your discipline must be devoted to securing that result. But if the end in view is the development of a spirit of social cooperation and community life, discipline must grow out of and be relative to such an aim. . .There is a certain disorder in any busy workshop; there is not silence; persons are not engaged in maintaining certain fixed physical postures; their arms are not folded; they are not holding their books thus and so. They are doing a variety of things, and there is the confusion, the bustle that results from activity. Out of the occupation, out of doing things that are to produce results, and out of doing these in a social and cooperative way, there is born a discipline of its own kind and type. Our whole conception of discipline changes when we get this point of view. (pp. 16–17)

Through Dewey's advocacy of progressive education, guidance began to be established in American educational thought.

MID-20TH-CENTURY INFLUENCES: THE DEVELOPMENTAL AND SELF PSYCHOLOGISTS

In the 20th century two distinct branches of psychology contributed to the progressive education movement and to the guidance tradition. In Europe, Jean Piaget brought together his distinct scholarship in the fields of biology and child study to provide the foundations of modern developmental psychology. In the United States, a group of psychologists integrated neo-Freudian thought and American humanistic psychology into a new branch of study, *self-concept* psychology, shortened in the present text to **self psychology.** These two distinct psychological fields gave articulation to many of the practices of today's guidance approach. Piaget's influence is introduced here and returned to in Chapter Two.

When the classroom becomes a "busy workshop," our conception of discipline changes.

Jean Piaget

Decidedly clinical in his orientation, Jean Piaget was the preeminent developmental psychologist of the 20th century. Writing in French, the Swiss psychologist shared with Montessori the precept that the developing child learns most effectively by interacting with the environment. Further, Piaget shared with Dewey a basic regard for the social context of learning—that peer interaction is essential for healthy development. Piaget agreed with both that education must be a cooperative endeavor and that discipline must respect and respond to this fact. In his landmark work, *The Moral Judgment of the Child* (1932/1960), Piaget stated:

> The essence of democracy resides in its attitude towards law as a product of the collective will, and not as some thing emanating from a transcendent will or from the authority established by divine right. It is therefore the essence of democracy to replace the unilateral respect of authority by the mutual respect of autonomous wills. So that the problem is to know what will best prepare the child for the task of citizenship. Is it the habit of external discipline gained under the influence of unilateral respect and of adult constraint, or is it the habit of internal discipline, of mutual respect and of "self government"?. . . If one thinks of the systematic resistance offered by pupils to the authoritarian method, and the admirable ingenuity employed by children the world over to evade disciplinary constraint, one cannot help regarding as defective a system which allows so much effort to be wasted instead of using it in cooperation. (pp. 366–367)

Subsequent generations of psychologists and educators have been influenced by Piaget's studies of how children develop. In the last few years, many of these "Neo-Piagetian" writers have focused on **constructivist education** (DeVries & Zan, 1995). In the constructivist educational model, the child builds knowledge by interacting with the social and physical environment. A foremost expression of the constructivist viewpoint is found in the acclaimed Reggio Emilia in Italy (Gandini, 1993). The schools have taken to new heights the idea of the child's innate ability to create meaning through expressive activity. The multimedia creations of even the very young at the schools are causing teachers the world over to rethink the creative and problem-solving potential of children in the classroom.

By redefining education from a *constructivist* perspective, developmental educators are changing the way professionals in the field look at teaching, learning, the curriculum, and discipline. This developmental and interactive view of the educational process blends well with the guidance tradition (DeVries, 1994).

A synopsis of the views of the pioneers in the guidance tradition, including Piaget, is provided in Figure 1–1.

The Self Psychologists

During the 1960s and 1970s the writings of such psychologists as Combs (1962), Erikson (1963), Maslow (1962), and Rogers (1961) brought attention to the developing self as the primary dynamic in human behavior. Combs'

Figure 1–1

Pioneers of the Guidance Tradition	
Friedrich Froebel 1782–1852	The teacher should see the natural impulses of the child not as a tendency toward evil but as the source and motivation for development that with guidance leads to character in the adult.
Maria Montessori 1870–1952	The child is in a process of dynamic development which the adult has attained. Children educate themselves through absorption in meaningful tasks in a process of self-discipline, leading to responsible decision-making.
John Dewey 1859–1952	Out of the occupation, out of doing things that are to produce results, and out of doing these things in a social and cooperative way, there is born a discipline of its own kind and type.
Jean Piaget 1896–1980	The modern ideal is cooperation—respect for the individual and for general opinion as elaborated in free discussion. Children come to this spirit of democracy through the practice of cooperation by adults who are able to make autonomous (intelligent and ethical) decisions themselves.

work was significant by furthering the idea that reality for the individual is what he or she perceives. Among other implications, this "perceptual field theory" pressed the need for educators to be aware of the feelings of children in the class. In agreement with Combs' constructivist-like leanings these psychologists maintained that to the extent children felt safe in their circumstances and valued as members of the group, they would see themselves positively and not need to act out against the world. Numerous studies of self-image (the collection of feelings about who one is) and self-concept (the conscious picture of who one is) were conducted. Collected in works by Purkey (1970) and Hamachek (1971), the trend in these studies was that children who felt better about themselves got along better with others and did better in school. Moreover, the studies found a high correlation between schooling practices and heightened or lowered self-esteem. Purkey stated:

[handwritten margin note: Constructivist - BUILDS knowledge SOCIAL/ PHYS. ENVIRON.]

> The indications seem to be that success or failure in school significantly influence the ways in which students view themselves. Students who experience repeated success in school are likely to develop positive feelings about their abilities, while those who encounter failure tend to develop negative views of themselves. (p. 26)

Purkey discussed schooling practices that reinforced failure and frustration:

> Traditionally, the child is expected to adjust to the school rather than the school adjusting to the child. To ensure this process, the school is prepared to dispense rewards and punishments, successes and failures on a massive scale. The child is expected to learn to live in a new environment and to compete for the rewards of obedience and scholarship . . . Unfortunately a large number of schools employ a punitive approach to education. Punishment,

failure, and depreciation are characteristic. In fact, Deutsch argues that it is often in the school that highly charged negative attitudes toward learning evolve. The principle that negative self-concepts should be prevented is ignored by many schools. (p. 40)

The **self psychologists** provided insights that assist educators with learners of all ages. In their time these ideas were valued especially in schools practicing "open education" and those serving preschool children. Since then, their ideas have bolstered the articulation of developmentally appropriate, culturally responsive educational practice. A main tenet of the self psychologists always has been that threat has no place in the classroom. From two decades of brain research, we are learning more about why: An intended or unintended threat in the classroom causes stress in children. Over time healthy brain development is impeded when children experience stress caused by threat (Shonkoff & Phillips, 2000). A message of the self psychologists still relevant today is that while "intense anticipation" is important for learning, teacher-induced stress is detrimental to it. Such writers as Dreikurs (1968) and Ginott (1972) adapted principles from self psychology for general classroom use, principles which are still studied and used today.

Rudolph Dreikurs

As an early proponent of the application of social science principles to classroom management, Dreikurs contributed much to a movement toward "positive discipline." A first contribution is Dreikurs' insistence that teachers need to be "leaders rather than bosses" in their work with children (1968). This emphasis on working with students, rather than being in opposition to them, is fundamental to a guidance approach—as the titles of Chapters Seven and Eight of the present text suggest. The idea of "teacher as leader" corresponds to the interactive view always central to progressive education.

A second contribution, perhaps not credited enough to Dreikurs, is his distinction between encouragement and praise (Dreikurs, Grunwald, & Pepper, 1982). Teachers who are leaders recognize the importance of sincere acknowledgment of a child's efforts and progress. Such encouragement is preferred to praise, which is often directed to the final product and is often public and shallow—"nice job . . . good talking." Encouragement gives specific information that assists the child to carry on; praise offers a "final judgment" about the product, often without helpful explanation. Ginott (1972) similarly distinguished between "evaluative praise" and "descriptive praise," although Dreikurs' terms have seen wider use. Encouragement instead of praise is a standard technique with teachers who use guidance; the issue is more fully discussed in Chapter Seven.

Many believe that Dreikurs' most substantial contribution is his explanation of the "goals" of misbehavior (1982). Building on his background in Adlerian theory, Dreikurs emphasized that all behavior is goal-directed and that the preeminent goal of behavior is social acceptance.

Behavior is purposive or goal-directed. . . . Humans are social beings with the overriding goal of belonging or finding a place in society. . . . The child's behavior indicates the ways and means by which he tries to be significant. If these ways and means are antisocial and disturbing, then the child did not develop the right idea about how to find his place. The antisocial ways or "mistaken goals". . . reflect an error in the child's judgment and in his comprehension of life and the necessities of social living. To understand a child, we must understand the child's purpose of behavior, a purpose of which the child may be unaware. (Dreikurs, Grunwald, & Pepper, 1982, p. 9)

In such books as *Psychology in the Classroom* (1968), Dreikurs developed a theory, using four levels, for why children misbehave. A clear synopsis of the "four mistaken goals of misbehavior" is provided in *Building Classroom Discipline* (1996) by C. M. Charles:

Dreikurs identifies four mistaken goals to which students turn when unable to satisfy the genuine goal [of social acceptance]: (1) getting attention, (2) seeking power, (3) seeking revenge, and (4) displaying inadequacy. . . . The

Repeated success experiences help children build positive feelings about their abilities.

goals are usually, though not always, sought in the order listed. If unable to feel accepted, individuals are likely to try to get attention. If they fail in that effort, they turn to seeking power. If thwarted there, they attempt to get revenge. And if that fails, they withdraw into themselves and try to show that they are inadequate to accomplish what is expected of them. (pp. 90–91)

As important as Dreikurs' theory is, it has not been correlated with recent understandings about the development of the young child. Neither has it received scrutiny for consistency with ideas about personality development contributed by the self psychologists. Stated in Dreikurs' writings, the "overriding goal" of children's behavior is acceptance by important others. This view differs from theory based on developmental research and the writing of psychologists like Maslow and Combs. In the view of developmental and self psychologists, social acceptance *is* a significant factor in children's behavior, but it is regarded more as a foundation for healthy personal development than an end in itself (Gartrell, 1995). Between three and eight years, children make tremendous strides in brain development and thinking processes, the communication of ideas and feelings, perceptual-motor skills, self-concept development, cultural identity, and social responsiveness. They are engaged in a process of *total development*. Yet with the natural insecurities of childhood and limited ability to understand the needs of others, children make mistakes. Social acceptance of each child even while addressing mistaken behavior, sustains *healthy personal development*, the primary goal in human behavior (Maslow, 1962; Purkey, 1970; Rogers, 1961).

In his insistence that adults can understand the purposes of unacceptable behavior, Dreikurs nonetheless has made a vital contribution to the guidance tradition in educational thought (Charles, 1996). Dreikurs' writings argue persuasively that unacceptable behavior is a result of mistakes that children make in the "purposeful" goal of getting along with others (1968, Dreikurs, Grunwald & Pepper, 1982). By placing misbehavior in the context of social acceptance, Dreikurs raised the discussion of discipline from judgments about children's morality to strategies for helping children learn acceptable alternative behaviors.

Haim Ginott

If Dreikurs has contributed to the theory of the guidance tradition, Ginott has contributed to its articulation. The opening lines from the chapter, "Congruent Communication" in his classic book, *Teacher and Child* (1972), illustrate the eloquent phrasing that typify Ginott's "psychology of acceptance":

Where do we start if we are to improve life in the classroom? By examining how we respond to children. How a teacher communicates is of decisive importance. It affects a child's life for good or for bad. Usually we are not overly concerned about whether one's response conveys acceptance or rejection. Yet to a child this difference is fateful, if not fatal.

Teachers who want to improve relations with children need to unlearn their habitual language of rejection and acquire a new language of acceptance. To reach a child's mind a teacher must capture his heart. Only if a child feels right can he think right. (p. 69)

Virtually all early childhood education texts written in the last 20 years have emphasized a need for management methods that respect the feelings and dignity of the individual child. Although Ginott's writings do not address the early childhood age group per se, they speak to adult-child relations at all levels and are in agreement with the tone and philosophy of the guidance approach. Ginott's words are cited frequently in chapters to come. His writings nurture the caring spirit that infuses the guidance tradition.

THE 1980s: GUIDANCE OR OBEDIENCE-BASED DISCIPLINE

Since the very first public school kindergartens in the 19th century, there has been much debate on what proper educational practice for young children entails. Traditional minded educators clung to an academic "drill-and-grill" emphasis, countered by the progressive views of associations such as the National Association for the Education of Young Children (NAEYC) and the Association for Childhood Education International (ACEI). During the 1980s, the educational pendulum swung in the direction of academics, even in early childhood education. With the need to keep normally active young learners in their seats and on-task, new, obedience-driven discipline systems became popular.

The Push-Down of Academics

During the 1980s, many of the criticisms of traditional education made by Froebel, Montessori, Dewey, Piaget, Ginott and others took on a new urgency. With the "back to the basics" emphasis of the late 1970s and 1980s, curriculum and teaching methods became more prescribed. Though the emphasis clashed directly with increased understanding about how young children learn (Bredekamp & Copple, 1997), the prescriptive academic influence meant increasing numbers of young children at school spending long hours in their seats, following directions passively, and completing endless numbers of work sheets. Teacher-directed education again had come to the fore.

In some kindergarten and many primary classrooms the prescribed academic program was not new—classrooms had always been run this way. However, on a broad scale, kindergarten programs were expected to become academic, and preschool programs felt pressures to "get children ready for kindergarten." The emphasis on academic programming with younger children lent itself to tightly controlled classrooms (Elkind, 1987).

Except for the occasional teacher who made human relations a priority, the interactive nature of the guidance approach did not fit the regimen of the prescribed, academic classroom. With the shift in educational priorities, discipline systems changed as well.

Assertive Discipline

Looking for methods to increase student compliance, administrators and teachers embraced new, "more effective" **obedience-based discipline** systems. Predominant among these programs was Canter's assertive discipline, "a take-charge approach for today's educator" (1976). A psychologist who worked with special education students in a clinical setting, Lee Canter actively marketed his discipline program for classroom use, and the program gained widespread use in school systems across the country (Canter, 1989). Although its effects were regarded by many educators as controversial, assertive discipline was widely used with kindergarten children and high school students, and even in some prekindergarten programs.

As followed in the 1980s, common practices under assertive discipline included:

- making rules and establishing consequent punishments and rewards with children;
- obtaining consent agreements from parents for use of the system;
- recording names, often publicly, of children who break rules;
- issuing "disciplinary referral slips" to repeat offenders—which commonly include trips to the principal, telephone calls home, and in-school suspensions;
- holding periodic popcorn parties or class outings as rewards for children who have complied with the system—and excluding those who have not.

By the end of the 1980s, debate about the effects of assertive discipline had become heated and ongoing (Canter, 1988, 1989; Curwin & Mendler, 1988/2000, 1989; Gartrell, 1987; Hitz, 1988; Render, Padilla, & Krank, 1989).

Canter (1989) points out that assertive discipline clearly establishes the authority of the teacher and the role of the student. The model teaches students to choose between the rewards of compliance and the consequences of disobedience. It provides a consistent system of rewards and punishments for teachers within a classroom and across a school or district. It involves parents. In the eyes of Canter and his adherents, his system "works."

Critics, including Brewer (1995), Curwin and Mendler (1989), Gartrell (1987), and Hitz (1988), argue that assertive discipline has negative implications for children and for teachers.

Effects on Children   Because rules and their consequences are cut in stone, the model does not allow for individual circumstances. Children who may make innocent mistakes suffer. The tendency toward public iden-

To reach a child's mind, a teacher must capture a child's heart.

tification of "culprits" causes humiliation and can begin a process of negative self-fulfilling prophecy. Students frequently identified and punished grow immune to the system and become stigmatized as "out-groups" in the classroom and school (Render, Padilla, & Krank, 1989).

Although the system includes positive recognition for compliance, even the public rewards set up "winners" and "losers" within the class. Classrooms in which teachers have become entrenched in the negative aspects of the system are unpleasant, anxious places to be. The emphasis on obedience in the assertive discipline classroom inadequately prepares children to function in a democracy (Curwin & Mendler, 1989; Render, Padilla, & Krank, 1989). Directing their comments to early childhood, Gartrell (1987) and Hitz (1988) assert that the Canter model is inappropriate for use with children during their most impressionable years.

Effects on Teachers   A second criticism is that the system seriously reduces the teacher's ability to use professional judgment (Gartrell, 1987). Because of the "obedience or consequences" emphasis, the teacher cannot react to the uniqueness of individual situations or individual children's needs. Neither can the teacher accommodate background, developmental, or learning style differences that manifest themselves in behaviors outside of acceptable limits (Hitz, 1988). Because the model is essentially authoritarian, it cannot adapt to democratic, interactive teaching styles necessary for developmentally appropriate practice; the system pressures the teacher to be an authoritarian. Where schools or districts have mandated the system, teachers are expected to use it even if they are uncomfortable with it; the danger is that teachers may become technicians rather than professionals (Curwin & Mendler, 1989; Gartrell, 1987; Render, Padilla, & Krank, 1989). In some situations, parents who object to use of the system may find themselves at odds with teachers and administrators charged with soliciting parental compliance. Often, parents who object are the very ones who might otherwise become productively involved (unpublished correspondence of parents with the author).

In their text, *Discipline With Dignity,* Curwin and Mendler say this about the "obedience models of discipline," such as assertive discipline of the 1980s:

> It is ironic that the current mood of education is in some ways behind the past. The 1980s might someday be remembered as the decade when admiration was reserved for principals, cast as folk heroes, walking around schools with baseball bats, and for teachers and whole schools that systematically embarrassed students by writing their names on the chalkboard. But we do have hope that the pendulum will once again swing to the rational position of treating children as people with needs and feelings that are not that different from adults. Once we begin to understand how obedience is contrary to the goals of our culture and education, the momentum will begin to shift. Our view is that the highest virtue of education is to teach students to be self-responsible and fully functional. (p. 24)

The very term "discipline with dignity" supports and reinforces the guidance approach.

THE TRANSITION FROM DISCIPLINE TO GUIDANCE

During the 1980s, pressures to sustain and renew an emphasis on the use of guidance were strong within two separate fields: early childhood and the growing field of conflict management education. The guidance tradition in early childhood had always been strong. By the end of the 1980s, this tradition was receiving renewed attention by writers who spoke directly about it and by new emphasis from NAEYC on the use of **developmentally appropriate practice (DAP).**

The Contribution of Early Childhood Educators

At the same time that obedience-based discipline systems were taking hold in many school systems, other forces were at work. Inspired by the nursery school movement earlier in the century and the work of the developmental psychologists, writers at the preschool level were declaring their independence from the conventional role and functions of classroom discipline. Textbooks in the nursery school tradition, such as Read (1950, tenth edition—1997), phrased the setting of the preschool as a "human relations laboratory" in which the teacher models positive guidance skills. In the writings of Stone (1978), Shickedanz & Shickedanz (1981), Cherry (1983), Marion (1998), Clewett (1988), and Greenberg (1988), careful distinction was drawn between positive and negative discipline practices. Teachers using negative discipline relied on punishment to enforce compliance or impose retribution (Clewett, 1988). Teachers using positive discipline, in contrast, worked to prevent problems and, when they occurred, intervened in ways respectful of the child's self-esteem (Gartrell, 1992; Greenberg, 1988; Wichert, 1989).

Significantly, after the debate about obedience-based discipline systems began, textbooks not specific to early childhood education also renewed the need for positive discipline practices. Albert's *Cooperative Discipline* (1996) emphasizes how to manage your classroom and promote self-esteem. Based on the theories of Dreikurs, the book stresses diagnostic and communication skills to build cooperative relations not just between teacher and student, but also between teacher and parent, teacher and teacher, and teacher and administrator (1996). Two other discipline texts, *Discipline with Dignity* (Curwin & Mendler, 1988/2000) and *A Guide to Positive Discipline* (Keating, Pickering, Slack, & White, 1990), are guidebooks that present specific classroom management approaches. Each offers a coordinated system that can be used schoolwide but still allows the teacher room for professional judgment while respecting the integrity of the learner.

The guidance approach addresses children's behaviors in ways that support self-esteem.

In early childhood literature, discomfort with the very term *discipline* emerged. Despite the claim that discipline is "value neutral" and an "umbrella term" (Marion, 1998), *discipline* still carries the baggage of negative connotations. The term to *discipline a child* suggests punishment, a practice unacceptable in the guidance approach. Gartrell (1997, 2001) points out that in problem situations, teachers tend to blur the distinction between punishment and discipline, and not to think about "guidance." He comments that unless handled so that a logical consequence is logical from the child's point of view, the child tends to perceive the act of discipline as punishment. For this reason, the teacher needs to emphasize guidance, which involves carefully teaching children about consequences and behavior alternatives (1997, 2001).

In *Guiding Young Children* (2000), Reynolds provides a problem-solving approach that begins with setting up the environment and includes specific communication and problem-solving strategies and techniques. Reynolds argues that the problem-solving approach precludes the necessity of the term *discipline*. She does not use the term in her text in order to avoid confusion and misinterpretation (2001). In fact, the term discipline generally is fading from early childhood literature, supplanted by *guidance.* For some teachers, unless the connection between the two terms is made, they may tend to think of *guidance* in one set of circumstances and *discipline,* perhaps lapsing into punishment, in another. The third edition of the present text continues the position that one can address any situation with the use of guidance. The term *discipline* is used sparingly and then with a "positive" modifier.

The Contribution of Developmentally Appropriate Practice

In 1987, the National Association for the Education of Young Children (NAEYC) published *Developmentally Appropriate Practice in Early Childhood Programs Serving Children From Birth Through Age 8* (Bredekamp & Copple). This now updated (1997) NAEYC policy statement* has synthesized prevailing trends in research and theory pertaining to the education of young children. Significant is the fact that chapters in the work are supported by 600 separate references to authorities in the child development and early childhood fields. The position statement advocates educational practices that allow for an interactive approach to learning and teacher-child relations. Developmentally appropriate practices discussed reflect the guidance-oriented approach to discipline advocated by Froebel, Montessori, Dewey, Piaget, and the self psychologists. Clearly espousing the guidance tradition, the NAEYC document cites positive guidance techniques that encourage the teacher to: establish routines and expectations understandable to children; use methods such as modeling and encouraging expected behavior; redirect behavior toward acceptable activity; and set clear limits

---

* Retitled *Developmentally Appropriate Practice in Early Childhood Programs.*

(1997, p. 129). "Teachers' expectations match and respect children's developing capabilities" (1997, p. 129). In addition:

> Teachers ensure that classrooms or groups of young children function as caring communities. They help children learn how to establish positive, constructive relationships with adults and other children. (1997, p. 123)

> Teachers provide many opportunities for children to learn to work collaboratively with others and to socially construct knowledge as well as develop social skills, such as cooperating, helping, negotiating, and talking with others to solve problems. (1997, p. 129)

According to the NAEYC document, *inappropriate* discipline practices are these:

> Teachers spend a great deal of time punishing unacceptable behavior, demeaning children who misbehave, repeatedly putting the same children who misbehave in time-out or some other punishment unrelated to the action. . . . Teachers do not set clear limits and do not hold children accountable to standards of behavior. . . . Teachers do not help children set and learn important rules of group behavior and responsibility. (1997, p. 129)

Guidance Defined

The NAEYC document, pertaining to children birth to eight, concretely contrasts **guidance** with discipline practices based on rewards and punishments,

---

Guidance Goes Beyond the Traditional Goals of Classroom Discipline
- Guidance means teaching children to learn from their mistakes, rather than punishing children for making mistakes; to solve their problems rather than punishing children for having problems they cannot solve.
- Guidance empowers the encouraging classroom in which all children feel fully accepted as capable members and learners.
- Guidance facilitates an interactive learning environment in which the adult functions as responsive leader and the child engages in an ongoing process of constructing meaning through developmentally appropriate activities.
- Guidance assists children to take pride in their developing personal and cultural identities and to view differing human qualities as sources of affirmation and learning.
- Guidance places healthy emotional, social, and cultural development at the heart of the curriculum.
- Guidance links together teacher, parent, and child as an interactive team.

Teachers facilitate the development of positive social skills at all times.

which are developmentally inappropriate. Building from this landmark document, a picture of guidance emerges.

Because so much of educational practice is now "outcome based," the goals for the use of guidance need to be stated. Note the difference between the proactive outcomes of guidance that follow, and the conventional expectation of traditional classroom discipline, "to keep children literally and figuratively in line" (Gartrell, 2001).

A guidance approach teaches children democratic life skills—the skills children need to function as productive citizens and healthy individuals:

- The ability to see one's self as a worthy individual and a capable member of the group.
- The ability to express strong emotions in nonhurtful ways.
- The ability to solve problems ethically and intelligently.
- The ability to work cooperatively in groups, with acceptance of the human differences among members.
- The ability to be understanding of the feelings and viewpoints of others.

Guidance and the Conflict Management Movement

From the country's beginnings, a peace tradition has been part of American religious thought, most often associated with the views of the Quakers. During the Vietnam Conflict, peace groups such as the Fellowship of Reconciliation in Nyack, New York, assumed a visible profile in the society. Following the conflict, in response to growing social awareness of what the Surgeon General termed "the epidemic of violence," such groups began to turn attention to child-rearing and the schools.

As early as 1973, the Children's Creative Response to Conflict Program trained teachers in the New York City area both to teach conflict resolution skills to children and to create a classroom atmosphere modeling the friendly community (Prutzman, 1988). In Miami, the Grace Contrino Abrams [Peace Education] Foundation also began working with teachers at about this time. Other groups followed, including the Community Board Program in San Francisco; Educators for Social Responsibility in Cambridge, Massachusetts; and School Mediation Associates in Belmont, California. The National Institute for Dispute Resolution, now merged with the National Association for Mediation in Education, became a national clearinghouse for conflict management materials.

Over the first half of the 20th century, John Dewey (1900, 1944) fundamentally altered views about education by advocating that the society should manifest its democratic ideals by making the classroom a "microcosm" of democracy. Democratic practice in the classroom (with the teacher as leader) remains a goal of educators who espouse the guidance tradition. Using a similar philosophy, groups working for a nonviolent society see the peaceable classroom as an important first step. In the book, *The Friendly Classroom for a Small Planet,* Prutzman (1988) states:

> We find that children develop positive self-concepts and learn to be open, sharing, and cooperative much more effectively when they become part of a [classroom] community in which these attributes are the norm. (p. 2)

Gradually the conflict management movement in American schools took root and established these important principles still gaining in acceptance today:

1. Each individual in the classroom, both child and adult, is to be treated with friendly respect;
2. All individuals, including young children, can learn to prevent and resolve problems by using words in peaceable ways;
3. Teachers create friendly classrooms both by modeling and teaching conflict management and by a philosophy of peace education throughout the entire school program.

With these principles and active training programs built around them during the 1980s, the peace organizations served as a counter trend to the practice of obedience-based discipline. Today, the conflict management movement continues to complement the practice of guidance. Perhaps the movement's foremost contribution is its friendly reminder that the primary vehicle for learning democratic life skills by the child is interaction with other children, facilitated by the teacher in the encouraging classroom.

PARENTS AND THE GUIDANCE TRADITION

Positive parent-teacher relations contribute at a fundamental level to the success of the guidance approach. A full history of parents and the guidance tradition would document events that have perpetrated both cooperative and coercive trends in parent-teacher relations. Noted here are a few major events that have supported each trend. Significantly, **parent-teacher partnerships** have a tradition in early childhood education going back to the last century.

Froebel's Kindergartens

Froebel's first kindergartens in 19th-century Germany called for cooperation between parents and teachers. As Lilley indicates, Froebel recognized the importance of the family in the education of the child:

> The child fully develops his driving need for creative activity only if the family, which is the vehicle of his existence, makes it possible for him to do so. (1967, p. 94)

Home visits were a part of the first kindergarten programs, and Froebel included parents in his vision of early childhood education:

> The plan [for the kindergarten] is primarily to provide games and means of occupation such as meet the needs of parent and child, educator and pupil, and possess interest and meaning for adults as they share children's play or observe children sympathetically and intelligently. (1967, p. 98)

In his writing Froebel called upon the mothers of Germany to take leadership in organizing kindergartens nationwide (Lilley, 1967). The original kindergartens, in Germany and then other countries, relied on parent involvement and began a practice that has continued in early childhood education ever since. The first kindergartens in America were run by immigrant parents who wanted the kindergarten experience for their own children. As the beginning point for K–12 education, kindergartens traditionally have enjoyed high levels of parent interest, allowing the opportunity for productive parent-teacher relations to this day.

Montessori's Children's Houses

Montessori (1964) no less than Froebel, encouraged parent involvement in the Children's Houses of Italy. Perhaps due to her standing as doctor, psychiatrist, and educator, Montessori saw the directress (teacher) as a consummate professional, providing a model for children and parents alike. Montessori's "Children's Houses" were located in tenement buildings and were attended by the children of the residents. Directresses lived in the tenements in which they worked. In the translation of her definitive work, *The Montessori Method* (1964) Montessori described the "modeling" role of the directress:

> The directress is always at the disposition of the mothers, and her life, as cultured and educated person, is a constant example to the inhabitants of the house, for she is obliged to live in the tenement and to be therefore a co-habitant with the families of all her little pupils. This is a fact of immense importance. (pp. 61–62)

Despite a professional-client emphasis in the relationship, an element of partnership was also present. The parent and directress met each week to discuss the child's progress at school and home. Moreover, Montessori reported that the parents felt a sense of "collective ownership" toward the Children's Houses, which she discussed this way:

> The parents know that the "Children's House" is their property, and is maintained by a portion of the rent they pay. The mothers may go at any hour of the day to watch, to admire, or to meditate upon the life there. (pp. 63–64)

The Nursery School Movement

Between 1890 and the 1930s, the child study movement, along with the growing influence of Freudian psychology, sparked new interest in humane child-rearing practices and child-oriented education. The nursery school movement in Britain and the United States was an expression of these values. Cooperative nursery schools, administered by parents, began in Chicago in 1916 and continue on a nationwide basis today (Osborn, 1980). The nursery school model, with parent governing boards and close parent-teacher relations, has proven popular in other types of early childhood programs, private "alternative" schools, and a growing number of public charter schools as well.

Head Start

By the 1960s new knowledge about the importance of the early years in development began to impact government policy. In 1965 Project Head Start began and parent involvement became an integral part of its operations. Head Start encourages cooperative parent involvement at several levels. In the home-based option, home visitors work with individual parents and children on a regular basis. In the center-based and home/center combination options, besides regular conferences with teachers and periodic home visits, parents are encouraged to volunteer in the classroom. Under all options, parents are given active policy roles on a local, agencywide and regional basis. Many trained Head Start staff began as parents with children in the program. In response to the rise in low-income working parents in recent years, Head Start nationally is putting new emphasis on serving infants and toddlers (Early Head Start) and supporting affiliated family and center child care programs.

Because the families served by Head Start are predominantly low-income, the contribution of Head Start to parent involvement in American education is significant (Gage & Workman, 1994).

The Public Schools

Notably, early childhood programs have had a positive influence on parent-teacher relations both in the areas of special and regular education. In many states early childhood special education teachers now establish contact with parents before the infant has left the hospital. Teachers in early childhood special education work with families in some cases for years before a child with a disability begins kindergarten. Parent-teacher collaboration is a hallmark of successful special education at all levels; the foundation often is being set by early childhood special education teachers.

In the last 20 years, a new generation of parent and child programs run through public schools are beginning to change the face of parent involvement. One national model is a statewide program in Minnesota that features weekly parenting classes held in conjunction with preschool activities. Minnesota's Early Childhood Family Education is available at no or low cost in virtually every school district in Minnesota, and last year served nearly 300,000 children and parents. Another model for bringing parents and teachers together is Georgia's school-based program for all four-year-olds, funded by gaming revenue, and similar "even start" and "school readiness" programs now beginning in several states.

Historically, many parents, especially from low-income and minority group backgrounds, have felt ill at ease at building and maintaining relationships with educators. Head Start, early childhood intervention and special education, and the new school-based child and parent programs are helping to raise parent-confidence at communicating with teachers and increasing the amount of parent involvement in their children's education and in the school system.

Aside from early childhood initiatives, public school personnel traditionally have assumed an authority-client relationship with parents. Between the end of the Civil War and 1920, the population of the United States more than doubled with many new citizens being non-English-speaking immigrants. Universal education got its start during this time. To "Americanize the aliens," kindergarten teachers especially were requested to make home visits and start mothers' groups (Weber, 1919). The practice of the Bureau of Education in the Department of the Interior (with the encouragement of business leaders) was to reach children in the school and mothers in the home so that immigrant and other non-mainstream families could be made "good citizens" (Locke, 1919). Although now somewhat outdated, this "melting pot" idea long was a part of American education.

With the advent of compulsory attendance laws, over time American schools have assumed a powerful role in their communities, as the institutions charged with socializing children to American society. One result of the schools' growing institutional power is that the opportunity for real parent

Parent-teacher partnerships are accepted practice in Head Start, as are early childhood family education, and other types of preschool programs.

input became limited, especially for parents "out of the mainstream" (Greenberg, 1989). Although the parents of children with disabilities have led the way, the determination and confidence necessary to advocate for one's child at school remains for many a daunting task. In most school districts, the individual teacher must build cooperative parent-teacher relations, largely on her own time. Indeed, individual teachers can make a difference, and teachers and parents together can change school policy.

From the perspective of the guidance approach, the situation will improve as schools give more recognition and resources to parent-teacher conferences, home visits, and innovative programs that help parents feel that they are valued partners in the education of their children. With the growing number of community-based schools, family learning centers, and neighborhood charter schools, models for this change are becoming established.

Parents and Developmentally Appropriate Practice

The NAEYC position document (1997) is significant because it ties together research about child development and appropriate teaching practice. As shown, the discipline methods are those in the guidance tradition. A dimension of the guidance approach is close, cooperative relations between parents and teachers. As discussed, Froebel and Montessori each recognized parents as the primary educators of their children. They involved parents in their programs to ensure that differences in values and lifestyle did not negate the purposes of their programs. Following through to today, NAEYC's "Developmentally

Appropriate Practices" identifies characteristics of parent-teacher relations that continue the guidance tradition:

> Teachers work in partnerships with parents, communicating regularly to build mutual understanding and ensure that children's learning and developmental needs are met. Teachers listen to parents, seek to understand their goals and preferences for their children, and respect cultural and family differences. . . . Teachers and parents work together to make decisions about how best to support children's development and learning. . . . Parents are always welcome in the program and home visits are encouraged. (p. 134)

For the guidance approach to be effective, the teacher develops a team relationship that includes the teacher, the parent, and the child. The parent-teacher partnership is part of a developmentally appropriate practice, and of the guidance tradition.

SUMMARY

1. Who were the pioneers of the guidance tradition?

Guidance has its roots in the history of Western education and is tied to the thoughts of progressive educators over the last two hundred years. During the 19th century, Froebel considered the child to be "unfolding" toward goodness but vulnerable to the negative influences of others. For Maria Montessori discipline is an extension of education itself—the purpose of which is to educate for the development of responsible decision-making on the part of the child. For Dewey, the classroom should be "a busy workshop," with teachers not enforcing silence, but teaching cooperation.

2. Who were mid-20th century influences in the guidance tradition?

As the foremost developmental theorist of the 20th century, Piaget argued that only when authority is shared by all members of the group can autonomous moral thought develop. Several self psychologists demonstrated the importance of supporting self-esteem in the classroom. Among them Dreikurs introduced the idea that children misbehave not because they are immoral, but because they adopt mistaken goals of behavior. Ginott's position that teachers must show acceptance of the child even while they address unacceptable behavior is at the heart of the guidance approach.

3. What was the significance of discipline trends in the 1980s?

During the 1980s many school systems placed an emphasis on "back to the basics" even at the early primary and preschool levels. To enforce compliance with these practices, schools began using new, obedience-based discipline systems at all levels of education. Proponents argued that such systems as *assertive discipline* permitted "the teacher to teach and the *student to learn*"; critics charged that undesirable side effects often resulted. By the end of the 1980s, vigorous debate about the use of obedience-based discipline in the nation's schools was occurring.

4. What is the state of the guidance tradition today?

A landmark NAEYC publication (1987, 1997) focused national attention on the need for education to be "developmentally appropriate"—responsive to the stage and needs of each child. Guidance rather than punishment empowered the active learning advocated by the NAEYC work. Some authors maintained that because of the punitive connotations attributed to *discipline,* the term should be replaced with *guidance,* or at least used with qualifiers. Authors generally agree that interactive, developmentally appropriate teaching techniques and guidance go together.

5. What is the role of parents in the guidance tradition?

Parent-teacher partnerships have been an important part of the guidance tradition. Building on the tradition of progressive nursery schools, Head Start and other modern early childhood programs have demonstrated the value of close parent-teacher relations. The "professionalization" of the public schools earlier in the 20th century gave rise to paternalistic attitudes toward parent-teacher relations at this level (Greenberg, 1989). New awareness of the importance of parent-teacher partnerships is serving to change the mind set of K–12 educators. The view that the child, teacher, and parent are on the same team, working together, is integral to the guidance approach.

KEY CONCEPTS

Autonomy

Conflict management

Constructivist education

Democratic life skills

Developmentally appropriate practice (DAP)

Encouraging classroom

Guidance

Obedience-based discipline

Parent-teacher partnerships

Self psychology

FOLLOW-UP ACTIVITIES

Note: An element of being a professional teacher is to respect the children, parents, and educators you are working with by maintaining confidentiality—keeping identities private. In completing follow-up activities, please respect the privacy of all concerned.

Discussion Activity

Think about a teacher at any stage of your education who most embodied guidance in her teaching. What qualities or skills characterize the teacher's approach? What is a main insight you have gained from the teacher who is assisting you in your professional development? How does this insight relate to what the chapter says about guidance and its use in the classroom?

Application Activities

Application activities allow students to interrelate material from the text with real-life situations. The *observations* imply access to practicum experiences; the *interviews,* access to parents and teachers. For an additional assignment, students might compare or contrast observations and interviews with referenced ideas from the chapter.

1. **Pioneers of the guidance tradition**
   a. Each of the pioneers advocated teaching practices that empower children to be active, involved learners. Observe a classroom in which such teaching is in practice. What kind of guidance/discipline practices do you see in use?
   b. Interview an early childhood teacher or college professor who has studied the work of Froebel, Montessori, Dewey, or Piaget. What does the person believe to be significant about how the pioneer educator thought about discipline issues?
2. **Mid-20th century influences in the guidance tradition**
   a. An emphasis of the self psychologists is support of the child's self-esteem. Observe an instance in the classroom when an adult supported a child's self-esteem. What did the teacher say and do? How did the child respond?
   b. Interview a teacher who values the ideas of either Dreikurs or Ginott. What is important to the teacher in the psychologist's writings?
3. **Discipline trends in the 1980s**
   a. Observe an instance in a classroom when a teacher intervened to stop a conflict or disruptive situation. Respecting privacy, how did the adult teach or fail to teach more appropriate social skills through the intervention? Did the teacher use guidance or traditional discipline? Why do you think so?
   b. One issue raised in the debate of the obedience discipline systems of the 1980s is the role of punishment. Interview a teacher about what she considers to be the difference between guidance and punishment. When, if ever, does the teacher believe punishment is justified?
4. **The guidance tradition today**
   a. Developmentally appropriate practice responds to the level of development and the needs of each child. Observe an instance of developmentally appropriate practice in a classroom. What are typical behaviors of the children? How does the teacher handle any problems that may arise?
   b. Interview two teachers at the prekindergarten to third-grade level who are familiar with the term *developmentally*

appropriate practice. How are the teachers' comments similar? How are the comments different?

5. **The role of parents in the guidance tradition**
   a. Observe an instance of productive parent-teacher relations at work. What seem to be the benefits of the productive relationship for the child in the classroom?
   b. Interview a teacher who has taught for five or more years. Talk with the teacher about how her views have changed/or stayed the same regarding parent-teacher relations.

What You Can Do

Empathize with a Child   Even if you are not the teacher in charge of a classroom, there are things you may be able to do to help children feel that they are worthwhile and accepted members of the class. Think about a child who has or had many conflicts in a particular classroom. Think about:

a. The child's view of life that would cause him to have these conflicts.
b. How the child views life in the classroom.
c. How the child views himself.
d. The interventions adults in the classroom use with this child.
e. The kinds of relationships of adults with the child.
f. How the interventions and relationships may be reinforcing or helping to improve the life perceptions of the child.
g. What you could do to help the child feel more worthwhile and more accepted as a member of the class.

After thinking about a–g, do what you can.

RECOMMENDED READINGS

Bakley, S. (1997). Love a little more, accept a little more. *Young Children, 52*(2), 21.

Carlsson-Paige, N., & Levin, D. E. (1992). Making peace in violent times: A constructivist approach to conflict resolution. *Young Children, 48*(1), 4–13.

Derman-Sparks, L. (1993). Empowering children to create a caring culture in a world of differences. *Childhood Education, 70*(2), 66–71.

DeVries, R., & Zan, B. (1995). Creating a constructivist classroom atmosphere. *Young Children, 51*(1), 4–13.

Elicker, J., & Fortner-Wood, C. (1995). Adult-child relationships in early childhood programs. *Young Children, 50*(1), 69–78.

Gage, J., & Workman, S. (1994). Creating family support systems: Head Start and beyond. *Young Children, 50*(1), 74–77.

Gandini, L. (1993). Fundamentals of the Reggio Emilia approach to early childhood education. *Young Children, 49*(1), 4–8.

Gartrell, D. (2001). Replacing time out, part one: Using guidance to build an encouraging classroom. *Young Children,* 56(1), 8–16.

Goleman, M. (1997). Families and Schools: In search of common ground. *Young Children, 52*(5), 14–21.

Porro, B. (1996). *Talk it out: Conflict resolution in the elementary classroom.* Alexandria, VA: Association for Supervision and Curriculum Development.

REFERENCES

Albert, L. (1996). *Cooperative discipline.* Circle Pines, MN: American Guidance Service.

Berger, S. K. (1991). *The developing person through childhood and adolescence.* New York: Worth Publishers, Inc.

Bredekamp, S., & Copple. (Eds.) (1997). *Developmentally appropriate practice in early childhood programs* (3rd ed.). Washington, DC: National Association for the Association of Young Children.

Brewer, J. A. (1995). *Introduction to early childhood education: Primary through the primary grades.* Needham Heights, MA: Allyn and Bacon.

Canter, L. (1988). Assertive discipline and the search for the perfect classroom. *Young Children, 43*(2), 24.

Canter, L. (1989). Let the educator beware: A response to Curwin and Mendler. In J. W. Noll (Ed.), *Taking sides: Clashing views on controversial educational issues.* Guilford, CT: The Dushkin Publishing Group, Inc.

Canter, L., & Canter, M. (1976). *Assertive discipline.* Seal Beach, CA: Canter and Associates, Inc.

Charles, C. M. (1996). *Building classroom discipline.* White Plains, NY: Longman Inc.

Cherry, C. (1983). *Please don't sit on the kids.* Belmont, CA: Pitman Learning.

Clewett, A. S. (1988). Guidance and discipline: Teaching young children appropriate behavior. *Young Children, 43*(4), 26–36.

Combs, A. W. (Ed.). (1962). *Perceiving, behaving, becoming: A new focus for education.* Washington, DC: Association for Supervision and Curriculum Development.

Curwin, R. L., & Mendler, A. N. (1988/2000). *Discipline with dignity.* Alexandria, VA: Association for Supervision and Curriculum Development.

Curwin, R. L., & Mendler, A. N. (1989). Packaged discipline programs: Let the buyer beware. In J. W. Noll (Ed.), *Taking sides: Clashing views on controversial educational issues.* Guilford, CT: The Dushkin Publishing Group, Inc.

deMause, L. (Ed.). (1974). *The history of childhood.* New York: Peter Bedrick Books.

DeVries, R. (1994). *Moral classrooms, moral children: Creating a constructivist atmosphere in early education.* New York: Teachers College Press.

DeVries, R., & Zan, B. (1995). Creating a constructivist classroom atmosphere. *Young Children, 51*(1), 4–13.

Dewey, J. (1900/1969). *The school and society.* Chicago: The University of Chicago Press.

Dewey, J. (1944/1966). *Democracy and education.* New York: The Free Press.

Dreikurs, R. (1968). *Psychology in the classroom* (2nd ed.). New York: Harper and Row, Publishers.

Dreikurs, R., Grunwald, B. B., & Pepper, F. C. (1982). *Maintaining sanity in the classroom.* New York: Harper and Row, Publishers.

Elkind, D. (1987). *Miseducation: Preschoolers at risk.* New York: Alfred A. Knopf.

Erikson, E. H. (1963). *Childhood and society.* New York: W. W. Norton and Company, Inc.

Gage, J., & Workman, S. (1994). Creating family support systems: Head Start and beyond. *Young Children, 50*(1), 74–77.

Gandini, L. (1993). Fundamentals of the Reggio Emilia approach to early childhood education. *Young Children, 49*(1), 4–8.

Gartrell, D. J. (1987). Assertive discipline: Unhealthy for children and other living things. *Young Children, 42*(2), 10–11.

Gartrell, D. J. (1992). Discipline. In L. R. Williams & D. P. Fromberg (Eds.), *Encyclopedia of early childhood education.* New York: Garland Publishing, Inc.

Gartrell, D. J. (1995). Misbehavior or mistaken behavior. *Young Children, 50*(5), 27–34.

Gartrell, D. J. (1997, September). Beyond discipline to guidance. *Young Children.*

Gartrell, D. (2001). Replacing time out, part one: Using guidance to build an encouraging classroom. *Young Children, 56*(1), 8–16.

Ginott, H. (1972). *Teacher and child.* New York: Avon Books.

Greenberg, P. (1988). Avoiding 'me against you' discipline. *Young Children, 43*(1), 24–25.

Greenberg, P. (1989). Parents as partners in young children's development and education: A new American fad? Why does it matter? *Young Children, 44*(4), 61–75.

Greenberg, P. (1992). Ideas that work with young children. How to institute some simple democratic practices pertaining to respect, rights, responsibilities in any classroom. *Young Children, 47*(5), 10–21.

Hamachek, D. E. (1971). *Encounters with the self.* New York: Holt, Rinehart and Winston, Inc.

Hitz, R. (1988). Assertive discipline: A response to Lee Canter. *Young Children, 43*(2), 24.

Keating, B., Pickering, M., Slack, B., & White, J. (1990). *A guide to positive discipline.* Boston: Allyn & Bacon.

Kohn, A. (1999). *Punished by rewards.* Bridgewater, NJ: Replica Books.

Lilley, I. M. (Ed.). (1967). *Friedrich Froebel: A selection from his writings.* London: Cambridge University Press.

Locke, B. (1919, July). Manufacturers indorse [sic] the kindergarten. *Kindergarten Circular No. 4.* Washington, DC: Department of the Interior, Bureau of Education.

Marion, M. (1998). *Guidance of young children.* Columbus, OH: Merrill Publishing Company.

Maslow, A. H. (1962). *Toward a psychology of being.* Princeton, NJ: D. Van Nostrand Company, Inc.

Montessori, M. (1912/1964). *The Montessori method.* New York: Schocken Books.

Osborn, D. K. (1980). *Early childhood education in historical perspective.* Athens, GA: Education Associates.

Piaget, J. (1932/1960). *The moral judgment of the child.* Glencoe, IL: The Free Press.

Prutzman, P. (Ed.). (1988). *The friendly classroom for a small planet.* Philadelphia: New Society Publishers.

Purkey, W. W. (1970). *Self-concept and school achievement.* Englewood Cliffs, NJ: Prentice-Hall, Inc.

Read, K. H. (1997). *The early childhood program: Human relationships and learning.* (10th ed.). Fort Worth, TX: Harcourt Brace Jovanovich.

Render, G. F., Padilla, J. E. N. M., & Krank, H. M. (1989). Assertive discipline: A critical review and analysis. *Teachers College Record, 90*(4). New York: Teachers College, Columbia University.

Reynolds, E. (2000). *Guiding young children.* Mountain View, CA: Mayfield Publishing Company.

Rogers, C. R. (1961). *On becoming a person.* Boston: Houghton Mifflin, Co.

Shickedanz, J. A., & Shickedanz, D. I. (1981). *Toward understanding children.* Boston: Little, Brown.

Shonkoff, J. P., & Phillips, D. A. (Eds.). (2000). *From neurons to neighborhoods: The science of childhood development.* Washington, DC: National Academy Press.

Standing, E. M. (1962). *Maria Montessori: Her life and work.* New York: The New American Library, Inc.

Stone, J. G. (1978). *A guide to discipline* (Rev. ed.). Washington, DC: National Association for the Education of Young Children.

Weber, S. H. (1919, December). The Kindergarten as an Americanizer. *Kindergarten Circular No. 5.* Washington, DC: Department of the Interior, Bureau of Education.

Wichert, S. (1989). *Keeping the peace: Practicing cooperation and conflict resolution with preschoolers.* Philadelphia: New Society Publishers.

For additional information on using the guidance approach in the classroom, visit our Web site at http://www.earlychilded.delmar.com

CHAPTER TWO

CHILD DEVELOPMENT
AND GUIDANCE
written with Lynn Gehrke

GUIDING QUESTIONS

- How do Piaget's ideas provide a foundation for the study of child development and guidance?
- What do Vygotsky's ideas contribute to the study of healthy personal development of the child?
- Why is Erikson's work a link between child development and guidance in the classroom?
- How do Gardner's theory of multiple intelligences and Goleman's concept of emotional intelligence contribute to guidance ideas?
- What are the implications of brain development for guiding personal development?
- How does the teacher create a climate for partnerships with parents?

A dults, and especially parents, have always thought long and hard about the process of "growing up." For most adults the nature of childhood—with its curiosity, exuberance, emotionality, decreasing dependence, and emerging sociability—has been an endless source of fairly profound mixed emotions! At least since Socrates, thoughtful observers have studied the developmental dynamic that transforms infants into adults. Although the process is universal, altered only somewhat by culture and time, for each individual the course of development is unique—the continuous interplay of genes, environment, and consciousness distinct for each human.

Given the complexity of life—which we know firsthand only for ourselves, and indirectly for all others—perhaps we should not be surprised at the difficulty in explaining, let alone guiding, development. The question of how we manage child development is crucial, of course, because for the sake of civilization, we need our children to grow up well. Over the last century, psychologists have made great strides in understanding child development. These psychologists have helped most of us go beyond views of the past that regarded children as amoral and uncivilized (deMause, 1974). The contributions of the developmental psychologists, both those mentioned here and many others, are assisting caregivers to understand more about the process it takes to assist children to become healthy individuals and productive citizens (the process defined in the previous chapter as *guidance*).

This chapter looks at key findings of noted developmental psychologists over the last 70 years. The focus in these discussions is what each has contributed to understanding about the healthy personal development of the child. By healthy personal development, I mean those aspects of development in the physical, emotional, cognitive, social, and cultural domains that lead to people becoming well individuals and productive citizens. (These would be people who have learned and are willing to use *democratic life skills*—defined in Chapter One.)

Before we begin, the reader might want to note two points. *First,* cognitive skills—the ability to turn information into knowledge—are part of the whole package of healthy personal development, not separate from or above it. An undisputed outcome of modern education should be intelligent citizens. But educating children to be intelligent, without at the same time being ethical, is building for the 22nd century without the hard lessons of the 20th century. In the words of Ben Thompson, a professor of the 20th century, there is a difference between knowing facts and being wise. Healthy personal development involves the ability to use information intelligently and ethically.

Second, let us briefly relate the terms *learning, education, personal development*, and *guidance*. *Learning* is what individuals do when they mentally construct meaning from information. (Learning is gained understanding across the physical, emotional, cognitive, social, and cultural domains.) The process whereby learning happens is *education*—in the home, the classroom, and all around. *Personal development* is what the individual does during the education process when she integrates learning into her developing self and makes it a part of her psychological and biological being. Personal development is the ever-changing product of those ongoing psychological and biological cross-influences in our everyday lives. The process that assists individuals to undertake healthy personal development is *guidance.* (These definitions may be a bit different from the conventional, but they work well for the intent of this book.)

Awareness of an unfolding human potential goes back at least to Socrates. Froebel, Montessori, and Dewey all wrote about the need to respect the dynamic of development within the child. Two mid-20th century psychologists, Jean Piaget and Erik Erikson, have added greatly to our understanding about development and its importance in teaching and learning. To bring the major contributions of Piaget and Erikson up-to-date, the interpretations of a "second generation" of developmental psychologists, notably Charlesworth (2000) and Elkind (1987, 1993), have been brought to the discussion of these two great authorities.

PIAGET: A FOUNDATION FOR THE STUDY OF CHILD DEVELOPMENT

Jean Piaget's clinical studies with his own and other children brought developmental theory into the forefront of 20th century psychology. Piaget discovered that in the process of growing and learning each person passes through "a biologically determined sequence of stages" (Charlesworth, 2000). Piaget identified four major stages of development. The common age span of each is included, although individual children may take more or less time to pass through the stages.

- Sensorimotor (birth to two)
- Preoperations (two to seven)
- Concrete operations (seven to eleven)
- Formal operations (eleven through adulthood)

In Piaget's view, the way a child responds to a situation is linked to her stage of development. Although a child's mode of thinking is limited by the psychological characteristics of the developmental stage, the process of learning is always active. The child constructs knowledge (derives meaning) through interacting with the environment. As each new stage is reached, the old ways of thinking are not lost but are integrated into the new ways (Charlesworth, 2000).

Charlesworth's interpretation of Piaget is helpful in understanding about the development of thought. Cognitive development begins during the sensorimotor stage as the infant forms schemata, or sensory impressions, of what she perceives. By the beginning of the preoperational stage, the toddler is linking similar schemata into preconcepts (Charlesworth, 2000).

The child constructs knowledge through interacting with the environment.

Preconcepts represent the start of symbolic thought and often contain *overgeneralizations*, calling all four-legged animals "kiki" (for kitty), and *overspecializations*, expressing shock at seeing a teacher in an unexpected setting like a store or church. (Charlesworth, 2000). During the preoperational stage, the child forms new preconcepts and refines existing concepts to increasingly accommodate the outside world.

Pat Sanford, a kindergarten teacher, mentioned in Chapter Six, tells this story about a child in her class that illustrates a child's contending with *overspecialization:*

> One Sunday my husband and I were ushers at church. Following the service, the mother of one of my kindergarten students said that her son had been so excited to see me in that capacity that he said, "I can't believe it! Pat's a gusher today!" (Gartrell, 2000)

Until concrete operations develop (between six and eight years), the child's perception process is limited by a tendency to focus on the outstanding elements of what is perceived. The young child does not yet have the ability to comprehend the complexities of situations. Within the limits of perceptual ability, however, the child notices and processes information with great efficiency. From the "Piagetian perspective," the role of the teacher is not to correct beginning concepts but to act as a guide and supply the necessary opportunities for the child to interact with objects and people (Charlesworth, 2000) and so construct knowledge for herself.

In a midwestern American Indian community, a Head Start class returned early from a trip to the beach on a very windy day. They were discussing why they had to leave early when the teacher asked, "What makes the wind blow anyway?"

A four-year-old named Virgil exclaimed, "Don't you know, teacher? The trees push the air."

With a smile the teacher commented, "You are really thinking, Virgil; how do you know that?"

Amused at the teacher's obvious lack of knowledge, Virgil explained, "Cause the leaves is fans, of course."

Undoubtedly Virgil's understanding of what makes the wind blow has changed since that experience. But to this day the teacher remains impressed with the boy's perceptive preoperational stage thinking.

As this anecdote illustrates, through experiences with peers, adults, and physical things, the learner perceives new, often conflicting information. The child learns by mentally processing this information and constructing knowledge from it. The need to reach **equilibrium,** harmony between perceptions and understanding, out of **disequilibrium,** dissonance between perceptions and understanding, is intrinsic. Piaget believed that the disequilibrium felt by the child is a primary source of the intrinsic motivation to learn (Charlesworth, 2000). However, he recognized that too much disequilibrium can be stressful. Keeping disequilibrium intriguing rather than threatening, is a big part of the early childhood teacher's job.

Jinada and Lorenzo were playing house. Jinada commented, "I'm the momma so I'll get breakfast."

Lorenzo retorted, "Poppas get breakfast, so I will get breakfast." A heated exchange followed.

Having heard the argument, the teacher intervened: "Jinada, you have a momma in your house and she makes breakfast. Lorenzo, you have a poppa in your house, and your poppa makes breakfast. Since you two are a momma and a poppa in the same house maybe you can make the breakfast together."

Jinada said "Yeah, and I will make the toast and the cereal."

Lorenzo added, "I will put them dishes and spoons on the table." The two children proceeded to "make" and "eat" breakfast. Afterward, the teacher was amused to hear Jinada say, "But we got to go to work so we'll clean up later." Lorenzo says, "Yeah," and the two went off to work.

The motivation to do a puzzle lies in the need to create equilibrium through putting the pieces in place from the disequilibrium of the missing pieces.

Developmental Egocentrism

In Piaget's developmental theory, a key idea is that young children show what the present author terms **developmental egocentrism.** Piaget believed that young children show egocentrism as a result of their limited development. Due to their still developing cognitive abilities, young children understand events from their own perspectives and have difficulty accommodating the viewpoints of others. Critics of Piaget's interpretation of egocentrism cite evidence that children in the preoperational stage are capable of "pro-social" acts. The capability is there, of course, but this view represents a misinterpretation of the meaning of egocentrism in the young child. Rather than implying that the child is capable only of selfish behaviors, egocentrism in the developmental sense refers to the inability of young children to understand the complexity of social factors at work in any situation, that is, their difficulty in seeing other points of view.

Take the situation of a preschooler who becomes terrified when a grasshopper lands on his shoulder. A second young child hears his screams, brushes the grasshopper off, and pats him on the back. The second child likely did not respond from high level empathetic analysis but from the discomfort she felt at the first child's distress. (She happened to notice the main elements of the situation, which were the first child's screams and "the big grasshopper.") The second child was indeed pro-social, but from reasoning that was developmentally egocentric. However, the acknowledgment that the second child might receive for being helpful is just the kind of reinforcement from significant others that can make social responsiveness a more conscious part of a child's behavior as she develops (DeVries & Zan, 1996). These two authors state the matter this way (1996):

> Young children often appear selfish when, for example, they grab objects from others and demand to be first in line or first in a game. This behavior often happens because young children have difficulty understanding others' points of view. Such selfishness in young children is not the same as selfishness in older children and adults. (p. 266)

Before children grow into concrete operations, their social understanding is limited. They see the world from their own perspectives—often blaming themselves or becoming upset when they do not understand the full set of social dynamics. Understanding developmental egocentrism, the role of the teacher is to adapt the curriculum so that young children can engage in meaningful social experiences. Building the encouraging classroom in which such experiences are possible takes hard work (Honig & Wittmer, 1996) and high level understanding (Charlesworth, 2000). Piaget knew then what researchers are reaffirming today: that healthy social, moral, and cognitive development will result (Piaget, 1932/1960).

Two student teachers organized a game of musical chairs with 12 preschoolers. To their amazement, the first child "put out" began to cry, the second moped, and the third swept a book off a shelf. The two noticed that as the remaining children left the game, none looked happy. The last child out complained that the winner pushed and "It's not fair."

After discussion with their supervisor, the student teachers realized that the children were unable to comprehend the rules of the game. The children probably thought they were being punished by being put out and felt hurt, frustrated, and guilty.

Not to give up, the student teachers organized the game on another day, but with different rules. The children helped to write and tape their names to chairs. They were then asked to suggest the names of animals and came up with "chickens," "dolphins," and "elephants." When the music stopped, the children proceeded to their special chairs; moving like the animal selected. The game continued for 40 minutes, all of the children participated, and all—including the student teachers—had a good time.

Autonomy

In Piaget's perspective, the challenge of development is for the child to build understanding about the perspectives of others and the capacity for intelligent decision making. Piaget referred to the individual's ability to make intelligent, ethical decisions as *autonomy*. For educators who take a Piagetian perspective, *intellectual* and *moral autonomy* are the most important goals of

Progress toward autonomy happens through adult guidance.

education (Kamii, 1984). *Autonomy* means being governed by oneself—as opposed to *heteronomy,* or being governed by others. Writing about moral autonomy, Kamii, a leading authority on the concept, states:

> Autonomy enables children to make decisions for themselves. But autonomy is not synonymous with complete freedom. . . . There can be no morality when one consider's only one's own point of view. If one takes the other people's views into account, one is not free to tell lies, to break promises, to behave inconsiderately. (1984, p. 411)

Early childhood education provides the first institutional experience for children in relation to issues of autonomy. Yet, young children's limited social experience and developmental egocentrism make instruction for autonomy an exasperating part of preschool-primary instruction. Charlesworth phrases the teacher's dilemma concisely:

> How often the adult says of the young child, "I know he knows better!" And the adult is right; the child does "know better," but is not yet able to reason and act consistently with his knowledge. It is not until the child is close to six that be begins to develop standards, to generalize, and to internalize sanctions so that he acts morally not just to avoid punishment but because he *should* act that way. (Charlesworth, 2000)

Clearly, given Piaget's discoveries about the course of development, mastering autonomy progresses throughout childhood and into adulthood. Teachers who recognize the young child's limited ability to conceptualize about moral decisions understand the importance of an approach that teaches rather than punishes, and so allows the child to develop in healthy ways.

At all levels of education, Piaget regarded authoritarian adult roles as un-helpful in the process of empowering autonomy (Piaget, 1932/1960). Interpret-ing right and wrong for children through the use of rewards and punishments reinforces *heteronomy* (Kamii, 1984, p. 410). Charlesworth cites DeVries as iden-tifying teaching practices of a "just community" (what we might call an en-couraging classroom), where opportunities to develop autonomy flourish.

A just community is a developmentally designed school democracy that stimulates moral and social advancement. Some of the approaches used are:

- encouraging student generated rule-making;
- providing support structures (such as clear rules, a system for taking turns, etc.);
- promoting group decision-making;
- using spontaneous interpersonal conflicts as the basis of discussion [conflict management];
- fostering a moral community;
- developing caring relations;
- promoting cooperative learning. (2000, p. 434)

For developmental psychologists, knowledge is not fixed and finite, to be transferred by teachers to the minds of passive students. Learning in both the intellectual and moral spheres is a *constructive process*, that is the learner constructs meaning from interactions with peers, adults, and mate-rials. From this perspective, social experience is fundamental to the educa-tional process. Through interactions with adults and classmates, the learner builds, alters, and integrates mental concepts and, in turn, contributes to the learning of others. A legacy of Piaget, like that of John Dewey, is the con-nection of the development of the child with the democratic functioning of society (Piaget, 1932/1960). The just community within the classroom be-comes the vehicle of society to further individual development and to re-plenish itself. The approach that adults use to teach the democratic life skills inherent in the just community is guidance.

VYGOTSKY: THE ROLE OF THE ADULT IN PERSONAL DEVELOPMENT

Over the last two decades, there has been increased interest in the work of Lev Vygotsky, specifically his studies of the effect of social interaction on cognitive development. Although he was a contemporary of Piaget, Vygot-sky's writings were not published until after his untimely death in 1934 at age 38, and not released by the Soviet government until 1956 (Crain, 2000). The translated writings of Vygotsky bring a focus on environmental and so-cial influences to the study of development. Of interest to early childhood educators is Vygotsky's insightful work on the importance of the interac-tion between the child and an adult or more experienced peer.

While Vygotsky recognized the importance of Piaget's theory that chil-dren construct knowledge by their interactions with the environment, as their development allows, he added "if children's minds were simply the products of their own discoveries and inventions, their minds wouldn't advance very far" (Crain, 2000, p. 232). In Vygotsky's view, children's actions on objects contribute to optimal development when they are included in a social context that emphasizes communication with others. This communication creates what Vygotsky termed a **zone of proximal development** in the child through which the adult or older peer supports learning by a process Vygotsky called **scaffolding.** We now look at Vygotsky's contributions regarding the zone of proximal learning and scaffolding, as well as his work on children's **private speech**—speech that is evident during play, which helps them control their behavior and thinking.

Zone of Proximal Development

In his theory of the zone of proximal development, Vygotsky attempted to give adults an explanation of how to recognize and empower a child's course of development. He defined the zone as:

> The distance between the actual developmental level as determined by independent problem solving and the level of potential development as determined through problem solving under adult guidance or in collaboration with more capable peers. (Vygotsky, 1935, p. 86)

In an encouraging classroom, where all children's interests and abilities are valued, a teacher who understands the distance between what a child can do alone and with help is in an excellent position to use effective teaching strategies. The challenge for the educator is to avoid what Piaget cautions as taking charge of the child's learning. Vygotsky believed that other people can and do affect what children learn, but, in agreement with Piaget, he was highly critical of direct instruction. In a classroom of young children, learning activities should be focused on interaction with others, both adult-child and child-child, to promote cognitive growth. To Vygotsky, these activities must be carefully planned to include interactions that are slightly higher than a child's current level of development. The teacher then uses finely tuned support, such as open-ended questions, to engage the child's interests and discovery. During the interaction, the teacher relinquishes control as soon as the child can work independently with the new information at hand (Vygotsky, 1935, p. 86).

Scaffolding

By scaffolding, Vygotsky meant the effective teaching necessary to move a child through the zone of proximal development. Scaffolding involves questions and prompts from adults or more experienced peers that help a child actualize potential development. Scaffolding helps children think about what they are doing by describing their activity, by providing clues to finishing that activity, by modeling the activity and/or by enlisting the aid of a peer as a "tutor" or partner in the activity. When the scaffolding has been successful, the child brings the activity to fruition and reaches her potential relative to the zone of proximal development at that time, constructing knowledge in the process.

A child in a mixed-age preschool classroom dumps a puzzle on the floor and begins to move the pieces around in an attempt to put it back together. The teacher notices the activity and from prior observation knows the child has not completed a puzzle of this complexity before, but sees her interest in the activity. The teacher sits down next to the child and says, "You are working on a puzzle. It looks like the Barney school bus puzzle." Another child joins the two on the floor. The teacher knows this second child is a capable puzzle solver and acknowledges that this child has done the puzzle before.

"I wonder if that piece with the bus tire fits here with the other part of the bus, see where the curves match?" asks the teacher.

"Yes," replies the puzzle expert. The young girl tries the suggested move and yells, "It fits! Let's do this one." She picks up another piece. This time the teacher asks what she sees on the piece. She replies, "Another tire."

"Do you see that round space there? Do you think the round tire will fit in that space?" The teacher points as he asks.

Again, the puzzle expert offers, "Yes, it does, I know it fits."

After successfully placing the piece, the teacher suggests that the two work together as he watches. The teacher's knowledge of the "expert's" ability to help and not take over is critical here. The new puzzle builder and the "expert" complete the puzzle and immediately agree to "do it again." The teacher backs out to let them work and continues to observe from a distance.

This anecdote demonstrates the notion of helping the child learn and develop at an activity level slightly higher than she could do on her own. The gentle support from this teacher provided the "scaffold" needed to lead development. The teacher relinquishes assistance as soon as the child demonstrates her new skill of fitting the puzzle pieces together. According to Crain (2000), Vygotskians oppose the image of human development as a lone venture for the child in which the child must figure everything out on his or her own. Instead, society has a responsibility to provide the child with the intellectual tools it has developed, and this means providing the child with instruction and assistance. Children simply cannot discover everything on their own. To develop their minds they need the help of adults and more capable peers (p. 243).

Private Speech

In his many writings, Vygotsky emphasized the importance of children's private speech as a guide to behavior and thinking. In fact, while children talk to themselves, they are trying out new ideas, actually acting as their own "teacher." Vygotsky said that private speech helps children plan and direct activities, to solve problems (Vygotsky, 1935). The link to scaffolding here is that when children work with an adult who supports their activity, they use more private speech after the adult leaves them to work independently.

Piaget had his own name for this kind of "self talk," which he called egocentric speech. The difference in view between Piaget and Vygotsky over private speech is well documented. Piaget's work suggests that children's egocentric speech will fade away, as they become less egocentric. Vygotsky disagreed and argued that it does not just fade away, but it becomes inner speech, the kind of discussions we often have with ourselves when we try to solve problems (Crain, 2000). "It is like saying that the child stops counting when he ceases to use his fingers and starts adding in his head" (Vygotsky, 1934, p. 230).

A preschooler was alone in the home living center of her preschool room busily caring for the baby dolls. "You need some breakfast." "I'm going to cook breakfast for you." "You sit in your high chair while I cook, don't cry now." The narration continues as she acts out this drama, talking to the baby and describing her actions.

This anecdote suggests what many early childhood professionals have observed. A child is solving problems in her head, creating a play situation, and even dealing with a variety of emotions. This use of private speech has been associated with greater mastery activities and so can be seen as a direct aid in learning (Berk & Winsler, 1995). In a key difference with Piaget, Vygotsky argued that language, through private speech and social interaction, is a dynamic in the development of the child, rather than a means of only representing what the child has already learned: language helps children learn rather than being only a product of learning (Schickedanz et al., 1998).

Vygotsky's Work Considered

Critics of Vygotsky argue that the zone of proximal development and scaffolding, as primary instructional strategies, tend to make children passive recipients of teacher-directed instruction. The strategies can be construed to mean that education is a lockstep process of assessing what a "group" knows, teaching to "the next level," testing the group to determine "achievement," and arbitrarily defining the next level of instruction. Vygotsky and his interpreters make clear that this interpretation is invalid (Berk & Winsler, 1995). The application of diagnosis-teaching-assessment techniques is different for each child, because what each child knows, can learn, and can integrate through development, is unique—especially in early childhood. Vygotsky's ideas correspond well to the **problem of the match** postulated by J. McVicker Hunt in 1965 (Schickedanz et al., 1998). Hunt spoke of the need to challenge children without overwhelming them—making learning intriguing but not threatening. By its lack of responsiveness to the individual, teacher-directed, group-focused instruction tends to be stressful to many and intriguing only to some.

When scaffolding is skillfully done, there is a pleasant partnership—a collaboration—between teacher and child. In the anecdote about the puzzle, the situation is often one of self-selected play by the child, and the cooperative problem solving with the adult tends to be play-like. As Berk and Winsler write, "During this collaboration the adult supports the child's autonomy by providing sensitive and contingent assistance, facilitating children's representational and strategic thinking, and prompting children to take over more responsibility for the task as their skill increases" (1995, p. 32).

For guidance in the encouraging classroom this difference is critical. Teacher-directed, group-focused instruction diminishes individual satisfaction levels among learners. These developmentally inappropriate techniques result in institutionally caused stress, frustration, and conflicts for many children in the class. As indicated in the previous chapter, discipline becomes inappropriately punitive under these circumstances. The consistent use of guidance becomes difficult. The classroom becomes discouraging (Elkind, 1997).

Another area of concern about "scaffolding to reach the zone" lies in Vygotsky's idea that scaffolding can be accomplished by "more capable peers." When a teacher keeps the practice of peers-helping-peers informal, and a situation—such as a new child entering a class—clearly lends itself to peer assistance, both children may gain from peer-scaffolding. Concern surfaces, however, when the "expert-novice" strategy becomes formalized, as in some "peer reader" programs. The concern is that classroom teachers may establish a core of "more capable peers" to help "less capable peers" (Schickedanz, 1998). When *patterns* of same-age children helping same-age children emerge, some in the class gain the reputation of *academic winners* and others become the *academic losers.* Teachers then find it difficult to maintain the appearance of unconditional positive regard and equality among learners in the class.

Schickedanz and her colleagues (1998) suggest strategies to address this dilemma. Based on the ideas of these authors and others, a logical arrangement in primary grade classrooms is the use of cross-age or cross-grade groupings. Recalling traditional care and education programs, family child care and Montessori programs always have used cross-age groupings; one-room schools always included teaching and learning across grade levels. Family groupings in preschool programs and multigrade classrooms in elementary schools are modern variations of these ideas.

Many years ago, Piaget documented the readiness of younger children to accept the authority of older children. Still today it is *natural* for older children

When older children help younger children, both benefit from the experience.

("experts") to help younger children ("novices"). A third grader with reading problems can still read a picture book with a kindergarten child. The younger child will gain cognitively and affectively from the experience. And the older child is likely to gain at least affectively—a boost in self-esteem from the experience. Teachers should recognize the need of the older child to have her own zone of proximal development tapped, of course, and as mentioned cross-age tutoring should not be the major part of the instructional program. As with all children, teachers scaffold with the veteran learners in the class, and also enlist adults, older students, and volunteers to make the classroom a place for multidimensional learning—and encouraging for all.

In early childhood classrooms the problem of the match is often solved by the accepted social nature of learning. Through informal **table talk,** children exchange ideas and challenge each other to solve problems. Interest centers promote interaction and spontaneous peer-assisted learning in any or all of the mathematical, linguistic, aesthetic, bodily-kinesthetic, social, and personal domains. Small-group activities, also provide for the mutual expression and development of ideas (Schickedanz et al., 1998). In teacher-facilitated small groups, the order listens, models, and extends for individual group members, guessing where each child may go with scaffolding ideas—and then often being surprised.

On a daily basis the interactive nature of a developmentally appropriate classroom raises the question of who is the expert and who the novice. In a kindergarten class, a teacher once held up Rita's name card and accidentally announced to the class it was Renee's (who was absent). When the teacher was immediately corrected, he said with a smile that he was just testing to see if the children could read their names—to which Rita replied, "Yeah, right."

Another time this teacher reported that while reading a book to Rita, he called an alligator a crocodile. After being corrected by the child, they looked up the difference—Rita was right. (Sometimes the child is a teacher, and the teacher is a learner. A sense of humor is important in an encouraging classroom.)

For many early childhood educators the question of who is the novice and who the expert is less important than how the learning of each is scaffolded by the other, as this anecdote suggests:

> Today in kindergarten, Dylan and Caleb were sitting at the art table during choice time making pictures. Caleb drew a box with a dot in the middle. He said to Dylan, "Look at this fly trap and I caught a fly."
>
> Dylan then said to Caleb, "I am going to draw a spider trap and catch a spider; then my spider is going to eat your fly."
>
> Caleb: "It can't eat my fly because it can fly away and spiders can't fly."
> Dylan: "If I draw wings on my spider, it will be able to fly and then it can catch your fly and eat it up."
>
> Their conversation, competitive yet friendly, continued for six more turns (Gartrell, 2000).

Without thinking, a teacher might have entered this situation and explained, "Because a spider can't grow wings it can't fly after the fly so Caleb is right. But then again, because the fly was caught in the trap, it couldn't fly away and so Dylan's spider would probably eat the fly, and so Dylan is right." My suspicion is the two would have left the table at this point to find something else to do. As even experienced teachers know, effective scaffolding is often more difficult than the adult anticipates.

Reflecting again on Piaget's ideas, when they scaffold teachers need to take care not to impose heteronomy (reliance on external authority) in the learning situation. It may be that the younger the child, the more difficult successful scaffolding is by the adult—younger children simply think differently than adults. Teachers are attentive and collaborative in learning situations, ever responsive to extending children's learning. But successful scaffolding takes personalization of the educational program, careful listening and thoughtful response. In this situation, maybe just observing Caleb and Dylan—and possibly following up with more spider/fly information later—would be appropriate.

In addition to his emphasis on a collaborative relationship between child and teacher, Vygotsky made a direct contribution to guidance in the area of private speech. Private speech serves as a vehicle for social problem solving, no less than in purely cognitive pursuits. Children who receive warm care and responsive support for their learning, are more effective in the use of private speech (Crain, 2000). By scaffolding children to their zones *in the use of private speech,* a teacher helps children to self-regulate their behavior—a primary goal in guidance. In these situations private speech becomes an aid in developing such skills as self-awareness, handling strong feelings, empathy, and social competence. Just as these abilities in children constitute democratic life skills, the teaching practices that underline them constitute guidance. One can easily imagine the guidance provided to Sean, and his resulting private speech, in this situation:

> Sean and Tevin are cousins in a center-based Head Start program. While in the active playroom, they both wanted the tricycle with the larger wheels. After a short pull-and-tug session, Sean overpowered Tevin and rode away. Tevin began to cry very loudly. Sean stopped, came back, and gave him the tricycle. Sean spotted the teacher watching their exchange and said, "He felt more bad than me and he was crying harder."

Beyond differences over the role of speech in development, Vygotsky and Piaget had important areas of agreement (Berk & Winsler, 1995). Both psychologists maintained that

- development results from an individual's interactions with his or her environment;
- psychological and social development are concurrent and overlap;
- major changes occur in children's thinking and use of language as they develop.

The theories of Vygotsky bring a focus on the role of the responsive adult to the study of child development. Vygotsky reminds us that despite the wonder of the developmental dynamic, children do not educate themselves by themselves. Vygotsky's depiction of the importance of adult-child interactions rings true with key ideas from brain research and attachment theory. As well, Vygotsky's ideas support Erik Erikson's theory regarding the need of children to encounter an environment in which they can grow toward trust, autonomy, initiative, and industry (Erikson, 1963).

ERIKSON: PERSONAL DEVELOPMENT AND THE CLASSROOM

The noted psychologist, Erik Erikson, framed an elegant concept of development across the life span in his much quoted work, *Childhood and Society* (1963). As a neo-Freudian, Erikson believed that healthy personal development comes from the resolution of inner conflicts (Trawick-Smith, 2000). Through life, Erikson wrote that each individual faces eight stage-

Table 2–1

Stage/Approximate Age	Life Conflict
1. Infancy/Birth to 18 months	Trust versus mistrust
2. Toddlerhood/18 months to 42 months	Autonomy versus shame and doubt
3. Preprimary/42 months to 6 years	Initiative versus guilt
4. Primary/6 to 12 years (Adapted from Erikson, 1963)	Industry versus inferiority

based crises, with mental health impacted by the ability to reconcile a fundamental conflict faced at each stage. From birth through the primary years, children go through four stages, and face four conflicts, as shown in Table 2–1.

Trust versus Mistrust

When an infant receives reliable, warm, and responsive care during the first 18 months, she has a good chance of finding the world reliable and worthy of trust. The security from this foundation allows the child to venture into life with openness toward learning. On the other hand, without stable and loving relationships, the infant is unable to develop trust in the world, and all subsequent development will be affected. A current depiction of the first life conflict, trust versus mistrust, is found in attachment theory (Trawick-Smith, 2000). During the first months of life, infants develop a long-term emotional bond (attachment) with primary caregivers—mothers, fathers, even other close family members such as grandparents. With secure attachments, the infant senses that the world is an all right place to be and feels relatively safe about venturing forth: "Securely attached infants tend to be more friendly and competent and have more positive views of themselves in later childhood" (Trawick-Smith, 2000, p. 178). If attachments are unhealthy—inconsistent, erratic, abusive, neglectful—the infant experiences deep unmet needs and may find future relationships difficult to form and future conflicts difficult to resolve.

Separation Anxiety Trawick-Smith cites studies that indicate roughly 70% of infants in the United States form relatively secure attachments with one or more adults. Between six and eight months, though, all infants begin to recognize who is and who is not that primary caregiver, and they begin to experience stranger concern and **separation anxiety.** Early experiences of short-term absence from primary caregivers and being with other adults—such as extended family members—tend to reduce these anxieties (Trawick-Smith, 2000). Parents aggravate separation fears when they show anxiety themselves and prolong transitions through lingering one-on-one contact.

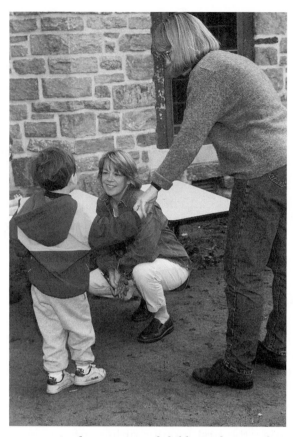

Transition times are easier for parents and children when teachers take the lead.

In contrast, research by Weinraub and Lewis (1977) and Lollis (1990) found that two-year-olds showed less upset at parents' departure in child care when the separation was explained to them clearly ahead of time. Separation was also found to be smoother if the departing parent suggested activities for the child to engage in during separation (Trawick-Smith, 2000, p. 177). At child care drop-off, parents and teachers often form a team, with parents setting the scene for the transition and suggesting activities. Teachers then follow through with individual support and getting the children involved.

For most children separation anxiety reaches its peak at about 14 months, and for many decreases markedly in the following months (Trawick-Smith, 2000, p. 177). With some children, though, a combination of the child's temperament and the pattern of parent-child interaction cause separation anxiety to become a learned behavior. In this case teamwork among the adults becomes really necessary, to nudge the child toward independence (while sustaining secure attachments). By helping very young children to form positive attachments outside of the immediate family, the adult may be assisting them in social situations for the long term (Kagan, 1997).

At separation—especially when care away from home is involved—many parents experience strong feelings: guilt about their parenting, worry about the child, and a sense of lost control. In the early childhood classroom, the teacher orients parents about the transition process and takes the lead at separation to assist the parent and the child. An important task of the early childhood teacher is to help young children and their parents feel that the classroom is a natural extension of their home lives:

> At 8 A.M. children and their parents were filing into the classroom. One little boy, Scott, and his dad came in. Scott resisted entering the classroom, and his dad was saying things like, "Come on, Scott, it's just like the other day. Daddy has to go to class." Scott's dad looked at his watch and said, "Scott, give me a hug and then I have to go. I'm late for class." Scott gave his dad a hug and cried, holding on tightly to his dad.
>
> The teacher walked over, took Scott from his dad, and said, "We will be just fine." The dad left Scott crying and went to class. The teacher sat down on a chair with Scott and held him. She said, "Don't worry, Scott, your dad will be back after his classes." Another child came over to try to comfort him, and Scott hid his face. The teacher asked the girl in a friendly tone to find something to play with while she talked to Scott for a minute. She proceeded to tell Scott, "I know you're embarrassed about crying, but that's okay; everyone misses their mom and dad sometimes, even teachers. She was just trying to help and tell you that it was okay. It really is okay to be sad when your dad leaves, but you know that he will come back as soon as his classes are over."
>
> She paused and Scott nodded. She said, "Would you like to sit here and cuddle for a little bit?" Scott nodded his head again. He sat there for about two minutes and then slid off of the teacher's lap and went to go play with the girl who had tried to comfort him. (Gartrell, 2000).

Autonomy versus Shame and Doubt

The issue of trust versus mistrust is reconciled in a basic (and hopefully positive) way during infancy. The trust-mistrust polarity is really a lifelong problem, though, one that shows itself in each of the other seven stages. In fact, Charlesworth (2000) reminds us that we never totally resolve the crises of any stage, but that relative success with one stage is likely to help us with the others. From the context of the rambunctious toddler, as the individual develops out of infancy, the crucial issue remains trust versus mistrust—it is just that the individual's attempts to resolve this crisis show themselves differently now that the toddler is walking and beginning to talk.

Parents know that infants have become toddlers and a new life conflict comes on the scene when:

"No!" sometimes with a smile, becomes a mantra.

A toddler sees a candy bar in a store, and a public tantrum ensues.

She washes her face, but gets soap in her eyes—and mouth.

She dresses herself, but won't put on socks.

She won't hold your hand, but will run ahead.

She accidentally falls into Aunt Jo's herb garden after you have warned her to be careful of Auntie's plants.

She perfects acts of competition for your attention when you are on the phone.

Ah yes, toddlerhood! The challenge for parents and caregivers is to sustain the child's trust in the adult-child attachment while at the same time keep the balance between the toddler's need for independence and need for safe limits. Would anyone deny that in the home and child care environments, looking after toddlers is a full-time job? Trawick-Smith (2000) provides some indicators of progress during the second stage:

> Once children are trustful of adults and know that their basic needs will be met, they are willing to venture out away from the safety of parents and family. They now wish to become individuals apart from those with whom they are bonded. In their striving for individuality, children often assert themselves, rebel against rules, and assume a negative affect when confronted with adult control. Erikson argues that the emotionally healthy toddler gradually acquires a sense of autonomy—a feeling of individuality and uniqueness apart from his or her parents. Children who are overly restricted or harshly punished for attempts at becoming individuals will come to doubt their individuality and suffer shame. Gradually, such children can become timid, lack confidence in their abilities and assume identities as mere extensions of their parents. (Trawick-Smith, 2000)

Initiative versus Guilt

The third critical age, *initiative versus guilt,* identifies the drive in young children to explore, to try, and to discover. Healthy development during this period depends on responsiveness of the adult to these needs. The adult structures the environment and provides guidance so that children can experience fully while learning nonpunitively about the limits of acceptable behavior. The saying, "The process is more important than the product," applies to this period, as children learn primarily from the doing and the gratification of *self-defined* results, in other words through play.

Erikson's encouragement of *initiative* in preschoolers parallels the findings of Piaget and Vygotsky. In fact, for years a standard of high-quality programs for young children has been the inclusion of large amounts of play—an "academic" definition of which is *self-selected, self-directed, self-realized learning activity.* These programs employ administrators and

The development of both a sense of initiative and belonging during early childhood
indicates the importance of this period.

teachers who understand the importance of play in the development of
children and incorporate large amounts of play in their programming
(Bredekamp & Copple, 1997). If we want children who are active learners,
who construct their own learning, who are intrinsically motivated to
learn, and who see themselves as capable learners, we must approach the
teaching of young children in developmentally appropriate ways—and
this means play every day.

As discussed in Chapter One, the swing of the pendulum in educational
thought toward the premature introduction of academics is counter to the
philosophy that a foremost characteristic of a developmentally appropriate
program is play. How do classrooms devoid of active, hands-on learning affect the young learner? How does a one dimensional, teacher-focused classroom affect the learning environment? A foremost interpreter of the
writings of Erikson as well as Piaget, David Elkind (1993) puts it well in his
essay, "Overwhelmed at an Early Age":

> Unfortunately, the child does not think or say, "Hey, you dumb grown-up, I am
> not ready to learn these things yet; wait a couple of months, and I will gobble it
> up like a candy bar." What the child is likely to think and say to herself is, "These
> all-wise, all-knowing adults say I should be able to learn this, but I can't. I guess
> there must be something wrong with me; I must be dumb!" (Elkind, 1993, p. 82)

This quote captures in a nutshell the opposite of a sense of *initiative:* feelings of guilt when a young child cannot meet the expectations of adults. The
uniqueness of preschoolers is their new awareness of how things are supposed to happen in the adult world, combined with their still limited ability
to make them happen as expected. What do we make of a preprimary child

who draws a purple pig? Do we criticize the lack of "realistic" colors, or do we accept that purple is an impressive color to a young child, and the pigs we saw at the farm yesterday were impressive animals? (And besides maybe purple is the only color the kid has available.)

A difficult task for many preprimary teachers is to recognize that art—like play—needs to be self-realized. Giving children interesting materials and occasional themes—but not models or our own parallel drawing—allows them to develop initiative in the graphic expression of ideas. After a snow, we do not have children draw our model of Frosty. We do have them make their own pictures that tell what they like to do outside in the snow (Bredekamp & Copple, 1997). If one child draws a complex city scene and writes "Sno frm de ski en ski scraprs," we enjoy the initiative taken. If another child covers blue paper with white chalk and tells us, "This is a bizzard and my dad's back there plowin, but you can't see him," we enjoy that also.

For the young child, art empowers creative thought. According to Erikson—and the findings of brain research to follow—our challenge is to encourage the child to explore many possibilities, not to narrow the child's focus to the one possibility the teacher has in mind (Newberger, 1997). What color is the sky? Think of all the possible colors, instead of "The sky is blue." Because in art the young child is not restricted by having to read and write, she can develop her ideas creatively and extensively. Over time children's initiatives will become more conventional; we need to encourage confidence in their own initiative-taking while they are young no matter how unanticipated the results.

Initiative and Belonging   In *Miseducation: Preschoolers at Risk,* David Elkind (1987) discusses factors in schooling that affect young children's development. Elkind interprets the third critical age by referring to it as "initiative and belonging versus guilt and alienation." Elkind explains:

> Erik Erikson describes this period as one that determines whether the child's sense of initiative will be strengthened to an extent greater than the sense of guilt. And because the child is now interacting with peers, this period is also critical in the determination of whether the child's sense of "belonging" will be greater than the sense of alienation. (1987, p. 115).

Elkind's inclusion of "belonging versus alienation" in the early childhood period is insightful. Studying the transition from preschool to kindergarten made by a sample of 58 children, Ladd and Price (1987) found that preschoolers who were liked by their kindergarten peers had fewer adjustment problems in kindergarten. A contributing factor to peer acceptance, and fewer anxieties around the transition, was the presence of friends made previously in the preschool setting.

In a second study,

> Ladd (1989) found that the number of new friendships children formed in the first two months of the school year predicted higher levels of social and academic competence, fewer absences from school, fewer visits to the nurse, and less behavioral disruptiveness. (Bukatko & Daehler, 1992, p. 669)

The value of friendships and the ability to make friends clearly are important skills, so important that they appear to be predictive of school success. Given these findings, the teacher who assists a prekindergarten to primary grade child with limited social skills to make friends contributes in a lasting way to the child's future.

Industry versus Inferiority

During early childhood, children, hopefully, have been immersed in *initiative* experiences with the social and physical world. Because of these early experiences, by the time they reach the next critical period, children are ready for more sophisticated social interactions and learning activities. Erikson's fourth critical period, *industry versus inferiority*, occurs mainly during the primary grade years. A characteristic of children during this time is that they are greatly affected by the judgments of significant others. They are acutely aware of the possibility of failure, and sensitivity in teacher feedback is critical.

The teacher who stresses evaluative comparisons and relies on competition creates social ranking in the class, with the implicit labeling of some students as "winners" and others as "losers." About these practices Honig and Wittmer comment:

> Competitive classrooms result in some children becoming tense, fearing failure, and becoming less motivated to persist at challenging events. (1996, p. 63)

Some children come to see themselves as educational failures and may well be hampered by this label in future learning endeavors (Kohn, 1999). In relation to Erikson's critical period the **conditional acceptance** of children, based on their performance and obedience, is a significant contributor to feelings of inferiority (Elkind, 1997).

Many teachers believe that classrooms predominantly cooperative in nature fail to teach children about the realities of life. A common view is that schools need to prepare children for "the competition of life" by "toughening them to it." To the contrary, public chastisement and evaluative comparisons are argued by Kohn (1999) to correlate with lower feelings of competence (i.e., inferiority). Teaching practices that lead to feelings of inferiority and low self-esteem include:

- Applying pressure tactics to "prepare students" for "high stakes" standardized testing.
- Relying on clearly defined ability groups—the Bluebirds, the Robins, and the Turkey Vultures. (As Bukatko and Daehler [1992] point out, the practice persists.)
- Using peer tutoring that formalizes a clearly defined tutor (the "smart kid") and "tutee" (the "dummy").
- Establishing teacher-domination of classroom transactions with children cast in passive and reactive roles.

As children approach middle childhood, they are greatly affected by the judgments of others.

- Ignoring children who show higher or lower levels of academic achievement.
- Showing indifference toward children who are unpopular with peers or who are from "nonmainstream" backgrounds.
- Giving negative attention to incorrect responses in written and oral exercises.
- Stressing "power tests" and other competitive evaluation procedures.
- Reacting punitively toward random mistaken behavior within the group.
- Using punishments repeatedly such as time-outs, in-school detentions, or exclusion of some children from special events.
- Distancing or reacting in other discriminatory ways toward the parents of some children.

In contrast, a corresponding list of teaching practices that promote industry in children includes:

- Use of authentic, observation-based assessment of learner progress.
- Multidimensional grouping arrangements—informal interest groups, cooperative learning groups, heterogeneous study groups, social style matched groups, collaborative peer pairings.
- A variety of means for achieving success available for children.
- Promotion of autonomy through opportunities to make decisions and contribute to the group.
- Cross-age tutoring, using a diverse population of older students.

- Inclusion of other adults in the classroom to maximize personal attention.
- Advocacy and support for unpopular and nonmainstream children.
- Specific, nonembarrassing teacher feedback.
- Low-key, supportive evaluation of children's work.
- Firm and friendly guidance orientation to mistaken behavior.
- Integration of conflict management skills and attitudes in the daily program.
- Collaborative, problem-solving orientation to serious mistaken behavior.
- Involvement opportunities for parents of all children.

As they enter middle childhood, teaching at its best nudges children toward a sense of industry—confidence in their ability to achieve successfully. Clearly, the principles of guidance are congruent with teaching practices that promote industry as children proceed through the primary grades.

Adults who have seen the curiosity, openness, and perseverance of young children recognize that a learning dynamic is intrinsic to the human species. As the writings of Jean Piaget, Lev Vygotsky, and Erik Erikson indicate, teachers can severely limit or fundamentally empower that dynamic. Teachers who seek to create an encouraging classroom recognize that teaching is about helping children to make the most of personal potential, regardless of labels the child might have received in the past due to birth order, cultural heritage, family circumstance, or personal reputation.

GARDNER AND GOLEMAN: NEW VIEWS ABOUT MENTAL ABILITIES

In his many writings Howard Gardner develops the case for a new way of thinking about mental abilities. Gardner maintains the notion is mistaken that an individual possesses a fixed, genetic entity called *intelligence* (Gardner, 1993). Instead, Gardner and his associates argue for multiple, separate intelligences, which have a genetic basis but can be developed. Gardner, along with other writers, finds much that is problematic in the *thought* and *social policy* of the last century regarding one-dimensional intelligence.

In relation to *thought* about intelligence, these new psychologists argue against the following commonly held assumptions:

- Intelligence is defined exclusively by the individual's ability to use verbal and numerical reasoning.
- Intelligence is determined by heredity.
- Intelligence is fixed through life.
- Intelligence can be measured by standardized tests.
- "Intelligence scores" can be compared and used in "utilitarian" ways (Gardner, 1993).

For Gardner and other psychologists these assumptions have been disproved by the longitudinal research of the 1950s and 1960s, and by the findings of cognitive psychology and brain research since (Schickedanz et al., 1998). The mid-century longitudinal studies demonstrated that environment had a profound effect on intelligence: Young children from enriched, caring situations were able to function more capably in youth and adulthood than young from deprived circumstances (Charlesworth, 2000; Schickedanz et al., 1998; Trawick-Smith, 2000). The conclusiveness of these studies gave rise to Head Start and other government programs intended to break "the culture of poverty."

As neuroscientists and cognitive psychologists became able to assess physical brain development in response to environmental influences, mounting research from these fields also supported the impact of enriched environments on intelligence (Newberger, 1997). With the notion of a single, genetically determined intelligence being debunked, new doors for discovery about mental abilities began to open.

In relation to *social policy* resulting from a theory of fixed intelligence, the new psychologists have joined with many others to decry clearly repressive social practices. One was the *Eugenics* movement, which planned "for the betterment of the human race by using various strategies for eliminating those thought to be genetically inferior" (Schickedanz et al., 1998, p. 6). The most horrendous examples were in Nazi Germany and more recently the Balkan nations, with large-scale attempts at genocide and "ethnic cleansing." Efforts at eugenics in the United States, largely before 1950, have been documented as well, ranging from the longstanding mistreatment of Native Americans to the sterilization of vulnerable minority group members, prisoners, the mentally ill, and the mentally disabled. Laws in 31 states—now largely repealed—forbade mixed-race marriages on the presumption that resulting children would be "genetically inferior" (Schickedanz et al., 1998).

Other mistaken policies stemming from a notion of fixed intelligence are found in American education. Placement of students in "ability tracks"—and in special education classes—frequently was done as a result of IQ test scores, often with little additional information (Gardner, 1993). Attempts have even been documented to end early childhood education programs like Head Start out of a false notion that not poverty but low intelligence keeps low-income populations from advancing (Schickedanz et al., 1998).

Schickedanz and her colleagues state that in recent years thinking about intelligence has undergone a transformation:

Today, most psychologists do not adhere to a strict genetic view of intelligence. Nor do they think of intelligence as a unitary or single factor. Instead, they consider intelligence to be the product of complex interactions between an individual's heredity and experience, and they think that intelligence can be reflected in a number of different domains. (1998, p. 7)

Multiple Intelligences

Multiple intelligences theories (there are more than one) have guidance implications for the classroom. Among these theories, perhaps the most noted is Gardner's construct of seven (now eight) intelligences. Gardner defined intelligence in a new way: "the ability to solve problems or to make things that are valued in a culture" (Gardner, 1993, p. 15). With this concept, he went beyond the conventional definition of intelligence, which essentially is the ability to use words and numbers in order to reason. He did so purposefully, by pointing to the limitations of the conventional definition in all but formal academic settings (Gardner, 1993).

> Gardner's objective is to free children from the narrow standardized test perspective and help them discover their own intelligences and use the information as a guide to vocational and recreational choices so that they can find roles where they feel comfortable and productive. (Charlesworth, 2000, p. 413)

The Intelligences Identified by Gardner
1. Musical intelligence—the ability to listen, to create, and perform music.
2. Bodily-kinesthetic intelligence—the ability to use large and small muscle activity to express ideas, solve problems, and produce results.
3. Logical-mathematical intelligence—the ability to use reason, logic, and mathematics to solve problems.
4. Linguistic intelligence—the ability to use written and oral language.
5. Spatial intelligence—the ability to perceive, orient oneself in relation to, graphically represent, and think creatively in relation to visual and spatial phenomena.
6. Interpersonal intelligence—the ability to perceive and interpret the behaviors, motives, feelings, and intentions of others.
7. Intrapersonal intelligence—the ability to understand one's own skills and their limits, motivations, self-perceptions, emotions, temperaments, and desires. (Gardner, 1993)
8. Naturalist intelligence—(the eighth intelligence, added later)—the ability to perceive subtitles and distinctions in the natural and people-made environment. (Shores, 1995)

Some religious philosophers argue for the inclusion of "spiritual/existential intelligence," (which Gardner may be considering). Aside from this caveat, a quick response to the multiple intelligences is that it looks like a modern effort to educate the whole child (the longtime goal of developmentally appropriate education). This conclusion is not far off. Gardner has retained basic findings of Piaget and Vygotsky, and the constructivist educators who came after them, in his recommendations for intelligences-friendly education. Developmentally appropriate education—using interest centers, theme-based instruction, and collaborative teacher-child relations (guidance)—all figure prominently in education models based on the multiple intelligences (Gardner, 1993).

Implications of Multiple Intelligences for Education

Significant in Gardner's conception is its perspective on mental abilities within a given culture. Different societies value some intelligences over others—logical-mathematical over bodily-kinesthetic, for instance, or inter-personal over linguistic (Gardner, 1993; Schickedanz et al., 1998). Each child is born with unique potential relative to the intelligences, and education be-comes a process of empowering those potentials in the context of, but not lim-ited by, cultural predisposition. We see these clashes of cultural values with individual intelligences in a British miner's son who would become a poet, for instance, or a daughter in Spain who would become a bullfighter.

Within this society Gardner and his colleagues oppose educators who over emphasize the "academic" areas—i.e., the linguistic and logical-mathematical intelligences, which comprise only part of healthy brain functioning (Gardner, 1993). Schooling must be accountable for more than the "academic child."

Multiple Intelligences and Early Childhood Education   Multiple intelligences theory is based on research in the fields of cognitive psychology and brain development. Principles of the theory directly affect education practices in early childhood. Adapted from the works of Charlesworth (2000), Gardner (1993, 1995), Schickedanz et al. (1998), and Shores (1995) some of these principles, and their importance for early education follow:

- The gifted artist, athlete, carpenter or teacher is no less intelligent than the theoretical physicist—just differently intelligent.
- Each kind of intelligence is relatively independent and involves the functioning of different parts of the brain.
- Children have different potentials for development in the eight intelligences, determined by the child's genetic makeup.
- Children make progress in developing all intelligences through those intelligences in which they are more comfortable and capable.
- Schooling must be opened up to educate children in each of the intelligences.
- Children make progress in developing their intelligences when they are intrigued (challenged positively) by learning opportunities, but not threatened by them.

- The teaching style needed for progress in the eight i[...] encouraging and interactive, not didactic and dict[...]
- As children construct meaning for themselves fro[...] developmentally appropriate classrooms, they ma[...] the eight intelligences.
- Assessment is for the purpose of assisting the developmen[...] children in the eight domains.
- Assessment is authentic to the everyday activity of the child, ongoing, and through a variety of collection mechanisms.

Schickedanz and her colleagues (1998) provide a chart adapted from Gardner (1995) delineating educational practices that foster the intelligences. In modified form, that information follows (Table 2–2). Notice its overlay with widely accepted views about developmentally appropriate early childhood education:

Table 2–2

Educational Practices That Foster Multiple Intelligences

Musical	Expose children to various types of music; use rhythmic and melodic instruments; encourage dancing, singing and song composing
Spatial	Provide opportunities for exploring spaces, varying arrangements of materials, fitting materials into spaces, working puzzles, mapping and charting, creative art experiences
Linguistic	Encourage writing, oral expression, vocabulary development, learning other languages; read to children and encourage reading
Logical-mathematical	Provide manipulatives for math; encourage puzzle and problem solving; encourage experimentation and prediction
Bodily-kinesthetic	Encourage dancing, creative movement, making things with hands, running, climbing, practicing large and small motor skills, sports skills
Interpersonal	Encourage social interactions, personal problem solving, conflict management; play games figuring out intentions and emotions of others and emphasizing cooperation
Intrapersonal	Encourage expression of emotions, preferences, and thinking strategies. Help with understanding of wishes, fears, and abilities
Naturalist	Encourage observation skills on field trips, in classroom activities, with classroom visitors. Encourage expression of observations through journals, artwork, discussions, and nonverbal creations

he Matter of Assessment

An overriding issue in education today is accountability, which many critics believe is inappropriately driving classroom practice toward preparation for standardized tests. The new psychologists argue the need to measure the performance of schools not by aggregate standardized test scores—tiny samples of performance in children's educational lives—but by the authentic assessment of children's progress in the multiple intelligences that are developing within each child. Gardner states it this way:

> Assessment, then, becomes a central feature of an educational system. We believe that it is essential to depart from standardized testing. We also believe that standard pencil-and-paper short-answer tests sample only a small proportion of intellectual abilities and often reward a certain kind of decontextualized facility. The means of assessment we favor should ultimately search for genuine problem-solving or product-fashioning skills in individuals across a range of materials. An assessment of a particular intelligence (or set of intelligences) should highlight problems that can be solved *in the materials of that intelligence.* (Gardner, 1993, p. 31)

The matter of assessment for educational accountability is a hot one just now, with contradicting trends on a nationwide basis becoming apparent. Most states now require standardized tests for students to graduate from high school, with preliminary assessments being used even in the primary grades. Moreover, with the threat of funding restrictions as a lever, the federal government may be heightening even further the "high stakes" nature of standardized testing by requiring the annual use of standardized tests.

Yet at the same time, the president of the State University System in California is joining the presidents of a growing number of independent universities at eliminating standardized college entrance exams as admission requirements. In a front-page article in the February 17, 2001 *New York Times,* the president's argument is that schools are feeling forced to train students to take such tests, rather than provide a reflective education that is broader in scope. For reasons of the unnatural pressures standardized testing puts on children, teachers, and parents, the position resisting standardized testing is developmentally appropriate and supports the use of guidance in the classroom.

Multiple Intelligences and Guidance

As a psychologist with an abiding interest in education, Gardner is a similar force on the scene to John Dewey, the philosopher and educator a century before. Just as Dewey faced forces in society that challenged his progressive educational ideas, so now does Gardner.

In Chapter One of this text, Dewey framed the issue of discipline in the classroom by writing that a new type of discipline (guidance) comes into play when educational practice is appropriate for children. Classrooms that allow for hands-on exploration, pursuit of individual interests, cooperative activity, and personalized levels of performance assessment remove tensions that are the cause of many difficulties for children at school.

Such classrooms are not without adult leadership direction with respect to children's behavior. But the techniques used respond to children's needs to learn about their own emotions and dispositions, and to understand and respond to others—in other words to develop their intrapersonal and interpersonal intelligences. The approach to education promoted by multiple intelligences theory is just the type of classroom that Dewey had in mind—the supportive educational environment in which the whole child is educated. The purpose of the classroom for Dewey, as well as Gardner, is to educate the child for intelligent and ethical living in democratic society.

Not surprisingly, teaching that empowers Gardner's interpersonal and intrapersonal intelligences resonates with the interactive teaching styles suggested by the other psychologists addressed in this chapter. Conventional discipline becomes less necessary, and guidance emerges, in classrooms where multiple intelligences provide the basis for curriculum, instruction, and assessment.

Emotional Intelligence

During the 1990s, Daniel Goleman's books on **emotional intelligence** were national best sellers (1995, 1998). Goleman gives credit to Gardner for the paradigm shift from a single intelligence to a multiple intelligences approach (Goleman, 1995). As anecdotal confirmation of the existence of multiple intelligences, Goleman states that both psychologists agree on the plausibility of the following scenario: A scientist with a 160 intelligence quotient (IQ) working as an employee for a successful CEO with an IQ of 100. Their conclusion is that the CEO must have skills in social competence unmeasured by the traditional assessment of intelligence.

Goleman also heralds Gardner's interpersonal and intrapersonal intelligences as a beginning in the explanation of the emotional aspect of intelligence (Goleman, 1995). His response to Gardner's two affective intelligences, though, includes a basic critique. He believes that Gardner's presentation of inter- and intrapersonal intelligence is slanted toward cognitive thought processes. By this he means that Gardner is more concerned about the reflective understanding of emotions than in the consideration of emotion as a driving force in behavior (Goleman, 1995). Goleman is more concerned about using emotions to shape behaviors.

Using the previous scenario to illustrate the difference, the scientist makes a discovery, and aware of the need to be objective, presents findings dispassionately. On the other hand, the CEO directly uses passion, generated by the importance of the discovery, to motivate others to finance the commercial development of the discovery. Goleman contends that due to his cognitive orientation, Gardner is more comfortable explaining the scientist's ability to understand (and so control) emotions than the CEO's direct use of emotion to influence others (Goleman, 1995).

Goleman argues that emotional intelligence means how individuals are able to use their emotions in their behavior. He presents studies of "Stars," successful individuals who have shown outstanding emotional intelligence, and he discusses environments—settings that promote *emotional literacy* (learning about the role of emotions in behavior), and so empower emotional intelligence (Goleman, 1995, 1998). He argues that education about the emotions needs to be central to modern family life and curricula—and cannot begin too early. For Goleman:

> "Emotional intelligence" refers to the *capacity for recognizing our own feelings and those of others, for motivating ourselves, and for managing emotions well in ourselves and in our relationships.* It describes abilities distinct from, but complementary to, academic intelligence, the purely cognitive capacities measured by IQ. (Goleman, 1998, p. 317)

In response to Goleman's stated differences with Gardner, the author's own response is that the two psychologists complement each other. Their work together advances the need to include emotional literacy in our classrooms—and the need for adults to model emotional intelligence in their interactions with children. Neither would argue that emotion and cognition together make us fully human. Both probably would find teaching democratic life skills, identified in Chapter One as the goal of guidance, congruent with education about feelings and their role in human relations.

Though Goleman has a particular perspective on the matter, the issue of separate intra- and interpersonal intelligences versus one "emotional intelligence" is to some degree a matter of semantics. Goleman's concept of emotional intelligence has separate within-self and with-other-selves competencies (Goleman, 1995). Still, the criticism can be made of Goleman's emotional intelligence that he seems to place undue emphasis on the "extroverted" personality, and the ability of the "emotional intelligent" person to persuade others. (A major advocate of Goleman's work seem to be members of the corporate world.)

In Piaget's concept of autonomy, the element that gives balance to (traditional) intelligence is personal ethics—the ability to incorporate into one's decisions the viewpoints, rights, and needs of others. Ethical decision-making involves empathy, the use of interpersonal intelligence, and integrity, the use of intrapersonal intelligence. As long as the wellspring of emotional intelligence is autonomy—by whatever name we give it—there is room for both Gardner's and Goleman's conceptions in contemporary thought about development. Certainly children need guidance in encouraging classrooms to engage in healthy personal and social development.

THE CONTRIBUTIONS OF BRAIN RESEARCH

In an often quoted article, "What Do We Know from Brain Research?", Wolfe and Brandt (1998) describe trends in research findings that directly impact the life of young children in the classroom. Citing Wolfe and Brandt, as well as Diamond and Hopson (1998), and LeDoux (1996), an adapted discussion of these findings follows:

1. *The brain is not fully formed and operational at birth, but develops physiologically in response to experiences throughout childhood.* With each experience, the brain of the young child transforms perceptions into trillions of new connections, called dendrites, across its neurons, the cells of the brain. Healthy development and maintenance of the dendrites is necessary for healthy brain functioning. The environment influences how these dendrites form, and the brain influences how the environment is interpreted. The brain is constantly changing its physical structure and functioning in relation to experiences (Wolfe & Brandt, 1998).

2. *Intelligence is not fixed at birth.* The child's environment is not neutral. Experiences either aid brain development by promoting dendrite formation, or hinder brain development by retarding dendrite formation—or even causing already formed dendrites to die off. This is why we say that mental abilities are the result of the interplay of heredity—the unique mass of brain neurons the infant is born with—and environment—the wiring of neurons with dendrites as the result of experiences.

As Head Start and subsequent generations of innovative early childhood programs have demonstrated, the need for society to improve the environments of children living in poverty is now generally recognized. Intervention programs that provide enriched environments for "impoverished" children can prevent children from the effects of hindered brain development, which is low mental functioning. In studies cited by Wolfe and Brandt, the most effective programs started with children when they were infants and directly involved parents (1998).

3. *The brains of children develop best in enriched environments* (Diamond & Hopson, 1998). Enriched environments have particular characteristics. They include the provision of:
  • consistent, positive emotional support that balances against both over- and understimulation;
  • nutrition and life circumstances that promote physical health;
  • a learning environment that is pleasurably intense (intriguing) but free of undue pressure and stress;
  • interest-based activities that encourage multiple aspects of development (physical, emotional, aesthetic, cognitive, language, social, cultural);
  • ongoing opportunities for children to construct personal meaning from their learning activities;
  • ongoing opportunities for children to relate their learning to what they already know;
  • ongoing opportunities for learning to be social by encouraging children to express, share, and scaffold ideas and to produce collaborative projects (Wolfe & Brandt, 1998).

4. *Most abilities are acquired more easily during certain sensitive periods, or "windows of opportunity" while the individual is young.* During the period of

birth to age ten, the trillions of dendrite connections among neurons proceed rapidly. During adolescence the process begins to drop, slowing down (significantly) but not stopping during adulthood. Certain abilities, eyesight for instance, develop only during windows of opportunity very early in life, while dendrite formation for that ability is most active. These abilities cannot develop if environmental deprivation occurs during the critical time (Diamond & Hopson, 1998).

For other abilities, such as a second language, the windows of opportunity do not close as quickly or tightly. The optimum time for learning additional languages is before adolescence. After about age ten, most individuals have trouble learning a second language without having an accent. A second language can be learned later in life, though usually not as easily.

Almost all windows of opportunity begin during early childhood. For this reason more attention needs to be paid to the development and education of young children by federal, state, and local programs. About 75% of children are in child care during the first five years. Yet, programs are underfunded and underregulated. Speaking of the need for early intervention instead of later remediation, the authors state: "With intense early intervention, we could reverse or prevent some adverse effects. It is possible that the billions of dollars spent on special education services might be better spent on early intervention" (Wolfe & Brandt, 1998).

5. *Emotions strongly influence learning by aiding or hindering brain development.* When heightened, *but not* stressful, emotions are attached to experiences, an individual forms stronger memory patterns around the experiences. Chemicals generated by the positively charged experience both generate potent processing of the information and facilitate healthy dendrite formation which fosters future learning (Wolfe & Brandt, 1998). In the encouraging early childhood classroom, teachers frequently guide toward, and in fact witness, such *peak learning experiences*. When the attention span of a child in an activity suddenly exceeds that of the adult, the child is fully learning from the activity, and the adult should sit back and smile.

In contrast, when children's minds are beset with stress—generated either by the classroom situation itself or pressures from outside the classroom— emotions negatively affect brain functioning. LeDoux in *The Emotional Brain* (1996) provides an authoritative analysis of how this happens: Sensing danger, the amygdala (the brain structure that processes experiences into emotions) sends out strong stress hormones to the hippocampus (the structure that mediates emotional reactions). If the experience is severe and prolonged, the hormones actually cause damage to the dendrites of the hippocampus. Healthy communication between the hippocampus and other parts of the brain, including those that mediate thought, is then disrupted. Memory and recall processes, essential for learning, become more difficult (LeDoux, 1996).

LeDoux states that if infrequent episodes of stress are discontinued, and the stress is not too severe, the hippocampus can repair its dendrites and resume normal functioning. However, in relation to long-term stress LeDoux states, "In survivors of trauma, like victims of repeated child abuse or

Vietnam veterans with post-traumatic stress disorder, the hippocampus is shrunken" (1996, p. 242). More so than others, these individuals must struggle to perform everyday thinking processes, made the more stressful by knowing they are struggling. One frequent side symptom is preoccupation with emotional memories of the traumatic events.

Emotional memories always have a strong unconscious component and often have a conscious component as well. Emotional memories of either type are difficult to extinguish on one's own (LeDoux, 1996).

> I remember a student in my education course who told of taking a math test in middle school and having her teacher publicly use her mistakes as examples for the class. She found the experience so painful that she had trouble completing math tests from then on. Our university requires college algebra. She failed the course twice, due to her scores on tests. She convinced herself that her failure in math would prevent her from becoming a teacher. With counseling, she took the course again, this time with a young woman instructor. The student explained the problem; the instructor said she would help and she did. On the day of the final exam, the student entered the classroom feeling "pretty drawn out." The instructor sat down next to the student and put her arm around the student's shoulder. The instructor sat there until the student was calm enough to take the test. This time the student passed.

Brain Research and Early Childhood Education

The book, *Rethinking the Brain*, by Rima Shore (1997), presents similar research on how a child's brain develops. In addition the book provides discussion of the environment, "the nourishment, care, surroundings, and stimulation," that influences how the synapses in the brain develop (Shore, 1997, p. x). Because learning experiences build neural connections, it is imperative that these experiences be positive and developmentally appropriate—both within and outside of the home. Shore emphasizes ways in which parents, families, and other caregivers can respond to the needs of young children and how they create a consistent, caring, and safe environment (1997).

Infants   A child's first experiences with the world revolve around the people who give her care. In daily interactions with her parents and caregivers, she begins to trust those adults and develop emotional security. "Neuroscientists are finding that a strong, secure attachment to a nurturing caregiver can have a protective biological function, helping a growing child withstand the ordinary stresses of daily life" (Shore, 1997, p. x). This attachment including consistent care teaches the baby trust and creates a sense of emotional security. And, by supporting synapse development, this consistency of care helps form the connections of healthy brain circuitry.

Bredekamp and Copple (1997) build on Shore's recommendations with discussion of the development of positive relationships in child care settings. They stress daily communication by teachers with parents of infants. Communication with the parent by the teacher helps develop trust between the two. Another reward of this relationship is that "when one discovers a care giving strategy that works, the other can follow suit. This creates continuity and reinforces the baby's ability to anticipate adult responses" (Bredekamp & Copple, 1997, p. 60). When babies can consistently anticipate adult responses, they build trust in their home and child care environments. With positive attachments in the home and child care setting, the infant feels secure and confident in her ability to make choices and to learn (Shore, 1997). In Erikson's terms, the infant has found basic trust and is ready to move toward autonomy.

Toddlers   Words and the social world fascinate toddlers. Toddlers are busy beginning to learn: to use words to express their feelings, to share/take turns and to act appropriately in different situations. A toddler's exploration of the world involves conflict with others, but by this conflict they begin to develop empathy for others (Shore, 1997). Even though this is a slow process and toddlers experience "age-related limits in their cognitive capacities, they also have enormous capacities to learn and often underestimated capacities to think, reason, remember, and problem solve" (Bredekamp & Copple, 1997, p. 115). If toddlers experience warm, responsive care as they did when infants, recent brain research shows that they are more empathetic with their peers. If they were responded to early in life, "they learned something basic about what it means to be connected with other people" (Shore, 1997, p. 31).

Young Children   As they continue to develop and sustain positive adult-child attachments, teachers nourish the brain development of young children in preschool and primary grade classrooms. But in doing so, adults shift their approach to accommodate the increasing purposefulness in young children's activity. Bredekamp and Copple define the teacher's task this way: Early childhood educators create and maintain an "environment of encouragement and genuine respect [through which] children are able to develop confidence and competence, not by being told how wonderful or special they are, but by being given chances to take initiative, experience success in performing difficult tasks, and figure things out for themselves" (Bredekamp & Copple, 1997, p. 116). Below is a "snapshot" of appropriate practices for creating warm, caring relationships between teachers and young children.

• Teachers provide opportunities for them to accomplish meaningful tasks and to participate in learning experiences in which they can succeed most of the time.

- Teachers know each child's abilities, developmental levels, and approaches to learning and design learning activities accordingly.
- Teachers help children learn how to establish positive, constructive relationships with adults and other children by supporting children's beginning friendships.
- Teachers facilitate the development of self-acceptance, social skills, and self-regulation by using positive guidance techniques (Bredekamp & Copple, 1997).

In *Rethinking the Brain* the point is made that the hallmark of quality non-parental care is not different from the quality care given by mothers and fathers: "Warm, responsive, consistent care-giving geared to the needs of individual children" (Shore, 1997, p. 59). Results of brain research indicate the following additional characteristics of quality child care:

- A sufficient number of adults for each child;
- Small group sizes;
- High levels of staff education and specialized training;
- Low staff turnover and administrative stability; and
- High levels of staff compensation (Shore, 1997, p. 59).

Dr. Brazelton Says . . .   These are exactly the characteristics of quality care recognized by the National Association for the Education of Young Children (Bredekamp & Copple, 1997).

From one additional perspective, Brazelton and Greenspan (2000) support the early time of life strongly and argue that one cannot ignore the importance of the caregiver's role in healthy brain development. "When there are secure, empathetic, nurturing relationships, children learn to be intimate and empathetic and eventually to communicate about their feelings, reflect on their own wishes, and develop their own relationships with peers and adults" (2000, p. 3). These responsive and secure relationships help children develop an ability to self-regulate their emotions and behavior. The study of early relationships and brain development has given us definitive research to support one of the key foundations of early childhood education—promoting social/emotional development in young children! Now we have the research to support what many in early childhood education have known all along. The authors phrase the issue this way:

> The notion that relationships are essential for regulating our behavior and moods and feelings as well as for intellectual development is one that needs greater emphasis as we think about the kinds of settings and priorities we want for our children. The interactions that are necessary can take place in full measure only with a loving caregiver who has lots of time to devote to a child. (Brazelton & Greenspan, 2000, p. 28)

In their statement about young children, Brazelton and Greenspan argue for small ratios in infant/toddler care, higher salaries for child care providers, and full-time child care only for children after age two. Within these parameters optimal relationships develop, followed by healthy brain development—and the self-regulatory skills, trust, autonomy, and cognitive abilities that healthy brain development engenders. One caveat in relation to their thesis emerges, however. In this day and age, even though most parents might like to, many simply cannot stay home with their infants and toddlers. Brazelton and Greenspan do well to remind us that this is the goal whenever possible and, if not, part-time care is preferential to full-time care. Even when the very young are in full-time care, however, the brain research tells us that positive attachments of children with non-parental caregivers are possible and desirable. The benefits (and real costs) of empowering positive adult-child attachments in early childhood settings need to be recognized outside of the early childhood profession.

A CLIMATE FOR PARTNERSHIPS WITH PARENTS

Teachers, directors, principals, and childcare providers are in positions that require them to create positive environments for young children. Just as crucial, they must find ways to articulate how significant parent-teacher partnerships are for the healthy development of their children. The beginning point for engendering this understanding is when the child is about to begin a program. Steps caregivers take to lessen separation anxiety in children and adults, by encouraging words and supportive actions, start the partnerships that will benefit the child, and family relationships, in the long run.

A young child's anxiety in a new school experience may be lessened if there is not an abrupt division between home and school. Children thrive when they feel a continuity between parents and teachers that can be present only when adults have reached out in an effort to understand and respect each other. Just as a teacher's first task in relating to young children is to build a sense of trust and mutual respect, the same task is important in working with parents. (Gestwicki, 2000, p. 126)

In school-related programs teachers use a variety of spring and summer activities to acquaint both children and parents with the new year's program. Examples of these activities include: a Head Start program that coordinates spring bus runs for children and parents to kindergarten classrooms the children will be attending the next September; transition journals that provide a dialog between the child and family, the preschool teacher, and the kindergarten teacher; and summer kindergarten transition classes held in the classrooms children will attend in September. In the days immediately preceding the beginning of school, teachers accelerate efforts at communicating with families. Several veteran kindergarten teachers from Minnesota have unique and effective approaches for building partnerships with parents during this period. The following case study is a composite of the practices of a few of these teachers, combined into the approach of one teacher, Juanita.

Before School Begins

Juanita views both the children and parents as her "customers." Her intent is to build "happy customers." Part of her approach is to reach the parents through the children. Another part is to reach the children through the parents. An axiom that she works with is "if the children are happy, the parents will be too." Juanita knows that parents who themselves had unhappy school experiences will be more likely to accept a teacher if they know that she cares about their kids. Juanita puts this idea to work even before the first day.

About two weeks before school, Juanita sends letters to both the child and the family. To the child she says how happy she is that the child is in her class and how many fun things they will do at school. The teacher encloses an animal sticker and tells each child to watch for that animal when they get to school. The animal emblem is prominently displayed by the classroom door, and Juanita wears a replica of the emblem during the first week. (See letters in Appendix B.)

In the letter to the family, Juanita says the same things but goes on to invite them to either of two orientation meetings (one late afternoon, the other at night) to be held during the second week of school. In addition, with permission of the principal, she offers each family the option of a home visit, "as a good way for you, your child, and I to get to know each other." She comments in the letter that not all parents are comfortable with a home visit, which is fine. She can make a visit later in the year, if they would like, and she will be telephoning each family a day or two before start-up to discuss any questions they might have. (See Recommended Resources.) Juanita intentionally sends the letter "To the Family of" so that if a parent is a nonreader, someone else in the family may read the letter to the parent.

After Start-Up

On the evening of the first day of school, Juanita telephones to make sure that children have returned home safely, to let the parents know how the child has adjusted, and to ask about any problems that may have occurred. Juanita has said that although she would rather be doing other things after the first day, like going to bed early, she regards these telephone calls as the best investment she makes all year in her relations with parents. For parents without listed telephone numbers, she makes a personal contact as soon as possible using notes or informal visits.

On the first day of school, Juanita always has a parent volunteer from the year before to help with separation problems. Juanita greets each child with a name tag as they arrive. Two classes of children attend on A days and B

The results of liberation teaching often speak for themselves.

days. At the request of Juanita and the other kindergarten teachers, the district allows half of each class to come in on separate days during the first week. This arrangement means that instead of 24 children attending on the two first days, 12 children attend on each of four days. Parents are always welcome in Juanita's class (and are put to use), although during the first two weeks or so, they are encouraged to let the children make the adjustment to school on their own, to the extent possible.

In the first days, Juanita allows a lot of exploration time, but she also gets the children used to numerous routines right away. She comments, "A lot of problems never happen if the children know and are comfortable with the routines." Juanita and the volunteer make sure that all children get on the correct buses at the end of the day. Before leaving the classroom, they have a "class meeting" to discuss how happy Juanita will be to see them the next time they come to school. Juanita gives an individual goodbye to each child as they leave, a practice she continues all year. After completing kindergarten, children receive individual letters saying how much she enjoyed having them in her class and wishing them the very best when they begin first grade next fall.

Juanita holds two orientation meetings (which she calls "Greeting Meetings"), and families can attend either one. She gets high school students who had her as a teacher to care for children who come with the parents to the greeting meetings. At the meetings, Juanita answers questions they might have and talks about the education program. To assist in the discussion, she provides each parent with a brochure entitled, "The Education Program in Our Class." (See the sample brochure in Appendix C.) The brochure discusses such matters as the role of play in the program, why

Parents are always welcome in Juanita's class and contribute in many ways.
(Courtesy, *The Bemidji Pioneer*)

manipulatives are used in math, why the art is creative, why a guidance approach is used, and the importance of parent involvement.

Juanita also asks the parents to fill out a brief survey. The one-page survey includes items about their and their child's interests, the child's family background, the kinds of activities the parents can help with during the year, and other information "that would help me to understand and work with your child." Completing the survey is optional but almost all parents fill it out. The responses provide useful information to discuss at the first conference later in the year. (See Appendix B for sample surveys.)

The teacher attributes the high level of attendance at the orientation meetings to the telephone calls, letters and home visits at the beginning of the school year. She says the first week is exhausting, but the investment is worth it. "That telephone call the first night of school really wins them over. I remember how I felt the first time my child left for kindergarten. I still get tears when I think about it."

Juanita tries hard to communicate with each parent and has even held a conference at a cocktail lounge, where a single parent worked afternoons and evenings. Juanita does have strong feelings about parents who she believes could be doing more for their children. She attempts to be friendly with these parents, nonetheless. She knows that some parents did not receive appropriate nurturing as kids and never had a chance to grow up themselves. She realizes that getting a parent involved may make a difference in that child's life.

She knows because she has seen some parents get involved and grow, and as a result their children's attitudes and behaviors change.

> It is not realistic to expect teachers to like all parents. However, it is essential and possible for teachers to respect all parents for their caring and efforts. In most cases, parents do care. This belief is the basis for all teacher interaction (Gestwicki, 2000, p. 126).

Juanita practices Gestwicki's words.

SUMMARY

1. How do Piaget's ideas provide a foundation for the study of child development and guidance?

The writings of Piaget document that children interpret experiences differently over time and their interpretations conform to the stage of development they are in. For teaching to be effective, it must be matched to the child's developmental level, base of experience, active learning nature, and limited social perspective. For Piaget the learning of autonomy, or principled and intelligent decision-making, is the purpose of education. Guidance in the encouraging classroom is the teaching approach that leads children to develop autonomy.

2. How do Vygotsky's ideas contribute to the study of the healthy personal development of the child?

Vygotsky studied the learning process of the child and concluded that the role of the adult is central to it. In any act of learning the child has a zone of proximal development, which is the psychological difference between what the child can learn on her own and with the help of a more capable other. Scaffolding, or sensitive interaction, guides the child through the zone. The child uses private speech, later internalized as conscious thought, to solve learning problems and self-regulate behavior. In the terms of Vygotsky guidance is the scaffolding process by which children learn the language and skills of cognitive and emotional problem solving.

3. Why is Erikson's work a link between child development and guidance in the classroom?

Erikson theorized that all humans go through critical periods, or stages, at each of which they face a central life conflict. During the first critical period of *trust versus mistrust,* the infant tries to develop feelings of basic trust in her world. During the second critical period of *autonomy versus shame and doubt,* the toddler begins to develop a distinct sense of identity. During the third period of *initiative and belonging versus guilt,* preschoolers need support for creative and social activity, through which they can define success for themselves. During the primary years, the critical issue is *industry versus inferiority.*

Through each of the critical periods, the teaching approach that encourages both productive learning and positive feelings about oneself as a learner is guidance.

4. How do Gardner's theory of multiple intelligences and Goleman's concept of emotional intelligence contribute to guidance ideas?

Gardner and Goleman are among a growing number of psychologists who have debunked the idea that intelligence is a single entity, determined by heredity and fixed for life. With others, Gardner has decried social policies that arose from the old viewpoint, including reactionary eugenics ideas and educational practices of "tracking" students based on IQ and other standardized test scores. Gardner's concept of eight multiple intelligences is intended to change how we look at child development, education, and social policies regarding mental abilities. To respond to all eight intelligences in the classroom, curriculum, teaching practices, and assessment methods need to be opened up and made developmentally appropriate. To assist children to develop their intrapersonal and interpersonal intelligences, teachers must model these intelligences and teach to them. Goleman's concept of emotional intelligence is similar, but not identical to, Gardner's intra- and interpersonal intelligence. Goleman's concept refers to the ability to use one's own emotions effectively in responses to others.

5. What are the implications of brain development for guiding personal development?

Over the last 20 years, important research findings have been made in relation to brain development. We now know that because the brain changes physiologically in response to the environment, intelligence is not fixed at birth. Enriched environments in early childhood empower optimal brain functioning and physical brain development. Teaching that aids brain development includes many opportunities for active, social, self-realized learning—opportunities that intrigue and engage the learner, but that minimize stress. Teaching that is based on guidance creates the encouraging classroom in which brain development can flourish.

6. How does the teacher create a climate for partnerships with parents?

Before and during the first days of school, the teacher does much to create a climate for partnerships with parents through the use of notes, telephone calls, home visits, and greeting meetings. Initiating partnership building eases the transition of the child from home to school. If parents know the teacher is working to build positive relations with both the child and themselves, they are more likely to become involved. Teachers cannot expect to like every parent, but by remaining friendly and accessible, parents may respond. Parent involvement in the education program can make a lifelong difference to the child and the family.

KEY CONCEPTS

Conditional acceptance
Developmental egocentrism
Disequilibrium
Emotional intelligence
Equilibrium
Multiple intelligences
Private speech
Problem of the match
Scaffolding
Separation anxiety
Table talk
Zone of proximal development

FOLLOW-UP ACTIVITIES

Note: An element of being a professional teacher is to respect the children, parents, and educators you are working with by maintaining confidentiality—keeping identities private. In completing follow-up activities, please respect the privacy of all concerned.

Discussion Activity

The discussion activity encourages students to interrelate their own thoughts and experiences with specific ideas from the chapter.

Think about an academic subject that you personally are quite comfortable *or* quite uncomfortable about. Trace your memories about that subject and the teacher(s) and try to pinpoint experiences that led to your present feelings. Analyze your thoughts, feelings, and experiences regarding the subject area in relation to the developmental ideas of one of the following: Vygotsky, Gardner, Goleman, or LeDoux's ideas about emotions and brain development.

Application Activities

Application activities allow students to interrelate materials from the text with real life situations. The observation imply access to practicum experiences; the interviews access to parents or teachers. For an additional assignment, students might compare or contrast observations or interviews with referenced ideas from the chapter.

1. **Piaget's foundation for the study of child development and guidance.**
   a. Observe two small groups of children in situations where they have to share materials with others: one group ages three or four, the other group ages five or six. Write down a sample conversation from each observation. What similarities and differences do you observe in the two groups in their actions and words? How much of what you observe can you attribute to developmental differences? to personality differences? Compare your findings to text material pertaining to Piaget's ideas.
   b. Interview an experienced teacher about the differences in what three- or four-year-olds and five- or six-year-olds understand about *cooperating with others*. Ask how the teacher would go about teaching the concept to each age group. What are the similarities and differences in the strategies the teacher would use? Compare your findings to text material pertaining to Piaget's ideas.

2. **Vygotsky's ideas contribute to the study of healthy personal development.**
   a. Closely observe a teacher using scaffolding with a young child. Record the age of the child in years and months. Write down as much actual dialog from the interaction as you can. Hypothesize about both the child's and adult's comfort levels during the experience. Did the scaffolding result in the learning that the adult expected? Why or why not? Compare your findings with text material regarding Vygotsky's ideas.
   b. Interview a teacher about the use of scaffolding with young children. Does the teacher use similar or different techniques with children of different ages? Why or why not? How does the teacher know when the scaffolding has been successful or unsuccessful? Compare your findings from the interview with text material regarding Vygotsky's ideas.

3. **Erikson—a link between child development and guidance in the classroom.**
   a. Observe a child who seems to you to be at one of the four of Erikson's childhood stages. Record actions and words in a fairly typical activity or situation for that child. Using the text material as a reference, analyze why you believe the child is at the stage you identify. Based on your observation, hypothesize about the child's apparent progress in dealing with the life conflict at that stage.
   b. Interview a teacher about two children, one who to the teacher seems to be progressing in terms of healthy personal development, and one who is having difficulties in making progress. Assuring that privacy will be protected, learn as

much as you can about each child from the teacher. Apply the findings from your interview to Erikson's ideas in the text about healthy personal development at the stage you believe the child to be in.

4. **Gardner's multiple intelligences and Goleman's emotional intelligence contribute to guidance ideas.**
   a. Observe a child who strikes you as having a high level of self-understanding and/or understanding of the feelings and needs of others. Record actions and words in a typical social situation for that child. Based on your observation, hypothesize about the child's use of intrapersonal and interpersonal intelligence. Relate your findings to Gardner's and/or Goleman's ideas in the text.
   b. Interview a teacher about the idea of emotional intelligence as separate from the traditional notion of "cognitive intelligence." Ask the teacher to discuss a child or two who seem to consistently make emotionally intelligent decisions. What seems to be "special" about these children in terms of their personalities, learning styles, and home situations? Putting together your interview and your reading, discuss what you have learned about intra and interpersonal intelligence.

5. **Brain development guides personal development.**
   a. The section on brain development discussed several major findings and program recommendations. Observe two or three children in a play situation (an activity that is self-selected, self-directed, and self-realized). Record as many words and actions from that situation as you can. Apply two generalizations you can make about the children's play to any two of the findings or recommendations in the text (one generalization for each finding/recommendation). Discuss the applicability (the "fit") between your observations and ideas about brain development and/or resulting program policy.
   b. Interview a teacher about brain development. Ask the teacher's response to the idea in the text that if children experience high levels of stress over time, their brain functioning and brain development are likely to be hindered. Ask about the teacher's approach when a child seems to be bringing high stress levels into the classroom. Compare the teacher's responses with the text material on brain development.

6. **The teacher creates a climate for partnerships with parents.**
   a. Interview a teacher about the steps he takes at the beginning of the year to build partnerships.
   b. Interview a parent about what is important for a teacher to do at the beginning of the year to create a climate for partnerships with parents.

What You Can Do

**Observe and Reflect about a Child's Intelligences; Try Scaf-
folding Strategies**   Select a child who seems to excel in one of Gardner's eight intelligences, but has a more difficult time progressing in
another one. Observe and think about:

a. The child's behavior in a domain (one of the 8 intelligences) in
   which he or she shows clear skill and ability intelligence. Decide
   whether you see more productive behavior or more mistaken behavior. Analyze why.
b. The child's behavior in a domain in which he or she shows difficulty making progress. Decide whether you see more productive
   behavior or mistaken behavior. Analyze why.
c. Decide a strategy (not a script) for scaffolding the child through
   the zone of proximal learning in relation to one of the child's intelligences (as observed in the situation).
d. Try the strategy. What did you learn about the child and the
   process of scaffolding from the experience?

RECOMMENDED READINGS

Berk, L. E., & Winsler, A. (1995). *Scaffolding children's learning: Vygotsky and
   early childhood education.* Washington, DC: National Association for the
   Education of Young Children.
Brazelton, T. B., & Greenspan, S. (2000). *The irreducible needs of children—
   what every child must have to grow, learn, and flourish.* Cambridge, MA:
   Perseus Publishing.
Diamond, M., & Hopson, J. (1998). *Magic trees of the mind: How to nurture
   your child's intelligence, creativity, and healthy emotions from birth through
   adolescence.* New York: Dutton.
Elkind, D. (1997, November). The death of child nature: Education in the
   postmodern world. *Phi Delta Kappan,* Vol. 79, 241–245.
Gardner, H. (1993). *Multiple intelligences: The theory in practice.* New York:
   Perseus Book Group.
Goleman, D. (1995). *Emotional intelligence.* New York: Bantam Books.
Kagan, J. (1997, February). Temperament and the reactions to unfamiliarity.
   Child Development, 139–143.
Lollis, S. P. (1900). Effects of maternal behavior on toddler behavior during
   separation. *Child Development, 61,* 99–103.
Newberger, J. J. (1997, May). New brain development research—A won-
   derful window of opportunity to build public support for early child-
   hood education. *Young Children,* 4–9.
Shores, E. F. (1995). Interview with Howard Gardner. *Dimensions of Early
   Childhood, 23*(4), 5–7.

Wolfe, P., & Brandt, R. (1998, November). What do we know from brain research? *Educational Leadership,* Vol. 56, 8–13.

REFERENCES

Berk, L. E., & Winsler, A. (1995). *Scaffolding children's learning: Vygotsky and early childhood education.* Washington, DC: National Association for the Education of Young Children.

Brazelton, T. B., & Greenspan, S. (2000). *The irreducible needs of children—what every child must have to grow, learn, and flourish.* Cambridge, MA: Perseus Publishing.

Bredekamp, S., & Copple, C. (Eds.). (1997). *Developmentally appropriate practice in early childhood programs* (rev. ed.). Washington, DC: National Association for the Association of Young Children.

Bukatko, D., & Daehler, M. W. (1992). Child development: A topical approach. Boston, MA: Houghton, Mifflin Company.

Charlesworth, R. (2000). *Understanding child development.* Clifton Park, NY: Delmar Learning.

Crain, W. (2000). *Theories of development—concepts and applications* (4th ed.). Upper Saddle River, NJ: Prentice Hall.

deMause, L. (Ed.). (1974). *The history of childhood.* New York: Peter Bedrick Books.

DeVries, R., & Zan, B. (1996). Assessing interpersonal understanding in the classroom. *Childhood Education, 72*(5), 268.

Dewey, J. (1900/1969). *The school and society.* Chicago, IL: The University of Chicago Press.

Diamond, M., & Hopson, J. (1998). *Magic trees of the mind: How to nurture your child's intelligence, creativity, and healthy emotions from birth through adolescence.* New York: Dutton.

Elkind, D. (1987). *Miseducation: Preschoolers at risk.* New York: Alfred A. Knopf.

Elkind, D. (1993). *Images of the young child.* Washington, DC: National Association for the Education of Young Children.

Elkind, D. (1997, November). The death of child nature: Education in the postmodern world. *Phi Delta Kappan,* Vol. 79, 241–245.

Erikson, E. H. (1963). *Childhood and society.* New York: W. W. Norton and Company.

Gardner, H. (1993). *Multiple intelligences: The theory in practice.* New York: Perseus Book Group.

Gardner, H. (1995). On multiple intelligences: ECT interview of the month. *Early Childhood Today, 10*(1), 330–332.

Gartreil, D. J. (2000). *What the kids said today.* St. Paul: Redleaf Press.

Gestwicki, C. (2000). *Home school, and community relations.* Clifton Park, NY: Delmar Learning.

Goleman, D. (1998). *Working with emotional intelligence.* New York: Bantam Books.

Goleman, D. (1995). *Emotional intelligence.* New York: Bantam Books.

Greenberg, P. (1989). Parents as partners in young children's development and education: A new American fad? Why does it matter? *Young Children, 44*(4), 61–75.

Honig, A. S. & Wittmer, D. S. (1996). Helping children become more prosocial: Ideas for classrooms, families, schools & communities, part 2. *Young Children, 51*(2), 62–70.

Kagan, J. (1997, February). Temperament and the reactions to unfamiliarity. *Child Development, 68,* 139–143.

Kamii, C. (1984). Autonomy: The aim of education envisioned by Piaget. *Phi Delta Kappan, 65*(6), 410–415.

Kohn, A. (1999). *Punished by Rewards.* Bridgewater, NJ: Replica Books.

Ladd, G. W. & Price, J. M. (1987). Predicting children's social and emotional adjustment following the transition from preschool to kindergartern. *Child Development, 58,* 986–992.

LeDoux, J. (1996). *The Emotional brain.* New York: Simon & Schuster.

Lollis, S. P. (1990). Effects of maternal behavior on toddler behavior during separation. *Child Development, 61,* 99–103.

Newberger, J. J. (1997, May). New brain development research—A wonderful window of opportunity to build public support for early childhood education. *Young Children,* 4–9.

Piaget, J. (1932/1960). *The moral judgment of the child.* Glencoe, IL: The Free Press.

Schickedanz, J. A., Schickedanz, D. I., Forsyth, P. D., & Forsyth, G. A. (1998). *Understanding children and adolescents.* Needham Heights, MA: Allyn & Bacon.

Shore, R. (1997). *Rethinking the brain.* New York: Families and Work Institute.

Shores, E. F. (1995). Interview with Howard Gardner. *Dimensions of Early Childhood, 23*(4), 5–7.

Trawick-Smith, J. (2000). *Early childhood development.* Upper Saddle River, NJ: Merrill.

Vygotsky, L. S. (1934/1986). *Thought and language* (A. Kozulin, Trans.). Cambridge, MA: MIT Press.

Vygotsky, L. S. (1930–1935/1978). *Mind in society: The development of higher mental processes* (M. Cole, V. John-Steiner, S. Scribner, & E. Souberman, Eds. and Trans.). Cambridge, MA: Harvard University Press.

Weinraub, M., & Lewis, M. (1977). The determination of children's responses to separation. *Monographs of the Society for Research in Child Development, 42* (Serial No. 172).

Wolfe, P., & Brandt, R. (1998, November). What do we know from brain research? *Educational Leadership,* 8–13.

For additional information on using the guidance approach in the classroom, visit our Web site at http://www.earlychilded.delmar.com

CHAPTER THREE

MISTAKEN BEHAVIOR

GUIDING QUESTIONS

- What is inappropriate about the term *misbehavior?*
- What is the concept of mistaken behavior?
- What are relational patterns?
- What are the three levels of mistaken behavior?
- Can mistaken behavior be intentional?
- How does the teacher communicate with parents about mistaken behavior?

BEYOND MISBEHAVIOR

As educators shift the paradigm away from traditional discipline toward guidance, they need to reevaluate widely used terms such as *misbehavior*. As commonly used,

"Misbehavior implies willful wrongdoing for which a child must be disciplined (punished). The term invites moral labeling of the child. After all, what kind of children misbehave? Children who are 'naughty,' 'rowdy,' 'mean,' 'willful,' or 'not nice.' Although teachers who punish *misbehavior* believe they are 'shaming children into being good,' the result may be the opposite. Because of limited development and experience, children tend to internalize negative labels, see themselves as they are labeled, and react accordingly." (Gartrell, 1995, p. 28)

When a child has difficulties in a classroom, the teacher who uses guidance has more important tasks than to criticize (and perhaps reinforce) children's supposed character flaws. For one thing, the teacher needs to consider the reasons for the behavior—a basic guidance technique. Was the behavior a result of a mismatch of the child and the curriculum, just a "bad day" for the child, or serious trouble in the child's life outside school? Equally important, the teacher needs to decide how she can intervene to teach the child a more acceptable way to solve the problem. By fixating on the child's *misbehavior*, the teacher may have difficulty in carrying out these important guidance tasks. The term suggests that the proper course of action may be retribution

How to share materials, as these kindergarten children are discovering,
takes time to learn.

against the misbehaver rather than guiding the child to learn a more productive way of behaving.

Teachers who use guidance work to free themselves of value judgments about the child. They do not view children as sometimes "good" and sometimes "bad," or being on balance "good children" or "bad children" (Greenberg, 1988). From the guidance perspective, teachers take a more positive view of human nature. These teachers align themselves with the findings of the developmental and brain psychologists of the last 70 years. They recognize the yet untold possibilities of optimum brain development for human development (LeDoux, 1996; Goleman 1995). These teachers understand that only with the assistance of caring adults can children learn and grow in healthy ways. When life circumstances permit them physical and psychological health, children are able to find personal meaning in everyday experiences, develop positive self-concepts, and grow toward social responsiveness.

Yet, at the same time, conflicts about property, territory, and privilege are so common in early childhood classrooms. If it is not "misbehavior," what explains the conflicts that young children frequently experience? Young children experience **conflicts**—differing points of view that clash—because they have not yet learned to solve the problems surrounding the conflicts. Effective social problem solving is complicated, and for most of us takes well into adulthood to master (if we master it then). When children start programs outside of the home, they typically are two months to six years in age. To put these ages into perspective, remember that even "big" seven- and eight-year-olds have lived only about one-tenth of the average life span. Four-year-olds have been around for fewer than 60 months. Young children are only at the beginning stages of developing their intrapersonal and interpersonal intelligences, and as they learn to solve social problems effectively they will make mistakes. In the guidance approach, this understanding is all-important. Guidance requires teachers to look at the conflicts that children have not as misbehavior, but as **mistaken behavior.**

This chapter provides a psychological basis for the guidance approach by developing the concept of mistaken behavior. It explains levels of social relations from which three levels of mistaken behavior can be understood. Teacher responses to each level of mistaken behavior—basic guidance techniques—are introduced.

THE CONCEPT OF MISTAKEN BEHAVIOR

In learning new skills and concepts of any kind, children make mistakes. Under the right circumstances, errors in the cognitive domain are accepted as part of the learning experience. Correction, when given, is responsive to the child's development and experience. It is offered in the form of helpful expansion or direction, and certainly is not given as criticism of the child's character. For example, a three-year-old child says, "I gots itchy feets." A sensitive teacher is likely to show acceptance of the child's comments, gently model the conventional language usage in her response, and offer to help: "You have itchy feet; are your socks making you itch? How about if we take a look?"

Perhaps because of the higher emotional stakes, adults have difficulty reacting similarly to children's mistakes in *behavior*. Missing the opportunity to teach a constructive behavioral lesson—one that affirms the child even as it guides to acceptable alternatives—adults often resort to punishment. The teacher may see disciplining as a "lesson the child has to learn," but for the child the only lesson is humiliation. That different, more constructive response could be used may not occur to the teacher, unless she becomes aware of the possibility.

> Inez and Hector were quarreling over who would use a car on the block road they had built. The teacher went to the children and declared: "You children don't know how to share the car properly, so I will put it away." As the teacher walked off with the car, Inez sat down at a table and looked sad. Hector frowned at the teacher's back, made a fist, and stuck one finger in the air. It was his index finger, but the sentiment was still expressed.

The teacher in this case was punishing the children for mistaken behavior, *not* teaching them how to solve their problem. As suggested by their responses, the likely message for the children was that they are incapable of playing together, solving their own problems, using school materials, and meeting the teacher's expectations. Because young children are actively engaged in self-concept development, consequences that result in perceptions of unworthiness need to be avoided.

In contrast, the teacher might have used guidance in the situation, specifically conflict management. Depending on the children, the adult might try active mediation: holding the car and coaching the children to agree about the problem and come up with a solution. Or, the adult might encourage the children to work the problem out themselves: "Look, you both want to use the same car. This is a problem. How can you solve the problem?" (The adult then looks on, ready to use active mediation if the children cannot solve the problem on their own.)

Teachers can reduce classroom conflicts with planning and responsive teaching (like having more than one popular car available). But, adults need to recognize that when a large number of small bodies are confined in a fixed space for long periods of time, conflicts are going to happen. Conflict management is an important guidance technique—whether the situation calls for active mediation or low-key encouragement. Conflict management teaches children that conflicts are not a source of shame, but experiences from which important life lessons need to be learned. Guidance means teaching children how to solve their problems rather than punishing children for having problems they cannot solve (Gartrell, 1995).

In candid moments teachers recognize that when conflicts occur they sometimes hold children to standards that they themselves do not always meet. Take the matter of "losing one's temper," a not unknown emotional state to most adults.

For a special first-grade cooking activity, the teacher planned to have two assistants and a parent come in, so the children could work in small groups. The principal reassigned assistants at the last minute, and the parent failed to make it. The teacher did the best she could with the whole class and later improvised when the music specialist went home with the flu. In an after-school meeting with the other first-grade staff, the teacher's proposal for more journaling and fewer worksheets was rejected. On the way home for a quick supper before an evening of parent conferences, the teacher got a speeding ticket. When she got home expecting supper to be ready, she discovered that her husband and children had forgotten to fix it. The teacher did not say, "That's OK, dear family; I'm sure you had a hard day too." (What would you say?)

The ability to manage and appropriately express strong emotions is a high-level skill. Perhaps the one skill that is more difficult is guiding children to learn it. Adults frequently operate from the misconception that children know how to behave and that mistaken behavior is the result of a willful decision to do "wrong." In truth, the decision to act out or defy is made because the child does not yet have the cognitive and emotional resources necessary for more appropriate responses. Children gain these resources over time through modeling and teaching by caring adults.

RELATIONAL PATTERNS: A MODEL FOR SOCIAL DEVELOPMENT IN THE CLASSROOM

Building from the work of the developmental and self psychologists, Steven D. Harlow has contributed a system for understanding children's social development in the classroom. Harlow's concept involved three levels of **relational patterns:** survival, adjustment, and encountering (1975). Although he directed his monograph to special education, Harlow actually provided a perspective about social development that pertains to all learners. Harlow's concept is helpful in that it also provides a model for understanding mistaken behavior. With Harlow's permission, portions of his monograph are presented:

As a way of viewing children's functioning in the classroom setting, it might be helpful to examine general relational patterns that individual children dis-

The adult accepts children as worthwhile individuals who, like all of us,
sometimes make mistakes.

close. By relational patterns, I mean ways in which children relate to situations, persons and things in the school environment. The patterns I would like to examine are: surviving, adjusting, encountering, all of which differ in their openness to experience, maturity, and their capacity to operate freely.

The most immature and the least open of the relational patterns is that of survival. A child operating at the survival level is concerned with merely getting through time and space without disturbing his established ways of satisfying needs. For whatever reason—perhaps he has learned that his environment is a dangerous and painful place, and cannot by his efforts be mastered—the child wishes to keep things constant and reduce the amount of change in his world. Accordingly, his behavior is extremely stereotyped and rigid. When confronted by a new situation, he will ignore its special demands and treat it as if it were no different than previous situations.

The second relational pattern is that of adjustment. At this level, the child is less pre-occupied with predictability and is far more open to others than was true of the survivor. The adjustor's concern is that of learning what is expected of him by others and then producing corresponding behavior. His sensitivity to a reference group's norms and expectations is characteristic of David Riesman's other-directed individual. His reinforcements and rewards come from the response of others to his behavior. . . . New ways of thinking and behaving are first sanctioned by an individual or reference group representing authority, before they are considered by the adjustor. . . .

The relational pattern of greatest maturity (and it should be added that maturity has little to do with chronological age) is that of the encounterer. Many educators and psychologists (among them Jean Piaget, Eric Erikson, and John Holt) have described the individual functioning at this level. In contrast with the adjustor and survivor, the encounterer is less concerned with security and certainty and much more occupied with what Erikson referred to as the inner mechanism that permits the individual "to turn passive into active" and to maintain and regain in this world of contending forces an individual sense of centrality, of wholeness, and of initiative.

In regard to the teacher's understanding of relational patterns, Harlow is clear that the teacher should not label children by the patterns they show. Instead, the teacher should consider how to assist children to progress to a more mature relational pattern. Harlow states:

> The purpose of the paradigm is to help describe and understand a child's functioning in order to encourage him to a higher level of functioning. Rather than a label that indicates to school personnel a condition of some endurance, the typology describes functioning that is amenable to change. Further, the paradigm permits a child to be described in different terminology, as the situation indicates, for example, a child may be a "survivor" in confronting reading activities but an encounterer during free class time. (p. 28)

Children at each relational level pose challenges and opportunities for teachers. The child at the survivor level is difficult for teachers to accept because of the nonsocial, at times antisocial, characteristics of the child's behavior. Yet, the trust made possible by a positive adult-child relationship empowers the child to progress to a higher relational pattern (Harlow, 1975).

Children at the adjustor level also can be challenging. Daily, teachers must respond to children, who fearing criticism, show anxiety over the completion of activities. Some children put off starting tasks, or don't start at all. Others ask the teacher or a friend to do it for them—or copy. Even when they have finished, many young children show taxing persistence in pursing the blessings of authority. As the following anecdote shows, teachers of young children must work hard to encourage progress from the adjustor pattern of relations.

After much encouragement by her kindergarten teacher, Emily completes a creative "family day" card for her mother.

Emily: Did I do it good?
Teacher: You worked hard, and your mother will love it.
Emily: But did I do it good?
Teacher: What's important is that you like it.
Emily: But is it good?
Teacher: Emily, I like whatever you make, just because you are you.
Emily: (Smiles) Now, I'm gonna do one for my sister.

Children who learn in ways that are creative and interactive learn best.
(Bottom photo courtesy of Michael Crowley, Family Service Center, Kootasca
Head Start, Grand Rapids, Minnesota)

Some teachers are notorious for preferring the obedience of children at
the adjustor level to the independence of children who relate as encounter-
ers. Yet, Harlow's concept indicates that children at the encountering level
are learning most effectively about themselves and the world (1975). As
psychologists ranging from Piaget (1932/1960) and Maslow (1962) to Gardner (1993) and DeVries and Zan (1994) have written, children need freedom to interact and problem-solve for healthy development to occur. The

Harry Chapin song, "Flowers Are Red," illustrates the effect an emphasis on conformity has on a young child. In the song a child wants to paint flowers every color of the rainbow. His kindergarten teacher admonishes that "Flowers are red, young man, and leaves are green." Later in a new school, the teacher asks the boy why his flowers are only red. The child responds with the words he was taught. The challenge to the teacher is to maintain harmony in the classroom at the same time she encourages the *autonomous* behavior of the children as they approach and enter the encountering level.

At any relational level, the cause of mistaken behavior in the young child is insufficient understanding about how to act maturely in the complex situations of life. With the internal need to go forward and to learn, but with limited ability to balance one's own needs with those of others, conflicts and mistaken behavior will occur. Harlow's model fits well with our current understanding of brain development. Children learn best when their minds are not beset by anxieties—when they are not punished for the mistakes that they make. Using Harlow's relational patterns, three levels of mistaken behavior can be derived. Knowledge of the three levels assists the teacher in understanding and working with children when they make mistakes.

THREE LEVELS OF MISTAKEN BEHAVIOR

Mistaken behavior results from attempts by inexperienced, developmentally young children to interact with a complicated, increasingly impersonal world. When mistaken behavior occurs, adults significantly affect what children learn from the experience. Guidance-oriented responses that encourage children to keep trying and to continue learning empower healthy self-concepts and full personal development. On the other hand, punitive responses coerce children to abandon the need to experience fully and to adopt instead defensive behaviors, usually in compliance with the teacher's expectations. Punishment can even create a well of unmet emotional needs and lead to survival level relational patterns; withdrawing from situations, reacting with overt or covert hostility, or showing anxiety (Kohn, 1999).

Adults help children toward healthy development if they regard mistaken behavior as an opportunity to teach and to learn, and if they realize that we all, including adults, make mistakes. The interactions of the adult and child together determine the path of the child's behavior in the educational setting, not the child alone.

Over many years of observing young children in classrooms, the author has noted patterns in mistaken behavior that parallel the levels of social relations discussed by Harlow. In fact, by extending Harlow's concept, a model for understanding and addressing mistaken behavior emerges, one that treats mistaken behavior as occurring at three different levels (Gartrell, 1995):

1. Experimentation
2. Socially influenced
3. Strong needs

Level One is **experimentation mistaken behavior.** Level One mistaken behavior is the equivalent of Harlow's category of encountering. Experimentation mistaken behavior occurs when the child reacts to one of two motives: *curiosity*—he acts to see what will happen; or *involvement*—the child's actions in a situation do not get the results expected (the "experiment" does not work out). In a previous anecdote Hector and Inez argued about a car; this incident illustrates experimentation mistaken behavior, as a result of their total *involvement* in the situation.

Corresponding to "adjustor" social relations is Level Two mistaken behavior, which is **socially influenced mistaken behavior.** Socially influenced mistaken behavior happens when children are reinforced in an action, sometimes unintentionally, by others important to them. Examples include a child's learning an expletive from someone at home, or being influenced by classmates to call another child a derogatory name. Often, Level Two mistaken behavior occurs when an experimentation mistaken behavior is reinforced by a significant other. Level Two mistaken behavior is learned behavior (Gartrell, 1995).

The social relations pattern of the *survivor* is close in concept to mistaken behavior at Level Three, **strong needs mistaken behavior.** Level Three mistaken behavior is the most serious. Children show Level Three mistaken behavior as a reaction to difficulty and pain in their lives that is beyond their capacity to cope with and understand. Most often, strong needs mistaken behavior occurs because of untreated health conditions, painful life experiences, or a combination of the two. Serious mistaken behavior happens because a child is reacting to strong unmet needs, acting out against a perceived hostile and uncaring world. Often a child acts out in the classroom because it is the safest place in her life.

Common Sources of Motivation

The relationship of Harlow's relational patterns and the levels of mistaken behavior is close. The motivational sources of each are the same. At the level of encountering *and* experimentation mistaken behavior, the motivation is curiosity or involvement. At the level of adjusting *and* socially influenced mistaken behavior, the motivation is the desire to please and identify with others. At the level of the survival *and* strong needs mistaken behavior, the motive is unmet basic needs. When a child at any of the three relational patterns acts in a way that is disruptive to the group or harmful to self or others, the child is showing mistaken behavior at that level. In other words, mistaken behavior is an expression *of* the child's particular level of relational pattern in a conflict situation. The common sources of motivation between the relational patterns and levels of mistaken behavior are indicated in Table 3–1.

An important point to remember about the relational patterns is that they are conceptualized around the relative mental health of the child. The same is true for the levels of mistaken behavior. The three levels of mistaken behavior indicate the degree that autonomy and openness motivate a child's actions versus heteronomy (dependency on others for moral direction) and

Table 3–1

Common Sources of Motivation
Relational Patterns and Levels of Mistaken Behavior

Motivational Source	Relational Pattern	Level of Mistaken Behavior
Desire to explore the environment and engage in relationships and activities	Encounterer	One: Experimentation
Desire to please and identify with significant others	Adjustor	Two: Socially influenced
Inability to cope with problems resulting from health conditions and life experiences	Survivor	Three: Strong needs

stress. In general, the conflicts of children at Level One will not be as violent, and certainly not as persistent, as the mistaken behaviors of children at Level Three. At Level Two, socially influenced mistaken behavior, young children may show a lack of concern for others' feelings, but again their behaviors will not tend to show emotional extremes.

Still, the levels are not meant as a gauge of the seriousness of the mistaken behavior so much as a point of understanding for the teacher in responding to the conflict. When teachers realize a child at Level One is upset, their goal is to help the child solve the problem and still support the mental health characteristic of children at this level. With Level Two mistaken behaviors, teachers work to kindle increased autonomy within the child and the feelings of self-worth and empathy that come with it. Teachers strive to help children at Level Three find the trust in relationships and reliability in the environment necessary for progress in emotional and social development.

In the chapters to follow, the levels of mistaken behavior serve as a reference for understanding children's behavior. The remainder of this chapter examines further each of the three levels of mistaken behavior.

Level One: Experimentation Mistaken Behavior

As children begin to master the social expectations of the classroom, the continuous process of making decisions results in mistaken behavior. In early childhood classrooms, children naturally do things to see what will happen, or because they are totally involved in a situation. For reasons of curiosity and involvement, all children who are responding at Harlow's encountering relational level occasionally show experimentation mistaken behavior.

(Level One mistaken behavior as a result of involvement)

At lunch in a Head Start classroom, three-year-old Rodney said to the teacher, "Gimme the bread."

With a serious look, the teacher responded, "What are the magic words, Rodney?"

Not hesitating for a moment, Rodney raised his arms, spread his fingers and chanted, "Abra-cadabra!"

Smiling about the response, the teacher passed the bread. She commented, "Those are great magic words, Rodney, but the magic words for the table are 'please' and 'thank you,' OK?" Rodney nodded, took the bread and said, "Thank you, please."

Sometimes there is an element of charm in mistaken behavior at this level, especially in young children. The novelty of children's responses in everyday situations is an elixir of great worth to many an early childhood teacher. The ability to understand that the child is trying to learn through experimental mistaken behavior is the hallmark of the guidance approach at this level. A sense of humor and the avoidance of overreaction are useful guidance techniques.

Some mistaken behaviors, such as the use of unacceptable words, can be shown by the child at any of the three levels. The intensity and frequency of the mistaken behavior tend to identify the level for the teacher. "Swearing" provides a useful illustration of this crossover pattern. An example of using unacceptable words at the experimentation level follows:

(Level One mistaken behavior as a result of curiosity)

A teacher passed by a child in the back of the room apparently talking to herself and grinning. He enjoyed having Karen in the classroom for her enthusiasm and spontaneity. A few minutes later Karen approached him and said with the same grin, "Shit, teacher."

Realizing the child had been involved in her own word recognition activity, he kneeled down, hid a smile, and responded, "Some words bother people, Karen, and this is one of them. You keep learning new words, though; that's important in kindergarten, but not that one, OK?" He looked her in the eye and she complained a bit, but nodded. He did not hear Karen use that word again.

In the anecdote, no moral issue was made, and the child was not punished for attempting to learn about the limits of acceptability in the classroom. Instead the teacher reinforced the limits in a matter-of-fact way without putting down Karen's efforts at "vocabulary development." Had the

A sense of humor and the ability to avoid overreaction are useful guidance techniques
during displays of innocent mischief.

teacher made this more of an issue, the word's power would have been reinforced, and Karen might have used it in a situation eliciting Level Two or
Level Three mistaken behavior. This possibility still existed but was reduced by the teacher's response. In line with the guidance approach, the
teacher let Karen know that her status as a member of the group was not in
question, even while he addressed Karen's mistaken behavior.

Level Two: Socially Influenced Mistaken Behavior

As mentioned, Level Two mistaken behavior is learned behavior. At the
second level, the child is reacting to the influence of others, repeating behavior that is modeled, taught, or suggested. In accord with Harlow's adjustment relational pattern, at Level Two children are conforming to the
authority of persons important in their lives. Typical sources of social influence—intentional or unintentional—that can result in Level Two mistaken behavior include:

- parents or other adult family members;
- siblings or other relatives;
- friends and neighbors;
- other children in the center or school;
- the teacher or caregiver;
- other adults in the center or school; and
- media "superheros" from television movies, the Internet, and computer games.

> (Level Two mistaken behavior as a result of family influence)
>
> Every so often Matt's dad got quite upset at home, especially when his handyman efforts went wrong. When dad got upset, he swore. In kindergarten, when Matt spilled too much glue on his paper one day, he used an expression quite familiar to him, "Damn it to Hell!"
>
> The teacher heard the comment and saw what happened. She quietly told Matt that she didn't blame him for getting upset. The teacher said that next time, he could use other words that don't bother people at school like "I'm upset I spilled my glue," then come to her for help.

Reality suggests that on occasion many adults use language not dissimilar to Matt's dad. By saying that Matt needs to learn words *that do not bother people at school,* the teacher avoided criticizing sources for the language outside of the classroom and perhaps putting Matt (and his dad) in an embarrassing position. Instead, the teacher focused on understanding Matt's frustration, even if his words were inappropriate, and on teaching Matt alternative words to use.

If the teacher had resorted to punishment, by putting Matt's name on the board or withholding a privilege, she would have made a simple problem into something possibly more lasting and serious. Of course, additional intervention is needed if Matt continued to use unacceptable language. As Ginott wrote in *Teacher and Child* (1972), firmness without harshness is essential in guidance. The guidance teacher is consistently friendly even if the situation dictates that she needs to be firm.

The difference in teacher response to Level One and Level Two mistaken behavior is often the degree of firmness. At the experimentation level, children are in the process of learning new behaviors. Teachers need to appreciate the tentative nature of this situation and not overreact. At the socially influenced level, teachers need to recognize that learning has already occurred and that the course of the learning needs to be changed. Children, like all of us, are more able to change if they know they are accepted, their efforts are appreciated, and there are definite expectations about their behavior. Children learn when they are taught what they can do instead and not just what not to do.

Sometimes, teaching to alter socially influenced mistaken behavior consists of reminders about limits and requests for alternate responses—as happened with Matt. Other times, the teacher works at consciousness raising to help children become more sensitive to a child or situation. The following anecdote involves children in a prekindergarten classroom. Notice the use of a class meeting, which is the guidance intervention of choice when mistaken behavior is decidedly social in nature—involves many in the group.

> (Level Two mistaken behavior as a result of peer influence)
>   Charlie had just progressed from crutches to a new leg brace. Several children noticed that the brace squeaked. By the end of the day, they were laughing among themselves about "Squeaky leg, Charlie."
>   The next day the teacher talked with Charlie and at a class meeting announced that he had something to show everyone. With a grin, Charlie pulled up his pant leg and announced, "Look, guys, I got a new leg brace. It squeaks some, but it works pretty good." With that he invited the children to come over and look at the brace close-up. He flexed his leg for them and made the brace squeak. The teacher then explained about Charlie's leg brace and how well he could walk with it. The children were impressed; the name-calling stopped.
>   The following day the teacher was absent. When she returned, the substitute called and reported, "I must tell you what happened yesterday. Just as I walked in the door, three children came up to me and said that Charlie has a new leg brace. They said it squeaks, but he gets around on it "really good."

The teacher adjusts to the situation, being firm about limits when needed, teaching alternatives, and raising consciousness. Teaching more so than "disciplining" is standard in the guidance approach. Being firm when necessary but consistently friendly is the key.

Superheroes and Socially Influenced Mistaken Behavior
One of the ironies of modern life is that children can be influenced to Level Two mistaken behavior not just by significant individuals and groups but also by media figures who are not even real! The **superhero syndrome** is well known in early childhood classrooms. Children actively identify with the current, most popular fictional character and engage in overly aggressive play. The superhero syndrome is not new—many generations of superheroes have entered and left the scene. In the author's youth, a popular superhero was the Lone Ranger—on the radio! For many younger adults, the action figures of choice were Superman, Wonder Woman, and the Incredible Hulk. The Ninja Turtles and Morphin Power Rangers have had

With friendliness and a smile, the teacher still can respond firmly
to a mistaken behavior.

quite a long-term run, and of course professional wrestlers dominate the
latest generation. The following anecdote is from a student teacher in a preschool in northern Minnesota:

The older preschoolers were outside on a summer day. I was with
some children in the sandbox when I heard Vernon yelling. I
went around the corner to where he was. Darnell was sitting on
Vernon, Rydell was trying to pull Vernon up, and Voshon was
trying to pull Rydell down! Vernon was still yelling, and since
Darnell was rather large, I didn't blame him.

I got the four separated and had them sit down, take deep
breaths, and we talked.

Me: What was happening over here? I heard
            somebody yelling.

Darnell:	We was playing wrestlers and Voshon and me was Earthquake and Hurricane. Rydell was Hulk Hogan and Vernon was Jesse the Body (smile)!
Vernon:	But I was not 'cause I didn't want to be no wrestler.
Rydell:	But you gotta be cause Hulk needs a partner!
Me:	OK, I've got it. You three were doing team wrestling and you wanted Vernon to be Rydell's partner, right?
Darnell:	Yeah, but Vernon wouldn't wrestle.
Me:	Well, we have a problem, because of the "No wrestling with other people rule." (They knew the rule, this was why they were around the corner.) OK, how's this? You either find something else to do that isn't wrestling, or you be one tag team and fight the invisible Phantom Wrestlers, but I don't know because they're kind of tough.
Darnell:	(Speaking as usual for the rest). Yeah, and you could too Vernon. (I left with all four wrestling the invisible wrestlers. It was hard to say who was winning!)

It seems like mainly boys have to get physical in their play. You can tell them no guns, but then they'll use blocks or Lincoln logs. They're going to do it anyway, so I guess you have to figure out how they can so nobody gets dragged in or hurt. The teacher liked how I handled this. Before long the four became firefighters fighting the fire in the skyscraper (the climbing gym) (Gartrell, 2000, pp. 98–99).

James, the student teacher in the anecdote, used conflict management to reinforce a previous class meeting held to resolve a media-influenced wrestling problem. To his credit James did not "discipline" the boys, but guided them to redirect their high-energy play in a less aggressive activity. In the article "Boys Will be Boys," Kantrowitz and Kalb make the point that boys especially are susceptible to the influence of fictional superheroes and have a definite physiological need for active physical play (1998).* These authors recommend that teachers tactfully limit aggressive play in boys— like James did in the anecdote—while at the same time allowing for large amounts of fully active play for boys and girls each day.

---

* Chapter Twelve discusses more fully the effects of television violence on children.

It can be argued that contrary to the conventional wisdom, children who experience much physical activity when young may have an easier time sitting and focusing in the primary grades. Early childhood teachers who restrict physical activity, perhaps from the misconception that this is proper training for boys to succeed at school, may be doing a disservice to all children. By failing to respond to the real needs of children in the class, the teacher may actually be causing mistaken behavior to occur. To reduce peer-induced mistaken behavior, teachers should work to substitute cooperative active play for the more aggressive variety.

Level Three: Strong Needs Mistaken Behavior

Stone (1973), Warren (1977), Honig (1986), McCracken (1986), Erickson and Pianta (1989), and Slaby et al. (1995) make the fundamental point that serious mistaken behavior is due to trouble in children's lives that is beyond their ability to cope with and understand. At Level One, a child might experiment with a swear word to see what the reaction will be. A child at Level Two will use an expletive learned from others to express a spontaneous feeling (that passes quickly unless a teacher overreacts). At Level Three, reacting from strong needs, a child might let loose a string of expletives over a simple frustration, having completely lost control. The primary sign of the strong needs level is repeated dysfunctional behavior with a definite emotional underlay—extreme behaviors that continue over time.

On occasion, any child (or adult) experiences a *Level Three day.* Anxiety, irritability, frustration, inattentiveness, hostility, withdrawal, or fatigue are common Level Three behaviors. Any of these can result from a short-term upset to an individual's physical or emotional health. With young children, Level One situations occasionally generate very strong reactions—children feel deeply about things. The teacher needs to watch for how quickly the child recovers from the upset and whether such episodes are infrequent or common. When serious mistaken behavior is repeated often and continues for more than a day, the teacher should be alert to the possibility that basic needs of the child are not being met.

Two sources of strong needs mistaken behavior operate independently or together. These sources are *physical discomfort*, due to a health-related problem, and *emotional discomfort*, due to neglect or abuse of a child's needs.

Health Factors and Level Three Behaviors   In their concern for the whole child, early childhood professionals sometimes detect chronic physical conditions missed by others such as vision or hearing disabilities, speech impairments, atypical developmental patterns, or perceptual-motor difficulties. Teachers of young children regularly observe acute conditions such as hearing infections, allergy flare-ups, and untreated illnesses. Teachers also have become more cognizant of possible neglect- and abuse-related conditions: hunger, hygiene problems, lack of sleep, pre-natal drug and alcohol involvement, and unexplained injuries. All these conditions, with

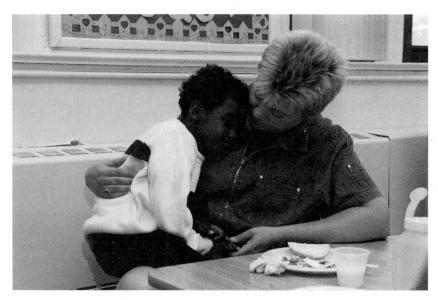

Stress and frustration are a part of life, even for young children.

physical etiologies and emotional ramifications, affect the behavior of children at school. A review process in which mistaken behaviors are evaluated for possible health-related causes is important in all programs serving young children. The process may be as informal as observing and asking the child a question, or as formal as a meeting that involves the parents, an assessment, and a resulting plan that might involve referral.

Emotional Factors and Level Three Behaviors   Like adults, young children experience Level Three days now and then. When these days occur frequently and serious mistaken behavior persists, it is likely that basic emotional needs are not being met. In the classic little book, *What About Discipline?* (1973), Stone discussed the connection between mistaken behavior and trouble in the children's life:

> People who persist in thinking of childhood as a time of happy innocence are fooling themselves. Every child's life includes some stress and frustration and it comes out in the child's behavior. Young children are not good at covering up their feelings or at expressing them in words.

> While most of these troubles fall under the category of normal stress, there are children whose lives are marked by deep unhappiness. Some children have to endure violence against themselves or other family members or the disruptive effects of drug dependency or mental illness by a family member. Children feel helpless at such times, as they do in the face of divorce, illness, and death.

> When people are going through trouble in their personal lives, most show it in other parts of their lives. Adults may be unable to concentrate, for exam-

ple. They may brood about their problems and not see or hear what is going on around them. They may try to deny their feelings but then get into arguments or fights because they are angry or worried. It is the same with children. (pp. 8–11)

Stone complements Harlow's discussion of the survival relational pattern. Harlow's words help the teacher to understand dynamics behind serious mistaken behavior in the classroom:

When problems arise, the survivor unsuccessfully attempts to meet them with generally inappropriate behavior. He may, for example, be prone to lash out destructively or withdraw completely when a problem presents itself. To the observer, it would appear that such behavior is self-defeating—and it is— but it serves the function of preventing the child from involving himself and opening himself to something in his environment that may prove overwhelming. Here, after all, is a child with little confidence in his ability to alter matters by direct action. (1975, p. 34)

Responding to Level Three Mistaken Behavior   When a child shows behavior that is disruptive or harmful, teachers need to enforce limits and protect the need for safety in the classroom. If mistaken behavior is serious, and especially if it continues over time, however, firm interventions in themselves will be inadequate to improve the situation. The "catch 22" with children behaving at Level Three is that although they need a helping relationship with a teacher the most, they are often the most difficult to work with and accept. A reminder from Warren applies here: The teacher must work to build a helping relationship with each child based on acceptance and respect. Such a relationship is essential if the teacher is to guide the child toward more productive patterns of behavior (1977).

The beginnings of such a relationship include efforts by the teacher to understand reasons for the mistaken behavior. Such efforts go beyond the common disclaimer, "He has a rough home life," to learning about the actual circumstances affecting the child.

After five weeks of school, a second-grade teacher noted the following pattern in a child's behavior. During the middle of the week, Wendy showed an interest in activities and cooperated easily with fellow students and the teacher. By Friday, however, Wendy was less able to concentrate, avoided contacts with other students and was irritable in dealings with the teacher. Usually, Wendy was not fully back into the swing of things until Tuesday of the following week.

The teacher contacted the mother who disclosed that she and Wendy's father had separated. Until a divorce was finalized, Wendy was living with her mother during the week and with the father on weekends in a new environment. Fortunately, in this case, the mother expressed confidence that the father was caring appropriately for Wendy. The teacher hypothesized that the separation and the transition from one home to the next were affecting her. The teacher encouraged each parent to help Wendy understand the situation and to assist her during the transitions. For the teacher's part, he became less judgmental about Wendy's behavior and did his best to support Wendy during times of greatest need. Over a few weeks, Wendy began to adjust and she became more attentive and responsive at the beginning and end of the week. Her mistaken behavior decreased.

As illustrated in the anecdote, the teacher seeks to understand what is going on with the child. Full understanding may not occur, but new information almost always is attainable and can help in building relations. Efforts to increase understanding should include discussions with the parent, other staff, and the child. Discarding the myth that the professional teacher works alone, she needs to communicate with other personnel (i.e., through teaming arrangements, staffings, and cross-agency collaborations). The more serious the mistaken behavior, the more the teacher may need to work with others to bring about a positive resolution.

Strong needs mistaken behavior then requires **comprehensive guidance,** a strategy that involves a clear but flexible plan. The plan should include components for: (a) getting more information; (b) building a helping relationship with the child; (c) preventing problem situations; (d) intervening in nonpunitive ways; and (e) teaching the child acceptable behavioral alternatives. In assisting Wendy to resolve issues causing her Level Three mistaken behavior, the teacher informally used a comprehensive guidance strategy. In fact, comprehensive guidance is often used informally, but generally has the components listed previously. Table 3–2 is a summary of how the plan was used with Wendy.

When the plan is working, in Harlow's words:

> What occurs then, over time, is that the survivor's need for predetermined constancy is replaced by a new network of dependable relationships, which are based upon his successful actions on, or mastery of, at least a portion of the classroom environment. . . . As the child begins to sense his powers of mastery, a new self-regard emerges. This self-regard enables the child to open himself to endeavors that before would have proven to be defeating. (1975, p. 34)

The discussion of Level Three mistaken behavior has been developed in some detail for a particular reason. Children at Level Three are the most challenging for teachers. Their situations are the most complex, and responses by the teacher need to be the most comprehensive (see Chapter Eleven).

Table 3–2

Using Comprehensive Guidance to Assist Wendy

a. Obtain more information	Teacher contacted parent
b. Build a relationship with child	Teacher became more understanding and less judgmental
c. Prevent problem situations	Parents helped child understand situation
d. Intervene in nonpunitive ways	Teacher actively supported child during transition days
e. Teach child alternatives	Child was able to show alternatives as her stress levels decreased

MISTAKEN BEHAVIOR AND INTENTIONALITY

Because the concept is new, readers may be tempted to associate mistaken behavior with "accidents" and misbehavior with acts "done on purpose." Mistaken behavior includes both accidents and intentional actions. A preschooler on a trike who runs over the toe of another child by accident has shown Level One mistaken behavior. The accident was the result of loss of control or failure to look where one is going. The accident was unintentional but was Level One because it was a mistake that arose from involvement.

A child may run over another's foot for a second reason related to Level One: The trike rider hits the other's foot "accidentally on purpose" to see what will happen. The lack of development of young children means that they have difficulty understanding how another child would feel under such circumstances. The act was intentional, but was done without full awareness of the consequences, and so is Level One mistaken behavior. The importance of the term *mistaken behavior* is that it reminds the adult that the trike rider needs guidance about human feelings and the consequences of actions, not punishment for making a mistake.

Of course, hitting another child's foot might also be a Level Two or Three mistaken behavior. At Level Two, one child follows another on a trike. The second rider sees the first swing close to a bystander and follows suit, but strikes the bystander's foot. At Level Three, a trike rider comes to school with feelings of hostility and acts out against an innocent child. When the teacher hypothesizes that Level Two or Level Three is involved, she reacts with increasing degrees of firmness while retaining the element of friendliness, which is at the heart of guidance. If the situation indicates strong needs mistaken behavior, the teacher follows up as suggested for Level Three. The follow-up is important because serious mistaken behavior is shown when children are victims of life circumstances that they cannot control. The acting out may have been intentional but the motive was not

With trust in the environment, the child succeeds at tasks that before
would have been self-defeating.

understood by the child. The mistaken behavior was an unintentional request for assistance, not punishment.

Whatever the level of mistaken behavior, the teacher responds to the immediate situation by using guidance. She first gives attention to the "victim." This action shows support for the child who deserves it; lets the trike
rider know the teacher is aware of what happened; and may help the
teacher calm down. The teacher then decides whether to use **conflict management** with the children together or a **guidance talk** with the trike rider.
This decision is based on the emotional state of each child and on the
teacher's idea of who needs to learn what in the situation.

If she uses conflict management, the teacher follows the five-step procedure outlined in Chapter Nine.

1. Helps all parties cool down enough to talk.
2. Asks the children to each tell their side and works for agreement
   on what happened.
3. Encourages the children to come up with possible solutions.
4. Guides the children to select a solution all can live with.
5. Facilitates and monitors the resolution process.

Strengths of mediation in a situation like the trike incident are that it empowers the child who was "victimized," nonpunitively teaches limits to
the trike rider, leads to an honest (as opposed to teacher-forced) reconciliation, and models for both children how to solve problems using words
(Wichert, 1989).

If the teacher chooses to use a guidance talk, she builds empathy by pointing out that the trike rider hurt the other child and that the teacher cannot let anyone, including the trike rider, be hurt at school. The teacher discusses with the trike rider how that child could avoid the problem next time. Although the teacher does not force an apology, she asks how the trike rider could help the child who was hurt feel better. The teacher then assists the trike rider to return to positive activity, which often includes helping the child to make amends (Gartrell, 1995). A strength of the guidance talk is that it shows that the teacher cares enough about the trike rider to believe the child can change.

Whether the teacher decides to use conflict management with both children or a guidance talk with one, she avoids the traditional discipline reaction. The teacher does not lecture about how naughty the behavior was or automatically put the trike rider in a time out. The teacher may or may not request the child to give up the trike, depending on the outcome of the guidance exchange. The goal is to help children learn from the mistake, not punish them for making it.

Again, the value of the term *mistaken behavior* is that it has different implications than the conventional term, *misbehavior. Misbehavior* tends to connote a judgment of character that leads to punishment. *Mistaken behavior* precludes character assessment and asks that the children involved be accepted as persons of worth by virtue only of their being in your class. A child may need to face consequences, but at the base of those consequences is guidance, so that the possibilities of change are maximized. Notice the response of the student teacher, Belinda, when Andy, in the following anecdote, intentionally spills his milk.

It was during my first week of student teaching. Andy was sitting at a table eating his snack and drinking his milk. I looked away for a minute and when I looked back at him, his cup was tipped just enough for the milk to spill out onto the floor. There was a puddle on the floor so he had spilled more than I first thought he did. He looked right at it, then at me, and turned away. When I asked him to help me wipe up the milk, he refused and walked away. Another teacher finally got him to help clean up the spill, but not willingly.

It seemed to me that Andy spilled the milk on purpose. He knew it was spilling, yet he didn't try to stop it. It's not like him to not cooperate, but today he sure didn't. He didn't want to clean up after lunch either. I think he was having a bad day or just wanted some attention. I was surprised that he refused to help me clean up the spill. He's usually friendly to me. I guess I haven't spent enough time with the kids to really know them all yet or how they typically behave.

Andy spilled his milk on purpose, testing how the new student teacher would respond. Sometimes young children ask for relationships with adults in peculiar ways. They need to know if an adult is "safe," and this is how Andy chose to find out. The student teacher reported that as she got to know Andy better, he stopped testing her and began to ask for her attention in more appropriate ways. Andy's act was a deliberate one, but it was still mistaken behavior. He made a mistake in judgment that could have resulted in a fairly serious conflict. *Because the lead teacher intervened and guided Andy with firm, low-key direction, he was able to understand the consequence of spilling the milk (cleaning up the spill), and the possibility of an improved relationship between he and Belinda was sustained.*

A premise in the guidance approach is that even "willful acts" that are done "on purpose" still constitute mistaken behavior. A child who deliberately bites or intentionally disobeys has made a mistake in judgment. The adult who is able to approach children as worthwhile individuals who make mistakes is in a philosophically strong position to guide them toward productive behavior and healthy development. Adults who have this understanding are able to operate from the position of "all guidance, all the time."

Visual Summary: Three Levels of Mistaken Behavior

Each of the levels of mistaken behaviors have distinct motivational sources. Behaviors that appear similar on the surface can be a result of differing motivations, and so be at different levels. The teacher must observe carefully to understand the motivation and the level of mistaken behavior in order to respond effectively. Table 3–3 illustrates how sample mistaken behaviors can be at different levels.

In the guidance approach, the teacher responds to children not just on the basis of the discrete behavior shown, but on a hypothesis about the meaning of the behavior for the child. This hypothesis making is a high-level skill that takes practice and sensitivity. The chapters to follow assist the adult in interpreting and responding to mistaken behavior in ways that enforce limits and teach alternatives, yet respect children's self-esteem.

COMMUNICATING WITH PARENTS ABOUT MISTAKEN BEHAVIOR

As teachers know, parents' views about their children and the subject of discipline vary a great deal: "My kid is basically a good kid who just needs some TLC." "My child can be willful and will try to get away with things unless you are right on him." Much of the expectations of parents go back to their own parents, and to the social, religious, and cultural views of their families. Once commonplace, the notion that children are to be "seen but not heard" has been replaced in many families by less authoritarian and more interactive parenting styles. Yet, the view that children are to be re-

Table 3–3

Sample Mistaken Behaviors by Level

Incident of Mistaken Behavior	Motivational Source	Level of Mistaken Behavior
Child uses expletive	Wants to see teacher's reaction	One
	Emulates important others	Two
	Expresses deeply felt hostility	Three
Child takes ball from another child	Wants ball; has not learned to ask in words	One
	Follows aggrandizement practices modeled by other children	Two
	Feels need to act out against world by asserting power	Three
Child refuses to join in group activity	Does not understand teacher's expectations	One
	Has developed a habit of not joining in	Two
	Is not feeling well or feels anxiety about participating	Three

spectful of and compliant toward the adults in their lives is still held firmly by a percentage of families in virtually any class. As well, some children come from home situations in which parents have not been able to establish consistent expectations at all.

In discussing children's behavior with parents, the teacher first seeks to understand how the parent views the child. The teacher works to be sensitive to differences in background that might make communication about the child more difficult. However else they differ, both parent and teacher share a priority of the well-being of the child. The teacher's job is to make the most of that common ground by remembering that whatever family values they espouse, parents want the best for their children (Gurham & Nason, 1997).

Parents who have positive views about their children generally accept the concept of mistaken behavior and its three levels. Out of an adult sense of fair play, however, parents neither want their child "to get away with things" nor other children to treat their child unfairly. In explaining behavior in terms of "making a mistake," the teacher needs to emphasize that the child is in a developmental process of learning more acceptable alternatives and that the teacher is providing guidance to help the child do so. With relatively mild mistaken behavior, the teacher might say that she doubts that the behavior will occur again but will continue to watch the situation.

Parents who feel positively about their children generally accept the concept of mistaken behavior.

Especially with more serious behaviors, the teacher must be clear to the parent that children, like all of us, make mistakes. At the same time, the child needs to learn from the mistake, and the role of the teacher is to help. Calling a hurting or disruptive behavior "a mistake" does not justify it. Guidance is not necessarily permissive. In the terms of Haim Ginott, "Helpful correction is direction":

> Frank, age five, pinched his friend, Sam. . . . The teacher who witnessed the event said to Frank, "I saw it. People are not for pinching." Frank said, "I am sorry." The teacher replied, "To be sorry is to make an inner decision to behave differently." "O.K.," replied Frank. He went over to Sam to resume his play (1972, p. 129).

Although Frank may not have understood the teacher's exact words, he got the message. The teacher modeled guidance by being firm, not harsh, and by clearly educating Frank about his actions.

The goal in communicating with the parent is to convey a stance of acceptance of the child and of appropriate guidance in relation to the child's behavior. The levels of mistaken behavior provide a helpful vocabulary for the teacher in working toward this goal. If a child is having problems, the teacher also needs to communicate about the effort, Guidance Tip, progress, and achievements the child has made. Parents, like all of us, accept suggestions for improvement more easily when progress is recognized.

At times, parents will be more critical of the child than the teacher. Parents can express skepticism about their children's behaviors and still be nurturing parents. Occasionally, however, a teacher encounters a parent who has overly negative views about the child or unrealistic reactions to

**GUIDANCE TIP FOR TALKING WITH PARENTS
ABOUT THEIR CHILDREN
(USING PREVIOUS ANECDOTE INVOLVING WENDY)**

Adults and children have an easier time with requests for change and improvement when the teacher recognizes their efforts, progress, and achievements. The compliment sandwich helps the teacher keep this goal in mind and is an important technique in general communication (see Chapter Eight). With parents a triple-decker compliment sandwich is the goal.

- The teacher compliments two indicators of efforts, progress, or achievement: Wendy likes books and reading and has close friends. (The compliments are discussed.)
- The teacher mentions the point needing discussion: We've noticed that on Mondays and Fridays she has a few difficulties concentrating and getting along. Is there anything you could share to help us understand this pattern? (Discussion follows.)
- The teacher follows up with another compliment: Wendy is so open and honest with her feelings. We really enjoy having her in class, and like you we want her to feel good about all she is accomplishing.

Compliment sandwich-conferences need to be sincere, and they should always convey the teacher's interest in working with the parent. See Chapter eight for a more detailed discussion of conducting parent-teacher conferences.

the child's mistaken behavior. One important comment needs to be made here. If a teacher believes that difficulties in parent-child communication are posing Level Three problems for the child, then the teacher needs to take a comprehensive problem-solving approach that includes collaboration with others. The teacher works with the family as well as with other professionals to solve difficult problems. Succeeding chapters discuss parent-teacher communication under these circumstances.

SUMMARY

1. What is inappropriate about the term *misbehavior?*

The complexity of teaching democratic life skills leads some adults to the misconception that young children know how to behave; they just choose "misbehavior." When conflicts occur, teachers who focus on misbehavior tend to label the child's character and attempt to shame the child into better behavior. Because of a lack of development and experience, a child may internalize the negative message and act out even more. Classrooms where teachers dwell on misbehavior tend to be tension-filled and become negative learning environments for all in the class.

2. What is the concept of mistaken behavior?

Teachers who use guidance see democratic life skills as difficult to learn, and they recognize that children are just at the beginning stages of democratic learning these skills. In the process of learning democratic life skills, children, like all of us, make mistakes. These teachers recognize that the decision to act out or defy is because the child does not yet have the cognitive and emotional resources for more mature responses. The concept of mistaken behavior frees the adult from the emotional baggage of value judgment about the child and allows the adult to focus fully on the problem, its causes, and its solutions.

3. What are relational patterns?

Steven D. Harlow has developed a system for understanding social development in the classroom, which he calls *relational patterns.* The three relational patterns Harlow identified are *surviving, adjusting,* and *encountering.* Because of a perception that the environment is a dangerous place, the child at the *survival level* resorts to extreme behaviors and may act out as a means of protection from perceived harm. A child at the *adjustor level* has a primary motive of desiring to please others, especially those in authority. A child at the *encountering level* is less concerned with security and approval and more occupied with exploring new ideas, materials, and experiences.

Children at each level of social relationship pose particular challenges for the teacher. In general, the teacher needs to avoid labeling children by relational pattern and assist children to progress through the differing patterns across the range of classroom experiences they share.

4. What are the levels of mistaken behavior?

The levels of mistaken behavior correspond to the three relational patterns. Level One is *experimentation mistaken behavior,* which corresponds to the relational pattern of encountering. Children show Level One mistaken behavior through curiosity and involvement. With Level One mistaken behavior, the teacher avoids overreaction but educates to more appropriate alternatives for problems solving.

Level Two is *socially influenced or learned mistaken behavior.* Children show Level Two mistaken behavior when they are influenced toward an inappropriate act by significant others, either peers, media figures or adults. With Level Two, the teacher acts in a firm but friendly manner to reinforce limits, raise consciousness levels, and teach alternative behaviors.

Level Three is *strong needs mistaken behavior.* Continuing serious mistaken behavior is caused by strong unmet needs that the child cannot cope with and understand. The source of the unmet needs might be health conditions that are untreated, emotional suffering from experiences either at home or school, or a combination of the two. To deal with strong needs mistaken behavior, the teacher takes a multistep approach called comprehensive guidance.

5. Can mistaken behavior be intentional?

Readers may be tempted to associate mistaken behavior with "accidents" and misbehavior with intentionality. *Mistaken behavior* includes both. Because young children do not yet possess the social awareness of the adult, they do not have the personal resources to act "properly" in all situations—especially when emotions are running high. For these reasons, teachers are better served by the term *mistaken behavior,* whether intention is inferred or not. By thinking in terms of mistaken behavior, the adult is more able to accept the child as a worthwhile, developing person. She is in a better position to guide, in firm but friendly ways, toward more appropriate behavior to use "all guidance, all the time."

6. How does the teacher communicate with parents about mistaken behavior?

For social, religious, and cultural reasons, parents' views about their children and the subject of discipline vary greatly. In communicating with parents, the teacher first seeks to understand how the parent views the child. Parents who see their children positively generally accept the concept of mistaken behavior and its three levels. Whether the teacher uses the term or not, she needs to convey to parents that children, like all of us, make mistakes. The teacher and parent just need to work together to help the child learn from mistakes that might be made.

KEY CONCEPTS

Comprehensive guidance

Conflict

Conflict management

Experimentation (Level One) mistaken behavior

Guidance talk

Mistaken behavior

Relational patterns

Socially influenced (Level Two) mistaken behavior

Strong needs (Level Three) mistaken behavior

Superhero syndrome

FOLLOW-UP ACTIVITIES

Note: An element of being a professional teacher is to respect the children, parents, and educators you are working with by maintaining confidentiality—keeping identities private. In completing follow-up activities, please respect the privacy of all concerned.

Discussion Activity

The discussion activity encourages students to interrelate their own thoughts and experiences with specific ideas from the chapter.

> Think back to a classroom incident that you witnessed or were a part of when a teacher intervened. Use references from the chapter to determine what level or levels of mistaken behavior were involved. Did the teacher respond as though the incident was misbehavior or mistaken behavior? Why did you reach this conclusion?

Application Activities

Application activities allow students to interrelate material from the text with real-life situations. The observations imply access to practicum experiences; the interviews, access to teachers and parents. Students may compare or contrast observations and interviews with referenced ideas from the chapter.

1. **Misbehavior, an inappropriate term**
   a. Respecting privacy, observe an incident in a classroom where a teacher intervened. Do you think the teacher regarded the situation as misbehavior or mistaken behavior? What difference did the teacher's decision make for the child or children involved? For the teacher?
   b. Respecting privacy, interview a teacher about common problems she sees involving children in the classroom. To what extent does the teacher seem to think misbehavior is involved? Mistaken behavior? Based on the teacher's responses and your reading of the chapter, what do you think are the main priorities of the teacher in leaning toward misbehavior or mistaken behavior?
2. **The concept of mistaken behavior**
   a. Observe a problem situation in a prekindergarten, kindergarten, or primary grade classroom. Analyze the situation using the concept of mistaken behavior.
   b. The concept of mistaken behavior is a new one for many teachers. Talk with a teacher about the concept. What parts of it are they comfortable with; what parts are they not sure about? Compare your findings from the interview with ideas in the text about mistaken behavior.
3. **Relational Patterns**
   a. Observe one child who is at two different relational patterns in two differing classroom situations. Which two relational patterns seem to be operating? Discuss differences in responses between the two children. Refer to the text to assist you in your responses.

   b. Briefly explain to a teacher the typical behaviors of children in each relational pattern. What for the teacher are the rewards and challenges of working with a child at each level? How do the teacher's comments compare with ideas from the text?

4. **The three levels of mistaken behavior**
   a. Observe an example of Level One, experimentation mistaken behavior. What did you observe that makes you think the mistaken behavior is at this level? In what ways does recognizing this level of mistaken behavior help you to understand the child?
   b. Observe an example of Level Two, socially influenced mistaken behavior. What did you observe that makes you think the mistaken behavior is at this level? In what ways does recognizing this level of mistaken behavior help you to understand the child?
   c. Observe an example of Level Three, strong needs mistaken behavior. What did you observe that makes you think the mistaken behavior is at this level? In what ways does recognizing this level of mistaken behavior help you to understand the child?

5. **Intentionality and Mistaken Behavior**
   a. Observe an act of harm or disruption by a child that you believe to be intentional. Try to analyze the situation using the concept of mistaken behavior. In what ways does the concept apply? In what ways does it not apply?
   b. Interview a teacher about the approach she takes when intervening in a problem situation. In what ways is the approach different if the teacher believes a child caused the problem by accident or on purpose? In what ways is the approach the same?

6. **Communicating with parents about mistaken behavior.**
   a. Talk with a teacher about the approach she uses when talking with a parent about a problem the child is having in the classroom. What is important to the teacher to convey to the parent? How does the teacher's approach relate to the concept of mistaken behavior?
   b. Talk with a parent about the approach she would like a teacher to use if the parent's child were having a problem in the classroom. How do the parent's comments relate to the concept of mistaken behavior?

What You Can Do

Practice Figuring Out Levels of Mistaken Behavior   Observe two children who have a conflict in the classroom. Record in as much detail as possible what each child says and does. Observe and think about:

a. Child One. What seemed to be the source of motivation behind the conflict? Was it a situation that simply got out of hand? Was the child imitating others in behaviors that led to the conflict or in the way the conflict happened? Did the child seem to be "acting out against the world" by behaviors before and during the conflict?

b. Considering your answers in (a), pull together other information about the child that might indicate if the mistaken behavior was Level One, Two, or Three.

c. Reaching a conclusion about the level of mistaken behavior, hypothesize a strategy you might use to help Child One when he is involved in a future conflict. Try the strategy if you get a chance.

d. Repeat steps a–c for Child Two.

e. What did you learn about using guidance from this project?

RECOMMENDED READINGS

Bernal, G. R. (1997). How to calm children through massage. *Childhood Education, 74*(1), 9–14.

Froschl, M., & Sprung, B. (1999). On purpose: Addressing teasing and bullying in early childhood. *Young Children, 54*(2), 70–72.

Gartrell, D. J. (1995). Misbehavior or mistaken behavior? *Young Children, 50*(5), 27–34.

Gartrell, D. (2000). *What the kids said today.* St. Paul: Redleaf Press.

Gurham, P. J., & Nason, P. N. (1997). Why make teachers' work more visible to parents. *Young Children, 52*(5), 22–26.

Kantrowitz, B., & Kalb, C. (1998). Boys will be boys. *Newsweek,* 54–60.

Parry, A. (1993). Children surviving in a violent world—Choosing nonviolence. *Young Children, 48*(6), 13–15.

Slaby, R. G., Roedell, W. C., Arezzo, D., & Hendrix, K. (1995). *Early violence prevention.* Washington, DC: National Association for the Education of Young Children.

Studer, J. R. (1993). Listen so that parents will speak. *Childhood Education, 70*(2), 74–76.

Weber-Schwartz, N. (1987). Patience or understanding? *Young Children, 42*(3), 52–54.

Zatorski, J. (1995). I am a mirror, I am a window, for a child who needs me. *Young Children, 48*(6), 18–19.

REFERENCES

Combs, A. W. (1962). A perceptual view of the adequate personality. In A. W. Combs (Ed.). *Perceiving, behaving, becoming: A new focus for education.* Washington, DC: Association for Supervision and Curriculum Development.

DeVries, R., & Zan, B. (1996). Assessing interpersonal understanding in the classroom. *Childhood Education, 72*(5), 268.

Erickson, M. F., & Pianta, R. C. (1989). New lunchbox, old feelings: What kids bring to school. *Early Education and Development, 1*(1), 35–49.

Gardner, H. (1993). *Multiple intelligences.* New York: Perseus Books Group.

Gartrell, D. J. (1995). Misbehavior or mistaken behavior? *Young Children, 50*(5), 27–34.

Gartrell, D. (2000). *What the kids said today.* St. Paul: Redleaf Press.

Ginott, H. G. (1972). *Teacher and child.* New York: Avon Books.

Goleman, D. (1995). *Emotional intelligence.* New York: Bantam Books.

Greenberg, P. (1988). Avoiding 'me against you' discipline. *Young Children, 43*(1), 24–31.

Gurham, P. J. & Nason, P. N. (1997). Why make teachers' work more visible to parents. *Young Children, 52*(5), 22–26.

Harlow, S. D. (1975). *Special education: The meeting of differences.* Grand Forks, ND: University of North Dakota.

Honig, A. S. (1986). Research in review. Stress and coping in children. In J. B. McCracken (Ed.). (1986). *Reducing stress in young children's lives.* Washington, DC: National Association for the Education of Young Children.

Kamii, C. (1984, February). Autonomy: The aim of education envisioned by Piaget. *Phi Delta Kappan,* 410–415.

Kantrowitz, B., & Kalb, C. (1998, May 11). Boys will be boys. *Newsweek,* 54–60.

Kohn, A. (1999). *Punished by rewards.* Bridgewater, NJ: Replica Books.

LeDoux, J. (1996). *The emotional brain.* New York: Simon and Schuster.

McCracken, J. B. (Ed.). (1986). *Reducing stress in young children's lives.* Washington, DC: National Association for the Education of Young Children.

Maslow, A. H. (1962). Some basic propositions of a growth and self-actualization psychology. In A. W. Combs (Ed.). *Perceiving, behaving, becoming: A new focus for education.* Washington, DC: Association for Supervision and Curriculum Development.

Piaget, J. (1932/1960). *The moral judgment of the child.* Glencoe, IL: The Free Press.

Slaby, R. G., Roedell, W. C., Arezzo, D., & Hendrix, K. (1995). *Early violence prevention.* Washington, DC: National Association for the Education of Young Children.

Stone, J. G. (1973). *What about discipline?* Cambridge, MA: Education Development Center.

Warren, R. (1977). *Caring: Supporting children's growth.* Washington, DC: National Association for the Education of Young Children.

Wichert, S. (1989). *Keeping the peace: Practicing cooperation and conflict resolution with preschoolers.* Philadelphia, PA: New Society Publishers.

For additional information on using the guidance approach in the classroom, visit our Web site at http://www.earlychilded.delmar.com

CHAPTER FOUR

GUIDANCE: THE BOTTOM LINE

GUIDING QUESTIONS

- What are the differences between a teacher who is a professional and a teacher who is a technician?
- How are positive teacher-child relations the basis of the guidance approach?
- How does guidance reduce the need for mistaken behavior?
- What does "guidance is solution-oriented" mean?
- Why is liberation teaching fundamental to the encouraging classroom?
- How are parent-teacher partnerships important in the guidance approach?

As discussed in Chapter One, guidance has a strong tradition in progressive educational thought. Infused by the work of the self psychologists, the approach builds upon the ideas of Ginott, Dreikurs, and others who articulated models of classroom management based on mutual respect. From Chapter Two, the writings of the 20th-century developmental psychologists illuminated the dynamic nature of the young child and demonstrated the need for responsive systems of adult leadership to ensure healthy personal development. The theories of multiple intelligences and emotional intelligence belied the extension of the early childhood curriculum into the social and emotional domains. The amazing findings in brain research have underscored the importance of positive adult-child attachment, and the need for a theory of behavior that directs adults to guide and to teach rather than to punish. Mistaken behavior, depicted through the three levels in Chapter Three, explained why guidance is more than "disciplining children for their misbehavior, shaming children into 'being good.' "

This chapter explores the principles of guidance and conveys the look and feel of classrooms in which guidance is used. The principles explain how guidance:

- *means the teacher is a professional, not a technician.*
- *depends on positive teacher-child relations.*
- *reduces mistaken behavior.*
- *takes a solution-orientation.*
- *includes liberation teaching.*
- *involves parent-teacher partnerships.*

Human motivations, relationships, and behaviors are complex, even when young children are concerned.

Each principle implies definite teaching practices, which combined constitute the guidance approach. Expanded discussions on each of these principles are found in later chapters.

GUIDANCE MEANS THE TEACHER IS A PROFESSIONAL, NOT A TECHNICIAN

In discussing discipline trends of the 1980s, Chapter One took the position that discipline based on obedience is *reductionistic* both of the child and the teacher. When using *obedience-based discipline,* teachers are reduced to the status of technicians, trained to follow a specific set of rules in predetermined inflexible ways. The guidance approach asks that the teacher be a *professional.* (Almy, 1975) How the teacher responds to situations in the classroom defines the difference between the teacher as technician and as professional (Gartrell, 2001) The **professional teacher:**

1. *Uses diagnostic skills to assess the situation.* The technician tends to determine only whether a rule has been violated or not. The professional recognizes that each situation is different and attempts to understand what actually is occurring.

2. *Makes judgments—actually hypotheses—about the situation and takes action based on the hypotheses.* The technician responds in an inflexible manner—X behavior happened, therefore punishment Y is called for. The professional uses a problem-solving approach. He works to resolve the conflict and to teach the child alternative behavioral patterns.

3. *Makes the effort to learn from the experience.* On a daily basis, the teacher makes quick assessments and takes quick actions. Even experienced teachers find that interventions do not always work out as intended. Professionalism means that even though the teacher does not always make the right decision, he endeavors to learn from the experience to improve the quality of relations with an individual child and the class.

Guidance supports the potential of the child to learn as well as the teacher. Although guidance provides no magic answers for teacher-technicians, it offers ideas to think about, try, and learn from—opportunities for teachers to feel better about who they are and how they are with children. Guidance offers the promise of professional growth, which is difficult for teachers locked into the technician role. Teachers who are professionals want to empower the learning and healthy development of young children and themselves.

GUIDANCE DEPENDS ON POSITIVE TEACHER-CHILD RELATIONS

In *Caring* (1977), Warren perceptively comments that teachers cannot feel love for each child and need not feel guilty when they realize this. Warren states, however, that the teacher does have an obligation to build positive

Productive human relations is an essential goal for the teacher.

relationships with all children and to help them feel a sense of belonging with the group. Building relations with persons we don't feel comfortable around is hard for all human beings. The task may be especially difficult when children show Level Three mistaken behaviors, which can be extreme and violent. Still, as Weber-Schwartz points out in her important article "Patience or Understanding," seeking to understand a child is an important step in increasing the level of acceptance (1987). Productive human relations is an essential life goal in a democratic society and an important professional goal for the teacher (Read, Gardner, & Mahler, 1993).

The early childhood teacher builds positive relations with children based on the role that he fills. The role is different from that of the parent whose relationship with the child is highly personal and subjective (Katz, 1980). The unique task of the early childhood teacher is to facilitate the transition of the child from the intense, private relationship with the parent to the more public and collectively driven relationship with the teacher (Daniel, 1993; Edson, 1994).

In early childhood education terms like *removed* and *impersonal* inadequately describe the teacher-child relationship. Adjustment to school is easier for children who feel positively about themselves in the school situation (Erickson & Pianta, 1989). The essential ingredient for this disposition is personal affirmation by the teacher, **unconditional positive regard** for the person of the child (Rogers, 1961).

Unconditional Positive Regard

The premise that discipline techniques should communicate respect for the child (Curwin & Mendler, 1988) is a critical element in guidance. Central to the approach is unconditional positive regard. Unconditional positive regard means full acceptance of the child as a developing human being despite mistaken behaviors that the child may show. While the teacher addresses the mistaken behavior, firmly if necessary, he simultaneously supports the intrinsic worth of the child as a member *in good standing* of the group (Ginott, 1972).

In the language of the conflict resolution movement, the teacher works to create a peaceable classroom (Kreidler, 1984), in which mutual respect and positive communication skills flourish (Girard & Koch, 1996). In the guidance tradition, the term encouraging classroom applies. In the encouraging classroom, the teacher has a positive expectation of productive, caring behavior from the class and shows active leadership to empower this behavior. A key technique in creating a classroom that is peaceable and encouraging is the rejection of punishment as a method of behavior control.

The Problem with Discipline

In the use of conventional discipline, teachers tend to blur the distinction between nonpunitive and punitive interventions. Children who *misbehave* have their names written on the board, are put into time-out, given detention, deprived of class rewards, or publicly embarrassed in other ways. Arguments for the use of punishment seem to be two. First, the teacher sends the message to the child that unless she behaves "properly," she will be ostracized from the group. Second, the teacher is letting the other children know that unless they behave, they too will be ostracized.

Teachers who use guidance reject the implicit reliance on punishment inherent in discipline. The problem they see with the *first argument* is that although the teacher believes that he is shaming the child into "being good," the result may be the opposite due to the **self-fulfilling prophecy** (Ginott, 1972). "Because of limited development and experience, children tend to internalize negative labels, see themselves as they are labeled, and react accordingly" (Gartrell, 1995).

> Early in the kindergarten year, Jamal got upset with another child and punched her in the stomach. The teacher became furious and marched Jamal to the time-out chair. Later in the day the principal gave him a "stern lecture." Two days later, Jamal got into another argument and hit again. As the teacher came toward him, Jamal walked to the time-out chair by himself and said, "I know. I'm going 'cause I'm no good." The teacher knelt beside him and explained that he did not upset her but that his behavior did. Afterwards, she worked to improve their relationship.

The danger with children who become stigmatized as troublemakers is that the threat of ostracism loses its power. These children not only come to see themselves negatively, but they may grow to care little about themselves in the school situation. A vicious cycle of "I am a trouble-maker, therefore I misbehave, therefore I am punished" is not one educators should want to introduce (Gartrell, 2001). Realizing this possibility, the teacher in the preceding anecdote realized she could only assist Jamal if she built a relationship with him. With this realization, the teacher moved from being a technician to a guidance professional. Yet, some fail to make this change.

Teachers who use guidance also disagree with the *second argument*. The emotional climate of classrooms where children are repeatedly reminded of the consequences of misbehavior tends to be negative. Tensions can become so intense that ordinary risks involved with learning become difficult challenges (Kohn, 1999). For children in these classrooms high levels of stress hormones may interfere with normal brain functioning (LeDoux, 1996). As mentioned in Chapter Two, high stress levels over time can have long-term implications for brain development.

A first-year teacher used a bit of guile to appeal to the pride of a group of very active boys in her third-grade class. By December, she had them functioning fairly well in the group and working fairly hard.

In January, the principal gave a staff training in a new discipline system he expected the whole school to use. Names were to be written on the board for *bad behavior*, and children were to be given disciplinary referral slips for repeat offenses. A roller skating party was to be held at the end of the winter term. Children with three disciplinary referral slips were to be excluded.

The teacher felt obligated to use the system and found she was writing the names of the boys on the board quite a bit. A few days before the class party, a popular member of the "rambunctious group" got his third referral slip. By the day of the party, the boy's friends also had gotten three slips; almost, it seemed to the teacher, on purpose. During the spring term, the teacher went back to her previous approach and worked hard to regain positive relations with the boys. She felt she almost got back to that point by the end of the year, but not quite.

Protecting Personality

Unconditional positive regard is a venerable idea that was used in the nursery school movement of the 1920s considerably before Rogers coined the term (Read, Gardner, & Mahler, 1993). In 1972, Ginott gave new articulation to the idea with his "Cardinal Principle." Since relationships grow from teachers' communication skills, then effective teacher-child communication is at the heart of the guidance approach. Ginott phrased his principle this way:

> At their best, teachers address themselves to the child's situation. At their worst, they judge his character and personality. This, in essence, is the difference between effective and ineffective communication. (1972, p. 70)

This principle is also the difference between guidance and punishment.

Cheryl spilled her juice for the second time in a week. The teacher *did not say*, "Klutzy Cheryl, you did it again. When are you going to learn to not be messy?"

The teacher *did say*, "It's OK, Cheryl, we all spill, even teachers. The sponge is in the bucket. If you need help, let me know."

Labeling   The teacher above recognized that "labeling is disabling," and avoided what Ginott calls "teaching at its worst" (Ginott, 1972). Labeling children, either intentionally or unintentionally, has two broad negative effects. First, as the self-fulfilling prophecy suggests, children learn to see themselves in the way they are labelled. The label is incorporated into the child's self-concept and may influence future behavior. Without fortunate counter experiences that tell the child, "I'm not like that," the child's views and feelings about self may be permanently affected (Elkind, 1993).

Second, the label causes adults to focus on the particular behavior they have come to expect. They fail to see other important patterns and qualities in the child. By labeling, adults limit their ability to work productively with children. Every child is greater than the sample of behavior that stands out to the teacher. So much development has yet to occur that the teacher must avoid constricting that development by labeling (Erickson & Pianta, 1989). The ability to value the child as a still developing person who naturally will make mistakes allows for teaching responses that truly are *liberating*.

A key understanding about labeling is that it occurs even when the adult does not specifically "call names." A teacher scolds a child by saying that what she did was "not nice." As a result of "developmental immaturity and limited experience," the child internalizes the message as "I'm not nice" (Erickson & Pianta, 1989). As Ginott suggests, the challenge is to convey to children that although the teacher is upset with what happened, he still accepts them as individuals of worth and welcome members of the group (Ginott, 1972). In other words, *teachers select their words carefully when they choose to intervene.* Assess for yourself which intervention is more supportive of the child's developing self:

"Kyle, you are being rowdy." "If you don't work more quietly, I will move you."

"The talking is too loud. You choose, Kyle; work quietly or find a different seat."

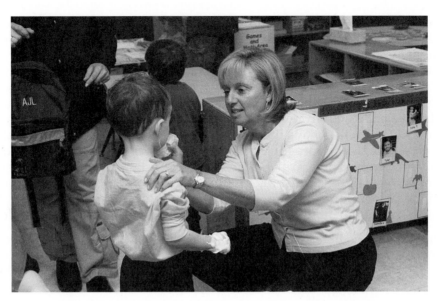

When teachers intervene, they select their words with care.

"Zach, don't you be lazy. You used the blocks. If you don't put them away, you won't go outside."

"Zach, all who used the blocks need to put them back. As soon as they're away, we can go out."

"Class, you are being antsy again. Story time is now over; go and take your seats."

"OK, everybody, we need a break. Let's stand up and stretch. When the music starts, let's all 'get the wiggles out.'"

After a few weeks of Head Start, a three-year-old named Jimmy began to show a strange behavior when he arrived in the morning: He began to kick the teacher in the leg! Sue, the teacher, tried an assortment of techniques none of which worked, but steadfastly refused to brand Jimmy with character references. Finally, she tried a new approach. When Jimmy first walked in the door, the teacher approached him quickly, gave him a hug and told him how happy she was to see him. After a few days of this new welcome, Jimmy would arrive, give the teacher a wide berth and say, "Hi, Teacher."

Four years later, Sue received a Christmas card from Jimmy and his mother. Written on the card were these words: "Dear Teacher, I'm having a nice Christmas. I hope you are. I still remember you. Do you remember me?"

Firm and Friendly   An erroneous criticism of a guidance approach is that it is permissive, sacrificing limits to maintain relations. In fact, positive relations with children depend on the reliability of limits, responsibly set and enforced (Hendrick, 1996). Children have the right to programming and practices that are appropriate for their development and personal backgrounds. Teachers have the responsibility to use guidelines that enable productive child activity.

Individual teachers have their own levels of tolerance and behavioral expectations. Such limits are for the teacher to decide. The guidance approach encourages appropriate firmness in a situation where a teacher intervenes, but it discourages the punishing effects of being harsh. In line with Ginott's **cardinal principle,** guidance calls for communication that is firm but friendly, maintains limits, but still supports the self-concept of the child:

> The teacher who uses guidance is not permissive; she does not let children struggle vis-a-vis boundaries that may not be there. Instead she provides guidance and leadership so that children can interact successfully within the reasonable boundaries of the classroom community. (Gartrell, 1995, p. 27)

GUIDANCE REDUCES MISTAKEN BEHAVIOR

Because of the intrinsic dynamic within their brains and bodies, young children normally come to school ready to learn and grow. When children have trouble in the school environment, two factors tend to be involved: (1) the challenges of childhood and (2) matching problems between the child and the program.

The Challenges of Childhood

The first factor has to do with the challenges of childhood. All young children bring insecurities—the fear of abandonment, the fear of failure—into the early childhood classroom. These anxieties, combined with only a beginning understanding of social expectations, mean that young children make mistakes (Greenberg, 1988). Many such mistakes are the product of everyday life in the classroom—not wanting to share the play dough, quarreling over a pencil—these the teacher monitors but may not prevent. Through learning to solve problems and resolve conflicts in a climate of positive regard, the child gains lifelong personal and social skills (Wittmer & Honig, 1994).

The teacher does not work to prevent all problems, but neither does he manufacture additional problems. The caring teacher may pose *challenges*, but only if he believes the child has a good chance to succeed in the face of the challenges. His role is to assist children in overcoming the anxieties they feel, and in learning to understand social expectations (Erickson & Pianta, 1989). The teacher bases decisions to intervene on the stress levels in, and the danger of harm among, the children involved.

A knowledge of the levels of mistaken behavior helps with guidance decisions. For example at Level One, experimentation, children are likely to argue over materials. The teacher may avoid a needless problem by providing an expanded choice of materials. Or, the teacher may help to resolve the dispute by encouraging the child to negotiate a compromise. If necessary, he mediates a solution or, with toddlers, redirects a child to another material.

At Level Two, social influence, a child may repeat a name used by others such as the timeless, "poopy butt." In this situation the teacher privately reinforces a guideline about name-calling and teaches "nonhurting" words to use. A "class meeting" may also be called, even at the preschool level, to discuss the need to appreciate each other and use nonhurting words. (Greenberg, 1992).

A child who frequently becomes upset over small frustrations is showing Level Three, strong needs mistaken behavior. As discussed in Chapter Three, children who show serious mistaken behavior have strong needs that they are unable to cope with on their own. The difficulties may be physical—health conditions and disabilities—and/or emotional, the effect of negative experiences and unhealthy attachments.

The teacher uses the multistep approach necessary with Level Three: reinforces limits nonpunitively, seeks more information about the child, builds a collaborative intervention strategy, and develops the relationship. The relationship helps the child develop trust in the school environment. The strategy assists the child to avoid problem situations and to express strong feelings in acceptable ways.

The challenge for the early childhood teacher is to be familiar with the kinds of mistakes children are likely to make, just because they are children. By preventing some problems and assisting children to resolve others, the teacher removes obstacles to the child's intrinsic construction of meaning based on successful experience (Carlsson-Paige & Levin, 1992).

The Match of the Child and the Program

A second factor in mistaken behavior lies in children's reactions to teaching practices that are developmentally inappropriate. A primary cause of inappropriate practice in early childhood education is an overreliance on teacher-direction. Pressures for a teacher-directed, academic program have always existed in schools. In the last 25 years or so, these pressures have come to affect even kindergartens and preschools (Elkind, 1993; Greenberg, 1992).

Willis (1993) has cited several pressure points for this trend. One is the nationalistic urge to keep up with other nations in the "education race." This pressure point began in 1958 when the former Soviet Union launched the first satellite, *Sputnik.* At present it continues with education critics citing low achievement levels of American eighth graders compared with students in other developed countries, especially in the areas of math and science (Willis, 1993).

A factor in reducing mistaken behavior is the relevance of the educational program to the child. Musical groups are a part of the lives of many young children.

Another pressure point cited by Willis is the misinterpretation of child development theory to mean that one can teach children anything at any age, if the methods are "right." A third source of this pressure is the notion that because more children are attending preschools and watching educational television, they are ready earlier for academic instruction. The present push to teach phonics to Head Start children is evidence of the continuation of this emphasis.

A fourth pressure for the push-down of an academic curriculum is the desire of some parents to have their children get an early academic advantage. How many teachers have experienced difficulty in helping parents understand that learning is more than the ABCs? A sign of the, strength of these pressures lies in programs intended to "get children ready to learn," or in its slightly more politically correct form, "ready for school." These programs can be beneficial, but only when their emphasis is not to prepare children for an academic life defined by accountability measure such as standardized tests.

Together, these influences have tended to "criminalize" the natural restless responses of young children to a sit down—controlled response "educational" program. Boys, young five-year-olds, especially youngest in group have been thought to "have short attention spans, perceptual/motor difficulties, and low frustration thresholds" (Charlesworth, 2000). Measures frequently taken include having children start kindergarten a year late, or placing them in "developmental" or "junior" kindergartens before "regular" kindergarten. Works ranging from Elkind (1997, 1993) to Bredekamp (1997) argue that programs need to be developmentally appropriate for all children not just for those who can sit still through formal academic programming.

Growing understanding about the importance of development in education is having an effect on how teachers interpret discipline issues. Behaviors that teachers previously regarded as immature and disruptive are now seen as an indication that programming is not appropriate for the development and learning style of a child. This new awareness shifts the responsibility for **institution-caused mistaken behavior** from the child to teachers and administrators.

A basic factor in reducing the need for mistaken behavior, then, is the relevance of the educational program to the child. To further healthy development, the teacher uses programming that has meaning for children and at which they can succeed. In this effort, developmental characteristics must be accommodated by appropriate curriculum and methods. Family backgrounds must be affirmed by culturally responsive teaching practices. As a professional, the teacher works with colleagues to improve the acceptance of these ideas in the center or school (Bredekamp, 1997).

Improving the Match   Within the classroom, the teacher designs and implements programming in line with accepted guidelines for appropriate and responsive practice. He monitors, and on occasion more formally assesses, the match between the needs and backgrounds of the children and the educational program. Deviations from expectations mean that revision may be necessary to improve the match (Hendrick, 1996). Modification of the program to improve learner-engagement is at the heart of reducing institution caused mistaken behavior (Bredekamp, 1997). The anecdotes that follow illustrate how two teachers fine-tuned music activities to respond more appropriately to the developmental and cultural needs of their children.

(Improving the developmental match with rhythm instruments) A kindergarten teacher was working for the first time with rhythm instruments. He held up the various instruments—tambourine, triangle, rhythm sticks, bells, blocks—and asked who wanted to use each. Many clamored for the "exotic" instruments; not many for the rhythm sticks. He observed that some children were crestfallen when they didn't get the choices they wanted, and others pressured those near them to trade.

After several minutes of stock market maneuvers, the teacher got the activity explained: He would start the cassette tape, call out the name of an instrument, and just that group would play. Unexpectedly, the children made rhythms at will, without much sense of either the beat or the instrument group called. The teacher saw that some adjustments were needed.

For the next three weeks during choice time, the music center materials included a set of each rhythm instrument. Five children signed up for the center each day, and all received two or three generous turns with the instruments. The children used the instruments each day while they listened to music on their headphones. After the three weeks of exploration, the teacher resumed the large group rhythm activity but with an expanded supply of instruments borrowed from another classroom. The rhythm band quickly improved its skills, and arguments over the instruments became much less.

(Improving cultural responsiveness with rhythm sticks) A teacher had been working with preschoolers using rhythm sticks for a few weeks when two Native American (Ojibwe) children joined the program. The teacher told D. J. and Cheyenne that they could participate with the group or sit and watch. The two boys watched, then noticed two extra sticks on a chair behind the teacher. They each picked up a stick, cupped one ear, and began drumming the sticks on the chair to the music. The teacher became upset, took the sticks, and told them to sit quietly for the rest of the activity.

Afterwards, a teacher aide who was also Ojibwe explained that the children were using the sticks as their older relatives did, to "beat the drum and sing like at a pow-wow." Embarrassed, the teacher asked the aide's help to organize a pow-wow for the preschool, which included the two boys' relatives as singers. D. J. and Cheyenne were proud to sit with the singers and dance with the rest of the class.

The teacher reduces the need for mistaken behavior by using practices that are developmentally appropriate and culturally responsive.

GUIDANCE TAKES A SOLUTION-ORIENTATION

Referring to child-rearing practices of the past, Berger states:

> Except for a few dissenters . . . most people were much more interested in disciplining children to keep them from becoming sinners or degenerates than in nurturing them so that they would preserve their natural curiosity and enthusiasm. (1986)

Only in the 20th century has empathy for the condition of childhood become a broad-based social value (deMause, 1974; Osborn, 1980). The understanding that children show mistaken behavior out of developmental immaturity and unmet basic needs is a surprisingly recent occurrence.

A guidance view of discipline holds that children should not be punished for having problems, but they should be assisted in developing the democratic life skills necessary to solve their problems (Gartrell, 1995; Honig & Wittmer, 1996). Rather than reinforce the labeling of children as good or bad, model students or rowdy, guidance is about helping all children to get along, solve problems, and express strong feelings in acceptable ways.

Even young children are put into situations where they must make moral decisions. This ability cannot be built through punitive discipline. Only a guidance approach empowers children to build the self-control *and* self-acceptance necessary to say yes or no "because it is the right thing to do" (Gartrell, 1997; Wittmer, & Honig, 1994). Rather than moralistic in tone, guidance is interactive. Guidance requires positive leadership. It requires teachers to make firm decisions. The decisions need to model ethical considerations, however, and be based not on an infallible sense of authority but on an understanding of young children and their needs. The NAEYC *Code of Ethics* (1989) provides invaluable guidance in the use of the teacher's authority (see Appendix A).

Conflict Management

In the guidance approach, the adult teaches techniques for *conflict management* as an ongoing part of the education program. Conflict management skills are critical in a democracy, but the widespread notion that children are incapable of solving their disputes peaceably is only now beginning to change. In 1984, Kreidler's landmark work, *Creative Conflict Resolution: More than 200 Activities for Keeping Peace in the Classroom,* provided a practical guide for a caring community in which children learn the skills of responding to conflict creatively. His text has been followed by many including in the early childhood field writings by Wichert (1989), Carlsson-Paige & Levin (2000), Levin (1994), Slaby, Roedell, Arezzo, and Hendrix 1995 and

Gartrell (2002). These writings demonstrate how even preschool children can be empowered to peaceably resolve disputes.

Although not the most recent work, Wichert's *Keeping the Peace: Practicing Cooperation and Conflict Resolution with Preschoolers* provides a usable construct for teaching young children to mediate their own problems. In Wichert's schema, children operate at one of three skill levels to resolve classroom difficulties. At *high adult intervention,* the teacher actively assists children to calm children, focus on the problem, and move toward resolution (Wichert, 1989). In *minimal adult intervention,* "children define the problem using their own language and the adult merely clarifies when needed" (Wichert, 1989, p. 56). At the level of *negotiation children take charge,* removing themselves from the situation to discuss and solve the problem (Wichert, 1989).

> Two preschool teachers in northern Minnesota set up *talk-and-listen chairs* in their classroom to help their children learn to settle conflicts. They introduced the concept to the class, and even modeled use of the chairs over a make-believe argument concerning play dough. (One talked, the other listened, and then they switched chairs and roles.) A week later two four-year-olds, Jason and Amber, pushed and shoved over use of the computer. Amaia (the teacher) got the children quieted down, brought them to the chairs, and in front of a few discrete onlookers, resolved the conflict.
>
> The following month, when Jason and Amber again argued over the computer, the two teachers held back and allowed the children to take charge. This time Amber said, "We gotta go use them chairs"! Jason said, "Yeah." This time the teachers were interested spectators as the children exchanged chairs twice, settled the problem, and used the computer together.

Views differ on the practice of having children leave the place of activity to resolve difficulties in a relatively formal fashion. The prospect of using the chairs—or engaging in other formal "official" mediation strategies—is often an incentive toward quick resolution in itself. Talk-and-listen chairs provide an example of a strategy that uses props to aid young children to resolve their problems. The anecdote illustrates clearly the direction of Wichert's approach—from high adult intervention to children taking charge.

The Teacher as Responsive Leader

If conflict management is to be used successfully, then adults must be sure about their role in the classroom. In distinguishing the democratic classroom from the autocratic, Dreikurs characterized the teacher as a leader winning cooperation in the one and a boss demanding compliance in the other. In the autocratic classroom, the teacher takes sole responsibility for

Frequently, the teacher waits to see whether children can resolve a difficulty on their own.

transactions and takes the position, "I decide, you obey." In contrast, the teacher in the encouraging classroom is more like a manager or coach who shares responsibility with the team (Dreikurs, 1972).

Many assistants or new teachers find difficulty learning the leadership that is required in the teacher's role. Out of concern for children's feelings, they confuse leadership with dictatorship (Hendrick, 1996). A teacher can be a friend to children, but the relationship must be that of an adult friend to a child. Even democracies need strong leaders.

In the encouraging classroom, the teacher creates a climate of mutual respect. Children reciprocate this feeling when they are empowered to make choices on their own and decisions with others (Hendrick, 1996; Wittmer & Honig, 1994). This is but one reason that play, self-selected work time, is important in the daily schedule. Play not only gives children the freedom to make mistakes and experience disagreements, but also the opportunity to resolve these difficulties as well. The teacher knows he is using conflict management well when children spontaneously use the communication skills on their own.

Crisis Intervention

Young children are just beginning to understand the complexities of social situations, and they feel emotions strongly. Even under the best of circumstances they will not always resolve problems with words. On occasion they need to be rescued from their own behavior. The test of guidance is when the adult must physically intervene to prevent harm. Although early intervention to head off a crisis is preferable, it is not always possible. When communication has broken down and physical or psychological harm is possible, the teacher must act.

In guidance, physical intervention is limited to brief periods of supervised removal to help a child calm down and, if a child has totally lost control, passive restraint. These are interventions of last resort, when harm and/or serious disruption occur. (Slaby, Roedell, Arezzo, Hendrix, 1995). If separation or other **crisis intervention** strategies are used often, teachers need to review their approach because (a) the techniques are not working and (b) the classroom atmosphere may be becoming more punitive than desired (Clewett, 1988).

The difference between these crisis interventions being guidance or punishment is the following. In guidance, removal and restraint are not done for their own sake, but are used to help the child regain enough control to talk about what happened (Gartrell, 2002). These discussions take the form of conflict management, if more than the one child is involved, or of guidance talks. In either case, when feelings have cooled, the teacher helps the child understand why the intervention was necessary, what the problem was, and how the child might respond differently next time. By asking how the child can help make the situation better (not by forcing an apology), the teacher helps the child in a low-key reconciliation process. Sensitive reconciliation assists the child to regain composure and self-esteem, and it models compassion.

Crisis interventions alone cannot "cure" the underlying reasons for crises. As discussed in Chapter Three, a teacher needs to use comprehensive strategies with children who repeatedly show strong needs mistaken behavior. But the tenor of the classroom is cast by how the teacher handles the crises that arise. (Later chapters address in depth the considerations discussed here.)

Learning While Teaching

In 1977, Kounin wrote about "with-it-ness" to describe a teacher's ability to identify those key situations in the classroom that need to be addressed. Discussed in Charles (1996), the term has become a staple in the literature of classroom management. From his classroom research, Kounin concluded that effective teachers—the ones with "eyes in the back of their heads"—have with-it-ness; ineffective teachers do not (Kounin, 1977).

With-it-ness, like other teaching skills, takes time to master, and even experienced teachers can be fooled. When teachers recognize that becoming fully informed is the goal, but that they must often act on less than complete information, then with-it-ness is put in its proper perspective. When teachers miscalculate a situation, then a sensible practice is to recognize both their fallibility and their potential to learn, and go on from there (Hendrick, 1996). In current terminology, teachers who have the ability to learn from their mistakes are proactive rather than reactive, professionals rather than technicians (Duff, Brown, & Van Scoy, 1995). The following anecdote from some years ago illustrates the difficulty in being a consistent guidance professional.

A circus was set up in a large room of a child care center. Different activities were occurring in various parts of the room, including a very popular cotton candy concession. Brian, age five, had a reputation as a "tough veteran" of the program. Brian was standing in line when he was pushed from in front. He accidentally bumped against and fell on a three-year-old who was hurt. A teacher arrived on the scene, looked over the situation, and told Brian to go to the end of the line for pushing. A few minutes later the teacher noticed that Brian was crying. A student teacher who had seen the incident explained what had happened. The teacher helped Brian get his place back in line, happily the next one to receive a wand of cotton candy.

Teachers often have difficulty knowing exactly what happened in a situation and how to intervene. These skills take continuing practice. An important guideline is that anytime a teacher can act more like a mediator in a courtroom and less like a police officer on the street, he is improving his chances of acting as a professional (Gartrell, 2001). Quick judgments sometimes are necessary, but a more positive resolution may come about if the teacher delays action to gather information and collect his thoughts (Hendrick, 1996).

In a Minneapolis kindergarten, Shad, a child who rarely initiated conversations, was using a truck during a choice time. The teacher did not see exactly what happened but heard Shad crying and saw Sharon pushing the truck to another part of the room. The teacher was tempted to confront Sharon, who was looking over her shoulder, but went first to Shad and quietly talked with him. When the teacher got up and walked to where Sharon was, the five-year-old did not argue that she had the truck first. Instead Sharon said, "I didn't mean to." This response allowed the teacher to assist Sharon to make amends. The time taken to comfort had helped Sharon decide what she had to do.

A task of the professional teacher is to develop techniques for understanding what is happening in a conflict situation. Another important task is to be as familiar as possible with the child in the situation. A teacher cannot always learn what is bothering a child, but the attempt to learn is likely to yield positive results. First, the teacher gains new information that may increase understanding about the child. Second, the *effort* to gain new information tends to improve the teacher-child relationship. From a modification in relations, the child may come to see school in a different light.

Accepting Our Humanness

Teachers need to monitor their own feelings to retain consistency in their communications with children (Hendrick, 1996). They watch out for their own Level Three days.

> After a night of little sleep, because her infant was teething and her husband was out of town, Marissa (who also happened to have a sinus headache) modified the plans for her first-grade class. This became a day of more reliance on an educational assistant, soft-pedaling expectations for the group (and individual children), an increase in self-directing activities, and use of an educational video that was scheduled for another day. The day proved long, but not as long as it might have been if she had not recognized her needs, changed her expectations, and made necessary adjustments. Her husband returned that evening and took care of the infant so she could get some much needed sleep.

Often when teachers are affected by personal circumstances, they let the class know. In a caring classroom even three-year-olds will make an effort to "help teacher feel better." (Teachers report, however, that this practice loses its effectiveness if used on a daily basis.) Teachers who keep a list of strategies and activities to help them through physically or emotionally

The teacher gains new information that assists in understanding behavior and building relations.

rough days have shown understanding about their importance in the lives of young children.

Despite the best of intentions and because they are human, teachers too make mistakes. They may misinterpret situations, overreact to a child, be punitive toward a group, or be unprofessional to an adult. Use of a guidance approach does not presume teaching perfection. Mastering the problem-solving orientation is a long process. In guidance, a teacher has a right to make mistakes, but what is important is that he learns from them. The professional teacher learns even while teaching.

GUIDANCE INCLUDED LIBERATION TEACHING

Many teachers have stated that their greatest challenge is working with the few children in a class who are difficult to like—or in the words of one frustrated first-grade teacher, who are "a pain in the butt." In any classroom, some children will be challenging to the teacher, who may have difficulty coping with, relating to, and understanding them. A necessary consideration for the encouraging classroom is that the teacher needs to figure out a way to accept every child in the class as a person of worth.

Children come into early childhood classrooms vulnerable in many ways. Many come from nontraditional family situations or from cultural groups different from the teacher's own. Other children may have "established disabilities" such as hearing loss or speech delay, less traditional disabilities such as fetal alcohol syndrome, or less easily diagnosed conditions such as pervasive allergies. Children may have unusual facial appearances, may be short or tall, or may be under-or overweight. Children may have unique learning styles, experience backgrounds, or developmental characteristics. They may possess a high need for attention or a strong need to act out or to be independent. Young children come into classrooms with a range of behavioral styles, social attributes, cultural backgrounds, physical characteristics, learning capabilities, and levels of self-esteem, any of which can impede or enhance a child's progress in the class.

The professional teacher learns how to respond positively to each child, given the mix of qualities that comprise that child's developing personality. As the most significant adult outside the family, the teacher has great influence. Responses that aggravate a child's need for security and acceptance and that deny growth are stigmatizing. In Goffman's terms (1963), receiving a **stigma** disqualifies an individual from full participation in the group and so greatly diminishes self-esteem. Children come to school at-risk for stigma in many ways. Teacher-responses that affirm the child's sense of belonging, worth, and competence empower the child toward growth. Teachers who do so liberate children from vulnerability for stigma. These adults practice **liberation teaching.**

A teacher can make a significant difference in children's lives by empowering them to grow.

Liberation teaching has its roots in the social psychology of Goffman (1963), the social commentary of such authors as Gottlieb (1973) and Boyer (1992), and the practices of countless caring teachers over the years. The term *liberation* is borrowed from such disparate sources as Catholic theology and the writings of Faber and Mazlich (1974).

The self psychologist, Maslow, has particularly contributed to the construct with his discussion of the dual human needs for safety and growth (1962). Within every learner there are two sets of needs, one for safety and one for growth. Of the two needs, the need for safety—security, belonging, identification, love relationships, respect—is the stronger. To the extent the child feels safety needs are unmet, she becomes preoccupied with meeting these needs and is likely to show mistaken behavior.

On the other hand, as safety needs are met, the child is empowered to address the need for growth through such qualities as openness, curiosity, creativity, problem-solving ability, responsiveness, and self-actualization (Maslow, 1962). In Maslow's terms, liberation teaching is the ability to assist the child to meet safety needs and to nudge the child toward growth.

Other psychologists also have contributed to the liberation concept. In Piaget's work *liberation teaching* is assisting the child to move toward autonomy (Piaget, 1932/1960) Vygotsky described scaffolding as the process of a teacher taking a child where she is and actively supporting her in the learning process. In Erikson's modified construct, liberation teaching is empowering the child to grow from shame, doubt, and inferiority to initiative, belonging, and industry (Elkind, 1993). For Harlow, cited in Chapter Three, liberation teaching is helping the child to rise from the social relations of survival and adjustment to encountering.

An enduring notion of the "real" teacher, sometimes attributed to Socrates, holds that she does not cram students' minds with facts but kindles enthusiasm in students by the knowledge of what they can become. Such descriptions clearly are not new. Why, then, use the term *liberation* when what is being described is plain old "good teaching"? The answer lies in the power of the teacher to affect the present and the future of the child. As the teacher makes the effort to "figure out" that hard-to-like child, to develop a helping relationship with the child, to assist the child in conquering mistaken behaviors and fitting in as a member of the class, that teacher deserves to know that she is engaged in a special process. In the practice of liberation teaching, the teacher has shown not just that to the child, but perhaps the family and to the other children, that this classroom is an encouraging place.

GUIDANCE REQUIRES PARTNERSHIPS WITH PARENTS

In a rural community in Minnesota, a principal informed a longtime third-grade teacher that she was assigned to a first-grade class the next fall. Taken by surprise, the teacher requested that she be allowed to invite parents into the class to help with activities. The principal reluctantly agreed but told the teacher the idea would never work.

By the end of October, the teacher had 75 percent of the parents, including working parents, coming into class on a regular basis. By December, the teacher reported that every parent had been into the classroom at least once. The principal responded warmly. She said she was sold on the idea the day a substitute had taught in the first grade and offered this reaction: Between the parents and the children, the classroom ran itself.

In a commentary in the NAEYC journal, *Young Children,* Greenberg discusses roadblocks to effective parent-teacher relations, including the issues of gender bias, racism, and classism (1989). Greenberg develops the argument that as the 20th century progressed, schools grew more "professional," and parents became less welcome in them—especially parents from cultural and income backgrounds different from school personnel. Moreover, the administrative structure of schools became male-dominated, making communication difficult for single parents, most of whom are women, and for the women teachers of young children (1989). Greenberg defines the resulting problem this way:

If, when they were children, parents had a great many frustrations and failure experiences in school, they may not like schools very much. This feeling can be contagious to their children. It can be true in any family. It seems to be particularly true of low-income minority families, though of course it's by no means always so. In this case, many children feel they have to choose to spurn the family and throw themselves into succeeding at school, or to spurn school success to win family approval. This is a tough spot to put a young child in! Children who have to buck school to avoid disapproval at home are often big-time discipline problems.

In further response to this issue, Greenberg concludes:

> Conversely, children whose parents expect them to cooperate and to do their best at school, and who are proud when they do, tend to have better self-discipline. [The children] are striving to achieve family approval; to do this they must earn the teacher's approval. Encouraging a high degree of family enthusiasm for their children's public schools and child care centers is one of the best ways in which teachers can . . . build children's self-esteem and reduce discipline problems. . . . (pp. 61–62)

For the reasons mentioned by Greenberg, partnerships with parents are integral to a teacher's use of guidance. Building such relations requires teachers to put aside biases and focus on what they and parents have in common, the well-being of the child (Brand, 1996; Kasting, 1994; see recommended resources). Exceptional teachers always have gone out of their way to make parents feel welcome and esteemed. Authorities in the field make the point that the responsibility to reach even hard-to-reach parents lies with the teacher (Galinsky, 1988; Gestwicki, 2000; Greenberg, 1989).

Whatever the existing practices of a school or center toward collaboration with parents, the teacher does well to note two generally accepted ideas in early childhood about parents:

- There is no more important profession for which there is so little preparation as being a parent.
- Parents are the primary educators of their children; teachers only help.

Writers such as Brand (1996) and Kasting (1994) are now answering Greenberg's call for prospective teachers to have more preparation in working with parents and for administrators to give more attention to parent-teacher relations. The child is an extension of the family unit. The teacher who knows and works with the family will be more successful in guiding the development of the child (Kagan & Rivera, 1991).

Awareness of the importance of parent involvement in their children's education is growing in the society. Despite busy schedules, many parents are willing to become involved. They need invitations, choices regarding their involvement, and support from the teacher. With increased parent participation, children learn they are supported at home and at school, mistaken behavior becomes less, and progress in the learning of democratic life skills becomes real.

SUMMARY

1. What are the differences between a teacher who is a professional and a teacher who is a technician?

Professionals use informed judgment formulated through continuing education and experience. They recognize that each child and each situation is unique. They adjust teaching practice on the basis of experience to improve the social and educational climate of the class. Professionals learn even as they teach. Technicians view teaching as the effective implementation of preset curriculum and discipline systems. They tend to react in rigid ways, determined by school traditions, administrative expectations, and inflexible classroom rules.

2. How are positive teacher-child relations the basis of the guidance approach?

As a professional, the teacher works to accept each child as a welcome member of the group. This *unconditional positive regard* does not mean that the teacher is permissive, but that he separates the mistaken behaviors a child may show from the personality of the child—addressing the behaviors while affirming personal worth. The teacher avoids singling children out either for criticism or praise. To maintain positive relations, the teacher practices the *Cardinal Principle,* avoids labels, is firm but friendly, and practices liberation teaching.

3. How does guidance reduce mistaken behavior?

The teacher recognizes that when children have trouble in the school environment, two factors tend to be involved. First are the challenges of childhood. The teacher accepts the fact that due to the anxieties of life and developmental inexperience, in the process of learning children make mistakes. The teacher assists children to learn from mistakes more effectively when he understands the three levels of mistaken behavior. A second factor lies in children's reactions when teaching practices are not developmentally appropriate. The teacher improves the match by using developmentally appropriate and culturally responsive teaching practices.

4. What does "guidance is solution-oriented" mean?

The teacher creates an environment in which problems can be resolved. He does so by teaching and modeling conflict-management skills. He does so as well by modeling democratic leadership skills. The teacher intervenes nonpunitively, using cooling down times and passive restraint only as methods of last resort when communication has broken down and harm is a possibility. After direct intervention, the teacher assists the child in reconciling with the group and salvages the child's self-esteem. The teacher practices such skills as with-it-ness but recognizes that teachers usually do not know all that has happened in a situation. The teacher improves chances for problem resolution to the extent that he can act more as a mediator and less as a police officer. Being models to children, teachers acknowledge their mistakes and learn from them.

5. Why is liberation teaching fundamental to the encouraging classroom?

The various physical, social, cultural, cognitive, and behavioral circumstances of children put them at-risk for stigma, negative separation from the group. A problem many teachers face is how to work with those children they find difficult to accept. To the extent that the teacher figures out how to assist children at-risk for stigma to meet their needs for safety and to move toward growth, he is practicing liberation teaching. Liberation teaching is a necessary condition for the creation of the encouraging classroom.

6. How are parent-teacher partnerships important in the guidance approach?

The teacher recognizes that being a parent is a difficult job and that many parents, for personal and cultural reasons, feel discomfort in communicating with educators. The teacher's job is to initiate relations even with hard-to-reach parents. Although busy, many parents respond positively to invitations to become involved in their children's education. The need for mistaken behavior diminishes when parents and teachers work together.

KEY CONCEPTS

Cardinal principle

Crisis intervention

Institution-caused mistaken behavior

Liberation teaching

Self-fulfilling prophecy

Stigma

Teacher as professional

Unconditional positive regard

FOLLOW-UP ACTIVITIES

Note: An element of being a professional teacher is to respect the children, parents, and educators you are working with by maintaining confidentiality—keeping identities private. In completing follow-up activities, please respect the privacy of all concerned.

Discussion Activity

The discussion activity encourages students to interrelate their own thoughts and experiences with specific ideas from the chapter.

> Identify the guidance principle (listed at the beginning of the chapter) that is the most important to you in your professional development. Relate the principle to an experience of yours as a student either before entering your teacher preparation program or since. Why is this experience important to you?

Application Activities

Application activities allow students to interrelate material from the text with real-life situations. The observations imply access to practicum experiences; the interviews, access to teachers or parents. Students may compare or contrast observations and interviews with referenced ideas from the chapter.

1. **The differences between a teacher who is a professional and a teacher who is a technician.**
   a. Observe a teacher you regard as a professional as he responds to situations in the classroom. Note an incident that you believe was handled effectively. Talk with the teacher about his responses.
   b. Interview a teacher you believe to be a professional. Discuss decisions the teacher has made to assist a child that might be construed as difficult, innovative, or even controversial. Ask about the teacher's reasons for the decisions.
2. **Positive teacher-child relations.**
   a. Observe an instance in which a teacher affirmed positive regard for a child. What did the teacher say and do? What did the child say and do? How do you think the child's behavior might be influenced by such an exchange?
   b. Talk with a teacher about a sensitive topic: Explain that your textbook says that teachers do not always have natural positive feelings toward every child. Ask the teacher how he builds relationships with children who are "more difficult to like or understand."
3. **Guidance reduces the need for mistaken behavior.**
   a. Observe an instance when a teacher acted to "head off" or resolve a problem in a firm but friendly manner. Think about what level of mistaken behavior was at work. Reflect about how the teacher showed understanding of the child or children involved.
   b. Observe an activity that seemed a "good match" between the levels of development of the children and what the activity asked the children to do. Discuss the amount of productive

behavior and/or mistaken behavior you observed in the activity.

c. Ask a teacher to discuss a change he has made to the curriculum or schedule to improve the match between the needs of the children and the expectations of the program. How did the change make the day "go better" for the children, and for the teacher?

4. **Guidance is solution-oriented.**

a. Observe an instance when a teacher assisted children to peaceably resolve a problem. What did the teacher say and do? How did the children react? What do you think they learned from the experience?

b. Ask a teacher to recall an instance when he successfully assisted children to resolve a classroom problem. Ask the teacher his feelings about the experience. What would the teacher do differently or the same if a similar situation were to arise again?

5. **Liberation teaching, fundamental to the encouraging classroom.**

a. Observe an example of liberation teaching when a teacher assisted a child who otherwise might be stigmatized. Focusing on the responses of the teacher and the child in the situation, decide why you believe liberation teaching was at work.

b. Ask a teacher to share an experience when he was successful in helping a child who was at-risk for stigma. Inquire about how the child was helped and how the teacher felt about the experience.

6. **Parent-teacher partnerships.**

a. Observe a classroom in which parents are participating as volunteers. What actions on the part of the teacher(s) seem to help the parents feel welcome? How are the parents participating?

b. Interview a parent who is actively involved in a program. Ask how the parent's involvement has affected the parent and the child. Ask how the parent's involvement has been received by the teacher.

What You Can Do

The Parent-teacher-child Team Something important can be learned from a parent, teacher, and child who seem to be "on the same page" and working together well. Interview and think about the responses of each team member:

a. Interview the teacher. How did she or he go about building the relationship? What were priorities for what the teacher wanted to communicate to the parent? What did the teacher want to learn about the child and family? Take notes and think about the teacher's responses.

b. Interview the parent. What did the teacher do and say to make a partnership seem inviting to the parent? How did the teacher communicate about the education program? How did the teacher communicate about the child's progress in the program? What difference did the child's attitude about the teacher make? Take notes and think about the parent's responses.

c. Interview the child. Ask the child what he or she likes about being in the teacher's class. Ask the child if he or she likes it that the parent and teacher are friends. Follow up with why or why not. Take notes and think about the child's responses.

d. Reflect about the possibilities and problems involved in building a parent-teacher-child team. What did you learn about building a team from this activity?

RECOMMENDED READINGS

Brand, S. (1996). Making parent involvement a reality: Helping teachers develop partnerships with parents. *Young Children, 51*(2), 76–81.

Carlsson-Paige, N., & Levin, D. E. (2000). *Before push comes to shove: Building conflict resolution skills with young children.* St. Paul, MN: Redleaf Press.

Gartrell, D. (2002). Replacing time outs; Part two: Using guidance to maintain an encouraging classroom. *Young Children, 57*(2), 36–43.

Kasting, A. (1994). Respect, responsibility, and reciprocity: The 3Rs of parent involvement. *Childhood Education, 70*(3), 146–150.

Kosnik, C. (1993). Everyone is a V.I.P. in this class. *Young Children, 49*(1), 32–37.

National Association for the Education of Young Children (1989). *The National Association for the Education of Young Children code of ethical conduct.* Washington, DC: Author. (Included as Appendix A.)

Weber-Schwartz, N. (1987). Patience or understanding. *Young Children, 42*(3), 52–54.

Wittmer, D. S., & Honig, A. S. (1994). Encouraging positive social development in young children. *Young Children, 49*(5), 4–12.

REFERENCES

Almy, M. (1975). *The early childhood educator at work.* New York: McGraw Hill Book Company.

Berger, S. K. (1986). *The developing person through childhood and adolescence.* New York: Worth Publishers, Inc.

Boyer, E. L. (1992). *Ready to learn: A mandate to the nation.* The Carnegie Foundation for the Advancement of Teaching.

Brand, S. (1996). Making parent involvement a reality: Helping teachers develop partnerships with parents. *Young Children, 51*(2), 76–81.

Bredekamp, S. (1997). *Developmentally appropriate practice in early childhood programs* (3rd ed.). Washington, DC: National Association for the Education of Young Children.

Carlsson-Paige, N., & Levin, D. E. (2000). Before push comes to shove, St. Paul: Redleaf Press.

Charles, C. M. (1996). *Building classroom discipline.* White Plains, NY: Longman, Inc.

Charlesworth, R. (1989). 'Behind' before they start? Deciding how to deal with the risk of kindergarten 'failure.' *Young Children, 44*(3), 5–13.

Charlesworth, R. (2000). *Understanding child development* (5th ed.). Clifton Park, NY: Delmar Learning.

Clewett, A. S. (1988). Guidance and discipline: Teaching young children appropriate behavior. *Young Children, 43*(4), 26–31.

Curwin, R. L., & Mendler, A. N. (1988). *Discipline with dignity.* Alexandria, VA: Association for Supervision and Curriculum Development.

Daniel, J. E. (1993). Infants to toddlers: Qualities of effective transitions. *Young Children, 48*(6), 16–21.

de Mause, L., ed. (1974). *The history of childhood.* New York: Peter Bedrick Books.

Dreikurs, R. (1972). *Discipline without tears.* New York: Hawthorn Press Books, Inc., Publishers.

Duff, R. E., Brown, M. H., & Van Scoy, I. J. (1995). Reflection and self-evaluation: Keys to professional development. *Young Children, 50*(4), 81–88.

Edson, A. (1994). Crossing the great divide: The nursery school child goes to kindergarten. *Young Children, 49*(5), 69–75.

Elkind, D. (1993). *Images of the young child.* Washington, DC: NAEYC.

Elkind, D. (1997, November). The death of child nature. Education in the postmodern world. *Phi Delta Kappan,* 241–245.

Erickson, M. F., & Pianta, R. C. (1989). New lunch box, old feelings: What kids bring to school. *Early Education and Development, 1*(1), 35–49.

Faber, A., & Mazlich, E. (1974). *Liberated parents, liberated children.* New York: Avon Books.

Galinsky, E. (1988). Parents and teacher-caregivers: Sources of tension, sources of support. *Young Children, 43*(4), 4–12.

Gartrell, D. J. (1995). Misbehavior or mistaken behavior? *Young Children, 50*(5), 27–34.

Gartrell, D. J. (1997). Beyond discipline to guidance. *Young Children, 52*(6), 34–42.

Gartrell, D. J. (2001). Replacing time-out: Part One—Using Guidance to build an encouraging classroom, *Young Children 56*(6), 8–16.

Gartrell, D. J. (2002). Replacing time-out. Part Two—Using guidance to maintain the encouraging classroom. *Young Children, 57*(2), 36–43.

Gestwicki, C. (2000). *Home, school, and community relations: A guide to working with parents* (4th ed.). Clifton Park, NY: Delmar Learning.

Ginott, H. G. (1972). *Teacher and child.* New York: Avon Books.

Girard, K., & Koch, S. J. (1996). *Conflict resolution in the schools: A manual for educators.* San Francisco: Jossey-Bass Publishers.

Goffman, E. (1963). *Stigma.* Englewood Cliffs, NJ: Prentice-Hall.

Gottlieb, D. (Ed.). (1973). *Children's liberation.* Englewood Cliffs, NJ: Prentice-Hall.

Greenberg, P. (1988). Avoiding 'Me against you' discipline. *Young Children, 43*(1), 24–31.

Greenberg, P. (1989). Parents as partners in young children's development and education: A new American fad? Why does it matter? *Young Children, 44*(4), 61–75.

Greenberg, P. (1992). Why not academic preschool? Part 2. Autocracy or democracy in the classroom. *Young Children, 47*(3), 54–64.

Hendrick, J. (1996). *Whole child.* Columbus, OH: Merrill/Macmillan.

Honig, A. S., & Wittmer, D. S. (1996). Helping children become more pro social: Ideas for classrooms, families, schools, and communities, Part 2. *Young Children, 51*(2), 62–70.

Kagan, S. L., & Rivera, A. M. (1991). Collaboration in early care and education: What can and should we expect? *Young Children, 46*(1), 51–56.

Kasting, A. (1994). Respect, responsibility, and reciprocity: The 3Rs of parent involvement. *Childhood Education, 70*(3), 146–150.

Katz, L. G. (1980). Mothering and teaching—Some significant distinctions. In L. G. Katz (Ed.), *Current topics in early childhood education.* Norwood, NJ: Ablex Publishing Corp.

Kohn, A. (1999). *Punished by rewards.* Bridgewaker, NJ: Replica Books.

Kounin, J. (1977). *Discipline and group management in classrooms.* New York: Holt, Rinehart and Winston.

Kreidler, W. J. (1984). *Creative conflict resolution: More than 200 activities for keeping peace in the classroom.* Glencoe, IL: Scott, Foresman.

Levin, D. E. (1994). *Teaching children in violent times: Building a peaceable classroom.* Cambridge, MA: Educators for Social Responsibility.

LeDoux, J. (1996). *The emotional brain.* New York: Simon & Shuster.

Mazlow, A. H. (1962). *Toward a psychology of being.* Princeton, NJ: Van Nostrand Company.

National Association for the Education of Young Children (1989). *The National Association for the Education of Young Children code of ethical conduct.* Washington, DC: Author.

Osborn, D. K., & Osborn, J. D. (1989). *Discipline and classroom management.* Athens, GA: Daye Press, Inc.

Piaget, J. (1932/1960). *The moral judgment of the child.* Glencoe, IL: The Free Press.

Read, K. H., Gardner, P., & Mahler, B. C. (1993). *Early childhood programs: Human relationships and learning.* Fort Worth, TX: Harcourt Brace Jovanovich College Publishers.

Rogers, C. R. (1961). On becoming a Person. Boston, MA: Houghton Mifflin, Co.

Slaby, R. G., Roedell, W. C., Arezzo, D., & Hendrix, K. (1995). *Early violence prevention: Tools for teachers of young children.* Washington, DC: National Association for the Education of Young Children.

Warren, R. (1977). *Caring.* Washington, DC: National Association for the Education of Young Children.

Weber-Schwartz, N. (1987). Patience or understanding. *Young Children, 42*(3), 52–54.

Wichert, S. (1989). *Keeping the peace: Practicing cooperation and conflict resolution with preschoolers.* Santa Cruz, CA: New Society Publishers.

Willis, S. (1993, November). Teaching young children: Educators seek 'developmental appropriateness.' *Curriculum Update,* 1–8.

Wittmer, D. S., & Honig, A. S. (1994). Encouraging positive social development in young children. *Young Children, 49*(5), 4–12.

For additional information on using the guidance approach in the classroom, visit our Web site at http://www.earlychilded.delmar.com

Building the Encouraging Classroom

PREVIEWS

CHAPTER FIVE

ORGANIZING THE ENCOURAGING CLASSROOM

GUIDING QUESTIONS

- What is an encouraging classroom?
- How does developmentally appropriate practice contribute to the encouraging classroom?
- How does physical layout make the classroom encouraging?
- How does thematic instruction at the primary grade level illustrate the encouraging classroom at work?
- How does the teacher encourage parents to be classroom volunteers?

P art One established guidance as the approach of choice in working for the healthy personal development of young children. Part Two develops the affective and cognitive environment in which guidance is used, the encouraging classroom. As the lead chapter in the unit, Chapter Five:

- defines the encouraging classroom.
- explains how developmentally appropriate practice is essential for the encouraging classroom.
- demonstrates how the physical layout supports the encouraging classroom.
- illustrates how thematic instruction at the primary grade level exemplifies the encouraging classroom.
- offers suggestions for encouraging parents to volunteer in the classroom.

Other chapters in this part address management of the encouraging classroom and the teacher's use of leadership skills with the group and the individual.

THE ENCOURAGING CLASSROOM

In *What the Kids Said Today* Gartrell discusses the encouraging classroom (2000). With a few adaptations, that discussion follows: The encouraging classroom is a place where children want to be even when they are sick, as opposed to not wanting to be there when they are well. It is a place where children feel at home when they are out of the home (Gartrell, 2000, p. 171). A textbook definition of an encouraging classroom is:

> The physical surrounds of a school, center or family child care program in which adults provide ongoing guidance in order to maintain an equilibrium between the needs of each developing member and the right of the learning community for mutual appreciation among its members. It involves the creation and sustenance of a caring community among children and adults for the purpose of furthering the learning and development of each member. (Gartrell, 2000, p. 171)

The encouraging classroom begins within the minds of its teachers. In the encouraging classroom, teachers work hard to sustain the dynamic balance between the changing needs of each individual (adults and children) and the right of the community for mutual appreciation—"of each other and yourself too." The equilibrium between the individual and the group is difficult to maintain because young children, with only months of total development and experience, still have trouble expressing and meeting their needs. Remember that expressing and meeting individual needs in socially acceptable ways are long-term democratic life skills. We work on these skills our entire lives. Young children are just starting this life's work (Gartrell, 2000, pp. 171–172).

In an encouraging classroom a teacher guides children to a good start even, and especially, when children make mistakes in the learning process—when they show mistaken behavior. Guidance, which is the approach teachers use to build the encouraging classroom, actively teaches children to express and meet needs acceptably. Unlike teachers who use traditional punitive discipline, in a guidance approach teachers do not threaten the child's membership in the community—such as with time-outs or suspension—to "motivate" better behavior. Instead, they build a positive relationship to ensure the child's acceptance in the class and provide freedom, within limits, to allow the child to relax and to grow. These teachers give the child positive reason to resolve problems peaceably. The child's place in the classroom community, except in rare situations that involve parents and usually other professionals, is not up for discussion (Gartrell, 2000, p. 172).

DEVELOPMENTALLY APPROPRIATE PRACTICE AND THE ENCOURAGING CLASSROOM

A current nationwide trend is "educational accountability," which means teachers need to be accountable for the education they are providing. Unlike more simple times in the past, we now are hearing terms of educational accountability used even in early childhood classrooms. Increasingly, early childhood teachers are familiar with words like "Work Sampling," "portfolios," "observational assessment," "anecdotal observations," and "out-

Informal pairings of "neighbors" for projects is one example
of multidimensional grouping.

come attainment." Educational accountability is vital at all levels of education, including in early childhood. One good that has come out of this movement is Developmentally Appropriate Practice (DAP), a priority of the NAEYC (Bredekamp & Copple, 1997).

A danger in the trend, however, is the confusion of **educational accountability** with **political accountability.** When officials put inappropriate pressures on schools and programs to "achieve," for the sake of reputation and appearances, they put both teachers and children at-risk. A main symptom of political accountability, the ever-increasing emphasis on testing, has pushed down academic lessons and reduced child-directed learning and play (Gartrell, 2000). As in the 1980s, teachers are again expecting too much of children and are using forced instructional techniques (Elkind, 1997).

Common inappropriate practices—such as long periods of sitting and listening, prescribed activities done to exacting standards, critical evaluation of children's work, and teacher-child communications that stigmatize— invite mistaken behavior. With the imposition of developmentally inappropriate practice, children become less able to meet teacher expectations. They

The presence of an intrinsic dynamic for learning is a given in the guidance approach.

Table 4–1

Increasing Appropriate Practice to Reduce Mistaken Behavior

Moving from Inappropriate Practice	To Appropriate Practice	Reduces Mistaken Behavior
Prolonged sitting and listening in large groups	Active, concise large groups; increased use of small groups	Restlessness, bothering neighbors, confrontation with adults
Prescribed activities done to exacting standards	Child-choice, creative, "no one right answer" activities	Acting out of feelings of failure, frustration, inferiority, boredom
Critical evaluation of children's work	Supportive evaluation of children's work	Mix of reactions to lowering of self-esteem
Ostracism of some children due to mistaken behavior	Acceptance of all children as group members	Acting out of feelings of rejection

experience frustration, resentment, and a sense of failure. Brain functioning and development may be affected (LeDoux, 1996). An encouraging classroom becomes difficult under these circumstances (Gartrell, 2000).

In the encouraging classroom, a professional teacher works to maximize children's engagement in the learning process. Such methods as integrated curriculum, daily child-chosen activities, creative art and journals (even before they can write conventional script or spell), manipulatives-based math, diverse small-group experiences, and active, concise large-group sessions allow children to find meaning and success in learning experiences (Brewer, 2000). Utilizing such practices, Table 4–1 illustrates how DAP can reduce mistaken behaviors.

School Readiness and Play

The NAEYC drafted its position statement on school readiness in July of 1990 and revised it in July 1995. In response to its adoption of the National Education Goals, specifically, "by the year 2000, all children will start school ready to learn," NAEYC maintains the following about **school readiness:**

1. Inequities in early life experiences should be addressed so that all children have access to the opportunities that promote school success;
2. Individual differences are recognized and supported among children including linguistic and cultural differences; and
3. Reasonable and appropriate expectations of children's capabilities are established upon school entry (NAEYC, 1995).

NAEYC also addresses school readiness in its Code of Ethical Conduct (see Appendix A). The NAEYC Code of Ethics, Ideals I-1.2 and I-1.5 state that it is essential:

- To base program practices upon current knowledge in the field of child development and related disciplines and upon particular knowledge of each child (I-1.2).
- To create and maintain safe and healthy settings that foster children's social, emotional, intellectual, and physical development and that respect their dignity and their contributions (I-1.5) (NAEYC code as cited in Feeney & Kipnis, 1999).

Current knowledge of child development and learning (discussed in Chapter Two) indicates that early education should be focused on the attainment of life skills outcomes pertaining to the whole child rather than on narrowly focused academic preparation. The premature introduction of academics is counter to this philosophy (Charlesworth, 1998). *Significant* learning (when the child constructs new personal meaning from the experience) has always been a part of early childhood education, but we now know definitively that such learning maximizes healthy brain development and the cultivation of multiple intelligences.

In this regard, an argument of Jean Piaget has stood the test of time. Piaget argued that the early years are "critical for determining whether the child would become a passive learner, mastering everything by rote, or become an active learner who gains new information by discovery and invention" (Elkind, 1993, p. 81). If we want children who are active learners, who construct significant learning, who are intrinsically motivated to learn, and who see themselves as capable learners, we must approach the teaching of young children in developmentally appropriate ways, a central component of which is play:

> Three kindergarten children are working hard at playing house. The children are Rachel, Jeremiah (Mia), and Sarah. Rachel is preparing a meal in the kitchen. She is wearing an apron and cooking on the stove with a frying pan.
>
> "Good morning, Honey," said Rachel as she smiled at Mia and continued to cook.
>
> "Good morning to you, Cupcake," said Mia as he walked up to Sarah. Mia asked, "How is our big girl doing today?"
>
> "Fine, Daddy," said Sarah as she held her baby doll.
>
> "Breakfast is ready, have Sarah sit down and it is time to eat," said Rachel. Rachel made a motion to have them sit and they did. I noticed that Sarah dropped her baby doll and started drinking

from a glass instead of the sipper cup that was on the table. Both Mia and Sarah were sitting at the kitchen table being served by Mom. Then they all said a prayer and began to eat.

"I'm filled," said Mia, "I am late for work." Mia grabbed a hard hat out of the toy box and he also gave Rachel a kiss good-bye (which was promptly wiped off!). When Mia was gone, Rachel started to clear the table, putting the dishes in the sink. Sarah walked over to the baby doll she had dropped and picked it up. She began holding the doll in her arms and wanted Mommy (Rachel) to play with her.

"I have to finish the dishes before I can go out and play," said Rachel.

"I want to play with you now," demanded Sarah.

"Barney is on now, go and watch him," said Rachel. Rachel continued to wash the dishes and Sarah went over to the TV and watched Barney. Mia also headed into the kitchen area; he had been just wandering around and fixing things in the playroom.

"Honey, I'm home," said Mia.

"You're home early," said Rachel. "Go back to work, I'm not done yet."

"I'm bored. I'm going to play with something different now," said Mia. All three children then left and found something else to do (Gartrell, 2000, p. 30).

Despite "typical family stereotypes," this anecdote is notable for the detail these kindergartners brought to the family situation—so much cognitive, language, social, emotional, and even physical learning comes from dramatic play like this. The anecdote is also notable because Arlene, the observing student, indicated that all three of the children came from single-parent families (Gartrell, 2000). Through play children expand their understanding about the world; sometimes imagining roles and situations that they may have little direct experience with.

One standard of developmentally appropriate early childhood classrooms is the inclusion of large amounts of play. These programs employ administrators and teachers who understand the importance of play in the development of children, ages birth through eight, and incorporate large amounts of play in their programming (Bredekamp & Copple, 1997). It behooves school districts to include play in the classrooms of young children and to hire teachers in preschool through third grade who understand how young children learn; practice and incorporate strategies in their classrooms that support significant learning; and recognize that those same strategies will create competent lifelong learners (Gronlund, 1995).

The gains possible through self-directing/open-ended activity (play) help children feel
positively about themselves in the classroom situation.

DAP in the Primary Grades

In many elementary schools, support is growing for teachers to use DAP to *supplement and modify* the traditional academic program. Such practices as integrated curriculum, outcomes-driven education, cooperative learning groups, teaching teams, and authentic assessment allow teachers to be fully professional and classroom practices to become developmentally appropriate (Bredekamp, 1992). In many schools, however, these changes have taken courage and ingenuity on the part of individual teachers.

> (Kindergarten). Despite a kindergarten teacher's statements that it was not developmentally appropriate, a principal decided that a worksheet-based arithmetic system had to be used. Being tenured and known as an individual, Ms. Cortez decided she would use the worksheets but in her own way. On the last Friday of each month, the class had a worksheet party. The teacher made plenty of popcorn, and everyone did worksheets. Having used manipulatives to teach the targeted math concepts during the month, Ms. Cortez reported that the children "whipped through the sheets, had fun doing them and took lots of papers home."

> (First Grade). Mr. Kelly, a first-grade teacher, felt compelled to use the basal series adopted by the school district but found that the reading program did not reinforce the children's excitement about learning to read. He supplemented the reading program with "super silent reading" times when he and the children read self-selected books. He introduced "just journaling and jotting" times, when he and the children recorded their own thoughts and feelings in journals. When Mr. Kelly discovered children reading and journaling *other* parts of the day, he concluded he now had an *emergent literacy program* that met his expectations.

Like the teachers in the anecdotes, for years individual teachers have been "psychologizing" the curriculum, as Dewey termed it (1900/1969). Many teachers have had to do so quietly, behind closed doors. Some—usually after receiving tenure—have done their own thing openly and endured the label from colleagues of being that "offbeat one at the end of the hall." As one teacher, known for being creative, commented, "I do as little of what I have to do and as much as I can of what I want to do in order to stay out of serious trouble." It is to be hoped that times are beginning to change.

Working Together for Change

Often, a committee can make a request for curriculum modification seem more studied and objective than an individual teacher. For this reason, two or more teachers who attend a workshop, conference, or course together may be successful in introducing developmentally appropriate practices into a school. When all teachers at a grade level, for instance, feel strongly about the need to modify practice, they may succeed by working together.

Tact, civility, and communication—starting with the modifications that are most feasible—are the watchwords. As textbook salespersons and inspirational speakers have long known, educators tend to be receptive to changes that are linked to the latest trends. Movement toward DAP is sometimes easier when it is linked with other buzzwords: *emergent literacy, computer literacy, manipulatives-based math, outcomes-driven education, graduation standards, performance assessment, integrated curriculum, theme-based instruction, inclusive education,* and/or *brain development.*

A noteworthy anecdote about riding the buzzword bandwagon is two first-grade teachers who are alleged to have gotten play into their programs by calling it a "self-selected, self-directed autonomous learning period." In many locations, the term *developmentally appropriate practice* in itself is fueling elementary school reform (Gronlund, 1995).

Role of the Principal

The stereotype of the elementary principal is of the middle-aged patriarch, the male secondary teacher who eventually got his administrator's license. A problem some teachers have experienced is that such principals neither have taught at the primary level nor seem to care about the needs of young children. As Greenberg has pointed out, sexism in the school sometimes confounds the communication process (1989).

Contrary to this image, many administrators are open to improvements in programming; they see becoming educated about early childhood education a part of their jobs. They ask only for a clearly spelled out rationale that the projected program will be cost effective and results-oriented (Goffin & Stegelin, 1992).

Now in a new century with a new generation of principals coming to the fore, an increase in administrators with backgrounds in early childhood education can be expected. Nonetheless, knowing the principal well as teachers work to introduce DAP into the school only makes sense. In some situations, she will be the teacher's best ally (Burchfield, 1996; Goffin & Stegelin, 1992). In others, the teacher without tenure should work closely with, but stay in the shadow of, teachers who do.

To modify practice in a school or district, teachers need to plan carefully and organize well. Inviting educators from other areas who are using interesting ideas is a useful technique. The DAP book and *Changing Kindergartens* (Goffin & Stegelin, 1992), both published by NAEYC, and articles such as Gronlund's (1995) and Burchfield's (1996) provide useful information for moving ahead.

> Two kindergarten teachers in an urban school became tired of worksheets and drills used to teach phonics and counting skills. They heard from a teacher at another school about alternate approaches using emergent literacy techniques and a manipulatives-based math program. The two teachers began attending workshops, collecting sample materials, and talking with other teachers. The teachers got the principal to agree that the new methods were more responsive to the developmental levels of kindergarten children. With the principal's support, the two teachers convinced the third kindergarten teacher to adopt a manipulatives-based math program to replace the use of worksheets. They currently are negotiating to use a new approach to beginning reading/writing, more child-active and less dependent on a preprimer phonics system. The first-grade teachers are taking notice of what is going on in the kindergarten. The kindergarten teachers plan to involve them further.

School Anxiety

If a child wants to go to school when ill, something is right; if a child does not want to go when well, something is wrong. Young children who are unhappy at school cannot easily work through anxieties with words. In some children, **school anxiety** shows in direct mistaken behavior—inattentiveness, frequent frustration, and/or irritability. In others, anxiety manifests in physical conditions situationally caused. Symptoms range from a twice-a-year stomach ache to actual ulcers, from occasional headaches to persistent allergies, from sporadic nervousness to high blood pressure and depressive reactions. Brain development and function can also be affected by school anxiety.

School anxiety can result from specific situations such as the morning bus ride or the afternoon power test. Also, the cause can be more pervasive—a general feeling of being:

- disliked by the teacher;
- alienated from other children;
- dislocated from the education program.

School anxiety is a major cause of Level Three mistaken behavior in children—strong unmet physical and/or emotional needs that children act out.

Educators sometimes miss school anxiety as a cause of serious mistaken behavior. With the plethora of problems besetting modern families, teachers tend to look first to the home situation. Previously, serious mistaken behavior and consequent punishment were rationalized by the la-

Young children cannot easily work through anxieties with words.

beling of a "bad child." More recently, educators attribute "a bad home life" to children who act out—and seek to provide the controls not provided at home.

Much Level Three mistaken behavior *is* caused by situations outside the school. However, teaching practice that fails to accommodate developmental levels and individual circumstances is a primary cause of mistaken behavior in many situations and a contributing factor in others. The use of DAP allows the teacher to interact with the child as an individual and empowers children to succeed (Gronlund, 1995). DAP reduces the occurrence of school anxiety and is fundamental to the encouraging classroom.

LEARNING CENTERS ORGANIZE THE ENCOURAGING CLASSROOM

There is no sacrifice of rigorous learning for personal development in the encouraging classroom (Wardle, 1999). Studies of developmentally appropriate practice consistently show that education can be responsive to the development and experience of individual children and still result in measurable, meaningful educational outcomes (Charlesworth, 1998). Similarly, the use of **learning centers*** in early childhood classrooms is not primarily for the purpose of practicing guidance. Rather, learning centers are the physical embodiment of developmentally appropriate practice as well as the encouraging classroom.

In the encouraging classroom, learning is not constricted by traditional academic priorities. Early childhood education always has been about educating for the *whole child*, including physical, cognitive, social, cultural, and personal domains. In current terms, learning centers cultivate multiple intelligences. Learning centers afford the full and positive engagement through which the child constructs knowledge and undergoes healthy brain development.

At the same time, centers engender ongoing interactions that allow for the practice and development of democratic life skills. Centers are used because they both assist teachers to guide children in the development of democratic life skills and place children in situations where meaningful cognitive learning can take place.

Learning Centers and Guidance

Teachers are sometimes reluctant to "open their classes" through the use of centers. The image of many busy little bodies actively encountering the materials of the classroom would seem to invite widespread mistaken behavior. The truth is that if carefully planned, even three-year-olds engage productively in center activities—and certainly second and third graders can. Centers in the classroom encourage what one teacher calls *play with a purpose*. Children aged three to eight are adept at this mode of learning and benefit from being able to select activities of relevance to them (Brewer, 2000). The self-selection and self-direction typical of center use promotes responsible and cooperative decision-making—even if some guidance is required.

If enough choices are present, center times tend to be busy, positive, and educational (Beaty, 1996; Brewer, 2000). Still, when centers are being effectively used, there will be mistaken behavior. But most of it will be Level One conflicts resulting from full involvement in the center activity. Because children are motivated by their engagement to resolve such conflicts, the teacher can use conflict management to turn mistaken behavior into learning opportunities. In fact, teachers know that they are using guidance effectively when they see the mistaken behavior that occurs at centers as opportunities to teach democratic life skills. For most children Level One conflicts diminish as they learn the routines of center use. When they do occur, conflicts become part of the curriculum between teacher and child, and not a distraction from it.

---

* *Learning centers are distinct areas within the classroom that provide a variety of related materials for children's use. Other commonly used terms are* learning stations, interest centers, *and* learning areas, *each with its own connotations. The term* learning center *is used in this text.*

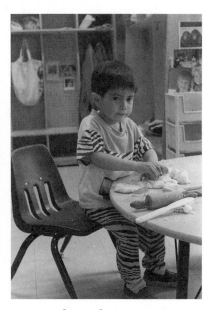

Even three-year-olds use learning centers productively.

At center time Cheyenne decided to play in the block area. Katrina decided she would play in the block area and the kitchen area. Cheyenne took out the Duplos. He started to build with them. Katrina began to play with the dishes in the kitchen area. After about ten minutes Katrina put away all the dishes and went over to the block area. Katrina approached Cheyenne.

Katrina: Can I play with you?
Cheyenne: No.

Katrina immediately ran over to Lorry (assistant teacher). Lorry was working on a puzzle with Roger Lee.

Katrina:	Cheyenne won't let me play with the blocks.
Lorry:	Let's go over and talk to him. Lorry took Katrina's hand and they walked over to the block area where Cheyenne was playing.
Lorry (to Katrina):	Please ask Cheyenne if you can play with him again.
Katrina (shrugged her shoulders):	Can I play here?
Cheyenne:	No.
Lorry (bent down by Cheyenne):	Could Katrina take some of the blocks and play over there? Lorry points to a spot about five feet away from Cheyenne.
Cheyenne:	Yes.

So Katrina picked up some of the blocks and took them to the spot Lorry had pointed to. Both children played in the block area until cleanup time.

The teacher knew that Cheyenne liked to "protect his territory" when he used the blocks. The teacher wasn't sure Katrina could persuade him on her own to let her play in the area. With the teacher taking the lead, Katrina began to learn she had a right to express her needs and Cheyenne began to learn he could share the space and blocks (Gartrell, 2000).

Still, there is one type of mistaken behavior that the teacher does try to reduce. The teacher needs to give enough thought to the design and management of learning centers to avoid the introduction of institution-caused mistaken behavior. The following considerations, discussed by many authors, reduce or eliminate mistaken behavior in center use that is caused or contributed to by the teacher (Beaty, 1996; Brewer, 2000; Essa, 1999; Zirpoli, 1995).

Consider Traffic Patterns and Noise Levels   Design center locations to prevent "runways." Typically beginning at doors into the room, runways invite the kind of large-muscle use that often is not quite what the teacher had in mind. If you are modifying an existing layout, look for runways. Place centers strategically so that children need to walk around one to get to another. Provide an active play area (see next subheading) that is open for at least some time each day, for "institutionally sanctioned" active play.

As well, when locating centers, block or building centers probably should not be in front of doorways. Active play areas probably should not be between library corners and computer centers. Be aware of the "spillover effect" where the natural activity of one center disrupts classroom traffic flow or obstructs the activity of a neighboring center.

Many teachers design classrooms so that centers with typically quiet activity are in one part of the room and centers with louder activity are in another. By using shelving, cupboards, movable bulletin boards, an occasional throw rug, and so on to create centers, noise to some extent can be buffered even in relatively small classrooms. A practical noise-level rating method for centers is the *3B system:* with (1) *bucolic* (tranquil, peaceful—smile), (2) *busy,* and (3) *boisterous.* Taking into account permanent features such as sinks and carpets, as well as traffic patterns, teachers typically locate the "mostly 1" centers at one end of the classroom, the "mostly 3" centers at the other end, and the "2 to 3" centers in between. If activity levels at bucolic and busy centers grow boisterous, the teacher needs to "check it out."

Range of Noise Levels in Typical Classroom Centers

Center	Range of Noise Levels
(Typical activity level given first)	
Library, science, technology, writing, music (headphone use)	(1) bucolic to (2) busy
Art, cooking, sensory table	(2) busy to (1) bucolic
Block-building, carpentry, music (with instruments), housekeeping, theme-based dramatic play	(2) busy to (3) boisterous
Active play center (climber, mini-trampoline, balance beam, large construction toys, hoppity-hops, indoor swing)	(3) boisterous to (2) busy

Accommodate the Active Nature of Young Children   As a parent volunteer in an early childhood classroom once commented, "They sure are active little critters, aren't they?" Busy-ness, not quietness, is the normal sound level in developmentally appropriate classrooms. Part of the natural fit of centers in early childhood classrooms is due to the busy level of child activity that centers accommodate.

Taking a broader perspective, obesity is a burgeoning problem in our society. In a traditional "sedentary" classroom, children may sit at desks or tables for five hours a day. What do most of these kids do when they get home? The average child watches television from four to six hours a day,

Active play encourages perceptual-motor development.

and computers used for entertainment may be increasing even further the relative inactivity of children (Pica, 2000).

Pica suggests that during early childhood, children begin to set lifelong patterns of activity or inactivity. Moreover, the argument can be made that young children who are physically active accomplish the physiological development that they need in order to be able to sit and concentrate for sustained periods when they are older. An irony of early childhood is that active play, and not sitting and being quiet, may be the best "rehearsal" for this traditional goal of classroom management.

If the school situation constrains active play, the teacher nonetheless figures out how to provide it each day. One kindergarten teacher in a fairly open school environment planned playtime with all centers open—including the most active—when the class next door was out of the room with specialist teachers. She had approached the other teacher about coordinating active play times across the two rooms, but the other teacher was not interested.

Although the recent spotlight on the need for increased physical activity has focused on young boys (Kantrowitz & Kalb, 1998), both girls and boys need opportunities each day to freely exercise their muscles (Pica, 2000). Daily aerobic activity at large-group times assists children (and teachers) to stay in shape. An active play area, with equipment such as a climber, balance beam, mini-trampoline, and hoppity-hops, is ideally located in an adjacent room and, as weather permits, outdoors. But the center is so important that if necessary, it is located in the "active end" of even small classrooms.

A Head Start program purchased a low mini-trampoline for about thirty dollars. The teacher oriented the preschoolers in its use: One child at a time; they could only jump so high unless an adult held their hands; they could strap jogger weights to their ankles if they wanted. The trampoline was available during every choice time all year. After a supervised training period, children received "licenses" to use it on their own. Several children bounced on the trampoline each day, but wait-times were brief. Few reminders were needed about its use. No injuries occurred. The mini-tramp proved especially helpful for a few very active children in the class. The trampoline became an accepted part of the classroom and was quieter than the teachers had expected.

Health studies consistently show the benefits of noncompetitive vigorous activity for stress reduction, hormone balance, and healthy development of all of the body's major systems (Pica, 2000). In our high-tech, low-activity society, learning centers can foster active lifestyles.

In a mixed prekindergarten-kindergarten class of 14 boys and 4 girls, many of the boys had summer and fall birthdays—and had trouble fitting into the teachers' initial program plans. The teacher and the assistant reduced large groups by substituting small-group activities led by the teacher, the assistant, and an inclusion special education teacher in the room for part of the day. One day, when they saw two of the boys lifting blocks like weights, the teachers decided to set up a *physical fitness center*. They enlisted the help of some families and came up with a manual treadmill, which they made a makeshift low railing for, a low weight table, some play barbells, and a stationary set of bike pedals that they put under a stool. They included a balance beam and occasionally mats for tumbling activities. They used hollow blocks for step exercises.

The children had to take a "course" and pass a "test" before they could use the equipment, and the area was only open when an adult "spotter" could be present. The center was so popular with both boys and girls that it became a permanent center for the rest of the year.

Build Centers Around the Interests of Children   In many classrooms the dramatic play center is usually set up as a home setting with kitchen furnishings, a table, a cabinet or two, and sometimes a bed. This center invariably is well frequented, as a previous anecdote illustrated. Increasingly, even in smaller classrooms, teachers are designing theme-based dramatic play areas, often adjacent to house settings. Usually, these centers change with themes, and the themes and centers are determined in line with the interests of the children in the group. The physical fitness center previously mentioned was an example of such a center. Three other examples follow:

1. Fishing is a big deal in many parts of the country. Near the beginning of fishing season, teachers in a Head Start program do a "fish week." Each center is equipped with fishing-related materials including fish books and computer games, water color "under water" picture making a rubber raft with actual fishing equipment (minus hooks), and a water table complete with minnows!

2. A child's parents operated a shoe store in the neighborhood. The class went to visit, and as a follow-up the teacher designed a shoe store. The two parents provided shoe boxes, a shoe stool, and foot measures. Other parents sent in lots of old shoes. The teachers added a cash register, play money, double-face receipt slips, and pencils.

3. The parents of some children in a kindergarten class were carpenters. A kindergarten teacher persuaded a reluctant principal to let her include a carpentry center in the classroom two afternoons a week. Besides a worktable with a vice, initial materials included soft pinewood scraps, eight former "household hammers," study 2-inch nails, and 12-inch "backsaws." Worried about accidents, the principal visited to view the center for himself. The principal arrived just in time to see Anita hit herself on the thumb with a hammer. Anita was about to cry. She noticed though that if she left the table to go to an adult, another child would take her place. With her thumb in her mouth, Anita continued to pound on the nail. The assistant supervising the table and the principal exchanged smiles. The principal occasionally returned to the classroom to visit the carpentry center, but out of interest, not concern.

Establish Routines for Center Selection and Use   Teachers have various names for the times children spend at centers: free play, play time, choice time, work time, or center time. At the preprimary level, two characteristics of center times mark appropriate practice. First, ample time must be allowed, at least 45 minutes—once during a half-day program, twice during a full-day program. Shorter periods prevent children from becoming fully involved (Rogers & Sawyers, 1988). Unfortunately, some teachers use brief play times as *buffer activities* (in between others), a practice that shows misunderstanding of the importance of the center experience (Beaty, 1996; Brewer, 2000).

Second, preprimary children need choice both in the centers they select and the activities they do. Some authors suggest methods for determining occupancy in centers such as hanging name tags on hooks or having a set number of chairs at the center (Zirpoli, 1995). These methods take the element of negotiation out of the process, but perhaps encourage self-regulation and adaptability—important for educational success.

The High/Scope Model takes the broader metacognitive view, maintaining that learning occurs in the selection and transition processes—and the child's reflection about them—as well as the center activity. In the famous "Plan, Do, and Review" procedure, children bring reflection, intentionality, and negotiation to the center learning experience (*Hohmann*, 1995). In small groups, children plan what they would like to do during "work time," with the adult and/or child "noting" the choices on paper. Children then "do" independent work times of about an hour, perhaps staying with their choices, perhaps not. Following work time, often during snack, children share what they did, with samples of work encouraged.

Plan, do, and review is just one part of the High/Scope Model. By its implementation of Piagetian thought and a solid research base, High/Scope has done much to legitimize the lasting benefits of child-initiated activity in early childhood (Schweinhart, Barnes, & Weikart, 1993).

A traditional center arrangement, used in some kindergarten classrooms, is for more quiet centers to be open in the morning "when children are fresh" and all centers—including carpentry, music, active play, blocks—during afternoon choice times. This arrangement fails to recognize the active nature of learning for the young child, but it does allow children self-selection among the open centers.

At the preprimary level, the rotation of groups through centers is not developmentally appropriate. The practice deprives children of the developmental benefits of self-selection and self-direction in learning activities. As Montessori discovered at the beginning of the 20th century, no one knows their level of learning better than the children themselves. For Montessori, the right of child-choice extends through the elementary years, a view still outside of the mainstream in American education.

CENTERS AT THE PRIMARY LEVEL

The use of learning centers in elementary schools remains a progressive idea (Brewer, 2000). After kindergarten, centers included in primary classrooms tend to be few and informally designed. Reading centers are fixtures, but less common are music, art, and writing centers. More classrooms

The center most commonly found in primary classrooms is the reading
or language arts center.

do have a computer or two, but in most settings well-stocked computer or
technology centers are a need that is just beginning to be met. As more
classrooms get on the Internet, the demand by educators for technology
will continue to grow. Although many classrooms do have informal science
areas, centers that encourage three-dimensional activity—blocks and other
building materials, dramatic play, carpentry, a variety of manipulatives,
abundant "sciencing" materials—are too seldom seen.

In the 20th century, Dewey, Montessori, and Piaget debunked the philosophical separation of mind and body within our schools. Yet, the view of
learning as a passive, teacher-controlled process, with discipline used to
enforce this view, persists. Educators appear to be telling children that
upon entering elementary school, they must foresake their bodies for long
periods of the day and use only their minds. With such an emphasis, educators abandon the natural and essential integration of movement and
thought that are so important for healthy development (Wade, 1992;
Williams & Kamii, 1986).

In an interview with Marilyn Hughes, an elementary teacher with years
of K–third teaching experience from Aspen, Colorado, Willis (1993) depicts
the "active learning" that occurs at learning centers:

Learning centers "allow for the broadest range of interactions," says Hughes.
Her own classroom featured 20 hands-on learning centers, which were run
on student contracts. Some of the centers were set up for independent work;

others, for pairs or small groups. Students could respond to the centers in a variety of ways: linguistic, visual, or kinesthetic. Hughes taught her pupils how to move independently through the centers, giving them a chance to pace themselves. The centers placed "hundreds of materials within the reach of the children." (1993, p. 90)

Independent Activity at the Primary Level

The values of self-directing/open-ended activity (play) for primary grade children are effectively discussed by Bredekamp and Copple (1997) and Perlmutter (1995). Daily child-choice manipulative activity is arguably necessary for children through the primary years (Brewer, 2000; Willis, 1993), though teachers feel hard pressed to find this time in their schedules. Certainly, the integrative values of play present a strong argument for this activity (Rogers & Sawyers, 1988). An expression among progressive educators is "Through play children learn what cannot be taught."

The thought, interaction, and expression that occur during self-directing/open-ended activity improves the satisfaction level of children in the primary classroom. Free for a time from external standards of evaluation, children can experience the gratification of learning for its own sake. With happier children, mistaken behavior decreases. For the professional teacher, the regular open-ended use of learning centers should outweigh any criticism that self-directed center activity is time spent "off task." Justification for the rationale of self-directing/open-ended activity at centers is perhaps the price of teaching progressively as schools begin the 21st century.

Learning Centers and Integrated Curriculum

Bredekamp and Copple (1997), Brewer (2000), and Diffily (1996) argue that DAP means shifting away from the study of isolated academic subjects during defined periods and toward the study of **integrated curriculum** in time blocks. Initiated by Dewey in laboratory schools at the beginning of the 20th century, integrated curriculum (often called the *project method*) has been a part of progressive education, including the nursery school movement, ever since (Diffily, 1996). Still, the changeover has yet to occur in most elementary schools, as Brewer (2000) points out:

> The most common approach to curriculum organization in schools in the United States, however, continues to be a subject-matter organization in which learning is segmented into math or science or language arts. You probably remember that in elementary school you had reading first thing in the morning, math right before lunch, and science in the afternoon. (p. 112)

Brewer states that in contrast to this fragmentation of the curriculum, a child's learning outside the school is whole and built around personally relevant experiences. She argues that integrating subject matter, as around themes, enables the child to find meaning in learning: "He recognizes that this information is personally useful, not something learned to please an adult, which has no other utility for him" (p. 112).

Nonstructured art illustrates the self-direction/open-ended use of learning centers.

A stringing demonstration preceded the work of these six-year-olds in a teacher-instructed/ exploratory activity.

The narration with cue to turn the page makes this cassette story a self-directing/self-correcting activity at the reading center.

Myers and Maurer (1987) have proposed a model for learning centers that includes their use in structured instruction as well as play times. The model of Myers and Maurer lends itself to the integrated curriculum. The authors assign three different functions to centers depending on instructional intent. The three functions are:

- Self-directing/open-ended
  At each learning center, children select and use materials according to their own interests and abilities.
- Teacher-instructed/exploratory
  The teacher motivates and models exploration of materials at the center according to a preset theme or concept. Children then investigate materials on their own.
- Self-directing/self-correcting
  Children use materials at the center that "have obvious and prescribed uses; the material tells the learner whether a given action is correct or incorrect" (1987, p. 24), that is, puzzles; object-to-numeral correspondence materials.

THEME-BASED INSTRUCTION IN A SECOND GRADE: A CASE STUDY

The promise of Myers and Maurer's model (1987) is that it enables the use of centers in a wide variety of primary grade activities. Foremost, in terms of integrated curriculum, the model lends itself to the thematic approach. Themes represent a practical application of integrated curriculum and allow for the full use of classroom learning centers. In the thematic approach, a topic of interest to the children is selected. A variety of activities, some large group, but many involving the use of centers, are planned, often by the use of webbing (Workman & Anziano, 1993) and undertaken by the children. The children share the results of their discoveries, and the teacher guides and monitors children's progress (Abramson, Robinson, & Anenman, 1995; Walmsley, Camp, & Walmsley, 1992).

The following case study illustrates the uses of learning centers suggested by Myers and Maurer (1987) in elementary school theme-based instruction. The teacher, Mrs. Ryan, is a composite of a few different Minnesota primary grade teachers. Note that the case study involves a second-grade class. In younger years, developmentally appropriate practice calls for teachers to be less prescriptive in their use of learning centers. For instance, children would be introduced to the centers and given their choice of which center activity to choose. Even at the second grade a teacher might allow for free choice involving centers a couple of times per week.

Mornings in Mrs. Ryan's second-grade class were reserved for specific skill development in the traditional subject areas. Afternoons, however, were spent in **thematic instruction** using an integrated curriculum approach. Mrs. Ryan

Centers lend themselves both to formal cooperative learning and informal table talk.

used the technique of **webbing** to conceptualize and organize themes (Workman & Anziano, 1993). On this day, she and the class decided on a large topic, rather than a specific concept, to plan the theme. The topic, signs of spring, grew from the children's frequent observations of the recent warm weather, flowers, and rain ("finally, 'stead of snow") that arrived in Minnesota (this year by the end of April). They decided to start with "a scientific field trip," a walk around the block to observe and collect specimens that showed spring had arrived. The first web was of activities related to signs of spring the children would do in small groups at different learning centers; Mrs. Ryan called this the "content web" and developed it with the children's input. The second web was of learner outcomes for the children at the different centers. The outcomes came from the school district's list for the second grade (Workman & Anziano, 1993). Mrs. Ryan developed the second web herself.

Mrs. Ryan waited until the end of the first week's activities to generate a third web, a "continued content" web, with the children. This web was the fun part of the theme for her, as the children and she together generated topics and activities to continue their study of the theme. (They would continue with the "signs of spring" as long as their mutual interest held out.) Later, she would construct a second learner outcomes web to correspond to the "continued content web" generated by the group.

Signs of Spring   To illustrate how Mrs. Ryan implemented the theme—using small-group teams, active learning, and learning centers—the first week's events are chronicled as follows:

Mrs. Ryan divided the class into four teams. (She established new teams for each theme.) The teams named themselves for animals that returned from migration or awoke from hibernation in the springtime: the bears, the hummingbirds, the bugs, and the skunks.

On Monday two parents, a college intern, and Mrs. Ryan took their four teams outside to tour the area around the school looking for signs of spring. With the snow recently melted, they collected samples of everything from insects to new grass to litter. (One parent drew the line at "beer cans"!) Each team recorded its observations.

Upon returning, the teams went to four different centers in the classroom. Each team cataloged their collections and pooled their observations. (Use of centers: teacher-instructed/exploratory.) Each team reported its findings to the rest of the class.

On Tuesday, the teacher oriented the class to the theme activities for the rest of the week. The four teams would rotate to a new center each day, with large group sharing at the end. Mrs. Ryan and the class decided to assign the teams alphabetically to centers for Tuesday. She made a chart to show the rotation pattern for the rest of the week. The bears started at center one; the bugs at center two; the hummingbirds at center three; and the skunks at center four.

Center one was a self-directed/self-correcting activity in the science center. The children sorted the entire collection of specimens into boxes labeled "plant things," "animal things," "natural things," and "people-made things." A list of

Teacher-directed exploratory activity at an art center is often used
in theme-based instruction.

sample items was attached to each box. They counted the items in each category. They decided which set of specimens had the "most" and the "least."

Center two was a teacher-directed/exploratory activity in the reading
center. The children studied a large collection of books about spring, including reports made by previous classes. They noted favorite parts of the
books and shared them. Although she monitored all of the goings-on, Mrs.
Ryan worked primarily with this group.

Center three was a second teacher-directed/exploratory activity in the
writing center. Each adult volunteer returned to class on the day his team
was at this center. With the adult's help, the children made their own dic-
tionary of words for specimens and other signs of spring (i.e., leaves, litter).
They then wrote their chapter of the class report on the topic.

Center four was a self-directing/open-ended activity in the art center.
Children made story-pictures of things they have done or would like to do
outdoors in the spring. They shared the story-pictures with the others in the
team. Later, Mrs. Ryan and a few volunteers displayed each story-picture
on the class-made bulletin board—the only kind of bulletin board she has
in the room.

Mrs. Ryan looks at the afternoon theme time as an opportunity to use integrated curriculum. Throughout the month she manages to include content in the following subject areas: science, social studies, math, language

arts, visual art, health, creative drama, music and physical education. She was able to get permission for the afternoon time blocks for Theme Time by documenting for the principal how she covers outcomes in all eight subject areas. Her preference would be for the children to have more freedom in selecting center activities (and not to rotate through) but, for this year anyway, the principal was adamant on this point. Mrs. Ryan has found Theme Time to be such an effective instructional vehicle that twice a week she can allow self-directing/open-ended activity at centers for a half hour at the end of the day.

Besides organization and management of the theme, Mrs. Ryan uses **performance assessment** with each child in relation to the school district's learner outcomes. She does so with a variety of **authentic assessment** tools including recorded observations, checklists, and examination of the children's written work kept in portfolios. She states that using the thematic approach "takes real work." However, she sees little mistaken behavior during the time block, "because the children are so busy." She mentioned that when she got volunteers involved the second year to assist with small group activities, "It really helped." Mrs. Ryan believes the children learn so much when they are involved with the themes that the effort is worthwhile.

ENCOURAGING PARENTS TO BE CLASSROOM VOLUNTEERS

In their parent involvement programs, educators tend to focus on one or a few of the following ways and measure success accordingly. Programs with a full range of family services, such as Head Start, might focus on all fifteen.

Ways Parents Can Be Involved in the Preschool or Primary Grade Program

1. Assist children with home assignments
2. Attend parent-teacher conferences
3. Attend parent meetings
4. Participate in home visits by staff
5. Contribute materials
6. Follow through with staff recommendations
7. Participate in "family journals"
8. Chaperone special events
9. Visit for observation purposes
10. Make presentations to the class
11. Volunteer to help on a regular basis
12. Help to organize special events
13. Assist other parents to volunteer
14. Sit on policy boards
15. Further their own development and education

Another method of gauging successful involvement is to first decide which of the ways are appropriate for the particular program, then assess success on a family-by-family basis (Rosenthal & Sawyers, 1996). For some parents, participation at levels 1–3 might constitute successful participation. For another family, criteria 1–7 might be used.

The number of parents working outside the home would seem to limit parent availability for in-class involvement (criteria 8–13). Nonetheless, with pleasant persistence, teachers can often prevail upon parents to find times when they can come into the classroom.

The present section focuses on those levels of involvement that pertain to the classroom, criteria 8–13. Specifically, the concern is how to help parents feel comfortable enough to volunteer on a regular basis. Previous chapters began the discussion about the importance of parent-teacher partnerships in the guidance approach. Gestwicki (2000) pre-sents the following advantages of encouraging parents to be classroom volunteers:

- Parents gain first-hand experience of a program, of their child's reactions in a classroom, and feelings of satisfaction from making a contribution;
- Children feel special when their parents are involved, feel secure with the tangible evidence of parents and teachers cooperating, and gain directly as parental understanding and skills increase;
- Teachers gain resources to extend learning opportunities, observe parent-child interaction, and can feel supported as parents participate and empathize with them (p. 293).

Roadblocks to Involving Parents

Despite these advantages, teachers sometimes encounter two roadblocks: (a) other staff are dubious about the merits of using parent volunteers, and (b) parents cannot find the time or they are not sure they can contribute (Gestwicki, 2000). In regard to the first situation, few programs and schools have policies forbidding the use of parent volunteers; such a practice is ill-advised. As mentioned in Chapter One, programs such as Head Start, cooperative nursery schools, and preschool/parent education programs have a rich tradition of including parents in the classroom. In a growing number of school districts, as well, parent volunteers are gaining in acceptance.

The teacher interested in including parents needs to determine what is policy and what simply has never been done. Talking with sympathetic teachers and speaking with the administrator are important first steps. The teacher is more likely to experience success by starting on a small scale and keeping a low profile, so that the effort does not become a "burning teacher's lounge issue." As Gestwicki suggests, determination on the teacher's part is likely to be the main ingredient for success (2000).

Parents volunteer in the classroom (and out) in many ways. (Courtesy, *Bemidji Pioneer*)

Helping Parents Feel Comfortable

In regard to the second situation Rockwell, Andre, and Hawley (1996) suggest that teachers work carefully with parents and not push them to levels of participation beyond their comfort levels. Ideas for creating the climate for partnership with parents were illustrated in Chapter Two. The following suggestions help parents feel more comfortable about volunteering in the classroom. Note that as a result of social and cultural differences, some families will respond to some of these suggestions, other families to others. When teachers work to get to know families at the beginning of the year, they then can tailor ideas to particular families.

1. Hold a "Greeting Meeting" for all parents. Distribute two fliers: (a) one that tells about your program, and (b) another that gives suggestions and guidelines for parent volunteers. (See samples in Appendixes C and D.) Go over each flier at the meeting. Stress that you encourage parents to visit and volunteer. Have a parent volunteer from the previous year share what he did. Mention

that you know many parents work outside the home and that finding time to get away is difficult. If possible, state that you are open to visits on the parents' time schedules.

2. At or after the Greeting Meeting, ask parents to complete a questionnaire (samples are provided in Appendix B). On the questionnaire, ask parents to check different ways they would be willing to participate. Include choices pertaining to the classroom. Don't ask *if* they would like to volunteer. Provide choices of ways that previous parents volunteered and ask them to check as many as they would like.

3. If the teacher makes home visits, mention volunteering at the home visit. During the first parent-teacher conference, refer to the questionnaire and discuss volunteering in the classroom.

4. Establish with parents when they are welcome. If you choose not to have a general "open house" policy, specify in the flier and at the meeting when parents can visit. Be flexible: parents working outside the home have limited time availability.

5. Let parents know that they have three ways to volunteer: (a) parents can participate on a regular basis (They only need to call if they cannot make it); (b) parents can informally visit or initiate a special event, such as a family sharing activity. (It is important that they call you first); and (c) parents can help with field trips, picnics, and so forth.

6. A brother or sister brought with a parent probably will not be as disruptive as a teacher might think. For some parents, permission to bring a younger sibling is necessary for them to visit at all. Make clear your policy about siblings accompanying the parent.

7. Some parents might like to volunteer but don't have transportation. Help parents work this out, such as by having two parents "buddy up." With staff encouragement parents in some Head Start programs ride the buses with their children.

8. When parents visit your classroom, treat them as you would like to be treated if you were visiting a class. Stop what you are doing and privately greet the parent. If the parent seems comfortable with the idea, introduce him to the children. Have a place where the parent can store any belongings. Talk with the parent about what he would be comfortable doing, and help the parent get started. Observe how things are going and provide assistance if needed. When the parent is about to leave, thank him for visiting; let the parent know that he is welcome back; if possible, have the children say good-bye.

The teacher assumes responsibility for relationships with parent volunteers. Teachers who view parent volunteers as a natural extension of the parent-teacher partnership will actively invite parents into the classroom. All stand to gain when parents become members of the teaching team (Stipek, Rosenblatt, & DiRocco, 1994).

Because this first grader's class is used to visitors, his younger sister does not disrupt the daily program.

SUMMARY

1. What is an encouraging classroom?

The encouraging classroom begins within the minds of its teachers. The encouraging classroom is defined as the physical surrounds of a school, center, or family child care program in which adults provide ongoing guidance in order to maintain an equilibrium between the needs of each developing member and the right of the learning community for mutual appreciation among its members. It involves the creation and sustenance of a caring community among children and adults for the purpose of furthering the learning and development of each member (Gartrell, 2000, p. 171).

2. How does developmentally appropriate practice contribute to the encouraging classroom?

Developmentally inappropriate practice—which tends to be teacher-directed, restrictively academic, and overly focused on standardized assessment and student compliance—leads to stress in many young children. Developmentally appropriate practice is rigorous teaching that engages each child in an interactive learning process geared to multiple learning domains and intelligences. Such instructional strategies as learning centers, integrated curriculum emerging from children's experiences, authentic (observation-based) assessment, child-directed activity (play), and guidance are indicators that teaching practices are developmentally appropriate.

3. How does physical layout make the classroom encouraging?

Learning centers mark the classroom environment that is developmentally appropriate. Because of the attraction of learning center activity, teachers can use the conflicts that arise in center use as opportunities to teach democratic life skills. To reduce institutionally caused mistaken behavior, consider traffic patterns and noise levels in organizing centers. Build centers around the interests of children. Develop daily routines in center selection and use that involve reflective selection criteria and allow sufficient time for center activity.

Learning centers make elementary education classrooms into learning laboratories. Tailor the types of learning activity in centers to the desired outcomes of the curriculum.

4. How does thematic instruction at the primary grade level illustrate the encouraging classroom at work?

Theme-based instruction promotes developmentally appropriate primary grade curriculum because it integrates academic subjects into topics of interest to the child, structures active learning through a variety of center activities, allows for individual and small-group learning experiences, and lends itself to observation-based assessment strategies. Teachers frequently use webbing to organize themes. They use large-group sessions to plan and assess theme activity with the children. Small groups in learning centers highlight the social nature of learning through themes.

5. How does the teacher encourage parents to be classroom volunteers?

Parents can be involved in their children's education in fifteen or more ways. Teachers need to measure the success of the parent involvement program by looking at what is possible for each individual family. Parents, children, and teachers all gain when parents volunteer in the classroom. With a positive attitude and friendly persistence, teachers can overcome most roadblocks to involving parents. Eight suggestions were provided for encouraging parents to visit classrooms and become regular volunteers.

KEY CONCEPTS

Authentic assessment
Educational accountability
Integrated curriculum
Learning centers

Performance assessment
Political accountability
School anxiety
School readiness
Thematic instruction
Webbing

FOLLOW-UP ACTIVITIES

Note: An element of being a professional teacher is to respect the children,
parents, and educators you are working with by maintaining
confidentiality—keeping identities private. In completing follow-up
activities, please respect the privacy of all concerned.

Discussion Activity

The discussion activity encourages students to interrelate their own
thoughts and experiences with specific ideas from the chapter.

> Recall from your experience as a student a theme or a classroom routine that
> you participated in and that means something to you in relation to your pro-
> fessional development. Compare or contrast that experience with relevant
> ideas from the chapter.

Application Activities

Application activities allow students to interrelate material from the text
with real-life situations. The observations imply access to practicum experiences; the interviews, access to teachers or parents. Students may compare or contrast observations and interviews with referenced ideas from
the chapter.

1. **The encouraging classroom.**
   a. Observe in a classroom that you believe to be encouraging.
      Select a child that you perceive to be vulnerable for stigma
      (negative separation from the group). Observe a situation
      with the child when a conflict is involved. Record the
      observation as objectively as you can. Compare the responses
      of the teacher and/or other children in the class to what the
      book says should happen in the encouraging classroom.
   b. Interview a teacher about the following: (1) what some
      characteristics are of children in the class who are particularly
      vulnerable for stigma; (2) how the teacher works with the
      group to be inclusive of these children; (3) how the teacher
      monitors her own responses with the identified children to

prevent stigma. How does what the teacher says go along with text material on the encouraging classroom?

2. **Developmentally appropriate practice.**

   a. Observe a small-group activity that you believe to be developmentally appropriate. Record as objectively as possible verbal and nonverbal responses that characterize one child's responses. Hypothesize what that child may be gaining from the activity in each of these developmental domains: physical, cognitive, language, social/cultural, and emotional. Discuss your findings with others in your class.

   b. Interview a teacher who uses developmentally appropriate practice. Ask how the teacher assesses children's progress in relation to outcomes or standards that might be required in the program or school. What key problems does the teacher encounter in assessing learning and discussing it with other adults? How does the teacher work to resolve these problems? Compare your findings to text material on developmentally appropriate practice.

3. **Physical layout.**

   a. Observe carefully the classroom of a teacher who uses learning centers. Diagram the classroom using as much detail as possible. Compare the pattern of center placement with considerations in the text for planning and using centers.

   b. In a small group of two or three, design a classroom using the centers listed under the consideration pertaining to traffic flow and noise level. Use the considerations listed in the chapter as criteria for center design and placement. Using hard copies, transparency projection, or computer projection, give a tour of your classroom to other members of your class. Remind them to use compliment sandwiches in their feedback to your group.

   c. Interview a teacher who uses learning centers. Discuss advantages and disadvantages of center use as the teacher sees them. How does the teacher see learning centers contributing to the atmosphere of an encouraging classroom? Compare your findings with what the text says about learning centers.

4. **Thematic instruction.**

   a. Observe a preprimary or primary class that is completing a theme. Note which of the following the teacher uses: webbing, learning centers, small-group activities, integrated curriculum. Note the children's level of engagement in theme activities. Compare the observations with what the text says about theme-based instruction.

   b. Interview a teacher who uses themes. Ask about the teacher's use of: webbing, learning centers, small-group activities, integrated curriculum. Note the children's level of engagement in theme activities. Compare the observations with what the text says about theme-based instruction.

5. **Classroom volunteers.**
   a. Observe a classroom where one or more parents volunteer. Note what the teacher is doing to help the volunteer(s) feel welcome. Compare or contrast your observations with ideas from the chapter about encouraging parents to volunteer.
   b. Interview a parent volunteer. What went into the parent's decision to volunteer in the classroom? What part did the teacher play in the parent's decision to volunteer? Compare what the parent said with ideas from the chapter about encouraging parents to be classroom volunteers.

What You Can Do

Design and If Possible Teach a Mini-Theme   For a classroom and an age group you are familiar with, decide on and design a theme:

1. Design a web for your theme. If possible use the children's input. The web should include a large-group introduction/orientation, and three to five learning center activities. Three of the centers might use Myers and Maurer's activity types. Decide how many adults you will have available in the classroom and which centers will require adult supervision.
2. Develop a schedule for your theme. Rather than rotating groups through the centers, allow children as much or as little time as they need—then they can choose another center.
3. Determine two to three concrete "process" objectives for each activity. "Process" objectives allow children to complete an activity at their various levels of achievement and still be successful. (Example: Children will make story-pictures about something they recall from our trip to the farm yesterday. Not—children will make a pig or a cow using these models.)
4. Think about how observations you make in relation to the objectives could give you important information about children's progress toward broader developmental outcomes. (Example: Children will show comprehension skills on paper through art forms and written symbols.)
5. What did you learn about the place of themes in an encouraging classroom from this activity?

RECOMMENDED READINGS

Burchfield, D. W. (1996). Teaching all children. Four different curricular and instructional strategies in primary grade classrooms. *Young Children, 52*(1), 4–10.

Diffily, D. (1996). The project approach: A museum exhibit created by kindergartners. *Young Children, 51*(2), 72–75.

Gronlund, G. (2001). Rigorous academics in preschool and kindergarten? Yes! Let me tell you how. *Young Children, 56*(2), 42–43.

Kohn, A. (2001). Fighting the tests: Turning frustration into action. *Young Children, 56*(2), 19–24.

Perlmutter, J. C. (1995). 'Play' as well as 'work' in the primary grades. *Young Children, 50*(5), 14–21.

Reisner, T. (2001). Learning to teach reading in a developmentally appropriate kindergarten. *Young Children, 56*(2), 44–48.

Rosenthal, D. M., & Sawyers, J. Y. (1996). Building successful home/school partnerships: Strategies for parent support and involvement. *Childhood Education 72*(4) 194–200.

Stipek, D., Rosenblatt, L., & DiRocco, L. (1994). Making parents your allies. *Young Children, 49*(3), 4–9.

Wesson, K. A. (2001). The "Volvo Effect"—questioning standardized tests. *Young Children, 56*(2), 16–18.

Willis, S. (1993, November). Teaching young children: Educators seek 'developmental appropriateness.' *Curriculum Update,* 1–8.

Workman, S., & Anziano, M. C. (1993). Curriculum webs: Weaving connections from children to teachers. *Young Children, 48*(2), 4–9.

REFERENCES

Abramson, S., Robinson, R., & Anenman, K. (1995). Project work with diverse students: Adapting curriculum based on the Reggio Emilia Approach. *Childhood Education, 71*(4), 197–202.

Beaty, J. J. (1996). *Preschool: Appropriate practices.* Fort Worth, TX: Harcourt Brace College Publishers.

Bredekamp, S., & Rosegrant, T. (Eds.). (1992). *Reaching potentials: Appropriate curriculum and assessment for young children.* Washington, DC: National Association for the Education of Young Children.

Bredekamp, S., & Copple, C. (1997). *Developmentally appropriate practice in early childhood programs* (3rd ed.). Washington, DC: National Association for the Education of Young Children.

Brewer, J. A. (2000). *Introduction to early childhood education: Preschool through primary grades.* Boston, MA: Allyn & Bacon.

Burchfield, D. W. (1996). Teaching all children. Four different curricular and instructional strategies in primary grade classrooms. *Young Children, 52*(1), 4–10.

Charlesworth, R. (1998). Developmentally appropriate practice is for everyone. *Childhood Education 74*(5), 274–282.

Dewey, J. (1900/1969). *The child and curriculum.* Chicago: The University of Chicago Press.

Diffily, D. (1996). The project approach: A museum exhibit created by kindergartners. *Young Children, 51*(2), 72–75.

Elkind, D. (1993). *Images of the young child.* Washington, DC: National Association for the Education of Young Children.

Elkind, D. (1997, November). The death of child nature: Education in the postmodern world. *Phi Delta Kappan* Vol 97, 241–245.

Essa, E. L. (1999). *Introduction to early childhood education* (3rd ed.). Clifton Park, NY: Delmar Learning.

Feeney, S., & Freeman, N. (1999). *Ethics and the early childhood educator using the NAEYC Code.* Washington, DC: National Association for the Education of Young Children.

Gartrell, D. J. (1997). Beyond discipline to guidance. *Young Children, 52*(6), 34–42.

Gartrell, D. (2000). *What the kids said today.* St. Paul, MN: Redleaf Press.

Gestwicki, C. (2000). *Home, school, and community relations: A guide to working with parents* (4th ed.). Clifton Park, NY: Delmar Learning.

Goffin, S. G. & Stegelin, D. A. (Eds.). (1992). Changing kindergartens. Washington, DC: National Association for the Education of Young Children.

Gordon, A. M., & Browne, K. W. (1989). *Beginnings and beyond: Foundations in early childhood education.* Clifton Park, NY: Delmar Learning.

Greenberg, P. (1989). Parents as partners in young children's development and education: A new American fad? Why does it matter? *Young Children, 44*(4), 61–75.

Gronlund, G. (1995). Bringing the DAP message to kindergarten and primary teachers. *Young Children, 50*(4) 4–13.

Hohmann, M., Banet, B., & Weikart, D. P. (1995). *Educating young children: Active learning practices in preschool and child care programs.* Ypsilanti, MI:The High/Scope Press.

Kantrowitz, B., & Kalb, C. Boys will be boys. *Newsweek,* May 11, 1998, 54–60.

LeDoux, J. (1996). *The emotional brain.* New York: Simon & Schuster.

Myers, B. K., & Maurer, K. (1987). Teaching with less talking: Learning centers in the kindergarten. *Young Children, 42*(5), 20–27.

National Association for the Education of Young Children (1995). Position statement on school readiness. Washington, DC: NAEYC.

National Association for the Education of Young Children (1995). Position statement: Code of ethical conduct. Washington, DC: NAEYC.

Perlmutter, J. C. (1995). 'Play' as well as 'work' in the primary grades. *Young Children, 50*(5), 14–21.

Pica, R. (2000). *Experiences in movement with music, activities, and theory.* Clifton Park, NY: Delmar Learning.

Rockwell, R. E., Andre, L. C., & Hawley, M. K. (1996). *Parents and teachers as partners.* Fort Worth, TX: Harcourt Brace Jovanovich College Publishers.

Rogers, C. S., & Sawyers, J. K. (1988). *Play in the lives of children.* Washington, DC: National Association for the Education of Young Children.

Rosenthal, D. M., & Sawyers, J. Y. (1996). Building successful home/school partnerships: Strategies for parent support and involvement. *Childhood Education, 72*(4), 194–200.

Schweinhart, L. J., Barnes, H. V., & Weikart, D. P. (1993). *Significant benefits: The High/Scope Perry Preschool study through age 27.* Ypsilanti, MI: High/Scope Press.

Stipek, D., Rosenblatt, L., & DiRocco, L. (1994). Making parents your allies. *Young Children, 49*(3), 4–9.

Wade, M. G. (1992). Motor skills, play, and child development: An introduction, *Early Report, 19*(2), 1–2.

Walmsley, B. B., Camp, A. M., & Walmsley, S. A. (1992). *Teaching kindergarten: A developmentally appropriate approach.* Portsmouth, NH: Heinemann Educational Books.

Wardle, F. (1999). In praise of developmentally appropriate practice. *Young Children, 54*(6), 4–12.

Williams, C. K., & Kamii, C. (1986). How do children learn by handling objects? *Young Children, 41*(8), 23–26.

Willis, S. (1993, November). Teaching young children: Educators seek 'developmental appropriateness.' *Curriculum Update,* 1–8.

Workman, S., & Anziano, M. C. (1993). Curriculum webs: Weaving connections from children to teachers. *Young Children, 48*(2), 4–9.

Zirpoli, T. J. (1995). Understanding and affecting the behavior of young children. Englewood Cliffs, NJ: Merrill/Prentice-Hall.

For additional information on using the guidance approach in the classroom, visit our Web site at http://www.earlychilded.delmar.com

MANAGING THE ENCOURAGING CLASSROOM

GUIDING QUESTIONS

- How does the teacher balance reliability and novelty in the daily program?
- What part do large group activities play in the encouraging classroom?
- How does managing transitions reduce mistaken behavior?
- How do routines help to build an encouraging classroom?
- Why is the teaching team important in managing the encouraging classroom?
- How can the teacher make use of parents and other classroom volunteers?

In the encouraging classroom, the goal of the teacher is to empower children to grow toward autonomy in Piaget's terms; toward initiative, industry, and belonging in Erikson's; and toward the encounterer level of social relations in Harlow's construct. In this effort, the teacher works to prevent some kinds of mistaken behavior and monitors, but does not necessarily prevent, other kinds. (Discussion about when and how to intervene when mistaken behaviors occur is the focus of Part Three.) One type of mistaken behavior that the teacher actively works to prevent is institution-caused mistaken behavior. This mistaken behavior is a result of a mismatch between the child and the expectations of the program—when the education program is developmentally inappropriate (Bredekamp & Copple, 1997). Seven common sources of institution-caused mistaken behavior are:

- Teacher judges children's worth by the behaviors they show (conditional rather than unconditional acceptance).
- Teacher judges misbehaviors instead of reteaching mistaken behaviors.
- Performance expectations for children are inappropriate (too demanding or not challenging enough).
- Lack of organization is shown in the classroom and teaching methods.
- Daily program lacks a balance of reliability and novelty.
- Large groups are too frequent, lengthy, and teacher-centered.
- Transitions lack planning and organization.

Part Two addresses creation of the encouraging classroom through the prevention of institution-caused mistaken behavior. Chapter Five discussed organization of the physical space and the curriculum to achieve the engagement of children in the learning process. Chapter Six continues the discussion by examining the daily program, the limits of large groups, the management of transitions, the place of routines, the benefits of the teaching team and the use of parents and other volunteers.

THE DAILY PROGRAM

In the daily program, children need both a sense of reliability and the promise of novelty. Too little of the former results in a lack of predictability and anxiety. Too little of the latter results in tedium (Hendrick, 2000). A set schedule that children are familiar with provides a useful baseline for both the informal *teachable moment,* the gerbil having babies, and the planned special event, a visit from Smokey Bear.

More than 100 years ago Montessori recognized that young children need a sense of order and continuity (Montessori, 1912/1964). A predictable schedule provides security. Much of life is beyond children's control, from the time they get up in the morning to the time they go to bed. Some choices, like which of two sets of clothes to wear, are good for chil-

When unscheduled events enable positive results, they add to the everyday program.

dren and add to their self-esteem. Other choices, such as whether to go to school or not, children are not in a position to make. When they cannot decide a matter for themselves, children benefit from understanding about a decision that is made for them. Understanding reasons helps children find reliability in the relationship with the teacher and in the classroom environment—necessary basic needs for personal growth.

The daily schedule is one of those decisions that young children don't make on their own but need to rely on. When unscheduled events enable positive results—celebration, delight, wonderment, enlightenment—they add immeasurably to the everyday program. An unpredictable program, however—whether it is just inconsistent or a nonending series of spontaneous teachable moments (basically unplanned)—makes children feel anxious and insecure. The teacher maintains a healthy balance in the schedule by monitoring the feeling level of the class—anxious, bored, interested, or engaged—and responding accordingly. By reading children's feelings and discussing reasons with them, the teacher may vary from the schedule. Returning to it allows children the security of knowing what is expected of them.

Three Sample Schedules

The sample schedules shown in Tables 6–1, 6–2, and 6–3 model developmentally appropriate programming, make full use of the classroom, and

Table 6–1

Prekindergarten Schedule

(Six-hour schedule, as in some Head Start programs. Half-day and full-day programs can be adapted.)

Time	Activity
8:15–8:30	Arrival. Teacher greets each child. Informal child-choice activity until all children arrive.
8:30–9:00	Breakfast in family groups of 8–10, each with a caregiver/teacher. At tables, the caregiver/teacher previews events; **Plan, do, and review** sequence used.
9:00–10:15	Center time. Self-directed/open-ended activity. All centers open. Clean up.
10:15–10:35	Snack in family groups. Review of "special things" done during center time.
10:35–11:00	Active play, inside or out.
11:00–11:15	Large group: music, story, movement activity, or occasional guest. (Sometimes replaced by longer small group activity that follows.)
11:15–11:45	Small group activities—art, cooking, creative drama, or walk outside.
11:45–1:00	Lunch in family groups. Rest.
1:00–2:00	Center time. Self-directed/open-ended activity. All centers open. Clean up.
2:00–2:30	Class meeting, song, and review of day. Get ready to go home.

Table 6–2

Kindergarten Schedule

(Full-day schedule. Half-day schedule can be adapted.)

Time	Activity
8:30–9:00	Arrival. Teacher greets each child. Breakfast available for all children. Informal child-choice activity as children arrive.
9:00–9:15	Morning class meeting. Quick preview of day.
9:15–9:30	Large group lead-in to center theme activities through use of discussion, story, song, object, or picture.
9:30–10:10	Small group theme activities using learning centers.
10:10–10:40	Snack time. Active play outside or inside.
10:40–11:45	Center time. Self-directed/open-ended activity at centers. Clean-up.
11:45–12:30	Lunch and child-choice activity inside or active play outside, depending on the weather.
12:30–1:00	Story. Reading, relaxing, resting.
1:00–1:45	Special Activity—gym, art, music, library, or computer. (Specialists extend these activities.)
1:45–2:30	Self-directed/open-ended activity; all centers open. Clean up. Occasional special event during part of this time.
2:30–3:00	Afternoon circle time—songs, movement activities, finger plays, and review of day. Get ready to go home.

Table 6–3

Primary Schedule

Time	Activity
8:15–8:45	Arrival. Teacher greets each child. Breakfast available for all children. Informal child-choice activity as children arrive.
8:45–9:00	Morning class meeting: business, discussion of important events and issues—brought up by children or teacher. Preview of **language arts focus** (time block). Assignment of small groups to centers.
9:00–10:00	Integrated language arts time block in small groups: book-read and share; journaling; language skills instruction; language skills follow-up; language arts choice—reading, journaling, or creative drama. (Groups rotate each day.)
10:00–10:30	Restroom, snack, and break/recess.
10:30–10:45	Transition large group—active to quiet; review of language focus; preview of math focus.
10:45–11:30	Math skill activities—manipulatives-based, in small groups; one small group each day has supervised computer use; every Wednesday, art specialist.
11:30–11:45	Review of math focus, story, and transition to lunch.
11:45–12:30	Lunch and recess.
12:30–1:00	Relaxation—relaxation activity or another story, quiet music, and reading; sometimes option of educational video.
1:00–2:05	Large and small groups work on integrative themes having a social studies/science emphasis. (See Mrs. Ryan case study in Chapter Five.)
2:05–2:15	Break, restroom, movement activity, and review of theme activities.
2:15–3:00	Monday: Continue work on themes; self-directing/open-ended activities.
	Tuesday: Alternating music and physical education specialist.
	Wednesday: Continue work on themes; self-directing/open-ended activities.
	Thursday: Continue work on themes; self-directing/open-ended activities.
	Friday: Theme presentations by small groups to class; self-directed/open-ended activities.
3:00–3:15	Afternoon class meeting. Happenings of the day—problems and accomplishments, brought up by children or teacher; future events introduced; preparations to go home.

provide a daily program through which interesting experiences can happen. Use of volunteers, as in the teaching team concept, will facilitate some small group activities. Schedules such as these attempt to balance the novel and the predictable so that children are involved but not overloaded—making mistaken behavior less likely. As Walmsley, Camp, & Walmsley note, flexibility in the schedule is a prerequisite for a developmentally appropriate program (1992). The schedules are for prekindergarten, kindergarten, and primary grade programs.

Tracking the Daily Schedule

To maximize the benefits of the schedule for children, the teacher can use a visual tracking method. Two such devices are the horizontal **period chart** and the circular **day clock;** either can be used with or without a movable marker or "hand."

These visualizations serve multiple functions. One function is to acquaint adults new to the classroom—with the daily program. A second function is assisting young children to begin to understand sequence and the passage of time. A third is to acquaint children with the idea of "telling time." Until they are seven or eight, children have difficulty understanding time concepts and frequently show *time confusion* (Elkind, 1976). In a helpful article on introducing time concepts, Van Scoy and Fairchild (1993) point out that in contrast to persons who are older:

> Young children's reasoning is tied to what they are seeing and experiencing; that is, young children are dependent on concrete, observable events . . . to help them 'figure things out.' Given this need for concreteness, it is understandable that time concepts—which cannot be seen, heard or felt—are difficult for young children to construct. . . . To help children understand the passage of time, we must relate time to physical objects and/or events that are meaningful to the children. (p. 21)

When used with a marker or hand, the period chart or day clock helps children to track events that are real to them—snack, center time, rest, time to go outside. When each time block is displayed by an illustration and a name on the chart or clock, children have contextual clues for building functional literacy. The use of a marker or a single hand helps children to begin telling time in the natural way that time passes—without the complexity of the conventional clock (more appropriate for children who have passed into concrete operations during the primary grades). If the chart or clock has a marker or hand, a daily "time-keeper" can move it. The teacher can use it during the morning meeting to introduce events of the day, including any "special events." He can refer to it during the day to remind children about the order in which events will happen: "Remember? Snack time comes after what?" By constructing time concepts that have personal meaning for them, children gain building blocks for the gradual mastery of the intricacies of chronology.

About midway through the year a teacher introduced a one-handed day clock to her class of four-year-olds. Gradually, during the day, children began to ask her "What comes next again?" Her standard response was, "go read the day clock." She knew the day clock idea was registering when Sam, an "experienced" four, told her, "Teacher, I know what comes next. Snack. So we gotta go wash our hands." A few days later, a naturalist spoke during large group about protecting the environment. After about fifteen minutes of his half-hour talk Sam, who was sitting by the teacher whispered, "Teacher, the clock says it's time for centers."

Mixing Active & Quiet Times

Young children learn most effectively through movement of large and small muscles (Wade, 1992). Much of the daily program should include activity at a busy activity level, with occasional excursions into the boisterous activity level ("with exuberance and high spirits") and the bucolic activity level ("peaceful, simple, and natural"). The center approach, discussed in Chapter Five, defines busy activity. **Table talk** (informal talking among children) and movement at and among centers are common in classrooms functioning at the busy level.

Boisterous activity is known to all—jumping on a mini-tramp, climbing on a climber, dancing to "The Pop Corn Rock," running, riding a trike. Bucolic activity includes attending in large groups, doing "seatwork," reading a book, watching a video, or resting.

Traditionally at the elementary level, educators have made bucolic the goal, with activity at the busy level occasionally acceptable, and boisterous activity only under special circumstances. The problem is that bucolic activity often lapses into *passivity*, the absence of engagement in the learning process. Without engagement children become bored and restless and mistaken behavior results.

When children experience difficulty in a program, adults often use common, sometimes trendy labels to describe their behavior: *immature, hyper, antsy, rowdy, strong-willed,* or *attention-deficit disordered.* Sometimes these behavior patterns have a physiological or psychological basis that needs to be diagnosed and remediated. But often such labels result from the mismatch between the program and the child—the program tending toward the bucolic level, and children needing to be actively engaged, *busy.* Rather than suppress the active learning style of the young, teachers do better to guide it and empower children through it (Gronlund, 1995; Wade, 1992).

Rest and Relaxation   Although busy sets the tone of the developmentally appropriate classroom (Brewer, 2000; Gronlund, 1995), neither children nor teachers can function all day at the busy level. For some years, books by such authors as Clare Cherry (*Think of Something Quiet*, 1981) and albums by such musicians as Hap Palmer (*Sea Gulls*, 1978) and Greg and Steve (*Quiet Moments*, 1983) have been helpful in promoting relaxation in the classroom. With modern family life-styles and the pressures of school and community, children, like adults, become tense, angry, and anxious. Cherry (1981) and Honig (1986) have pointed out that children do not always have the ability to relax on their own. Marion (1999) discusses teaching children specific relaxation techniques to help them cool down and become more receptive to guidance from adults.

In the encouraging classroom, the normal activity level is busy.

The traditional naps in preschool, the rest periods or naps in kindergarten, and quiet periods in elementary grades—when done nonpunitively—all serve to restore a sense of equilibrium for children and teachers. Stories too, when done on a daily basis in a relaxed atmosphere, have regenerating values. The relaxation materials mentioned previously go a step further, however, by providing activities to specifically reduce stress in young children. A few topics in the Cherry text, for instance, are:

- creating wholesome environments;
- responding to stress;
- developing inner awareness;
- learning to relax muscles (pp. v–vii).

Think of Something Quiet is now as old as some students reading this book. No work in the early childhood literature that I know of has replaced it; more attention needs to be given to the matter of relaxation and children at school.

In full-day programs for young children, nap times can be challenging. Children have different rest needs and show differing behaviors when adjusting to nap time (Saifer, 1990). When children of different ages share the same room for rest, problems can be compounded. The "fingertip guide" shown in Table 6–4 provides suggestions for helping staff meet nap challenges.

Table 6–4

Fingertip Guide to Happy Napping

Challenge	Suggestion
Many children have trouble settling down.	Review: (a) Activity level prior to nap—relaxing, quiet? (b) Method of creating mood—story, music, relaxation activity used? (c) Environment—comfortable temperature, low lighting, enough space? (d) Role of adults—present, speaking quietly, lying with children, rubbing backs?
Children rest, but many are ready to rise too early.	Assess length of nap time. Consider shortening. Start early risers doing quiet activities.
Older children don't sleep; ready to rise before others.	Move older children to different room or separate area. Allow to read books on mats. Allow to rise early and do quiet activities.
Individual child doesn't sleep; ready to rise. Doesn't seem tired.	Check with parent about child's sleep schedule and habits. Some children need less sleep than others. If willing, try solution above for older children; note how child responds.
Individual child doesn't sleep; ready to rise. Does seem tired.	Separate from others. Primary caregiver rubs back, lies by child. At another time talk with child about problem. Talk with parent about child's sleeping habits.
Individual child not ready to rise with others.	Let child sleep. Monitor health of child. If pattern continues, talk with parent about possible reasons.
Early risers in buffer activity get too active.	Review selection of activities. Allow to read books or make pictures, but *not* watch videos. Young children watch hours each day at home as it is. Review placement of children: too near sleepers? too close together?

Adults help children to nap when they create a relaxing mood and setting. Maintaining a firm, friendly, and quiet response style is important. Staff who take a problem-solving approach can most often improve the situation (Saifer, 1990), often within a week or two.

One group in a child care center had preschoolers along with part-time kindergarten children who arrived from school each day at noon. The kindergarten kids felt they were "too old" for naps, and the younger children were affected each day by their arrival. "Rest" was proving difficult.

> One day an assistant teacher asked a kindergarten child to rub the back of his younger brother to help the three-year-old get settled. It worked. The preschool staff got to talking about this and decided to try something new. They had each kindergarten child rub the back of a selected preschooler. After the preschooler fell asleep, the kindergartners lay down on their mats behind a long book shelf. On their mats the "k" kids looked at books or listened to relaxing music. In just a few days, rest time at the center changed completely.

These days changing family dynamics, mean that more children are coming to classrooms with sleep deprivation. A health-related condition, sleep disruptions can result in classic Level Three mistaken behaviors that hinder individual development and community building. Any child can arrive at school overtired, for any number of reasons. Sometimes, the best thing that teachers can do is help a child leave the group and get some rest—and perhaps contact the parent. If sleep deprivation continues, the teacher should work actively with other staff and the family to address the situation.

Active Play   For teachers to use boisterous activity productively, three ideas are important.

1. Throughout the age range, movement to music activities refreshes participants and renews their ability to concentrate. A common practice in Asian programs, some American schools now begin the day with movement to music. Pieces by Steve and Greg, Hap Palmer, and various current "aerobics for kids" artists are piped into classrooms over the loudspeakers. Teachers as well as the children move to the music. As enjoyment and not skill is the purpose, each person moves in her own way.
2. The teacher should not rely only on scheduled active play times or physical education periods to meet children's need for vigorous activity. At the preprimary level, include an active play center—a climber, mini-tramp, adapted exercise equipment, etc.—that is open each day.
3. Effective vigorous play activities involve children without the need to compete or take turns. Young children run for the sake of running, skip for the sake of skipping, and climb for the sake of climbing. The rules and complexities of competitive games tend to confuse young children and cause hurt feelings (Honig & Wittmer, 1996). As well, wait times between turns are often frustrating and limit the opportunity for physical activity that is the main reason for the activity. When all participate enjoyably, everybody wins.

An early childhood teacher became tired of the usual active game in her class, Duck, Duck, Grey Duck. A large portion of the game was spent in squatting down. Once the children began running, the teacher noticed most did not want to stop. The inability of some children to catch the others also detracted from the fun. The teacher ended the game. Instead, she adapted Red Light, Green Light for her group by requiring different ways to move each time the "green light" showed and declaring the whole class winners as soon as the last child crossed the finish line. The game became the new favorite of the children, especially when the teacher taped a red light to her front and a green light to her back, jumped around, and enthusiastically called out directions.

Teachers who take the guidance approach need to consider the balance of active and quiet times in the daily programs. Distinct from traditional practices, the general noise level of classrooms should be *busy*, with planned periods that are *boisterous* and *bucolic*.

THE LIMITS OF LARGE GROUPS

A hallmark of encouraging classrooms is that they accommodate the entire range of developmental responses that any group of children will show. A productive *center* such as a reading center accommodates developmental diversity by providing a variety of materials from picture books to "early readers" to elementary science tests. Productive *materials* such as blocks and clay accommodate developmental diversity by allowing children to construct whatever they will, from a simple stack to a castle, from a simple clay ball to a bird sitting on its nest of eggs. Productive *activities* also are developmentally inclusive. In the area of art, for instance, the teacher avoids predrawn forms and craft projects but instead motivates children to work creatively with the materials provided so that each child can succeed at her level (Bredekamp & Copple, 1997; Edwards & Nabors, 1993).

Likewise, productive **grouping patterns** encourage children to function effectively at their various levels of development. A problem with overreliance on large group, teacher-directed activities is that they easily exceed children's developmental levels and attention spans (Brewer, 2000). Very few preschoolers, only some kindergarteners, and many—but not all—primary grade children are capable of sitting, listening, and following directions for any length of time (Bredekamp & Copple, 1997; McAfee, 1986).

An argument for frequent large groups is that young children need to get used to sitting and listening to succeed at school. However, the physiology of preprimary children prevents them from sitting comfortably for long periods.

Children play actively without the need for adult direction, even under less than
ideal conditions. (Courtesy Michael Crowley, Family Service Center,
Kootasca Head Start, Grand Rapids, Minnesota)

To the comment that young children must learn to sit and listen, the response
is that young children are not developmentally ready; they will become more
ready as they get older (Brewer, 2000). In fact, even though the development
of primary grade children means that they attend longer, the DAP research indicates that even primary grade children learn more effectively when they are
actively doing and interacting (Bredekamp & Copple, 1997; Brewer, 2000;
Dunn & Kontos, 1997; Gronlund, 1995). The reality is that for some teachers
large groups offer a sense of predictability and control. As the following anecdote indicates, the opposite is often the case:

On a sunny spring afternoon, a first-grade class went to the library.
While there, they silently read/looked at books, then heard the li-
brarian read quite a long story. When they arrived back at the class-

room, a parent who was scheduled to read a book that morning arrived and asked if he could read then. The teacher felt this was important and agreed. She and the student teacher sat with the children and worked hard to keep them focused on the story.

The next scheduled activity was another large group; the student teacher was to do a lesson on friendship with a puppet named Charlie. After three tries at starting the lesson, the student teacher whispered to the teacher. Then, the Puppet announced, "Boys and girls, Charlie thinks that listening is hard to do right now because you have had to sit so long. When I call your name, line up to go outside." Charlie called out the names *very* rapidly. After a half hour outdoors, the teacher and student teacher again had "happy campers." The class came in and worked industriously on their daily journals.

Throughout this age range, children learn best when they engage in many independent activities, frequent small groups, and *limited* large groups that are friendly, participatory, relevant to the children's experiences, and concise (McAfee, 1986). Brewer (2000) and McAfee (1986) recommend that teachers review standard large group practices for such criteria. From the perspective of the encouraging classroom, this section examines some traditional large group practices: taking attendance, calendar and the weather, show and tell, and large group instruction and, presents suggestions for making them more effective when engaging young learners.

Taking Attendance

Attendance can be done efficiently if teachers greet children individually when they arrive and ask them to "register" right away. One way of registering is to have them log in on a computer program. A lower-tech method is to laminate "mushrooms" with each child's name, a child-made design, and the child's photo. After learning their names, the children take their own mushrooms from slots in one tagboard sheet and put them in the slots with their names on a second sheet. At a morning class meeting, the teacher quickly reviews the charts with the class, and those absent and present are noted. Even three-year-olds quickly recognize their names.

An alternative, which many teachers enjoy, is to sing an attendance song that mentions each present child by name. Such songs may have made-up words to familiar tunes and sometimes use name cards, such as the "mushrooms" to encourage functional literacy. Songs make taking attendance more participatory, an objective for successful large groups. Teachers who use greeting songs seem to overcome two minor difficulties with them: (a) with a large class, long verses take a lot of time; (b) some children get embarrassed and

Primary grade children, like younger children, learn more effectively
when they are doing and interacting.

may not want their names sung. Short verses and a matter-of-fact approach
with individual children make this method of greeting successful.

Calendar and the Weather

Many teachers like calendar and weather activities because they introduce
children to new vocabulary and sequencing. But these activities too easily become rituals rather than conceptual learning experiences (McAfee, 1986). As
mentioned, until middle childhood children experience **time confusion,**
which means they have difficulty understanding time concepts (Elkind, 1976).
A first-grade teacher was amused to discover time confusion when he asked
his students two questions: What season is the month of November in? How
old they thought he was? He got answers that included *salty, 18,* and *62!* In
their article about time, Van Scoy and Fairchild (1993) say this about typical
time activities such as the daily calendar:

> Time is often taught to children by having them recite social labels such as
> the days of the week or months of the year. Children who recite labels in this
> way are being given an opportunity to construct social knowledge about
> time. . . . Social knowledge is knowledge of an arbitrary set of symbols and
> behaviors common to a society. Children who recite labels are not having
> experiences that will help them develop an understanding of the passage of
> time. (p. 21)

A common experience many teachers recognize at calendar time is for children to sing a "recognition" song involving days or months and still not be able to name the day or month. And still they continue the ritual.

Weather concepts also are more abstract to children than adults may realize. Two partly cloudy days following two cloudy days simply is not an every day topic of conversation for five-year-olds. When the selected "weatherperson" goes to the window and looks hard at what's going on outside, she may notice one small cloud and announce that the day is cloudy; see snow on the ground & declare it snowy. If the child gives a "wrong" report, the teacher has to engage in "damage control," especially with the two others who thought they should have been picked to be the weatherperson to begin with.

Many teachers use alternatives to the ritualistic treatment of the calendar and the weather. In a morning class meeting, an alternative is to ask four or five questions that encourage children to think about time and weather concepts in ways that have personal meaning for them. Sample questions include:

- Who can remember what you had for supper last night?
- Who knows what you will do after school today?
- Who can remember three things you saw on the way to school this morning?
- Was it hot or cold outside today? How could you tell?
- It is windy today. Who saw the wind push something?
- It is raining today. Who hopes it is still raining after school today? Why? Why not?

These questions relate directly to the children's experience. If children know that all interpretations of questions are welcome and not just one answer that the teacher may have in mind, they will participate readily. Through engagement in interesting discussion, children gain in observation powers, thinking skills, and communication abilities (McAfee, 1986). They will have a foundation in personal experience that will help them master adult weather and time concepts later.

Despite the criticism that conventional calendar and weather tend to be more meaningful to teachers than children, many teachers would rather not give them up. They value the social development that occurs through a positive group experience and maintain that the exposure to weather, day, and date vocabulary has its own value. I remember visiting a classroom of three-year-olds in a child care center where the children clearly enjoyed singing a "days of the week" song, and the weatherperson's report was appreciated whatever it turned out to be. These activities helped the children feel a sense of belonging, reliability, and accomplishment—important for young ones away from home. The suggestion here is that young children may not understand as much from these activities as the teacher may think. A compromise is to do calendar and the weather in a way that is concise, positive, and as relevant as possible to the children's own experience. Then move on to activities that have more intrinsic interest for the audience.

Show and Tell

Show and tell often is criticized as "bring and brag" (Brewer, 2000). The thought behind show and tell seems to be that if children bring in familiar objects, they will feel comfortable showing them in a large group and so use communication skills. One problem with show and tell is that it is materialistic. Focusing on object possession, children expect one another to bring in interesting items. Then they judge each child on the basis of the items shown (Brewer, 2000). A second problem is that the child may not have a lot to say about the item. The teacher then has to become an interviewer, and the rest of the group may tune out. Passivity is likely to increase if all in the group are expected to share (Saifer, 1990), and after a few months of following the same show and tell routine (McAfee, 1986).

Teachers handle problems with show and tell in various ways. Most directly, some teachers have ended the practice. They spark discussions in the circle time instead that lead to a fuller sharing of thoughts and feelings. Open-ended questions that children can personally relate to are a superior medium for developing communications skills. The kinds of questions mentioned under the calendar and weather heading are examples. A few others include:

- Who can tell us about a time when you went swimming?
- Who can share about when you were in a snowball fight?
- Who knows about an interesting pet that someone owns?

Such questions lead well into themes and learning center activities that may follow the large group. They arouse interest and focus on *ideas* rather than *things*.

For teachers who do not wish to end show and tell altogether, Saifer (1990) provides ideas for dealing with "bored children during show and tell." Useful ideas include:

- Do show and tell in small groups (such as during center time, for those who are interested);
- Schedule show and tell on a rotating basis with only some children sharing each day;
- Directly encourage other children to ask questions; stand behind the child to direct the group's attention;
- "Have children share family experiences, a picture they made, or what they did earlier in the day at school. Sharing themselves rather than things, helps children who have no item to share; develops the children's ability to review; and makes for more personal, meaningful sharing" (Saifer, 1990, p. 22).

Some teachers have successfully linked show & tell to ongoing themes. The main idea is to replace a competitive materialistic focus (on things) with a spirit of community that the sharing of thoughts, feelings and experiences can inspire.

Using Stories with Children

The traditional method of delivering stories is the large group. When doing stories in a large group, to preserve lines of sight, teachers frequently sit on low chairs. Children sit on rug samples or other markers, which reduces crowding and the frequent complaint that "I can't see." The technique is efficient but results in a separation between adult and children. An alternative in story delivery is the small group. With children on the adult's lap or all lying on stomachs around a book, an important closeness results, which the McCrackens term the lap technique (McCracken & McCracken, 1987). Ideally, the lap technique begins early in the child's life at home. To encourage an appreciation of books and reading, the lap technique is an important method to use but difficult to accomplish in the large group. (See anecdote, page 210.)

Of course, a role remains for stories in large group settings (McCracken & McCracken, 1987). Two different purposes for using stories in large groups may be helpful to note: First, encourage appreciation; second, encourage personal expression. By focusing on the particular intention of the story experience, the teacher can reduce mistaken behavior.

Reading to Encourage Appreciation   The long-standing goal of reading for appreciation is to teach children to enjoy the rhythm and flow of language and plot. Teachers who wish to encourage appreciation of books and stories want the experience to be relaxing and engaging for the children. Usual times when the teacher reads to foster enjoyment are after sustained activity for a calming effect; and to set a relaxed mood for an activity to come such as lunch, nap, or going home. Adults can use various methods to establish an engaging story setting. The techniques listed in Figure 6–1 are the author's top ten suggestions.

Reading to Encourage Personal Expression   Although reading to encourage children's appreciation of stories is common in early childhood, there is a second function, *the encouragement of personal expression.* Some teachers are able to integrate the two functions quite effortlessly in the group setting, but others struggle especially with the second.

Reading for personal expression means encouraging discussion during and after the story. At key points while he is reading, the teacher asks open-ended questions and welcomes children's responses. He uses a technique called *discussing inclusively.* Discussing inclusively means that when a child makes a comment that doesn't seem to relate to the discussion, the teacher realizes that the comment *does relate for the child.* The teacher responds in a friendly way and tries to include the comment in the conversation. When discussing inclusively, he does not focus on *correct* or *incorrect* answers but allows the discussion to build, based on the shared and unique experiences of the children. When the teacher thinks it is appropriate, he steers attention back to the book and continues to read.

Figure 6–1

Top 10 Techniques for Encouraging Appreciation of Books and Stories

1. **Choose books carefully.** Select books appropriate for the age and backgrounds of the children and that will engage and hold their interest. Think about the children's attention spans and interests when previewing books you will read. Consider whether stories reinforce or go beyond stereotypes pertaining to culture, gender, and disability.

2. **Select books that match themes and special events.** Many "read aloud," "story stretching," and theme books have bibliographies of relevant books. Preread such books for appropriateness to ages and interests of group. Discuss with the children whether or not they like a book you have just read.

3. **Use "big," oversized picture books** so that all children can see the important details. Videos of children's literature *perhaps* also have their place, but they cannot be as easily personalized by the teacher.

4. **Select books you can read with expression.** If you are not familiar with the story, practice reading it aloud first. Use dramatic tones when you read; animate your usual speaking voice. When you are "into" the story, the children will be.

5. **Station co-teachers and volunteers near certain children** who may need extra support to stay engaged. If other adults are not available, quietly seat children who need extra support close to you. Establish that all children can see and that children need to stay seated where they are so that they can continue to see.

6. **Use a brief finger play, movement activity, or engaging introduction** to help children get ready for the story. If an anticipatory set is not established, some children may not focus enough to pick up the story line. Avoid simply starting the book without first gaining the children's attention; otherwise, you may never have it.

7. **Allow children to read their own books while you read.** Many children can attend to two things at once, and this will help *independent learners* keep occupied. The practice sounds unorthodox, but it is in line with the outcome of appreciation for reading and books. Typically, only some children choose to read their own books; these readers stay with their books until the teacher gets to a "good part." Then they look up and follow the teacher's story. These children are often the ones who have trouble attending in the large group.

8. **Tell stories as well as read them.** Some current or historic folktales of cultural relevance to your group may not be accessible in written form. Telling stories takes fortitude the first few times, but children adjust quickly to this "radio way of learning." Ask children to close their eyes and see the pictures in their minds. Having children spread out and lie down adds to the success of this experience and makes the technique useful at rest time.

9. **Gauge your time.** Avoid selecting books that will be too long for the available time block. You can sometimes shorten stories to fit the time but be prepared to be corrected if the children know the story already.

10. **Have backup activities planned.** Be ready to shorten the experience, change books, or switch to another activity if many children lose interest.

Through the technique of discussing inclusively, the teacher fosters a number of desirable learner outcomes, including the practice of listening and speaking skills, comprehension abilities, engagement in the learning process, enjoyment of literature, and comfort at speaking in front of others. A fear of speaking in public is widespread and too often gets its start in elementary classroom discussions that are handled insensitively. Teachers need not, and should not, restrict inclusive discussions to children's books, but reading for personal expression provides an excellent opportunity to build a classroom where all feel their ideas are welcome.

Often, teachers use reading for personal expression as a lead-in for related expressive activity such as creative drama, journaling, story-pictures, or more free-flowing discussion. Effective follow-up depends upon the teacher finding topics to which the children can relate. Often the most effective follow-up is in small groups, which the teacher may or may not have previously planned.

After a snowfall, a kindergarten teacher was reading the classic, *A Snowy Day*, when Clarise raised her hand: "Teacher, me and Cleo went sliding and she got snow down her pants!" (General laughter.)

Teacher: That must have been cold. What did she do?
Clarise: She went inside but Paul and me kept sliding. It was fun.
Teacher: Thanks for sharing, Clarise; did anyone else go sliding last weekend?

After several children shared, the teacher commented, "You had lots of good times sliding and skiing. Now let's see what's going to happen to Peter."

At the end of the book, the teacher announced: "It sounds as if you like to do lots of fun things in the snow just like Peter. Right now, when I call your name, you are going to tell me which "snowy day" center you are going to today, and I will note your choice. Remember that when one center is full, you can pick another. Either today or tomorrow, everyone will get to go to the centers they want." The teacher then quickly had the children chose between four "snowy day" learning centers, including a story-picture activity at the writing center where they created stories about what they liked to do outside in the snow.

As a final note, display books you have read to the class in the library center for children to look at by themselves and use in small-group activities. When they use stories to spark follow-up activity, teachers encourage a fuller appreciation of the literature they have shared and literacy development.

Large groups work well to orient children to interactive follow-up experiences on an individual basis or in small groups.

Large Group Instruction

Teaching in large groups seems normal because it is the way most teachers themselves were educated, kindergarten through college. In traditional large group instruction, the teacher transmits information and then solicits repetition or application of the information from "volunteers" who give an indication of group understanding.

The basic criticism of this "didactic method" is that children are "over taught and under practiced" (McCracken & McCracken, 1987). They absorb the information but don't have the opportunity to construct their own knowledge from it. They are not fully able to "own" the learning, make sense of it, and value it. Common signs that children are unable to engage in the learning process include glassy eyes, inattentiveness, and restlessness (Gronlund, 1995). With prolonged exposure to the passivity of large groups, feelings of inadequacy build, and chronic mistaken behavior—tuning out as well as acting out—tend to result.

Contrasted with traditional large group instruction, the DAP position is that learning is *interactive.* The teacher provides opportunities for the child to integrate learning through expression in creative endeavor—art, music, play,

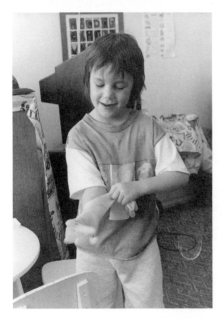
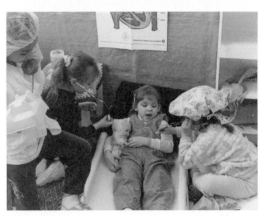

Stimulated by a teacher in surgical garb, children follow up large group discussion with hospital play, complete with doctors, patients, and even a "new baby."

creative drama, construction, and discussion (Bredekamp & Copple, 1997). When carefully planned, large groups work well for orienting children to an interactive learning experience called establishing an **anticipatory set.** The child then moves to a follow-up activity, either individually or in a small group. Using large groups to establish an anticipatory set *is* developmentally appropriate (Barbour & Seefeldt, 1992).

Whenever a large group is to be the sole vehicle for instruction, however, the teacher needs to proceed with caution (Bredekamp & Copple, 1997; McAfee, 1986). Successful large group experiences tend to include a series of short activities—a concise presentation or demonstration, a brief story, a movement activity or song, class business—each of which is *less than five minutes.* A quick pace to the large group, followed by a crisp transition, reduces passivity. To reiterate an earlier statement, for large groups to be a part of an interactive learning program, they should be friendly, participatory, relevant to children's experiences, and concise.

A teaching team in an early childhood class held three 20-minute large groups each day; as soon as all the children arrived, before lunch, and before time to go home. The team, frankly, was having problems with the large groups. The teachers tried preventive methods such as placing themselves strategically in the circle to help children stay focused. Still, many of the children grew restless, and the teachers found themselves calling for attention as much as conducting activities.

The lead teacher met with the team, and they reorganized the day. The teachers continued the morning large group but reduced it to singing a single attendance song and doing a "slow transition" game while children washed hands for breakfast. They dispensed with the large group just before lunch; instead, staff read stories to the children in three family groups. The groups also ate lunch together. Brief singing and a transition activity comprised the large group in the afternoon. The class went from one hour of large group each day to about 15 minutes.

With the change the teachers found that mistaken behavior decreased, and more children seemed engaged in productive activity. Though they had to "sell" the new program to a supervisor and parents, the team was pleased with the results.

MANAGING TRANSITIONS

Transitions, changes from one activity to the next, have the potential to be disruptive. One classic transition dilemma occurs at cleanup between individual activity and large group. A conventional approach is to get most of the children into the circle and then call out, "We're waiting for Ryan and Sonya." Such an approach often embarrasses the targeted children and may make others in the circle wonder who is going to get "nagged" next.

Instead, the professional teacher uses alternative strategies that get children to the group on time but do not undercut self-esteem. Here are some basic guidance strategies for transitions. Some are more appropriate for preprimary classrooms; others pertain throughout the age range.

1. Give a notice five minutes before the transition. Some children—like adults—get so involved that they may need an additional "two-minute" notice.

For large groups to be developmentally appropriate, they are friendly, participatory, relevant, and concise. (Courtesy, *Bemidji Pioneer*)

2. Model enthusiasm for the cleanup process. Make the process a game with comments like, "I need some strong kids over here who can carry lots of blocks. Who is strong enough?" Participate in the cleanup.

3. Give generous encouragement to the group who are conscientious about cleaning up (Saifer, 1990). Ignore or use private matter-of-fact comments to children who are slow to participate. Avoid accusations and debates.

4. Sing a cleanup song with the children. Make up words and put them to a familiar tune. Children capture moods more easily than adults. Songs, or even popular pieces of recorded music, identify the transition and get children into the mood.

5. Make up and sing a song in the large group naming children who are there. (To your own tune:)
   "We're happy to see you, see you, see you.
   We're happy to see Cathy, at circle time today."
   Be sure to include all children, including the late-comers when they arrive so that no one feels left out. The song is likely to

Recognize that even after a five-minute notice, children sometimes will need a bit longer to finish. Some activities can be returned to later in the day.

speed up the transition and serves as a buffer activity, an activity that uses time productively while waiting. (One of the fringe benefits of teaching young children is they don't care if you can't carry a tune, just if you don't sing.)

6. With enthusiasm start the large group before all have arrived. The magnetism of an exciting large group will attract the rest of the children. No comment about anyone who is late is needed.

Waiting

A primary consideration in managing transitions is the reduction of time children spend waiting. Young children live in the here and now (Elkind, 1976). Although most will do it better as they get older, children under seven or eight years do not wait well. Strategies the teacher uses to reduce wait times prevent many problems.

Natasha, a student teacher, was in charge of "art time" in a kindergarten class. Her projects were all open-ended and creative (and so developmentally appropriate). She ran into problems, though, with the wait time before the children could do the projects. First, she had the children sit at the tables while she gave directions. Then she handed out the materials to each table. The problem was the children grabbed for the materials at the same time and mini-chaos resulted.

After talking with her cooperating teacher, Natasha made some changes for "next time." She had all materials out on the tables when the children came in from recess. This time they began using the materials before she could introduce the project, so the theme was lost.

Finally, she used a two-step approach. She set the materials out on the tables but had the children sit at the large group circle when they came in. She discussed the project with them at the circle. Then she dismissed them to their tables a few at a time by the color of clothing they wore: "All wearing purple or yellow may get up and slowly walk to their tables." The student teacher did not interrupt the flow by challenging children who had interesting interpretations of purple or yellow; the purpose was to get them to the tables efficiently without a stampede or hurt feelings.

Buffer Activities

A **buffer activity** keeps children occupied during wait times. A song in a large group before everyone arrives is an example. At the primary level, a teacher often has alternative activities for children who finish first. Such activities range from "working quietly at your desk" to use of selected learning centers. Although these types of buffer activities are useful, they should not be so attractive that they encourage hurried completion of the main lesson. Such a pattern discourages thorough work habits and discriminates against children who work slowly or find the task difficult. Popular activities sometimes used as buffers should be available at another time of day for all to enjoy. With thought, the teacher can use buffer activities to reduce significant amounts of mistaken behavior.

Children at a Head Start center were having problems each day just before lunch. The schedule called for them to come in from outdoor play, line up to use the restroom, and wash hands. During this time, the lead teacher prepared the tables for lunch, and the assistant teacher monitored the lines. Waiting in line with nothing to do was difficult for many of the children. Pushing and fights were becoming more frequent.

The teaching team reviewed the situation and tried a new arrangement. The teacher brought in a few children early. They washed their hands first and helped the teacher set the tables and bring in the food on carts. When the rest of the children came in, they sat at the reading center near the restroom and sink where they looked at books together. During this buffer, the assistant teacher had small clusters of children use the facilities and rotate back to their books until lunch. The waiting in line was eliminated and with it the mistaken behavior.

A first step in creating a successful buffer activity is awareness that mistaken behavior can be situationally caused by prolonging the time that children are waiting. With this awareness, the second step follows: adapting the program to better accommodate the children's development. Buffer activities, sometimes planned, sometimes spontaneous, help in this effort.

Learning to Live with Lines

Young children and lines—like large groups—are not a natural match. Moving big groups of little people is always a hazardous business. In many preschools, formal lines are not used. Out-of-building excursions are safest when the ratio of adults to children is at least 1:4 and lines are not needed. This ratio is so important, especially on busy streets, that staff should do their utmost to recruit additional volunteers for these occasions. An unsafe alternative is the old-time use of ropes with loops that each child holds. Besides the "chain gang" appearance, anyone who has seen one child stumble and all lose their balance knows this is one piece of equipment that should be retired.

Preschools located in public school buildings sometimes experience difficulty with movement of the group through halls. The concept of two-by-two lines is not a natural one for three- and four-year-olds. School administrators should not expect the same "hall expertise" of preschoolers that they expect of third graders. Discussions with administrators about their expectations are important even before preschools locate in school buildings.

When having children line up, teachers learn quickly that more is needed than simply stating, "Everyone line up at the door." Instead, teachers need "creative alternatives," methods for lining up in a quick but orderly fashion. The methods should *not* violate the principle of unconditional positive regard—"Millie, you've been quiet; you can line up first today." This practice results in hurt feelings among the others who have been quiet and weren't selected. "Chance-based" criteria such as "Everyone whose first name begins with a C or K may quietly line up," are more appropriate. Chance-based criteria remove the appearance of favoritism from the line-up procedure and get the job done efficiently.

A common point of contention is who will be the "leader" (and sometimes "trailer") when lines form. Some programs have a Very Important Kid or Star of the Week who leads the lines for a designated period. Another method is to have a large chart with each child's name. A marker, moved each day, indicates who will lead. (Perhaps the child who led the previous day could be

Buffer activities, sometimes planned, sometimes spontaneous, reduce the mistaken behavior caused by waiting. (Courtesy, *Bemidji Pioneer*)

the "caboose.") Other markers could be placed on the chart to identify other "classroom helpers." This practice makes selection systematic and visible and eliminates "I was first!" "No, it's my turn!" controversies. (A child with the name Zelda Zyzkowitz can count how long before she gets a turn. List criteria should perhaps not always be alphabetical from A to Z.)

Here are two other considerations about line procedures, one controversial, the other, "common sense." In agreement with the ideas of anti-bias curriculum (Derman-Sparks, 1989), the author recommends lines that do not pair girls and boys. This practice needlessly exaggerates differences between the sexes in an era when cross-gender cooperation needs to be encouraged. Healthy cross-gender interactions become more difficult in programs that institutionalize gender differences (Derman-Sparks, 1989).

Instead, the teacher should work to create an atmosphere in which gender is accepted as just another element in who each child is. As *Anti-Bias Curriculum* points out, teachers have more say about reducing sexism in the classroom environment than they might think (Derman-Sparks, 1989). Comfortable cross-gender relations are in keeping with the encouraging classroom and should be reflected in line-up procedures as well as in all other parts of the program.

The commonsense suggestion is in relation to helping young children wait and move in lines cooperatively. Whenever a teacher can make such time an enjoyable experience, he is showing skill at preventing mistaken behavior. Having finger plays and songs ready for when children in line must wait is sound preventive practice. Simple songs that use the children's names are effective buffer activities.

Similarly, when children walk in lines, stimulating their imaginations can work wonders.

A particular kindergarten teacher used the children's imaginations to move her class efficiently. On one day she whispered: "Today, we are the elephant mommies and daddies. We need to tiptoe quietly so we don't wake up the sleeping baby elephants. Let's very quietly tiptoe down the hall." When the principal came out of her office to compliment the class, one of the children told her, "Ssh, you'll wake up the babies."

ROUTINES IN THE ENCOURAGING CLASSROOM: A TEACHER'S PERSPECTIVE

Familiarity with the classroom and full use of its many resources help children to become confident, productive learners. Pat Sanford, an experienced kindergarten and primary teacher in northern Minnesota, offers these thoughts about effective use of the classroom.

Pat says that the secret to classroom management lies in getting children used to **routines.** For example, she shows them how to store their boots, under their coats with the heels to the wall. This way, the boots won't get knocked over and mixed up with someone else's. Mittens go inside one sleeve. Then children will always know where they are. She makes sure they know where the restroom is (early on the first day) and how to use it.

Materials go back in boxes and on shelves just where they were. Clearly marked labels with pictures and words help the children decide this. Books are to be read and valued; they go back in the bookcase right-side up, facing out. She dislikes the word, "cubby," so each child has a storage bin and knows how to keep papers and belongings there. The children understand that messes during activities are perfectly OK. They also know that cleaning up afterwards is not an optional chore; it is a part of kindergarten life. After commenting about her management style, Pat adds, "Now, if my home only looked like my classroom. . . ."

As a professional, Pat does some things differently than other teachers. For most activities during the day children sit at tables wherever they wish. She comments:

Adults like to sit wherever they want; kids should be able to also. Like adults, kids settle in next to someone they're comfortable by. Usually, this is not a problem. If it looks like it might be, I just talk with them privately.

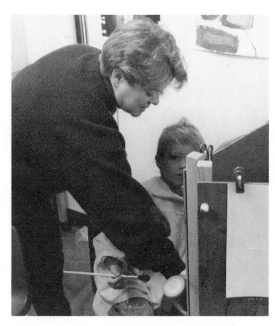

Pat sees her role as not preparing children for first grade but as providing the best possible kindergarten experience for each child.

Pat believes that not "institutionalizing" individual space encourages a more comfortable atmosphere. The same goes for the name the children use with their teacher. She makes it clear to the children that she does not want to be called "Teacher" ("Because I am a person"). Some call her "Mrs. Sanford," but most call her, "Pat."

Although she believes that helping children get used to routines is important to future school success, she brings a sense of humor to her managerial style. For Pat, the mixture of elementary school rituals and early childhood innocence often brings a smile:

> One day I was supervising a student teacher in Pat's classroom. With a grin, Pat sent me over to stand by a boy for the Pledge of Allegiance. With a hand on his heart he said loudly and with total confidence; I pledge Norwegians to the flag. . . ."

Finally, Pat is definite about her role as a teacher. "My job is not to prepare children for first grade. My job is to help them have the best kindergarten experience it is possible for them to have." Pat attributes the absence of discipline problems in her classroom to helping the children get used to kindergarten routines, "but in a way respectful to each child."

Helping children know that asking for assistance is all right is a part
of Pat's approach to teaching routines.

Whether readers agree with all of her ideas about managing the classroom, Pat offers some thoughtful suggestions that teachers of children aged three to eight would do well to consider. Enjoyment of the children, each and every day, is at the top of her list.

GUIDANCE MEANS TEAMWORK WITH OTHER ADULTS

A myth that still afflicts education is that the teacher handles all situations alone. Perhaps the myth goes back to the one-room schools of rural America's past and the expectations upon the teachers who taught in them. Many adults wanted no part of the teachers' job, which was seen as making unruly, undisciplined youth sit obediently and master the three Rs. Depending on their demeanor and perceived success, teachers were revered as saintly, like the first Montessori directresses in the tenements of Rome; respected for their iron discipline, like the school masters of British boarding schools; or made the butt of jokes, like the fabled Ichabod Crane. In any case, the adult community expected teachers to sink or swim on their own with minimal support from administrators, other teachers, or parents.

A remnant of the myth of the self-sufficient teacher still can be seen in relation to the first year of teaching. Some administrators remain oriented more to performance reviews than mentoring relationships. Happily, this trend is beginning to change. Early childhood educators are among those who have pointed out the need for new teachers to be eased into the profession by working with mentors. A new consciousness about the importance of family and community involvement for educational success is further indication that the myth of teacher as "supermarm" may be coming to an end.

Team-Teaching

There is **team-teaching** and then there is the **teaching team.** The two concepts are different. Team-teaching is the practice, mainly at the K–12 level, of having two similarly licensed teachers working together with the same group of children. Thornton (1990) provides a useful account of the problems and promise when two teachers work together. For Thornton, mutual trust is a prime ingredient and this quality takes hard work, communication, and time.

When the relationship is established, the benefits are many. Cooperative planning, implementation, and evaluation of the program take pressure off each individual. Through teamwork, developmentally appropriate, active learning experiences are easier to initiate. The choice of two personalities with whom to relate can be empowering both for the children and for their parents (Thornton, 1990). By virtue of their differing personalities, two teachers can respond more effectively to the wide array of learning and behavioral styles represented in any group of young children. When team-teaching is working, each member has a built-in support system.

The Teaching Team

The technical name for the teaching team is differentiated staffing, or the use of adults with differing credentials and experience bases to serve the same group of children. The traditional teaching team format is the teacher and the assistant teacher or the educational assistant. In actuality, classroom volunteers as well as staff can comprise the team. In modern educational settings, a teacher may work with volunteers, staff assistants, Title I teachers, special education teachers, and other specialists, all in the same class—a comprehensive staffing arrangement to be sure.

When the adults work together as a team, the teacher provides supervision for the learning environment, but the assistant works with small groups, individual children, and on occasion with the full group. In other words the assistant also teaches. Conversely, if the situation warrants, the teacher may wipe up a spill or help a child change clothes (Read, Gardner, & Mahler, 1995).

In classrooms where a strict separation of professional and assistant roles is maintained, the general assumption is that only the teacher does the teaching. Despite appearances, this view is incorrect. In reality, all adults in a classroom serve as models for young children, and so all are teachers. The adult who accepts this premise accepts the concept of the teaching team.

When a teaching team concept is used, children and adults benefit.

The advantages of the teaching team are similar to those of team-teaching, but the teaching team goes further in its model of democracy. When children see adults in differing social roles converse and work together, they learn that social and cultural differences need not be threatening. The teacher-parent relationship is the most direct example and offers the most benefit to the child. Nonetheless, when a teacher and assistant work together amicably, the child's expanding social world becomes that much more reliable and friendly. The children are likely to follow the lead of the teacher and feel respect for all the adults in the classroom.

When the efforts of the assistant are appreciated, he feels affirmed. Negative feelings that result from being "stigmatized" (disqualified from full membership in the group) do not arise. Disagreements do not become conflicts but get resolved. Like children, assistants who feel accepted participate fully (Read, Gardner, & Mahler, 1995).

Of course, not all assistants are prepared to function as "associate teachers" on the team. Using the criteria of state regulations, program policy, and personal readiness, the teacher, as team leader, determines how much responsibility other team members are to be given. Unpressured discussion about roles, along with ongoing communication about duties, are important to make teaming work.

Over the last 25 years, a variety of terms have been used to describe teaching team members. The terms usually reflect the educational programs completed by the member and the roles defined by the program or district. Such terms as *volunteer, educational assistant, teacher-aide, teacher assistant, associate teacher, Child Development Associate, teacher, lead teacher, center supervisor,* and *early childhood educator* illustrate the complexity of the mix of roles. In 1994, the National Association for the Education of Young Children (NAEYC) issued a position statement titled, "A Conceptual Framework for Early Childhood Professional Development," which is helping to clarify the role definitions for both programs and educational institutions. The point of the teaching team is that it is comprised of adults of various education levels and backgrounds working together, with mutually respectful communication and trust. The positive atmosphere in such classrooms radiates to the children.

The Teaching Team in the Primary Grades   On the surface, the teaching team concept seems to have less relevance to K–3 classrooms. In most schools the system is set: one teacher, twenty to thirty-five children. When an educational assistant is present, it is usually for a small part of the day. The assistant likely has "paraprofessional" duties specified in the "master contract."

Primary grade teachers who wish to incorporate a team concept into their classrooms sometimes have limited options, but it is happening. The growing practice of **inclusion,** or broad-scale integration of children with disabilities in the "regular" classroom, is advancing the teaching team concept by bringing special education teachers and assistants into the classroom. Some teachers recruit parents, college students, or senior citizens to come into classrooms on a regular basis. These volunteers read to children, supervise learning situations, work with small groups, or otherwise lend their experience. In a growing number of schools, students from the upper grades assist in prekindergarten, kindergarten, and primary classrooms. Where such efforts are organized and supervised, programs run smoothly, and both older and younger children benefit.

Teacher as Team Leader   With the use of a teaching team, the teacher's role changes. He no longer undertakes all teaching transactions. Instead, he manages an active learning laboratory, teaching and modeling continuously, but also supervising others who are helping. The complexity of the team leader or "lead teacher" role makes it an uncomfortable one for many new teachers just entering the profession and for others, steeped in the traditional notion of what a teacher does.

We are still learning about the teacher's role in the differentiated staffing situation, and about the effects of the teaching team for the classroom and children's behavior. In some ways the role poses additional new tasks for teachers. In others it offers new freedoms and possibilities—in particular the ability to reach children who in the old system might have passed through unaided. Here is the connection with guidance. With more adults in the classroom on a regular basis, the chances for positive relations with adults increases, and the need for mistaken behavior diminishes.

Working with Other Professionals   Besides team members in the classroom, the teacher communicates with other professionals: administrators and specialists in the program or school; specialists from other agencies. As Kagan and Rivera point out (1991), the "buzzword" for such

The growing practice of inclusion is advancing the teaching team concept.

communication is **collaboration.** The word is a useful one if it has the meaning the authors intend:

> We have defined collaborations as those efforts that unite and empower individuals and organizations to accomplish collectively what they could not accomplish independently. (Kagan & Rivera, 1991, p. 52)

In early childhood settings, collaborations typically revolve around two criteria: (a) specifics of the program itself—resources, scheduling, content, methods; and (b) matters pertaining to the children in the class. When children show serious mistaken behavior, collaboration is often required. Information exchanges within the school or center, professionally done, assist the teacher to better understand the child and the situation. As Hendrick points out, however, discussions involving formal diagnosis or possible referral should not be effected between professionals by themselves (2000). Professional ethics, and often statute and policy, warrant the involvement of parents. (See NAEYC Code of Ethics, Appendix A.)

When parents, the teacher, and other professionals meet for a possible referral or special services, the teacher assists the collaboration by remaining sensitive to the discomfort that many parents feel in the presence of professionals. Such collaborations are strengthened when representatives of all concerned programs participate, such as day care staff with the kindergarten teacher, or Head Start personnel with early childhood special education teachers. The promise of collaboration is that the process allows for a comprehensive and unified plan that can assist a troubled child. The use of the teaching team makes many of the ideas in this book work more easily for the guidance teacher.

PARENTS AND OTHER CLASSROOM VOLUNTEERS

A premise of this chapter is that the shift away from large groups toward small group and individual activities promotes an encouraging classroom. Moving to a **multidimensional environment** though, does pose challenges for the teacher. In the multidimensional environment, the teacher is a classroom manager as well as a teacher. The teaching team concept, is not an absolute requirement in this classroom environment, but it does make the teacher's tasks easier.

Depending on the skills and comfort level of the teaching team members, staff and volunteers perform a variety of functions in the classroom. The teacher's goal is to have volunteers working with individual children, reading stories, leading small groups, being in charge of centers, and presenting on occasion to the full group. Children gain from the role modeling, encouragement, support, and teaching that caring adults working as a team can provide.

In a kindergarten with an effective volunteer program, five parents visit the class once a week at center time. (One attends each day.) They usually help with the same center each week, where an index card (work card) provides them with instructions. Occasionally, Mona (the teacher) will ask a parent to go to a different center or help with a particular project, like making cookies with a small group. Several other parents have visited to share a hobby, interest, or item of family heritage with the class. Many parents have come in on their child's birthday and on monthly class field trips. Parents know they are welcome, and some have brought younger brothers or sisters when they have visited.

Mona is an exception in her school, and developing the program has taken a few years. Some parents each year have chosen not to participate. Not all the teachers approve, though more are including parents than in prior years. It has taken extra work, but Mona believes firmly that involving parents in the classroom is worthwhile for the increased individual attention the children receive.

Helping Parent Volunteers Feel Welcome

The key to working successfully with parent volunteers is to help them feel welcome. At whatever point a parent enters, she should be greeted by the teacher and usually introduced to the children. Taking time to orient the parent briefly is important. A "parent's corner," though not always possible in

"Oh, yes, Joanie's parents—I recognized you from her drawings!"

Joanie's Parents (Courtesy of Mrs. Ray Morin)

the classroom, provides a great home base. A bulletin board, checkout library, pamphlets and fliers, a collection of newsletters, and a place the parent can leave belongings should be included. One teacher set up a corner behind a tall book stand in the reading center. When not used by the teacher at story time, a rocking chair was kept in the "corner."

In addition to parent helpers with parties and field trips, parents who share knowledge or skills with a class are important "special events" volunteers. One teacher asked three families per month to share a favorite dish, the vocation of a family member, a family interest (including the interest of an older brother or sister), and/or a bit of family heritage. The social studies program for the year was taken care of on this basis. Parents working in nontraditional gender roles are a particularly important resource. A male nurse, a female firefighter or police officer, an in-home working dad all raise children's consciousness levels and horizons.

On the first visits for parents who may become regulars, the teacher encourages the parent to walk around, interact, and observe but not take on undue responsibility (Gestwicki, 2000). The teacher is aware that the busyness of the developmentally appropriate classroom will draw in the parent. Sitting and talking with a group as they work, reading a book to children, and helping a child get a coat on closely resemble parenting tasks—tasks that parents generally find nonthreatening in a home or classroom.

Some children feel strong emotions when parents enter the room or leave for the day. Teachers often cite this drawback for not encouraging parent involvement (Gestwicki, 2000). The teacher addresses this possibility before hand by providing reassurance that she will work with the parent to handle any problems that arise (Gestwicki, 2000). Allowing the child to sit with the parent shows sensitivity to the child's feelings. Reassurance and diver-

Classroom volunteers often include foster grandparents, college interns, students from older grades, and parents. (Top left photo courtesy, *Bemidji Pioneer*)

sion to activities are standard at the time of separation. As children adjust to frequent visitations by parents, their own included, the need for their parents' undivided attention subsides.

Regular Volunteers   When a few parents have begun to volunteer regularly, the teacher may want to meet with them after school. Such meetings can be useful in further acquainting the parent with the education program or with observation techniques to better understand children's needs (Kasting, 1994). "Old hands" might be invited to attend to share suggestions and sometimes to educate about DAP as well as the teacher. (An important example is educating parents to let children do their own artwork.) If a parent needs extra guidance about volunteering, the teacher needs to find a way to provide it (Gestwicki, 2000). Open and timely communication can prevent the unusual circumstance of asking a parent to come in less often.

The teacher will know that a volunteer is a true "regular" when ongoing communication becomes unnecessary. Teachers then can begin to rely on the skills of the volunteer by assigning a center and providing a work card, as Mona did in the previous anecdote. Gestwicki sums up the process of helping parents become productive in the classroom by stating:

Parents (and grandparents) who share knowledge or skills with a class are important "special events" volunteers. Here, John helps two children make pinecone bird feeders.

As teachers invite parents to participate in classroom learning activities, they need to concentrate on their skills for working with adults. Teachers need to be able to relax and enjoy the contribution of others to their classrooms and not feel threatened by any attention transferred from themselves to a visiting adult. It is important to remember that as more specific information is given to parents, parents will feel more comfortable knowing what is expected of them. (p. 308)

Perhaps the most important reason for involving parents in the class-room is that it encourages them to be active in their children's education (Rockwell, Andre, & Hawley, 1996). Each year as a result of parent in-volvement, families become more interested in their children's success at school—and the children respond. This reason is enough, but annually as well, many parents become interested in personal and professional ad-vancement as a result of a successful volunteering experience.

Parents like feeling that they're making a valuable contribution to a class-room. Many parents will try to find the time for a visit if they feel truly needed and wanted. A note of appreciation from the teacher and children af-terwards, pictures of the event displayed on a bulletin board, a mention of the event as a classroom highlight in the next newsletter—all these convey to par-ents that their time was well spent. (Gestwicki, 2000, p. 309)

The most important reason for involving parents is that it encourages them to become more active in their children's education.

SUMMARY

1. How does the teacher balance reliability and novelty in the daily program?

The schedule provides a base line of predictability for the children about the program. When unscheduled events enable positive results for children, they add to the everyday program. The teacher maintains the balance between predictability and novelty by reading children's behaviors and discussing reasons for changes with them. Though "busy" sets the tone for the classroom, children and teachers also need periods of rest and relaxation. Relaxation activities and a thoughtful approach to rest times rejuvenate spirits in children and adults alike. The teacher provides opportunities for vigorous activity each day. Movement-to-music during large group activities refreshes children and renews their ability to concentrate. Effective vigorous activities avoid formal rules, competition, and taking turns.

2. What part do large group activities play in the encouraging classroom?

A problem with overreliance on large groups is that they easily exceed children's developmental levels and attention spans. For this reason, large groups should be used selectively and not as a matter of institutional routine. Teachers who want to use large groups effectively do well to reassess the effectiveness of traditional large group practices: taking attendance, calendar and the weather, show and tell, reading, and large group instruction. A

Movement activities fit the criteria for developmentally appropriate
large group experiences.

developmentally appropriate use of large groups is to establish an *anticipatory set* for interactive follow-up activities done either independently or in small groups. For large groups to be a part of an interactive learning program, they should be friendly, participatory, relevant to children's experiences, and concise.

3. How does managing transitions reduce mistaken behavior?

Transitions, changes from one activity to the next, can be disruptive. The professional teacher develops and implements strategies for transitions that get the job done but do not undercut self-esteem. A primary consideration in managing transitions is the reduction of time that children spend waiting. One strategy to reduce waiting is through buffer activities. When lines prove necessary, teachers need to plan strategies for lining up and waiting in lines that support each member of the group and capture children's imaginations.

4. How do routines help to build an encouraging classroom?

Pat Sanford, an experienced kindergarten and primary grade teacher, believes that the secret to managing the encouraging classroom lies in getting children used to routines. Pat begins teaching routines on the first day of school. She teaches that making a mess during activities is fine, but returning materials and cleaning up are parts of kindergarten life.

Although Pat states that learning about routines is important, she believes in creating a warm classroom atmosphere, with a minimum of institutionalization practices. She states that her job is not to prepare children for "next year," but to provide the best possible "present year" for the children in her class.

5. Why is the teaching team important in managing the encouraging classroom?

Children benefit from positive relations with all adults who may be in the classroom. Effective communication among adults allows for comprehensive strategies for working with mistaken behavior. For these two reasons, the myth that the teacher handles all situations alone needs to come to an end. In the guidance approach, the teacher moves toward a teaching team model in the classroom and involves fellow staff and volunteers of diverse backgrounds to provide responsive programming. The teacher collaborates with other professionals: administrators and specialists in the center or school as well as specialists in other agencies. Through collaboration adults can accomplish together what they might not be able to do alone.

6. How can the teacher make use of parents and other classroom volunteers?

In the multidimensional learning environment the teacher is a manager of the daily program as well as a lead teacher. The use of staff and volunteers as a teaching team contributes to the success of the program. Depending on the skills and comfort level of the team members, staff and volunteers perform a variety of functions in the classroom. A first step in working with volunteers in the classroom is to make them feel welcome. The teacher helps the volunteer find tasks she is comfortable with such as fastening coats or reading to a small group that a parent might do at home. The most important reason for involving parents in the classroom is that the experience encourages them to become more active in their child's education, although the parent stands to benefit in personal/professional ways as well.

KEY CONCEPTS

Anticipatory set

Buffer activity

Collaboration

Grouping patterns

Inclusion

Multidimensional classroom

Period chart/Day clock

Routines

Table talk

Teaching team

Team teaching

Time confusion

Transitions

FOLLOW-UP ACTIVITIES

Note: An element of being a professional teacher is to respect the children, parents, and educators you are working with by maintaining confidentiality—keeping identities private. In completing follow-up activities, please respect the privacy of all concerned.

Discussion Activity

The discussion activity encourages students to interrelate their own thoughts and experiences with specific ideas from the chapter.

Think about a classroom you have visited as a part of your preparation program. Recollect a regular activity or routine during the day in which more mistaken behavior occurred than at other times. Referring to the chapter for possible ideas, how would you change this part of the daily program to reduce the mistaken behavior and make the classroom more encouraging?

Application Activities

Application activities allow students to interrelate material from the text with real-life situations. The observations imply access to practicum experiences; the interviews, access to teachers or parents. Students may compare or contrast observations and interviews with referenced ideas from the chapter.

1. **Reliability and novelty in the daily program.**
   a. Observe an instance of the "teachable moment" when a teacher deviated from the schedule to provide a special experience. How did the teacher manage the change of routine? What did you notice about the children's behavior before, during, and after the special event?
   b. Talk with a teacher about the daily schedule he uses. What parts of the schedule is the teacher pleased with? If the teacher were going to modify the schedule, what parts would he change? Why?
2. **Large group activities.**
   a. Observe children in a large group activity. If most children are positively involved, what about the large group seems to be holding their attention? If several children look distracted, or are distracting others, what do you think are the reasons?

   b. Interview a teacher about large group activities. How does the teacher plan large groups to hold children's attention? While teaching, what techniques does the teacher use to hold children's attention?

3. **Managing transitions.**
   a. Observe a transition to or from an organized activity. How does the teacher prepare the children? How does the teacher manage the physical movement of the children? How does the teacher get the new activity started?
   b. Interview a teacher about how he handles transition situations. Ask about what he does when some, but not all, children have finished an old activity and are ready to begin the new activity. What suggestions does the teacher have for when he and the class have to wait for an event; when he and the class have to walk in a line?

4. **Routines in the encouraging classroom.**
   a. Observe a classroom where there are definite, well-accepted routines. What are the likely effects of the routines on the children? On the teacher? How do Pat's comments about routines compare or contrast with your observations? When you teach, would you use routines similar to or different from what you observed? Why?
   b. Interview a teacher about his use of routines. How does the teacher believe the use of routines assists with classroom management? Ask the teacher how he knows when insufficient use is made of routines in a classroom, or when overreliance is placed on routines. How do Pat's comments in the chapter match with what the teacher said about routines?

5. **The teaching team.**
   a. Observe a productive teaching team in operation. Note the kinds of communication that occur between the team members—verbal and nonverbal. What seems to characterize the communication you have observed?
   b. Interview a lead teacher and/or another member of a teaching team. Ask what is important to each in maintaining positive relations between the adults and a positive atmosphere in the classroom. Compare your findings with what the text says about the teaching team.

6. **Parents and other classroom volunteers.**
   a. Observe a teacher working with staff or volunteers in the classroom. What is typical in how the teacher communicates with the other adults? How much of the teacher's attention is directed to working with the other adults? How much to working with the children?
   b. Interview a teacher about having other adults, staff, and volunteers in the classroom. What benefits does the teacher

see in the arrangement? If there are difficulties, what are they? What would the teacher recommend for working through some difficulties that might arise?

What You Can Do

The Teaching Team   Something important can be learned from interviewing members of a successful teaching team about how they work together. Interview and think about the responses of each team member:

   a. Interview the teacher. Ask how that teacher works with other staff members to build an effective team. How does the teacher take personalities, roles, and education levels of members into account? What has worked well for the teacher and not so well in building a team? Take notes and think about the teacher's responses.
   b. Interview a staff member who is an assistant on the team. What did the teacher do and say to make the teaching team concept seem inviting to the assistant? How did the teacher communicate about the education program and the assistant's role in it? How did the teacher address communicating with other adults who might be members of the team?
   c. Interview a staff member who is a specialist (such as a special education teacher) on the team. (Ask the same questions as in b. above.) What did the teacher do and say to make the teaching team concept seem inviting to the specialist? How did the teacher communicate about the education program and the specialist's role in it? How did the teacher address communicating with other adults who might be members of the team?
   d. Interview a regular parent volunteer who seems to be part of the team. (Ask the same questions as in b. above.) What did the teacher do and say to make the teaching team concept seem inviting to the parent? How did the teacher communicate about the education program and the parent's role in it? How did the teacher address communicating with other adults who might be members of the team?
   e. Compare your findings in the interviews with comments from the text about the teaching team. What did you learn from completing steps (a) through (e) about building and maintaining a teaching team?

RECOMMENDED READINGS

Barbour, N. H., & Seefeldt, C. A. (1992). Developmental continuity: From preschool through the primary grades. *Childhood Education, 68*(5), 302–304.
Educational Productions Inc. (1990). Video: Give yourself a hand: "Guidance techniques for successful group times," Program 2 in video

training series: Super Groups: Young children learning together. Portland, OR: Educational Productions Inc.

Edwards, L. C., & Nabors, M. L. (1993). The creative art process: What it is and what it is not. *Young Children, 48*(3), 77–81.

Gottschall, S. M. (1995). Hug-a-Book: A program to nurture a young child's love of books and reading. *Young Children, 50*(4), 29–35.

Gronlund, G. (1995). Bringing the DAP message to kindergarten and primary teachers. *Young Children, 50*(5), 4–13.

Kasting, A. (1994). Respect, responsibility, and reciprocity: The 3Rs of parent involvement. *Childhood Education, 70*(3), 146–150.

Pica, R. (1997). Beyond physical development: Why young children need to move. *Young Children, 52*(6), 4–11.

Rockwell, R. E., Andre, L. C., & Hawley, M. K. (1996). *Parents and teachers as partners: Issues and challenges.* Fort Worth, TX: Harcourt Brace College Publishers. (See Chapter 10, Parent and Community Volunteers.)

Van Scoy, I. J., & Fairchild, S. H. (1993). It's about time! Helping preschool and primary children understand time concepts. *Young Children, 48*(2), 21–24.

Willis, S. (1993, November). Teaching young children: Educators seek 'developmental appropriateness.' *Curriculum Update,* 1–8.

REFERENCES

Barbour, N. H., & Seefeldt, C. A. (1992). Developmental continuity: From preschool through the primary grades. *Childhood Education, 68*(5), 302–304.

Bredekamp, S., & Copple, C. (1997). *Developmentally appropriate practice in early childhood programs* (3rd ed.). (Washington, DC: National Association for the Association of Young Children.

Brewer, J. A. (2000). *Introduction to early childhood education: Preschool through primary grades.* Boston, MA: Allyn & Bacon.

Cherry, C. (1981). *Think of something quiet.* Belmont, CA: David S. Lake Publisher.

Derman-Sparks, L. (1989). *Anti-bias curriculum: Tools for empowering young children.* Washington, DC: National Association for the Education of Young Children.

Dunn, L., & Kontos, S. (1997). What have we learned about developmentally appropriate practice? *Young Children, 52*(5), 4–13.

Edwards, L. C., & Nabors, M. L. (1993). The creative art process: What it is and what it is not. *Young Children, 48*(3), 77–81.

Elkind, D. (1976). *Child development and early childhood education: A Piagetian perspective.* New York: Oxford University Press.

Gestwicki, C. (2000). *Home, school, and community relations: A guide to working with parents* (4th ed.). Clifton Park, NY: Delmar Learning.

Gronlund, G. (1995). Bringing the DAP message to kindergarten and primary teachers. *Young Children, 50*(5), 4–13.

Hendrick, J. A. (2000). *Whole child.* Columbus, OH: Merrill Publishing Company.

Hohmann, M. (1997). *Study guide to educating young children.* Ypsilanti, MI: High Scope Press.

Honig, A. S. (1986). Research in review. Stress and coping in children. In J. B. McCracken (Ed.), *Reducing stress in young children's lives* (pp. 142–167). Washington, DC: National Association for the Education of Young Children.

Honig, A. S., & Wittmer, D. S. (1996). Helping children become more prosocial: Ideas for classrooms, schools, and communities. *Young Children, 51*(2), 62–70.

Kagan, S. L. & Rivera, A. M. (1991). Collaboration in early care and education: What can and should we expect? *Young Children 46*(1), 51–56.

Kasting, A. (1994). Respect, responsibility, and reciprocity: The 3Rs of parent involvement. *Young Children, 70*(3), 146–150.

McAfee, O. D. (1986). Research report. Circle time: Getting past 'two little pumpkins'. In J. B. McCracken (Ed.), *Reducing stress in young children's lives* (pp. 99–104). Washington, DC: National Association for the Education of Young Children.

McCracken, R. A., & McCracken, M. J. (1987). *Reading is only the tiger's tail.* Winnipeg, Canada: Perguis Publishers Limited.

Marion, M. (1999). *Guidance of young children.* Columbus, OH: Merrill Publishing Company.

Montessori, M. (1912/1964). *The Montessori method.* New York: Schocken Books.

Palmer, H. (1978). *Sea gulls.* Topanga, CA: Hap-Pal Music.

Read, K. H., Gardner, P., & Mahler, B. C. (1993). *Early childhood programs: Human relationships and learning.* Fort Worth, TX: Harcourt Brace Jovanovich College Publishers.

Rockwell, R. E., Andre, L. C., & Hawley, M. K. (1996). *Parents and teachers as partners.* Forth Worth, TX: Harcourt Brace College Publishers.

Saifer, S. (1990). *Practical solutions to practically every problem: The early childhood teacher's manual.* St. Paul, MN: Redleaf Press.

Scelsa, G., & Millang, S. (1983). *Quiet moments with Steve and Greg.* Los Angeles, CA: Youngheart Records.

Thorton, J. R. 1990. Team teaching: A relationship based on trust and communication. *Young Children 45*(5), 40–42.

Van Scoy, I. J., & Fairchild, S. H. (1993). It's about time! Helping preschool and primary children understand time concepts. *Young Children, 48*(2), 21–24.

Wade, M. G. (1992). Motor skills, play, and child development: An introduction. *Early Report, 19*(2), 1–2.

Walmsley, B. B., Camp, A. M., Walmsley, S. A. (1992). *Teaching kindergarten: A developmentally appropriate approach.* Portsmouth, NH: Heinemann Educational Books.

For additional information on using the guidance approach in the classroom, visit our Web site at http://www.earlychilded.delmar.com

LEADERSHIP COMMUNICATION WITH THE GROUP

GUIDING QUESTIONS

- How does the teacher establish leadership in the encouraging classroom?
- Why are guidelines, not rules, important in the encouraging classroom?
- Why is encouragement more appropriate than praise?
- Why is discussing inclusively important?
- How do class meetings build the encouraging classroom?
- How does the adult teach friendliness in the encouraging classroom?
- How does leadership communication with parents build and maintain partnerships?

Mistaken behavior is often the result of a mismatch between the child and the education program and/or miscommunication between the child and teacher. Previous chapters discussed reducing this institution-caused mistaken behavior by building a developmentally appropriate educational program. Retaining the main idea of Part Two that "prevention is the best medicine," Chapters Seven and Eight shift focus to the communication skills of the teacher. In these chapters, **leadership communication** defines the communication techniques used by the teacher to positively manage the group and to build positive relations with each child and so reduce mistaken behavior.

Chapter Seven examines leadership communication that is *group-focused*. Elements of group-focused leadership communication include:

- Establishing leadership by being firm and friendly
- Creating guidelines instead of rules
- Using encouragement instead of praise
- Discussing inclusively
- Holding regular class meetings
- Teaching friendliness

The chapter concludes with a discussion of communication techniques teachers use to build and maintain partnerships with parents.

ESTABLISHING LEADERSHIP

Previous chapters established the need for positive teacher-child relations as a guidance principle. The teacher works to accept each child unconditionally, even as she endeavors to help children learn alternatives for mistaken behavior. The environment in which children feel individual acceptance and growing social capability is the encouraging classroom. The ability to create this feeling of community in the classroom takes particular leadership on the part of the teacher, leadership that is democratic and authoritative (Dreikurs, 1968; Wittmer & Honig, 1994).

Building an encouraging classroom environment begins in the first days that the teacher is together with the class. The teacher establishes leadership by acquainting the class with routines and guidelines. Children benefit from knowing what is expected of them and what the limits of acceptable behavior are. The teacher is clear, firm, and friendly in this communication effort. When teachers blur the distinction between *firm* and *strict*, friendliness drops out of the formula. In this matter, the guidance approach differs from conventional discipline.

Conventional thought about discipline holds that the teacher is *strict* at the beginning of the school year, in order to "take charge of the classroom" (Canter, 1988). Then, with the teacher's "right to teach" established, she eases up in demeanor. From the guidance perspective, this position has pitfalls. The teacher may fixate on the assertion of will and lose faith in more positive teaching practices. Children and teacher alike get used to the

Through the program and the communication skills used,
the teacher reduces mistaken behavior.

teacher in the role of disciplinarian. She becomes a disciplinarian as part of a permanent teaching style. This unfortunate situation is epitomized by the proverbial teacher who meant only "not to smile until Christmas"—and didn't smile for 40 years (Gartrell, 1987).

Even if the strict teacher gradually does "lighten up," children suffer from negative encounters in the interim. Working with limited experience to develop feelings of initiative and belonging, children who have conflicts early in their school careers may receive lasting damage to self-esteem (Gartrell, 1995). A "law and order" environment in the classroom affects even model children who do not normally "get into trouble."

Early in September, a parent who was also a health professional noticed her first grader seemed bothered by something. Shirley asked her daughter what was the matter. The first grader, an early reader, had seen a word on the chalkboard and asked what it was: "D-E-T-E-N-T-I-O-N." Shirley explained, and her daughter then asked several other questions:

"Where is detention?"
"Do the children get to go home?"

"Why do Jarrod and Paula go there?"
"Are they bad children?"
"Will the teacher put me there?"

Shirley commented that she saw concern in her daughter's face that she had never seen during kindergarten. Shirley went in and talked with the teacher who said, "The children need to know that I am here to teach, and they are here to learn. I will not let individual children keep this from happening."

Shirley wondered about a classroom where the first words children learned to read were the names of friends being punished. She monitored her daughter's feelings closely and talked with the teacher several more times that year. Shirley felt her work with the teacher did make the year go a bit better for her daughter. The following spring she worked with the principal to place her daughter with a second-grade teacher whom Shirley knew to be more positive.

Guidance and Routines

No matter how anxious a teacher is about beginning the school year, children are more anxious. In the first days, the teacher sets a precedent for children's education that makes it either a welcome event, or an event arousing ambivalence and negative feelings. The following anecdotes illustrate this difference.

During the first week of kindergarten, teachers responded to a similar situation differently. Trying to acquaint their groups with desired routines, each teacher instructed children to put away the materials they were using and come to the circle for large group instruction.

Teacher one reminded Juan, who was building a road, to put away the blocks; she then directed the group into a circle. She was set to begin when she noticed that Juan was still quietly building. From her place at the head of the group, the teacher said loudly, "Get over here, young man. In this classroom, children listen to the teacher." After waiting for Juan to join the group, she explained the daily schedule to the children.

When *teacher two* was about to begin large group, she noticed that Lumey—whom she thought she had asked to pick up—was still playing with blocks. Then teacher walked to Lumey, smiled and held out her hand. She began speaking in English, but when he looked confused, she commented in Spanish. "You can finish your building after circle time. We need you to join us right now." Back in the circle, the teacher introduced the children to the daily schedule, sprinkling her speech with Spanish phrases.

Teacher two was showing leadership no less than teacher one. She reacted differently, though, to the notion that the teacher must "be tough from the beginning." Teacher two recognized that children in the first days of school can become overloaded and that they readily identify with materials that seem "safe." She recognized that a child for whom another language is natural may need extra assistance. Teacher two did not equivocate with a guideline for her classroom, but took a guidance approach by educating to the guideline. She used guidance measures so that Lumey (and the rest of the class) would not develop doubts about themselves and fears about school, but they would learn classroom routines.

GUIDELINES, NOT RULES

A point of agreement about guidance over the years is the importance of establishing clear expectations with children. Standards for behavior, understood by all, are important in any educational setting. Insufficient attention has been given, however, to differences between rules and **guidelines**. In making the case for guidelines as a part of the guidance approach, this section looks anew at the conventional use of rules.

Rules tend to be stated in negative terms: "No running in the classroom"; "No gum chewing in school." Frequently, punishments are predetermined for the transgression of a rule:

- No talking out of turn or your name goes on the board;
- No unfriendly words or you sit in the time-out chair;
- No homework and you stay after school.

The conventional thinking about rules with known consequences is that they convey clear conditions for citizenship and teach children about governance by law in adult society (Dreikurs & Cassel, 1972). This view presents two difficulties.

First, rules with defined consequences institutionalize the use of punishment in the school or center. The negative phrasing of rules suggests that teachers expect children to break them. Spelled-out consequences underscore this perception. Reason, cooperation, and caring become secondary when educators enforce preset standards that may or may not fit actual situations. The teacher who reacts with an automatic response often shows less

In the first days of school, children identify with materials
that are familiar and seem safe.

than full understanding of the event. If teachers choose "to make an exception" and not enforce a predetermined punishment, their leadership comes into question. In either case, the teacher is functioning as a technician and not as a professional, as discussed in Chapter Four.

A second problem lies in the effects of punishment itself. Punishment tends to reduce human interaction from the educational to the moralistic. The factor of developmental egocentrism in young children makes this issue critical. Developmental egocentrism means the younger the age, the less the child understands about social expectations (Elkind, 1976). Because of lack of experience and development, young children have difficulty understanding that when they are punished for breaking a rule, the punishment is the result of their *actions*. They tend instead to internalize the shame associated with the punishment and to feel that they are being punished because they are "bad children." Diminished self-esteem results (Gartrell, 1995; Kohn, 1999). The child has been influenced away from feelings of initiative, belonging, and industry, and toward shame and self-doubt (Elkind, 1987).

Logical Consequences

With his writings, Dreikurs raised discipline practice to a level above the reliance on punishment (Dreikurs, 1968; Dreikurs & Cassel, 1972). Dreikurs suggested that misbehavior has **logical consequences,** responses taken by adults that "fit" a child's mistaken act. Logical consequences differ from punishment because the redress imposed is a logical extension of the mis-

A logical consequence of climbing on a divider is to choose between staying on the floor in the same area or moving to the "real climber" that is safe.

behavior itself. For example, if a preschooler marks on a table, he cleans it off. If a second grader neglects doing homework, he completes it in a timely fashion. This consequence contrasts with the punishment of detention whether the child finished the assignment during the day or not.

The use of logical consequences fits a guidance approach if two conditions are met: (a) the consequence is logical to the child as well as the adult; and (b) the consequence is *not* set out beforehand.

(a) In reference to the first condition, note the difference between these statements:

"You get a sponge and wipe that mark off the table right now."
"It's OK, your marker just went off the paper. Let's get a sponge and clean it off."

An adult may have thought the first statement was a "logical consequence," but it was most likely perceived as punishment to the child.

(b) In reference to the second condition, a primary grade child may have legitimate reasons for not completing homework such as a family emergency. In a guidance approach, a teacher uses professional judgment to evaluate an event before discussing a logical consequence. The teacher acting as a professional recognizes that every situation is different.

In a current interpretation of Dreikurs' theories, Linda Albert (1996) carefully handles the use of logical consequences. The method is included more as a last resort than the "first line of defense," as it was treated in the past (Charles, 1996). Dreikurs maintained that his approach to discipline was a democratic one. In new interpretation of his work, emphasis is placed on communication *before* problems arise—an effective use of democratic leadership.

The Benefits of Guidelines

For children in the classroom standards are necessary for building understanding about the requirements of social living. Like rules, guidelines set those standards. Unlike rules, guidelines accomplish this understanding in a positive way. As suggested in the previous section, an admonishment such as "Don't interrupt" (run, hit, etc.) is likely to make a child feel that he is "bad" in the teacher's eyes. Moreover, from this enforcement of the rule, young children often fail to recognize what the teacher is really asking them to do. *By using guidelines, adults teach what productive behavior is; they do not just admonish against mistaken behavior.* Because their message is positive and instructive, guidelines are more developmentally appropriate in educational settings than are rules. Guidelines contribute to the encouraging classroom. Contrast the following guidelines from a third-grade classroom with conventional classroom rules:

- We use words to solve problems;
- Sometimes we need to stop, look, and listen;
- We all help to take care of OUR room;
- We appreciate each other and ourselves;
- Making mistakes is OK—we just try to learn from them.

Guidelines and Different Age Levels

Teachers working with different age groups use guidelines differently. The NAEYC document on developmentally appropriate practice maintains that standards (guidelines) should not be used formally with children under four (Bredekamp & Copple, 1997). The document points out that three-year-olds do not easily understand or remember rules. Instead, teachers should use "guidance reasons (guidelines) that are specific to a situation and repeated with consistency in similar circumstances." Examples are "Friendly touches only" and "Use your words to tell him."

A difference at the preschool, kindergarten, and primary levels is the number of guidelines used. Experts often comment that there should not be too many rules. This recommendation applies as well for guidelines. The exact number of guidelines depends on the teacher and the group, but usual practice is two to three guidelines in prekindergarten classes; three to four in kindergarten; and four to six in the primary grades. These numbers are arbitrary, however. A well-known trio of guidelines, often used at the kindergarten level, is "Be kind," "Be safe," and "Be smart."

As to when to introduce guidelines, some teachers choose not to "present" them as a set procedure at the beginning of the year. Instead, these teachers construct guidelines with children as situations arise, usually through the mechanism of class meetings. This constructivist approach serves to personalize and maximize the meaning of guidelines for children, a practice in keeping with the developmental nature of the encouraging classroom. Other teachers use guidelines as part of the beginning orientation for the children. This is a matter of professional preference.

Creating Guidelines

Castle and Rogers (1993) present many benefits of having children create guidelines in a democratic classroom atmosphere. The authors point out that children usually make the same rules that adults would, but respect the rules more because they feel ownership of them. They comment that "Engaging children in classroom discussions on creating rules leads to: active involvement, reflection, meaningful connections, respect for rules, sense of community, problem solving through negotiation, cooperation, inductive thinking, and ownership" (pp. 77–78)—certainly all attributes of the encouraging classroom community.

Although the authors do not distinguish between rules and guidelines, the same benefits of guideline formulation certainly apply. With preprimary children, the teacher may need to take more of a lead in the discussion process. Even if very young children do not actually formulate the guidelines, they develop ownership of a guideline like "Friendly touches only" by discussing it—why the guideline is important; why we might not always remember to follow it; what we can do if we forget and make a mistake. Certainly primary grade children, the main focus of the Castle and Rogers article, can significantly participate in the formulation process. The idea is that by replacing external control with democratic leadership, children are likely to take more responsibility for their own (and each other's) behavior. Castle and Rogers conclude:

> Teachers who commit time and effort to the process have found it benefits children's relationships and increases understanding of what it means to participate as a constructive member of a classroom community. (1993, p. 80)

As we have discussed, a first reason for using guidelines is that they supportively educate children to standards of behavior. A *second reason is that guidelines allow teachers a range of choices and so empower them to be professionals.* Rules with set punishments force teachers to act as technicians. Rules fail to encourage teachers to be professionals who can use their store of experience to help children settle problems wisely. In contrast to rules, guidelines create neither hierarchies of authority that young children feel compelled to challenge nor lines of morality that children feel pressed to cross. Guidelines contribute to an environment where mistaken behavior is seen by the leader as a problem to solve. Note the difference in the teachers' roles in the following anecdotes:

(Teacher working with rules.) At recess on a rainy day, second graders Clarence and Rubey first argued, then fought over a "friendship bracelet." Mrs. Cleary came into the room, separated the children, and declared, "You know the rule in here about fighting. I am taking you both to the principal's office."

The principal asked Mrs. Cleary what the punishment was for fighting. Mrs. Cleary stated that it was detention and sitting out the class's next popcorn party. When the two children returned, others in the class made fun of them. The two looked miserable as they sat in detention. Rubey did not attend school the next day when the class party was held.

(Teacher working with guidelines.) At recess on a rainy day, a second-grade teacher, Mrs. Drewry, entered her room to find two children fighting. She separated the children and had them each cool down at their desks. She then asked Cosby and Marla to "a private meeting" to each tell their side of the problem. Marla said she brought some cookies to eat at recess, and Cosby tried to take them. Cosby said he didn't either. The teacher acknowledged what each child said and felt. She then requested to hear how they would keep from fighting next time. Marla told Cosby he should bring his own stuff to eat. Cosby said his mom wouldn't let him.

The teacher paused and said to Cosby: "Our guideline says 'We use words to solve problems.' If you want Marla to share, you need to ask with words. Cosby, I've got an idea. Why don't you save an apple or roll from breakfast in the lunch room? Then, you will have something to eat at recess." Cosby shrugged and Marla looked relieved. The teacher ended the meeting by stating firmly, "Remember, Cosby, in this class we use words to solve problems. I will talk to the kitchen staff and see what we can do for a recess snack, OK"? Cosby nodded and told Marla he was sorry.

When young children have disputes, they gain if they are helped to work through the difficulty. To the complaint that the teacher should not be a "referee," the response is that the adult is teaching conflict management skills, the ability to solve problems with words. The use of guidelines enables the teacher to act as a mediator and teach conflict management. Learning how to manage conflicts may be the most important democratic life skill of the 21st century.

ENCOURAGEMENT

Perhaps the most basic guidance technique is that of *encouragement*. It bridges two dimensions of the teacher's communications in the classroom—with the class and with the individual child. How the teacher uses encouragement in the one dimension influences the other. For this reason, both dimensions of encouragement, group focused and individually directed, are discussed here.

Encouragement More than Praise

A basic difference between encouragement and praise is that encouragement empowers the efforts of the child; praise gives approval to the achievements (Hitz & Driscoll, 1988). With the process-orientation young children bring to activities, encouragement is important if only for this reason. Encouragement is preferable to praise for other reasons as well.

A typical example of praise is, "Children, see what a good worker Joshua is." Writers such as Dreikurs (1968), Ginott (1972), Hitz and Driscoll (1988), and Kohn (1999) believe that a comment like this one creates several problems:

- The statement is made more to elicit conformity from the group than to recognize the individual child.
- Others in the class feel slighted because they were not praised for working hard.
- Class members feel resentment toward Joshua for being praised.
- All children in the class are reinforced toward dependency on the teacher for evaluation of their efforts rather than being taught to evaluate efforts for themselves.
- The class is uneasy about whom the teacher will single out next and what she will say.
- Joshua experiences mixed emotions: pride at being praised, embarrassment at being publicly recognized, worry about how others will react, uncertainty about exactly what he did that was *right,* and concern about what the teacher will say to him next time if he is not "a good worker."

Praise stresses the traditional definition of successful achievement—"winning," "doing the best." When this emphasis is strong, children become anxious about the possibility of not living up to the adult's expectations—of becoming "losers" or "failures" (Kohn, 1999). This use of praise leads to a classroom with an environment of conditional acceptance: Children who meet the teacher's criteria for success feel like winners and enjoy the social trappings of winning; other students feel the humiliation and resentment that accompanies their more marginal social status. Teachers who use encouragement have learned that support is usually needed more during a task than at its completion—the accomplishment frequently being its own reward. They

The child knows that encouragement given privately is truly meant for him.

have learned that all children in a class deserve full acceptance and support and that is what an encouraging classroom is about.

Encouragement happens in two primary ways, publicly directed to the entire group, privately directed to the individual. A teacher says to her kindergarten class, "You are working very hard on your journals today. Many special story-pictures are being made. I am proud of you all." Strengths of this **public encouragement** include:

- The group has received clear feedback and knows their efforts are being appreciated.
- The teacher has not made a value judgment about "the class personality" but has given a **self-report:** She has described the event being recognized and given an **I message** or personal response to it.
- No children feel the ambivalence of being singled out.
- The teacher has avoided institutionalizing "winners" and "losers" (in-groups and out-groups). She has eliminated the negative social dynamic of differential treatment.
- The group feels a positive group spirit, a sense that "we are doing together and we are succeeding."
- The teacher has allowed room for children to evaluate their efforts for themselves (Ginott, 1972). She is empowering a sense of competence in the members of the class.

Many of the same benefits apply to **private encouragement** given to an individual child. Note this teacher's response to Julia when the four-year-old tells the teacher she is building a castle: "You *are* building a castle, Julia. It has towers and walls and windows and doors. I am impressed."

From this one comment, Julia knows what the teacher has noticed in her work. Julia sees that encouragement really was meant for her. Julia was allowed to draw her own conclusions about her building ability, without undue expectations on her for the next time. Julia feels that she and her work are appreciated by the teacher. She feels positively about building again.

(From the journal of a student while completing a practicum in a kindergarten classroom.) I decided to use both types of encouragement, publicly directed to the entire group and privately directed to the individual. In the second observation, I use (C) for the specific child, and (S) for me.

Public Encouragement, Directed to the Entire Group

Students were working on story-pictures to send to some survivors of the Oklahoma City bombing disaster. I made a point of going around to look at each child's creation, not making any specific comments; then I stood in front of the class and said, "You are all working very hard on your story-pictures. I'll bet that you are proud of your work." Some children smiled, and they all seemed pleased with this comment. They worked very hard. I noticed a few children even made comments to other children on how nice their story-pictures were. By saying something positive to the group, they all wanted to share in that feeling; it was like the domino effect.

Private Encouragement, Directed to the Individual

Later the children were involved in center play, and one child in particular was drawing. I went over to him and looked at his creation.

S: You are really working hard on that picture.
C: Yeah, I'm using brown, 'cause that's the main color of it. Can you smell it? (giggle)
S: (Smile) No, does it smell?
C: No, not for real. It's a piece of garbage under a microscope. I'm gonna color it lots of colors 'cause that's how it looks.
S: Wow! You have drawn an enlarged piece of garbage. I see that it has many points, curves, and corners. It really looks like it would look under a microscope. Your picture is impressive.

After this last comment the child gave me a very large smile and continued to draw using lots of colors all mixed together. Later I learned the child had been exposed to a microscope by an older sibling, but he applied the idea of garbage under the microscope by himself. I was impressed.

Encouragement—What to Say

When they are beginning to use encouragement, teachers sometimes do not know what to say. If a child's product is "pre-representational" or is not what was expected, teachers find themselves especially at a loss for words. A strategy is to use a **starter statement** that elicits a response from the child; the encouragement then comes from the interaction.

An effective starter statement used by the practicum student in the previous anecdote was: "You are really working hard on that picture." The idea is to begin a starter statement with *you* or *we* and then describe what the teacher sees that indicates effort or progress. The teacher is developing skill in the use of encouragement when she can pick out details in the child's or group's efforts and positively acknowledge them. *In fact, the ability to notice details and comment positively about them ends the "loss for words"—problem.*

Encouraging Statements Are Simple, but They Can Have an Immediate and Positive Effect

- You have made a real start on that puzzle.
- You have printed almost your whole name.
- Everyone is working so hard to clean the room today.
- We're almost ready for the story.
- You got eight of the ten problems correct.
- You have all the letters right in that word but one.
- You slid down the slide all by yourself.
- You stayed calm all day and didn't get upset once.

An effective starter sentence tells a child that the teacher is interested, cares, is willing to help. Listening is a big part of the act of encouragement. Frequently, the child's response will be a smile, new resolve to continue the activity, or discussion of a problem encountered.

The support has registered when the child says something like:

Yep, that's a picture of my baby brother. You can't see him 'cause he's hiding under the covers.

or

Yes, and I'm going to make another froggy for *you* to take home.

In contrast to encouragement, statements of praise like "good job" neither give specific feedback nor invite interaction (Bredekamp & Copple, 1997). Such statements do not take as much concentration by the teacher and are mental shortcuts; they are quick and easy "fixes" for the teacher (Kohn, 1999). Mastering specific encouragement requires conscious practice over time. The boost in student self-confidence, persistence on-task, and even

In the course of a day there are many opportunities
to offer encouragement.

Cartoon courtesy of American Guidance Service, p. 8 of "Teaching and Leading Children"
by Dinkmeyer, McKay et al. © 1992.

acceptance of others' efforts makes the effort worthwhile. A teacher who
uses encouragement will not hear this complaint, when she told a child he
did a good job: "Teacher, you say that all the time."

Stickers and Smiley Faces: Basically Bribes

Stickers and stamped smiley faces have become traditions in early childhood education. The following *nontraditional* comments are intended to encourage thought about the use of these *reward tokens*.

Stickers in most uses are praise rather than encouragement (Kohn, 1999).
They reward achievement rather than acknowledge effort. They fail to tell
the child exactly what the teacher likes about the achievement. Keeping the
use of stickers private is quite difficult. If they are given to some but not all,
children make mental comparisons about who gets how many, how often.
When used in evaluation of behavior or achievement, stickers reinforce an
impression of differential treatment by the teacher—"who the teacher
likes." They are easily interpreted by young children as judgments about
personality. Because they are extrinsic rewards, stickers build dependency
upon the teacher. They demean the intrinsic worth of the learning activity
(Bredekamp & Copple, 1997). If it is developmentally appropriate, no external reward should be necessary. If the activity is not developmentally appropriate, the teacher should not be doing it.

Personal encouragement instead, either spoken or written, is more appropriate for young children. To a first grader, the teacher could either
whisper or write, "You got all of your Ms on the line." If written, the teacher

might read the notation to the child; *that* will be a paper likely to be taken home. Written encouragement, even to kindergartners, is a sure inducement to functional literacy. Supportive rather than judgmental feedback supports an environment in the classroom in which each child is encouraged to try.

Interestingly, no other section of the first edition of this text was more controversial than this one with students in my classes. For those teachers and prospective teachers, stickers and smiley faces remain a popular tradition. For those insistent on the use of these reward tokens, here are two suggestions:

1. **Save the use of stickers for children with pronounced needs** (who are showing Level Three mistaken behaviors). Use the stickers only in defined situations to help the child master a specific behavior such as not taking home small figures in play sets. Give the stickers as privately as possible and explain to the child why you are giving them each time. (Explain the reason as well to children who notice; they can understand more than teachers sometimes realize.) Phase out sticker use as soon as the child is making noticeable progress but keep giving encouragement.

2. **Use stickers to celebrate not evaluate.** Give everyone in the class a sticker when you are proud of the group's accomplishments. Celebratory use should not be every day, just on special occasions. Older kids will compare stickers, so make them as equivalent as possible—not smelly stickers to some and not to others. Another practice is to have an accessible-to-all sticker box so that children can use stickers as they choose, and not the teacher. Use stickers that do not glorify violent "superheroes," but convey friendly and happy themes.

When Praise Is Appropriate

Praise is not *always* inappropriate, though it does need to be given with care. On occasion a solid rationale exists for having the class recognize an individual child. One reason is to acknowledge achievement after a child has struggled publicly and persevered. The class can appreciate in any child a hard fought victory.

A second example is the practice in some classrooms of recognizing a "Star of the Week" or "Very Important Kid." If using this practice, the teacher needs to ensure that children know they will all have a turn. One way to designate turns is the chart with each child's name and a movable marker. The children might be listed in order of age, with the youngest child the first "Very Important Kid." When praise is done carefully in select situations, both the individual and the group benefit. The child receives a boost in self-esteem, and the class a boost in empathy levels toward individual members. Appropriate praise and encouragement both take conscious thought and decision-making by the teacher. It should be noted that one teacher-acquaintance scoffs at this practice. She says, "In my class every kid is important every day."

DISCUSSING INCLUSIVELY

When doing stories, Chapter Six introduced the idea of **discussing inclusively** with children. In discussions of all kinds, of course, the teacher listens. She does not discard comments that seem out of context. On the surface, what sounds like inattentiveness may indeed be careful listening and hard thought—but from a perspective different than the teacher's.

> With the coming of spring, a kindergarten class had finished a dinosaur unit and was well into hatching chicken eggs. In a discussion the class talked about how baby chickens know to peck for food. The teacher asked if anyone knew what the word *instinct* meant. One child raised her hand and announced, "That's like dinosaurs 'cause they're not alive any more." The teacher started to call on another child, then turned to the first child and thanked her for the comment. With an impressed smile, the teacher explained to the class the difference between *instinct* and *extinct*. In an instant the child's expression changed.

The teacher in this anecdote knew that the kindergarten class would not gain a full understanding of the terms from her brief explanation. (Some children may even have heard the word *extinct* as *eggstinct*.) However, she never could have anticipated the association made by the child. The teacher might have passed over the remark as having no connection to the present discussion—in fact she almost did. Instead, the teacher's open-ended expectation of progress was rewarded because of her willingness to listen. The teacher was discussing inclusively.

What can the teacher do, however, when children really do *not* listen? The conventional practice has been to call on a child who is "chatting" or daydreaming to force renewed focus. The implication of the guidance approach is that the teacher *needs to make the discussion interesting so that children will want to participate.* On average, by the time children have begun kindergarten, they have watched nine months to a year of television, including perhaps a month of *public television.* From television—as well as from the family—they have acquired a host of receptive experiences to work through and share. The days are fading when teachers could force compliance to didactic instructional methods, focused on retrieval of a series of "right answers." Fewer children now come from "children are seen and not heard/think before you speak" home environments that prepared them for the traditional classrooms of the past.

Children learn willingly when ideas are interesting to them. They fail to learn, in significant ways, if content and delivery have no relevance (Wing,

1992). When discussions repeatedly require a "right" answer that children may not know, many develop defensive strategies—playing "dumb," making jokes, acting belligerent—to escape the embarrassment of public correction (Holt, 1964). Discussions that accommodate a diversity of ideas and opinions mean that the teacher has mastered the skill of discussing inclusively. The atmosphere in such classrooms is likely to be both encouraging and intellectually stimulating. The two go together.

> A teacher was reading the classic *Harry the Dirty Dog* to her new first-grade class. A girl the teacher hadn't gotten to know yet raised her hand and said, "Teacher, we got a canary at our house."
>
> The teacher decided to use reflective listening and repeated the girl's comment, "Rita, you have a canary?"
>
> "Yes," said Rita, "And last night it was dirty so me and my dad gave it a bath, and then it was cold, so we put new newspapers in its cage and put it by the radiator, and this morning its feathers was soft and warm and fluffy." The teacher noted Rita's "application of relevant ideas," and thanked her.
>
> Another child then chipped in, "Guess what, teacher, we have two canaries!"
>
> The teacher, who knew this, said, "Yes, Ramon, you do." She then added, "You know what, everybody? Let's see what's going to happen to Harry, because he needs a bath just like Rita's canary did. As soon as we finish the book, we'll talk more about pets and whether you give them baths."
>
> She finished the book, and resumed the discussion, beginning with Ramon. She then had the class write and/or draw in their journals about when they gave or might give a pet a bath. The children worked hard on their journals, and shared them at language arts focus time the next day.

In reflecting about the activity, the teacher was pleased with Rita's comment. The impromptu discussion gave Rita a chance to successfully share an experience in front of the class. Rita had to use comprehension, sequencing, syntax, and vocabulary skills (canary, cage, newspapers, feathers, fluffy) in telling her story. At a receptive level, the rest of the class similarly gained. In addition, a teachable moment occurred that made the book come alive for the children in a way that the teacher had not anticipated. What was to be a simple story about a dog that needed a bath became a multidimensional language arts experience.

Mattie, the teacher, modified a traditional practice when reading books to children: The teacher reads and the children listen. She commented that if less time was available or the story had been more compelling, she might have reacted to Rita the way she did to Ramon, accepting the comment and gently steering attention back to the book. She would have made a point, though, to return to Rita, either in the large group or later individually. Not all teachers would react as this one did, of course, but Mattie showed that she knew the importance of discussing inclusively.

CLASS MEETINGS: HOW THEY BUILD THE ENCOURAGING CLASSROOM

Class meetings are different from circle times. In many cases circle times emphasize the traditional routines of the early childhood classroom: opening activity, weather, calendar, lunch count, finger plays, songs, stories, and lead-in for the day's academic program. As Harris and Fuqua suggest, when teachers keep circle times concise and engaging, children are more likely to be attentive participants (Harris & Fuqua, 2000). Circle gatherings have long been used by Native Americans and other cultural groups for matters of public deliberation in a spirit of equality. Circle times in the classroom go back to Froebel's first kindergartens in Germany. For Froebel, the circle represented the nonbeginning/nonend of the universe and the eventual unity of humankind with God. Whether or not modern teachers work from this symbolism, the circle suggests the equality and worth of each individual and lends itself to the community spirit that is the objective of the class meeting. A circle formation is common to both.

On occasion circle times flow into class meetings and vice versa. But, class meetings (sometimes called *community meetings*) have a different focus, transcending daily routines to deal with life in the classroom. The class meeting is expressly designed for the active involvement of each child; its purpose is to encourage reflection and sharing by children and teachers about their experiences, needs, concerns, and triumphs. About the meeting—McClurg says:

> The purpose of the community meeting is to create an intentional community devoted to a common project: learning to live with and take in the realities and perspectives of others. Here young children encounter and learn to acknowledge multiple realities, discover that they have choices, and realize that they are responsible for their decisions. (McClurg, 1998)

Teachers choose to hold class meetings in order to establish a sense of belonging within the group, conduct class business, and to solve problems that arise. Whatever the immediate purpose, guidelines such as these apply:

- Anyone can talk.
- Take turns and listen carefully.
- Be honest.
- Be kind.

Developing these guidelines, and the reasons for them, may well be the subject of one or more early class meetings.

In an encouraging classroom children come to value class meetings.

In addition to class guidelines, the teacher might have personal guide-lines for class meetings:

- Support each child in the expression of his or her views.
- Maintain a positive, caring focus.
- Personal situations may require private remedies.
- Meetings are to solve problems, not create them.
- Build an encouraging community that includes everyone.

McClurg points out that meetings help teach the skills of group living that adults generally want all children to learn:

> Some children may be too self-conscious; others may need to become more self-aware. Some may need to take control, while others are learning how to give. It is good news that, with a little leadership from an understanding adult, young children can learn these and many other things from each other. (McClurg, 1998, p. 30)

Teachers use class meetings to establish a sense of belonging, conduct class business, and to solve problems that arise.

Class meetings, then, become a primary method for teaching democratic life skills. Each time a meeting occurs, children are reminded the classroom is a community that includes each one of them as well as each adult. As learning centers do, class meetings help to define the encouraging classroom.

Class Meetings/Magic Circles

William Glasser is credited with popularizing the use of *class meetings* (1969), sometimes also called "magic circles." In Glasser's model, class meetings are held to identify problems and work toward solutions. The meetings center around behavior issues, curriculum matters, or student concerns. Glasser is adamant that the class meeting occurs without blame or faultfinding by participants. Honest opinions stated and respected are the keys that make the method work. When children know they have a say in how the program goes and how it can be made better, they feel like they belong and want to contribute.

In a 1989 account of the writing of Glasser on building "a sense of togetherness" within the class, Charles states:

> To foster a sense of togetherness, the teacher should continually talk with the class about what they will accomplish *as a group,* how they will deal with

the problems they encounter as a group, how they will work together to get the best achievement possible for every individual in the group. In order to bring this about, responsibilities are given and shared, students are encouraged to speak of their concerns while the class attempts to find remedies, and the teacher takes special steps, when necessary, to incorporate every student into the ongoing work of the class. (p. 142)

Wolfgang (1999) points out that in Glasser's classroom meetings, there are no wrong answers; every child can successfully participate without fear of correction. The teacher works for this goal with direct teaching about the meeting process, but also with ongoing verbal and nonverbal support. To reduce her own personal judgments during meetings, the teacher might use reflective statements that affirm what a child has said or meant:

Child: Den the snow wented down my back! Brrrr.
Teacher: The snow went down your back? It must have felt very cold!

The teacher also may use nondirective statements:

Child: I could write it in a story, but I don't know how to.
Teacher: Well, you think about how to do it and let me know if you
           come up with an idea.

Just as much as supportive comments, the teacher relies on the staple nonverbal responses of *nods and smiles,* allowing the children as much as possible to guide the discussion's flow (Wolfgang, 1999).

For Glasser, there were three types of classroom meetings: open-ended, educational/diagnostic, and problem solving (Wolfgang, 1999). The open-ended meeting was to discuss hypothetical life problems—What if you saw a child had left a quarter on his desk. What would you do? (Experience sharing is a modern, very open early childhood variation of this type of meeting.) The second type, educational/diagnostic, is for the purpose of conversing about educational ideas—such as the topic of missing teeth when a dentist is coming to visit. The third type, problem solving, is for the purpose of discussing real problems occurring in the classroom. For instance, holding a class meeting with preschoolers when play on a climber has gotten too rambunctious. Discussion about this third type of class meeting, integral to the guidance approach, continues under another heading.

Holding Class Meetings

Writers have different ideas about how often to hold class meetings. McClurg suggests a weekly meeting of at least a half-hour for a first-grade class (McClurg, 1998). In contrast, at a kindergarten/first-grade level, Harris and Fuqua recommend three meetings a day. Harris and Fuqua state: "Twenty minutes, three times a day spent in building a sense of community, we predict, will have an impact on all aspects of the day and make all other times more productive with less time spent in overt management" (Harris & Fuqua, 2000).

Because they are central to the encouraging classroom, the author rec-ommends one or two 5- to 15-minute meetings a day—after arrival and/or just before going home—both at the prekindergarten and primary grade level. The teacher can also call a special meeting if something eventful hap-pens that needs immediate discussion.

The morning meeting might follow a concise, interactive circle time. A segue might be special events, reported by any child, such as a new pet or a visit to the doctor's. The teacher too might contribute a topic at this time, perhaps one that ties in with a theme or topic of the day. She must take care, however, to share the discussion with the children, for the essence of the class meeting is a sharing of authority with the class. (Harris & Fuqua, 2000; McClurg, 1998). With knowledge of the group, such discussions are not dif-ficult to spark. At a morning class meeting, before a child's visit to the den-tist a first grade teacher asked: "I wonder. Have you or someone that you know ever lost a tooth?"

Special event discussions should be handled with sensitivity. Some ex-periences, such as a hospital stay or death of someone close to a child, may be painful for a child to discuss. It is important for the teacher to know the children and their families well enough to discuss such matters with them privately first. We cannot always know everything beforehand, though. Sometimes young children do share the darndest things; this comes with the territory:

> In my kindergarten I had a little boy named Dean who was very shy. One day in group he raised his hand and quietly mumbled, "I had to wear these shoes today because I got b'ture on my good ones."
>
> I asked him what he had said. He again mumbled it. I said, "You got what?" He looked with frustration at me and said loud and clear, "Cow shit!"

(Sometimes a teacher has to accentuate the positive, especially when you've put your foot in it yourself.) "Oh, Dean, now I know what you said! You got cow manure on your shoe. That's not much fun, is it?" One wide-spread phobia in the United States is a fear of public speaking. When a child speaks up in a class meeting, as in any group situation, we need to be in-clusive of his comments—even when they are embarrassing—so he still feels part of the group and will feel comfortable sharing in the future. Any-way, who has not gotten manure of one kind or another on his shoe? (Gartrell, 2000).

A second time for holding scheduled class meetings is just before going home. The purposes of the meeting are to review the day and discuss com-ing events. Children might share something they learned or enjoyed doing, or something that did not go right. When a teacher or child experiences a problem, the end of the day meeting is a time to discuss it (Greenberg, 1992; Harris & Fuqua, 2000). The teacher, or a child, may bring up the messy classroom restroom or inappropriate behavior involving members of the group. If an afternoon meeting becomes too involved, the teacher asks the class to think about it overnight so that "we can discuss it in the morning when we are fresh." The teacher works to end class meetings on a positive note.

Meeting to Solve Problems

A vital use of the class meeting is to resolve conflicts that affect the group (public, often Level Two, mistaken behaviors). Examples include when an activity gets out of hand, or a word like *butt head* is catching on and driving a teacher "bananas."

According to Glasser (1969), the teacher models and teaches during class meetings the following discussion skills:

1. The dignity of individuals is protected;
2. Situations are described, not judged;
3. Feelings are stated as *I* messages;
4. Suggestions for solutions are appreciated;
5. A course of action is decided, tried, and reviewed.

Class meetings that focus on problems provide an excellent opportunity for learning human relations and conflict management abilities. Some of the most important learning that the class and teacher will do occurs during class meetings:

> In Vicki's kindergarten class, Gary wet his pants. A volunteer took Gary to the nurse's office where extra clothes were kept. Vicki overheard some of the children talking about Gary and decided it was time for a class meeting. She explained to them what had happened. She then told a story about when she was a little girl, she wet her pants too and felt very embarrassed. She said people sometimes have accidents, even adults, and it's important that we be friendly so they don't feel badly. Vicki then paused and waited for a response.
>
> The children began to share similar experiences they remembered. When Gary came back to the room, another child smiled at him and said, "It's OK, Gary; last time I wet my pants too."
>
> Other children said, "Me too." Looking greatly relieved, Gary took his seat. The class got back to business.

The reader might assume that the discussion of class meetings is directed more to the elementary than to preschool levels, but this is not the case.

Hendrick (1992) discusses using class meetings to teach "the principles of democracy in the early years" (p. 51). She comments that one part of the process is "learning to trust the group" (p. 52). Hendrick states, "Even four-year-olds can participate successfully in making simple group decisions that solve social problems" (p. 52). She goes on to say:

> Together, for example, they might plan ways to stop children from running through the room. They might also discuss which special outside activity to do—would they rather take a snack and ride their trikes around the block or get out the wading pool for a swim? As children move on to kindergarten and first grade, opportunities of greater magnitude arise. (pp. 52–53)

Class Meetings and Level Three Mistaken Behaviors

A particularly difficult problem that every teacher faces is how to explain to the rest of the class serious mistaken behaviors that one child shows. The teacher must balance the right of the child for the dignity of privacy with the need for other children to express their concerns about the behavior and to try to understand. There is no magic answer to this dilemma. In a course journal, a teacher once shared that she felt she had no alternative but to "go public" when a child over time had many and violent conflicts in her first-grade class. Here is her account, slightly adapted:

> One day, after Jon calmed down from a tantrum, I told him that we had to have a class meeting and called the children together. After seating Jon beside me, I explained to him and the class that he had been hurting others and himself for days, and he needed to hear from the other children how that made them feel. With the mutual respect I had been stressing with the children, each child told Jon how his actions made them feel sad, mad, or scared. When one child said, "I want to be your friend, but I'm scared 'cause you hit me," Jon hung his head and whispered he was sorry.
>
> I thanked the class and told them that Jon was trying hard to use his words and be friendly and that maybe the other boys and girls could help him. I stayed close to Jon the rest of the day, and helped him into class activities. Outside of class I worked with the parents and the special education teacher to get Jon additional assistance. Whereas before, most class members were actively avoiding Jon, some now sought to include him—warily to be sure, but they tried. Jon's struggles became less, but I am still not completely sure I did the right thing.

"Going public" about conflicts concerning an individual child is a difficult choice, though Glasser makes the case that this is a valid use of class meetings (Glasser, 1969). Teachers who do so open themselves and their children to fairly complex social dynamics. At any point the teacher must be prepared to step in to retain a spirit of mutual respect. The following anecdote was recorded by a student teacher in a rural, multicultural primary grade classroom. Upon graduation, the student received a contract from the school, where she is still teaching:

One of the children that we'll call Chris exhibited mistaken behavior on a regular basis. He did things like tipping over his desk, laying on the floor, getting up from his desk on impulse, and other types of mistaken behavior. On this day, Chris started out on the wrong foot, and things grew progressively worse as the day wore on. Right before lunch, after a series of crises, I ended up having the special education teacher physically remove Chris from the classroom.

I knew the children were bothered by what they had seen. After lunch when we returned to the classroom, I held an unscheduled class meeting. I started out by saying "Sometimes when we come to school, we don't feel good about something that is going on at our home or with our friends. Many of us go to our parents or to someone we trust and talk about how we feel. Sometimes when we haven't been able to let our feelings come out, they start to sneak out in ways that maybe we don't want them to. I think that is how Chris is feeling today. I think he has some feelings that he needs to get out because they are starting to sneak out in ways he can't help. Before lunch today, Mrs. O. helped Chris down to her office so that she could maybe help him get rid of some of those scary feelings."

One child raised a hand and said, "Yea, one time I was so mad at Joe I could have hit him, but I went home and talked to my Mom and that helped."

Another child says, "So you mean that Chris doesn't tip his desk over on purpose?"

I said, "Yes, that is what I mean."

Another student raised her hand and said, "But sometimes I get mad and I don't tip my desk."

Her neighbor said, "Maybe you aren't mad like Chris."

We had just finished an Ojibwe story about a boy and a butterfly. The story was an analogy about people and their feelings. The last comment made was by one of the girls and she said, "Chris is like the butterfly with the broken wing."

It was so sweet I could have cried. I said, "Yes, Chris has a broken wing." We ended the class meeting and I felt like the children had a better understanding of their classmate.

> I can honestly say I have learned a great deal each time I had to deal with a problem, not only about solving problems, but about kids as well. I think the biggest thing I learned here was how effective a class meeting can be at helping children understand their classmates. The class meeting allowed them to really think about how Chris felt. I saw this when the one child related his story of being so angry at Joe that he wanted to hit him. By discussing this they had a better understanding of Chris. I also felt they needed to know that Chris was not out there tipping his desk over for the fun of it. Deep down inside, Chris is a hurt little boy trying to cope with a problem that is bigger than he is. I wanted the class to try to see that in him. When Leah made that reference to the butterfly, I knew I had succeeded in that area.
>
> Another thing that I learned was how effective a class meeting can be at solving a class problem that could have gotten worse. If we didn't have that talk, maybe some of the kids would have teased Chris when he came back into the room. Instead they treated him with respect. I was very pleased to see this response when he did return. Chris did continue with his mistaken behavior during the remainder of the day, but the kids ignored it. They seemed to understand that Chris was having a bad day and needed his space (Gartrell, 2000).

A basic guidance principle is that to avoid embarrassment, a teacher tries to keep her interventions with a child private. Real life, however, means the teacher must balance this principle with the right of the class to a sense of well-being. In this anecdote, and the previous journal entry as well, the teachers worked hard to preserve the dignity of the child, in his own eyes and in the eyes of the group. Notice that when involved in such a situation, children accustomed to the class meetings do respond. Through these meetings, the community of the encouraging classroom is sustained, and the learning of democratic life skills occurs.

The Value of Class Meetings

As class meetings become established in the encouraging classroom, children come to value them. The teacher will know that community meetings are having an impact when children take more responsibility for running them, and the teacher is almost able to sit back and watch (McClurg, 1998).

> Over time, children will begin to care for one another, solve their own problems, feel more empowered and more in control of their learning, and come to view all in the community as their "teachers." It will be time well spent when the teacher sees what happens during [class meetings] coming around again and again. (Harris & Fuqua, 2000)

At a workshop a teacher from a small high school once shared this story: The daughter of the superintendent, in the teacher's social studies class, had her bike thrown in a creek by some classmates. The student, who tried hard to get along with everyone, asked the teacher if she could hold a private meeting with the class. The teacher was unsure about this prospect, but gave the student 10 minutes—a very long time to be pacing outside your own classroom. At the end of the time, the student came out and with a slight smile, thanked the teacher, and said the meeting was over. Nothing more was mentioned about the incident—apparently nothing had to be— and the student reported no more problems with her classmates. Class meetings can be held successfully with (and by) young children, high schoolers, and college students alike. Such meetings are at the heart of the encouraging classroom.

ENCOURAGING FRIENDLINESS

The encouraging classroom fosters friendliness, or an *ethic of caring* among all members of the classroom community. An ethic of caring means that members are open to forming inclusive relationships with other community members. The process that drives the ethic of caring is effective communication as individuals work and play together (Mecca, 1996). The purpose of creating an ethic of caring is to assist children in learning how to build relationships with others.

Lawhon (1997) points to studies that show children who lack the opportunity to have close personal relationships are more likely to experience long-term mental and physical health problems. She mentions that unhealthy social development can begin in infancy when parents and children fail to build positive attachments (Lawhon, 1997). By their behavior in the classroom, such children are vulnerable for stigma—further social separation. Because the window of opportunity for social development extends through early childhood, however, teachers can make a significant difference in children's lives by encouraging friendliness among all in the class (Scharmann, 1998).

Friendships and Friendliness

Lawhon says this about friendship:

> Friendship is a mutual involvement between two people that is characterized by affection, satisfaction, enjoyment, openness, respect, and a sense of feeling important to the other. . .While most of these alliances are healthy, some are not. Negative associations are restrictive, while healthy relationships allow for freedom. Each pair determines what is acceptable for the relationship. The most healthy relationships will inspire feelings of autonomy, initiative, and industry (1997, p. 228).

Friendliness helps bring everyone together in the class.

Most teachers have seen friendships between children of both kinds. For this reason the teacher works to encourage friendliness among all in the class, both within and outside of friendship patterns Lawhon suggests that the following questions help a teacher decide whether a friendship is healthful or harmful:

- Is each child being treated fairly in the relationship?
- Does this friend get the other child into trouble?
- Is the relationship healthful for both children?
- Will others be excluded as a result of this new friendship?
- Does this friendship endanger either child (Lawhon, 1997, p. 230)?

These questions are important. At the same time, teachers need to recognize that children are just learning how to be friends. In this endeavor, like others, they make mistakes. For instance, the offer, "I'll be your friend if you let me have the truck," may not be an ideal opening line, but it probably represents the child's developmental understanding "of the sharing that is involved in friendship" (Burk, 1996). Though not as common as same gender relationships (Lawhon, 1997), boy-girl friendships are important in encouraging classrooms and may need special support. The expectation that "In our class girls and boys can be friends and work and play together" reflects a goal for our society no less than the classroom.

Addressing Cliques and Squabbling   Friends who frequently squabble or exclude others from their play present a problem for many teachers, (Barkley, 1998), Three quick strategies follow:

1. Use class meetings and your curriculum to teach friendliness. Discuss real situations. Dramatize, as with puppets, hypothetical

situations that the children can then discuss. Many great books—
including the classic, *Swimmy*—can anchor projects and themes
that teach social cooperation (Mecca, 1996).

2. Establish a guideline of *friendliness* such as, "We cooperate with
others in our work and play." Actively teach the word *cooperate*; it
will become a useful tool for you. "You s'posed to 'coperate'"!

3. Use your leadership to structure small group experiences that
transcend the usual social circles. (We are not talking "ability
groups," of course; it is time to retire "the bluebirds, robins, and
turkey vultures.") Instead use grouping strategies that show
your awareness of existing social dynamics. One way to overcome prejudice toward others is do something successfully with
them. Led if need be by members of the teaching team, diverse
small groups can model and teach the ethic of caring.

The Difference Between Being Friends and Being Friendly

When teachers make responsiveness to social dynamics a part of their teaching, things can get complicated. One result is that we occasionally confuse the
need for children to be friendly with the need for children to be friends.

> One day Roan's teacher thought he needed a reminder and said,
> "You need to be nice to your friends."
>   Roan replied, "But he's not my friend."
>   The teacher said, "We're all friends in this class."
>   Exasperated, Roan stated, "Chip's not my friend. Forrest is."
> "Chip's my mate"! With that Roan and Chip resumed playing as
> though nothing had happened. The teacher was about to con-
> tinue the discussion, then stopped and thought about how chil-
> dren—and, adults—distinguish between friends and classmates.

In a previous case study concerning how Pat introduced routines to her
kindergarten class, she expressed concern about not "over-institutionalizing."
Pat let children hang their coats where they wanted and sit next to whomever
they chose. Pat understood a basic point about human nature: children, like
all of us, need to choose their own friends. The issue of inclusion is a hot one
right now, due to the society's awareness of the extremes that can happen
when some children at school become chronically stigmatized. Yet, at the
same time, Roan had an important message for the teacher. We can and
should encourage friendliness among all classmates ("mates" or "neighbors"), but we need to allow children the right to choose their own friends.

Burk concludes her article with this important thought about friendliness:

We are finding more evidence to support Piaget's position that children are
social beings and they do not develop in cognitive isolation from others. If we
focus our attention on cognitive development without consideration for the
social realm, we may inhibit development in both realms. . . .By recognizing

and appreciating children's relationships, teachers show respect for children as members of the social world (1996, p. 285).

How One Teacher Brought Friendliness to Her Classroom

Tessa Logan (1998), in an important article in *Young Children,* set a clear direction for how to bring friendliness to the classroom:

> I had always felt uneasy about small groups of children purposely excluding other children from their play. Exclusions, I had observed, are often motivated by assumptions about particular students, not by anything related to the specific requirements of the play or project.

> [In class meetings] I explored with the children how they felt when they were left out and whether or not they thought it was fair for children to be told no and others yes in answer to their request to play. We decided that telling someone she could not play was a type of put down. We agreed that anyone who wanted to play at school would be allowed to do so, unless that child was treating people or materials badly and would not stop when asked. (pp. 22–26)

Logan was able to introduce and sustain these ideas in class meetings, also discussing such topics as how to express strong emotions and still be friendly (1998). As well, she used community-building activities, teacher-assigned grouping, and conflict management to further the theme of inclusiveness in her kindergarten classroom. She encouraged children to realize that reporting a concern regarding exclusiveness was not tattling, but a learning opportunity in creating a kindergarten community. After nearly a year of everyday effort, Logan commented:

> In summary, the issues of sexism and exclusion are still with us. That cannot change until the society at large changes. But the practice of divisive behaviors has lessened a great deal in my classroom. The atmosphere of the group is one of caring attachments. The children send out letters when people are sick. They ask after absent children. They raise a cheer when their classmates return. Their arms go around people who are hurt. Our classroom is a *nice* place to be. (Logan, 1998)

Teaching friendliness is really teaching the language arts and social studies skills. Teaching friendliness is essential curriculum in the encouraging classroom.

LEADERSHIP COMMUNICATION WITH PARENTS

The responsibility for communication with parents lies with the teacher (Sturm, 1997). Parents depend on teachers, even those younger than themselves, to initiate contacts and maintain relations. Most parents respect and appreciate even beginning teachers who enjoy working with young children and take pride in their programs. This section discusses leadership communication with parents to keep communications open and solve problems before they become serious.

Previous chapters discussed the importance of building partnerships with parents to encourage greater involvement in the education of their own children and increased participation in the educational program of the class. Specific activities toward these goals included the following:

1. Send welcome letters (Appendix B) to children and parents before the start of school. When possible, make home visits. When a visit is not possible, make introductory telephone calls to the home.
2. Begin the program on a staggered schedule with half the parents and children attending each of the first two days or on alternating days for the first week. Give a special invitation to parents to attend on these days.
3. Telephone each family on the first night of school. Check with the family about any problems the child had that the teacher might help resolve.
4. Hold an orientation meeting (greeting meeting) on two occasions during the first week or two—ideally on a late afternoon and evening. Invite parents to attend either meeting. Go over a brochure about your education program (Appendix C) at the meeting; discuss policies and highlight opportunities for parent involvement. Ask parents to complete optional surveys during or after the meeting to provide information about the child and family and their preferences for how to be involved (Appendix B).
5. Have parent conferences during the first month. Use the conferences to get to know each parent, referring to the survey if appropriate.
6. Invite parents to be involved in the program. Make sure parents know they are welcome to volunteer in the classroom. Help them feel welcome and useful when they visit (Appendix C).
7. Assist parents to find tasks in the classroom that they are comfortable doing.
8. Send thank-you notes—from the class if possible—affirming the value of the visit for the parent.

For parents to feel comfortable with any of these activities, they must feel comfortable in their relationship with the teacher (Sturm, 1997). Rosenthal & Sawyers (1996) refer to building positive relations with parents as joining. Joining means establishing the idea in parents' minds that the teacher accepts them and is working together with them on behalf of the child. Leadership communication is the tool of the teacher in building partnerships. Discussion now focuses on five basic types of leadership communication helpful in maintaining positive parent-teacher partnerships and preventing serious problems: written notes, electronic communication, telephone calls, parent meetings, and parent-teacher conferences.

Written Notes

Many parents associate notes home with criticisms of their children's behavior. In the guidance approach, notes home are neither for the purpose of punishment nor correction. The reason is straightfoward: notes do not allow for discussion. The written message is, as it were, cast in stone. When a critical note arrives, the parent has a limited range of responses which frequently come down to becoming upset with the child, and/or feeling "dumped on" by the school.

When sending personal notes that discuss a child, the teacher uses *encouragement*. The note is either an occasional, unsolicited "happygram" or a statement of progress, perhaps as follow-up to a conference. Because children wonder about the content of personal notes from the teacher, she does well to read them to the child beforehand. If the tone of the note is encouraging, most children will take pride in seeing that it is delivered. If the matter is serious, it probably is best handled not by a note but by a conference.

During the first few weeks to alleviate anxiety about notes home, the teacher might send a happygram or two with each child, reading the note to the child beforehand. Such notes give the child a "real idea" about what the teacher thinks; lets the parent know that the teacher is "on the child's side," and helps children feel positively about carrying notes home in general. Those early happygrams actually may improve the rate of note delivery for the rest of the year.

Regarding routine notes that provide information about events, the teacher needs to be aware of three factors:

1. Delivery rates by children are seldom 100 percent;
2. Some parents will forget or misplace the note; and
3. Some parents are nonreaders.

Regarding the third point, when she knows that a parent is a nonreader, the teacher can either telephone or deliver the message personally. If she has a relationship with nonreading parents, the teacher may be able to send home taped messages or coded pictographs. For cultural reasons, some nonreading parents take offense if notes are sent home with an older child to be read to them. Others find the insinuation that they are "illiterate" derogatory. Being identified as a nonreader in modern society often leads to stigma. When parents confide in a teacher that they are nonreaders, it is important to appreciate and respect the trust they are showing in the relationship.

E-Mail and Web Sites

Although surprising to some, more and more families with young children are accustomed to using e-mail and the Web.

In virtually any class, some parents will be regular e-mail/Web site users. In greeting meetings at the beginning of the year, and in informal parent survey letters (see samples, Appendix B), teachers can discover which parents are and are not comfortable with this technology. Fairness suggests that in mixed "yes-no" groups, the teacher needs to make sure technology users will not be "advantaged" in teacher-parent communication. One idea is to ask parents if they would prefer hard copy notes home or e-mails; hard copy newsletters or a regularly updated Web site. Then be a split-medium teacher—though if all parents and the teacher are "techies," the sky is the limit.

E-Mail   The hard copy alternative for e-mail is the note home. Yes, e-mail is more interactive, but it is also potentially more powerful in causing miscommunication. Probably everyone who uses e-mail has had at least one conversation go in an unanticipated, even bothersome, direction. Parents have high emotional investment in their children, and a blithe comment by a teacher easily can be "overinterpreted." It is difficult to take back a message that either should not have been sent, or should have been sent with different wording—just as can happen with a note. The difference is that with e-mail the teacher is more likely to receive directly the parent's negative reaction. Until a teacher has an ongoing relationship with a parent, similar precautions pertain to e-mail letters as to notes home: send happygrams; send routine kinds of information, but hold off on serious communication until you can meet face-to-face.

The upside of e-mail is that due to the possibility of dialog, teachers can get to know parents through its use. It is unusual for a parent to respond with a thank-you note to a hard copy happygram. Much more common with e-mail, a parent might reply: "Please let me know what you are feeding my child at school. I'd like to give him some of that same 'food' at home." The teacher probably would *not* respond, "It's not the food; it's the tranquilizers," but nonetheless a relationship is developing. In fact, e-mail relationships blossom so easily that the teacher may need to monitor e-mail use to make sure she is not conversing too much with a few parents. (The goal is to decrease, rather than widen, the *digital divide*.)

Web Sites   The hard copy equivalent of the Web site is the newsletter. Both inform families what is going on in the class, what projects children are doing, what themes and events are coming up, what parents can do to help out. Web sites perform these tasks with flare—such as by including digital video from the *Three Little Pigs* play. Web sites can also provide in-depth information about the educational program, and because it is electronic, more parents might read the information. Undoubtedly, Web sites will continue to flower as a medium in teacher-parent-child communication. Many articles—hard copy and electronic—are being written on this topic even now. (See the Web sites listed for each chapter in the Electronic Accompaniment to this text.)

A consideration for teachers about Web sites, again, is that not all parents may be able to access them. Training sessions for interested family members who are novice computer users might really be appreciated. But other parents will not have Web capabilities in the foreseeable future. A new generation of newsletters is appearing that uses such electronic assists as digital photographs of individual children doing activities. Technology can make hard copy newsletters more attractive and readable in many ways. The really resourceful teacher will figure out how to coordinate hard copy materials and electronic communication in ways that cut down effort and expense, and still reach all parents.

Telephone Calls

Telephone calls allow for personal conversation but not for physical proximity and face-to-face contact. For this reason, unless the teacher knows the parent, telephone calls should be used in a similar fashion as notes home. In other words, under normal circumstances a teacher should not attempt a serious conference on the telephone. Telephone conversations are helpful in underscoring the need for special conferences. They are helpful for personally delivering happygrams, following-up conferences, and inviting parent participation in special events.

When requesting a conference regarding a child's behavior over the telephone, the use of a *compliment sandwich* is important, (See Chapter Eight for more on compliment sandwiches.) If the teacher is upset, the compliments help the teacher put the behavior in perspective. For the parent, they convey the message that "my child is not a total problem because the teacher sees at least some 'good' in him." Note the difference between these two calls home regarding Jeremy, a four- and-a-half-year-old.

Call One:	Jeremy was a total monster today. He hit two children, bit one, and threw a book at me. We will have to talk about his behavior tomorrow because I've had it. How is eight o'clock?
Call Two:	Jeremy has been working hard on his behavior, but he had a rough morning. He had conflicts with two children that I had to help him resolve. After that he settled down, and the rest of the day went better. He's making progress, but I think we need to talk. What are some times that would be good for you tomorrow?

Phone calls and conferences are two important ways to communicate with parents.

Telephone calls also are well suited to giving positive feedback after a conference. If the teacher wants to communicate more directly than with a note, a call like the following would mean a lot:

> I just wanted to let you know how Jeremy did this week. No hitting or kicking at all. He only got upset once, but he used his words. He was also playing more with the other children. I'm really pleased. How are things going for him at home?

Parent Meetings

Regular meetings offer an important vehicle for parent involvement, but they can be difficult to accomplish with complete success. Foster (1994) provides several ideas for successful **parent meetings,** incorporated into the six suggestions shown in Figure 7–1. (See Foster's article, "Planning Successful Parent Meetings" in Recommended Resources.)

As Figure 7–1 illustrates, meetings add to the time demands on busy staff as well as busy parents. Parent meetings should be held for a reason, not just because they *should* be held. Once the purposes for the meetings are clear, the work in planning and carrying them out becomes worthwhile.

Figure 7–1

Suggestions for Successful Parent Meetings

---

1. Consider convening a parent committee to help plan meetings. Teachers might ask parents who are familiar with the program to serve on the committee. This step is not an automatic guarantee of success, but it shows respect for parent involvement and helps build parent ownership of the meetings (1994). Some teachers prefer to plan the topic and have the committee help to make the logistical arrangements. Others prefer to make the arrangements themselves.

2. Assess parents' interests and needs. Asking parents to complete the optional questionnaire, contacting parents at the beginning of the school year, and polling the parent committee can help with this determination. Topics selected should be high priorities for the parents.

3. Make specific arrangements for the meetings by considering the following:
   a. Date, time of day, and length of the meeting; plan for when most parents can attend. Specify both a starting and ending time so that parents know when the meeting will be over. Keep the meeting concise; under an hour and a half.
   b. Meeting location; an informal location comfortable to the parents is best.
   c. Transportation options; bus line availability; car pool possibilities.
   d. Free on-site child care; takes work to arrange, but it makes a difference. As Foster points out, "Babies should be welcomed and allowed to stay with their parents if need be" (p. 79).
   e. Refreshments; good food brings people together and helps bring them back (1994).

4. Get the word out about the meeting. A useful advertising strategy is to have a "hook" that will draw in people. Teachers need to use their imaginations to attract parents. One center borrowed a camcorder, videotaped the children in activities, and sent home notices saying, "See your kids on TV." Other ideas often used are potluck meal meetings held early in the evening and activity nights where parents, or parents and children together, do typical class activities or make-and-take projects.

5. Keep in mind key elements of the meeting:
   a. A short greeting is given that includes thanks to presenters, meeting organizers, and parents in attendance. Include a concise overview of the program.
   b. An icebreaker activity—perhaps parents telling stories about their children—helps participants relax.
   c. Whether it is a lecture, panel discussion, open discussion, or video, the presentation needs to be interesting and keep in mind fatigue levels. A useful technique is to follow a concise presentation with small group discussions. The large group then reconvenes for small group sharing, questions of the presenter, and a summary statement. Refreshments and informal conversation follow.
   d. Parents go out the door with make-and-take projects or handouts, fliers about the next meeting, and many thanks for attending.

6. Include the parent committee and/or all involved in the planning to assess how the meeting went and decide any changes for future meetings.

Serious discussions occur best in the face-to-face setting of the conference.

With successful meetings, the classroom community is expanding to include home and school together.

Parent-Teacher Conferences

Conferences provide the most direct link between teacher and parent, and much has been written in recent years about them. Gestwicki devotes a chapter to conferences in her text, *Home, School and Community Relations* (2000). Others who have written about conferences are Bjorklund and Burger (1987); Rockwell, Andre, and Hawley (1996); and Rosenthal and Sawyers (1996). This section discusses using conferences to build partnerships for the prevention of problems. Conferencing to remediate problem situations is discussed in Chapter Eight.

Gestwicki suggests that successful conferences consist of three phases: *preparation, conduct,* and *evaluation* (2000). In preparing, the teacher needs to make sure the parent knows the reasons for the conference. A statement about conferences might be included in a brochure about the program (Appendix C) and repeated in a note home. Time options are helpful for the parent, including both night and daytime slots if possible. An informal private setting, in which parent and teacher can sit side by side at a table, is preferable to conversing over a desk. Likewise, adequate time is preferable to the "get them in; get them out" atmosphere common in some schools.

The teacher should have a folder for each child with samples of the child's work over time. Dated observational notes are helpful. Some teachers may include video clips of the child. A form to record notes from the conference, in preparation for a later written summary, rounds out preparation (Gestwicki, 2000).

There is considerable agreement about the *conduct* of the conference. The teacher begins with a positive *I* statement about the child, such as: "I really enjoy having Maybelle in class. She works hard and has such a sense of humor." The teacher goes over materials she has prepared, and invites parent discussion about them. She asks about items the parent would like to discuss. The teacher paraphrases comments the parent makes and uses **reflective listening,** which means repeating back the thoughts and feelings the parent is expressing (Gestwicki, 2000). The compliment sandwich is another useful communication technique. If a follow-up plan comes out of the conference, the teacher writes it out and sends it to the parent for approval. The teacher ends the conference on a positive note (Gestwicki, 2000).

Gestwicki includes a list of pitfalls to avoid during conferences:

- Technical terms and jargon. Use terms parents can understand.
- The "expert" role. Describe events and trends rather than make broad judgments.
- Negative evaluations of a child's capabilities. (Use compliment sandwiches.)
- Unprofessional comments: talking about others, becoming too personal or, taking sides. Respect the principle of confidentiality.
- Flatout advice. Offer alternative suggestions "that have worked for other parents," for the parent to consider.
- Instant problem-solving. Decide instead on a cooperative plan of action that will be reviewed (2000).

Gestwicki concludes her discussion of conferences with this important paragraph:

> It should be remembered that nonattendance at a conference does not necessarily indicate disinterest in the child or the school. Instead, it may be a reflection of different cultural or socioeconomic values, of extreme pressures or stress [on the] family or work demands. A teacher's response to nonattendance is to review the possible explanations. . . see if different scheduling or educational action will help, persist in invitations and efforts, and understand that other methods of reaching a parent will have to be used in the meantime (2000).

Following the conference, the teacher reviews notes and completes a brief summary, perhaps on a prepared form. She files the original form and when a cooperative plan has been decided upon, sends a copy to the parent. The teacher also reflects in personal terms about the success of the conference, takes agreed upon follow-up actions, and notes possible changes in approach for conferences to come (Gestwicki, 2000).

SUMMARY

1. How does the teacher establish leadership in the encouraging classroom?

An encouraging classroom is one in which the teacher sets and maintains clear limits at the same time as reinforcing a sense of belonging, self-esteem, and self-control. As soon as the teacher and class come together, the teacher establishes leadership, but in a way that values children and teaches them to value each other. In such an environment, much mistaken behavior becomes unnecessary.

2. Why are guidelines, not rules, important in the encouraging classroom?

Rules tend to be stated in negative terms and have preset consequences. Rules institutionalize the use of punishments, fail to respond adequately to the complexities of situations, and reduce the role of the teacher to a technician. Guidelines educate children toward productive behavior. Helping to formulate guidelines increases children's ownership of the guidelines and their sense of belonging in the class. Guidelines allow the teacher the range of choices appropriate for a guidance professional.

3. Why is encouragement more appropriate than praise?

Praise rewards achievements, often is used to manipulate the group, and fails to distinguish between personalities and deeds. Encouragement empowers effort; does not single out or evaluate personalities; gives specific, positive feedback; and builds an encouraging environment. Encouragement is public when directed to the group and private when directed to an individual. Teachers are mastering the technique of encouragement when they can comment on details in children's efforts in ways that encourage interaction with the child.

4. Why is discussing inclusively important?

In group situations, as well as with individuals, the teacher listens. She goes beyond a preoccupation with *right* or *wrong* answers and who is and is not listening. Instead, the teacher works to make class discussions opportunities for engagement by children through welcoming all perspectives in a mutually respectful atmosphere. By discussing inclusively with children, the teacher is building an encouraging environment in the classroom.

5. How do class meetings build the encouraging classroom?

Class meetings are held to maintain a sense of community, carry on the business of the class, and solve classroom problems. Scheduled class meetings occur most often at the beginning and end of the day. The teacher calls unscheduled meetings when events cannot wait. Guidelines such as the need to be respectful of others make class meetings positive and productive experiences. Even with preschoolers, class meetings build the encouraging classroom.

6. How does the adult teach friendliness in the encouraging classroom?

Beginning with class meetings, the teacher acquaints children with the pain of being stigmatized by others. Building on the ideas of the teacher offers a strong rationale for expecting children to learn to include each other in all of their play. The teacher continues using class meetings, organized activities, teacher-directed small groups, and conflict management to teach children that while they can choose their own friends, they need to be friendly to all.

7. How does leadership communication with parents build and maintain partnerships?

Leadership in communication with parents lies with the teacher. An overriding goal of the teacher in communication with parents is *joining,* or establishing with parents that the teacher wishes partnership with them on behalf of the child. Five types of leadership communication with parents were highlighted: notes home, electronic communication, telephone calls, parent meetings, and parent-teacher conferences. Notes, e-mails, and telephone calls are best used to deliver happygrams that recognize children's progress, provide necessary information to the parent, and set up conferences. Telephone calls can also be used as conference follow-ups. Parent meetings take planning, often done with a parent committee. Parent conferences have three phases: preparation, conduct, and evaluation.

KEY CONCEPTS

Class meetings
Discussing inclusively
Guidelines
I messages
Leadership communication
Logical consequences
Parent meetings
Private encouragement
Public encouragement
Reflective listening
Self-report
Starter statements

FOLLOW-UP ACTIVITIES

Note: An element of being a professional teacher is to respect the children, parents, and educators you are working with by maintaining confidentiality—keeping identities private. In completing follow-up activities, please respect the privacy of all concerned.

Discussion Activity

The discussion activity encourages students to interrelate their own thoughts and experiences with specific ideas from the chapter.

Think of a time when you were embarrassed by praise a teacher gave you, or when you embarrassed a child by giving praise. Compare or contrast that experience with what the chapter says about praise. How might the teacher, or you, have given encouragement in that situation instead? What difference do you think giving encouragement might have made?

Application Activities

Application activities allow students to interrelate material from the text with real-life situations. The observations imply access to practicum experiences; the interviews, access to teachers or parents. Students may compare or contrast observations and interviews with referenced ideas from the chapter.

1. **Leadership in the encouraging classroom.**
   a. Observe an example of what you believe to be positive leadership shown by a teacher. What was the situation? What did the teacher say and do? What did the children say and do in response? Using ideas from the chapter, why do you believe this was an example of leadership communication?
   b. Interview a teacher who shows what you believe to be positive leadership in the classroom? Ask the teacher to share how she goes about establishing leadership at the beginning of the school year. How do the methods of the teacher agree or disagree with what the chapter says about leadership communication?
2. **Guidelines in the encouraging classroom.**
   a. Whether she uses the term *rules* or *guidelines,* observe how a teacher uses standards in the classroom. Is the use of standards closer to that of *rules* or *guidelines?* Document your conclusion.
   b. Interview a teacher about how she uses standards with young children. (The use of the term *guidelines* is new, so she may use the term *rules.*) What developmental considerations does the teacher make in creating and using the standards? How is the class involved? Is the use of standards closer to that of rules or guidelines? Explain why you think so.
3. **Encouragement more than praise.**
   a. Observe a teacher giving feedback to a child or to the class. What did the teacher say and do? How did the children respond? Was what you observed more like praise or encouragement? Why do you think so?
   b. Interview a teacher about her priorities when giving positive feedback to an individual child and to the class. Write down what the teacher said. How do her ideas correspond to the text ideas about encouragement and praise?
4. **Discussing inclusively.**
   a. Observe a teacher in a discussion or activity with the class. How does the teacher respond to questions or comments that

do not seem to "fit"? How has your understanding of discussing inclusively changed by what you observed and read in the text?

b. Interview a teacher about her priorities in discussions with the class. Ask how the teacher generally responds to comments that do not seem to "fit" the topic or activity. How do the teacher's comments correspond to the text ideas about discussing inclusively?

5. **Class meetings.**
   a. Observe a class meeting as distinct from a "Circle Time." Determine whether the meeting was scheduled or unscheduled and the purpose of the meeting. How do the purposes and conduct of the meeting correspond with ideas from the chapter?
   b. Interview a teacher who uses class meetings as distinct from circle times. Does the teacher use scheduled class meetings, unscheduled, or both? What does the teacher believe to be the reasons for holding class meetings? How do the reasons identified by the teacher correspond with ideas from the chapter?

6. **Friendliness in the encouraging classroom.**
   a. Observe a classroom that encourages friendliness. Record an instance of teacher-child interaction and/or child-child interaction that you believe typical. Compare your findings from the observation(s) with what the text says about teaching friendliness.
   b. Interview a teacher about the efforts she makes to encourage friendliness toward one or a few children by other children. Ask the teacher to give you an informal "case study" based on recent experience. Compare your findings from the interview with what the text says about teaching friendliness.

7. **Leadership communication with parents.**
   a. Observe how a teacher uses notes, e-mails, telephone calls, meetings, or conferences with parents. How does the teacher's use of these communication methods correspond with ideas from the chapter?
   b. Interview a teacher about using notes, e-mails, telephone calls, meetings, or conferences as communication techniques with parents. How do the teacher's priorities correspond with ideas from the chapter?

What You Can Do

The Class Meeting   Something important can be learned from observing and analyzing a class meeting:

a. Ask a teacher if you can record by video, audio, or notes a class meeting in which a classroom problem is addressed. Assure the teacher that the recording will be used only for your private analysis and will be destroyed or given to the teacher afterward.

  b. Attend and record the class meeting. Ask the teacher to introduce
     you to the children. If taking notes, ask if the children can wear
     name tags with first names only.
  c. What can you tell from your observations about the number of
     children who were engaged in the meeting; the number who
     were not?
  d. What can you tell from your observations about the level of mu-
     tual respect among class members during the class meeting?
  e. What can you tell from your observations about the balance of
     leadership between the teacher and the children during the class
     meeting?
  f. Based on your observations and readings about class meetings,
     what are your thoughts about the contributions of class meetings
     to the social, emotional, and learning climates of the classroom?
     (Remember that your observation was only of one meeting.)

RECOMMENDED READINGS

Barkley, S. (1998). On teasing, taunting, and "I can do it myself." *Young
     Children, 53*(2), 42.
Burk, D. I. (1996). Understanding friendship and social interaction.
     Childhood Education, 72(5), 282–285.
Castle, K., & Rogers, K. (1993). Rule-creating in a constructivist classroom
     community. *Childhood Education, 70*(2), 74–80.
Foster, S. M. (1994). Planning successful parent meetings. *Young Children,
     50*(1), 78–81.
Harris, T. T., Fuqua, J. D. (2000). What goes around comes around: Building
     a community of learners through circle times. *Young Children, 55*(1),
     44–47.
Kohn, A. (1999). *Punished by rewards: The trouble with gold stars, incentive
     plans, A's, praise, and other bribes.* Somerville, NJ: Replica Books.
Lawhon, T. (1997). Encouraging friendships among children. *Childhood
     Education, 73*(4), 228–231.
Logan, T. (1998). Creating a kindergarten community. *Young Children, 53*(2),
     22–26.
McClurg, L. G. (1998). Building an ethical community in the classroom:
     Community meeting. *Young Children, 53*(2), 30–35.
Mecca, M. E. (1996). Classrooms where children learn to care. *Childhood
     Education, 72*(2), 72–74.
Rockwell, R. E., Andre, L. C., & Hawley, M. K. (1996). *Parents and teachers as
     partners: Issues and challenges.* Fort Worth, TX: Houghton Mifflin
     Company.
Rosenthal, D. M., & Sawyers, J. Y. (1996). Building successful home/school
     partnerships: Strategies for parent support and involvement.
     Childhood Education, 72(4), 194–200.

Scharmann, M. W. (1998). We are friends when we have memories together. *Young Children, 53*(2), 27–29.

Wing, L. A. (1992). The interesting questions approach to learning. *Childhood Education, 69*(2), 23–26.

REFERENCES

Albert, L. (1996). *A teacher's guide to cooperative discipline.* Circle Pines, MN: American Guidance Service.

Barkley, S. (1998). On teasing, taunting, and "I can do it myself." *Young Children, 53*(2), 42.

Bjorklund, G., & Burger, C. (1987). Making conferences work for parents, teachers, and children. *Young Children, 42*(2), 26–31.

Bredekamp, S. (Ed.). (1987). *Developmentally appropriate practice in programs serving children from birth through age 8* (2nd ed.). Washington, DC: National Association for the Education of Young Children.

Bredekamp, S., & Copple. (1997). *Developmentally appropriate practice in early childhood programs* (3rd ed.). Washington, DC: National Association for the Education of Young Children (NAEYC).

Burk, D. I. (1996). Understanding friendship and social interaction. *Childhood Education, 72*(5), 282–285.

Canter, L. (1988). Viewpoint 1: Assertive discipline and the search for the perfect classroom. *Young Children, 43*(2), 24.

Castle, K., & Rogers, K. (1993). Rule-creating in a constructivist classroom community. *Childhood Education, 70*(2), 74–80.

Charles, C. M. (1996). *Building classroom discipline.* New York: Longman.

Dreikurs, R. (1968). *Psychology in the classroom.* New York: Harper and Row.

Dreikurs, R., & Cassel, P. (1972). *Discipline without tears.* New York: Hawthorn Books.

Elkind, D. (1976). *Child development and education: A Piagetian perspective.* New York: Oxford University Press.

Elkind, D. (1987). *Miseducation: Preschoolers at risk.* New York: Alfred A. Knopf.

Foster, S. M. (1994). Planning successful parent meetings. *Young Children, 50*(1), 78–81.

Gartrell, D. J. (1987). Assertive discipline: Unhealthy to children and other living things. *Young Children, 42*(2), 10–11.

Gartrell, D. J. (1995). Misbehavior or mistaken behavior? *Young Children, 50*(5), 27–34.

Gartrell, D. J. (2000). *What the kids said today: Using classroom discussions to become a better teacher.* St. Paul, MN: Redleaf Press.

Gestwicki, C. (2000). *Home, school and community relations: A guide to working with parents.* (4th ed.). Clifton Park, NY: Delmar Learning.

Ginott, H. (1972). *Teacher and child.* New York: Avon Books.

Glasser, W. (1969). *Schools without failure.* New York: Harper and Row.

Greenberg, P. (1992). How to institute some simple democratic practices pertaining to respect, rights, responsibilities in your classroom without losing your leadership position. *Young Children, 47*(5), 10–21.

Harris, T. T., & Fuqua, J. D. (2000). What goes around comes around: Building a community of learners through circle times. *Young Children, 55*(1), 44–47.

Hendrick, J. (1992). Where does it all begin? Teaching the principles of democracy in the early years. *Young Children, 47*(3), 51–53.

Hitz, R., & Driscoll, A. (1988). Praise or encouragement? New insights into praise: Implications for early childhood teachers. *Young Children, 43*(4), 6–13.

Holt, J. (1964). *How children fail.* New York: Pitman.

Kohn, A. (1999). *Punished by rewards: The trouble with gold stars, incentive plans, A's, praise, and other bribes.* Somerville: Replica Books.

Lawhon, T. (1997). Encouraging friendships among children. *Childhood Education, 73*(4), 228–231.

Logan, T. (1998). Creating a kindergarten community. *Young Children, 53*(2), 22–26.

McClurg, L. G. (1998). Building an ethical community in the classroom: Community meeting. *Young Children, 53*(2), 30–35.

Mecca, M. E. (1996). Classrooms where children learn to care. *Childhood Education, 72*(2), 72–74.

Paley, V. (1992). *You can't say you can't Play.* Cambridge, MA: Harvard University Press.

Rockwell, R. E., Andre, L. C., & Hawley, M. K. (1996). *Parents and teachers as partners: Issues and challenges.* Fort Worth, TX: Houghton Mifflin Company.

Rosenthal, D. M., & Sawyers, J. Y. (1996). Building successful home/school partnerships: Strategies for parent support and involvement. *Childhood Education, 72*(4), 194–200.

Scharmann, M. W. (1998). We are friends when we have memories together. *Young Children, 53*(2), 27–29.

Sturm, C. (1997). Creating parent-teacher dialogue: Intercultural communication in child care. *Young Children, 52*(5), 34–38.

Wing, L. A. (1992). The interesting questions approach to learning. *Childhood Education, 69*(2), 23–26.

Wittmer, D. S., & Honig, A. S. (1994). Encouraging positive social development in young children. *Young Children, 49*(5), 4–12.

Wolfgang, C. H. (1999). *Solving discipline problems.* NY: John Wiley & Sons.

For additional information on using the guidance approach in the classroom, visit our Web site at http://www.earlychilded.delmar.com

<hr />

CHAPTER EIGHT

<hr />

LEADERSHIP COMMUNICATION WITH THE INDIVIDUAL

GUIDING QUESTIONS

- How do teachers' listening skills encourage young learners?
- How are contact talks a useful guidance method?
- What is a compliment sandwich and how does it work?
- Why is friendly humor an important guidance strategy?
- Is friendly touch still a viable guidance technique?
- How can teachers care for themselves so they can care for the children?
- How do teachers use leadership communication in the parent-teacher conference?

Children show mistaken behavior because they do not know how else to act; others have influenced them to act in a particular way; or they are driven to act out because of strong unmet needs. When adults get beyond **childism,** the naive belief that childhood is a rosy time without stress and hardship, they realize that sometimes the opposite is the case (Chenfield, 1997). Without the positive attachment and social supports of families, many children come to school with pronounced needs and are unsure of how to cope with the uncertainties of the classroom. When children understand that the teacher will listen to their needs and cares about them, they will feel that they belong in the class. They want to be there, fit in, and do well. Almeida (1995) phrases the idea this way:

> Teachers need to care more about their students as the focal point of the classroom, and less about the curriculum. Without question, the curriculum is important, but if students sense that you're more concerned about finishing a spelling lesson than you are about them, they'll be less likely to behave the way you'd like them too. . . .Teachers must care about their students as children (p. 89).

Chapter Eight presents five skills for leadership communication with individual children. The five skills are: listening to life experiences, contact talks, the compliment sandwich, friendly humor, and (although controversial) the use of appropriate touch. The skills build upon the general guidance priority of encouragement, introduced in previous chapters. In contrast to Chapter Seven, the skills focus on leadership communication with the individual child. The chapter concludes with a discussion of leadership communication with parents in the setting of the parent-teacher conference.

LISTENING TO LIFE EXPERIENCES

A teacher using the guidance approach recognizes that young children who are unhappy cannot easily express their anxieties in words. Unless teachers are able to show they care by **listening to life experiences,** children's pent up feelings tend to show as serious mistaken behaviors. The co-existing environments of the child: the school, the home, and the neighborhood all can be sources of child stress. In listening to children, the teacher must be attuned to problems emanating from each source.

Listening for School-Related Stress

In many children, the symptoms of school-related stress manifest themselves in feelings of ill-health (Novick, 1998). Symptoms range from the twice-a-year stomach ache to actual ulcers, from occasional headaches to hypertension and depressive reactions. The causes of school anxiety can be related to specific situations, such as the morning bus ride or the afternoon "power test," or be more pervasive—a child's general feeling of being a failure or being disliked. A remedy for many school-related anxieties is making the education program more developmentally appropriate. At an interpersonal level, as Almeida (1995) suggests, the teacher who understands school-related stress is alert to the individual support that children sometimes need.

(From the journal of a student teacher.) We were cleaning the tables for breakfast when Raul walked into the room. He stood over by his cubby with his head down. Tami [the teacher] went over, knelt down beside him, and said, "It looks like you might be a little tired this morning." Raul shook his head no. She asked him if anything was wrong. He told her that someone on his bus hit him with a backpack and he felt really bad. Tami affirmed that wasn't a good way to start the day and asked if they could do something together. She suggested a book and he agreed. They sat down on the bean-bag chair and read. She encouraged him to say the words from the book with her. He smiled as he helped her read the book. Later the teacher and Raul talked with the bus driver about the incident.

Listening for Stress Related to the Home and Neighborhood

From an early childhood perspective, several writers have discussed the increasing complexities of family life (Bullock, 1993; Furman, 1995; Rich, 1993; Sang, 1994). The rising numbers of dual working parent families, single-parent families, blended families, and families in various states of transition and crisis are by now well known. In previous times, grandparents, aunts, uncles, and other family members were available to lend support in times of need. Now, not only are many children without access to the extended family, but they are experiencing the trauma of unsafe and violent conditions outside in their neighborhood, as well as within their home. Children can be *resilient*, but they need, at minimum, at least one significant adult who cares about them. That caring adult more and more is the teacher.

The authors mentioned above discuss the effects of unsafe home and neighborhood situations on children, and supportive steps teachers can take, in the classroom. Bullock (1993) discusses factors that lead to children being lonely and rejected. She says that "Observing is the key to detecting feelings of loneliness in children" (p. 56). Assisting children to express their feelings through open-ended activities and helping them to build social skills can make a lasting difference in their lives.

Furman (1995) suggests that stresses are unavoidable and may offer opportunities for education. He states that, in turning the challenge into an opportunity, teachers can help children deal with their feelings and develop cooperative working relations with parents.

Sang (1994) describes her mental health consultation role in a kindergarten class as the "worry teacher." She recounts how working with children who need help immediately relieves behavioral demands on the teachers, gives the children in need the opportunity to express and work through their feelings, and models for the teacher therapeutic teaching techniques. Today, the values of ongoing mental health consultation in a classroom cannot be underestimated.

Rich (1993) discusses how she worked with "Harry," who showed ongoing disruptive behavior in her kindergarten classroom. Rich was able to get a teaching team member to cover her class for the first ten minutes of each day, and spent the time "for more than a month" talking with Harry in a quiet corner of the hall. They sat in two chairs, and as time went on, Harry began "thinking of things that he wanted to talk about" (p. 52). As a result of this "talking time," the relationship grew and Harry's impulsive talking and acting out in the class diminished. Rich concludes that "talking time" might not work for every child like Harry, but for him, "talking time was the simple, positive nudge into a calmer, more richly communicative life" (p. 52).

Following a similar strategy, Bowling and Rogers (2001) state that:

> The most powerful way we have found to help children heal emotionally is to give them complete focused attention with no interruptions. This works especially well one-on-one. We call this *special time* and talk about when it will be and for how long. . . . If there is one thing we really want to share with children, it is this: It's OK to be angry. It's OK to be sad. It's OK to cry. You are loved and are lovable, no matter how you are feeling (pp. 79–81).

Novick (1998) provides a structure for "fostering resiliency and emotional intelligence, by way of a *comfort corner.* The comfort corner is available to children who are referred for its use by staff and/or parents. Staffed by a Child Development Associate, the comfort corner provides open-ended activities and one-on-one attention, whenever a child feels the need. Capitalizing on the research that for children to be resilient, they need a positive attachment with at least one person, time in the comfort corner affords this special relationship (1998).

(Student teacher observation.) Marsha was sitting at the breakfast table and tapped Lois (the teacher) on the arm. Lois turned to her and said, "Yes?"

Marsha said, "My privates hurt." Lois asked her if she had to go potty. Marsha said, "No, they always hurt when I go to my daddy's." Lois did not pursue the conversation any further at that point. Later in private Lois talked to Marsha and did a report on possible child abuse. I was glad Marsha said it to Lois and not me. I'm glad Lois stopped the conversation at the table because all the other children were listening intently, and that she took Marsha aside later.

The key to helping any child faced with difficult circumstances is to have already developed a trust relationship when the crisis arises. Marsha went to Lois here because Lois was her teacher. In addition, every school and center should have a well-understood working policy for reporting suspected abuse, which is required in all 50 states. The teacher in this classroom followed the program's established policy for reporting. Extreme family situations require a planned response by a team of educators, sometimes including outside social service professionals. Teachers do not intervene on their own in such situations, but work as part of the team (Gartrell, 2000). The teacher plays an essential role, though, by maintaining the helping relationship—one that begins and ends with listening.

Using Greetings to Read Children's Feelings

On any given day, teachers do well to "read" children's feelings when they first enter the classroom. If the teacher prepares for the day ahead of time and allows for open activity when children first arrive, he is able to listen to as well as greet his students. The teacher may then be able to give a little attention to the child, or ask other members of the teaching team—assistants, volunteers, or other staff—to do so. When the teacher is able to show caring at the beginning of the day, the teacher and child may be able to reduce or avoid serious mistaken behavior that may show up later on.

> In a first-grade class, the children each drew in their own way three faces—happy, sad, and angry—on large paper plates. With help, they labeled each face and attached dials to their "face plates." When children came in each morning, they set the dials according to their moods. The teacher and an assistant made a point of noticing each child's setting and attended to those children who might need an adult to listen. In a class meeting, the children talked about how sometimes they felt more than one mood. They decided they could put their dials in between faces on these days. (One said that between sad and angry, though, "was the worsetest.")

> When a third-grade teacher witnessed Jordan tear up his arithmetic paper and say, "I hate this damn stuff," he reacted with a friendly hand on the shoulder and some kind words. The teacher might have reacted differently except for a talk he had with Jordan earlier that morning:
> "Hi, Jordan, you're not smiling today." When the boy looked down and shook his head, the teacher asked, "Something you'd like to talk about?"

Jordan said no, then fighting back tears shared, "Last night a guy hit Bumpers with his truck. We thought he was gonna be OK, but we took him to the vet. The vet took X-rays and said his whole back end was broken. We had to put him to sleep. That guy did it on purpose too."

The teacher said, "Oh, Jordan, I'm so sorry. I know what Bumpers meant to you. Do you want to talk more about it?" Jordan said no, but the teacher knew that for this child it would be a long day.

The following morning at class meeting Jordan shared about his dog. The other children listened carefully and during the day some seemed to go out of their way to show Jordan they cared.

Boyer (1992) comments that an increasing challenge to our schools is the pressure on personnel to be social workers as well as educators. In agreement with Almeida (1995), the four authors mentioned earlier argue that individual support for personal development is a central part of the modern teacher's role. The early childhood teacher is not licensed to be a psychologist or a social worker, but every day he does perform some of these functions. In the presence of Level Three mistaken behaviors caused by stress within or without the school setting, the teacher collaborates with parents, colleagues, and other professionals to help the child solve the problem. Whether comprehensive collaboration is needed or not, the teacher uses a listening ear to assist children to work through anxieties, build social skills, and gain self-esteem. Beginning when they arrive, the teacher makes time for listening to individual children each day.

CONTACT TALK

Contact talk is the practice of "quality time," adapted for the classroom. Teachers continually must battle the clock to make personal contacts. The point is that even a very short time matters to children; it tells them they are valued so much that their busy teacher takes time to talk with them.

On the surface, contact talk may sound similar to the tactic of "catch them being good," but the two are different. The "catch them" practice involves a one-way conversation with the teacher giving praise. Specific recognition of productive behavior (using encouragement) *is essential* with children, but it is not the main reason for contact talk.

With contact talk, the teacher has the motive of getting to know a child. The teacher initiates, or allows the child to initiate, a conversation. He responds as the child defines the course of the conversation. For the time that

The teacher uses a listening ear to assist children to work through anxieties,
build social skills, and gain self-esteem.

the teacher can give, he is a good listener. Children are generally eager to
have contact talks with adults. The teacher's role is pivotal in deciding that
a contact talk will happen. He does so by putting aside other work, moving
to the child's level, and conversing openly with the child.

Examples of contact talks were given in the previous section, at the preschool level with the teacher who helped Raul get over an unhappy experience on the bus, the kindergarten level with the teacher who scheduled
talking time with Harry, and the primary level with the teacher who gave
Jordan permission to express his feelings about his dog. Contact talks need
not be of great length. They do not even have to be of a serious nature, but
they do need to happen with each child in the class on a regular basis.

The sun was shining warmly and the children could play inside
or out until all arrived. Mavis bounded in the door of Head Start,
ran a circle around the teacher, and announced, "Me gots new
shoes, teacher!"

Looking down at Mavis' pulled up pants, the teacher exclaimed, "Oh, Mavis, those are sure some colorful sneakers."

Indignant, Mavis replied, "Not sneakers. 'Lectic shoes!"

Grinning broadly, the teacher corrected herself, "I'll bet you
can sure run fast in those athletic shoes." With a nod over her
shoulder, Mavis galloped out the door to the playground.

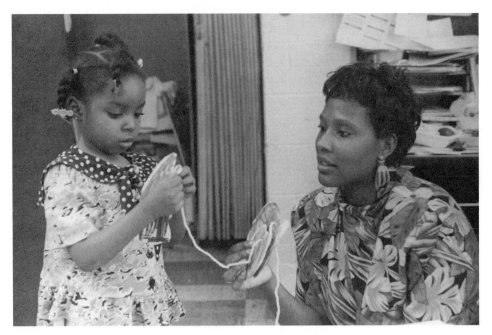

The teacher decides that a contact talk will happen by putting aside other work, moving to the child's level, and conversing openly.

As time is precious during the day, the teacher must look for opportunities for contact talks to occur. Some likely moments in the daily program include:

- before other children arrive,
- during a choice time,
- unstructured active playtimes (inside or out),
- at lunch,
- during a break in the day,
- after a self-directing activity has begun,
- after school.

Contact Talks at the Preschool Level

The following anecdotes, from the journals of student teachers, illustrate contact talks at lunch and during choice time in two separate Head Start centers.

> (Lunch time) Karly and I were eating at the lunch table. Some children at the table were talking about what they had done on Easter, where they had gone, etc. Karly quietly said, "I didn't see my Daddy at Easter."

I said, "Oh?"

She then said, "He isn't good with kids. He doesn't like them either. My Grandma and Grandpa don't like kids either."

I said, "I'm sorry, Karly. I'll bet you have other grown-ups who like kids."

She smiled and said, "Yes, I do! My other Grandma and Grandpa love me. And Uncle Tim and Aunt Judy like to play with me. And my Mom really loves me."

I said, "It's OK to still miss your dad, but you are a very lucky girl to have so many people who love and care for you." she nodded seriously, and that ended the conversation.

(Choice time) I heard the words, "Shut up," and walked around the corner to the restroom to find out who said them. Shayna was sitting in the corner crying. I asked, "Shayna, why are you crying?"

She said, "Amanda and Christina said they aren't my friends anymore." I asked her if she told them to shut up. Shayna said yes.

I told her I was sorry that what they said made her feel sad and angry, but we don't use those words in our classroom because they hurt people's feelings. (Amanda and Christina had been watching and listening to us talk.) I added that maybe next time she could tell the girls that hearing that they didn't want to be her friend made her sad. I told Amanda and Christina that Shayna was feeling sad. They came over to Shayna and gave her a hug and said they were sorry.

Shayna walked over to the table where I was sitting. She started crying again. I asked, "Is something making you feel sad, Shayna?"

She said, "I miss my daddy." (Her father was killed in a car accident a few months before.)

I asked if she would like to sit on my lap, and when she did, I said, "Shayna, my daddy died when I was a little girl, and I was very sad too. I am so glad you told me why you were crying." We sat by each other until snack.

Shayna went to the housekeeping area after snack. Later in the day, she came up to me and said, "I'm over my daddy now."

I said, "Shayna, feeling sad about missing your daddy is OK. I still miss my dad. If you need a hug or want to talk, you come and tell me."

The advantage in staffing arrangements of preschools is that contact talks can occur more easily. In the supportive prekindergarten classroom, a reasonable goal is *at least* one contact talk with each child every day. Teachers of three- to five-year-olds can hardly escape contact talks, and of course shouldn't.

Contact Talks in the Primary Grades

Because of typical staff-to-child ratios in the primary grades, regular contact talks are often more difficult. A system that allows every child to be reached is critical. Here is where use of the teaching team can help. If the teacher can bring other adults into the classroom, more contact talks can occur (Rich, 1993). With only one adult in the room, a teacher might only be able to have a few conversations a day—still better than none at all. Elementary teachers who work to increase the number of contact talks tend to be rewarded.

In his first year of teaching, Clay felt hampered because he was only able to relate to his 30 third graders as "students." He decided to try an after school program that he called "Get to Know Our City." He got approval from the principal and sent home letters with permission forms. One day each week, he took a carload (five) of the third graders to visit interesting places.

By the end of the school year, all children had gone with him at least once. Most had gone a few times. Clay found the experience had helped him gain new understanding about the children. When one child who usually did not say much asked him if his toothache was better, Clay discovered that the other children were also getting to know him. Of course, the entire class learned more about the city. And, quite important to Clay, the program especially helped his relations with a few children he had mainly known before as "strong-willed."

For a workshop assignment, Gayle, a kindergarten teacher, made a chart of the children's names set against a four-week calendar. Daily, the teacher made a point of having two-minute personal conversations with at least five children and noted these conversations on the chart. With alternate day programming, Gayle was able to have at least one contact talk with each child every two weeks—and with most children more than one.

After the month, Gayle decided to continue the practice. The teacher discovered she was becoming more familiar with the children, especially those who were less outgoing. She found she was not only getting to know the children better, but they were also getting to know her. Gayle felt there was a change of atmosphere in the classroom.

The value of contact talk is that as teachers and children get to know each other,
trust builds, and mistaken behavior lessens.

The value of contact talks is that as teachers and children get to know
each other, trust builds, and the need for mistaken behavior lessens. Studies have shown that teachers tend to talk most with children who are talk-
ative and from backgrounds similar to their own (Derman-Sparks, 1989;
York, 1991). A chart may seem mechanical, but it ensures that all children
(and the teacher) receive the benefits of contact talks.

THE COMPLIMENT SANDWICH

At a workshop, Dr. Julie Jochum came across the idea of the **compliment
sandwich.** Jochum developed the concept as a feedback technique for teacher
education majors when journaling with children (Jochum, 1991). As adapted
from Jochum's usage, the spoken or written compliment sandwich provides
a focused way of giving encouragement. The technique is useful with children
or adults for preventing or resolving problems. (The technique even works
with family members, though sometimes a "triple-decker" is needed.)

The compliment sandwich has these parts: at least *two* statements of encouragement; *one* suggestion, recommendation, request, or question. The
encouragements recognize effort, progress, or interim achievement. (They
are the pieces of "bread.") The peanut butter in the middle guides the child
toward further progress. The ratio is important as some research has shown

that two positives per negative is the barest minimum for a child to feel supported (Kirkhart & Kirkhart, 1967). In other words, three pieces of bread ("triple-decker encouragement") is desirable. If the teacher considers adding a second request or recommendation, she makes a new sandwich.

What do compliment sandwiches sound like? The reader can tell very quickly what is and is not a compliment sandwich. Let us "overhear" two second-grade teachers, one during language arts, the other during math time.

> *Language arts:* You are being careless again. Look at how those sentences wander over the page. You forgot your periods. This is messy work. You will need to do it again.
>
> *Math:* You have seven of the problems exactly right. This assignment is hard, and you are really staying with it. Use your counters again and see if you can get different answers for the other three. You can do it.

By using the compliment sandwich—as opposed to "character assassination"—the second teacher was probably helping to prevent math anxiety. The technique is self-explanatory—for whatever change the teacher requests, she recognizes two or more indicators of progress or effort. The math teacher's use of the technique was in an academic situation. The compliment sandwich also applies in other classroom situations. Here are examples of compliment sandwiches, first with a group and then with an individual child:

> *Preprimary:* You have put away all the blocks and the books. We just have the table toys to finish and then we can go outside.
>
> Jamie, you have your coat hung up and your boots off; you just need to put the boots under your coat, and you're all set.
>
> *Primary:* Class, you read lots of books in the library today, and you sat very quietly for the story. Coming back through the hall, though, was a little too noisy. Who has ideas for how to make the walk back more quiet next time?
>
> Sondra, you stayed in your seat and didn't have any problems with your neighbors. That's real progress! Now, how can we help you to remember to use that "inside voice"?

Encouragement that is a part of the compliment sandwich reassures children that the teacher is on their side. (It is always easier to improve when the coach is pulling for you.) With serious mistaken behavior, the compliment sandwich also helps to remind the *teacher* of this fact. With parents, the compliment sandwich helps establish a spirit of cooperation, that the parent and teacher are working together for the benefit of the child. (References to use for the compliment sandwich in this setting can be found in Chapter Two and Seven.) The technique is an important one, an essential ingredient of leadership communication with children and adults in the encouraging classroom.

FRIENDLY HUMOR

The use of **friendly humor** affirms positive relations with children and affords a friendly atmosphere in the classroom. An attraction of teaching young children is the delightful unpredictability in their responses. Teachers who find themselves refreshed by the reactions of young learners know why they are practicing at this age level. In light of the difficulties classroom teachers face each day, the ability to find humor in situations adds to the positives of the profession.

> A student kept a journal of her practicum experiences throughout her teacher education program. A few of the enjoyable statements she recorded:
>
> When I was helping a boy in kindergarten fold his paper in half, Cody said, "I can't fold very good because I'm from Tenstrike, and people in Tenstrike don't know how to fold."
>
> While I was helping a four-year-old button her coat, Ashley said, "My grandpa can't snap the buttons very good because his hands are old."
>
> As I read kindergartners a story, Amanda said as I paused to catch a breath to keep reading, "Miss Curb, you have bags under your eyes." (Kids are so honest—you gotta love it)
>
> During a practicum at St. Philip's Preschool, While five of us education majors were doing a theme project with the children, the teacher asked the three- to five-year-olds if they could do anything to help us. One little boy piped up and asked, "Should we pray?" We smiled at each other because it wasn't such a bad idea.
>
> At a practicum in a day care center, A little girl arrived late, just in time to pass the "Easter Bunny" on the sidewalk. The Bunny, who had just visited our center, was in a hurry to get to his next visit. The little girl watched wide eyed as the Bunny got in his car and drove off. She walked into the center shaking her head and muttering, "I didn't know the Easter Bunny could drive a car"!

The ability to find humor in situations adds much joy to a teacher.

Different kinds of situations are apt to make teachers smile. One such occasion is when teachers hear their own words echoed by children:

> A teacher was at first amazed, then amused when a four-year-old made the following request: "I am having a difficult morning, so I need kindness." The teacher remembered making a similar comment in jest earlier in the week.

The fact that children interpret words quite literally can be a source of enjoyment for adults and children alike:

> It began raining heavily outside the windows of a kindergarten class. The teacher exclaimed, "Why, it's raining cats and dogs out there."
>
> The children looked out of the windows intently. Then one child turned to the teacher and said with a smile, "Teacher, it's raining elephants even."

A classroom atmosphere in which humorous moments are enjoyed by all is a positive atmosphere. Teachers who see humor even in trying moments can defuse problems effectively. Curwin and Mendler suggest the use of mildly self-effacing humor as a remedy for power struggles (1988). This use of humor can be challenging for a teacher, but it has its rewards.

> In front of the class, a fearless third grader said to his male teacher, "Boy, Mr. D., you sure are hairy."
>
> The teacher, who had forgotten to shave, said, "You're right, Willie. I couldn't find my razor today, so I hit my whiskers in with a hammer and bit them off inside. Guess I missed some." The class, including Willie, shook their heads and laughed. The moment was quickly forgotten as Mr. D. started a project.

Finally, we teachers are often bemused, sometimes delighted, by the creative imagination any child might show at any time in an encouraging classroom:

> The theme this week in our school-age care classroom was "animals in our backyards." As part of the theme, we asked the children who came to the dramatic play center to dress up like animals and we would guess which ones they were. Cheyenne, a quiet and studious first grader, found an old brown coat and a floppy brown hat. She also put on some enormous sunglasses. After no one guessed what animal she was, I asked Cheyenne if she would tell us. With a big grin she said, "Sam, don't you know? I am an owl out in the daytime"!

Humor helps in sustaining positive teacher-child relations. However, humor can also be used against children, by a teacher who needs to control through humiliation. Dr. John Halcrow, an education professor in human relations, has this to say about the use of humor:

We need humor in the classroom but let's be careful about it. Humor can be a two-edged sword. Some rules for humor: Never use it as a weapon, nor to chastise or correct. Never make a student the butt of a joke, and remember not to take yourself too seriously.

We need fun, hope, even frivolity in the classroom. If we put too much focus on the mechanics of what we're teaching, we kill the joy. Work students hard, then let them play with what they've learned. Let them talk to each other, try out their ideas and correct their own errors along the way. (1988)

A sense of humor in teachers is much appreciated by learners of all ages. Humor makes learning meaningful because it makes it fun.

FRIENDLY TOUCH

Along with humor, another practice that conveys warmth in relations is the use of **friendly touch.** Unfortunately, the use of warm physical contact (hugs and friendly touches) by teachers, so accepted in times past, has become controversial today. Now in some school districts, teachers ask permission of a child before giving a pat on a shoulder or a hug. In many situations, teachers must communicate with fellow staff, administrators, and parents before doing what before came so naturally. Every teacher must make personal decisions regarding touch. This section cites Curwin and Mendler (1988) and Hendrick (2000) in supporting the use of friendly physical contact within the limits of reasonable policy.

Curwin and Mendler (1988) recommend the use of hugs and touching in communicating with children. They decry the fallacy of prohibition against touch because of sexual misunderstanding, but they seem to assume that this proscription pertains only to teachers of older students (1988, p. 16). Yet, Hendrick points out that recent sensationalized court cases have made early childhood teachers as well "uneasy about touching or cuddling youngsters lest they, too, be accused" (2000, p. 107). The article, "Vanishing Breed: Men in Child Care Programs," (Robinson, 1988) points out that male teachers of young children are particularly susceptible to such suspicions.

A practice that conveys warmth in relations is the use of touch.

Given the value of nurturing touches for children, physical closeness should not be deleted from the teacher's repertoire. Rather, as Hendrick points out (2000), educators need to maintain written policies that allow open visitation by parents, require clear understanding among all staff regarding physical closeness, and conduct criminal background checks for prospective employees. The rationale for the guideline "friendly touches only" needs to be fully communicated to children, parents, and staff. Such practices are becoming necessary for the continuation of this important teaching technique as a legitimate expression of human caring.

A teacher worked to develop a sense of belonging with her class. In her own words, she was "a hugger," and talked with the new principal early in the year about his policy regarding physical closeness. The principal commented that his policy was, "Friendly physical contact is acceptable in the public confines of the classroom with the written permission of the parents and the verbal permission of the child." Bothered but undeterred by the new policy, the teacher explained the situation to parents at the September orientation meeting. Almost all the parents signed the written permission slips allowing the teacher to use "friendly touches, hugs, and sitting on my lap."

With her kindergartners, the teacher held a class meeting. The class decided that at arrivals and departures if children wanted a hug, they would give two thumbs up; if they wanted a friendly wave or comment only, they would put up one thumb. The teacher also made sure that they knew they could put up one or two thumbs during other times of day, if they needed to.

Stationing herself by the door each morning, she greeted each child with a one thumb or two thumb hello. She noticed that some children were "everyday huggers," and some children wanted a hug seldom or once in a while. All the children, though, responded warmly to her daily greeting. The teacher believed that putting her preparations aside for the greetings helped each day go better.

The teacher also gave a one or two thumb farewell at the end of the day. She noticed that more children elected a hug at the end of the day than at the beginning. She talked with the one or two children whose parents had not signed the slips, and gave these children special smiles and verbal comments. Though she saw the policy as a bother, she concluded that it was worth it to make her classroom a friendly place.

Physical closeness accomplishes what words cannot in forming healthy attachments with children (Curwin & Mendler, 1988). As Hendrick points out, children "require the reassurance and comfort of being patted, rocked, held, and hugged from time to time" (2000, p. 107). Hendrick states:

> Research as well as experience supports the value of close physical contact. Montagu (1986) has reviewed numerous studies illustrating the beneficial effect of being touched and the relationship of tactile experience to healthy physical and emotional development. Investigations documenting the link between touching and the development of attachment confirm those findings. (2000, p. 107)

Brain research suggested by Wolfe and Brandt (1998), Diamond and Hopson (1998), and LeDoux (1996) provides the psychological link to explain the beneficial nature of friendly touch. Tactile calming promotes helpful hormone secretion and harmonious brain functioning, assisting the child to feel acceptance and trust in the encouraging classroom. Considering the benefits of touch for children, teachers should not dismiss this technique, but use it carefully and with open communication to the full extent that program policies allow.

BE THERE FOR THE CHILDREN, BE THERE FOR YOURSELF

Gruenberg (1998) mentions that "Stress is widely acknowledged to be a problem of our times and early childhood caregiving, while joyful and satisfying is one of the most stressful types of work. . . ." To open yourself to the experiences and needs of children, required for guidance leadership, the teacher must be attuned to his own needs and circumstances. Gruenberg mentions that a common pattern among early childhood professionals is **overfunctioning:** feeling one must be all things to all people. She comments that it is important to be cognizant about one's situation and to recognize that "a disproportionate workload does not have to occur."

Honestly confronting in oneself the cause of the stress is a first step to making life more manageable. Gruenberg (1998) explains that without this reflection, the symptoms of stress sneak up on us and show in one or more reaction patterns such as:

Body: headaches, body aches, illness, weight gain or loss, sleeping problems

Emotions: anger, frustration, fear, anxiety, depression, overreaction

Actions/behavior: withdrawal, aggression, impulsivity, feeling victimized, casting blame, stigmatizing others

Mind: disorganization, distraction, rigid thought patterns, compulsive organization, need to control

While anyone can have a day or two with such symptoms, a pattern over time indicates a problem that the teacher needs to address. The adult may

turn to friends and family, fellow staff, counselors, and other helping professionals to understand and address the source of the stress. Either with
help or on one's own, Gruenberg suggests options for alleviating stress reactions that include purposeful behaviors like:

- exercising, relaxing strategies,
- setting reasonable limits,
- taking a break,
- practicing flexibility,
- prioritizing tasks,
- breaking big tasks down into little ones,
- letting oneself be silly,
- actively collaborating,
- creatively solving problems (1998).

Gruenberg maintains that regular practice at these tasks helps and often
can be done in an enjoyable way (1988). Again, a personal support system
is important in this effort, Gruenberg states:

> Belief in one's own ability to cope with the situation makes all the difference
> in taking charge and making healthy choices. . . .Whatever we do to support
> our own health contributes to the well-being of our relationships and com-
> munities, including our relationships with children, parents, and colleagues
> in our early childhood communities (Gruenberg, 1998, pp. 41–42).

LEADERSHIP COMMUNICATION IN THE PARENT-TEACHER CONFERENCE

Chapter Seven emphasized five basic teacher-parent communication
techniques useful in creating positive relationships: notes home, telephone calls, electronic communication, parent meetings, and parent-
teacher conferences. Chapter Eight focuses specifically on the
parent-teacher conference and what Rosenthal and Sawyers argue is
the overriding goal of conferences, the accomplishment of *joining,* or
helping parents understand that the teacher accepts them and wants
to work with them on behalf of the child (1996).

Joining with Parents

The traditional setting for the conference is the classroom, though sometimes parents feel more comfortable with the teacher in a setting outside the
school—the home, a community center, a child care or Head Start building,
or a restaurant. (One of my favorite stories is of the teacher who, after several attempts at reaching a single mom, finally located her at a lounge

A main purpose of the conference is to help parents understand that the teacher accepts them and wants to work with them on behalf of the child.

where she worked as a cocktail waitress. The two had a conference in a booth during the mom's coffee break. She later become a classroom volunteer.) The teacher needs to give consideration to the site of the conference and its likely meaning for parents.

> In her second year of teaching first grade, a teacher created a "parent corner" in her classroom by placing a cardboard divider, decorated by the children, between her desk and a corner of the room. The corner was small, but it had enough room to squeeze in two chairs, a small table and coffee pot, a bulletin board, a fledgling resource library, and a coat hook with a plastic carton below where parents could stow their belongings. After talking with a parent volunteer, the teacher decided to have her conferences in the parent corner. She noticed that the parents felt quite comfortable having the conferences in "their" area. Unlike the previous year, many of the conferences proved downright fun, and holding the conferences in the corner seemed to increase the number of parents who came into the classroom to volunteer. Two other teachers set up parent corners the next year and conducted their conferences in them.

Wherever the site of the conference, Rosenthal and Sawyers offer a list of suggestions important for the process of **joining** (building partnerships) **with parents:**

1. Speak the language of the family; use their words and definitions.
2. Understand the family's rules and rituals.
3. Try to keep jargon to a minimum—especially at first.
4. Monitor your own level of discomfort; do you resort to becoming the "expert" when you become uncomfortable?
5. Try to build a collaborative, rather than an adversarial, system.
6. Ask the family to suggest solutions [and contribute ideas].
7. Recognize signs of a power struggle (1996, p. 197).

Listening to Parents

In an article included in the Recommended Resources, Studer (1993) offers suggestions to better enable teachers to "listen so that parents will speak." The following discussion incorporates Studer's ideas.

An essential part of communication is listening. Studer points out four reasons for why teachers may not listen as effectively as they might (1993). First, the teacher may have negative attitudes about the parent. For instance, if the teacher believes that the parents do not care about their child's education, he may not even attempt communication intended to build partnerships. Second, when persons such as teachers are in "power" positions in conversations, they tend to think ahead to the next point they want to make. Instead, the teacher needs to listen to what the other is saying. Third, in a similar fashion, the teacher may finish the comments of parents, or otherwise "politely" interrupt, rather than give the respect of fully listening. Fourth, prejudging a person and anticipating what that person is going to say may keep the teacher from listening effectively (p. 74).

For teachers to be effective in communications, they need to listen fully and reflectively (what Studer terms *active listening*). Real listening involves both body placement and the honest effort to understand (Studer, 1993). The teacher sits side by side with the parent or in chairs across from one another; faces and even leans toward the parent in an open posture; and when culturally appropriate, makes eye contact and uses light touch.

When listening, the teacher respectfully acknowledges what the parent says, avoids giving quick advice, and involves the parent as a full partner in the discussion. Notice the difference in the following dramatized reactions of two teachers when Mrs. Dillworth comments that her son, Cory, has complained about two children picking on him.

> *Teacher one* sits behind a desk with arms folded, leans away, and looks out the window. Interrupts when he has heard "enough." Speaks in a "lecture" voice: "You know, Mrs. Dillworth, when I was a kid, I had that problem and what I did was join a karate club. Get Cory enrolled in a karate club, Mrs. Dillworth. Your kid has to learn to take care of himself."
>
> *Teacher two* sits next to Mrs. Dillworth, faces her, and lets her fully express what is on her mind. He reflects back what he has heard, how Mrs. Dillworth must be feeling, and what she probably would like to see happen (Studer, 1993). "Cory has shared that two boys in the class have been picking on him? You must be bothered by that idea, and you'd like this problem addressed. Tell me more about what Cory has said and then we'll figure out what we can do about this problem."

In the first scenario, a parent might well assume they weren't going to get very far, thank the teacher for the time (maybe), and leave still feeling upset. In the second, the teacher has listened to what the parent has said and joined with the parent as a team member. By doing so, he has improved the chances that a positive action will result from the conference and that the problem will not be escalated.

One reaction tendency of many teachers to situations like the one in the anecdote is defensive: "Doesn't happen in my classroom." These thoughts, the result of feeling threatened by the parent, may not be directly expressed, but they come through indirectly in defensive communication styles. By staying calm and remembering that the parent, child, and teacher are all on the same team, the teacher is in a better position to invite cooperation from the parent and prevent problems in parent-teacher relations. Studer concludes her article in this way:

> Teachers must remember that parents have special needs and special concerns. Conferences need to be approached with an attitude of sharing and learning, as well as a willingness to consider parents' observations. Such a cooperative attitude between home and school can be paramount to a child's achievement (1993, p. 76).

Such an attitude will also result in parents who are not adversaries but allies, because the conference has allowed joining to occur.

SUMMARY

1. How do teachers' listening skills encourage young learners?

With the complexities of modern life, many children feel tension, stress, and anxiety. These feelings may be school-related or related to the child's experiences in the home or neighborhood. Unless they are able to express and work through their feelings and concerns, their unmet needs may cause children to show Level Three mistaken behavior. With larger problems, the teacher works with other adults in a collaborative approach. In many cases, however, by listening and helping children to express and cope with the stress they feel, teachers bolster self-esteem, boost feelings of safety and belonging, and promote the development of life skills.

2. How are contact talks a useful guidance method?

Contact talk is the concept of quality time adapted to the classroom. The purpose of contact talks is neither to preach nor to "catch the student being good." Rather, contact talks are for the purpose of the teacher and the child getting to know each other. Contact talks need not be long nor especially serious, but the teacher needs to find the time and take an action such as moving to the child's level to ensure that they happen. In the process of the contact talk, the teacher learns more about the child and how to work with the child more effectively. The child learns that the teacher cares and that the classroom is an encouraging place to be.

3. What is a compliment sandwich and how does it work?

The compliment sandwich allows teachers to make a request for change or further progress effectively by coupling the request with two or three statements of encouragement. When a teacher is bothered by a child's behavior, the compliment sandwich assists the teacher to phrase the concern positively. Adults as well as children respond more easily to requests for change when the listener concludes that both individuals are on the same side. For this reason, the compliment sandwich has uses with colleagues and parents as well as with children.

4. Why is friendly humor an important guidance strategy?

For children and teachers alike, friendly humor eases tense situations and makes classroom transactions more enjoyable. One important benefit of being a teacher of young children is the delightful things that they say. The ability to enjoy the freshness and unpredictability of children adds much to the profession. When laughter is not used against children but with them to create a feeling of community, humor becomes an important guidance strategy. Learners of all ages appreciate teachers who use friendly humor.

5. Is friendly touch still a viable guidance technique?

Some educators reject using touch with children because they fear the innuendo of sexual abuse. Such attitudes are unfortunate. Children experience the world through touch even more than other senses and brain development is fundamentally enhanced by frequent friendly touch. For younger children and older ones alike, appropriate touch is fundamentally reassuring; it tells children in ways that words cannot that the teacher cares. Programs need to be clear about their guidelines for touch, when and what kind of touch is appropriate, and they need to negotiate these guidelines with parents. Within established guidelines, touch tells children that they are cared for and they belong.

6. How can teachers care for themselves so they can care for the children?

Stress is an unavoidable part of the early childhood teacher's life. Unless teachers are active in confronting sources of stress, over time they are likely to experience the effects of impaired mental and physical health. Having a support system is important, as is following through on strategies that may include counseling, exercising, setting personal limits, letting oneself be silly, working more closely with others, and creatively addressing problems. When we can make ourselves healthy, we can be there effectively for the children in our lives.

7. How do teachers use leadership communication in the parent-teacher conference?

The main purpose of communicating with parents is *joining,* or helping parents understand that you are working with them cooperatively on behalf of the child. A main vehicle in the process of building partnerships is the parent-teacher conference. The teacher endeavors to make the conference setting comfortable for the parent. In the conference, the teacher must be sensitive to any prejudices toward the family and listen without interrupting or giving quick advice. Listening to parents is crucial in the communication process of the conference. To listen effectively, the teacher takes an open body position and uses eye contact and light touch as culturally appropriate. In a supportive tone, the teacher reflects on what the parent says and states what he thinks the parent is getting at. With confirmation, the teacher involves the parent in a shared resolution of the issues at hand.

KEY CONCEPTS

Childism
Compliment sandwich
Contact talk
Friendly humor
Friendly touch
Joining with parents
Listening to life experiences
Overfunctioning

FOLLOW-UP ACTIVITIES

*Note: An element of being a professional teacher is to respect the children,
parents, and educators you are working with by maintaining
confidentiality—keeping identities private. In completing follow-up
activities, please respect the privacy of all concerned.*

Discussion Activity

The discussion activity encourages students to interrelate their own thoughts and experiences with specific ideas from the chapter.

Think about a time when a child needed to say something to you and you listened. Compare the dynamics of this experience with what the chapter says about listening skills and contact talks. What did you learn about working with young children by making the decision to listen?

Application Activities

Application activities allow students to interrelate material from the text with real-life situations. The observations imply access to practicum experiences; the interviews, access to teachers or parents.

1. **Listening skills.**
   a. Observe an adult in the classroom who is sympathetically listening to a nonacademic experience a child is sharing. What do you notice about how the adult is using listening

skills? What seems to be the child's demeanor at the start of the conversation, at the end?

b. Interview a teacher about the priority he gives to listening to individual children's personal experiences. Ask the teacher if he can remember an experience when he helped a child by listening. How does the teacher cope with the "time problem" that listening to individual children entails?

2. **Contact talks.**

a. Observe a teacher having what appears to be a contact talk with a child. What did the teacher do to be available for the talk? Who is doing more talking? How is what you observe similar to or different from what the text says about contact talks?

b. Interview a teacher about contact talks. Explain the term if necessary. What does the teacher believe the place of contact talks should be in the daily program? How does the teacher's position agree or disagree with the discussion of contact talks in the text?

3. **The compliment sandwich.**

a. Observe a teacher talking with a child about a behavior that the teacher would like the child to improve. Did he use a compliment sandwich? Why or why not?

b. Interview a teacher about the compliment sandwich. Explain the term if necessary. What value does the teacher see in using contact talks? How do the teacher's ideas compare with the text?

4. **Friendly humor.**

a. Observe an instance of humor used by a child in a classroom. How did the other children respond? The teacher respond? Observe a second instance of humor, this time used by the teacher. How did the children respond? What have you learned about humor in the classroom from these observations?

b. Interview a teacher that you believe to have a sense of humor. What is important to him about using humor in the classroom? Ask for an example or two of events that the teacher found humorous. Compare what the teacher says about humor with the text position.

5. **Friendly touch.**

a. Observe two instances when a teacher used touch in the classroom. What seemed to be the effect on the child in each case? How does each child's reaction correspond to what the text says about touch?

b. Interview a teacher that you know uses friendly touch. Ask the teacher how he deals with the concerns that some adults have about touch. Ask if the program has any policies or guidelines regarding touch. Ask what the teacher believes to be important about the use of touch with children. Compare the teacher's ideas with the text.

6. **Teachers caring for themselves.**
   a. Select a teacher who seems to you to cope well with stress. Observe that teacher's interactions with others in a potential "high stress" situation. Decide particular strengths the teacher shows. Which of the options for alleviating stress reactions listed in the text does the teacher seem to be using?
   b. Interview a teacher about how he deals with job-related stress in order to remain positive in situations. If you and the teacher are both comfortable, ask also how the teacher deals with life-related stress outside of the classroom. Compare your findings with what the text says about stress, its symptoms, and options for alleviation.
7. **The parent-teacher conference.**
   a. Observe a parent-teacher conference. Identify some listening behaviors used by the teacher. How do the behaviors used by the teacher correspond to the recommendation for effective listening in the text?
   b. Interview a teacher experienced in parent-teacher conferences. Ask the teacher to discuss how he communicates during the conference to make it productive for both the parent and the teacher. How do the communication ideas mentioned by the teacher correspond to the recommendations for effective listening in the text?

What You Can Do

Leadership with the Individual   Something important can be learned from observing a teacher who uses leadership skills with individual children:

   a. Ask a teacher whom you know to use leadership skills with individual children if you can observe him for a day. Arrive early before the children get there and stay until the last child goes home.
   b. Observe and record all instances of the following communication techniques that you see: listening to life experiences, contact talks, compliment sandwiches, friendly humor, and friendly touch. To the best of your ability record the words and actions of the teacher and the primary child involved.
   c. Watch the resulting behaviors of the child after each interaction and throughout the rest of the day.
   d. Select a few of the interactions and ask the teacher to discuss them with you.
   e. Comparing your findings to ideas from the text, what did you learn about using leadership skills in the classroom with individual children?

RECOMMENDED READINGS

Almeida, D. A. (1995, September). Behavior management and "the five C's." *Teaching Prek–8,* 88–89.

Bowling, H. J., & Rogers, S. (2001). The value of healing in education. *Young Children, 56*(2), 79–81.

Bullock, J. R. (1993). Lonely children. *Young Children, 48*(6), 53–57.

Furman, R. A. (1995). Helping children cope with stress and deal with feelings. *Young Children, 50*(2), 33–41.

Gootman, M. E. (1993). Reaching and teaching abused children. *Childhood Education, 70*(1), 15–19.

Gruenberg, A. (1998). Creative stress management: Put your own oxygen mask on first. *Young Children, 53*(1), 38–42.

Novick, R. (1998). The comfort convex: Fostering resiliency and emotional intelligence. *Childhood Education, 74*(4), 200–204.

Rich, B. A. (1993). Listening to Harry (and solving a problem) in my kindergarten classroom. *Young Children, 48*(6), 52.

Robinson, B. E. (1988). Vanishing breed:Men in child care programs. *Young Children, 43*(6), 54–57.

Sang, D. (1994). The worry teacher comes on Thursdays. *Young Children 49*(2), 24–31.

Studer, J. R. (1993). Listen so that parents will speak. *Childhood Education, 70*(2), 74–77.

Sturm, C. (1997). Creating parent-teacher dialogue: Intercultural communication in child care. *Young Children, 52*(5), 34–38.

REFERENCES

Almeida, D. A. (1995, September). Behavior management and "the five C's." *Teaching Prek-8,* 88–89.

Bowling, H. J., & Rogers, S. (2001). The value of healing in education. *Young Children, 56*(2), 79–81.

Boyer, E. L. (1992). *Ready to learn: A mandate for the nation.* Princeton, NJ: The Carnegie Foundation for the Advancement of Teaching.

Bullock, J. R. (1993). Lonely children. *Young Children, 48*(6), 53–57.

Chenfield, M. (1997). *Creative experiences for young children.* San Diego, CA: Harcourt Trade Publishers.

Curwin, R. L., & Mendler, A. N. (1988). *Discipline with dignity.* Alexandria, VA: Association for Supervision and Curriculum Development.

Derman-Sparks, L. (1989). *Anti-bias curriculum: Tools for empowering young children.* Washington, DC: National Association for the Education of Young Children.

Diamond, M., & Hopson, J. (1998). *Magic trees of the mind: How to nurture your child's intelligence, creativity, and healthy emotions from birth through adolescence.* New York: Dutton.

Furman, R. A. (1995). Helping children cope with stress and deal with feelings. *Young Children, 50*(2), 33–41.

Gartrell, D. J. (2000). What the kids said today: Using classroom conversations to become a better teacher. St. Paul, MN: Redleaf Press.

Gruenberg, A. (1998). Creative stress management: Put your own oxygen mask on first. *Young Children, 53*(1), 38–42.

Halcrow, J. (1988). *Laughter in the classroom.* (Professional education document). Bemidji, MN: Bemidji State University.

Hendrick, J. (2000). *The whole child.* Englewood Cliffs, NJ: Merrill/Prentice Hall.

Jochum, J. (1991). Responding to writing and to the writer. *Intervention, 26*(3), 152–157.

Kirkhart, R., & Kirkhart, E. (1967). The bruised self: Mending in the early years. In K. Yamamoto (Ed.), *The child and his image: Self concept in the early years.* Boston: Houghton Mifflin Company.

LeDoux, J. (1996). *The emotional brain.* New York: Simon & Schuster.

Novick, R. (1998). The comfort corner; Fostering resiliency and emotional intelligence. *Childhood Education, 74*(4), 200–204.

Rich, B. A. (1993). Listening to Harry (and solving a problem) in my kindergarten classroom. *Young Children, 48*(6), 52.

Robinson, B. E. (1988). Vanishing breed: Men in child care programs. *Young Children, 43*(6), 54–57.

Rosenthal, D. M., & Sawyers, J. Y. (1996). Building successful home/school partnerships: Strategies for parent support and involvement. *Childhood Education, 72*(4), 194–200.

Sang, D. (1994). The worry teacher comes on Thursdays. *Young Children, 49*(2), 24–31.

Studer, J. R. (1993). Listen so that parents will speak. *Childhood Education, 70*(2), 74–77.

Wolfe, P., & Brandt, R. (1998, November). What do we know from brain research? *Educational Leadership,* 8–13. Vol 56.

York, S. (1991). *Roots and wings: Affirming culture in early childhood programs.* St. Paul, MN: Redleaf Press.

For additional information on using the guidance approach in the classroom, visit our Web site at http://www.earlychilded.delmar.com

PART THREE

Solving Problems in the Encouraging Classroom

PREVIEWS

Nine   **Using Conflict Management to Solve Social Problems**
Chapter Nine explores how the adult can model and teach conflict management and negotiation skills so that children learn to solve social problems. Discussion is given to conflict management basics for teachers; using an understanding of children's development to assist in conflict management; a five-finger formula for using and teaching conflict management; and the process of teaching conflict management skills to children. The final section explores how parent involvement at St. Philip's School in northern Minnesota helped to build a peaceable school community.

Ten   **Problem-Solving Mistaken Behavior**
Chapter Ten presents strategies for the teacher to use to resolve mistaken behavior. Strategies include making the decision to intervene, responding to behaviors reported by children, using quick intervention techniques, and intervening when follow-up is necessary. A question answered is, "Why take the time to find solutions"? The final section discusses building cooperation with parents through non-biased communication.

Eleven   **Guidance Through Intervention**
Chapter Eleven offers information to help prospective and practicing teachers cope with and remediate strong needs mistaken behavior. Conditions that make intervention necessary are examined. Methods of crisis management and of handling feelings of anger are discussed. Strategies and case studies in working with Level Three strong needs mistaken behavior are presented. The

chapter concludes with considerations for when teachers and parents disagree.

Twelve **Liberation Teaching: A Guidance Response to Violence in Society**

Chapter Twelve develops the concept of liberation teaching as a guidance response to violence in society. The chapter begins with a look at societal violence and its effects on children in the classroom. The discussion then turns to defining liberation teaching and discussing how liberation teaching responds to violence in the classroom. A section investigates recent research on bullying, and the liberating teacher's response to bullying. The relation of liberation teaching to anti-bias education, guidance, and peace education is explored. The chapter ends with application of the concept of liberation teaching to relations with parents.

CHAPTER NINE

USING CONFLICT MANAGEMENT TO SOLVE SOCIAL PROBLEMS

GUIDING QUESTIONS

- What conflict management basics do teachers need?
- How does understanding young children's development assist in conflict management?
- What is the five-finger formula for conflict management?
- How does the adult teach conflict management skills to children?
- How have parents helped to shape the peaceful problem-solving program at a model school?

Thanks to Sarah Pirtle of Discovery Center, Shelburne Falls, Massachusetts; and to Sue Liedl of St. Philip's School, Conflict Management Program, Bemidji, Minnesota, for contributing to this chapter.

> (From the journal of a student teacher) *Observation:* Starre came to Head Start one day with a buzz haircut—quite a change from her longer hair. Starre went up to her friend, Aisha, and asked, "Do you like my hair?"
>
> Aisha looked at her and started to say that she didn't like it, but caught herself and with a quizzical smile said, "I'm not used to it yet."
>
> Starre replied, "Yeah, me neither."

No less than parents, educators want children, as they mature, to be able to make *autonomous* (ethical and intelligent) decisions. With young children such as Aisha this social problem-solving includes a bit of self-control and beginning empathy for the other person. In adolescence, when faced with peer pressures regarding vandalism, cigarettes, alcohol, drugs, and premature sex, the young person's ability to make autonomous decisions requires individual strength, a healthy conscience, and well-practiced problem-solving skills.

Slaby et al. (1995) define *social problem solving* as "The skills needed to manage social conflict successfully. . . ." Sometimes, as in Aisha's case in the previous anecdote, the management of conflict means having the skills to prevent conflict from happening. In fact, this ability might be considered a central "learner outcome" of teaching social problem-solving skills. More often, though, and especially with young children, social problem solving is needed after one child has objected to an action of another, and the conflict is escalating. This is when the teacher steps in to model and teach conflict management skills.

Some writers emphasize "self-regulation"—children's ability to regulate their own behaviors—as the primary goal in social development (Bronson, 2000). For this writer, the term "self-regulation" has a connotation that is a bit puritan—"just say no" to emotion. The term neglects the full complexity of social learning. Clearly, the skills children need to get along include self-regulation (or self-control) *as one component*. But a *cluster* of skills is needed to manage conflict situations (Wittmer & Honig, 1994). Various names for this cluster have been discussed—"emotional intelligence," "intra- and interpersonal intelligence," and "democratic life skills." In conflict situations, the active ability to solve social problems in a peaceful manner seems a more inclusive developmental goal.

Chapter Nine explores how adults in the encouraging classroom model and teach conflict management. Conflict management basics are discussed including how understanding children's development assists in conflict management, and how a five-finger formula can be used in applying conflict management skills in everyday settings and in teaching these skills to children. The chapter concludes with the case study of a school in northern Minnesota that as a result of parental input, has made conflict management and peace education its way of life.

The response of the teacher to societal violence is to make social problem solving central in the educational program. A key element of social problem solving is conflict management, the teaching of democratic life skills when emotions are high.

CONFLICT MANAGEMENT: THE BASICS

In the encouraging classroom conflict is different from violence. Conflict occurs when persons express differing views about an action taken. Violence happens when the person with more power in the situation asserts his or her will without regard for the rights and worth of the other. Advocates for the use of classroom conflict management argue that conflicts are opportunities for learning. Conflicts become negative only when they degenerate into violence (Girard & Koch, 1996; Slaby et al., 1995).

From this viewpoint, even teachers can cause violence by imposing moralistic "solutions" in conflict situations that result in punishment to one or more of the parties. Teachers do so for a variety of reasons: emotional discomfort caused by the conflict; need to maintain control; desire to teach certain children "a lesson"; and/or frustration at distraction from "time on task" (Carlsson-Paige & Levin, 1992; Dinwiddie, 1994). These teachers fail to see the important life lessons that individual children and the full group can gain from the modeling and teaching of conflict management skills.

Teachers who regard conflict management as basic to the developmentally appropriate curriculum strive to respond to conflicts in ways that teach. Taking time to intervene is not time "off task." These teachers know that as children begin to learn democratic life skills, conflicts will take up less of their classroom time, and the classroom community will become a more effective learning environment for all children (Levin, 1994).

An ideal is for children in the encouraging classroom to be able to talk together in friendly ways that keep conflicts from escalating: "Oh, you are not yet done with the computer? I surely want you to have your full turn; so I will read this book until you are finished. Be sure to take your time." (Smile.) Or at least, "I am not used to your haircut yet." The everyday reality, though, is that conflicts get emotional, even in the most encouraging classrooms.

Social problem solving is the application of democratic life skills: using intelligence and ethics to solve problems in ways all can accept. Conflict management is social problem solving when emotions in a situation run high. There is a broad cultural reason for why conflict management skills are important: When we teach young children, older children, young adolescents, and older adolescents to solve tough social problems in a peaceful manner, we reduce violence in the society. By reducing violence, we further society's democratic ideals. Lofty? Accepted. To bring us back to the classroom, it all starts when preschoolers won't share the play dough.

Conflicts provide opportunities for teachers to help children understand important life skills.

Claire, Teagan, and Mathilde were busy with yellow and blue play dough. Thomas came over to the table and asked for some.

Claire: But you can't have any 'cause there isn't any more.

Thomas: But you got some and you have to share.

Teagan: But not now 'cause you are too late.

With this comment, Thomas grabbed some yellow play dough from Mathilde and tried to play with it. Mathilde began to wail. Teagan tried to wrestle the play dough back from Thomas, who kicked at her from his chair.

Katrina, the teacher, arrived and said, "We have a problem with this play dough, and we need to solve it with words. Teagan, please sit down. Thomas, please give me the play dough to hold or put it in front of you on the table."

Thomas put it down, but kept one hand on it.

Katrina: First, everyone take three deep breaths to cool down. Ready? One. . .two. . .three. . . That's better. Now I need to hear from each of you what the problem is. Mathilde, you first.

Mathilde: Thomas took my play dough when I didn't give him any.

Teagan: Yeah, he was too late 'cause we were using it.

Katrina:	How did that make you feel, Mathilde?
Mathilde:	Sad, 'cause he just took it.
Thomas:	I just wanted some play dough to make grass from the ocean and sun.
Katrina:	What?
Thomas:	If you mix the sun play dough and ocean play dough, you get grass play dough.
Katrina:	You're right, you do! Yellow and blue together make green. It looks like there is enough play dough for everyone to share. Does anyone have an idea how we can help Thomas make grass play dough?
Mathilde:	He could have that yellow, but no more.
Claire:	He could have some of my ocean play dough.
Katrina:	Teagan? I think Thomas could use just a little more sun play dough. Could you let him use some of yours?
Teagan:	It's not sun, teacher, it's yellow, and he could have just a little bit, 'cause I'm not making no grass.
Katrina:	Thanks, Teagan. I think we almost solved this problem, but is there something more you could say, Thomas?
Thomas:	Thanks. I won't take no more.
Katrina:	If there is a problem next time, do you all remember what to do?
Kids:	Talk about it. Get you, teacher.
Teagan:	But I'm not making grass. I'm making green play dough.

The four children mix the play dough and talk together. They sit at the table for about 20 minutes.

The teacher in this anecdote was experienced, and the children had been coached in conflict management for three months. As well, none of these children were dealing with serious violence issues. Katrina recognized that time spent in conflict management is essential to social studies and the language arts. She realized that as children learn the dynamics of conflict management, in future conflicts she will spend less time mediating their problems. For this teacher, the time spent in conflict management is an investment in the quality of life of the encouraging classroom.

This is a successful scenario of how conflict management works in many classrooms. Let us analyze what Katrina did and said in this situation and set some guidelines for teaching conflict management to children.

Guidelines for Using Conflict Management

Guideline 1: **The teacher intervenes firmly, not as a "moral authority" but as a democratic leader.** Notice that Katrina did not act as a "moral authority," making judgments about the not sharing, grabbing, and kicking that resulted in punishment. She intervened firmly, but put aside who was right and wrong. Instead, she used her leadership to solve the problem in a way beneficial for all (Dinwiddie, 1994). This approach is consistent with guidance interventions going back to Ginott (1972): The teacher addresses behavior but protects personality; assists to solve the problem, but does not punish the child for having a problem he cannot solve. Conflict management provides the teacher with a tool for guiding children in the development of democratic life skills—something that punishment cannot do.

Guideline 2: **The teacher is mediator in charge.** The process of mediation involves an outside party assisting two or more persons to resolve a conflict they cannot resolve on their own (Porro, 1996). In the anecdote Katrina involved each child, starting with the child who perhaps had lost the most, Mathilde. Teagan and Thomas did more talking, but all children have an equal opportunity for input. As a measure of the success of the mediation, the children accepted the solution.

Being "mediator in charge," the teacher manages power sharing with and among the children. It is the power sharing that enables all to feel ownership of the solution. Over time, as children show experience in using conflict management, the teacher shares more of the actual mediation with the children as well. This process, explored later in the chapter, is termed moving from high-level mediation to low-level mediation to child-managed negotiation. The teacher decides when and how to nurture this important shift (Gartrell, 2002).

Guideline 3: **The teacher cools down all parties before starting.** It is difficult for anyone to use civil words when upset. Katrina assisted the children to *de-escalate* their emotional involvement in two ways. First, she requested the four children take deep breaths. Counting to ten is another method. Second, she asked Mathilde, the child most upset, to share how she felt when her play dough was taken. When children can vent their feelings, they feel respected and are more likely to engage themselves in the mediation.

Two other comments apply. First, if children are too upset for the mediation they may need to sit down for a *cooling-down time* until mediation can be started. Different from a "time-out," a cooling-down time is not punishment, but preparation for social problem solving. (See Chapter Eleven for the differences between time out and cooling down time.) Second, after witnessing harm, the teacher must calm (*herself*)—by taking deep breaths, counting to ten, or even herself utilizing a cool-down time. The teacher provides the even keel necessary for conflict management—even in rare occasions by asking another adult to mediate.

Guideline 4: **The teacher supports the right of personal expression in all children involved.** A trade-off for not imposing "retribution" on a child who did harm is offering the suffering child the justice of *protected response.* Thomas listened when Mathilde said, "Sad, 'cause he just took it." Understanding how the other child felt helps build empathy in a child who did harm (Wittmer & Honig, 1994). This empathy building especially happens when the protected response does not stigmatize, but is part of the solution process. While preventing one child from being stigmatized for showing mistaken behavior, the teacher at the same time prevents another child from becoming a victim with no institutional recourse. The teacher ensures mutual respect through honest communication during the conflict management process.

Through conflict management, personal expression flows into effective communication. Children make substantial cognitive and linguistic gains when they put feelings into words, analyze social problems, cooperatively generate solutions, and verbalize acceptable alternatives for the future. These are skills that some adults have not mastered, and with guidance young children handle them so competently! Conflict management is not a diversion from the educational program, but central to it, especially in relation to social studies, language arts, and sometimes even science: "If you mix the sun play dough and the ocean play dough, you get grass play dough."

Guideline 5: **The teacher need not mediate perfectly for children to learn social problem-solving skills** (Dinwiddie, 1994; Wichert, 1989). In matters of high emotions with young children, the adult cannot expect to resolve problems perfectly (Gartrell, 2002). Even with imperfect mediation, done in a positive manner, children still will be learning the following problem-solving skills: the ability to evaluate consequences; the ability to generate nonviolent solutions; and the ability to predict the consequences of their behavior in advance (Dinwiddie, 1994).

Besides, although the basic process of mediation is widely agreed upon, writers differ in the number and kinds of steps they recommend teachers use (Pirtle, 1995). A teacher who follows the four steps suggested by Kreidler (1994), would not be following perfectly the six steps suggested by High/Scope (1996), or the ten steps suggested by Slaby et al. (1995). Slaby and his colleagues point out that expecting children to master each of several specific conflict management steps is unrealistic. They suggest that adults model mediation steps during conflicts, but focus instead on the intent and the general problem-solving approach.

DEVELOPMENTAL CONSIDERATIONS IN USING CONFLICT MANAGEMENT

Teachers need to understand developmental characteristics of young children that lead to conflicts—and successful resolutions. Dinwiddie (1994) points out that:

> Children have conflicts over property, territory, or privilege. The younger the child, the more likely the conflict is to concern property: toys, clothes, even people can be viewed by young children as their own personal property. (p. 15)

Property tends to be the most frequent source of conflict in the preprimary years, and the kind of dispute adults most often have to mediate. As teachers know, the concepts of sharing materials or taking turns with them are not natural ones for preprimary children. These concepts take time to learn.

When children begin to play in groups, problems of territory arise (Dinwiddie, 1994). These problems involve whether a child gets to join others in the dramatic play area, where a child can play when joining another, and so on. In some ways, territorial disputes seem easier to mediate than property disputes because "negotiable" space rather than a single object is the issue. However, a child already in an area often defines fairly shared spaced differently than the other child *and* the adult. In territorial mediation, the adult frequently has to work hard to see the issue as the child already in the area does.

Problems of privilege emerge as children's awareness of social subtleties continues to grow. Privilege conflicts such as who gets to line up first or who gets to sit next to the teacher are often seen in sophisticated preschoolers as well as in primary grade children. Dinwiddie (1994) points out that conflicts even can be over a combination of the three types of disputes. The challenge for the teacher is to understand the issue for each child and thereby mediate a successful solution for all.

Carlsson-Paige and Levin (1992) frame the developmental factor in teaching social problem solving as follows. Young children

> tend to see problems in the immediate moment and in physical terms. They also see problems from their own point of view. Only with age and experience do children slowly learn to see problems in a larger context; in more abstract terms that involve underlying motives, feelings, and intentions; and from more than their own point of view. Until they are able to do this on their own, therefore, the teacher needs to help. (1992, p. 7)

Carlsson-Paige and Levin suggest guidelines for teaching social problem solving to young learners (1992). The object of such mediation is to present problems encountered in terms that make sense to each child. The following items are an adaptation of their suggestions:

- Help children define problems in simple terms: physical objects and specific actions.
- Use the concrete situation to reinforce that their problems have two sides.
- Encourage children to see the whole problem and how their behavior contributed to it.
- Encourage children to suggest their own solutions. Adult solutions tend to be "fair," but they are cast from an adult's point of view. Often children's solutions are more creative than the adults. Although not always as fair in adult terms, they may be more satisfactory because the children arrived at them themselves. Carlsson-Paige and Levin call these *inclusive solutions.*
- If children cannot think of winning solutions, suggest alternatives and help them find, try, and evaluate a solution.

If children cannot solve the problem, the teacher helps them find,
try, and evaluate a solution.

- Over time nudge children from mediation (the teacher serves as
  mediator) to negotiation in which children resolve problems by
  themselves. The teacher provides only as much mediation as the
  children need to negotiate the rest for themselves (pp. 7–10).

One morning in a child care center, two three-year-olds decided
they both wanted to use scissors for free-form cutting in the art
center.

Only one chair was at the table, and they raced to the chair and
began pushing each other for possession of it. Both children were
getting increasingly upset as the teacher arrived.

She knelt down, put an arm around each child, and said, "You
two are upset because you both want this chair."

Sheila said, "Me had it, and her tried to take it."

Button didn't say anything, but she continued the wailing she
had just started. The teacher comforted Button and then said,
"What can we do so that you can both have a chair?" The girls
just frowned at each other so the teacher suggested, "Sheila,
there's another chair right over there. Why don't you get it? Then
you can both have one." Sheila didn't move, she just bit her lip.
Just then, Button (in a complete mood change), exclaimed, "We
could both use this one"!

The teacher was about to say this wouldn't work when to her amazement, the two girls sat side-by-side, each on half of the chair. They cut together for 15 minutes. (Educational Productions, 1997).

Peace Props

To build on the concrete world of young children, some conflict mediation models use **peace props.** An established peace prop is the use of *talk-and-listen chairs.* Other common props are the *peace table,* the *talking stick,* and *problem (or peace) puppets* (Janke & Penshorn Peterson, 1995; Kreidler, 1984).

Talk-and-listen chairs and the peace table are both formally designated places in the classroom where children and adults go to resolve disputes. Children follow established guidelines such as: *respectful words only; explain, don't attack; take turns talking;* and so on. The talk-and-listen chairs assist in the "taking turns" guideline by having as a policy that the children actually switch chairs to talk and listen.

A prop popularized by Janke and Penshorn Peterson (1995) is the talking stick. Teachers introduce the talking stick as a "sacred tool" for helping children talk and listen to one another. Often, it is passed around in class meetings, where the person holding the stick expresses thoughts and feelings, and all others listen. The talking stick is passed until the problem or issue facing the group is resolved, or the group decides they have "counseled" enough for one sitting. Another use is in an exchange between individual children locked in a dispute. The teacher calms and mediates as necessary to remind the children that the stick is a peace prop and not a weapon. With modeling and practice, even preschoolers will seek the talking stick and resolve a problem on their own.

During April, a student teacher in an early childhood classroom recorded in her journal an anecdotal observation of two children, "Charissa" and "Carlos":

Observation: Charissa and Carlos were building with blocks. Charissa reached for a block, and Carlos decided he wanted the same one. They both tugged on the block and then Carlos hit Charissa on the back. Charissa fought back tears and said, "Carlos, you're not s'posed to hit, you're s'posed to use the talking stick."

Carlos said "yeah" and got the stick. I couldn't hear what they said, but they took turns holding the stick and talking while the other one listened. After only a minute, the two were playing again, and Charissa was using the block. Later I asked her what the talking stick helped them decide. She said, "That I use the block this time. Carlos uses it next time." (Smile.)

Reflection: I really got concerned when Carlos hit Charissa, and I was just about to get involved. I was surprised when Charissa didn't hit back but told Carlos to get the talking stick, and he did! Then, they solved the problem so quickly. "DeeAnn" [the teacher] told me that she has been teaching the kids since September to solve their problems by using the talking stick. Usually she has to mediate, but this time they solved the problem on their own. It really worked!

Puppets are another conflict management prop that Kreidler discussed (1984) and that are still in use today. Whether they are called *peace puppets, power puppets,* or *problem puppets* (Janke & Penshorn Peterson, 1995; Kreidler, 1984), hand puppets have almost magical properties and can instruct in ways that adults by themselves could only hope to do. Like the talking stick, puppets can be used both to instruct and to help resolve problems. Because puppets "come alive" for young children, they can draw children into communication in ways that other props cannot. Kreidler (1984) and Janke and Penshorn Peterson (1995) have many suggestions for their use. (See Recommended Resources and anecdote, p. 40.)

THE FIVE-FINGER FORMULA FOR CONFLICT MANAGEMENT

When emotions are high and teachers want to manage the situation effectively, a specific model is useful to follow. Alluded to earlier, several conflict management models are out there (see Recommended Resources), each having its own steps for teachers to follow. A classic is Kreidler's ABCD procedure (1994): ask what's the problem; brainstorm solutions; choose the best; do it.

Many model variations exist, though, including among others a three-step model (Guth, 1995), a six-step model (Wichert, 1989), a seven-step model (Janke & Penshorn Peterson, 1995), and a five-step model that includes 16 substeps (Pirtle, 1995). This text is going to feature a five-step "formula" that is an informal composite of several. Because most people have at least five fingers to count on—and an additional cool-down step makes Kreidler's model more complete—this author is suggesting the following five steps when using conflict management with children, the **five-finger formula:**

1. **Thumb:** Cool down, if needed (all of you, the adult too).
2. **Pointer:** Discuss and agree what the problem is.
3. **Tall Guy:** Brainstorm solutions all can live with.
4. **Ringer:** Select one that seems reasonable to all.
5. **Pinkie:** Try it out, with the adult's guidance if needed.

To remember the five steps for social problem solving, some adults post them on the wall. Some actually do count them off on their fingers. Whatever method you use, remember that in many mediation situations, the adult may not formally follow each step. Whether informally combined or formally kept separate, these five steps tend to be present when an adult mediates a conflict or when children negotiate it for themselves (Gartrell, 2000). Notice how Katoshi, an exchange student completing a practicum in an American early childhood classroom, helped two children, Ennis and Callie, manage this conflict. (We will follow the anecdote with an analysis using the five steps.)

One day when I was observing, two children were fighting over time at a keyboard with earphones in the music center. Ennis was upset with Callie because he felt she was taking too long in the area. Ennis said that Callie had forgotten to set the time for ten minutes and had been there a lot longer.

Callie: I set the timer. Look at it if you don't believe me.
Ennis: You just set it a few minutes ago when I asked you how much time!
Callie: I'm staying until the time is up.

Ennis then hit Callie on the back. Callie hit at Ennis from her chair and her earphones fell around her neck. I had been observing during the entire argument and was staying close, but not too close in hopes that maybe these children would be able to work out their own problem. I went over, got them both sitting on chairs and calmed them down. I asked Ennis what happened. He told me his version of the story, what I had seen. I said, "That is a problem, but I can't let you hit other students, and I won't let them hit you. Let's hear what Callie has to say." She told me her side.

I told her she should set the timer before she starts playing the keyboard so that she doesn't forget because other children do not want to be left out. I asked, "How can we fix this so you don't fight?" The two children seemed bummed out, so I said, "How about if Callie sets the timer for five minutes to finish up and then Ennis can set the timer for the full ten minutes?" They agreed, and I said that next time they should remember to set the timer right away during their turn. A few minutes later I observed Callie give the earphones to Ennis when the timer rang.

The dispute was over privilege—who has the privilege of using the keyboard for how long. As mentioned earlier, when teachers try to mediate conflicts, they don't need to do things perfectly. Considering that Katoshi was trying conflict mediation for the first time, she deserves compliments. Let us explore how Katoshi followed the five steps of conflict management:

1. *Cool Down (All of You).* She didn't go into detail (like having each child take deep breaths), but she did calm them down enough so they could discuss the problem.

2. *Discuss and Agree What the Problem Is.* Katoshi heard both children's versions of what happened. She explained to each child why the hitting was mistaken behavior. She did this in a way that did not punish, but guided the children about what they needed to do differently. The children didn't dispute what she said. They pretty much agreed what the problem was; the agreement was apparent later when they went along with the solution.

3. *Brainstorm Solutions All Can Live With.* She invited the children to give ideas for "how to fix this so you don't fight." The children were not ready to suggest solutions, so she proposed one, which they accepted. (This is called "high-level" mediation, which is discussed in the next section.)

4. *Select a Solution.* A key difference between conflict mediation and traditional discipline is that the teacher does not force "a solution." Katoshi proposed a solution that the children accepted. If the children don't agree to a solution, the teacher goes back to step 3. Step 4 is a common time for a guidance talk. Here, rather than step 2, Katoshi might have reminded them about hitting and kicking being unsafe and to use words instead. She did get them set up with an imaginative solution to try, however, and this is key in step 4.

5. *Try It Out, With the Adult's Guidance if Needed.* Katoshi observed the children put the solution into practice. Reinforcement for how the children are solving the problem peaceably is also a common follow-up. That the two children did what was agreed to indicates the success of the mediation. Step 5 is the other time for a guidance talk, sometimes with one or both children separately. (Gartrell, 2000. With permission of Redleaf Press.)

Often, when teachers use conflict management successfully, children get back together after the conflict as though nothing has happened. Note that children getting back together is not due to a teacher saying, "Now you go apologize." Forced apologies are false apologies for adults as well as children. As a part of step 5, teachers might ask, "Now how can you help him feel better?" Or, "Can you figure out how to play together again?"

Children may decline, though more often they figure out a way to make up—most kids are better at this than grown-ups. If they do decline to reconcile, accept this, but keep watching. They may very well do something together in a low-key way before the day is through (Gartrell, 2002). The chances of authentic reconciliation are not 100 percent after conflict management, of course. "If anything goes exactly the way you expect in early childhood education, something's wrong." But the chances are good—and certainly better than if you punish a child for having a conflict and then tell him to go say he is sorry. By teaching children how to use democratic life skills in the tough times, conflict management epitomizes the encouraging classroom.

TEACHING CONFLICT MANAGEMENT SKILLS

The goal in social problem solving is to move children from dependency on the teacher to reliance on themselves. Although Wichert's *Keeping the Peace* (1989) is not the most recent work on the issue, the text provides a clear introduction to three levels of teacher response designed to achieve this objective. In an adaptation of Wichert's terminology, the teacher guides children to progress from **high-level mediation to low-level mediation to child negotiation.**

High-level mediation involves direct, guiding intervention by the adult including, if necessary, articulation of the problem, possible solutions, and trying a solution—agreed to by the children. At the high mediation level, the adult does not impose interpretations and actions. Instead, the adult offers suggestions and works for agreement by the children. The adult provides active leadership in the resolution process, a role similar to that of a coach.

In *low-level mediation,* the adult suggests that children negotiate the conflict, but stands by to offer assistance as needed. Low-level mediation has been achieved when the children in dispute are able to define the problem, generate a solution, and bring about a resolution with minimum adult assistance. The adult is on hand to provide verbal and nonverbal encouragement, but moves from being a coach to a facilitator.

Child negotiation occurs when children take charge of resolving a conflict by themselves. An illustration of negotiation was the anecdote about Charissa and Carlos. An irony of social problem solving is that many young

A teacher can act as a coach to assist children to find solutions.

Guided in the conflict management process, many young children can negotiate conflicts.

children, guided in the conflict management process, can negotiate conflicts successfully, while many older students, who have not been so guided, cannot.

Before turning to case studies of the three levels of conflict resolution, it is useful to note that the levels of mediation are different from, and somewhat independent of, the three levels of mistaken behavior. Sometimes a child experiencing Level One mistaken behavior might be so upset that the teacher needs to use high-level mediation. On the other hand, in an encouraging classroom where a child who often shows Level Three mistaken behavior feels accepted, low-level mediation or even child negotiation can sometimes work—not always, but sometimes.

Case studies follow, taken from the journal entries of student teachers in two kindergarten classrooms and one prekindergarten classroom. (Anecdotes from "beginners" are being used to illustrate that one need not be experienced and an expert to make conflict management work.) Analysis of each anecdote follows, including these parts:

Defining the Problem

Reaching the Solution

Bringing Successful Closure

Notice that the three student teachers and the children did not use a specific conflict resolution model, but instead flowed through the five-step process quite informally. A point made earlier bears repeating: Conflict management skills need not be used perfectly to assist children with conflict resolution.

High-Level Teacher Mediation

During a project involving seeds, the teacher instructed kindergarten children to wrap a bean inside a saturated paper towel and place it into a plastic baggie with their name on it. After doing this, the children were supposed to take their baggies and tape them on the window. About half the class had their baggies taped on the window when I noticed two boys arguing about putting their baggies in the same spot. I listened for about a minute and decided to intervene because I felt that the arguing was becoming more heated (they were pushing each other), and they would not be able to resolve this issue without outside guidance.

Heather: I think we have a problem. You both want your baggies taped up in the same spot.

Justin: Yeah! (nodding).

Brian: I was here first, and Justin just came up and stuck his right there too.

Heather: Okay, we need to think up some ideas to try and solve this problem. Can you boys help me think of something that we can do?

Justin: We could put the bags on top of each other.

Heather: We could, but then I don't think we would be able to see whose baggie is whose, and you wouldn't be able to see your bean grow. Let's try it and see.

Brian: Now I can't see my name.

Heather: We should see if we can try something different. Can you think of something else?

> Brian: He could put his on the wall next to mine.
> Heather: That might work, but remember about what we learned this morning about what plants need in order to grow. Do you think that Justin's bean would get any sunlight if it was taped up on the wall?
> Brian: No.
> Justin: I know! He can tape his up here, right here (points to a spot above his own).
> Heather: What do you think, Brian?
> Brian: Okay.
> Heather: It's settled. We will tape Brian's baggie right above Justin's. I'm so glad that you boys can use your words to solve problems. Thank you.

> The boys didn't seem to be upset with each other after they talked out their conflict. Later that morning I saw them playing with the plastic zoo animals together.

Defining the Problem   Heather recognized that the conflict was over territory. She approached the situation calmly and neutrally. She stated that "we" have a problem and identified it for the two children in a way that they could accept. The way that she described the situation gave the children confidence to proceed to the step of sharing information.

Some procedural models have the mediator ask permission of the children to conduct the mediation. In the Peacemaker program (Janke & Penshorn Peterson, 1995), the children agree to participate in mediation as a part of the program. In the *I to I* program (Guth, 1995), children are given the choice of *using their power* to solve the problem by mediation or *giving up their power* to adult authorities who would then solve the problem for them. As in the case of the anecdote, children in classrooms where the choice of mediation is not a formal issue are usually relieved to participate in the process. If one or all involved children are agitated, the teacher may request a *cooling-down time*.

The mediation procedure of High/Scope (1996) stresses the acknowledgement of feelings at the beginning of negotiation as a way to calm down children. If the mediator believes children need to cool down before "talking it out," options are Wichert's suggestion, "Take a deep breath and be quiet for a minute," or reflective statements suggested by the High/Scope procedure, such as:

"You don't like it that. . . ."

"You feel . . . because. . . ."

"You feel . . . because . . . and you feel . . . because. . . ."

The acknowledgement of feelings releases emotions so that the children become calm enough to discuss the problem.

Reaching a Solution   In the anecdote, the clear statement of the problem by Heather enabled the children to share the details of what happened. A lengthy rehashing of the problem did not seem necessary. She moved them directly to thinking about solutions by asking, "Can you boys help me think of something that we can do?" She then helped them test two solutions they came up with without imposing her own, the mark of effective mediation.

In other situations, the teacher gains information and achieves an objective restatement of the conflict for two reasons. Sometimes the adult will not know what the issue is, and of course she needs that information to facilitate a solution. As well, when children are given an opportunity to explain what happened from their own perspectives, they feel that their side has been heard, and they are more willing to participate in the process.

A challenge for many teachers in high-level mediation is to *avoid imposing a solution*. By the time the mediation has progressed to the point when the problem is identified and the participants accept the description, the teacher has an idea of how to solve the problem. Often by this point the participants also have reached a degree of reconciliation, and the problem has become less of "an issue." An imposed solution by the teacher allows the children to get on with things they would rather be doing, often together. As mediation unquestionably takes time, imposing a solution also saves time for the teacher.

The reason for encouraging children to come up with their own solutions is that the resolution process becomes empowering for them. The children more fully realize that they can solve their own problems. If the teacher does decide to help with solutions, she needs to be conscious about whether the solution is only suggested or imposed. This difference is illustrated by asking, "Now, how do you think you can help him feel better?", instead of demanding, "Now, shake hands and say you're sorry." Sometimes no action more than a matter-of-fact reconciliation is needed to solve the problem.

Bringing Successful Closure   Heather confirmed the solution with both children and then affirmed their use of management skills by saying, "I'm so glad that you boys can use your words to solve problems. Thank you." She also was undoubtedly prepared to give follow-up if needed, but it was not, confirmed by her observation that they played together later in the morning. The success of this experience is likely to reinforce the children's continuing willingness and ability to use problem-solving skills.

Low-Level Teacher Mediation

Dakota and Chante were in the classroom store. Dakota was using the cash register, and Chante was "talking to a customer" on the telephone. Dakota picked up another telephone and started talking to her. Chante turned to him and yelled, "Shut up!"

Dakota looked very sad. I knelt down and asked if he could tell Chante how that made him feel. He turned to her and said, "I felt really, really sad and bad when you yelled at me."

Chante responded, "I'm sorry, Dakota. I didn't mean that, I guess. I was talking to a 'custmer.'"

I asked, "Chante, I think Dakota wants to talk on the telephone with you."

Chante said, "Yeah, but he's not a 'custmer.'"

I suggested, "I wonder if Dakota could take the telephone to the house and be a customer?"

"I could call you from the house," Dakota said.

"Yeah, you need lots of stuff," said Chante (getting into it). "Go over and tell me what you need."

Dakota, smiling, "phoned" from the house. Chante had the "stuff" ready for him when he came to pick it up. He gave her some make-believe money, and she even gave him change!

Defining the Problem   Camille (the student teacher) approached the situation calmly and had a calming effect on Dakota by kneeling down and speaking directly to him. She acknowledged his feelings, then encouraged him to tell Chante how what she said made him feel.

The student teacher did not begin a formal conflict resolution procedure that involved acknowledging Chante's feelings and asking each child to describe what happened. Some educational programs prefer the teacher to follow the mediation procedure more formally so that the steps in the mediation not be lost. Instead, Camille made the decision that encouraging Dakota to express himself was important and that the chances were good that a satisfactory resolution would occur if he did.

Reaching a Solution   Again, the student teacher did not follow the formal steps of gathering information, restating the problem, and asking for possible solutions. Both children understood the situation. When Dakota let Chante know how he felt, Chante offered a first solution: apologize. When Camille helped Dakota understand how Chante was using the telephone, Dakota enabled a second solution: talk on the telephone in a way that fit Chante's purpose. Camille observed the children as they negotiated and made two comments, but she let them reach the solutions by themselves.

Bringing Successful Closure   Typical of a successful low-level mediation, the children basically solved the problem themselves and went back to playing as if nothing had happened. The reflection portion of Camille's journal indicated how pleased she was that they solved the problem. Camille states, "These kinds of instances just prove to me that these children will solve their own problems. Sometimes all they need is a little guidance."

Child Negotiation

Nakisha and Suel Lin were caring for a variety of dolls in the kindergarten housekeeping area. They both reached for the last doll that had to be fed, bathed, and put to bed. They started yelling that they each had it first, and Suel Lin took Nakisha's arm and started squeezing it.

"Stop, that hurts," exclaimed Nakisha. "Use your words"!

"I can't," yelled Suel Lin.

"Then get Power Sock," Nakisha demanded. Both girls, still holding part of the doll, walked over and got Power Sock. "I will wear him, Suel Lin, and you tell Sock."

Suel Lin said to Sock, "Baby needs a bath, but we both want to do it."

"Both do it," said Sock.

The two girls put back Power Sock and returned to the housekeeping area, both holding the doll. One girl washed the top half, the other the bottom half. Then Suel Lin held the doll and fed it while Nakisha read a story to the other dolls already in bed. Suel Lin said, "Here's baby, do you want to read another story?"

"Yeah," said Nakisha, who read another story while Suel Lin rubbed the babies' backs as they lay in their beds.

Defining the Problem   Nakisha acknowledged her feelings calmly enough that Suel Lin could agree to negotiate with her by using the Power Sock. Suel Lin forgot a guideline by squeezing Nakisha's arm. Conventional discipline would call for a punishment such as a scolding or even sitting on a time-out chair. The result would have been Suel Lin feeling upset and Nakisha feeling victimized. Because the student teacher refrained from intervening, she opened the door for negotiation and the opportunity for the children to find a mutually satisfactory solution.

Reaching a Solution   Nakisha and Suel Lin used a prop introduced by the teachers to reach a solution. Nakisha was more experienced with Power Sock than Suel Lin and took the initiative to request Sock to help in the negotiation. The solution did not involve a high level of verbal articulation and probably evolved as the children got back into their play. Nonetheless, their solution was creative and peaceable and would have made many teachers smile. The self-esteem of each child seems to have been sustained.

Bringing Successful Closure   The two children continued to play together and did so with a high level of cooperation. In contrast to conventional discipline successful negotiation reduces the buildup of residual resentment and continued conflicts in the future. The ability of children to negotiate conflicts indicates the important goals of an encouraging classroom are being attained.

First Year

St. Philip's is a prekindergarten through eighth grade private school of 270 students in downtown Bemidji, a town of 15,000, including tourists, university students, and truck drivers passing through. One spring day, Sue Liedl's second-grade son told her of a playground game called, "smear the queer." It was a kind of dodgeball game in which if you hit others with the ball, you got to call them names. The game bothered her son, and it bothered Sue. A social worker having several years of experience with youth-at-risk, Sue looked at the problem as a chance to prevent some of the life situations that she saw oppressing the kind of youth she worked with.

Shortly thereafter Sue left her job and began to volunteer hours at the school, on the playground and in classrooms. In the school office she came across a brochure on conflict management, read it, and located more materials. During May with the support of the principal, Sue met with the 23 staff members to discuss whether they would be interested in a **peer mediation** program at St. Philip's the following year. The staff expressed interest in Sue's beginning the program. *Peer mediation* is a system of conflict management in which trained upper elementary students assist other students who may be having conflicts, such as on the playground. Sue reports that peer mediation was the most popular form of conflict management used at the time of this story.

Second Year

In September with the principal's support, Sue called a meeting of the 190 families in the school; 70 parents attended. She introduced them to peer mediation and asked for and received their support for a program

at St. Philip's. She recruited a core committee of three parents, all interested in working with the teachers and children. Sue attended peer mediation training and then trained the parent committee. The committee
wrote grant proposals, collected resources, contacted other Minnesota
schools, and mapped out a plan for sharing the training with staff and
students.

During the winter the committee prepared the teaching staff for the program, and on Martin Luther King Day, January 19th, the four parents introduced the idea to the third- through eighth-grade classes by presenting
a play. (Drama has been a continuing part of the St. Philip's program.) This
play, like most, actively involved the students and illustrated the importance of respectful communication skills.

The upper elementary children (by themselves) selected two peer mediators per classroom. The peer mediators had two days of training away
from the school. To supplement the work of the peer mediators, the parent
committee returned to each classroom once a week for four weeks to present the program. The peer mediators were active at the school throughout
the spring and conducted 35 mediations; about half the cases seemed to be
students "testing the system."

Third Year

Over the summer, Sue held the first of what have become annual leadership camps, attended by the peer mediators and teachers, and conducted
by St. Philip's parents. In September, the parent committee reviewed the
peer mediation program and came to a surprising conclusion: They decided that the focus of peer mediation was too specialized to meet their
goals for the school. The committee's goal was to make every student a
"peaceful problem solver." The peer mediator program continued into the
school year, but the parent committee, with some new members, discussed
their conclusion with the school staff. The staff agreed, and over the third
year the conflict management program began to take a new direction.

The parent committee held a series of meetings during the year with
families to discuss the new emphasis. At the same time, two of the parent
committee went into each of the classes weekly for eight weeks, involving
all the students actively in conflict management instruction. Puppets frequently were used to teach such skills as communicating feelings productively, using the *I to I* process, achieving win-win solutions, and keeping
friends despite disagreements.

During the third year, each of the upper elementary classes took a specialized topic and method of presentation. In teams of four or five, they re-
hearsed their puppet play, real-life skit, or game sequence. The older
students presented their plays for younger students, frequently involving
them in the productions, and the whole school got involved. On a night in
mid-winter, the school put on their program for the families, and over 90
percent of the parents attended. Each team put on their performance for

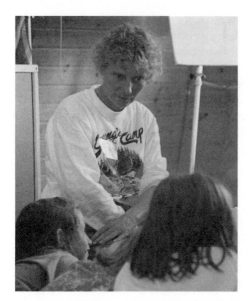 

Sue and fellow parents introduced summer leadership camps to orient new third graders to conflict management projects.

their own parents; then the family—children and family together—would visit other classrooms and participate in other productions.

Sue reported that the family night more than any other activity sparked parent interest in the conflict management philosophy. She commented, "Every child in the school participated. If their children are involved, parents will attend; that's what gets parents involved."

Fourth Year

Over the summer, the new fourth-grade class participated in the summer "leadership training camp." Their teacher attended the training with the class, which made for strong attachments right from the beginning of the school year. In September the fourth-grade teacher began by reviewing with the children the skills they learned at the leadership camp. The class then received additional training over ten weeks and attended a two-day retreat. The fourth graders learned to do puppet plays illustrating the basics of conflict resolution. They performed the plays for the younger children, actively involving the younger children in discussion about the plays. This emphasis on active participation, with children teaching other children, has been a hallmark of the program. By this time, the *I to I* model, developed by Guth (1995) had replaced the peer mediation model, and the whole school was participating.

During the fourth year, an initiative was also started with the seventh graders. Another St. Philip's parent began a media literacy program, educating these older students about the effects of violence and commercialism in the public media. Guests from outside the school helped students at various levels connect peacemaking efforts with music and the martial arts (Liedl, 1996). Sue and the planning committee actively wrote grant proposals to support bringing in guests for brief residency periods. Another grant enabled St. Philip's School to make a video documenting elements of the program, shown as a demonstration piece in other schools in the region.

Fifth Year

Again in 1996, the fourth-grade class attended leadership camp. A special project was prepared for the year. The fourth grade teamed in groups of four or five with parent volunteers. The teams specialized in a topic and prepared participation-productions relating their topic to conflict resolution. After much practice, the teams served as trainers for other classes at St. Philip's and public schools in the area.

A second project, also begun over the summer in a two-day "theater camp," continued in the fall. Sue, with a group of fourth through eighth graders, created a six-scene play illustrating differences between families with high and low social problem-solving skills. Aided by a professional director from the town, the players put the play on several times, polishing their production between performances.

One special performance included a role created for Arun Gandhi of the M. K. Gandhi Institute for Nonviolence in Tennessee. Mr. Gandhi was in the area participating in a three-day community-wide residency that included events at the local university, school district, and offices of law enforcement and human services personnel, as well as St. Philip's School. The cooperative that organized and gained funding for this event, including both public and private agencies, was begun by Sue Liedl and other parents at St. Philip's.

One parent began and ran this innovative "peaceful problem-solving" project. Working with other parents, and with the active support and encouragement of school staff and administrators, this one parent was able to make a difference in not just a school, but a community. When schools choose to involve parents and use their particular skills, there are few limits as to what can happen.

SUMMARY

1. What conflict management basics do teachers need?

Five guidelines for using conflict management are: (1) The teacher intervenes firmly, not as a moral authority, but as democratic leader. (2) The teacher is mediator in charge. (3) The teacher cools down all parties before starting. (4) The teacher supports the right of personal expression and the skill of effective communication. (5) The teacher need not mediate perfectly for children to learn social problem-solving skills.

2. How does understanding young children's development assist in conflict management?

The three most common sources of conflict in young children are issues dealing with property, territory, and privilege. The younger the child, the more likely the dispute is to be over property. Young children tend to see problems in immediate and physical terms, and from their own point of view. Children learn to see problems in a broader, more socially responsive context only over time, with development and experience. Teaching children conflict management skills at a level they can understand, such as by the use of peace props, helps them to progress with an important lifelong skill.

3. What is the five-finger formula for conflict management?

A model is a practical, consistent method of practice. By providing specific steps in high-emotion situations, models of conflict management can be helpful for the teacher. In early childhood education many conflict management models are available, using various numbers of steps ranging from 3 to more than 20. The five-finger formula includes the essential steps addressed by many models. The ready availability of this particular set of "props" can help teachers through the sets when emotions are running high.

4. How does the adult teach conflict management skills to children?

Through modeling and encouragement, the teacher moves children from high-level mediation, with children dependent on the teacher, to low-level mediation, with the teacher providing support, to child negotiation in which children take charge of solving problems for themselves. A "developmental timetable" does not exist for learning social problem-solving skills. With guidance four-year-olds negotiate many conflicts themselves; without guidance many eight-year-olds do not.

5. How have parents helped to shape the peaceful problem-solving program at a model school?

An interview/case study discloses how a parent, Sue Liedl, brought the spirit of peace education and practicality of conflict management to a small private school in northern Minnesota. A parent at St. Philip's School, Sue Liedl became uncomfortable with a playground game her son told her about. Rather than complain, she began a five-year program that got children, parents, and teaching staff involved. The program began and has developed as a result of the receptivity of the staff of St. Philip's School to working closely with parents. St. Philip's has become a center for conflict management and peace education in northern Minnesota.

KEY CONCEPTS

Child negotiation
Five-finger formula
High-level mediation
Low-level mediation
Peace props
Peer mediation
Social problem solving

FOLLOW-UP ACTIVITIES

Note: An element of being a professional teacher is to respect the children, parents, and educators you are working with by maintaining confidentiality—keeping identities private. In completing follow-up activities, please respect the privacy of all concerned.

Discussion Activity

The discussion activity encourages students to interrelate their own thoughts and experiences with specific ideas from the chapter.

Recall a conflict situation in a classroom resolved by the use of conflict management. Referring to the chapter, was the process used high-level teacher mediation, low-level teacher mediation, or child negotiation? Analyze the possible effects for each individual involved (including the teacher if present) in relation to self-esteem and life skills.

Application Activities

Application activities allow students to interrelate material from the text with real-life situations. The observations imply access to practicum experiences; the interviews, access to teachers or parents. Students may compare or contrast observations and interviews with referenced ideas from the chapter.

1. **Conflict management basics.**
   a. Observe and record an instance of conflict management that you believe to be handled effectively by the teacher. Referring to the text, which of the guidelines for conflict management did you see the teacher using during the mediation? Which did you not see?
   b. Interview a teacher who uses conflict management regularly in the classroom. Ask the teacher to discuss each of the

guidelines. What are her thoughts about the importance of each in the mediation process? Compare the teacher's comments with what the text says about the guidelines.

2. **Young children's development and conflict management.**
   a. Observe a typical conflict in a classroom and record it. Using the text as a reference, decide whether the primary cause of the dispute was property, territory, privilege, or some other cause. What did you learn about young children from your observation and analysis?
   b. Interview a teacher about the three types of disputes in the text. Ask the teacher to select one of the types. In conducting conflict management in relation to the type of dispute what is the teacher's basic approach? What does she try to teach through the mediation?
   c. Interview a teacher who uses a peace prop to aid in conflict management. Find out as much as you can about how the teacher uses the prop. Using the text for comparison, what did you learn about the use of peace props in conflict management with young children?

3. **The five-finger formula.**
   a. Conduct the mediation of a conflict using the five-finger formula. Record what you and the children said and did. Referring to the text, which of the steps did you find easier to follow? Which of the steps were more difficult to follow? What did you learn from this experience that may help you when you mediate a conflict in the future?
   b. Interview the teacher about the steps she follows in conducting conflict management. Record the main points from the interview. Which of the five steps did the teacher mention? Compare your findings from the interview with what the book says about conflict management.

4. **Teaching problem-solving skills to children.**
   a. Observe an instance of high-level mediation, low-level mediation, or child negotiation. Which do you believe it is? Why? How effective was the process of social problem solving that you observed? How successful was the solution reached?
   b. Interview a teacher about her views on the relative importance of teacher-led mediation versus teaching children to negotiate. What surprised you about the teacher's comments? Which of her comments were what you expected? How do the teacher's comments compare or contrast with the text?

5. **Parents shape a peaceful problem-solving program.**
   a. Observe an instance of any activity or program in a classroom (simple or comprehensive) put on by one or more parents. What did you learn about parent-led programs from what

you observed? How did what you observe compare or contrast with events in the chapter?

    b. Interview a teacher or a parent about a specific parent program in a classroom. What does the person think is important for successful parent programs? How did the ideas shared compare or contrast with events in the chapter?

What You Can Do

Correlating Levels of Mistaken Behavior with Levels of Conflict Management   Something important can be learned from determining what levels of mistaken behavior typically require which levels of conflict management. When conflicts occur, one might expect that children who frequently show experimentation mistaken behavior would be able to use child negotiation; children who frequently show socially influenced mistaken behavior would require low-level mediation; and children who frequently show strong needs mistaken behavior would require high-level mediation. But what if children who show different levels of mistaken behavior experience a conflict? What if a child usually at Level One in conflict becomes very upset? This project will ask you to use your observation and analysis skills to begin to answer these questions, and perhaps others of your own. (Don't forget to use the text as a resource in your analysis.)

    a. Over a few days or visits to a classroom, watch for and observe one or two examples of each level of conflict management. Record as specifically as you can the words and actions of each child in each situation—and the words and actions of adults if involved.

    b. Analyze the levels of mistaken behavior for each child in each conflict. (Remember that Level One is experimentation—immediate experiences that get out of hand. Level Two is socially influenced—one or both children are influenced to show the behavior by others—real or media figures, present or not present. Level Three is strong needs—one or both children are acting out as a result of life circumstances that are causing them big problems.)

    c. Match the level(s) of mistaken behavior shown by each child with the level of conflict management you determined from each observation.

    d. Note any patterns in the matches you made.

    e. Given that your observation sample is small, what can you conclude about the relationship of levels of mistaken behavior with the levels of conflict management? (Note from Dan: I'd be interested in hearing from you on this project. We are only beginning to collect information in this area.)

RECOMMENDED READINGS

Carlsson-Paige, N., & Levin, D. E. (2000). *Before push comes to shove: Building conflict resolution skills with children.* St. Paul MN, Redleaf Press.

Dinwiddie, S. A. (1994). The saga of Sally, Sammy, and the red pen: Facilitating children's social problem solving. *Young Children, 49*(5), 13–19.

Gartrell, D. J. (2002). Replacing time-out, Part 2: Using guidance to maintain the encouraging classroom. *Young Children, 56*(3) QA9-12.

Guth, J. T. (1995). *Teacher P.A.L.S. A classroom guide to the peaceful alternatives and life skills program.* Brainerd, MN: Mid-Minnesota Women's Center, Inc.

Head Start Bureau. (1997). *Head Start Bulletin: Conflict Management Issue,* Spring 1997 (61). Washington, DC: U.S. Department of Health & Human Services.

Janke, R. A., & Penshorn Peterson, J. (1995). *Peacemaker's A, B, Cs for young children.* Marine on St. Croix, MN: Growing Communities for Peace.

Kreidler, W. J. (1994). *Teaching conflict resolution through children's literature.* New York: Scholastics Professional Books.

Pirtle, S. (1997). *Linking up: Building the peaceable classroom with music and movement.* Boston: Educators for Social Responsibility.

Slaby, R. G., Roedell, W. C., Arezzo, D., & Hendrix, K. (1995). *Early violence prevention.* Washington, DC: National Association for the Education of Young Children.

Wichert, S. (1989). *Keeping the peace.* Philadelphia: New Society Publishers.

REFERENCES

Bronson, M. B. (2000). Research in review: Recognizing and supporting the development of self-regulation in young children. *Young Children, 55*(2), 32–37.

Carlsson-Paige, N., & Levin D. E. (1992). Making peace in violent times: A constructivist approach to conflict resolution. *Young Children, 48*(1), 4–13.

Carlsson-Paige, N., & Levin, D. E. (2000). Before push comes to shove: Building conflict resolution skills with children: St. Paul, MN: Redleaf Press.

Department of Health and Human Services. (2001). Report of the Surgeon General's Conference on Children's Mental Health: A National Action Agenda. http://www.surgeongeneral.gov/cmh/childreport.htm

Dinwiddie, S. A. (1994). The saga of Sally, Sammy, and the red pen: Facilitating children's social problem solving. *Young Children, 49*(5), 13–19.

Educational Productions. (1997). *Doing the groundwork: From stopping misbehavior to teaching skills* [video]. Beaverton, OR: Educational Productions.

Gartrell, D. J. (2000). *What the kids said today: Using classroom conversations to become a better teacher.* St. Paul, MN: Redleaf Press.

Gartrell, D. J. (2002). Replacing time-out, Part 2: Using guidance to maintain an encouraging classroom. *Young Children, 56*(3), 36–43.

Ginott, H. (1972). *Teacher and child.* New York: Avon Books.

Girard, K., & Koch, S. J. (1996). *Conflict resolution in the schools.* San Francisco: Jossey-Bass Publishers.

Guth, J. T. (1995). *Teacher P. A. L. S. A classroom guide to the peaceful alternatives and life skills program.* Brainerd, MN: Mid-Minnesota Women's Center, Inc.

High/Scope (1996). *Problem-solving approach to conflict: Two-day workshop participant guide.* Ypsilanti, MI: High/Scope Press.

Janke, R. A., & Penshorn Peterson, J. (1995). *Peacemaker's A, B, Cs for young children: A guide for teaching conflict resolution with a peace table.* Marine on St. Croix, MN: Growing Communities for Peace.

Kreidler, W. (1984). *Creative conflict resolution: More than 200 activities for keeping peace in the classroom.* Glenview, IL: Scott, Foresman.

Kreidler, W. J. (1994). *Teaching conflict resolution through children's literature.* New York: Scholastics Professional Books.

Levin, D. L. (1994). *Teaching young children in violent times: Building a peaceable classroom.* Cambridge, MA: Educators for Social Responsibility.

Liedl, S. (1996). *We dream; mediation news.* [Spring 1996 Newsletter]. Bemidji, MN: St. Philip's School.

Pirtle, S. (1995). *Conflict management workshop guide.* Shelburne Falls, MA: The Discovery Center.

Pirtle, S. (1997). *Linking up: Building the peaceable classroom with music and movement.* Boston: Educators for Social Responsibility.

Porro, B. (1996). *Talk it out: Conflict resolution in the elementary classroom.* Association for Supervision and Curriculum Development.

Slaby, R. G., Roedell, W. C., Arezzo, D., & Hendriz, K. (1995). *Early violence prevention.* Washington, DC: National Association for the Education of Young Children.

Wichert, S. (1989). *Keeping the peace.* Philadelphia: New Society Publishers.

Wittmer, D. S., & Honig, A. S. (1994). Encouraging positive social development in young children. *Young Children, 49*(5), 4–12.

For additional information on using the guidance approach in the classroom, visit our Web site at http://www.earlychilded.delmar.com

PROBLEM-SOLVING MISTAKEN BEHAVIOR

GUIDING QUESTIONS

- What goes into the decision to intervene?
- What are five quick intervention strategies?
- How does the teacher respond to mistaken behaviors reported by children?
- What are five strategies when interventions require follow-up?
- Why take the time to problem-solve mistaken behavior?
- How does the teacher build cooperation with parents?

When mistaken behavior occurs, mediation is the guidance strategy of choice. Sometimes, however, the teacher may not be sure that mediation is feasible in a particular situation. Chapter Ten considers the full range of decisions teachers make when they encounter all but the most serious mistaken behavior. Dealing with serious, strong needs mistaken behavior is the focus of Chapter Eleven.

A beginning note needs to be made about a matter of vocabulary. In Chapter Nine, the word *conflict* was often used. Conflict is a disagreement over an action, verbal or physical, one or more parties has taken (Girard & Koch, 1996). In the case of children, the action usually involves property, location, or privilege (Dinwiddie, 1994). We also learned in Chapter Nine that conflicts need not be negative. If through mediation or negotiation children come to a solution peacefully, the conflict actually has a positive result.

In guidance terms *mistaken behavior is a conflict* where the action usually is taken by a child or children, and the person disagreeing with the action usually is the teacher. The teacher may react with punishment, in which case the mistaken behavior has a negative outcome, or with guidance, in which case the mistaken behavior more likely has a positive outcome.

Another possibility also exists, of course, that the teacher may initiate a conflict, and the child may object to the *teacher's* mistaken behavior. This remote possibility with readers of this book is also addressed in Chapter Ten.

THE DECISION TO INTERVENE

Beginning teachers especially feel concern about the decision to intervene because of fear of alienating the children in their charge. In response to a basic question about the role of the early childhood teacher, he *is* a friend to children—but as an adult and a child must be friends—with the adult as leader and guide.

In intervention situations, the adult retains the element of friendliness, even if circumstances call for responses that are firm and that children may not like. Feelings change, and there will be time after the intervention for the adult and child to "make things right." Writers about child behavior from Glasser (1969) to Reynolds (1996) share the view that children need to know the limits of acceptable behavior.

The teacher acts with firmness if safety or well-being are endangered. Guidance rests upon the authority of the teacher to protect the learning environment for all. Children feel secure when clear limits are consistently reinforced. Note, however, that punitive discipline practiced with consistency is still punitive discipline. Teachers using guidance need to appreciate the difference between firmness and harshness (Clewett, 1988; Gartrell, 1997; Greenberg, 1988).

As well, firmness as an *overriding* personal characteristic of a teacher limits other important personality dimensions, such as flexibility. The professional

By being proactive and non-punitive, the teacher makes life easier for the child.

teacher is sometimes permissive and sometimes firm, depending on the judgments he makes about each situation. As long as children know when the teacher will smile and when he will be firm, *consistency* has been achieved.

Kounin's concept of *with-it-ness* (synonymous with "eyes in the back of the head") is an important teaching skill (1977). Yet, in a guidance approach, teachers recognize that the judgments they make are more appropriately thought of as *hypotheses.* Teachers must react quickly and firmly to situations, but the professional teacher does not hold judgments as infallible. Instead, he continues to learn even during the situation.

In an early childhood classroom, a four-year-old named Sharisse was playing with Kiko, also four, at the water table. After a few minutes, Sharisse stormed over to the teacher and said, "Kiko spilt water on me." She had a spot of water on her overalls. Upset, the teacher walked over to the water table. Kiko turned around. His shirt and pants were soaked and he was crying silently. The teacher got down to Kiko's level and asked what happened. After listening to him and talking with Sharisse, she figured out that Kiko had dropped a bottle and it splashed up on Sharisse. Sharisse then dumped a bowl of water on his front.

> The teacher helped Kiko get a change of clothes. She then talked with Sharisse and Kiko together. Kiko had been having a rough week with frequent displays of mistaken behavior and the teacher was pleased when Sharisse told him she was sorry. The teacher felt fortunate that she had gotten additional facts.

In this situation the teacher was able to collect information that helped her modify her original hypothesis. Anytime a teacher can act less like a police officer on the street and more like a mediator, he is in a better position to make informed decisions.

Another important part of with-it-ness decision making is to determine the number of children involved in a situation. With only a few children, child guidance responses are called for; with several, group management responses are needed. Child guidance responses involve intervention in the least obtrusive way possible to bring the child's behavior within guidelines while protecting self-esteem. Frequently, the teacher uses mediation to solve the immediate problem and *guidance talks* to guide toward alternative behaviors in the future.

Group management responses address the entire group and avoid calling attention to individuals. A key to group management, of course, is prevention of *institution-caused* mistaken behaviors by using the ideas discussed in previous chapters. The class meetings and intervention techniques discussed later in Chapter Ten augment the many prevention aspects of positive group management previously discussed. When a teacher is able to keep the class busily on-task, he is better able to give extra guidance to those few children who seem to require so much of a teacher's time—the children facing Level Three difficulties. With-it-ness is an important skill that, even for "experienced" teachers, takes ongoing effort. Daily, professional teachers make decisions about the ever-changing situations that they face. In addition to judgments about the level of mistaken behavior and whether child guidance or group management responses are necessary, the teacher makes two other important determinations now discussed:

1. Whether to intervene at all;
2. The degree of firmness to use in the intervention.

Whether to Intervene

A first decision is whether to intervene. In cases of serious mistaken behavior, the teacher has no choice; he must enter the situation. In other cases, the decision is not so clear. Three situations that require thought about whether to intervene are **marginal mistaken behaviors,** *"bossy" behaviors,* and *arguments.*

Marginal Mistaken Behaviors   Teachers have different comfort levels with minor mistaken behaviors. One teacher intervenes; another does not. Because no one way is the only way to use guidance, this human difference is to be expected.

An important question to ask is if the behavior is bothersome only to the teacher and not particularly to the group. When this is the case, care should be taken in the intervention decision. Unless the intervention is matter-of-fact and nonthreatening, the intervention may constitute more of a disruption than the mistaken behavior itself. In such a case, the degree of firmness is mismatched with the situation.

> During rest time in a child care center, a teacher witnessed the following event. Four-year-old Missy, who "never misbehaved," reached out and tugged a neighbor's hair. Then, she rolled over and pretended that she was asleep. The neighbor, a three-year-old, sat up, rubbed his head, and complained. He then lay back down and closed his eyes. The teacher *did not* wade through the sleeping bodies and scold Missy. Instead, she smiled at this unusual event and commented later to a colleague that she thought Missy was finally feeling comfortable at the center.

The child care teacher decided that Missy's Level One mistaken behavior did not warrant intervention. To do so would have embarrassed a child with high personal standards and disrupted a group of sleeping preschoolers. The teacher did make a point of watching Missy's behaviors more closely, involving Missy in more activities, and building the relationship with her.

Marginal mistaken behaviors are the sort that some teachers may react to one day but not the next. *Consistency* in teacher response is needed both by the child and the group. Consistency provides reliability in the environment and facilitates trust between child and teacher. In determining whether to intervene, the teacher references behavior to the guidelines that have been established, the specifics of the situation, and the personalities of the children involved. Ultimately, the teacher must make intervention decisions by relying on his professional judgment. Reflection after the event helps the teacher decide whether adjustments are necessary for "next time."

Bossiness   Many teachers experience negative feelings about the marginal mistaken behavior of bossiness. A democratic society depends on citizens with leadership abilities. When young children show beginning leadership behaviors, they do so with the developmental egocentrism that they show in all behaviors. As a sense of fair play is strong in most teachers, they need to check tendencies to come down quickly on "bossy" behavior.

Teachers positively acknowledge and encourage beginning leadership.

At choice time four kindergarten girls were playing cards. The game went like this: Lisa, who frequently organized play situations, stacked and dealt the cards. All four children picked up their cards and giggled, then put them back on the table. Lisa stacked the cards again and re-dealt.

The teacher, who was watching, fought a tendency first to teach the children a "real game" and second to have each girl get a turn stacking and dealing. As it was, none of the other children pressed to have a turn, and the game went on as it was for almost half an hour!

Children learn about leadership and group participation from experience with peers. Teachers may need to remind a child to give others a chance; this is understandable. At the same time, they should positively acknowledge and encourage "beginning leadership." The children themselves provide an indication of how leadership is showing itself. If others willingly associate with the leading child, intervention should be minimal. If other children shy away, the child probably needs guidance. Teachers frequently can help a child feel less need to dominate by building a personal relationship and help-

Table 10–1

Problem-Solving Classroom Arguments with Children Aged Three to Eight

Situation	Teacher Response
1. Reasonable chance children can work out difficulty.	Monitors, but may not intervene. If needed, uses low-level mediation.
2. Argument proving disruptive to a focused group activity.	Teacher intervenes. Redirects parties to class activity. States that he will help them solve problem later. Teacher follows up.
3. Argument becoming heated. Children don't seem able to resolve on own. Perhaps one child dominating.	Teacher mediates. May use props like talking sticks, talk-and-listen chairs, or puppets. Has each talk in turn and uses high-level mediation to assist children to resolve problem.
4. One child reports argument to teacher; wants assistance.	Teacher avoids taking sides. Determines whether #1, #2, or #3 above applies. Responds accordingly.
5. One or both have lost control; children are yelling or fighting.	Teacher intervenes. Separates children for cool-down time. Uses high-level mediation and often guidance talks when tempers have cooled.

ing the child feel more secure and accepted by the group. Teachers also model and teach cooperation over competition through general teaching practices, specific curriculum activities, and games (Pirtle, 1995).

Arguments   Teachers generally feel a need to intervene when children quarrel. In the guidance approach, the teacher uses with-it-ness skills to analyze the situation and takes any of several possible courses of action, as Table 10–1 suggests.

As presented in Chapter Nine, children who learn to solve problems with words are gaining a life skill of lasting value (Wichert, 1991). Using words to solve problems can be learned by prekindergarten children no less than by third graders.

> Head Start teachers, Tammy and Connie, had a stock phrase whenever children had a disagreement: "We have a problem. How can we solve this problem?" At the beginning of the year, they helped children settle arguments on a daily basis with the phrase. As the year went on, the two needed to use it less and less. The reason was that other staff (including a teenage assistant) and the children themselves began to say: "We have a problem. How can we solve this problem?"

Firmness of Intervention

Besides deciding whether to intervene, the teacher must determine the level of firmness to use if intervention is necessary. Matching firmness to the seriousness of the mistaken behavior is a practice usually taken for granted. Part of practicing with-it-ness should be conscious thought about the degree of firmness to use.

As Ginott points out, "Children are dependent on their teachers, and dependency breeds hostility. To reduce hostility a teacher deliberately provides children with opportunities to experience independence" (Ginott, 1972, p. 76). The teacher avoids communication that pits his authority against children (Greenberg, 1988). Instead, he invites, requests, or commands choices. The teacher does so in factual nondemeaning ways, because children "resist a teacher less when his communications convey respect and safeguard self-esteem" (Ginott, 1972, p. 77).

The strategy of putting choices to children illustrates how to use degrees of firmness in teacher responses. A first degree is **inviting choices:**

> "I need some strong helpers to put the blocks away."

For some teachers, a mild invitation in situations like this is all that is needed. For others (and in other situations for all teachers) increased firmness is needed. A second degree is **requesting choices:**

> "As soon as the blocks are picked up, we can go outside."

or

> "The blocks need to be picked up before we can go out."

Suggesting a reward after a task has been done is known as the "grandma principle" (Jones, 1993). (As Grandma says, "Eat your peas, and then we can have dessert"—applied to "nonfood" situations in the classroom.) When requesting cooperation, the tone of voice as well as the words convey a confident determination that the task be done.

The third degree of firmness is **commanding cooperation:**

> "Children, I am bothered that you are pushing and using loud voices. Stop now and we will discuss how to use the computer together, or please find something else to do."

When commanding choices, the teacher sometimes includes an *I message* to underscore the seriousness of the situation. Notice use of the I message, a factual report, and firm direction in the teacher's statement. There is a clear expression of disapproval in these words, but the teacher is addressing the situation, not attacking the personalities of the children involved—he is using Ginott's cardinal principle. Some teachers may be uncomfortable with the particular choice given—stay here and discuss this or do something else. For some children, the decision to leave an argument is a positive choice in this situation. For others, who perhaps need assistance with assertiveness, the teacher may word his response differently and not offer an "out" before the mediation process.

When putting choices to children at any degree of firmness, an objective is to make the *in-choice* attractive. The *in-choice* is the one the teacher hopes the child will make. The teacher must be prepared, though, for the occasional *out-choice*. The *out-choice* is the less preferred option for the teacher, but one he can still live with. Sometimes even in encouraging classrooms, children select the out-choice because they need to feel significant in the situation. Other times, the out-choice just sounds better to them. The teacher accepts either choice the child makes, and helps the child understand that the consequences the child has chosen are real and logical in this situation. Life is choice-making, and choices have consequences—sometimes not what one wants, but always to learn from.

(From a student teacher journal) *Observation.* Eric [a new child at Head Start] was climbing over the playground fence. By the time the lead teacher realized what he was doing, she only had time to grab and hold him until I went around to bring Eric back. Eric didn't want to go back. He said, "Teachers don't make the rules. The kids do." I explained to him how the kids get a choice in some situations, but not in all of them.

Meanwhile, the lead teacher had come around the fence and taken over. She said, "Eric, you have two choices: One, you can walk back into the playground by yourself or, two, you can be carried back in."

I could tell the lead teacher expected Eric to say walk, but he replied, "Carried."

The lead teacher didn't miss a beat. She said. "You want me to carry you over my shoulder like a sack of potatoes?" Eric confirmed this statement, so the lead teacher picked him up and carried him over her shoulder like a sack of potatoes back into the playground. While carrying Eric, she made jokes about him being a sack of potatoes. Eric enjoyed being carried back into the playground. He didn't try the "trick" again, but played for awhile, and then the lead teacher talked with him about the incident. When it was time to go in, they walked in together.

Reflection. The lead teacher gave Eric a choice of what he wanted to do and responded to the choice he made. Since he picked a way that might have caused him embarrassment, the teacher decided to make carrying him fun and nonthreatening. It saved him from being embarrassed in front of the other kids and didn't allow him to get upset at the teacher for carrying him back into the playground. I think this was a respectful and appropriate way to handle this situation, but the teacher got quite a workout!

Offering choices is basic in the guidance approach, but the skill takes practice. Sometimes, beginning teachers offer a choice that is too open-ended, or where choosing really is not warranted; for example: "Do you want to wash your hands for lunch?" Children need to know what the teacher wants them to do in order to cooperate. Sometimes a task gets done with minimum fuss if, instead of a choice, a matter-of-fact request is given: "It's time to wash hands for lunch now."

QUICK INTERVENTION STRATEGIES

Unlike marginal mistaken behaviors, teachers generally agree that serious classroom situations require intervention. When teacher-time is limited, the resolution of problems becomes more difficult. Nonetheless, the objective is still to solve the problem, and effective techniques for resolving problems quickly are among the most important for teachers to learn. With quick and effective intervention, little problems tend not to become big ones, and the spread of mistaken behavior to other children—socially influenced mistaken behavior—is prevented. Quick intervention strategies are: **negotiation reminders, humor, nonverbal techniques, brevity,** and **describe-express-direct.**

Negotiation Reminders

When a child complains about a conflict with another, a common teacher phrase is

"I understand that bothers you, can you use your words to tell him?"

or

"You need to tell him how you feel."

When conflict management is a part of the everyday program, this friendly reminder is often enough to stimulate child negotiation. Though it might not seem so, the message to a child in these statements appears to be, "I had a complaint, and the teacher listened." Having told the teacher and been heard, children often feel less need to press the issue with the other child. If a child does confront the other, it is often with righteous indignation rather than belligerence. The other child, usually taken aback (and aware that the teacher has been consulted), tends to respond in interesting ways:

(From a student teacher journal) *Observation.* Aureole, Amber, and Kendra were decorating doilies with sequins and other materials. After a couple of minutes, Amber came up to me and said, "Teacher, Aureole keeps telling me what to do. She's bossy."

With quick intervention, little problems tend not to become big ones.

I got down on my knees, looked her in the eye, and said, "Could you tell her how that makes you feel?" Amber nodded her head, returned to Aureole, and said, "I don't like when you tell me what to do. That makes me sad."

"Sorry," replied Aureole, "I won't be bossy no more, OK?" Amber smiled, "OK."

Reflection. These children are very used to using their words and are comfortable with it. It was extremely effective for Amber to explain how she felt after telling me about it. Aureole was receptive to her feelings and they were able to continue working together just like nothing had happened.

A stock phrase like the student teacher used is not a panacea, but it does tend to remind children that they can handle many issues for themselves.

Sue Liedl, in the case study at the end of Chapter Nine, has reframed a classic negotiation reminder attributed to Marshall Rosenburg (Pirtle, 1995). Designed more for elementary than for preschool children, Liedl's *sentence frame* is as follows:

I feel _____

when _____.

Next time _____.

Sue points out that many accidental or mostly accidental things happen when groups of children are in confined spaces for long periods of the day. She teaches the children to use this response before getting more serious, such as by asking a teacher to mediate. This way of framing the statement opens the door to solving the problem in a relatively nonconfrontational way; for example:

Sentence frame: "*I feel* really sad *when* you bumped my arm 'cause I'm writing. *Next time* try to be more careful, OK?"

Response: "Well, I didn't mean to, but OK."

Sometimes, children just do not know what to say or how to respond in a conflict situation. Taking the time to teach a specific response like this (perhaps as a part of a lesson) gives the teacher another helpful reminder: "Did you use your sentence frame?" A teacher is occasionally rewarded for repeated modeling of the frame when he hears a child use it on her own.

Humor as Tension Reliever

Just as good-natured humor prevents mistaken behavior, it also diffuses problems that do occur. The ability to see humor in a difficult situation relieves tension. When not at the expense of a child, a sense of humor complements well the firmness teachers show, and helps children and teachers alike put mistaken behavior in perspective.

In a child care center, the preschoolers were making a footprint mural. An assistant at one end of a five-foot strip of butcher paper helped children step into a bin of red paint and pointed them in the right direction. The teacher at the other end assisted as the children stepped into a bin of soapy water and onto an absorbent towel.

Two children waiting in line began to push, and the assistant went back to mediate. A three-year-old decided not to wait for the assistant's help. She stepped into the paint, walked onto the paper, and took an abrupt left turn. The teacher at the receiving end was busy with another child and looked up to see red tracks leading to the restroom, just as the door closed. The two adults looked at each other, grinned, and shook their heads. The assistant stayed with the waiting line while the teacher, still smiling, retrieved the three-year-old.

Some years ago a teacher in an elementary school classroom was also the part-time principal. The children knew that when she

> was out of the room, silence was to reign. On one occasion when Mrs. Kling returned, she was dissatisfied with the noise level and demanded, "Order, please!"
>
> From the back of the room a reply was heard: "Ham and eggs!" The young man (whose voice sounded a lot like the author's) was greatly relieved at the teacher's response: She laughed with gusto.

Using humor in a difficult situation is the teacher's choice. For some teachers, humor comes easily and helps all to function comfortably in the classroom. For others, humor takes work; it requires that the teacher look freshly at events when "the pressure is on." Young children, because they look freshly at all situations, make humor an obvious tool to use. The challenge is for teachers not to take themselves too seriously and to remember that shared laughter can make long days seem not so long.

Nonverbal Techniques

The advantage of using nonverbal techniques (also called body language) is that they remind children about guidelines without causing undue embarrassment. Charles comments that nonverbal techniques typically include eye contact, physical proximity, body carriage, gestures, and facial expression (1996). In an encouraging classroom, smiles and a friendly facial expression are, of course, the basic nonverbal techniques. Also important, physical proximity is useful both in prevention and intervention with young children. In the active, developmentally appropriate classroom, the teacher is constantly moving about and establishing physical proximity. Locating by children who have a problem is frequently enough to refocus attention. The skillful teacher does so without disrupting the flow of the activity or lesson.

Fredric Jones is known for his writing about body language as a method in positive classroom discipline (1993). For purposes of intervention, Jones' nonverbal techniques apply mainly to children in the *primary grades and up*. Preprimary children are so involved in situations that they tend to be oblivious to all but the most direct nonverbal techniques—physical proximity with friendly physical contact. A proviso about nonverbal techniques is that eye contact and some touches, such as a pat on the head, may be appropriate with European American children, but not with children of some other cultural backgrounds. Knowledge of the cultural expectations of the families one works with is important.

As they progress through the primary grades, children become attuned to the teachers' use of body language. Appropriate with this age group, a multi-step strategy for addressing mistaken behavior follows, building from the work of Jones (1993). Although the final steps involve words, the words are private, carefully chosen, and follow from the nonverbal foundation.

Step one: *Eye contact*
The power of eye contact, the age-old stare, is remembered by most adults from their own school days. Generally, making eye contact involves less embarrassment than if the teacher calls out a child's name or writes it on the board. A slight smile lessens the intensity of Step one.

Step two: *Eye contact with gestures*
A slow shake of the head with a gesture such as the palm up or an index finger pointed up at about shoulder height reinforces the message of the eye contact. Jones maintains that holding eye contact until the child resumes attention is important (1993).

Step three: *Physical proximity*
Mistaken behavior occurs most often away from the teacher. An important finding of Jones (1993) was that nearness of the teacher to children is effective at reestablishing limits.

Step four: *Proximity with general reminder*
Having moved close to children, the teacher makes a general reminder such as "I need everyone's attention for this." (A quick glance at the children makes this step more emphatic.)

A caring expression communicates acceptance and support for a child in need.

Step five: *Proximity with direct comment*
After establishing proximity, the teacher makes eye contact and privately requests the behavior expected. (The teacher protects self-esteem by speaking in a low but determined tone.) A follow-up conference sometimes is warranted.

Jones has contributed to intervention practices with his emphasis on body language. According to Jones, body carriage even more than spoken words tells children about the teacher's sureness of professional calling and comfort level with the group (1993). The basic element of body language, of course, is facial expression. About facial expression, important for all teachers of young children, Charles (1996) says the following:

> Like body carriage, *facial expressions* communicate much. Facial expressions can show enthusiasm, seriousness, enjoyment, and appreciation, all of which tend to encourage good behavior; or they can reveal boredom, annoyance, and resignation, which may encourage misbehavior. Perhaps more than anything else, facial expressions such as winks and smiles demonstrate a sense of humor, the trait students most enjoy in teachers. (p. 133)

Brevity

Among writers about teacher-child relations, none discusses the use of language more constructively (or elegantly) than Ginott (1972). Ginott states:

> Teachers like parents, need a high degree of competence in communication. An enlightened teacher shows sensitivity to semantics. He knows that the substance learned by a child often depends on the style used by the teacher. (1972, p. 98)

About the use of language during intervention, Ginott speaks of the importance of **brevity**. Young children have difficulty understanding lengthy explanations. Concise statements by the teacher that address the situation and motivate toward change are the objective.

When Justin spoke to a neighbor for the third time during a class discussion, the teacher moved over to him and did **not** state: "Justin, you certainly have a lot to say today. Your mouth and your ears can't work at the same time. When you're talking, others can't hear either, and the class can't have important discussions. Do you think you could sit quietly for the rest of the group? You can talk all you want to the other children when you're out on the playground. Now, let's see you use your listening ears. Do you have them on? I am certainly glad that you do."

Table 10–2

Examples of Quick Encouragement to Reinforce Guidelines

Toddlers:	You made it all the way to the potty chair. Next time I bet you'll get your pull-ups down! (As adult comforts toddler who was intent on using the potty chair.)
Preschoolers:	You two are both holding on to the tray. Just have to keep it steady while you walk. (As teacher gently steadies tray that the children were starting to rock.)
Primary grade children:	Decide at break whose pencil it is. Use my "loaner" pencil for now so you can both get started. (As teacher approaches two children arguing over a pencil at start of assignment.)

> Establishing proximity, the teacher **did** say (quietly but firmly), "Justin, only one person talks at a time so we can hear. You have good ideas to share, but you need to wait for a turn."

The brief use of encouragement along with reinforcing a guideline captures well Ginott's sense of the positive power of words (Table 10–2).

Being Direct

Confrontation as an intervention technique must be used with care. The line between earned authority and forced authority is crucial in the guidance classroom. This is why the use of negotiation reminders, humor, and nonverbal strategies anchor quick guidance interventions. When the teacher does not have time for mediation, matching firmness to the behavior by using choices (previous section) is a key concept. A set of ideas from Ginott (1972) provides another alternative when harm or serious disruption are imminent, and the teacher is on the verge of becoming upset. Ginott suggests the following trio of ideas (1972):

- Describe without labeling;
- Express displeasure without insult;
- Correct by direction.

Describe Without Labeling   The teacher accepts the individual, but he need not accept the individual's mistaken behavior. In a paraphrase of other Ginott words: address the situation, do not attack personality. The teacher describes what he sees that is unacceptable, but does so without labeling personalities, because "labeling is disabling" (1972). *Example:* "Stefan, you have a right to be upset, but we don't hit in our classroom. Hitting hurts. Use words to tell him how you feel."

Express Displeasure Without Insult   Anger leads to mistaken behavior, in children and in adults. For this reason, even obedience based discipline models maintain that "teachers should never act out of anger." As Ginott points out, anger is an emotion that all teachers feel; they either manage it or are controlled by it (1972). Since they assist children to express emotions in acceptable ways, professional teachers need to model the management of anger themselves. The careful use of displeasure, to show that you mean business but will not harm, is a necessary teaching skill. Ginott advocates the use of *I* messages, to report feelings without condemnation. *Example:* "I am really bothered that you two are fighting. You will sit down in different places. We will use words to talk as soon as both of you and I have cooled down."

Correct By Direction   This statement echoes another guidance basic: "Don't just tell children what not to do; tell them what to do instead." Direct children to alternate, acceptable behaviors. The difference is between intervention that is punitive and intervention that is educational. Young children are still learning "what to do instead" and have a need for and a right to this guidance. (If you won't tell them, you cannot expect them to know.) *Example:* "Voshon, I cannot let you hit anyone, and I will not let anyone hit you. You need to use words to tell him how you feel. He doesn't know until you tell him."

Using the Ideas Together   The describe-express-direct intervention techniques recommended by Ginott need to be used with care. They are guidance-oriented only when they address mistaken behaviors and at the same time support self-esteem. Note that the teacher expresses displeasure only when she feels bothered by events and needs to get personal feelings "on the table." *Describe* and *direct* are sufficient to move many behaviors back within guidelines, and to sustain an encouraging classroom. Expressing the teacher's feelings tends to "up the ante." Notice the difference in the types of intervention in Table 10–3. The teacher chooses when to express feelings. Sometimes he feels children need to know how their teacher feels—that adults have

Table 10–3

Using Directness to Guide to Redirect Mistaken Behavior

Type of Intervention	Examples of Technique
Describe-Direct	• Many outside voices are being used. Inside voices instead please. • It sounds like a bunch of professional wrestlers over here. Please solve the problem quietly.
Describe-Express-Direct	• I have difficulty listening when many children are using outside voices. I am bothered by the noise. Inside voices only. • You two sound like Hulk and the Rock on a bad night. I am really upset about this. You choose. You play the game peacefully or choose separate activities.

feelings too. Other times, he may want to model the labeling of feelings—angry, sad, upset—for children. Self-reports tend to convey a sense of disapproval—a response that needs to be used with precision in the encouraging classroom. As a communication technique, expressing one's feelings is useful, but the teacher should not take the technique for granted as being guidance.

BEHAVIORS REPORTED BY OTHER CHILDREN

"Tattling" bothers most teachers. They would prefer that children "attend to their own affairs" and solve their own problems. In some classrooms, children are punished for tattling. In others, a child who chronically tattles acquires a label such as "busybody."

Child-report (an alternate term for *tattling*) is difficult to deal with because the motives of children are not always what they seem. The reasons for a child-report range from a legitimate concern to a need for attention to a desire to manipulate the teacher. From a guidance perspective, teachers have two reasons for neither banning nor disparaging child-report.

First, sometimes a teacher wants a child to report, for instance, when:

- a child has wandered from the playground;
- children are fighting, and one has been seriously hurt;
- a child has been injured in an accident;
- a child is having a seizure or is otherwise ill;
- others are acting inappropriately toward a child.

Children should be encouraged to report such incidents. In a class meeting, the teacher may discuss with children what such an emergency is and what children should do in the event of an emergency. The well-being of children and the professional integrity of the teacher are supported by children acting as "concerned citizens."

Second, a report by a child is a request for a response by the teacher. Children need positive contact with teachers even if they don't always know how to ask for contact appropriately. The teacher models acceptance of the child by responding even when he sees an event differently than the child. One technique that attempts to balance the priorities of teachers and the needs of children is a "report box." Children who have concerns that are not emergencies can write or draw out the problem on prepared "report forms" and put them into the box. The teacher consults the box daily, reads the name the child has put on the "name line," and talks with the child about the concern. Follow-up actions to address the concern, such as a class meeting, may result, though often a little individual attention is enough to resolve the situation.

When children report, the teacher does well to take a moment and consider which of several possible motives may be operating. A first motive is that they have experienced a problem and have come to the teacher for assistance. A second motive is that they have witnessed a problem and believe the teacher should know about it. A third motive is to make contact with the teacher for

Table 10–4

Teacher Responses to Child Report

Suspected Motive of the Child	Suggested Response of Teacher
Child has legitimate difficulty in relations with another child.	Teacher encourages children to solve on own—"tell him how you feel about that"—or mediates to extent necessary.
Child honestly reports problem situation involving other children.	Teacher thanks child for being a "caring citizen." Monitors situation. If necessary, intervenes taking a guidance approach.
Child reports only once or twice to get teacher's attention or see what teacher will do (Level One mistaken behavior).	Teacher reassures child that things are under control. Monitors situation in low-profile manner "just in case." Notices whether reporting child seeks attention in other ways. Works on building relationship with child. Gives attention in other ways.
Child reports minimal problems on a regular basis (Level Two mistaken behavior).	Teacher thanks child for concern but explains that teacher is watching and other children can take care of themselves. Tells child what the serious problems are that child can report. Builds relationship. Gives attention in other ways.
Child reports either to manipulate teacher or get another child into "trouble." Does so on a regular basis (Level Three mistaken behavior).	As in all cases, teacher avoids "charging into the situation." Keeps open mind about children involved. Monitors "reporter" for other Level Three mistaken behavior. If necessary, follows procedures for working with this level.

attention. A fourth motive is that they report to find out what the teacher will do. A fifth motive is that they wish to control the teacher's reactions. A sixth motive is that they wish to put another child in a difficult situation.

As Table 10–4 indicates, teachers respond differently depending on the suspected motive of the child.

Why should teachers bother with the complex, troublesome interactions that are a part of child-report? By using guidance adults teach children to resolve their own conflicts; to respect others' efforts at problem solving; and to come to the aid of peers who are genuinely in need. These capabilities are desirable in citizens of any age in the 21st century. From this perspective, "tattling" too becomes a teaching opportunity.

INTERVENTION WHEN FOLLOW-UP IS NEEDED

When adults disagree, the immediate resolution of differences is not assured. Yet, with children who lack the resources and experience of adults, instant resolution frequently is expected. In academic settings that emphasize decorum

Child report can be for many reasons—including a legitimate request for assistance.

and academic achievement, many view teachers who mediate difficulties as using time unproductively.

Time is required if differences are to be settled in ways from which all can benefit. In the mutually satisfactory resolution of problems, all learn (Wichert, 1991). In the peaceful resolution of difficulties, teachers enhance children's self-esteem and their faith in school—their will for educational success (Greenberg, 1988).

Ginott (1972) recognized that in many situations there should be "no hurried help." He wrote that when the teacher quickly "solves" problems for children, they feel inadequate. In anticipation of the conflict management movement to come, Ginott states:

> The teacher listens to the problem, rephrases it, clarifies it, gives the child credit for formulating it, and then asks, "What options are open to you?" "What are your choices in this situation?" Often the child himself comes up with a solution. Thus, he learns that he can rely on his own judgment. When a teacher hastily offers solutions, children miss the opportunity to acquire competence in problem-solving and confidence in themselves. (p. 92)

Sometimes, situations can be addressed quickly with nonverbal or verbal responses that sustain self-esteem and increase understanding. In these cases, follow-up is not necessary. In other cases, speedy resolution is not realistic. When the teacher must give time to a situation, he does so either at the moment of the occurrence or later in the day. (Response at a later time is due to conflicting demands on the teacher at the moment, the need for a *cooling-down time* if emotions are high, or the need for privacy.)

This section addresses teacher responses when follow-up is necessary. Four follow-up strategies are explored: *teacher-child negotiation, reflective listening, including children's ideas,* and *reconciliation.*

Negotiating Teacher-Child Conflicts

Chapter Nine primarily discussed teaching social problem solving to children. Child-child conflicts tend to be the main focus of writers about social problem solving. With the active learning encouraged by developmentally appropriate practice, child-child disputes are a natural focus. Yet, a higher concern among many beginning teachers are teacher-child conflicts.

Teacher-child conflicts occur more frequently when the education program is less responsive to the developmental needs of children. Such programs place an expectation on children that they may not be ready for, and create a mismatch situation that can lead to defiance, anxiety, and frustration. The teacher reduces this mistaken behavior, of course, by making the program more developmentally appropriate.

Still, even in encouraging classrooms, differences of opinion will occur between teacher and child. Moreover, children with serious needs will show Level Three mistaken behavior regardless of classroom climate, and sometimes the teacher will be the target.

When two individuals resolve a conflict between themselves without an outside mediator, they have *negotiated* a solution. The idea of *teacher-child negotiation* makes some teachers uncomfortable because the term seems to imply communication at a peer-to-peer level. The reasoning is that if negotiation can only happen between peers, teachers would have to relinquish their leadership role and compromise their standards! In fact, probably the leaders that people look up to most—whether they are teachers, administrators, supervisors, or political figures—frequently negotiate.

The choice to negotiate is the teacher's, and he may elect not to negotiate depending upon the circumstances. But sometimes, the best action a teacher can take *is* to negotiate. When the teacher so decides, he does not give up the mantle of leadership, just uses it with dignity and mutual respect. The *thought* of negotiating with a child can be unsettling. However, for many teachers who use guidance, the action is not a "big deal"; teachers negotiate routinely.

(From a student teacher journal) *Observation.* It was the end of independent learning time in a first-grade class. Miles had been running around for most of free time already. He ran over to the window and noticed that some wheat berries, planted by the class, had sprouted. "Look, teacher, they're growing," he screamed. He then went around showing the sprouts to anyone who would look.

When he was back by the window, the teacher met Miles, kneeled with hands gently on his shoulders, and said, "Miles, I can see you are very interested in the wheat berries that are starting to grow. If you come to the writing table where your group is starting, maybe we can write down a plan about how we could plant some different seeds tomorrow." Miles went to the table with the teacher.

Reflection. I was impressed with the teacher's response. Miles, who gets enthusiastic about a lot of things, just noticed the sprouting seeds for the first time. The teacher realized that and let him know she understood what he was feeling. She was then able to get him back on task at the writing table by writing a plan that he was very interested in making. (Later, I asked her if she had been planning to plant more seeds the next day. She smiled and said, "We are now.")

When a teacher disagrees with a child's behavior, he uses the same problem-solving steps as when he mediates child-child conflicts. The teacher guides the child and himself through the five-finger formula: (1) cooling down; (2) agreeing what the problem is; (3) cooperatively arriving at a solution to try; (4) implementing the solution; and (5) supportively monitoring the solution. The advice of most writers on conflict management is worth heeding in negotiation. Stay calm and attempt to be calming. If remaining calm is difficult, just as the teacher might ask two children to take a cooling-down time, the teacher might need to cool down as well.

The ability to settle differences cooperatively is a cornerstone both of individual mental health and the functioning of a democracy. The teacher who takes time to negotiate is modeling problem solving in the way most likely to impact children. When the situation involves the teacher as participant, he must model caring leadership despite emotional involvement. One of the challenges for teachers who use conflict management is that it is often easier to resolve problems that are between children. The teacher can be an objective (and authoritative) outside party who mediates or encourages child-child negotiation. When the teacher is directly involved in the conflict, the emotional stakes are higher. Although the opportunity for significant learning is high, both for the child and adult, the outcome is not assured. The measure of the teacher's commitment to the civil resolution of conflicts, and to the encouraging classroom, is his growing ability to use teacher-child negotiation, as opposed to traditional classroom discipline.

Using Reflective Listening to Teach Impulse Control and Self-Calming

Referred to several times in the text, a key tool in social problem solving is *reflective listening* (called by some "active listening"). Reflective listening means that the teacher articulates or rephrases the child's feelings and perceptions. The teacher does so to show the child he understands and to model the use of helpful language in stressful situations. By having feelings and perceptions articulated and affirmed by the teacher, the child calms down and is more open to discussion. This *release function* of reflective listening is illustrated in many of the text anecdotes and is the common use of reflective listening.

Another way of thinking about reflective listening is that it is the effective use of "describe" in the *describe-direct* intervention. Following reflective listening with directions for behavior makes the technique an anger management tool as well. Slaby et al. (1995) point out that some children in particular show mistaken behavior as a result of still-developing systems for **impulse control.** They act on an impulse, lose control of the situation, and become upset. By listening and directing, the teacher assists children to build strategies by which to manage impulses as well as calm themselves down (Table 10–5).

The technique is straightforward, but is effective only when we have built relationships with children and they are willing to listen to us. Used as *describe and direct,* this intervention is crisis management. Our goal is for the child to internalize our cueing suggestions and use them to prevent harm. Children's internalization of self-cueing to manage an impulse or to calm down takes time to master. With individual children who need this strategy, teachers model the technique regularly and consistently. Teaching children to practice self-calming skills "provide[s] a foundation for more independent self-control skills in later childhood and adulthood" (Slaby et al., 1995). Often after the listening-directing cue, the adult engages in extended reflective listening as part of conflict management or a guidance talk to resolve the problem.

Table 10–5

Cueing to Teach Impulse Management and Self-Calming

Situation	Cueing Example
• Preschooler upset that doll has been taken. Teacher intercepts:	• "You are upset and that is OK. Take five deep breaths and we will make this better."
• First grader thinks another child has stolen his quarter. Is approaching the suspect with an angry expression. Teacher arrives:	• "Your quarter is gone and you are angry. Think aloud what you can do instead of fight. I am right here to help."

Including children's ideas during negotiation sustains their involvement
in the problem-solving process.

Les was building a barn with blocks when Craig accidentally knocked it over. Les had fists clenched and teeth set when the teacher arrived. The teacher said, "Craig didn't mean to, Les, but it's too bad about your building, and it's OK to feel upset about it." Les remained upset and kicked the remaining blocks, a unit smacking the teacher on the ankle. Les saw what had happened and looked like he was about to cry.

The teacher grimaced silently, then said, "Les, take deep breaths please so that you will feel better . . . in and out, that's right." She put her arm around Les' shoulder and continued, "It's OK, Les, that only hurt a little, and I'm not upset because I know you didn't mean to. You're not having a very good day, are you?" Then Les did cry. The teacher held him until he felt better, and the two picked up the blocks together. Later they talked about what he could do next time when he felt upset.

In the anecdote, the teacher heroically modeled the use of reflective listening while remaining calm. She used *I messages,* or *self-report,* to reassure the child she was staying with him in an effort to make the situation better. Self-report, that affirms a guidance intent helps the teacher as well as the child. For the teacher self-report affords personalized reflective listening as well as a self-assist with his own impulse control. Self-report enables the teacher to stay focused on the problem-solving effort, despite an aching ankle.

Including Children's Ideas

Another tool helpful in both mediation and negotiation is *involving children in the solution process.* When children contribute to the solution, they feel capable as problem-solvers. Including some suggestions of Ginott, questions like these empower children to "work things out":

- What options are open to you?
- What are your choices in this situation?
- How can we solve this problem?
- Who has an idea about what we can do?
- What can we do about it?
- How could you solve this differently?
- Maybe the two of you can solve the problem together?
- What words could you use next time?

These questions are useful both in conflict management and individual guidance situations. When children are asked for their views, ideas, and assistance, they are encouraged to show initiative and to work for a cooperative solution. The leadership of the adult here is critical (Wichert, 1991), as the following example of teacher-child negotiation illustrates.

Third grader Elaine had a difficult time concentrating during large group activities. She visited with neighbors and showed inattentiveness to topics being discussed. At a break-time, the teacher talked with the child:

Teacher: Elaine, we need to talk about a problem we are having during large group. I have to remind you to pay attention too many times.

Elaine: Well, the other kids are always talking to me.

Teacher: Yes, I know; it is hard to listen when too many people are talking. What can we do about it?

Elaine: (long pause) Maybe I could move.

Teacher: That sounds like an idea. Why don't you choose? Where could you sit where you wouldn't be bothered by other children?

Elaine: By Renee, maybe.
Teacher: All right, let's try it. But remember our guideline,
            one person talks at a time, OK?
Elaine: OK, teacher

The teacher followed through by making sure Elaine sat where
they agreed and by using nonverbal techniques, including
smiles, to hold her attention. Two days later the teacher complimented the progress that Elaine has shown.

Teacher-child negotiation, which actively seeks children's input, can be
used with groups as well as individuals. In fact, many class meetings are
called so that teachers and children can negotiate solutions to problems together. The leader is the teacher, who is perhaps bothered by an event, and
calls a class meeting to request the children's input in solving the problem
(Hendrick, 1992).

Reconciliation   Teacher-child negotiation, reflective listening, including
children's ideas, and reconciliation are all parts of conflict management, class
meetings, and guidance talks that are basic guidance strategies. To review a
key idea in **reconciliation** the teacher does not force apologies. Children no

In a group setting, a request to solve a problem becomes part of a class meeting, or a
negotiation between the teacher and the class.

less than adults know when they are ready to apologize and when they are not. (To their credit, children tend to forgive more easily than most adults.) Instead, the adults ask the child for ideas about "how to help the other child feel better." Children come up with creative solutions when they are encouraged to make amends on their own. Teachers often hear ideas like:

"Tell her I'm sorry."

"Tell him I would be his friend again."

"Put a wet towel on it."

The teacher then uses the suggestion to encourage the child to get the relationship back on track. Children are more willing to apologize when they know that their feelings and points of view have been respected—which is what social problem solving is about.

In the most serious conflict situations, teachers physically restrain or remove children to prevent harm (see Chapter Eleven). In these cases, the primary focus of the child's anger may be the teacher. Whatever the focus of blame for a conflict, the teacher is the one who initiates reconciliation. The principle of unconditional positive regard means that the teacher works for reconciliation as a part of daily practice. In the guidance approach, the teacher recognizes that the act of reconciling comes not from weakness, but from strength. Guidance differs from punitive discipline in this regard (see Table 10–6).

Table 10–6

Steps in Problem-Solving Conflicts

A. Identify the problem.
  1. Decide that time should be taken to solve the problem.
  2. Establish that the purpose is to resolve a problem, not blame or label individuals.
  3. Enable each party to express views and feelings about the problem, using reflective listening to clarify points.
  4. Summarize differing viewpoints, checking for accuracy of interpretation with participants.
B. Generate possible solutions.
  1. Request cooperation in seeking a solution.
  2. Encourage the suggestion of solutions.
  3. Appreciate that each suggestion was made, even if others have difficulty with it.
C. Agree on a solution to be tried.
  1. Work for consensus on a course of action.
  2. Avoid accusation of vested interest. Instead, point out that "others see the situation differently" and encourage further discussion.
  3. If necessary, point out that perfect solutions are not always possible, but this one is worth trying.
D. Reach successful closure.
  1. Facilitate implementation of the solution.
  2. Provide encouragement (compliment sandwich if necessary).
  3. Affirm the participant(s) for reaching the solution.
  4. Discuss alternative behaviors for next time.

WHY TAKE THE TIME?

The criticism can be made that the intervention methods discussed in Part Three take time away from "actual" teaching. The author's response is that teaching children democratic life skills is at the heart of what good education is about. Lillian Katz's reference to the need for a "1st R" in education practice: *Relationships* (Kantrowitz & Wingert, 1989) is a response to the findings of those who have noted a steady decline in self-esteem of children as they pass through school. Curwin and Mendler discuss Mitchell's findings in this regard:

> Mitchell found that 80 percent of children enter first grade with high self-esteem. By the time they reach fifth grade, only 20 percent have high self-esteem. By the time they finish high school, the number having positive self-esteem has dropped to a staggering 5 percent. (1989, p. 26)

An accepted principle in social psychology is that self-esteem is greatly influenced by the degree of acceptance given the individual by the reference group. In other words, children who feel accepted "as members in good standing" of the class think better about themselves (Nansel et al., 2001). Children who are prevented from full group participation (stigmatized), by teachers and/or classmates think less of themselves. The factors that cause teachers and children to stigmatize individuals are negative perceptions about academic ability (marked over- or underachievement), physical appearance, social and cultural status, and/or behavior. Negative thoughts about who one is lead to self-defeating and acting out behaviors (Surgeon General's Report 1999).

The encouraging classroom is about helping all children in the class feel they are members in good standing. In line with Katz's recommendation, the encouraging classroom makes relationships the 1st R. Through using guidance to solve problems of mistaken behavior, the adult is teaching children the skills children need to function as productive citizens and healthy individuals. As a reminder, those democratic life skills include:

- The ability to see one's self as a worthy individual and a capable member of the group.
- The ability to express strong emotions in nonhurting ways.
- The ability to solve problems ethically and intelligently.
- The ability to work cooperatively in groups, with acceptance of the human differences among members.
- The ability to be understanding of the feelings and viewpoints of others.

These outcomes of guidance in the encouraging classroom can also be put in terms of developmental outcomes; the child gains in:

- emotional development through the ability to express feelings acceptably and resolve problems constructively;

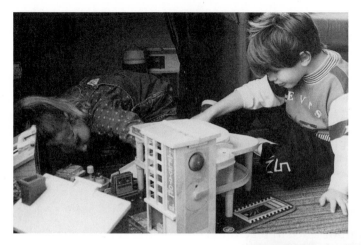

Guidance discipline is a part of an interactive teaching approach
that includes the "1st R," relationships.

- language development through the vocabulary, phrasing, and functional communication necessary for the resolution of difficulties;
- cognitive development by the critical thinking inherent in problem solving;
- physical development through freedom from the effects of stress, tension, and hostile feelings when problems remain unresolved or become aggravated;
- social development by learning life skills important for productive functioning as a member of the group and a democratic society.

A Matter of Ethics

There is an inherent importance in teaching children the skills they need to be productive, mentally healthy adults. Still, another reason to take the time needs discussion. Assisting children to learn alternatives for mistaken behavior is *a matter of ethics.*

A new teacher in a group of three-year-olds noticed one large boy who showed the following pattern of behavior. When he wanted something or became upset, he would strike out at the nearest child. The new teacher took a problem-solving approach to the boy's behavior that included learning more about him. She discovered that he had limited language development, and could not easily use words to express his needs. She noticed that he seemed to get a "glint in his eye" before he would hit out. She noted that the other teachers would give him a time-out after he hit, talk briefly with him, and get him to say he was sorry. They would then leave him alone until the next episode. The teacher noticed a similar pattern being followed by the child and the other teachers over several days.

After talking with the other teachers and not getting much response, the teacher took her notes to the director. She suggested to the director that a more comprehensive response was needed, involving the child's parents and perhaps other professionals. The director told her she was new in the center; this is how the boy was; and that the parents were not to be involved. She was told to let the more experienced staff handle the situation.

The teacher concluded that the director and staff turned a "blind eye" to the situation because they didn't want to do anything that might cause the family to drop the program. The teacher stayed with her observations and noted that the child's behavior, if anything, became more extreme. As a professional, the teacher felt bound to continue pressing the issue. Because of her actions, the director asked her to leave.

The Code of Ethical Conduct   The National Association for the Education of Young Children has published a **Code of Ethical Conduct,** included as Appendix A of this text. The Code "provides a shared conception of professional responsibility that affirms our commitment to the core values of our field." One important use of the Code is to provide guidance when practitioners face ethical dilemmas. The new teacher was acting ethically, and the director and other staff unethically, in relation to key statements in the Code, especially principles P-1.1 and P-2.5:

> **P-1.1**—Above all, we shall not harm children. We shall not participate in practices that are disrespectful, degrading, dangerous, exploitative, intimidating, psychologically damaging, or physically harmful to children.

Harm was being done to other children who were victimized by the child, and to the child himself, by not being guided to alternative behaviors and communication skills. The director apparently did not recognize she was under an ethical mandate. Her duty was to prevent the harm that this child, at Level Three mistaken behavior, was causing and experiencing.

> **P-2.5**—We shall inform the family of accidents involving their child, or risks such as exposures to contagious disease that may result in infection, and of events that might result in psychological damage.

Whatever the staff did or did not say to parents of the other children, the family in question was denied information about events that were causing psychological harm to their son and to others in the class. In not communicating with the parents about the problem, the director failed to act in the best interests of the family. The director denied the family an opportunity to cooperate in a plan that would have improved prospects for the child's healthy development and for a healthy climate in the class.

As an "afterword," the teacher thought about reporting the incident to the state licensing agency, but concluded that nothing but added grief for herself would come of it. If the National Association had accredited the program for the Education of Young Children—the Association responsible for the Code of Ethical Conduct—she could have reported the incident to NAEYC. In the end, the teacher did what many dedicated young teachers do when encountering frustration in the field. She returned to a university for more education.

The teacher has now completed a master's program in early childhood education. She is the author of a handbook to educate parents and teachers about ethics in early childhood education and the importance of liberation teaching. She is still a professional in the field, though more on her own terms and with less dependence on administrators and staff who act as technicians rather than guidance professionals.

BUILDING COOPERATION WITH PARENTS

As a professional, the teacher cooperates with parents in the education of the child. Many factors make cooperation with parents a challenge (Galinsky, 1988). Parents and teachers have distinct roles and perspectives, and often their values differ from each other. Parents:

- have a strong emotional investment in their own child;
- at times question their own effectiveness;
- have views about acceptable behavior and discipline influenced by their backgrounds more than formal education (Galinsky, 1988);
- may regard the teacher as a "superior" who will be unreceptive to efforts at communication (Greenberg, 1989).

Unless teachers accept these role-based qualities, they may take personally contacts with parents that seem defensive or unfriendly.

To accommodate the difference in roles and viewpoints, Galinsky recommends: "Rather than the dispenser of correct information, the professional builds an alliance in which the parent's own expertise is strengthened" (1988, p. 11). Galinsky (1988) and Morgan (1989) provide useful suggestions for taking this collaborative approach. The following discussion builds upon points made by the authors. Today as when first written, these six steps guide the teacher toward achieving cooperation with parents.

Create a Team Concept

When parents and teachers work together, children benefit in many ways—this idea is central to guidance in the encouraging classroom. Teachers discern when parents and teachers have joined together in a team. Parents convey trust in relations. They speak openly about their child and family dynamics that may affect the child at school. Teachers appreciate the active interest parents show, act on their ideas, and at all times respect the family's privacy. Joining with parents on behalf of the child begins as soon as the teacher learns the child will be in his class. The teacher initiates and sustains communications that accept and build upon parents' emotional ties to the children, the natural bond between parents and teachers.

Your Feelings Toward the Family

Teachers sometimes feel uncomfortable around some families. One reason for ambivalent feelings is the view that a family has not met implicit "minimum expectations" that the teacher has about parenting or lifestyle (Galinsky, 1988). In this event, the teacher needs to understand circumstances within the family that may make his expectations unrealistic. For instance, a family of a dif-

Establishing relationships early on helps parents and children feel supported
by your role as the teacher.

ferent cultural heritage may seem to the teacher to be "male-dominated," with
the wife and a daughter who is in the class kept in apparent subservient roles.
The teacher who discerns this difference in cultural—rather than strictly
moral—terms is in a better position to still accept the common bond he has
with the family, work for the well-being of the child, and treat all members of
the family respectfully in working toward this goal.

Cultural, economic, and social factors contribute to family situations and
parenting styles often different from the teacher's. When the teacher perceives discomfort about a family, his challenge is to increase understanding
so that he can engage in team building around what he and the parents
have in common: the child. On occasion, the effort can and does result in
heightened cross-cultural understanding for both.

Understanding Parent Development

About this topic Galinsky states:

> It is much easier to understand parents if you know the normal course of
> parental growth and development. For example, before decrying the super
> baby phenomenon, it helps to know that all parents want perfection for their
> children—that is normal. It is their definition of perfection you want to alter,
> not their desire for the best for their child. (Galinsky, 1989, p. 10)

Single parents in their late teens or early twenties are still growing into
adulthood, without the customary support system—though hopefully
with support nonetheless. The needs of these parents might be considerably different from parents in their late thirties who have achieved relative

stability in their professional and/or family lives. Parents in the first category may need a mentor in education or development processes—both for their children and themselves. The latter parents may be more interested in the teacher's competence and vision for his educational program.

The task of balancing work or school with parenthood provides ample challenges for many parents, whether just starting out or established. Teachers might be attuned to expressions of attachment by the child for the family and make a point of relaying these to the family. Parents who hear from a teacher how much they mean to the child tend to be encouraged and to recognize that the teacher understands. Working parents who are just starting out with a new baby need early childhood teachers to be active in the support role. The teacher avoids the appearance of a "substitute parent" and portrays instead who he is, a caring professional who works as a team member with parents.

Parents who stay at home with their young children often feel strongly about their identities. The early childhood teacher accepts the identity that this parent feels. If the parent is willing, the teacher invites the parent to extend her interest in her own children to the class by becoming a volunteer. The development of parents is affected not just by their age, but by the roles they define for themselves in the home, workplace, and community.

Choose Words That Avoid Value Judgments

Describing without labeling is a basic of the guidance approach that pertains to parents no less than children. Galinsky and Morgan use examples that may sound familiar. Here is a tongue-in-check variation of an example used by Morgan (1989):

Instead of:	Karla turned into a real terror this afternoon. It was "isolation corner" for her today. After that she shaped up, and she is being a good girl now.
Say:	Karla's morning went well, but this afternoon she had a conflict with two children. She needed a cool-down time, but we talked about it and she is having an easier time now.

Note the nonjudgmental tone and the recognition of progress included in the second statement, which is a compliment sandwich. As a contrast, in the first statement the use of "value laden" language is clear. The compliment sandwich, *I* message, and reflective listening all provide alternatives to value judgments, and are useful in communications with parents as well as with children to encourage cooperation.

Use Support Services

Galinsky identifies a crucial role for the teacher as referring families to other services (1988). She states, "It is just as important to know when to say no and to refer as it is to know when to say yes" (p. 10). The teacher is not

Understanding parents is much easier if the teacher understands the normal course of parental growth and development.

a therapist or a social worker, but he can refer a family to a needed service and be supportive through the referral process.

Head Start has led the way in assisting families to access health and social agencies as well as educational services. Increasingly, schools and other programs are coming to realize that not just the child, but the family is the unit of service in early childhood programs (Boyer, 1992; Heath, 1994). The ability to work with families to remove the stigma of special education or social service assistance is a goal of the teacher (Coleman, 1997).

In making referrals, to the extent possible teachers should know the agencies in their area and individuals at the agencies who will be helpful. Rosenthal and Sawyers (1996) provide a list of steps important in making a referral:

1. Know the agencies in your area.
2. Know competent people with whom you can work at these organizations.
3. Refer to specific people, not just an organization.

4. Get an agreement from the family preferably in writing that they will participate.
5. Ask the family to predict what might prevent them from participating and ask for solutions (such as transportation and child care).
6. Check on families' ideas about solutions and arrangements.
7. Make sure you provide for a follow-up meeting (p. 199).

Head Start staff might be comfortable helping with more of these steps; a child care professional or an elementary school teacher might be comfortable with fewer of the steps. Often, the individual teacher should not think in terms of taking referral actions on his own. Instead, working with other staff as a team, teachers can and should endeavor to make referrals, including the preliminary step of learning as much as possible about the services available. Families who are helped with successful referrals tend to strengthen their commitment both to their children and to the classroom staff. The success of the referral process almost always depends on the quality of the teacher-parent relationship.

Problem Solving with Parents

Teacher-parent negotiation often becomes necessary when a child's mistaken behavior grows serious. Galinsky suggests a six-step approach to *teacher-parent problem solving.* The goal is to convert "unhealthy tension" to "healthy tension" in relations (1988). The six steps are similar to the processes suggested earlier for helping children solve problems in the classroom. The steps include:

1. Describe the situation as a problem to be solved. Avoid accusations or the implication that the source of the problem resides in the personality of the parent or the child.
2. Generate multiple solutions. Parents and professionals should both do this, and no one's suggestions should be ignored, put down, or denounced.
3. Discuss the pros and cons of each suggestion.
4. Come to a consensus about which solutions to try.
5. Discuss how you will implement these solutions.
6. Agree to meet again to evaluate how these solutions are working so that you can change your approach, if necessary (p. 11).

On occasion, communication with parents may prove difficult and negotiation needs to give way to third-party mediation. As Galinsky comments, "Having others to turn to when there are tensions is crucial in working effectively with parents" (1988, p. 10). Seeking a senior staff member to assist in the problem-solving process is a mark of maturity for the guidance teacher (Koch & McDonough, 1999). A source of support for the teacher outside of the immediate situation—preferably both a fellow staff member and a friend or family member—is equally important. The person serving as the support base should recognize the need for a teacher to privately "vent" with no repercussions. Hopefully, the source of support can also assist the teacher to plan a constructive course of action regarding the situation.

The teacher cannot separate the child's life at school from the child's life at home. The child's life at home is the family. Through cooperating with the family, the teacher gains the parents' trust and assistance in helping the child.

SUMMARY

1. What goes into the decision to intervene?

The teacher is a friend to children, but he is an adult friend who accepts the responsibility of leadership. The adult works to understand situations by practicing "with-it-ness." He determines the level of mistaken behavior, and whether problem situations involve one or two children or a number of children. The teacher then decides whether to intervene and the degree of firmness of the intervention. The strategy of inviting, requesting, or commanding choices illustrates the use of different degrees of firmness and at the same time grants children a measure of independence.

2. What are five quick intervention strategies?

Quick intervention strategies that resolve problems but still protect self-esteem are important in guidance. Negotiation reminders that cue children to use their own developing social skills are a first strategy. Humor is a second strategy by which the teacher can relax children in tense situations. A third strategy is nonverbal communication that includes using facial expressions and establishing proximity. Brevity is a fourth strategy, an effective alternative to moralizing and "lectures." A fifth strategy is direct intervention through the "describe, express, and direct" and the "describe and direct" sequences.

3. How does the teacher respond to mistaken behaviors reported by children?

Child-report (an alternate term to *tattling*) is difficult to deal with because the motives of children are not always what they seem. Teachers should neither ban nor disparage child-report for two reasons. A teacher wants a child to report when safety is threatened. Also, child-report can be a request for contact with the teacher. Children need positive contact even if they don't always know how to ask for the contact appropriately. Suggestions were provided to help teachers determine motives for child-report and take an appropriate course of action.

4. What are four strategies when interventions require follow-up?

Time is required if conflicts are to be settled in ways in which all can benefit. In the event of teacher-child conflict a first strategy is to negotiate. This negotiation is not at a peer level; the teacher uses his authority to problem-solve civilly with the child, using the principles of conflict resolution. A second strategy, reflective listening, is an effective tool in both negotiation and mediation. The technique assists children with emotional control by helping them express their feelings in ways acceptable both to themselves and to other children.

A third strategy is to include children's ideas in the problem-solving effort. By including children's ideas, children feel ownership of the resolution process and are more likely to participate fully in it. A fourth strategy is the reconciliation process, a chief point of difference between guidance and conventional discipline.

5. Why take the time to problem-solve mistaken behavior?

Assisting children to develop democratic life skills is a valid part of the curriculum for the 21st century. Individual children and the society both benefit when teachers take the time to problem-solve mistaken behavior. The NAEYC Code of Ethical Conduct specifies that teachers must work to prevent harm to the children in their care. Guidance enables the teacher to reach and teach children who are the victims of their own or others' mistaken behavior.

6. How does the teacher build cooperation with parents?

Collaboration with parents is sometimes difficult for teachers because of differences in perspective and values. To accommodate these differences, Galinsky (1988) suggests that the role of the teacher is to foster an alliance in which the parents' own expertise is strengthened. To do so, the teacher builds positive relationships, monitors feelings toward the family, understands parent development, chooses words that avoid value judgments, and makes referrals for support services. The teacher uses a six-step problem-solving approach in collaboration with parents to solve problems that may arise. When communication becomes difficult, third-party assistance both in problem solving and providing a support base for the teacher are important.

KEY CONCEPTS

Brevity as quick intervention

Child-report

Code of Ethical Conduct

Commanding cooperation

Describe-direct

Describe-express-direct

Humor

Impulse control

Inviting choices

Marginal mistaken behaviors

Negotiation reminders

Nonverbal intervention

Reconciliation

Requesting choices

FOLLOW-UP ACTIVITIES

Note: An element of being a professional teacher is to respect the children, parents, and educators you are working with by maintaining confidentiality—keeping identities private. In completing follow-up activities, please respect the privacy of all concerned.

Discussion Activity

The discussion activity encourages students to interrelate their own thoughts and experiences with specific ideas from the chapter.

Recall an incident when you or a teacher intervened in a situation that required follow-up. What strategies did you or the teacher use that are identified in the chapter? How did one or two principles from the NAEYC Code of Ethical Conduct (Appendix A) apply to the intervention?

Application Activities

Application activities allow students to interrelate material from the text with real-life situations. The observations imply access to practicum experiences; the interviews, access to teachers or parents. Students may compare or contrast observations and interviews with referenced ideas from the chapter.

1. **The decision to intervene.**
   a. Observe a situation when a teacher had to decide whether to intervene. Respecting the privacy of the teacher, how did the decision correspond to the discussion about intervention in the chapter? Refer to the issues of with-it-ness, the intensity of the mistaken behavior—marginal to serious—and the degree of firmness of the intervention.
   b. Interview a teacher about how he decides whether intervention in a situation is needed. Does having one or two children or a larger group involved make a difference in the intervention strategy he likely would use? How does the teacher decide how firm to be during the intervention?
2. **Five quick intervention strategies.**
   a. Observe one of the five strategies in use. How did the teacher use the strategy? How did the child or children respond? What did you learn from the observation and the text about the intervention strategy?
   b. Interview a teacher about which of the five strategies he regularly uses. What are the teacher's thoughts about each

strategy? How comfortable is the teacher with each strategy?
Why? For any one strategy, compare your findings from the
interview with the text.

3. **Mistaken behavior reported by children.**
   a. Observe an instance of child-report. Referring to the text as a
      guide, what seemed to be the motivations of the child in
      making the report? How did the teacher handle the situation?
      What seemed to be the effect on the child who reported?
   b. Interview a teacher about "tattling" or child-report. How
      does the teacher handle child-report? How do the teacher's
      views compare or contrast with the material on child-report
      in the text?

4. **Strategies when interventions require follow-up.**
   a. Observe an instance of serious mistaken behavior. Which of
      the follow-up strategies did the teacher use? How did he use
      them? What did you learn about working with serious
      mistaken behavior from your observation and the text?
   b. Interview a teacher about his approach when intervening
      during serious mistaken behavior. What does he try to
      accomplish at the point of the conflict? After the parties
      involved have cooled down? Which of the four follow-up
      strategies did the teacher discuss? How did his comments
      about them compare to the text?

5. **Why take the time.**
   a. Observe an instance when you believe a teacher took a
      problem-solving approach to mistaken behavior. What
      seemed to be the outcome for the children involved? Using
      your observations as a guide, explore the text position that
      problem-solving mistaken behavior is worth the time.
   b. Interview a teacher who takes a problem-solving approach to
      mistaken behavior. What are the priorities of the teacher
      when he intervenes? What does the teacher want children to
      learn when he intervenes? How do the teacher's priorities
      compare with principles from NAEYC's Code of Ethical
      Conduct in Appendix A?

6. **Cooperation with parents.**
   a. Observe, and if possible participate in, an instance of
      teacher-parent communication outside the classroom—a
      conference, parent meeting, home visit, and so on. How did
      the teacher's practices compare with those of the chapter?
      What seemed to be the result in terms of teacher-parent
      cooperation?
   b. Interview a teacher about a family that he was uncomfortable
      with or had trouble understanding. How did the teacher
      communicate with the family to build cooperation? How
      satisfied was the teacher with the success of the effort?

What You Can Do

Applying the Code of Ethical Conduct   Something important can be learned from studying the connection of guidance practices to ethical standards in early childhood education. The purpose of this activity is to observe guidance-related practices and relate these practices to sections of the Code. Over a few days or visits to a classroom, watch for and observe an example of what you believe to be guidance-related teaching practice to as many of the four sections of the Code as possible: Children, Families, Colleagues, and Community/Society.

   a. Observe an example of a guidance teaching practice that relates to the profession's Ethical Responsibilities to Children, Section I. Record in as much detail the words and actions of the teacher and child or children involved. Reference the teacher's responses to the Ideals and Principles of Section I of the Code. How do the teacher's responses coordinate with the Code?
   b. Observe an example of a guidance teaching practice that relates to the profession's Ethical Responsibilities to Families, Section II. Record in as much detail the words and actions of the teacher and a parent or other family member. Reference the teacher's responses to the Ideals and Principles of the Code. How do the teacher's responses coordinate with the Code?
   c. Observe an example of a guidance teaching practice that relates to the Ethical Responsibilities to Colleagues, Section III. Record in as much detail the words and actions of the teacher and a colleague. Reference the teacher's responses to the Ideals and Principles of the Code. How do the teacher's responses coordinate with the Code? Note any patterns in the matches you made.
   d. Observe an example of a guidance teaching practice that relates to the Ethical Responsibilities to Community and Society, Section IV. Record in as much detail the words and actions of the teacher and relevant others. Reference the teacher's responses to the Ideals and Principles of the Code. How do the teacher's responses coordinate with the Code?
   e. What have you learned about the NAEYC Code of Ethical Conduct? What have you learned about the relevance of guidance practices with children, family members, colleagues, and the community to the Code?

RECOMMENDED READINGS

Curry, N. E., & Arnaud, S. H. (1995). Personality difficulties in preschool children as revealed through play themes and styles. *Young Children, 50*(4), 4–9.

384   Part Three   Solving Problems in the Encouraging Classroom

Gartrell, Daniel J. (2000). *What the kids said today.* Using classroom conversations to become a better teacher. St. Paul, MN: Redleaf Press.

Koch, P. K., & McDonough, M. (1999). Improving parent-teacher conferences through collaborative conversations. *Young Children, 54*(2), 11–15.

Logan, T. (1998). Creating a kindergarten community. *Young Children, 53*(2), 22–26.

McClurg, L. G. (1998). Building an ethical community in the classroom: Community meeting. *Young Children, 53*(2), 30–35.

Rosenthal, D. M., & Sawyers, J. Y. (1996). Building successful home/school partnerships: Strategies for parent support and involvement. *Childhood Education, 72*(4), 194–199.

REFERENCES

Boyer, E. L. (1992). *Ready to learn: A mandate for the nation.* Princeton, NJ: The Carnegie Foundation for the Advancement of Teaching.

Charles, C. M. (1996). *Building classroom discipline.* White Plains, NY: Longman.

Clewett, A. S. (1988). Guidance and discipline: Teaching young children appropriate behavior. *Young Children, 43*(4), 26–36.

Coleman, M. (1997). Families and schools: In search of common ground. *Young Children, 52*(5), 14–21.

Curry, N. E., & Arnaud, S. H. (1995). Personality difficulties in preschool children as revealed through play themes and styles. *Young Children, 50*(4), 4–9.

Curwin, R. L., & Mendler, A. N. (1989). *Discipline with dignity.* Alexandria, VA: Association for Supervision and Curriculum Development.

Dinwiddie, S. A. (1994). The saga of Sally, Sammy, and the red pen: Facilitating children's social problem-solving. *Young Children, 49*(5), 13–19.

Galinsky, E. (1988). Parents and teacher-caregivers: Sources of tension, sources of support. *Young Children, 43*(3), 4–12.

Gartrell, D. J. (1997). Beyond discipline to guidance. *Young Children, 50*(5): 27–34.

Ginott, H. (1972). *Teacher and child.* New York: Macmillan Publishing Company.

Girard, K., & Koch, S. J. (1996). *Conflict resolution in the schools.* San Francisco: Jossey-Bass Publishers.

Glasser, W. (1969). *Schools without failure.* New York: Harper and Row.

Greenberg, P. (1988). Ideas that work with young children. Avoiding 'me against you' discipline. *Young Children, 44*(1), 24–29.

Greenberg, P. (1989). Ideas that work with young children. Parents as partners in young children's development and education: A new American fad? Why does it matter? *Young Children, 44*(4), 61–75.

Heath, H. E. (1994). Dealing with difficult behaviors—Teachers plan with parents. *Young Children, 49*(5), 20–24.

Hendrick, J. (1992). Where does it all begin? Teaching the principles of democracy in the early years. *Young Children, 47*(3), 51–53.

Jones, F. H. (1993). *Instructor's guide: Positive classroom discipline.* Santa Cruz, CA: Fredric H. Jones & Associates.

Kantrowitz, B., & Wingert, P. (1989, 17 April) How kids learn. *Newsweek,* 50–56. New York: Newsweek, Inc.

Koch, P. K., & McDonough, M. (1999). Improving parent-teacher conferences through collaborative conversations. *Young Children, 54*(2), 11–15.

Kounin, J. (1977). *Discipline and group management in classrooms.* From first edition (p. 259). New York: Holt, Rinehart and Winston.

Morgan, E. L. (1989). Talking with parents when concerns come up. *Young Children, 44*(2), 52–56.

Nansel, T. R., Overpeck, M., Pilla, R. S., Ruan, W. J., Simons-Morton, B., & Schiedt, P. (2001). Bullying behaviors among U.S. youth. *Journal of the American Medical Association 285*(16): 2094–2100.

Pirtle, S. (1995). *Conflict management workshop guide.* Shelburne Falls, MA: The Discovery Center.

Reynolds, E. (1996). *Guiding young children: A child-centered approach.* Mountain View, CA: Mayfield Publishing Company.

Rosenthal, D. M., & Sawyers, J. Y. (1996). Building successful home/school partnerships: Strategies for parent support and involvement. *Childhood Education, 72*(4), 194–199.

Slaby, R. G., Roedell, W. C., Arezzo, D., & Hendrix, K. (1995). *Early violence prevention: Tools for teachers of young children.* Washington, DC: National Association for the Education of Young Children.

Surgeon General. (1999). *Surgeon General's report on mental health.* Washington, DC: Department of Health and Human Services.

Wichert, S. (1991, March). Solving problems together. *Scholastic Prekindergarten Today,* 46–52.

For additional information on using the guidance approach in the classroom, visit our Web site at http://www.earlychilded.delmar.com

CHAPTER ELEVEN

GUIDANCE THROUGH INTERVENTION

GUIDING QUESTIONS

- What conditions make intervention necessary?
- What are three methods of crisis management?
- What are strategies for working with Level Three strong needs mistaken behavior?
- What techniques assist the teacher to manage personal feelings of anger?
- What are considerations when teachers and parents disagree?

From early experiences in baby-sitting or high school child development classes, some young adults gravitate toward early childhood education in college. After teaching in the upper grades, other adults shift to early age groups, feeling they can relate more comfortably with young children. The opportunity to be fully nurturing within the teaching role, and the rewards for being so, motivates many women and a small but growing number of men toward early childhood education.

Teachers want to be friendly and supportive toward young children. Aware of the trust that is placed in them, early childhood teachers take seriously the decision "to discipline." They worry about hurting feelings, impairing development, and losing children's friendship. They are concerned about what they or a child might do when confronted. They wonder how intervention will affect other children and the atmosphere of the class. They fear the self-doubt and shame that occurs if they overreact. They may feel anxiety as well about what a child may say to a parent, and what the parent may do in response.

Still, sometimes intervention is necessary, and timely intervention is the measure and foundation of the authenticity of the teacher (Brewer, 2001; Gartrell, 1997). Enforced limits provide security for the child, other children, and the teacher (Slaby et al., 1995). To paraphrase Dreikurs (1972), reluctance to intervene in the face of harm or serious disruption marks an unproductive level of teacher permissiveness, as distinct from democratic discipline [guidance].

The opportunity to be nurturing within the teaching role motivates
many toward early childhood education.

A premise of Part Three is that even in crisis situations, intervention techniques remain problem solving in nature, intended to guide and not to punish. Chapter Ten examined strategies for solving "routine" problems in the classroom. The strategies discussed were for those situations that could be resolved without undue difficulty, either immediately or with follow-up. Chapter Eleven examines serious mistaken behavior, when strong emotions make solving problems difficult.

CONDITIONS THAT MAKE INTERVENTION NECESSARY

Varying tolerance levels toward mild mistaken behaviors mean that teachers differ in responses to these situations. To maintain consistency in response to mild mistaken behaviors, teachers do well to link interventions to established guidelines, work to understand the child and the situation, and self-monitor moods and response tendencies. In contrast to mild mistaken behaviors, a large majority of teachers choose to intervene when:

1. children cannot resolve a situation themselves, and the situation is deteriorating;
2. one or more children cause serious disruption to the education process;
3. the danger of harm exists.

In the event of serious mistaken behavior, often two or all three of these conditions are present; virtually all teachers would then intervene.

Whenever possible, if the teacher can control the situation with intervention strategies discussed in the previous chapter—negotiation reminders, body language, humor, brief comments, inviting or requesting choices, describing situations, and directing behaviors—such strategies are desirable. They minimize classroom disruption, cause minimum upset to children, and restore equilibrium effectively. When children have lost control, however, the nature of the intervention becomes more involved. The teacher then uses a *combination of intervention strategies* for the purpose of resolving the conflict.

1. **Deteriorating situation:** Nigel was in the space under a four-sided climber playing by himself. Dinee opened the door and started to come in. Nigel pushed against the door and said, "You can't come in here." Dinee pushed her way in, and the two were yelling at each other when the teacher arrived.

With firmness she said to both: "You are having a problem, so let's see if we can solve this problem, or you can play somewhere else." Nigel made a fist at Dinee, who hit his fist and then pushed him back. The loud voices got louder. The teacher, halfway in the

When children have lost control, the teacher uses a combination of intervention strategies.

door, put a hand on each child's shoulder and stated: "You have decided. Please separate, and we will talk about this later."

Dinee left, but Nigel lay down and began to cry. Outside the climber, the teacher sat by him for a bit and got him started on a favorite puzzle. Later, the teacher talked with the children about how they felt they might handle the problem "next time," and how they could be friends again.

2. **Serious disruption:** Although the teacher had given a "five-minute warning," Randy was not ready to stop using the Legos™ as cleanup began. The teacher asked him to help put the Legos away, but Randy instead grabbed several loose ones and brought them to where he was building. The teacher went over to Randy and told him he could leave his structure for later, but he would have to put the new Legos away. Randy became upset and began to throw them. After ducking and bobbing, the teacher approached

Randy, looked him in the eye and stated firmly, "Randy, I know you are angry, but Legos are not for throwing. Let's go sit so that you can cool down." She looked at the assistant teacher who nodded and took over supervising cleanup. The teacher took Randy's hand, and the two sat down. After he calmed down, the two talked about what happened and what he could do differently next time. At the end of cleanup, the teacher made sure that Randy successfully joined the next activity.

3. **Danger of harm:** Darwin and Rita were painting on opposite sides of an easel. Darwin peeked around the side and painted some red on Rita's blue sky. Rita painted blue on Darwin's bare arm. Darwin dropped his brush and pushed Rita down. Rita yelled and while sitting began to kick Darwin's ankles. Looking furious, Darwin was in the act of pouncing when the teacher arrived and restrained him.

Darwin struggled with the teacher to get loose until he realized that he couldn't. After a few minutes in the teacher's "bear hug," with the teacher speaking soothingly to him, Darwin quieted down. When she felt she could leave him, the teacher tended to Rita, who was still sitting on the floor. She followed up later with the children together. She asked each to explain what happened and how they felt. She let them know how she felt about the conflict, and got them to agree on a nonviolent course of action they could take next time.

In these three situations the teacher chose to resolve conflicts by non-punitive intervention. In each case, the teacher worked to establish limits, order, reconciliation, and acceptable behavior alternatives for the future. During a conflict, all involved are at risk for psychological and often physical harm. For this reason, crisis intervention is neither easy nor pleasant. When any or all three conditions are present—a situation deteriorates, serious disruption occurs, the danger of harm exists—intervention becomes necessary. Firm, friendly *non-punitive intervention* is the measure of the value the teacher places in the guidance approach.

CRISIS MANAGEMENT TECHNIQUES

Crises are conflicts that get out of hand. Crises occur when emotions are running high, and the communication process is breaking down. In crisis intervention, the teacher makes a final effort to restore communication so that mediation can occur. If this is impossible, the teacher works to restore order, so that guidance techniques can be used when emotions have cooled down.

The three previously illustrated situations constitute typical early childhood classroom crises. Among the intervention techniques the teachers used were *commanding cooperation, separation,* and *physical restraint.* These procedures are fundamental crisis management techniques and each is discussed further.

Commanding Cooperation

In a guidance approach, the teacher matches the intensity of the intervention to the seriousness of the mistaken behavior. Chapter Ten introduced *giving choices* as a useful intervention procedure. At a prevention level, the teacher frequently works to *invite cooperation:* "I need some superstrong helpers to move the chairs." At a problem-solving level, the teacher *requests cooperation:* "As soon as the books are on the shelves and the blocks are in the box, we can go outside." At the crisis level, the teacher sometimes *commands cooperation:* "Brett, you choose: Use words to express your feelings, or go to another part of the room and cool down."

When commanding cooperation, the teacher is not making an ultimatum— "Either you shape up, or I will make you." Ultimatums set up adversarial relationships between teachers and children that undermine mutual trust (Greenberg, 1988). Instead, the adult requests children to choose a personal course of action and teaches them that they have some control in the situation. The child may not like the options, but the fact that he can choose retains dignity, in contrast to the "do it or else" alternative imposed by a threat.

Referring to Anecdote 1, Dinee and Nigel may choose to use words—the in-choice. In this case the communication process is restored and mediation becomes possible. If the children continue to use violence, they have elected to separate from the situation—the out-choice—their decision is respected, and the teacher later uses guidance methods to teach them more effective behavior alternatives.

Among crisis techniques the command for cooperation is a *method of first resort* because it holds out the possibility of mediation to resolve the difficulty. This method remains nonpunitive, however, only if the out-choice is a logical consequence of the behavior and if guidance is later offered. What seems a logical consequence to a teacher in the midst of a crisis may really be punishment, so the teacher should pose the "out" alternative with care. In a preprimary setting, an out-choice for continued reckless play on a climber might be to go to a different activity; it would not be to stay off the climber for a week. A guidance talk that follows up by discussing consequences and teaching more acceptable behaviors are a key part of the procedure.

Some authors criticize the use of commanded choices, as by itself the technique does not help children realize the immediate and long-term benefits of mediation (Carlsson-Paige & Levin, 1992). Liedl, of the St. Philip's School program, teaches children that if they choose to stay and mediate,

A common command for cooperation is that children discuss a conflict
or play elsewhere. The teacher stands by to mediate to resolve the difficulty,
or initiates a guidance talk later. The guidance talk makes the "out-choice"
less punitive, and so less likely to hurt self-esteem.

they "keep their power" to be a peacemaker. If they choose not to use
words, they lose their power—or rather, they give their power over to the
teacher. (It's better, she emphasizes, for them to keep their power.) When
one or both parties elect the out-choice, the teacher brings them together
later, when feelings have cooled, and engages in a guidance talk. The
follow-up is what keeps commanding choices in the "guidance camp." Notice, also that teaching management techniques like "keeping your power"
outside of conflict situations assists children when crises occur, and is fundamental in crisis-centered guidance (Wittmer & Honig, 1994).

Separation

Separation from the group is the crisis intervention technique of next-to-
last resort. Whenever possible, the teacher uses the least disruptive form
of separation: diversion to an alternative activity in another part of the
room—*redirection*. The teacher uses redirection when she decides not to
mediate a problem. Even when separation is "only" redirection, the
teacher usually opts to follow-up with a guidance talk to ensure that
young children understand the events and maintain composure. Redirec-

tion is often used with preschoolers, especially ages three and younger, but in certain circumstances it has its place with older learners as well. The likelihood of embarrassment is present with redirection, as with more severe forms of separation, so the follow-up is especially important.

In-room isolation—commonly known as the **time out**—occurs when a child is removed from a situation and placed alone in a separate part of the room, usually with no alternative activity. (Isolation in either a closed-off portion of the room or outside the room, unless in the company of an adult, is an inappropriate and harmful intervention practice.) The time-out has received criticism for overuse in early childhood classrooms (Betz, 1994; Clewett, 1988; Gartrell, 2001, 2002; Marion, 1999; Slaby et al., 1995). Introducing a note of practicality (maybe levity), Betz (1994), writes:

> I think that Time-Out should be used either for fairly serious matters, such as when a child is wildly out of control and repeatedly hurting others, or when a child has exasperated you beyond endurance and, if you *didn't* have the child take Time-Out, you very possibly would slug him. Time-Out should be thought of as a Last Resort. (p. 11)

Actually, if a teacher is this upset with a child, the *teacher* may need a time out. But, Betz makes the point well: that putting a child on a "time-out chair" should be anything but an automatic occurrence.

Traditionally, in-room isolation has been used for two distinct purposes:

- punishment for perceived misbehavior;
- a cooling-down time for when a child has lost control, before a guidance talk can occur (Gartrell, 2001 & 2002).

Insufficient distinction often has been made between these two practices, with *time-out* being the general term used. The distinction needs to be made clear.

The Time-Out   In sports, a time-out is a break from the game for the purpose of substitution and strategy. For young children the time-out should be a break from a tense situation for the purpose of regaining composure. In his clinical studies, Piaget (1960) has documented that young children—due to developmental egocentrism—have difficulty conceptualizing the intricacies of social situations. The ability of young children to "think about what happened" is limited, especially when put on a chair by themselves. During the time out, young children do not logically "analyze the consequences of their actions," even if directed to do so (Katz, 1984, Schreiber, 1999). Instead, they are likely to internalize the shame of being separated, while sometimes simultaneously relishing the negative attention received from the teacher. This developmental reality means that periods of isolation fail to teach children "how to get along better." Even when considered a "logical consequence" by the teacher, the effect on the child is not logical; it invariably is punishment.

As Clewett maintains (1988), isolation reinforces a teacher's sense of power by forcing conformity to his expectations. Isolation also pressures the child toward diminished self-esteem and negative feelings toward the teacher and the education environment (Marion, 1999). **When isolation is used in retribution for unacceptable social activity, the separation becomes punishment and is conventional discipline rather than guidance.**

Unless a child has lost control, mediation or one of the quick but non-punitive interventions methods should be used. Separation before this point is often done for the teacher's convenience—to avoid the "bother" of mediation, or to rely on the "standard discipline practice" for when a child "misbehaves." In some classrooms the use of time-outs—meaning in-room isolation—still is taken for granted. Teachers attest that it is successful in "getting a child to behave" at the time, but fail to notice that they have to use it several times a week with the child for this purpose.

The mark of an effective intervention technique is that it reduces the mistaken behavior. Ongoing use of the time out for one or a group of children indicates that the technique is not working (Slaby et al., 1995). In moving toward a guidance approach, teachers need to realize that methods sometimes taken for granted may be more punitive than commonly thought (Marion, 1999). Teachers need to be professionals rather than technicians.

Cooling-Down Time   Separation to help a child regain equilibrium is a logical consequence of loss of control. Usually the adult sits with the child during the **cooling-down time.** As the child regains composure, the adult talks with the child about what happened, what the child might do differently next time, how the child can help the other feel better, and helps the child rejoin the group. The difference between separation as punishment and separation as cool-down time is one of teacher disposition. The self-check for this difference is a straightforward question: **Am I isolating this child because he deserves to be punished or because he needs to regain control?**

Classrooms using a guidance approach resort to the *time-out chair* seldom if at all (Marion, 1999), and to *cooling-down times* only in serious situations. Guidance-oriented teachers start with developmentally appropriate, individually responsive programs that reduce the need for mistaken behavior. They prefer the intervention techniques discussed to this point, including mediation, requesting choices, and redirecting to alternative activity (Gartrell, 2001, 2002; Marion, 1999, Schreiber 1999).

To distinguish further *cooling-down time* from *time-out,* here are some additional considerations:

1. The use of a time-out chair or worse, a "naughty chair," institutionalizes separation as a form of punishment in the classroom. The chair becomes a place of negative value, and children made to sit on the chair are at risk of being stigmatized. Like sitting in a corner or on "think-about-it" steps, a time-out chair should never be used.

2. Children need a cool-down time when they have lost emotional or behavioral control. Generally, an adult stays with a child while the child regains composure. On rare occasions, if she believes

her presence is reinforcing mistaken behavior, the teacher may have the child sit alone (Slaby et al., 1995). If the child is unaccompanied, the time of separation should be brief; a simple guideline is no more than one minute per year of age—that is, three minutes for a three-year-old. If more time is needed, the adult should be there (Betz, 1994).

3. The purpose of the cool-down time is to help the child regain emotional control so that guidance follow-up can happen. The follow-up typically is conflict management and/or a guidance talk. With this follow-up the child is able to gain in understanding about what happened, how all parties felt during the conflict, and how to settle the conflict using words. Without guidance follow-up the child is deprived of the positive expectation that he is capable of changing his behavior.

4. The guidance talk is one part of the *reconciliation* process at the conclusion of the cooling-down time. A second part is assisting the child to rejoin the group. Often, the teacher facilitates the transition by steering the child to a quiet activity alone or with one or two other children, often those involved in the now-settled conflict.

5. Reconciliation does not mean forcing a child to say that he "is sorry." Premature apologies contradict honest feelings and do an injustice to this important convention. Instead the adult may ask a child, when she believes the child is ready, how the child feels he might make amends. If children are helped to understand their feelings and know that they are supported by the teacher, they will reconcile on their own—usually more quickly and fully than adults.

6. When it is part of the reconciliation process and not forced, *restitution* is a valuable part of reconciliation. With the teacher's assistance, a child might help clean up a mess that was made, rebuild a house that was knocked down, or get a wet towel for a bump on the head. Children can often think of ways to help another child "feel better."

7. Two common practices for concluding traditional time-outs have been the use of a timer and the child's own judgment about when to rejoin the group (Slaby et al., 1995). In agreement with Clewett (1988) and Marion (1999), the cooling-down separation is a serious enough experience that direct teacher assistance is important for reconciliation. Timers and the child's unsupported judgment should not substitute for teacher involvement.

Four kindergarten children were sitting down to "supper" in a housekeeping center. The pretend food was a large quantity of styrofoam "peanuts" used in packing. Mark, a developmentally delayed five-year-old, arrived to join the group. The table was too small and before Ina, the teacher, could arrive to mediate the problem, the children told Mark he couldn't play. Irate, Mark swept the bowl of "peanuts" on the floor and began to scream. He was in the act of dumping the four plates upside down when Ina arrived. She stooped, put her arm around Mark, and guided him to an unoccupied beanbag chair. Sitting by him, Ina stroked Mark's head until he quieted down.

The teacher reminded Mark to come to her when he had a problem and told him the children felt sad about what had happened. She asked Mark what he could do to make things better. Mark said, "Pick up."

Mark and the teacher went over and helped the children who were already picking up the styrofoam. When they were done, Ina asked the children if Mark could join them for supper. "OK," said Shelley, "Mark can be the little kid." Shelley then measured carefully the "peanuts" they put onto his plate. Mark smiled at being included.

Self-Removal   In a published research summary, Bronson (2000) points out that during the preschool years, children make great strides in regulating emotional responses, complying with external requests, controlling behavior and attention-getting responses, and engaging in self-directed thinking and problem solving. She cites studies to show, however, that the capacity to develop these abilities is somewhat affected by innate factors such as temperament and greatly affected by the child's environment (Bronson, 2000). As every teacher knows, due to the combination of genetic and environmental factors, some children have considerable difficulty managing their emotions.

A child who "loses it"—whether in relation to other individuals, one's self, or the world at large—is upsetting for all in the encouraging classroom. When repeated over time, the raw expression of emotions is a classic Level Three mistaken behavior. As such, the child needs the comprehensive approach to strong needs mistaken behavior described later in the chapter. Essential components—though usually not enough by themselves—are the immediate steps of crisis intervention: halting the impulse (often by the describe-direct strategy), cooling the child down, engaging in conflict management, and guidance talks.

The major order of business is moving the child toward self-management of emotions. The strategy requires an adult who has positive relations with the child to serve as "point person." When the child has lost control, this teacher is the one who intervenes, actively coaching the child to deescalate emotions and solve the problem using words. For teaching self-management of emotions, the guidance talk is key. When the child has cooled down, the primary caregiver, in a deliberate eye-to-eye discussion, discusses the problem and negotiates alternatives to the emotional outburst that the child can use next time. The adult then works with the child to implement the emotions-management strategy and enlists the team to provide encouragement and compliment sandwiches. As strong as the child's emotions are, the teacher needs to be stronger in firm but friendly persistence that the child learn alternative behaviors.

The process of teaching and learning emotions-management is interactive. As long as designated alternative behaviors are sensible to the child, they may change over time:

> I remember a resourceful teacher who was guiding a child to manage his anger. One day when I arrived at the classroom, Jamal was standing with the teacher outside a closed side door yelling into the wind. Another day, Jamal walked over to the teacher and said, "Teacher, I am so mad"!
>
> The teacher responded, "I can see you are, Jamal. Thank you for coming and telling me. How about if you go into the restroom, close the door, and spit in the sink as long as you want." Three minutes later, emotions cooled, Jamal walked out of the restroom and headed right for the water fountain. He was a dry little kid! After quickly cleaning the sink, the teacher then complimented Jamal for removing himself from the situation and handling his anger. She talked quietly with him and helped him rejoin the group.
>
> An outcome for Jamal was impulse control by removing himself from stressful situations. His teacher watched as he learned to do this, helped him cool down, and then had a guidance talk with him. Crisis intervention was not all the lead teacher and staff did to help Jamal with his problems. Jamal had been transitioned to foster care and then back home as his mother progressed in drug therapy. The staff worked hard to build relations with the Mom. In the classroom each staff member, and especially the lead teacher, spent quality time with Jamal each day, to build his trust and their relations with him. Over time, Jamal progressed in his ability to manage his emotions.

Self-removal is an intermediate objective in the long-term goal of teaching children to use nonhurting words to solve their problems. Self-removal is an important accomplishment for some children, however. Teachers know when a child is using self-removal effectively, and mark it as progress with a child facing unmet needs.

Observation: We were making a video for the parents and during one of the songs Nick chose to take himself out of the singing. He said, "I don't want to sing this song."

I asked, "What are you going to do, Nick?"

His comment, "I'll sit on a chair."

I followed with, "That would be fine, as we want to finish singing for the movie."

Nick sat out for two songs and then when we started with the instruments he stated, "I want to play."

I remarked, "If you are ready to come back, that is fine."

Reflection: Nick has had a lot of difficulty over the year controlling his impulses and participating in activities planned for the group. We teachers have been working both with him and his parents to help him increase his impulse control. Choosing to sit out for a few minutes has helped him so that he didn't get into trouble with other students and to get his composure back. He was told at the beginning of the year when he was ready to return to what the other students were doing, he could. He was given the opportunity to monitor himself, and now in April he has made a giant step when we were making the video, to sit down and not interrupt the other children. I hope he is in Head Start again and that we can continue to help him with his social development (Gartrell, 2000).

Over time teachers may notice a child beginning to use self-removal less as impulse control and more as a learned behavior to get out of everyday activities. If so, they should smile. The child is progressing from Level Three mistaken behavior to Level Two. Guidance talks should continue, but in addition the staff works to make involvement in activities more meaningful for the child.

Finally, one reviewer of this text suggested a novel approach to the whole matter of self-removal—available to staff as well as children. A class made one corner of their classroom into "Australia." The corner was equipped with a map on the floor, a palm tree, stuffed koala bear, music, sitting pillows, and a beach towel. (The inflated crocodile proved too stimulating and was removed.) When adults or children are having a "Level Three day," and need to relax, they go to Australia! (The author wonders if classrooms in Australia have a "North Dakota" or a "Canada" corner.) The teachers watch for "visitors" and provide assistance to them in quiet but friendly ways.

Physical Restraint

Physical restraint is part of an active intervention strategy to halt and discourage the continued use of aggression by a child. Some children experience aggression in their lives, and as a result of Level Three needs, use it against others. The payoff for aggression can be reinforcing for a child, and teachers must use firm but friendly words and actions to discontinue "an upward spiral of violence" (Slaby et al., 1995). The foundation of guidance is undermined if teachers allow children to hurt others. At the same time, the encouraging classroom promotes nonviolence in adults as well as children. The adult intervenes actively but neither punitively nor violently. "Grownups as well as children are *never* allowed to hurt anyone in the classroom" (Slaby et al., 1995, p. 93).

The Crisis Prevention Institute (CPI, 1994) offers training "on how to use minimal-force restraint techniques that are appropriate, effective, and safe in given situations" (Slaby et al., 1995, p. 93). Especially with older children, CPI training is helping teachers learn to cope in violent situations. The following discussion of physical restraint, *the passive bear hug*, has been used by teachers of young children for many years.

Physical restraint is the crisis management technique of *last resort*. It is *not* any of the notorious methods of subtle or not so subtle corporal punishment used on children over time. Physical restraint is *not* paddling, spanking, slapping, ear pulling, hair yanking, back-of-the-neck squeezing, knuckle whacking, retribution child-biting, mouth taping, or binding to a chair. Neither is it pushing or pulling a child nor (in contrast to one author's view) holding a child upside down (Cherry, 1983).

Physical restraint means holding a child, including arms, legs, and perhaps even head, so that the child cannot harm you, other children, or himself. Physical restraint is used when a child has lost control, physically and emotionally. A child in need of restraint may be attacking another child, the teacher, or another adult. The child may also be having a tantrum and showing such behaviors as hitting body parts against a floor or wall.

Once the teacher decides that physical restraint is necessary, the commitment is total. Quickly removing the child's shoes is a helpful survival strategy. Sitting down and clamping arms around arms and legs around legs is what physical restraint is about. Children generally will react strongly and negatively to being restrained. The teacher stays with it and often speaks soothingly to the child (Clewett, 1988). With many children calm words or even quiet singing or rocking helps; other children calm down more easily with silence.

With the realization that the teacher is providing needed behavioral and emotional controls, the child calms down. Gradually, the child finds the closeness comforting and, strange as it might seem, the passive restraint sometimes ends as a hug. (Who needs the hug more at this point is an open question.) If the child becomes able to talk about the event at the time, the teacher provides guidance. Otherwise, guidance talk is provided at a later time. After physical restraint, children (and adults) are drained. Helping the child into a quiet activity, like reading a book, promotes reconciliation. A follow-up self-check by the teacher later in the day is needed: Did the teacher use a level of force necessary to prevent further harm and not cause more? Many programs have a written report system for when crisis intervention such as passive restraint is used. Supportive discussion with other staff members is also important, as is witnessing use of passive restraint by fellow staff.

> For the third time Dean had his block structure knocked down. This time the child was Andy, and Dean began shouting. Dean threw blocks at Andy and then hit and kicked at him. Diane, the teacher, approached rapidly, said firmly "You're upset, Dean, but no hurting." When he began hitting out at her, Diane took hold of his arms and legs, and sat down on the floor.
>
> Dean shouted for Diane to let him go, but she held on and began to say quietly, "Dean, I can't let you hurt anyone, and I won't let anyone hurt you. I am holding you so that no one will be hurt."
>
> After struggling, Dean realized that the teacher would not let go and gradually became more quiet. Diane told him that it was no fun to have things destroyed by others and that he had a right to be upset. She encouraged him to next time use words and to come to her right away. After a few minutes, she suggested that Dean do some puzzles, which he did. Dean later asked to sit by Diane during snack—much to the teacher's relief.

The crisis management techniques discussed here support children so that self-esteem is not further deflated by punitive teacher reaction. When serious mistaken behavior continues, however, crisis management techniques in themselves are not enough. A comprehensive strategy for addressing Level Three mistaken behavior follows.

STRATEGIES FOR WORKING WITH STRONG NEEDS MISTAKEN BEHAVIOR

Serious (Level Three) mistaken behavior is due to strong needs that a child feels, cannot meet, and acts out in relation to. The strong needs arise from physical or emotional factors, or a combination of the two. Often, the causes of strong needs mistaken behavior lie outside the classroom. Untreated *physical and health conditions* that bother a child are one source. To the list of

Non-punitive physical restraint provides a child who has lost control
with the limits needed to regain composure.

long-standing health conditions, such as obvious physical disabilities, illness, hunger, and lack of sleep, teachers have seen an increase in less "traditional" conditions: attention deficit-hyperactive disorder, fetal alcohol
syndrome, chronic allergies, abuse-related injuries, and environmental illnesses, among others. Any of these conditions, undiagnosed and untreated,
can cause the persistent behaviors, ranging from withdrawal to aggression,
that constitute Level Three.

In recent years teachers have gone beyond the stereotype of "a bad home
life" to address more openly the *emotional sources* of strong needs mistaken
behavior of children in their charge. Due to life circumstances, for instance,
some children show a fear of abandonment, more severe than that commonly felt by many young children. Other children may show the psychological effects of abuse: both victimization by the act and internalization of
aggression as a relational style due to modeling of the act (Slaby et al.,
1995). The difficulty these children sometimes experience in developing a
conscience and empathy for others is a particular challenge for educators.
Teachers are also seeing an increase of *post-traumatic stress syndrome*, due to
violence perpetrated on children themselves or others in their presence.
Once thought to affect mainly soldiers in war, experts now recognize that
violence in families and neighborhoods can impact severely the sensibili-
ties of young children (Rogers, Andre, & Hawley, 1996). Too often in our society, the effects of these traumatic conditions cause chronic stress,
undermine healthy brain development, and generate the extreme behavior
that is characteristic of Level Three.

The teacher must react firmly to serious mistaken behavior, for the well-being of all concerned. Because young children who have problems easily internalize guilt, however, strategies for assisting them cannot be reactive alone. Discipline is not enough. Experts from many related fields have recognized that a comprehensive approach is needed with children having strong unmet needs. In the last twenty years, writers from the differing contexts of preschool, elementary, middle school, secondary, and special education have advocated a comprehensive or *collaborative* approach (Boyer, 1992; Curry & Arnaud, 1995; Surgeon General's Report, 1999).

At the preschool level, Head Start has given impetus to looking at children's behavior from an **ecological perspective** (Lombardi, 1990) that includes the social, cultural, economic, health, and behavioral circumstances affecting the family. The nursery school movement also has tended to view behavior from the broader child and family context (Moore & Kilmer, 1973). Such writers as Heath (1994), Curry and Arnaud (1995), Reynolds (1996), and Honig (1986) have recognized the importance of comprehensive strategies for addressing the behavior of young children having problems.

At the elementary/secondary levels, the Teacher Assistance Team procedure articulated by Chalfant et al. (1979) has become a widely accepted model "for within building problem-solving." Strengths of the model are its encouragement of teacher collaboration and nonjudgmental approach to the problems of children and teachers alike.

The Contribution of Special Education

Because of the nature of serious learning and behavior problems, special educators have developed systematic assessment, planning, and intervention strategies to assist children with disabilities. In use nationwide since the 1970s, the Individual Education Plan (IEP) is collaborative—in that it involves the input of a range of staff, as well as parents—and comprehensive, tailored to the complexity of needs identified through the IEP assessment.

Labeling or Diagnosis   Despite its promise, special education has suffered from an "image problem" that has worked against its effectiveness in the lives of young children. A widespread criticism of special education intervention is that children "must be labeled to be served." The intentions behind this sentiment are humane. Reacting to the idea that "labeling is disabling," the belief is that a child labeled with a behavioral disability probably will suffer more from a negative self-fulfilling prophecy than gain from the special education assistance.

The difficulty in this view is its confusion of the processes of **labeling** and **diagnosis.** A label is a judgmental shortcut that others use to put a child in a behavioral category: *hyper, rowdy, withdrawn,* and so forth. Labels do injustice because they blind adults to other behaviors and qualities of the child. By adult fixation on the labeled behaviors, the child becomes stigmatized and is undermined in the effort to grow and change.

Diagnosis is the process used by helping professionals to determine systematically the nature of a child's difficulty in order to guide the child to overcome it. Adults have the power to interpret diagnoses in different ways. Some are legitimate such to determine insurance coverage, special education funding, and remediation services. A special education diagnosis only becomes detrimental when adults use the diagnosis as a label.

As an illustration, the difference is between a child who receives a diagnosis of attention deficit-hyperactive disorder through special education assessment and a child who acquires the label of "hyper" from his teachers. In the first case the child receives counseling, program modifications and perhaps diet restrictions or prescribed mediation. Classroom staff, special education teachers, and parent(s) actively monitor the situation; and in most cases the child's behavior changes. In the second case, teachers only resort to isolating the child's desk, requiring enforced seatwork, and using frequent time-outs. The behavior does not change and remains disturbing to teachers and peers alike.

At its best, special education intervention involves close collaboration between classroom staff, specialists, parents, and the child (McCormick & Feeney, 1995). In such situations adults work together to assist children to cope with the problems that result from learning and behavioral disabilities. The guidance approach builds from the special education experience to construct similar comprehensive, nonjudgmental therapeutic strategies.

Special Education and Guidance   Over the years, a problem in many schools has been denial of the causes of stress that surround children who show Level Three mistaken behavior. Educators instead have tended to punish these children, thinking that what they need is strict external control. In truth, punishment reinforces the negative feelings the children have about themselves and world around them. Either immediately or later in life, the emotional difficulties and the acting-out behaviors tends to become worse.

In more fortunate circumstances, special education teachers are brought in, an assessment and IEP process are undertaken and the downward spiral is lessened and hopefully reversed. Drawing upon the special education perspective, practitioners of guidance hold that **children showing serious mistaken behavior need comprehensives assistance, not the stigma of a one-dimensional discipline approach.** In fact, a basic guidance practice is the more serious the mistaken behavior, the more comprehensive the intervention program and the more people likely to be involved in the solution.

Many children showing strong needs mistaken behavior in schools today do not meet the criteria for a diagnosis of "emotionally/behaviorally disturbed." The Surgeon General's Report (1999) however clearly makes the case that these children need comprehensive guidance. The IEP procedure provides a model for addressing strong needs mistaken behavior. When classroom staff, parents, and other professionals collaborate, the groundwork is set for an effective problem-solving strategy to improve the mental health of children who are having serious difficulties.

Comprehensive Guidance and the Individual Guidance Plan

Children who show Level Three mistaken behavior pose difficult challenges for the encouraging classroom. Gootman (1993), Heath (1994), and the Surgeon General's Report (1999) point out that a comprehensive guidance strategy with a child having strong unmet needs is likely to be more effective than traditional discipline responses. Teachers may have to remind themselves more than once that the time and energy the child requires is an investment in the future. On the "up side" teachers do not need specialized licenses or advanced degrees to use **comprehensive guidance** successfully.

The strategy for comprehensive guidance we will examine here was introduced in Chapter Four and mentioned in various other chapters of the text. Of necessity, the strategy starts with intervention to prevent harm and disruption—the crisis intervention techniques discussed earlier in this chapter. The plan also calls for learning more about the child, collaborating with all adults concerned in a coordinated response, improving the level of teacher-child relations, and enhancing opportunities for the child to experience success.

Comprehensive guidance includes some or all of the steps that follow. In many situations not all of the steps are necessary—such as the conference and written plan. In other situations, when informal application is not working, a formalized procedure may be needed, including a conference and development of an **Individual Guidance Plan** (IGP). The steps of comprehensive guidance follow:

1. *Build Relations With the Child and Family Prior to Crises.* From the beginning of the year the teacher develops relationships both with the child and family. Independent of crisis management, this knowledge helps the teacher understand the needs, interests, learning qualities, and response styles of the child. This information is invaluable should a child show strong needs mistaken behavior. There is no substitute for positive relations already formed in the event that comprehensive intervention becomes necessary.

2. *Use Crisis Intervention Techniques.* In the event of strong needs mistaken behavior, the teacher uses the crisis intervention techniques discussed in Part Three: describe-express-direct, commanding choices, cool-down time, physical restraint, conflict management, and guidance talks. One teacher, often the primary caregiver, may take charge in crisis situations, providing consistent limits, interventions, and follow-ups for the child.

3. *Obtain Additional Information.* The teacher seeks to understand the child's behavior and the child more fully. Incidents of mistaken behavior are charted against days of the week, times of the day, and the daily schedule. Actions for gaining more information include talks with the child, discussions with staff, and a conference with the family.

4. *Hold an Individual Guidance Plan (IGP) Meeting.* If the first three steps do not result in resolution of the problem, a meeting is held with parents,

An increasing practice is special education staff working alongside regular teachers in the classroom. Where staffing is adequate, inclusion allows service for many children with disabilities in the classroom.

teaching staff, and other relevant adults to develop an IGP. The team uses the problem-solving process outlined to develop the plan. In writing the IGP, the team uses forms such as the worksheet included in Appendix E. The team involves the child in the IGP or shares the plan with the child.

5. *Implement the Guidance Plan.* The team works together to put the IGP into operation. Consistent, nonpunitive crisis intervention is a part of the plan. A component of most plans is improvement of the relationships between the child and adults. Another is adaptation of the program to increase the child's opportunities for success. Referral for assessment by special education or other professionals may be part of the IGP. Counseling or other services may then be included. If special education services are warranted, an IEP may supersede the IGP.

6. *Monitor Guidance Plan.* The staff continues observations, reviews the plan, communicates with parents, and makes modifications as needed. If necessary, the staff holds follow-up IGP meetings.

Each of the following three case studies uses comprehensive guidance differently. In the first case study with Sherry the staff did not follow the formal six-step procedure, but did use a comprehensive approach that reflected the steps. In the second case study, the teachers used the IGP more formally, and the steps were followed. The third case study follows the steps, but a telephone call replaced a face-to-face meeting. These cases illustrate the flexibility of comprehensive guidance procedures. They also indicate the possibilities and complexities of using comprehensive guidance with young children and their families.

Case Study One: Individual Guidance Plan, Used Informally With Sherry, Age 4

Sherry had few friends at the Head Start center. She occasionally joined children in the housekeeping area, but stayed only for short periods before leaving to play by herself. Sometimes arguments precipitated her leaving; other times Sherry simply drifted off. The two teachers often had to coax her to stay on task during directed activities. Sherry got restless easily during large groups.

Sherry liked reading stories in small groups with a teacher. She also enjoyed small animal and people figures and engaged in extensive play with the figures. During September, Sherry's first month at the center, the teachers had to talk with her privately several times about putting the figures in her jacket pockets to take home. The teachers discussed the problem in a staff meeting. They agreed that the mistaken behavior was a symptom of a larger problem, and before confronting Sherry, they decided to try to learn more about her situation.

The teachers established that Sherry was the second youngest of nine children from a low-income family. One remembered from teaching an older brother that the father was a truck driver and was often away from home. The mother sometimes had seemed overwhelmed in the family situation and perhaps was a nonreader. The children often had to fend for themselves.

The two teachers met with the mother, as they tried to meet periodically with each child's parents. The staff did not directly discuss their main concern, the fact that Sherry was taking things home from the center. They believed that the parents would react punitively to this information. Instead, they used a compliment sandwich, mentioning that Sherry really seems to like reading, playing "house," and using miniature figures. They shared that they would like to see Sherry gain confidence in relating with other children because she tends to stay by herself. The teacher and mother discussed how the family could help Sherry gain confidence. The staff suggested that an older member of the family might begin reading to Sherry each day. The parent identified an older sister that Sherry was close to and said the sister could start the practice. The staff set up a system with the mother by which Sherry would take home a "special book" each day and return it the next.

The teachers commented that they also would begin to spend more individual time with Sherry, reading stories and having contact talks. They agreed the teacher would call the parent in two weeks to discuss Sherry's progress.

In a separate staff meeting, the teachers decided that one teacher would check Sherry's jacket at the end of each day. She would use guidance talks to reinforce that the figures are needed at the center, and compliment sandwiches to note Sherry's progress. One of the teachers hypothesized that Sherry might be taking things as a way of looking after herself, by "giving herself presents," as others didn't seem to give Sherry all the attention she needed.

Each day the staff informally noted how Sherry was doing and after a week agreed that she was building an attachment especially with one teacher. By two weeks, her "taking things" decreased, and Sherry seemed happier at the center. She shared with the teacher that her sister was reading her the books she took home, "and the other kids read 'em too." The teacher called the parent and expressed pleasure over the progress Sherry was making. The mother mentioned that she and her husband were trying to spend more time with the children; she commented that other children in addition to Sherry were enjoying the daily story time.

Case Study Two: More Formally Used Individual Guidance Plan with Gary, Age 5

The playground supervisor reported to Ms. Martin, Gary's kindergarten teacher, that Gary "had a real chip on his shoulder." The supervisor had noticed that on more than one occasion when Gary thought someone was teasing him, he charged and pushed the child down. In the classroom, Ms. Martin noticed that Gary became restless easily and would need to pace for a while before he could settle down. Ms. Martin also noticed that Gary shied away from any kind of physical contact. Gradually, Gary's reactions became more aggressive. On one occasion when Ms. Martin quietly asked him to resume his seat, Gary swept boxes off a shelf and sat under a table.

Ms. Martin began having daily contact talks with Gary. She used cooling-down times, but he reacted strongly to being removed. On two occasions she had to restrain him in the isolation location. She felt that he was distancing himself from her despite her efforts to be nonpunitive.

Ms. Martin took two actions. First, she asked a special education teacher to observe Gary. During the observation, Gary had no difficulties. The special education teacher said she would come back another time.

Second, Ms. Martin called Gary's mom. Ms. Martin had met Gary's mom at the class orientation, and the two had talked. Gary's mom had said she was a single parent who was working at a liquor store and going to a technical college part-time. In the telephone call, Ms. Martin explained that she respected Gary's independent spirit, but that he was having difficulty managing his emotions. She asked if there were anything Gary's mom could share that would help her in working with him. Gary's mom hesitated then said that when Gary was four, he had been abused by her past boyfriend. Ms. Martin asked if she and the special education teacher could meet with the mom. Though reluctant, the mother agreed.

The mom did not show up for the first meeting. Ms. Martin called again, and the mom said she had to complete a late assignment for a class. The meeting was rescheduled after Ms. Martin emphasized that the meeting would only be about helping Gary. The meeting was held. Because of the abuse factor, Ms. Martin had reported the telephone conversation to the principal. The school social worker determined from county Social Services that the abuse had been verified—it had been against both mother and child. At the meeting, the mother insisted that she did not want Gary to receive special education "testing" because she was afraid he would be labeled as disturbed. She said any informal support would be all right.

They agreed that a teacher aide would spend time with Gary each day. The mother was encouraged to seek counseling for her son through Social Services. The teacher would set up some "pace space" for Gary and a cubicle he could go to when he needed to be alone. The teacher suggested that when the aide was not present and Gary needed to, he could visit the special education teacher, who was just two doors down from the class. The teacher and aide would work on helping Gary express strong feelings more acceptably, steering him to open-ended activities and coaching him in self removal and the use of words.

The plan was put into place. Ms. Martin held a class meeting. She explained that sometimes children need special help to get along in school. She matter-of-factly mentioned that she and the aide would be working closely with Gary and sometimes they would do things differently with him. The teacher said that if the other children felt that they ever needed special help they should come and tell her; she would try to help them too. The children accepted the arrangement. Some of the children had been afraid of Gary, and the special assistance made sense to them.

Gary got so he liked both the teacher aide and the special education teacher. He developed enough trust in the teacher that he would come to her often when he was upset and verbally vent, which everyone thought was an improvement. He continued to pace and react violently at times when he felt threatened.

After two weeks, Gary stopped coming to school. The teacher tried to reach the mom by telephone, first at home, then at work and the college. She learned through the school social worker that Gary and his mom had suddenly left the community perhaps to escape from the boyfriend. Gary stayed on Ms. Martin's mind. One day after school a teacher called from another town. The teacher had Gary in her class, and the mom had told her she could call Ms. Martin for background. The two teachers kept in touch every week or so for the rest of the school year.

Case Study Three: Telephone-Based Individual Guidance Plan with Wade, Age 7

After a few weeks of second grade, Wade began to have difficulties. He was in three fights in a week and showed inattentiveness frequently during his studies. The teacher, Mr. Harper, had to remind him to stay on task, and his homework assignments—a new happening for Wade—often went undone.

Two of the three fights occurred in the classroom. The first happened just as Mr. Harper returned to the classroom from lunch. The teacher quickly intervened. He described what he saw, told the two children how he felt about it, and separated them for a cooling-down time. He talked with each child, and then the two of them together. Wade felt that another boy had taken his "GT Racer," and a fight had resulted. The situation was resolved after Wade found his GT car in his desk. Mr. Harper similarly used mediation with the other fight that occurred.

Mr. Harper observed Wade and noticed that while Wade excelled in reading, he was having a difficult time with written assignments. Mr. Harper noted that Wade became frustrated quickly if he made a simple error. Small muscle control, particularly in penmanship, seemed to be a problem. Mr. Harper started regular contact talks with Wade. The teacher learned that his older sister and brother teased him about "doing baby work" and "writing like a baby." From previous meetings with the parents, the teacher thought that his father might have inappropriately high standards for Wade as well. Because the source of Wade's unmet needs seemed to include his family, the teacher decided contact with the parents was important.

Wade's parents both worked, and setting up a meeting with them at the school proved difficult. Though not his preference, Mr. Harper decided to have a "two-part" meeting. Part one was with the student teacher and foster grandparent in Mr. Harper's class. Both shared concern about Wade's situation. They agreed that the foster grandparent and student teacher would have daily individual contact with Wade to improve his confidence and relations with him. At the student teacher's suggestion, the teacher agreed that they should do more open-ended art activities that didn't invite comparative attention to neatness. The team also came up with a few suggestions for Wade's parents.

Part two of the meeting was a telephone conversation with Wade's mom during her break at work. The teacher used a compliment sandwich, saying that Wade really liked reading and worked hard at tasks, but that lately he was showing quite a bit of frustration. Mr. Harper added that Wade seemed sensitive about his penmanship, and he was worried that some of Wade's assignments were not getting done for this reason.

Teacher and mom agreed that the family should be more encouraging toward Wade's written assignments. Mr. Harper suggested that new pencils with better erasers might help Wade to make corrections. Mr. Harper also mentioned the teaching team's ideas and got the mother's feedback about them. At the conclusion of the telephone call, the mother agreed that Mr. Harper would call back with a progress report and that she and her husband would come in for a follow-up meeting in three weeks.

Wade came to school with the new pencils. He and Mr. Harper had a guidance talk about how the teacher, the family, and Wade were all going to work together to make school go better for him. He mentioned that Bill, the foster grandparent, and Kendra, the student teacher, would each be visiting with Wade to see how things were going. Kendra especially gave Wade lots of encouragement about his writing skills. The teacher asked for new pictures to hang on the "kids art" bulletin board each week. Bill got

Teachers who use the guidance approach work to accept children
and view them nonjudgmentally.

Wade to volunteer his fall collage and his "whatever you like to do outside in the fall" picture.

Mr. Harper provided private encouragement to Wade about his written assignments. Instead of stickers on his papers, the teacher gave more specific feedback in the form of written compliment sandwiches. On occasion, Wade still expressed his frustration graphically, but he used words and there were no more fights. Mr. Harper called the mom and shared his progress. The mother stated that she was working on the rest of the family to be more encouraging of Wade's efforts.

In the follow-up meeting with the mother and father, Mr. Harper remarked about the progress that Wade had made. He explained to the parents that Wade had high standards and had convinced himself that he could not meet them. The teacher commented that Wade did not respond well to classroom criticism and that instead he needed encouragement to succeed. For the father, who was concerned about "spoiling the boy," the teacher showed Wade's portfolio with sample assignments from early in the year and the preceding day. Dad could see a difference, and grudgingly agreed that the "positive approach" should be continued. Mr. Harper left the meeting feeling that progress had been made.

IGP Afterthoughts

In these case studies, immediate intervention was given to address the mistaken behavior shown by each child. Beyond immediate intervention, however, the teachers recognized the mistaken behavior as symptomatic of larger problems in the children's lives. Comprehensive guidance intervention, used informally or formally, allowed the teachers to learn more about the child. Such information is crucial if the teacher is to build a relationship and alter the environment in ways that allow the child to overcome mistaken behavior and to grow. Involving family caregivers is a crucial part of developing and implementing the guidance plan. Notice that in all three case studies the teachers sensitively included the parents.

Teaching that uses comprehensive guidance can be difficult; it calls for teachers to go beyond their immediate feelings and reaction tendencies and to view children—and family situations—nonjudgmentally. Sometimes, as happened in Case Study Two, an IGP will not work out as a teacher would wish. We may not be able to change life circumstances for children, but in the time they are with us we can make their lives easier. The professional teacher does not win every battle, but learns as she tries and contributes to the life of the child, and sometimes the family, in the effort.

WHEN TEACHERS FEEL ANGER

Because teachers are human and cannot always accomplish what they want, they feel anger. The source of the anger may be the children themselves—a child who manipulates or harms others—or a group that too many times fails to live up to expectations. The source may be outside of immediate teacher-child transactions, such as a parent who does not follow through, a fellow staff member who does not agree, or a friend or family member who lets us down. In 1972, Ginott pointed out that teacher preparation programs rarely educate about anger and how to handle it—a shortcoming still widely true today.

The teacher of young children may feel particularly guilty about anger—because consistent nurturing is such an expected part of the role. Yet, teachers of young children no less than secondary teachers face anger within themselves. The issue is not feeling guilty about the reality of this emotion; the issue is how we manage the anger we feel.

Teachers generally can improve their management of anger through three steps:

1. monitoring feelings and making adjustments;
2. using safeguards when expressing anger;
3. practicing reconciliation.

Monitor Feelings; Make Adjustments

An effective anger management strategy begins before a crisis occurs. Teachers need to *self-monitor* moods and predispositions. For physical and emotional reasons, all teachers occasionally function at the "survival" level. Perhaps later in the 21st century, more teaching contracts will include adequate paid

A long-used coping strategy for down days is free time for children, outside when possible.

personal leave policies ("mental health days") to allow for this aspect of the human condition. In the meantime, teachers—both men and women—do well to prepare contingency plans for when they are emotionally or physically "down." The following coping strategies were suggested by participants in early childhood classes and workshops in the upper Midwest.

1. Aware of DAP guidelines about the use of videos, a kindergarten teacher only uses them for two special purposes: to tie the video directly into the curriculum or to provide emergency relief for the teacher. He talks regularly with the children about their favorite videos and for the second purpose has a few favorites on hand, using them only two or three times a year.

2. A third-grade teacher keeps a list of high-interest, largely self-directed activities to use when she is overtired or has a sinus headache and cannot take sick leave.

3. Three first-grade teachers have an agreement among themselves and with their rotating teacher aide that for "special occurrences," the aide spends more time in a particular classroom.

4. In several preschool programs, teachers and associates work as "teaching teams," rather than in sharply defined professional and paraprofessional roles. As needed, one or the other adult can assume more leadership on a particular day.

5. In both preschool and elementary school classrooms, on Level Three days one member of a teaching team asks another to work with a child who shows frequent mistaken behavior. (One

kindergarten teacher stated: "I have a good relationship with the special education teacher who works with three children in my room. Most days, I work fine with a particular 'active-alert' child. Once in a while, I rely on Jan to help with this child. We have become a real team.")

6. A first-grade teacher, on days when he is overly tired, intentionally soft-pedals expectations for two children in his class, whom he otherwise "might come down hard on." (On these days he also fights the teacher's occupational hazard of hoping one or both of these children won't be in school—and the guilty feelings connected to this wish.)

7. A principal from the province of Ontario has a policy in her school that if any teacher ever needs a break, she will stop what she is doing and take over the teacher's class. She says it took a while for teachers to ask, but now she gets a request every week or two. She states the teachers like this policy—and teachers from other schools have asked to transfer to hers.

8. Teachers in a particular school have a buddy system. The system was set up carefully to match teachers who get along. If a teacher feels that a day will be challenging, the two might talk for a while before the children arrive or go for a walk off school grounds during a break.

9. The most frequent comment of workshop participants is that they let children, even preschoolers, know how they are feeling. In classrooms where concern for the well-being of all is modeled by the teacher, children respond in kind. Even three-year-olds have been known to tiptoe and whisper, " 'cause teacher's not feeling good."

Ongoing problems that keep teachers from being at their best need attention. Just as it is important to understand the reasons for the behavior of children, it is also important for adults. Teaching is a difficult occupation. The teacher who seeks a friendly ear, counseling, or therapy to improve her work in the classroom is acting as a true professional.

Use Safeguards

By monitoring feelings and adjusting the program on Level Three days, the teacher reduces the risk of losing emotional control. But on *any* day, a teacher may become justifiably—or at least understandably—angry, even when teaching young children. Ginott provides guidance on the expression of anger (1972). His contention is that anger cannot always be controlled but that it can be managed. He states:

The realities of teaching—the overloaded classes, the endless demands, the sudden crises—make anger inevitable. Teachers need not apologize for their angry feelings. An effective teacher is neither a masochist nor a martyr. He does not play the role of a saint or act the part of an angel. . . .When angry, an enlightened teacher remains real. He describes what he sees, what he feels, what he expects. He attacks the problem, not the person. He knows that when angry, he is dealing with more elements than he can control. He protects himself and safeguards his students by using "I" messages. (pp. 72–73)

In his discussion, Ginott referred to the communication basic, "describe, express, and direct," introduced in Chapter Ten. This safeguard steers the teacher toward the problem, rather than the child's personality. If two children are fighting, the safeguard might well result in the comment: "You are hitting and not using words. I do not like what I see. You will separate and sit down. Then we will talk." The teacher backs up the words by establishing physical proximity and indicating where the children are to sit. As soon as feelings have "cooled," she and the children use mediation and/or guidance talk.

I messages express strong feelings relatively non-punitively and focus children on the teacher's concerns. Ginott discusses the use of *I* messages this way:

"I am annoyed," "I am appalled," "I am furious" are safer statements than "You are a pest," "Look what you have done," "You are so stupid," "Who do you think you are?". . .When Mrs. Brooks, the kindergarten teacher, saw five-year-old Alan throw a stone at his friend, she said loudly, "I saw it. I am indignant and dismayed. Stones are not for throwing at people. People are not for hurting." (p. 73)

Talking to the situation and not to the personality of the child is a most important safeguard. This "cardinal principle" pertains in many situations, but especially in the expression of anger. Ginott's contention is that when teachers express displeasure but still observe the safeguards that protect self-esteem, children listen. By using words effectively, teachers not only manage their anger, but model nonviolent self-expression and conflict-resolution much needed in society.

Practice Reconciliation

Teachers, like all of us, make mistakes. For this reason as the leaders of the classroom, when teachers overreact, they need to model reconciliation (Gartrell, 1997). Under normal circumstances, children are resilient and bounce back (Hendrick, 2001). They also forgive easily, more easily than most adults. Because teachers are important in their lives, children want to be on friendly terms with them.

Soon after a conflict, the teacher needs to reassure children that they are accepted for who they are and as members of the group. The importance of reestablishing relations is recalled by readers who can remember a conflict with a teacher when they were students. If on the following day, the teacher acted as if nothing had happened, the reader probably recalls a feeling of relief. If from that day on things never seemed the same, the year probably seemed a long one indeed.

After a cool-down time, reconciliation often occurs with the follow-up guidance talk.

Reconciliation is a matter of timing and inviting. No one is ready immediately after a confrontation to apologize and make amends. This is as true for children as it is for adults. Children may not be ready to reconcile with a teacher until they have had time to work through their feelings. After a cool-down time, reconciliation often occurs with the follow-up guidance talk. Children are ready to talk when they are not actively resisting the conversation. Sometimes, though, they will show reluctance, unsure of their standing with the teacher.

By the teacher's *inviting* reconciliation, children are more apt to oblige. The guidance techniques discussed in Chapter Eight, including reflective listening and the compliment sandwich, are important. With young children, apologies, and acceptance of apologies, are often expressed nonverbally. A hug says a lot, "Please forgive me" and "I forgive you" all at once.

R. J. was holding a door open for his first-grade class while they walked to another room for a special activity. He began swinging the door toward children as they passed, making believe he was closing it. As Kaye walked by, R. J. lost his grip and the door banged into her, knocking her down. After tending to Kaye, the teacher looked for R. J., but he had disappeared. She asked an aide to take the class into the room for the activity and, getting more upset by the minute, went to look for R. J. She found him in the furthest corner of their classroom, looking anxious.

Teacher: (Loudly) You banged the door on Kaye, and I am really upset about it.

R. J.: (Crying) I didn't mean to.

Teacher: (Surprised at his reaction) What can we do about it?

R. J.: Tell her I'm sorry?

Teacher: All right. Anything else?

Still crying, R. J. shakes his head no. The teacher decides not to pressure him. After helping R. J. feel better, she suggests that they join the group. When they sit down with the class, R. J. leans against the teacher. They both sit quietly for a short while. After the activity, R. J. apologizes to Kaye.

A difficult challenge for any teacher is when she has overreacted and crossed the boundary between firmness and harshness, between guidance and punishment. The frailty of our humanness means that this sometimes happens. Because the skills of expressing strong emotions acceptably and getting along with others take effort, even for experienced adults, teachers occasionally do express anger in ways that hurt.

Perhaps a first step in learning to recover from a bad episode is to recognize our feelings and forgive *ourselves.* Only then can we figure out how to make the best of the situation and to forgive the other. Thoughts in the middle of the night may be part of this healing process and talks with others important to us certainly are (Jersild, 1985). Children are forgiving and *need* us to be firm. If the undercurrent of our firmness is appreciation of the worth of each individual child, reconciliation offers the possibility of fuller understanding and more productive relations. As Ginott suggests in *Teacher and Child,* true reconciliation means change (1972). For professional teachers who care about young children, change means learning and growing.

WHEN TEACHERS AND PARENTS DISAGREE

At one time or another, teachers and parents will have differences in viewpoints about program priorities, program content, teaching style, behaviors of the parents' own children, or the actions of other children. Boutte et al. (1992), Galinsky (1988), Lightfoot (1978), and Powell (1989) make similar points about such differences: They need not become **negative dissonances** but can serve as **creative conflicts,** which retain the possibility of being solved (Lightfoot, 1978).

Lightfoot distinguishes between these terms by stating that *negative dissonance* is the result of differences that alienate the parent from the teacher. In such cases, the teacher typically asserts the power of the education institution over the parent, often on the basis of the parent's social or cultural background. Views, values, and communication styles of the parent are considered of lesser importance than those of the teacher, as an "official representative" of the school or center (Powell, 1989).

Creative conflicts arise from the diversity of life in a complex, pluralistic society in which the right of the individual to his own views is accepted (Lightfoot, 1978). The teacher who respects parents, whatever their background, realizes that differences in values or viewpoint need not terminate positive teacher-parent relations. The common ground of the child whose life they share makes differences an opportunity for creative communication, and possible resolution, not inevitably a point of division (Galinsky, 1988; Jacobs, 1992; Manning & Schindler, 1997).

Yet, the reality remains that some parents are difficult to communicate with, and many teachers feel underprepared for this part of the job (Boutte

At one time or another teachers and parents will have differences in viewpoints. (Courtesy of Richard Faulkner, Family Service Center, Kootasca Head Start, Grand Rapids, Minnesota)

et al., 1992; Jacobs, 1992). The tendency to support parents selectively, depending on the teacher's feelings toward them, leads to the "negative dissonance" that is important to avoid (Powell, 1989).

In the article, "Effective Techniques for Involving 'Difficult' Parents," Boutte et al. (1992) identify and provide suggestions for working with parents when conflicts arise. (See Recommended Resources.) Teachers who find that they are in disagreement with parents engage in the basic negotiation process discussed in Chapter Ten. Seven additional guidelines assist in a variety of situations when teachers and parents disagree.

1. *Encourage Mutual Respect.* Warren (1977) makes the case that parents who seem unworthy were children whose unmet needs have prevented them from a healthy adulthood. The teacher who does not let personal judgments get in the way of involving parents in their children's education understands the importance of Warren's words.

Parents from backgrounds different from the teacher's have legitimate points of pride and values that their children share. Remaining open to learning about customs and lifestyles new to the teacher conveys respect for the family and the child.

At the same time, the teacher can take pride in being a professional and need not be defensive about educational practice that she knows to be appropriate. Regardless of differences in age or experience, self-respect is a right of the early childhood teacher. As a professional, the teacher uses appropriate practice in relations with parents, no less than with children. Appropriate practice means an invitation to parents to become involved and to collaborate in the education process of the child (Boutte et al., 1992; Rogers, Andre, & Hawley, 1996).

2. *Model Reflective Listening.* When parents feel strongly to the point of anger or confrontation, the teacher needs to listen, allow them to cool off, and not dispute or "block out" what they say (Boutte et al., 1992). To ensure the parent that the teacher is listening, she repeats the substance of what the parent has said, the basic element in reflective listening. The teacher is flexible about accepting specifics in the argument, but stops personal abuse, redirecting communication to the point of the meeting. Use of parents' ideas when deciding on follow-up shows that listening was at work. As part of the listening process, reiterating that everyone wants what is best for the child is important. Invitation for another contact in the future communicates that the teacher is serious about having parents involved. Parents who know they are being listened to become more likely to listen in return (Rogers, Andre, & Hawley, 1996).

3. *Talk to Situations.* In conferences the teacher should have specific, objective information on hand about the child and the situation being discussed: observations, samples of the child's work, and written accounts of situations. The teacher describes events and does not judgmentally evaluate the child, the child's behaviors, or the child's family background. Citing a workshop she attended, Galinsky notes,

Honestly meant, open-ended questions make conversations with parents more friendly.

Certain statements tend to create distrust and worry rather than an alliance. For example: If a teacher says, "Is something going on at home?" the parent may feel accused. Instead, try, "Did Arthur have a hard time getting up to-day? He seems tired." (1988, p. 11)

Basic guidance communication techniques like compliment sandwiches highlight progress and pose problems constructively. Honestly meant, open-ended questions make conversations more friendly. A goal is to generate possible solutions to problems together, discussing the pros and cons of each (Rogers, Andre, & Hawley, 1996).

4. *Invite Continued Involvement.* For parents who are assertive, the teacher works to accommodate their perspectives. Positive strategies include: providing current literature to discuss later, encouraging attendance at parent meetings, and seeking active involvement in the classroom. Such measures give the parent a respectful opportunity to learn more about, and contribute to, the program. As Boutte et al. state:

> Parents usually will feel less alienated and will be more willing to participate if they are involved more in the decision making regarding their children. All parents should be allowed to contribute to the program in some significant way. (1992, p. 20)

In inviting continued involvement in the child's education, the teacher makes hypotheses about the level and type of involvement the parent may accept. She adjusts expectations as necessary to keep the communication going. The teacher who works around a point of difference and wins an ally has truly mastered the principle of "creative conflict" (Manning & Schindler, 1997).

5. *Communicate with Staff and Consulting Professionals.* When a teacher suspects a problem may arise with a family, and certainly if a problem occurs, she should discuss the situation with other staff (Rogers, Andre, & Hawley, 1996). The communication may range from asking for information from a colleague who knows a parent to discussing the matter with an administrator. Venting to trusted others may be important for the teacher's mental health, but communication about families needs to avoid the "teachers' lounge phenomenon" (gossip). Beyond fellow staff, a consulting professional can also be a valuable resource (Manning & Schindler, 1997). In the complex world of today, teachers need collaboration to extend their ability to assist children, and their parents, to learn and to grow.

6. *Switch to Mediation.* In some situations, negotiation with parents will not prove successful. In the event that productive communication grows impossible, the teacher takes the initiative to bring in a third party. The teacher may even realize this in the midst of a conference, in which case she terminates, the conference. A mediator makes it easier for all parties to understand and sets a process for rescheduling that the disagreement is not a "personal grudge" or a personality conflict. When emotions are high, the mediator can help teacher and parent focus on the facts and on a strategy for positive resolution (Koch & McDonough, 1999). Teachers sometimes feel that they are "failures" if they have to call on a third party. For the benefit of the child and relations with the family, this request is among the most professional a teacher can make.

7. *Collaborate for Safety.* When dealing with serious family situations, the teacher needs to collaborate with colleagues for another reason: her own safety. In some circumstances, such as suspected child abuse, the teacher

must by law report to authorities. In rare occasions a teacher may feel a need to assist in an emergency, such as a battering or a stalking situation. The teacher may feel vulnerable as a result of such acts.

The teacher is not a social worker, but is a member of a team of professionals helping the child and family. As soon as a problem appears more serious than the teacher handles in everyday duties, she needs to cease being the "point person" and collaborate with other staff and administration. Serious decisions regarding the health and safety of the child, or another member of a family served, must be made by a team led by a person trained in this area. Communication with the family at this point is to come *not* from the teacher, but from the appropriate team leader (Manning & Schindler, 1997).

Sometimes, in an effort to save a child from harm, the possible wrath of a family member must be risked. From the beginning of the school year, the teacher works with the family to prevent creative conflicts from becoming negative dissonances. In the event of a deteriorating situation, however, the teacher informs the principal or administrator and collaborates with others to prevent needlessly standing out and being affected by an action. Whenever a teacher begins in a new school or program, she needs to determine the policy for handling serious situations. The teacher should discuss the policy with all parents as part of a parent orientation or "greeting meeting." The teacher then follows the policy, gaining the assistance of other staff and administrators as necessary. When in doubt about a situation involving family members, collaborating with other staff is the key.

SUMMARY

1. What conditions make intervention necessary?

Three conditions make intervention necessary:

- Children cannot resolve a situation themselves and the situation is deteriorating;
- One or more children cause serious disruption to the education process;
- The danger of harm exists.

In these situations the teacher uses nonpunitive crisis management techniques in order to reestablish limits, mediate the conflict, and accomplish reconciliation.

2. What are three methods of crisis management?

Commanding cooperation is the method of first resort because it holds out the possibility of mediation to resolve the difficulty. Not an ultimatum, the teacher uses the method to encourage the child to mediate. When the child selects the "out-choice," the teacher follows up with guidance.

Separation is the crisis intervention method of second resort. If mediation seems impractical, the teacher may opt to redirect the child to a different location. If the child has lost control, the teacher uses a *cooling-down time*, as distinct from a time-out. After the child is calmed, the teacher follows up with conflict management and/or a guidance talk. With children who have difficulty managing their emotions, the adult may teach self-removal.

Physical restraint is the method of last resort. The passive bear hug communicates to the child that the teacher will reestablish limits. Physical restraint is exhausting but important to use with a child who has lost complete control. The adult self-checks the level of force used in the restraint and discusses the event with fellow staff.

3. What are strategies for working with Level Three strong needs mistaken behavior?

When working with children who show serious mistaken behavior, the teacher uses a comprehensive guidance. That may include an Individual Guidance Plan (IGP). Formally or informally, the comprehensive guidance strategy has some or all of the following steps:

- Develop relationships with the child and family;
- Use consistent guidance intervention techniques;
- Obtain additional information about the child;
- Hold an IGP meeting;
- Implement the guidance plan;
- Monitor the guidance plan.

The more serious the behavior, the more comprehensive the response, and often the more persons that need to be involved. Parents are central parties in the use of the IGP.

4. What techniques assist the teacher to manage personal feelings of anger?

An effective anger management strategy begins before a crisis occurs, as the teacher *self-monitors feelings* and *makes adjustments* in the program. Teachers do well to prepare contingency plans for when they are emotionally or physically "down" and are at risk for loss of control.

The teacher practices *safeguards* in the expression of anger. The teacher uses *I* messages that express feelings without humiliating others. She uses the describe-express-direct technique to address the problem without disparaging personality.

The teacher *practices reconciliation*. Teachers on occasion may overreact. Reconciliation initiated by the teacher testifies to the need of the professional to change and to grow, no less than the child.

5. What are considerations when teachers and parents disagree?

At one time or another, teachers and parents will have differences. The teacher works to avoid having those differences become divisive. *Negative dissonances* occur when the teacher asserts the authority of the institution over the parent. Such division happens most often when parents are of differing social or cultural circumstances than the teacher. Instead, the teacher uses strategies to keep positive relations with the parent because the goal of each is the same, the best interests of the child.

KEY CONCEPTS

Comprehensive guidance
Cooling-down time
Creative conflicts
Ecological perspective
Individual Guidance Plan
Labeling versus diagnosis
Negative dissonances
Physical restraint
Self-removal
Separation
Time-out

FOLLOW-UP ACTIVITIES

Note: An element of being a professional teacher is to respect the children, parents, and educators you are working with by maintaining confidentiality—keeping identities private. In completing follow-up activities, please respect the privacy of all concerned.

Discussion Activity

The discussion activity encourages students to interrelate their own thoughts and experiences with specific ideas from the chapter.

Identify a situation involving serious mistaken behavior shown by a child in a classroom you are familiar with. Referring to the chapter, what parts of the individual guidance plan approach did the teacher use in addressing the problem? What parts did the teacher not use? What would you do that is similar to what the teacher did to resolve the problem? What would you do that is different?

Application Activities

Application activities allow students to interrelate material from the text with real-life situations. The observations imply access to practicum experiences; the interviews, access to teachers or parents. Students may compare or contrast observations and interviews with referenced ideas from the chapter.

1. **When is intervention necessary?**
    a. Observe an instance when a teacher chose to intervene in a situation. How do the apparent reasons for the intervention correspond to the reasons for intervening presented in the chapter?
    b. Interview a teacher about the reasons she has for when to intervene. Compare the reasons with the reasons given in the chapter.

2. **Three methods of crisis management.**
   a. Observe an incident when a teacher intervened in a crisis. Were the methods the teacher used any of the three mentioned in the chapter? Why or why not? In what ways did the intervention help to resolve the crisis?
   b. Interview a teacher about how she uses separation. Ask about this crisis intervention method and other methods the teacher uses when children's emotions are running high. How are the teacher's views similar or different than the text?
3. **Strategies for Level Three mistaken behavior.**
   a. Discuss with a teacher how she worked with fellow staff, or other professionals, to help a child overcome Level Three (serious) mistaken behavior. Which steps of the comprehensive guidance were formally or informally followed? How was the child's family involved?
   b. Interview a teacher who worked successfully with a parent to help a child overcome Level Three mistaken behavior. Which steps of the strategy were formally or informally followed?
4. **Techniques for managing anger.**
   Talk with a teacher about the following:
   a. Adjustments they make on days when they are encountering physical or emotional difficulties.
   b. How they manage angry feelings toward a child or a situation.
   c. How they work for reconciliation after they have intervened in a crisis situation when feelings are high.
   How are the teacher's responses similar or different from each other? From the text?
5. **When teachers and parents disagree.**
   a. Interview a teacher about a time that she and a parent disagreed. Reminding of the importance of protecting identities, discuss how the teacher tried to resolve the disagreement. Did the teacher feel the effort was successful? Why or why not? What does the teacher think is important to successfully resolve a difference with a parent?
   b. Interview a parent you are comfortable with and who will give you open feedback. Reminding of the importance of protecting identities, talk about a time the parent disagreed with a teacher. Discuss whether the parent felt the disagreement got resolved successfully. Why or why not? What does the parent think a teacher should do to resolve a difference with a parent?

What You Can Do

IGP Case Study   Something important can be learned from doing your own case study of comprehensive guidance at work. Over a few days or visits to a classroom talk with a teacher about an ongoing situation involving a child who shows Level Three mistaken behaviors in the classroom. Safeguarding privacy, and working under the supervision of the teacher, use the steps in the Individual Guidance Plan as a format for learning about comprehensive guidance.

    a. *Establishing relations with parents.* Interview the teacher about her relations with the family caregiver(s). How does the teacher feel about efforts at building relations, beginning when the child started in the class?

    b. *Guidance intervention techniques.* Interview the teacher about and observe interventions with the child to prevent or resolve conflicts. How do the techniques used match ideas from the text?

    c. *Obtain additional information.* Under the supervision of the teacher find out what staff members have learned about the child. Observe the child, and if possible interview staff and parents. Summarize information gained.

    d. *Find out if a formal or informal IGP meeting has been held.* If so, determine as much as you can about the meeting and the strategies decided. If a meeting has not been held, work cooperatively with the teacher to determine if a formal or informal meeting might take place. Attend the meeting if possible. What were the results of the formal or informal IGP meeting?

    e. *Follow the implementation of the plan.* Talk with staff members as they implement the plan. To the extent possible observe interventions, relationship building, partnering with parents, and so on. Record, perhaps in journal form, your specific, objective observations.

    f. *Analyze what you learned from this experience about assisting young children who have problems to resolve those problems.* Compare your findings with the case study results from the text.

RECOMMENDED READINGS

Betz, C. (1994). Beyond time out: Tips from a teacher. *Young Children, 49*(3), 10–14.

Boutte, G. S., Keepler, D. L., Tyler, V. S. & Terry, B. Z. (1992). Effective techniques for involving 'difficult' parents. *Young Children, 47*(3), 19–24.

Curry, N. E., & Arnaud, S. H. (1995). Personality difficulties in preschool children as revealed through play themes and styles. *Young Children, 50*(4), 4–9.

Heath, H. E. (1994). Dealing with difficult behaviors—Teachers plan with parents. *Young Children, 49*(5), 20–24.

Jacobs, N. L. (1992). Unhappy endings. *Young Children, 47*(3), 23–27.

Manning, D., & Schindler, P. J. (1997). Communicating with parents when their children have difficulties. *Young Children, 52*(5), 27–33.

McCormick, L., & Feeney, S. (1995). Modifying and expanding activities for children with disabilities. *Young Children, 50*(4), 10–17.

McDermott Murphey, D. (1997). Parent and teacher plan for the child. *Young Children 52*(4), 32–36.

Schreiber, M. E. (1999). Time-outs for toddlers: Is our purpose punishment or education? *Young children 54*(4) 22–25.

REFERENCES

Betz, C. (1994). Beyond time out: Tips from a teacher. *Young Children, 49*(3), 10–14.

Boutte, G. S., Keepler, D. L., Tyler, V. S., & Terry, B. Z. (1992). Effective techniques for involving 'difficult' parents. *Young Children, 47*(3), 19–24.

Boyer, E. (1992). *Ready to learn.* Princeton, NJ: Carnegie Foundation for the Advancement of Teaching.

Brewer, J. A. (2001). *Introduction to early childhood education: Preschool through primary years.* Boston: Allyn & Bacon.

Bronson, M. B. (2000). Recognizing and supporting the development of self-regulation in young children. *Young Children, 55*(2), 32–37.

Carlsson-Paige, N., & Levin, D. E. (1992). Making peace in violent times: A constructivist approach to conflict resolution. *Young Children, 48*(1), 4–13.

Chalfant, J., Pysh, M., & Moultrie, R. (1979). Teacher assistance teams: A model for within building problem-solving. *Learning Disabilities Quarterly, 2*(3), 85–96.

Cherry, C. (1983). *Please don't sit on the kids.* Belmont, CA: David S. Lake Publishers.

Clewett, A. S. (1988). Guidance and discipline: Teaching young children appropriate behavior. *Young Children, 43*(4), 25–36.

CPI (Crisis Prevention Institute). (1994). *Managing the crisis moment* (catalog). Brookfield, WI: National Crisis Prevention Institute.

Curry, N. E., & Arnaud, S. H. (1995). Personality difficulties in preschool children as revealed through play themes and styles. *Young Children, 50*(4), 4–9.

Dreikurs, T. (1972). *Discipline without tears.* New York: Hawthorn Books, Inc.

Galinsky, E. (1988). Parents and teacher-caregivers: Sources of tension, sources of support. *Young Children, 43*(3), 4–12.

Gartrell, D. (1997, September). Beyond discipline to guidance. *Young Children, 52*(6) 27–34.

Gartrell, D. (2000). *What the kids said today.* St. Paul, MN: Redleaf Press.

Gartrell, D. J. (2001). Replacing time-out part 1: Using guidance to build an encouraging classroom. *Young Children, 56*(6), 8–16.

Gartrell, D. J. (2002). Replacing time out part 2: Using guidance to maintain an encouraging classroom. *Young Children, 57*(2).

Ginott, H. (1972). *Teacher and child.* New York: Avon Books.

Gootman, M. (1993). Reaching and teaching abused children. *Childhood Education 70*(1), 15–19.

Greenberg, P. O. (1988). Ideas that work with young children: Avoiding 'me against you' discipline. *Young Children, 44*(1), 24–29.

Heath, H. E. (1994). Dealing with difficult behaviors—Teachers plan with parents. *Young Children, 49*(5), 20–24.

Hendrick, J. (2001). *The whole child.* Columbus, OH: Merrill Publishing Company.

Honig, A. S. (1986). Research in review: Stress and coping in children. In J. B. McCracken (Ed.), *Reducing stress in young children's lives.* Washington, DC: National Association for the Education of Young Children.

Jacobs, N. L. (1992). Unhappy endings. *Young Children, 47*(3), 23–27.

Jersild, A. S. (1985). *When teachers face themselves.* New York: Columbia University Press.

Katz, L. (1984). The professional early childhood teacher. *Young Children, 39*(5) 3–10.

Koch, P. K., & McDonough, M. (1999). Improving parent-teacher conferences through collaborative conversations. *Young Children, 54*(2), 11–15.

Lightfoot, S. L. (1978). *Worlds apart: Relationships between families and schools.* New York: Basic.

Lombardi, J. (1990). Head Start: The nation's pride, a nation's challenge. *Young Children, 45*(6), 22–29.

Manning, D., & Schindler, P. J. (1997). Communicating with parents when their children have difficulties. *Young Children, 52*(5), 27–33.

Marion, M. (1999). *Guidance of young children.* Columbus, OH: Merrill Publishing.

McCormick L., & Feeney, S. (1995). Modifying and expanding activities for children with disabilities. *Young Children, 50*(4), 10–17.

Moore, S., & Kilmer, S. (1973). *Contemporary preschool education.* New York: John Wiley and Sons.

Piaget, J. (1960). *The moral judgment of the child.* Glencoe, IL: The Free Press.

Powell, D. R. (1989). *Families and early childhood programs.* Washington, DC: National Association for the Education of Young Children.

Reynolds, E. (1996). *Guiding young children: A child-centered approach.* Mountain View, CA: Mayfield Publishing.

Rogers, R. E., Andre, L. C., & Hawley, M. K. (1996). *Parents and teachers as partners: Issues and challenges.* Fort Worth, TX: Houghton Mifflin.

Schreiber, M. E. (1999). Time-outs for toddlers: Is our goal punishment or education? *Young Children, 54*(4) 22–25.

Slaby, R. G., Roedell, W. C., Arezzo, D., & Hendrix, K. (1995). *Early violence prevention.* Washington, DC: National Association for the Education of Young People.

Surgeon General (1999). *Surgeon General's report on mental health.* Washington, DC: Department of Health and Human Services.

Warren, R. M. (1977). *Caring.* Washington, DC: National Association for the Education of Young Children.

Wittmer, D. S., & Honig, A. S. (1994). Encouraging positive social development in young children. *Young Children, 49*(5), 4–12.

For additional information on using the guidance approach in the classroom, visit our Web site at http://www.earlychilded.delmar.com

CHAPTER TWELVE

LIBERATION TEACHING: A GUIDANCE RESPONSE TO VIOLENCE IN SOCIETY

GUIDING QUESTIONS

- How are children in the classroom affected by violence in society?
- How is liberation teaching a response to societal violence?
- What is the liberation teaching response to bullying?
- What is the connection between liberation teaching and other education practices?
- How does liberation teaching apply to relations with parents?

C ompared with the Western European democracies, Canada, and Japan, ours is an exceedingly violent society (Surgeon General's Report, 1999). Either through direct victimization or indirect media exposure, few children escape societal violence. Writers who believe that our education system must respond to violence generally agree on these facts: (1) Social conflicts—disagreements, disputes—happen all the time; they are part of life for children and adults. (2) Popular culture glorifies violence in ways that make civil problem solving difficult to teach and learn. (3) Some children, touched deeply by violence, are affected for their whole lives—unless they experience comprehensive intervention while they are young. (4) If we as a society are to increase our capacity to resolve conflicts peacefully, we need to educate children toward this end, beginning while they are young, in the home and in school (Carlsson-Paige & Levin, 1992; Girard & Koch, 1996; Kreidler, 1984; Levin, 1994; Slaby et al., 1995; Surgeon General's Report, 1999).

Violence in society is a significant cause of classroom mistaken behavior. This statement becomes more clear if we take a broad definition of violence, to include acts of neglect and aggression that result in arousal of stress with attendant emotions of anxiety, anger, fear, and confusion. Violence results in debasement of the child's self-concept and impairment of healthy brain development. Implied is the assertion of will by a more powerful individual against a less powerful individual, without regard for physical and psychological well-being. These conditions occur in degree depending on whether the exposure to violence is direct or indirect and on the ability of the individual child to cope. Even with "mild" exposure children's behavior is affected in the classroom. For society to become more peaceful, a paradigm shift is necessary in how we look at education. Teaching for emotional development—stressing resiliency, interpersonal and intrapersonal intelligence, character education, democratic life skills—whatever terms one is comfortable with—is becoming at least as important as scores on standardized tests. Yet, this change will only occur as families demand it, and much parent education about violence has yet to happen.

Chapter Twelve looks at violence in society, its effects on children in the classroom, and the guidance response to violence: liberation teaching. **Liberation teaching** (activist teaching much like anti-bias education) is the pivital concept of the chapter. In particular, liberation teaching is discussed as a response to the "hot discipline topic", "bullying." The concept's relationships to other teaching practices—guidance in the encouraging classroom, anti-bias education, and peace education—are also explored. Liberation teaching, as a guideline for relations with parents, concludes the chapter.

THE VIOLENCE PYRAMID

Most children experience violence vicariously through television and also through related recreational activities. On average, American children between the ages of three and six view four hours of television each day, often including a diet of violent cartoon shows (Levin, 1994). By age 18, they will have watched the equivalent of seven years of TV, exclusive of videotapes and video games (Levin, 1994). Between the ages of 5 and 15, children typically will have viewed in excess of 13,000 TV murders (Carlsson-Paige & Levin, 1992).

Although parents often believe they are screening what their children watch, a large portion of shows, videotapes, and video games that children are exposed to are actually designed for older viewers. In addition, toys and books based on action figures, as well as generic play weapons, flood the market for children to read and play with along with the television and computer screen. As they get older, children become aware as well of popular youth culture and the violence attendant to it (Carlsson-Paige & Levin, 1992).

Most children in the society experience violence at least indirectly by exposure to these sources. Through her construct, the **continuum of violence in children's lives** (Figure 12–1), Levin points out that smaller numbers of children have more direct and intense exposure to violence. For instance, children from low-income situations tend to view more television than their middle-income counterparts (Levin, 1994) and experience more direct violence in the neighborhood (Carlsson-Paige & Levin, 1992). Some children at all income levels are exposed to violence in the home. Levin comments:

> The more frequent, varied, and extreme the violence children experience, the more likely their ideas and behavior will be affected by that violence, and the more help they will need from adults in working through the harmful effects of that violence in learning how to be nonviolent themselves. (p. 15)

With a still developing ability to understand, young children face conflicting messages about violence, experiencing it through television at the same time as receiving contradictory messages from adults: "don't hit," "play nice," "stand up for yourself" (Levin, 1994). Pirtle (1997) points out that along with the increase in television viewing, parents are having young children participate more in formal, organized activities such as team sports, gymnastics, and music lessons. Less time is available for the informal, unstructured neighborhood play that in the past has been instrumental in helping children to learn social problem-solving abilities (Pirtle, 1997). Unless taught otherwise by adults, children today easily acquire "unrealistic and superficial beliefs" about violence as the way to handle conflicts (Slaby et al., 1995).

For children to learn democratic life skills, they need a coordinated, encouraging learning environment and specific, positive teaching. While this instruction needs to happen in the home, through the encouraging classroom teachers too have an important role in it. New educational programs such as *Linking Up* (Pirtle, 1997) are designed to help educators use the expressive arts to assist children in developing positive social skills. Literature, music, movement, art, and creative drama are useful instructional tools for educating about feelings, cooperation, and problem solving.

Effects of Violence in the Classroom

At the top of Levin's continuum of violence, the child is a victim of direct acts of violence—physical and emotional. (Such victimization happens as well by witnessing violence done to others.) Lower on the pyramid, the

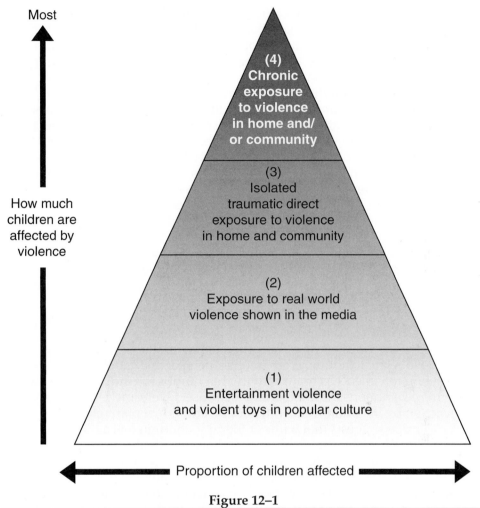

Most

How much
children are
affected by
violence

(4)
Chronic
exposure
to violence
in home and/
or community

(3)
Isolated
traumatic direct
exposure to violence
in home and community

(2)
Exposure to real world
violence shown in the media

(1)
Entertainment violence
and violent toys in popular culture

◄── Proportion of children affected ──►

Figure 12–1

The Continuum of Violence in Children's Lives

Reprinted with permission from *Teaching Young Children in Violent Times,* by Diane E. Levin ©
1994. Published by Educators for Social Responsibility. For more information call 1-800-370-2515.

child is exposed to indirect "background" violence, largely through media
and violent toys. Yet, how does exposure to violence, apparently so widespread, show itself in the classroom? Behavior for any individual is the
complex product of development, personality (including disposition), past
experiences, and perceptions of present circumstances. To conclude that a
mistaken behavior is due to societal violence, an adult needs to know the
child and the child's circumstances very well.

   There are patterns of classroom mistaken behavior, however, that are
more likely to occur when violence is present in a child's life (Lowenthal,
1999). In fact, the effects of violence are seen in children's behavior every day

in early childhood classrooms. Violence in all of its forms is perhaps the major cause of serious mistaken behavior. The effects especially of direct violence (affecting children at the top of the pyramid) are striking. In a recent review of the literature, Lowenthal (1999) provides a graphic summary:

- **Difficulty in managing emotions.** Past experiences may overwhelm the child's ability to handle emotions, especially those associated with traumatic events. For these children, gaining a measure of self-regulation—learning to manage anger—is an important first step in learning democratic life skills. At times, one-on-one assistance becomes necessary. Such programs as "worry teachers" and "comfort corners" address these situations.
- **Avoidance of intimacy.** Loss of trust causes children to view intimate relationships as increasing their vulnerability and lack of control. "To avoid intimacy, children may withdraw, avoid eye contact, be hyperactive, or exhibit inappropriate behaviors" (Lowenthal, 1999). A motivation for mistaken behaviors, then, may be to avoid forming close relationships, which in the past the child has found unreliable and profoundly painful.
- **Provocative behaviors.** Violent reactions may be the main form of adult attention the child has known. For these kids, provoking negative reactions becomes a learned behavior. It is how they have come to relate to adults. From another perspective, a defensive reaction to violence is brain activity that numbs the individual to the extreme emotions these experiences arouse. Over time this defensive reaction by the brain wears off, and the emotional pain returns. Lowenthal suggests that without therapy, children feel a human need to again numb themselves. By acting "provocatively and aggressively," children seek to produce the extreme reactions that cause renewal of the "self-anesthetizing" process. (Later drug use may serve the same purpose.) For early teachers who use guidance, these understandings bring new meaning to the need to "keep your cool."
- **Disturbances in the attachment process.** The attachment process is the long-term bond that forms between a child and primary caregivers. Abuse and neglect make attachment difficult, due to children's feelings of mistrust, unworthiness, anger, and anxiety. These feelings may cause children to become hostile toward adults who genuinely wish to build positive attachments. Building attachments under such circumstances becomes a challenging but essential task.
- **Effects on cognition and learning.** Over time violent experiences cause children's emotion-based brain reactions to overwhelm cognitive processes. Mental functions involved in learning become more difficult (LeDoux, 1996). At the same time, self-perceptions tell the child that she is incapable of learning and unworthy of teacher assistance, lowering motivation levels. "On average, abused, maltreated, or neglected chidden score lower on cognitive measures and demon-

strate poorer school achievement compared to their non-abused peers of similar socioeconomic backgrounds" (Lowenthal, p. 206).

This list of reactions to violence is daunting indeed. Gootman (1993) agrees with Jackson (1997) that teachers must step forward and be *enlightened witnesses* for children who have experienced violence. Teachers who are enlightened witnesses affirm the goodness within each child and that the child is not to blame for the violence experienced (Gootman, 1993). Such teachers work to build positive attachments and make the classroom a trustworthy place where learning can happen. By encouraging **resiliency**—personal strength that promotes self-healing—they practice **liberation teaching.**

Assessing the Effects of Violence, by the Levels

Using the three levels of mistaken behavior as guideposts, the following classroom behaviors are typical of children who have been affected by violent experiences. Applying Levin's pyramid concept, note that mistaken behaviors at Levels One and Two are more common in children who have experienced indirect "background violence." Level Three mistaken behaviors are typical of children directly victimized by violence in the home or community. Included are brief considerations for interpreting these mistaken behaviors.

Level One: Experimentation Mistaken Behavior   The following behaviors are Level One if they are shown once in a while by a child, but not on a repeated, emotionally "driven" basis: A child makes play guns and weapons out of "nonviolent" materials such as blocks, Lincoln logs, Legos, and so on. A child draws pictures with violent themes. A child initiates *rough-and-tumble play*—perhaps linked to superheroes—such as wrestling, chase, and "guns" (Boyatzis, 1997). A child "plays rough" with puppets, dolls, and miniature figures. A child is surprisingly competitive in play situations. (These behaviors become mistaken, of course, only when they threaten harm or serious disruption in the class.)

Considerations: Jackson indicates that part of the human condition is to fear and to desire mastery of that fear (1997). In the relatively powerless position of childhood, children imagine themselves less vulnerable and more powerful through play that involves make-believe. Children often use art, individual dramatic play with figures for this purpose.

"Action" (rough-and-tumble) play also helps accomplish this goal. At the same time, action play actually may assist children to build friendships, establish dominance patterns (which can actually reduce conflict by defining power structures within a group), and facilitate social skills—such as interpreting one's own and others' emotions (Boyatzis, 1997). A child who makes a situation competitive and "wins" asserts personal power. Children at Level One are showing reactions to violence experiences that may be worrisome to them but are not overwhelming.

Level Two: Socially Influenced Mistaken Behavior   Societal violence sometimes shows in children who are *influenced by others* to engage in rough-and-tumble play and "mischief." Superhero play, in which children identify with action heroes and play more roughly than they would otherwise, is a variation of rough-and-tumble play (Boyatzis, 1997). Another example of socially influenced mistaken behavior is the stigmatization of other children—excluding from play, calling names, bullying—done by members of an "in" group. Children who stigmatize others often have learned this behavior by being stigmatized themselves.

Considerations: Unless the teacher can create a spirit in the classroom where mutual affirmation is ongoing, some children are likely to assert their power by affiliating with others in mistaken power acts. When stigma occurs, direct violence is happening in the classroom, and the teacher must show firm leadership—often by class meetings, ethics instruction, and conflict management (Gootman, 1993). Teachers also need to actively support children who are particularly vulnerable for stigma, often because of differing appearances or abilities.

Level Three: Strong Needs Mistaken Behavior   A major cause of Level Three mistaken behavior is direct violence experienced by a child. The harm may be physical, psychological, or both. When the emotional motivation for a behavior is intense and continues over time, any of the types of mistaken behavior mentioned previously can be an indication of strong unmet needs and so be Level Three. Examples are violent pictures drawn repeatedly, rough-and-tumble play that often becomes aggressive, bullying that is continuing and severe. Other common indicators are children who repeatedly lose emotional balance, try to harm others, influence others to serious acts, continually withdraw from situations and relationships or show marked anxiety (Gootman, 1993).

Considerations: Our goal with children who are the victims of violence is to help them build resiliency. A first step in this process is to establish an attachment with the child in order to help her find trust in the classroom environment (Gootman, 1993). Interventions must be firm but friendly to retain the child's sense of trust. A child who has experienced violence may have lost any ability to define and meet limits. When we enforce limits nonpunitively, the child eventually will appreciate the safety that our limits provide. Children who show Level Three behaviors require comprehensive guidance strategies (discussed in Chapter Eleven) that involve teachers, family members, and often other professionals (Gootman, 1993). Liberation teaching occurs in the active support, encouragement, and guidance of all children showing vulnerabilities in the classroom, but especially children showing Level Three mistaken behavior.

LIBERATION TEACHING: THE GUIDANCE RESPONSE

In the "olden days" of teacher preparation, an instructor sometimes told education majors: "You can divide any class into three groups. The top third will learn even if they are not taught. The middle third will learn if they are well taught. The bottom third will not learn however they are taught." Today, this callous view of education is rejected by early childhood teachers.

Liberation teaching means that the teacher does not give up on any child. In Ginott's terms, the teacher who practices liberation teaching sees children beyond the frailties they may show (1972). The methodology of liberating teachers is developmentally appropriate, culturally responsive, and guidance-oriented. The teacher realizes that the child is an extension of the family system and works with the family to benefit the child. Much like what anti-bias teaching is to multicultural education, liberation teaching is the activist application of guidance principles.

As introduced in Chapter Four, liberation teaching has its roots in the social psychology of the 1960s and 1970s. The term derives from such disparate sources as liberal Catholic theology and the writings of Faber and Mazlich (1974). Maslow (1962) provides a useful dynamic for the concept in his statement that all individuals have two sets of needs, one for safety and one for growth. To the extent that children feel that safety needs— security, belonging, self-esteem—are unmet, they are likely to feel stress and exhibit mistaken behavior. Personal development then becomes difficult. Unmet needs can be caused or aggravated in the classroom. In Maslow's terms liberation teaching is assisting the child to meet safety needs and empowering the child toward growth. Liberation teaching means extending the encouraging classroom environment to each and every child.

The work of other psychologists also applies to the liberation concept. In Piaget's terms liberation teaching is teaching for autonomy (Kamii, 1984; Piaget, 1960). In Elkind's refinement of Erikson's work, liberation teaching empowers the child to move away from shame, doubt, and inferiority toward initiative, belonging, and industry (1989). For Harlow, cited in Chapter Three, liberation teaching is assisting the child to rise from the social relations of survival and adjustment toward encountering. In the guidance theory of this text, children benefiting from liberation teaching show significant gains in the ability to understand, develop, and use democratic life skills.

Specific to the issue of violence, liberation teaching assists children to find the inner resources for resiliency—to begin a healing process. The challenge to the teacher in nurturing resilience lies in the harm done to these children by the effects of violence.

Stigma Versus Liberation

A form of psychological violence, **stigma** happens when a leader or group members act in a way that prevents another individual from full group participation. In the classroom stigma occurs in two ways. The first way is when a teacher fixates on a vulnerability of a child and separates the child from the group. The separation at times may be physical (such as timeouts), but at the source is psychological, first in the mind of the teacher, and then, by social influence, in the minds of the class (Goffman, 1963). The children are influenced by the teacher to show a Level Two mistaken behavior toward the excluded child.

The second way is if some members of the class fixate on a child's vulnerability and exclude the child from full membership. (There are many names for this event: oppression, rejection, exclusion, stigmatization, bullying.) In this case the teacher may ignore the act of stigma, fail to notice it, or even contribute to it. Either way that stigma happens, psychological violence has found its way into the classroom. The child feels debasement of the self-concept and confusion in relation to social identity. Unless helped by a teacher, the child may experience a life at school that is marked by frustration and failure. It is from this dynamic that the victim of violence may become violent in later years (Nansel et al., 2001).

Children most at-risk for stigma are those who show frequent mistaken behavior. These are the children who need a positive relationship with the teacher the most, but often are the most difficult for the teacher to like and accept. There is an irony here. Young children at Level Three are already victims of difficult if not violent life circumstances. Through the mistaken behavior they show in the classroom they are vulnerable to further victimization by the teacher and/or peers' act of stigma.

While mistaken behavior is a primary cause of stigma, children come into the classroom vulnerable for other reasons. (These are noted here because a child who experiences stigma for any reason experiences classroom violence.)

1. *Personality qualities.* Children with unique temperaments, learning capacities, learning styles, verbal abilities, and attention needs can be a bother and difficult for some group members to accept.

2. *Disabilities.* Children having disabilities still pose challenges for those peers and teachers who find human differences uncomfortable. The kinds of disabilities some children face have grown in recent years. In addition to the "established disabilities" such as cerebral palsy, developmental delays, and sensory impairment, some children suffer from more recently identified disabilities such as attention deficit-hyperactive disorder and fetal alcohol syndrome, and less commonly recognized conditions such as allergies and frail health syndrome. Children who are HIV positive or have AIDS are most vulnerable for stigma.

3. *Physical factors.* Children who are of differing racial characteristics, of unusual facial appearance, short or tall, underweight or overweight, or unclean may cause some to feel a "discomfort of association." Gender differences may constitute a common source of stigma in some early childhood classrooms.

4. *Social factors.* Children from family backgrounds different from the norm in terms of income, religion, family structure, child-rearing priorities, parent careers, or family lifestyles may make children vulnerable for stigma. Typically in early childhood, adults before children would distance themselves from a child of differing social background. Examples are a family whose religious preferences are markedly different from a teacher's, a family that has a member who is a prominent citizen, or a family of mixed-race parents, same sex parents, or a caregiver who is not a parent.

5. *Cultural factors.* Children are vulnerable for stigma if they are from cultural and ethnic backgrounds that may be emotionally charged for teachers or classmates. An example would be children of Mexican families who have come to a midwestern town to work in a meatpacking factory, and are perceived as a threat to local workers.

Whatever the child's behavior patterns, personality, physical condition, social background, or cultural heritage, stigmatizing responses in the classroom aggravate a child's need for safety, undermine the possibility of growth, and increase the likelihood of mistaken behavior.

Teacher Behaviors that Stigmatize   Stigmatizing behaviors by a teacher can be intentional or unintentional. Stigmatizing behaviors are those which:

- fixate on a vulnerability as a limiting factor in the child's development;
- establish psychological distance between the teacher and the child;
- tolerate or tacitly encourage stigmatizing responses by other children or adults;
- fail to alter the physical or social environment to include the child;
- stress competition and establish patterns of winning and losing (winners and losers) in the group;
- show preference for some in the class over others on the basis of social, cultural, academic, or behavioral criteria;
- ignore or disparage the background, lifestyle, and language of the family of a child;
- use forms of discipline that punish and fail to teach conflict resolution skills.

Teachers are apt to show stigmatizing behaviors especially if they feel marginal acceptance in the teaching situation. When support is inadequate, teachers are likely to find reasons that children do not "perform." If the reason is "the child's fault" or "the family's," then the teacher is "not to blame." Administration sensitivity to the difficulty of the job is an essential first step in assisting the teacher to overcome tendencies toward stigma. Support systems for teachers are important.

Liberating Responses   With the practice of liberation teaching, the teacher helps each child to feel accepted as a welcome member of the group. Supported through the encouraging classroom—children come to accept perceived vulnerabilities as a part of—but not dominating their identities. With acceptance assured through positive teaching, children become more understanding of the human qualities of others (Greenberg, 1992; Honig & Wittmer, 1996).

Liberating responses also can be unintentional or intentional. Liberating responses:

- show clear acceptance of the child as a worthwhile individual and member of the group;
- empower the child's abilities;

One way to encourage the acceptance of differing human qualities
is through the use of puppets.

- educate both the child and the class away from rejecting responses
  and toward accepting responses;
- adapt the physical and social environment so that all are included;
- facilitate cooperative and individual activities so that each child
  can experience success;
- appreciate the child's family background;
- sensitively incorporate elements of the child's family background
  and language into the program;
- use forms of discipline that guide rather than punish and that teach
  conflict management skills;
- help the class understand and cope with challenging behaviors
  from the child.

The teacher is effectively using liberation teaching when differing human
qualities do not polarize the class, but instead they become opportunities
for personal affirmation and mutual enrichment. The classrooms of liberating teachers are encouraging, caring communities.

Liberation Teaching and Resiliency

In an important article on *resiliency mentoring*, Weinreb (1997) makes a statement similar to Levin's about the effects of violence:

> When children are faced with multiple issues such as family violence and
> substance abuse, compounded by the risks of living in poverty, they are more
> likely to be adversely affected; these issues intensify each other. (p. 14)

In such children, factors of post-traumatic stress syndrome, suppressed conscience, and violence as modeled behavior combine to make the child susceptible to Level Three mistaken behavior and for stigma. In the face of this bleak prospect both for the child and the teacher, Weinreb (1997) reports consistent findings that some children "exposed to various forms of adversity grow up to enjoy productive, normal lives, even though some may suffer silent anguish and emotional wounds in some area of their lives." These children are considered *resilient*, in the definition of Werner and Smith, possessing "the capacity to cope effectively with vulnerabilities" (Weinreb, 1997).

Three dynamics that promote resiliency seem to be personality factors in the child, characteristics of the family, and the social environment. Liberating teachers contribute to resiliency in relation to all three of these dynamics. Weinreb (1997) mentions that self-esteem and the ability to find meaning in activities and hobbies are two important personal characteristics that help children surmount adversity. In the encouraging classroom, the teacher empowers the child at risk for Level Three mistaken behaviors to experience success in classroom transactions.

Despite even the situation when a teacher builds positive relations with a child, he alone cannot turn around a child's life circumstances. This is a factor of discouragement and even despair for many early childhood teachers (Weinreb, 1997).

> Sharon, a student teacher, developed a positive attachment with a child who previously had been unable to connect with other adults in the classroom. At the teacher's suggestion, Sharon spent contact time with Tyrell on a daily basis. After just a few days, the boy began to seek Sharon out and sit by her so she could recognize his accomplishments. On a Friday afternoon as dismissal approached, Tyrell unexpectedly hugged Sharon's leg and cried for her to take him home. Over the next few days, this behavior repeated itself. Sharon was bothered by the unknown circumstances that would cause Tyrell to express this need so strongly. She talked with the teacher and the principal about the child. Her student teaching ended a short time thereafter, but Sharon says Tyrell is not a child she will soon forget. She has kept in touch with her cooperating teacher since and always asks about him.

Teachers cannot become substitute parents or social workers for the children in their classrooms, but they can do their best in the classroom and work with others, including the parent as much as possible, to make home circumstances safe and secure. As schools and centers work more closely with other community resources such as neighbors and religious and community leaders, the social environments of children at risk can be significantly improved.

A teacher's leadership can help a child overcome his vulnerabilities.

Weinreb (1997) comments that teachers: "Need to collaborate, cooperate and acquaint ourselves with other community efforts. Such collaboration, whether informal or formal, supports families, is cost-effective, and prevents burnout in teachers" (p. 18).

In a review of research about teachers' interactions with children, Kontos and Wilcox-Herzog (1997) conclude that "children exhibit higher levels of stress when teachers are harsh, critical and detached" (p. 11). In contrast, when teachers develop positive attachments with children, through sensitivity to their needs and consistent positive interaction with them, children's development, including socioemotional development, is enhanced. This finding dovetails with that of Weinreb (1997) that the single most important factor in the classroom is the early childhood teacher. By the practice of liberation teaching, the teacher provides a **protective buffer** that prevents the vulnerable child from being stigmatized and teaches the democratic life skills that enable the child to overcome vulnerabilities. (To encourage resiliency, the teacher must help the child to meet *both* the need for safety and for growth.)

Weinreb points out that not all vulnerable children show resiliency. Moreover, as in the case of Tyrell, the limitations of classroom situations sometimes prevent the full provision of a protective buffer. Still, the practice of liberation teaching, in collaboration with others, increases this possibility. "Few studies have explored the role of teachers as protective buffers; those that do exist concur that teachers of young children can have an enduring and profound effect on the children they teach" (Weinreb, 1997, p. 19).

THE GUIDANCE RESPONSE TO BULLYING

Bullying has become a much studied topic in American education, and with good reason. Recent studies, including a large study from the National Institutes of Child Health and Human Development (Nansel et al., 2001) indicates that youth who bully have more behavior problems, regard school more negatively, and are at greater risk for legal problems as adults. Children who are bullied "generally show higher levels of insecurity, anxiety, depression, loneliness, unhappiness, physical and mental symptoms, and low self-esteem. Witnesses to bullying as well are affected." While the national study focused on adolescents rather than young children, Froschl and Sprung (1999) discuss bullying in early childhood education. These authors emphasize the importance of comprehensive prevention and intervention with young children to prevent the onset of the long-term consequences of bullying.

This discussion of **bullying as violence** has three parts. Part one discusses bullying as the classic example of child-initiated stigma in the educational setting; part two analyzes bullying in relation to the three levels of mistaken behavior; and part three emphasizes the importance of a comprehensive approach to prevention and intervention rooted in liberation teaching.

Bullying as Violence that Causes Stigma

The national study on bullying gives an often-quoted definition:

> Bullying is a specific type of aggression in which (1) the behavior is intended to harm or disturb, (2) the behavior occurs repeatedly over time, and (3) there is an imbalance of power, with a more powerful person or group attacking a less powerful one. (Nansel et al., 2001)

This definition is similar to one offered earlier in the chapter in relation to violence: acts of neglect and aggression that result in arousal of stress with attendant emotions of anxiety, anger, fear, and confusion; debasement of the child's self-concept; and impairment of healthy brain development. Implied is the assertion of will by a more powerful individual against a less powerful individual, without regard for physical and psychological well-being.

While the definition of bullying emphasizes events over time, Nansel et al. (2001) and Froschl and Sprung (1999) indicate that even single occurrences of bullying can have detrimental effects. Significantly bullying is a form of violence that happens in the education community itself. In fact, it is the classic example of classroom stigma in two respects: Children already stigmatized tend to be the targets of bullying. Bullying further stigmatizes the targeted child.

Children are bullied more if they are isolated from others in the classroom or if their own behavior is overly aggressive. (The national study expresses particular concern about children who both bully and are the victims of bullying.) Children stigmatized due to physical appearance—being frail, small, or overweight—or due to a disability are also more likely to be bullied.

Froschl and Sprung point out that in one study 78 percent of K–3 children who initiated bullying were boys, though girls and boys equally were likely to be the targets (1999). This finding was similar in the national study, which provided the additional data that bullying by boys was more likely to deteriorate into physical aggression while the bullying of girls was more likely to include taunting, exclusion, and gossip (Nansel et al., 2001).

Bullying as Levels of Mistaken Behavior

Level One is experimentation level mistaken behavior. A child picks on another child, calls another child a name, or excludes another child from play in order to find out what will happen. From the statistics, children who initiate bullying are likely to be boys. Level One bullying may happen "out of the blue," and in fact be a first occurrence for the child. Yet, this is not a time for the teacher to conclude, "It is just once and boys will be boys." According to Froschl and Sprung (1999), a common adult response to bullying is to ignore it. Adults condone bullying when they fail to recognize it or deny the importance of intervention when they do recognize it (Froschl & Sprung, 1999). The child who tries out bullying and is not helped to learn from the experience may be reinforced by bullying behavior. For this child, the teacher may cause bullying to become a Level Two mistaken behavior.

Level Two is socially influenced mistaken behavior. As suggested, bullying becomes Level Two when a child has been reinforced for bullying behavior. This happens most frequently when a teacher ignores, and so condones, experimentation bullying. It also can happen if a teacher overreacts with punishment to the child doing the bullying. The child then learns that bullying is a way of achieving attention, albeit negative, from the teacher and may repeat its use.

A second way that children show Level Two bullying is if they are influenced by peers to join in the stigmatization of a vulnerable child. Group bullying through name-calling, ostracism, or even aggression is a pernicious, if common, form. By identifying with a group against a child, participating children feel a sense of belonging and power—which they may be denied in teacher-led, organized activities. Conflict management is the intervention of choice in the event of one-on-one bullying. (Mediation gives the targeted child a chance for needed self-assertion and teaches the child doing the bullying that friendly behaviors only belong in the classroom.) When bullying becomes evident in a group, class meeting interventions as well are called for. Prevention, by activities promoting the friendliness and acceptance of the encouraging classroom, also are needed. Parents may be enlisted to bring the message of friendliness "home" to children as well.

Level Three, strong needs mistaken behavior, is due to trouble in a child's life that is beyond her capacity to cope with and understand. Chil-

Bullying has detrimental effects on the child who bullies as well as the child who is bullied.

dren at Level Three often show "classic bullying" with the emotional intensity and persistence that are associated with this act. If children at Level Three are often out of control, they may as well become the targets of bullying—the group of high concern in the national study. With more social savvy, some older children at Level Three instigate others to join in the bullying, bringing to the clique an emotional intensity that elevates annoyance bullying to the pernicious.

Bullying and Liberation Teaching

Liberation teaching is being an activist in the use of guidance principles. Writers (of books and articles) about bullying agree that the key to solving problems of bullying in the classroom lies with the teacher. They agree that the teacher's responses must show active leadership and be comprehensive (Beane, 2000; Froschl & Sprung, 1999; Hoover & Oliver, 1996; Nansel et al., 2001). The tasks of the liberating teacher in response to bullying are now discussed concerning the class, the child, the staff, and the parents.

With the class, the liberating teacher works on *prevention* by talking and teaching about bullying and the need for friendliness (Bullock, 2002). The teacher uses children's books (see Recommended Resources); puppet and role plays, story-pictures, experience charts, journals, and class meetings to teach children the importance of empathy and inclusion (Beane, 2000; Froschl & Sprung, 1999; Hoover & Oliver, 1996). The teacher and children together make guidelines, as much as possible in the children's words, to define the spirit of encouragement. The teacher foregoes competitive practices in instruction and games that set children against each other and put an artificial premium on performance. He designs activities and encourages cooperation and relationships that go across genders, "because anyone can be friends in our classroom, girls and girls, girls and boys, boys and girls, and boys and boys" (Froschl & Sprung, 1999).

The teacher holds class meetings to assess and further the development of a cooperative group spirit. To lessen tension and aid in group problem solving, he may use relaxation activities, and soothing sound effects, like flowing water, (Froschl & Sprung, 1999). The prevailing intent of the meetings is to accept and celebrate human differences in the class, not to "divide and conquer" because of them. The adult teaches children that if they cannot stop it themselves, it is all right to report bullying. In the encouraging classroom, bullying does not have a "code of silence."

The adult may teach the use of de-escalating words or actions—such as the sentence frames in Chapter Ten—for children to use. (When a toddler got into a habit of biting to get her way, a teacher taught the other children, if threatened by the child, to hold up their hands and say "Stop"! This defensive action disrupted the impulse of the child who was biting, and alerted the teachers to intervene. They encouraged the child to use her words too.) The adult teaches that children have a right not to be bullied, and at the same time a child who is bullying needs to be accepted as a full member of the class. The child just has a problem that she needs help in solving. This challenging balance is at the heart of liberation teaching, the belief that all children can learn democratic life skills.

With the child, the liberating teacher uses his developing relationship with the child to assess whether the bullying is the result of experimentation, social influence, or deep unmet needs. He also uses his relationship to help a child prone to bullying find a sense of belonging and self-esteem through creative and cooperative activities in the educational program. He knows that bullying is an expression of a lack of perceived power, and the child has chosen mistaken behavior as a way to gain power and prestige. He uses conflict management to teach children involved in a situation that they both have rights, they just need to express them in friendly ways.

For children at Level Three who are bullying, teachers use the crisis intervention techniques and comprehensive intervention strategies discussed in Chapter Eleven. The teacher intervenes in firm but friendly ways (using conflict management and guidance talks), seeks more information, develops the relationship with the child, helps the child find success in the program, involves fellow staff and parents, and, if necessary, implements a formal plan (Bullock, 2002).

Most of all, the teacher is vigilant, ever aware of the possibility of bullying behavior. In fact, the liberating teacher has a zero tolerance for bullying. But he also has a zero tolerance for disqualifying any child from full participation in the class. When he sees bullying, he acts to make it a teaching opportunity because he knows that all children can learn democratic life skills. Some children will just take longer to learn than others.

I walked out onto the playground and immediately saw that a child from another room was hitting Kevin. Kevin stood against the fence with his arms up over his head. I hurried over and arrived at the same time as the teacher of the other child. She pulled the child off of Kevin, and we both knelt down, holding each child, to talk to them. Before either of us said anything, Kevin looked at the other child and said, "It made me very mad when you hit me." He told the other boy, "You're supposed to use words, not hit." The boy from the other class did not respond in any way during the discussion. I thanked Kevin for using his words and not hitting back. The teacher stayed to talk with the other boy. She later told me that she and her teaching team had scheduled a "staffing" concerning him that day and would meet with the parents soon (Gartrell, 2000).

With staff, liberating teachers work for a unified, program-wide approach to bullying (Bullock, 2002). If all teachers in a school or program team together to build encouraging classrooms, develop positive relations with parents, handle mistaken behavior with guidance, and take a planned approach to bullying that includes both systematic prevention and intervention, stigmatizing behaviors will decrease (Beane, 2000; Hoover & Oliver, 1996). Policies addressing bullying/friendliness issues need to be clear to children and adults alike, and enforced in firm but friendly ways (Beane, 2000). Administrators need to be visible regarding their leadership with guidance policies in relation to bullying. Both students and teachers need to participate in the policy-guidelines process. "Cohesiveness among the teaching staff and the principal [or director] relates to less violence" (Beane, 2000, p. 6). Working with fellow staff, the liberating teacher accomplishes what he cannot on his own.

With parents the liberating teacher starts from the beginning of the year to build positive relations and to communicate that parents and teacher are on the same team. He makes guidance priorities, including teaching democratic life skills, known to parents right away. He shares guidelines with parents that he and the class have developed. He involves parents in simple activities with their children that encourage empathy building and the acceptance of human differences (Froschl & Sprung, 1999).

When problems involving bullying become serious, the liberating teacher communicates with parents. He holds conferences for face-to-face discussion, using reflective listening, compliment sandwiches, and social problem solving. If differing viewpoints about bullying grow evident, the teacher works to make them creative differences rather than negative dissonance. He may involve a third party to mediate differences and to take leadership in implementing an individual guidance plan. A support system with fellow staff, family, and friends allows the teacher to persist in the risks and challenges of liberation teaching. Reaching a child who bullies, is bullied, or both—and helping the child to overcome—is the goal and reward of liberation teaching.

Jeremiah was almost three when I started teaching at the center. He was one of those very physical kids, whose feelings and thoughts always moved through his body first. He'd had a turbulent life and when I came to the center, he was living mostly with his mom, and some with his dad. They were separated and neither made very much money. Jeremiah was a shiningly bright kid, curious about and interested in everything, who loved stories and connected with others with his whole heart. He knew so much about the natural world and was observant and gentle with animals, insects, and plants.

When I first started working with Jeremiah, he had a lot of angry outbursts. The center used time-out at that point (the dreaded "green chair") and Jeremiah spent considerable time there. While I was at the center, we moved away from using time-outs. Instead we introduced a structured system of problem solving called "peer problem solving" developed by a Montessori teacher in New Hampshire. By the time Jeremiah graduated to kindergarten, we had been using the system for three years, and he was one of the experts.

One day, I overheard a fracas in the block corner. I stood up to see what was going on, ready to intervene. The youngest child in the room, who was just two and only talking a little bit, and one of the four-year-olds were in a dispute over a truck. There was an obvious imbalance of power, and I took a step forward, ready to go to their aid. Then I saw Jeremiah approach them.

"What's going on?" he asked (my standard opening line). He proceeded to facilitate a discussion between the two children that lasted for five minutes. He made sure both kids got a chance to speak; he interpreted for the little one. "Jordan, what do you think of that idea?" he asked. Jordan shook his head and clutched the truck tighter. "I don't think Jordan's ready to give up the truck yet," he told the four-year-old.

It was amazing. Jeremiah helped the kids negotiate an agreement, and then he walked away with a cocky tilt to his head I'd never seen before. His competence was without question; his pride was evident (Gartrell, 2000. Thanks to Beth Wallace for this anecdote.)

LIBERATION TEACHING AND RELATED EDUCATIONAL PRACTICES

As the active implementation of guidance, liberation teaching has much in common with the concept of **anti-bias curriculum.** As defined by Louise Derman-Sparks (1989), *anti-bias* means:

> An active/activist approach to challenging prejudice, stereotyping, bias, and the "isms." In a society in which institutional structures create and maintain sexism, racism, and handicappism, it is not sufficient to be nonbiased (and also highly unlikely), nor is it sufficient to be an observer. It is necessary for each individual to actively intervene, to challenge and counter the personal and institutional behaviors that perpetuate oppression. (Derman-Sparks, 1989, p. 3)

Curriculum in this sense means that the anti-bias disposition is institutionalized in the educational program of the school or center. Derman-Sparks comments that anti-bias curriculum incorporates the positive intent and awareness of **multicultural education,** but avoids the surface treatment of other cultures—such as using the "Mexican Hat Dance" to "study" Mexico—which she regards as **tourist curriculum** (Derman-Sparks, 1989, p. 7). The author adds:

> At the same time anti-bias curriculum provides a more inclusive education: (a) it addresses more than cultural diversity by including gender and differences in physical abilities; (b) it is based on children's tasks as they construct identity and attitudes; and (c) it directly addresses the impact of stereotyping, bias and discriminatory behavior in young children's development and interactions. (pp. 7–8)

A feature of anti-bias curriculum is its active involvement of parents in planning and implementing the program and its problem-solving approach to differences between parent and teacher (Derman-Sparks, 1989; McCracken, 1992; Neuman & Roskos, 1994; Wardle, 1992; York, 1991).

Liberation Teaching, An Additional Step

Liberation teaching is in harmony with the activist nature of anti-bias curriculum. The basis of the anti-bias approach is the creation of an affirming environment in the classroom, in which children learn to appreciate others and themselves. This too is the goal of liberation teaching. Liberation teaching goes beyond the definition—though not the spirit—of anti-bias curriculum in one respect. Along with factors of race, gender, and disability, liberation teaching focuses on an additional element that leads to stigmatization in the classroom—behavioral and personality characteristics of the individual child.

According to Bullock (1992), aggressive behavior is the most prevalent reason for stigmatization in the classroom. Children who are withdrawn and lack social skills also tend to experience the "passive oppression" of being ignored (Bullock, 1992). Though Bullock found differences for children "rejected" versus "neglected," her review of the research indicates that "many adolescents who drop out of school experience poor peer adjustments in their earlier years of school" (p. 93). Oppression (stigma) as a result of cultural, physical, or *behavioral* factors is not acceptable in the encouraging classroom. Liberation teaching seeks to reduce the effects of stigma, both to children oppressed by the mistaken behavior of others *and* to children showing the mistaken behavior themselves. Teachers who assist children to build ties with peers may both reduce bullying and enable better school adjustment (Ladd, Kochenderfer & Coleman, 1996). These teachers extend the promise of anti-bias curriculum.

The Contribution of Anti-bias Curriculum

In the anti-bias view, the teacher is an activist who intervenes to halt discriminatory acts. In her discussion of the *power of silence,* Stacy York criticizes teaching practices that prevent open discussion of tacitly oppressive behavior:

> Teachers and schools create "no-talk" rules for classrooms. Controversial situations occur, and questionable things are said or done. A Euro-American child calls a Native American child a "dumb Indian." Three boys in the block corner won't let a Laotian boy join them. They chant, "Go away, poopy boy. You talk funny." Everyone in the classroom hears it and sees it. Children may even look at each other as the situation occurs, but nothing is said then or thereafter.
>
> Many times, people feel paralyzed and make no response. [Teachers] have told us that they fail to act because they are uncertain of the right thing to say; or they fear making a mountain out of a molehill; or because they feel they should not be influencing children with their ideas. But the silence only serves to reinforce the hurt, pain, fear, hatred, and distorted thinking. (York, 1991, pp. 197–198)

York's examples illustrate the overlap of mistaken and stigmatizing behavior. In such situations, teachers need to intervene. Using nonpunitive, problem-solving techniques, they explain the unacceptable behaviors and teach prosocial alternatives. They may follow up as well with a class meeting, a planned activity, or a discussion with a parent to reinforce the message that different human qualities are not to be feared or scorned, but learned from and understood. The activist message in anti-bias curriculum offers much to guidance by empowering teachers to be liberating.

> In a kindergarten classroom some boys were playing "fireman," using the climber for their station and the dramatic play areas for the "house on fire." Charlene asked to play, but was told, "You can't 'cause you're a girl. Only boys can be firemen." Charlene tried to get on to the climber anyway, but the boys pushed at her and began yelling.

Oppression as a result of cultural, physical, or behavioral factors is not acceptable in the guidance-oriented classroom.

The teacher intervened: "Hey, guys, do you remember our book about firefighters? Men and women can both be firefighters. That's why we call them firefighters instead of firemen. How can Charlene help you as a firefighter?"

The other boys didn't object when Steve said, "OK, Charlene, you can steer on the back." The teacher watched as the four got on their long wooden "fire truck" and "sped off" to the fire. Charlene turned a make-believe steering wheel in the back, helped to fight the fire, and even found a baby that needed to be saved. After the fire was out, the boys included Charlene on the climber fire station, " 'cause Charlene saved the baby."

That Friday a female firefighter, who was a friend of the teacher, visited the class. She arrived in street clothes and with the class's participation discussed, put on, and demonstrated her gear. No one commented the next week when Charlene and Della played firefighter with two boys.

Liberation Teaching and Guidance

Traditionally, discipline systems have been used to support the content of the educational program. The purpose of discipline was to keep children in line so that the teacher could present lessons without distraction. Guidance

Liberation teaching engenders an appreciation of human qualities in one's self and others.

rises a notch above the usual support function. The reason is that the guidance approach actively teaches democratic life skills: appreciating one's self and others, making decisions intelligently and ethically, expressing strong feelings in acceptable ways, cooperating with others, and resolving problems through the use of words. As the world grows more complex and interconnected, these life skills become paramount. The skills learned in the encouraging classroom are the skills of social studies and the language arts, practice for life in a democracy.

Liberation teaching raises the importance of guidance further. Liberation teaching links the prevention of oppression occurring in mistaken behavior with the cultural and physical factors that also cause children to be stigmatized. If guidance encourages democratic life in the encouraging classroom, liberation teaching provides a foundation for that democracy in human relations—the appreciation of human qualities in the self and the other.

By empowering the child to overcome a vulnerability for stigma—and helping others to see the child as a worthwhile class member—the teacher models a precept of democracy: acceptance of the humanity of the other, with differing human qualities not a source of anxiety, but of affirmation. Human relations abilities are becoming ever more important in our culturally diverse society. Modern education serves no higher purpose than to nurture this basic outcome. In the encouraging classroom through the use of guidance and liberation teaching, children learn human relations skills.

> In a suburban first grade, Tom, a member of an all European-American class, approached his teacher, an African American. Without looking directly at her, but with some emotion. Tom declared: "Teacher, somebody's different in here."
>
> The teacher responded, "Do you mean me, Tom? My skin is a darker color than yours and that's one of the special things that makes me who I am." Tom frowned and shook his head, but the teacher thought that her skin color was probably what Tom had on his mind.
>
> The next day Tom's mother, an occasional classroom volunteer, called the teacher and said; "Annie, I just have to tell you what happened last night. Tom and I were in the supermarket when an African-American woman went by with a shopping cart. Tom turned to me and said, "Look, Mom, there goes a teacher."

Liberating teachers accept the child beyond the behavior. In refusing to demean, they model human relations and life skills that encourage the child to learn and to grow. Guidance, the encouraging classroom, and anti-bias curriculum infuse liberation teaching. Liberation teaching contributes an appreciation for the humanity of each child to the guidance approach.

Liberation Teaching and Peace Education

The goal of liberation teaching, to help the child at risk for stigma overcome vulnerabilities, is the goal for all children in **peace education.** When conflict occurs, teachers tend to regard children according to their role in it: *aggressor* and *victim*. A child who is seen as an aggressor is at risk for stigma because even if the teacher is able to control negative feelings, others in the classroom may avoid or reject the child (Bullock, 1992). Significantly, the child who is the victim is also at risk. Some children, perhaps victimized often in early childhood, suffer from low self-esteem and feel incapable in social situations. They may find themselves assuming a generalized "victim role" and continue to be a target of acting out behaviors by others.

Conflict management empowers children to overcome the labeling phenomena and find success in their efforts at peaceable communication. It allows children victimized in conflict situations to express their feelings, participate in an equitable resolution process, and achieve vindication. At the same time, the child who is growing in the ability to understand the perspectives of others is in a profound way being liberated from the vulnerabilities inherent in the use of violence. Peace education, like liberation teaching, elevates all members of the encouraging classroom and teaches that mutual respect shows itself most fully in the peaceful resolution of social problems. Peace education is an important concept for prospective and practicing teachers. In their adaptation of Harris' 1988 work on the subject, Janke & Penshorn Peterson (1995) set out eight tasks of peace education. Peace education:

- draws out from people their desires to live in peace;
- provides awareness of alternatives to violence;
- consists of teaching skills, content, and a peaceful pedagogy;
- examines the roots and causes of violence;
- empowers students to confront their fears of violence;
- helps build a peaceful culture to counteract militarism;
- challenges violent ways of thinking and acting;
- promotes loving behavior towards oneself, others, and the environment.

Readers may react to some of these issues as being political as much as philosophical: such an interpretation is definitely the consumer's right. Nonetheless, the tenets of democratic life skills have much in common with the priorities of peace education. Given the violence prevalent in modern life, teachers today can hardly engage in character education without addressing the issues of peace and the need for peace education. Peace education, like guidance in the encouraging classroom, takes liberating teachers.

LIBERATION TEACHING AND PARENT INVOLVEMENT

The practice of liberation teaching means that the teacher accepts the fundamental connection between the life of the child and the family. The teacher works with and seeks to understand the family in order to benefit the child (Neuman & Roskos, 1994). The sections of previous chapters addressing parent involvement are based on this premise of liberation teaching. Liberation teaching with parents means that the teacher encourages the maximum involvement in the education of the child possible for each family. Over time, as trust builds between teacher and parent, parent involvement grows. Recapping information from previous chapters, a strategy for increasing parent involvement is suggested, using the following progressions:

1. Sharing of information
2. Active involvement
3. Policy participation
4. Personal/professional development

Liberation teaching with parents means that the teacher encourages
their maximum participation in the education of the child.
(Courtesy of Richard Faulkner, Family Service Center, Kootasca Head Start,
Grand Rapids, Minnesota)

Progression One—Sharing Information

At the beginning of the school year, the teacher introduces parents as well
as children to the program. The teacher becomes acquainted with each family and seeks ways to involve the family in the child's education. Families
differ in the level of participation that they are ready to accept (Coleman,
1997). Most families are at least willing to receive information. The teacher
makes the most of this willingness, recognizing the two sources of information the parent will have: the teacher and the child.

On the teacher's part, he uses the methods of communication discussed
in previous chapters—phone calls, happy-grams, electronic communication, orientation meetings, home visits, and parent conferences. The teacher
works for three outcomes at this level of involvement:

- understanding by the parent that the teacher accepts and appreciates the child;
- comfort felt by the parent in communicating with the teacher about
  family background, including information about the child;
- willingness on the part of the parent for increased involvement.

The child is the second source of information for the parent. If the child
wants to come to school when sick, the foundation is set for further parent involvement. If the child does not want to come to school when well,

participation beyond the passive receipt of information may be the best the teacher can expect. Through the foundation provided by a successful program for the child and active inviting by the teacher, parent participation is encouraged at additional levels.

Progression Two—Active Involvement

The nature of active involvement will differ for each parent and for each program. Working parents may not be able to come into the classroom, except on a special occasion. They may be able to contribute materials, read or do other enriching activities with children at home, or arrange for a nonworking family member to attend the class. The use of a home-school journal—a running dialogue by hard copy or e-mail between the teacher and parent—is a clear indication of active involvement with some parents who cannot participate with the group.

With parents who can come into the classroom, McCracken (1992) suggests a **tossed salad approach** in which parents from differing backgrounds add to the program in informal but important ways. Rather than focus on parent presentations around holidays or specific customs, parents interact informally with children and other adults—with friendships and discovered mutual interests providing incidental educational opportunities. As McCracken points out, when the families served are diverse, the tossed salad approach allows for multicultural education in a natural and supportive way. For such a program to work, parents must feel welcome and comfortable in the classroom—the job of the teacher, as leader of the teaching team (McCracken, 1992).

Another approach, a bit more formal, is to ask each family to have members come into class and share something of their heritage and their interests (Gestwicki, 2000). Every family would be asked, not just those with an "exotic" heritage, and the members could share anything that was important to them, such as a shared activity. The teacher might ask families already familiar to him to share at the beginning of the year. Use of the tossed salad approach would help other parents become used to the classroom before being asked to present. As mentioned, working parents might be able to have a nonworking member participate.

With planning and coordination, the teacher can provide follow-up activities for children around the topics of individual family visits. For instance, integrated curriculum activities could be set up around pets if one or more parents brought pets to share. One benefit of a family-share program is that it introduces cultural differences in functional ways for the children—even two Swedish American families would have different items and interests to share. (The author recalls a Swedish American family in northern Minnesota that ran a Mexican take-out restaurant.) A second benefit is that it allows each child to bridge the gap between home and school in personally satisfying ways. Some parents, who came only to share, might be encouraged to come back to the class at other times. A third benefit is the creation of a basis for an emergent social studies program across the year.

One method of parent involvement is to invite families to share with the class something of their heritage and interests. (Courtesy, *Bemidji Pioneer*)

Progression Three—Policy Participation

Progression Three is participation in policy activities: program committees, advisory councils, policy boards. Some parents start at Level One, but prefer policy participation to educational participation. Each parent is different and progress to either Progression Two or Three should be supported. The importance of policy participation is that it means the parent is taking a leadership role in the education of *all* children in the school or center. If the parent has begun at Level One and progressed to Level Three, the children, the program, and the parent all stand to benefit.

The model that Head Start has provided for encouraging low-income, often low-esteem parents, to become active participants in their children's education is one of liberation teaching on a broad scale (Collins, 1993). A parent who over time comes to a meeting, volunteers in a class, gets elected to a policy council and positively influences the program is what liberation teaching with families is about. The gain in confidence levels in such parents is impressive. The parent who says, "I sent my child and hoped that she would benefit, but I have benefitted as much or more," indicates liberation teaching at its best.

Progression Four—Professional Development

One contribution of successful early childhood programs, and encouraging classrooms in elementary school, is parents who experience successful involvement and as a result prepare for and enter a professional field. Whether these parents become paid teacher assistants, family child care providers, Head Start staff, elementary grade teachers, special education teachers, or professionals in another field such as business or human services, the success of the parent involvement program for them cannot be denied. They began "only as parents" whom a teacher took an interest in, and over time improved life circumstances for themselves and their families.

(Journal of a graduate student) Margaret was a parent volunteer in the Head Start classroom I observed. (She had volunteered in the center previously.) A staff member said "Good morning" when Margaret arrived. "We are glad you could come today. How are you feeling?"

Margaret said, "My mouth is still sore, but it feels better than yesterday." (She had two teeth pulled.)

The teacher said, "If you don't feel well, Margaret, you can come in another day." Margaret indicated that she would stay. She hung up her coat and, without any direction from the teacher, went out to meet the second group of children who arrived on the bus. Margaret waited with the children while they hung up their coats, walked with them to wash their hands, and then sat down to breakfast with them. She reminded them how to open their milk and quietly asked Calvin to keep his feet still.

After breakfast, the teacher asked Margaret if she would like to play the alphabet fishing game that she brought. Margaret played the game with three children and had to ask four others to wait for a turn. The teacher came over to the table and said, "Margaret, the children are enjoying the game so much." Margaret smiled. Margaret then helped the children with brushing their teeth. The teacher asked Margaret if she could sit close to Ray during story time. She said, "He needs some extra attention today." Margaret sat down by Ray, and he crawled onto her lap.

Later, I interviewed Margaret and asked her what went into her decision to volunteer in the classroom. Margaret said, "At first, I volunteered because I wanted to make Alicia (her daughter) feel more comfortable. Alicia was with us most of the time and wasn't used to being with groups of children without us. I felt more relaxed if I knew she was happy at school. Then I got used to being with the kids, and it was a lot of fun being with them, so I came back to volunteer. My hours changed, and I got put on part time, so I could volunteer more easily."

I asked Margaret what part the teacher played in her decision to volunteer. Margaret said, "On the first home visit, the teacher encouraged us to volunteer in the center, but she wasn't pushy about it. When I came into the center, I felt welcomed by the teachers. There was always a 'Hi' or 'Good morning.' The kids all said 'Hi' or gave me a hug. I felt like I was really contributing, giving more attention, and sometimes, like on the playground, making it safer for the kids. The teachers always thank me for helping out when I leave. When someone is appreciated, it makes them want to come back. If someone's not appreciated, they're not going to come back. Now, I know this is what I want to do. My family has seen a change in me. I'm starting college this fall to become a teacher. They weren't for it at first, but now they're all for it." Margaret paused, then said, "Just because the teacher got me to volunteer."

Many teachers in Head Start programs, as well as child care centers and schools, have success stories like this one with parents. The long-term societal benefits of early childhood education in the area of parent involvement have not been fully realized. In fact, measures of the success of early childhood education in general have focused too narrowly on the immediate measurable gains of children. When educators see the classroom more broadly, as an encouraging community involving parents no less than children, the full potential of guidance will begin to be realized.

SUMMARY

1. How are children in the classroom affected by violence in society?

Virtually all children are touched by societal violence. At the low end of Levin's continuum of violence, large numbers of children are exposed to many hours each week of violent television programming (often meant for adults), computer games, books, action toys, and play weapons. In addition to this indirect or background violence, smaller numbers of children, at the upper end of the continuum, experience violence directly in their homes and neighborhoods. The more extensive and intensive the exposure to violence, the more direct the affect of violence on children in the classroom.

2. How is liberation teaching a response to societal violence?

Liberation teaching is the activist application of guidance principles. The concept derives from the work of many educators and psychologists during the 20th century. Specific to the issue of violence, liberation teaching assists children to find the inner resources for resiliency—to begin a healing process. Because of behavior, physical appearance, and sometimes social and cultural factors, some children are vulnerable for stigma—or negative separation from the group in ways that prevent full participation. The effects of stigma—which is psychological violence in the education setting—are the effects of violence on the child.

3. What is the liberation teaching response to bullying?

Bullying is a classic example of violence in the classroom, taking the form of child-initiated stigma. Children already stigmatized tend to be targets of bullying. Bullying further stigmatizes the targeted child.

The response of liberating teacher to bullying is a comprehensive one that involves both educational prevention and guidance intervention and includes the class, the children directly involved, fellow staff, and parents. Reaching a child who bullies, is bullied, or both—and helping the child to overcome—is the goal and reward of liberation teaching.

4. What is the connection between liberation teaching and other education practices?

Anti-bias curriculum teaches alternatives to oppressive behaviors that perpetuate sexism, racism, and handicappism. Anti-bias curriculum incorporates the positive intentions of multicultural education but addresses more than cultural diversity by including gender and differences in physical abilities. Liberation teaching is in harmony with anti-bias curriculum, but goes a step beyond by addressing additional factors that lead to stigmatization: behavioral and personality characteristics. Liberation teaching infuses guidance with a foundation in human relations. Peace education, like liberation teaching, elevates all members of the encouraging classroom and teaches that mutual respect shows itself most fully in the peaceful resolution of social problems.

5. How does liberation teaching apply to relations with parents?

The practice of liberation teaching means that the teacher accepts the fundamental connection between the life of the child and the family. The teacher encourages the maximum participation acceptable to each family, and over time, as trust builds, invites increased participation. The teacher encourages the parent to move from the sharing of information to active educational involvement to participation in program policy decisions to personal/professional development. Liberation teaching broadens the encouraging classroom to a community that includes children and adults together.

KEY CONCEPTS

Anti-bias curriculum	Protective buffer
Bullying as violence	Resiliency
Continuum of violence	Stigma
Liberation teaching	Tossed salad approach
Multicultural education	Tourist curriculum
Peace education	

FOLLOW-UP ACTIVITIES

*Note: An element of being a professional teacher is to respect the children,
parents, and educators you are working with by maintaining
confidentiality—keeping identities private. In completing follow-up
activities, please respect the privacy of all concerned.*

Discussion Activity

The discussion activity encourages students to interrelate their own
thoughts and experiences with specific ideas from the chapter.

Referring to the text, identify a guiding principle important to you in the
practice of

- teaching friendliness as a response to bullying;
- liberation teaching;
- resiliency mentoring;
- anti-bias curriculum;
- peace education;
- levels of parent involvement.

Discuss the importance of these principles to you in your professional
development.

Application Activities

Application activities allow students to interrelate material from the text with
real-life situations. The observations imply access to practicum experiences;
the interviews, access to teachers or parents. Students may compare or contrast observations and interviews with referenced ideas from the chapter.

1. **Effects of societal violence on children in the classroom.**
   a. Observe a child whose behaviors seem to show the effects of
      indirect or direct violence. Assuring confidentiality, interview
      a teacher who knows the child about the child's life outside of
      school. Record your observation and interview and compare
      your findings to what the text says about the effects of
      societal violence on classroom behavior.
   b. Interview an experienced teacher about whether he believes
      that societal violence is a major factor in conflicts and
      mistaken behavior in the classroom. Record your interview
      and compare your findings to what the text says about the
      effects of societal violence on classroom behavior.
2. **Liberation teaching: a response to societal violence.**
   a. Record an observation of what you believe to be liberation
      teaching with a child who is vulnerable for stigma. Why do you
      think the child is vulnerable for stigma? Referring to the text,
      why do you think the teacher's responses were liberating?
   b. Interview a teacher about liberation teaching. Ask the teacher
      to remember an instance of liberation teaching in his
      professional career. Compare your findings from the

interview with what the book says about liberation teaching being a response to societal violence.

3. **The liberation teaching response to bullying.**
   a. Record an observation of bullying behavior, including the words and actions of all involved. Compare specifics from your observation with what the text says about the reasons for bullying and the levels of mistaken behavior shown in bullying behavior. If you were to intervene in this situation, what would you say and do?
   b. Interview a teacher about bullying and his response to it. Do some children seem to bully more than others? Are some children more likely to be targets? How does the teacher work with the class to prevent bullying? How does he intervene when bullying occurs? Compare your findings from the interview with what the text says about these questions.

4. **The connection between liberation teaching and other education practices.**
   a. Record an observation of when a teacher intervened to halt stigmatizing behavior that seemed to be done for reasons of cultural, racial, gender, or ability differences. Which factors above seemed to cause the stigmatizing behavior? How did the teacher respond? Comparing the teacher's response to the text, what have you learned about the connection of liberation teaching to anti-bias education?
   b. Interview a teacher about an experience of stigmatizing behavior in the class based on cultural, racial, gender, or ability differences. Record the interview and compare your findings with the text regarding the connection of liberation teaching with anti-bias education.

5. **Liberation teaching and relations with parents.**
   a. Interview a parent whom you believe to be participating successfully in a classroom or program. Ask what the parent believes that she is gaining personally from the experience. Ask in what ways, if any, the experience has changed the parent's view of her personal development, education, or career aspirations.
   b. Discuss with a teacher a situation in which he helped a parent overcome initial reluctance to be involved and the parent ended up growing from the participation. Ask the teacher to reflect about the likely effect of the experience for the parent, the child, and the teacher.

What You Can Do

Liberation Teaching   Something important can be learned from interviewing teachers about their experiences with liberation teaching.

   a. Select a teacher at any level whom you had as a teacher and whom you respect. Define liberation teaching and the effects of stigma for the teacher. Ask the teacher to recollect the clearest example of liberation teaching he can think of. Ask about the difficulties and conflicts the child was experiencing when she entered the teacher's class. Ask about the challenge she posed to the teacher and the other children. Ask about the teacher's approach to the child and to the family. Over time what signs of resiliency did the teacher see in the child? What progress did the child make in relation to democratic life skills? What was a frustration the teacher experienced in working with the child? What were the accomplishments the teacher felt were made?

b. Repeat this full interview process with a different teacher from the prekindergarten level.

c. Repeat this full interview process with a different teacher from the kindergarten or primary grade level.

d. What was similar in what the teachers had to say?

e. What did the teachers say that was different?

f. What did you learn about liberation teaching from this project?

RECOMMENDED READINGS

Agassi, Martine. (2000). *Hands are not for hitting*. Minneapolis, MN: Free Spirit Publishing.

Beane, A. L. (2000). *Bully free classroom*. Minneapolis, MN: Free Spirit Publishing.

Boutte, G. S., & McCormick, C. B. (1992). Authentic multicultural activities: Avoiding pseudomulticulturalism. *Childhood Education, 68*(3), 140–144.

Bullock, J. R. (2002). Bullying among children. *Childhood Education, 79*(3), 130–133.

Clark, L., DeWolf, S., & Clark, C. (1992). Teaching teachers to avoid having culturally assaultive classrooms. *Young Children, 47*(5), 4–9.

Coleman, M. (1997). Families and schools: In search of common ground. *Young Children, 52*(5), 14–21.

Froschl, M., & Sprung, B. (1999). On purpose: Addressing teasing and bullying in early childhood. *Young Children, 54*(2), 70–72.

Jackson, B. R. (1997). Creating a climate for healing in a violent society. *Young Children, 52*(7), 68–70.

Koeppel, J., & Mulrooney, M. (1992). The sister schools program: A way for children to learn about cultural diversity—When there isn't any in the school. *Young Children, 48*(1), 44–47.

McCracken, J. B. (1992). Tossed salad is terrific: Values of multicultural programs for children and families. In *Alike and different: Exploring our humanity with young children*. Washington, DC: National Association for the Education of Young Children.

Neuman, S. B., & Roskos, K. (1994). Bridging home and school with a culturally responsive approach. *Childhood Education, 70*(4), 210–214.

Weinreb, M. L. (1997). Be a resiliency mentor: You may be a lifesaver for a high-risk child. *Young Children, 52*(2), 14–19.

York, S. (1991). *Roots and wings: Affirming culture in early childhood programs*. St. Paul, MN: Redleaf Press.

REFERENCES

Beane, A. L. (2000). *Bully free classroom.* Minneapolis, MN: Free Spirit Publishing.

Boyatzis, C. (1997). Of Power Rangers and v-chips. *Young Children, 52*(7), 74–79.

Bullock, J. R. (1992). Reviews of research: Children without friends. *Childhood Education, 69*(2), 92–96.

Carlsson-Paige, N., & Levin, D. E. (1992). Making peace in violent times: A constructivist approach to conflict resolution. *Young Children, 48*(1), 4–13.

Coleman, M. (1997). Families & schools: In search of common ground. *Young Children, 52*(5), 14–21.

Collins, R. C. (1993). Head Start: Steps toward a two-generation program strategy. *Young Children, 48*(2), 24–33; 72–73.

Derman-Sparks, L. (1989). *Anti-bias curriculum: Tools for empowering young children.* Washington, DC: National Association for the Education of Young Children.

Elkind, D. (1989). *Miseducation: Preschoolers at risk.* New York: Alfred A. Knopf.

Faber, A., & Mazlich, E. (1974). *Liberated parents, liberated children.* New York: Avon Books.

Froschl, M., & Sprung, B. (1999). On purpose: Addressing teasing and bullying in early childhood. *Young Children, 54*(2), 70–72.

Gartrell, D. (2000). *What the kids said today: Using classroom conversations to become a better teacher.* St. Paul, MN: Redleaf Press.

Gestwicki, C. (2000). *Home, school and community relations: A guide to working with parents* (4th ed.). Clifton Park, NY: Delmar Learning.

Ginott, H. (1972). *Teacher and child.* New York: Avon Books.

Girard, K., & Koch, S. J. (1996). Conflict resolution in the schools. San Francisco: Jossey-Bass Publishers.

Goffman, E. (1963). *Stigma: Notes on the management of spoiled identity.* Englewood Cliffs, NJ: Prentice-Hall, Inc.

Gootman, M. E. (1993). Reaching and teaching abused children. *Childhood Education, 70*(1), 15–19.

Greenberg, P. (1992). Ideas that work with young children. How to institute some simple democratic practices pertaining to respect, rights, responsibilities, and roots in any classroom (without losing your leadership position). *Young Children, 47*(5), 10–21.

Harlow, S. D. (1975). *Special Education: The meeting of differences.* Grand Forks, ND: University of North Dakota.

Honig, A. S., & Wittmer, D. S. (1996). Helping children become more prosocial: Ideas for classrooms, families, schools, and communities. *Young Children, 51*(2), 62–70.

Hoover, J. H., & Oliver, R. (1996). *The bullying prevention handbook.* Bloomington, IN: National Education Service.

Jackson, B. R. (1997). Creating a climate for healing in a violent society. *Young Children, 52*(7), 68–70.

Janke, R. A., Penshorn Peterson, J. (1995). *Peacemaker's ABCs for young children.* Marine on St. Croix, MN: Growing Communities for Peace.

Kamii, C., (1984). Autonomy: The aim of education envisioned by Piaget. *Phi Delta Kappan, 65*(6), 410–415.

Kontos, S., & Wilcox-Herzog, A. (1997). Teachers' interactions with children: Why are they so important? *Young Children, 52*(2), 4–12.

Kreidler, W. J. (1984). *Creative conflict resolution: More than 200 activities for keeping peace in the classroom.* Glenview, IL: Scott, Foresman.

Ladd, G. W., Kochenderfer, B. J., Coleman, C. (1996). Friendship quality as a predictor of young children's early school adjustment, *Child Development, 67,* 1103–1118.

LeDoux, J. (1996). *The emotional brain.* New York: Simon & Schuster.

Levin, D. L. (1994). *Teaching young children in violent times: Building a peaceable classroom.* Cambridge, MA: Educators for Social Responsibility.

Lowenthal, B. (1999). Effects of maltreatment and ways to promote children's resiliency. *Childhood Education.* 75(4), 204–209.

Maslow, A. H. (1962). *Toward a psychology of being.* Princeton, NJ: D. Van Nostrand Company, Inc.

McCracken, J. B. (1992). Tossed salad is terrific: Values of multicultural programs for children and families. In *Alike and different: Exploring our humanity with young children.* Washington, DC: National Association for the Education of Young Children.

Nansel, T. R., Overpeck, M., Pilla, R. S., Ruan, W. J., Simons-Morton, B., Scheidt, P. (2001). Bullying behaviors among U.S. youth: Prevalence and association with psychosocial adjustment. *Journal of the American Medical Association, 285*(16), 2094–2100.

Neuman, S. B., & Roskos, K. (1994). Bridging home and school with a culturally responsive approach. *Childhood Education, 70*(4), 210–214.

Piaget, J. (1932/1960). *The moral judgment of the child.* Glencoe, IL: The Free Press.

Pirtle, S. (1997). *Linking up: Building the peaceable classroom with music and movement.* Boston: Educators for Social Responsibility.

Slaby, R. G., Roedell, W. C., Arezzo, D., & Henriz, K. (1995). *Early violence prevention.* Washington, DC: National Association for the Education of Young Children.

Surgeon General. (1999). *Surgeon General's report on violence.* Washington, DC: Department of Health and Human Services.

Wardle, F. (1992). Building positive images: Interracial children and their families. In *Alike and different: Exploring our humanity with young children.* Washington, DC: National Association for the Education of Young Children.

Weinreb, M. L. (1997). Be a resiliency mentor: You may be a lifesaver for a high-risk child. *Young Children, 52*(2), 14–19.

York, S. (1991). *Roots and wings: Affirming culture in early childhood programs.* St. Paul, MN: Redleaf Press.

For additional information on using the guidance approach in the classroom, visit our Web site at http://www.earlychilded.delmar.com

The National Association for the Education of Young Children Code of Ethical Conduct

This Code of Ethical Conduct and Statement of Commitment was prepared under the auspices of the Ethics Commission of the National Association for the Education of Young Children. The Commission members were Stephanie Feeney (Chairperson), Bettye Caldwell, Sally Cartwright, Carrie Cheek, Josué Cruz, Jr., Anne G. Dorsey, Dorothy M. Hill, Lilian G. Katz, Pamm Mattick, Shirley A. Norris, and Sue Spayth Riley.

Preamble

NAEYC recognizes that many daily decisions required of those who work with young children are of a moral and ethical nature. The NAEYC Code of Ethical Conduct offers guidelines for responsible behavior and sets forth a common basis for resolving the principal ethical dilemmas encountered in early childhood education. The primary focus is on daily practice with children and their families in programs for children from birth to 8 years of age: preschools, child care centers, family day care homes, kindergartens, and primary classrooms. Many of the provisions also apply to specialists who do not work directly with children, including program administrators, parent educators, college professors, and child care licensing specialists.

Core Values

Standards of ethical behavior in early childhood education are based on commitment to core values that are deeply rooted in the history of our field. We have committed ourselves to:

- Appreciating childhood as a unique and valuable stage of the human life cycle
- Basing our work with children on knowledge of child development
- Appreciating and supporting the close ties between the child and family

- Recognizing that children are best understood in the context of family, culture, and society
- Respecting the dignity, worth, and uniqueness of each individual (child, family member, and colleague)
- Helping children and adults achieve their full potential in the context of relationships that are based on trust, respect, and positive regard.

Conceptual Framework

The Code sets forth a conception of our professional responsibilities in four sections, each addressing an arena of professional relationships: 1) children, 2) families, 3) colleagues, and 4) community and society. Each section includes an introduction to the primary responsibilities of the early childhood practitioner in that arena, a set of ideals pointing in the direction of exemplary professional practice, and a set of principles defining practices that are required, prohibited, and permitted.

The ideals reflect the aspirations of practitioners. The principles are intended to guide conduct and assist practitioners in resolving ethical dilemmas encountered in the field. There is not necessarily a corresponding principle for each ideal. Both ideals and principles are intended to direct practitioners to those questions which, when responsibly answered, will provide the basis for conscientious decision making. While the Code provides specific direction for addressing some ethical dilemmas, many others will require the practitioner to combine the guidance of the Code with sound professional judgment.

The ideals and principles in this Code present a shared conception of professional responsibility that affirms our commitment to the core values of our field. The Code publicly acknowledges the responsibilities that we in the field have assumed and in so doing supports ethical behavior in our work. Practitioners who face ethical dilemmas are urged to seek guidance in the applicable parts of this Code and in the spirit that informs the whole.

SECTION I: ETHICAL RESPONSIBILITIES TO CHILDREN

Childhood is a unique and valuable stage in the life cycle. Our paramount responsibility is to provide safe, healthy, nurturing, and responsive settings for children. We are committed to supporting children's development by cherishing individual differences, by helping them learn to live and work cooperatively, and by promoting their self-esteem.

Ideals:

I-1.1 To be familiar with the knowledge base of early childhood education and to keep current through continuing education and in-service training.

I-1.2   To base program practices upon current knowledge in the field of child development and related disciplines and upon particular knowledge of each child.

I-1.3   To recognize and respect the uniqueness and the potential of each child.

I-1.4   To appreciate the special vulnerability of children.

I-1.5   To create and maintain safe and healthy settings that foster children's social, emotional, intellectual, and physical development and that respect their dignity and their contributions.

I-1.6   To support the right of children with special needs to participate, consistent with their ability, in regular early childhood programs.

I-1.7   To ensure that children with disabilities have access to appropriate and convenient support services and to advocate for the resources necessary to provide the most appropriate settings for all children.

Principles:

P-1.1   Above all, we shall not harm children. We shall not participate in practices that are disrespectful, degrading, dangerous, exploitative, intimidating, psychologically damaging, or physically harmful to children. **This principle has precedence over all others in this Code.**

P-1.2   We shall not participate in practices that discriminate against children by denying benefits, giving special advantages, or excluding them from programs or activities on the basis of their race, religion, sex, national origin, or the status, behavior, or beliefs of their parents. (This principle does not apply to programs that have a lawful mandate to provide services to a particular population of children.)

P-1.3   We shall involve all of those with relevant knowledge (including staff and parents) in decisions concerning a child.

P-1.4   When, after appropriate efforts have been made with a child and the family, the child still does not appear to be benefitting from a program, we shall communicate our concern to the family in a positive way and offer them assistance in finding a more suitable setting.

P-1.5   We shall be familiar with the symptoms of child abuse and neglect and know and follow state laws and community procedures for addressing them.

P-1.6   When we have evidence of child abuse or neglect, we shall report the evidence to the appropriate community agency and follow up to ensure that appropriate action has been taken. When possible, parents will be informed that the referral has been made.

P-1.7   When another person tells us of their suspicion that a child is being abused or neglected but we lack evidence, we shall assist that person in taking appropriate action to protect the child.

P-1.8   When a child protective agency fails to provide adequate protection for abused or neglected children, we acknowledge a collective ethical responsibility to work toward improvement of these services.

P-1.9   When we become aware of a practice or situation that endangers the health or safety of children, but has not been previously known to do so, we have an ethical responsibility to inform those who can remedy the situation and who can protect children from similar danger.

SECTION II: ETHICAL RESPONSIBILITIES TO FAMILIES

Families are of primary importance in children's development. (The term *family* may include others, besides parents, who are responsibly involved with the child.) Because the family and the early childhood educator have a common interest in the child's welfare, we acknowledge a primary responsibility to bring about collaboration between the home and school in ways that enhance the child's development.

Ideals:

I-2.1   To develop relationships of mutual trust with the families we serve.

I-2.2   To acknowledge and build upon strengths and competencies as we support families in their task of nurturing children.

I-2.3   To respect the dignity of each family and its culture, customs, and beliefs.

I-2.4   To respect families' childrearing values and their right to make decisions for their children.

I-2.5   To interpret each child's progress to parents within the framework of a developmental perspective and to help families understand and appreciate the value of developmentally appropriate early childhood practices.

I-2.6   To help family members improve their understanding of their children and to enhance their skills as parents.

I-2.7   To participate in building support networks for families by providing them with opportunities to interact with program staff and families, community resources and professional services.

Principles:

P-2.1   We shall not deny family members access to their child's classroom or program setting.

P-2.2   We shall inform families of program philosophy, policies, and personnel qualifications, and explain why we teach as we do.

P-2.3   We shall inform families of and, when appropriate, involve them in policy decisions.

P-2.4   We shall inform families of and, when appropriate, involve them in significant decisions affecting their child.

P-2.5   We shall inform the family of accidents involving their child, of risks such as exposures to contagious disease that may result in infection, and of events that might result in emotional stress.

P-2.6   We shall not permit or participate in research that could in any way hinder the education or development of the children in our programs. Families shall be fully informed of any proposed research projects involving their children and shall have the opportunity to give or withhold consent.

P-2.7   We shall not engage in or support exploitation of families. We shall not use our relationship with a family for private advantage or personal gain, or enter into relationships with family members that might impair our effectiveness in working with children.

P-2.8   We shall develop written policies for the protection of confidentiality and the disclosure of children's records. The policy documents shall be made available to all program personnel and families. Disclosure of children's records beyond family members, program personnel, and consultants having an obligation of confidentiality shall require familial consent (except in cases of abuse or neglect).

P-2.9   We shall maintain confidentiality and shall respect the family's right to privacy, refraining from disclosure of confidential information and intrusion into family life. However, when we are concerned about a child's welfare, it is permissible to reveal confidential information to agencies and individuals who may be able to act in the child's interest.

P-2.10   In cases where family members are in conflict we shall work openly, sharing our observations of the child, to help all parties involved make informed decisions. We shall refrain from becoming an advocate for one party.

P-2.11   We shall be familiar with and appropriately use community resources and professional services that support families. After a referral has been made, we shall follow up to ensure that services have been adequately provided.

SECTION III: ETHICAL RESPONSIBILITIES TO COLLEAGUES

In a caring, cooperative work place human dignity is respected, professional satisfaction is promoted, and positive relationships are modeled. Our primary responsibility in this arena is to establish and maintain settings and relationships that support productive work and meet professional needs.

A—Responsibilities to Co-workers

Ideals:

I–3 A.1 To establish and maintain relationships of trust and cooperation with co-workers.

I–3 A.2 To share resources and information with co-workers.

I–3 A.3   To support co-workers in meeting their professional needs and in their professional development.

I–3 A.4   To accord co-workers due recognition of professional achievement.

Principles:

P–3 A.1   When we have concern about the professional behavior of a co-worker, we shall first let that person know of our concern and attempt to resolve the matter collegially.

P–3 A.2   We shall exercise care in expressing views regarding the personal attributes or professional conduct of co-workers. Statements should be based on firsthand knowledge and relevant to the interests of children and programs.

B—Responsibilities to Employers
Ideals:

I–3 B.1   To assist the program in providing the highest quality of service.

I–3 B.2   To maintain loyalty to the program and uphold its reputation unless it is violating laws and regulations designed to protect children and the provisions of this Code.

Principles:

P–3 B.1   When we do not agree with program policies, we shall first attempt to effect change through constructive action within the organization.

P–3 B.2   We shall speak or act on behalf of an organization only when authorized. We shall take care to note when we are speaking for the organization and when we are expressing a personal judgment.

P–3 B.3   We shall not violate laws or regulations designed to protect children and shall take appropriate action consistent with this Code when aware of such violations.

C—Responsibilities to Employees
Ideals:

I–3 C.1   To promote policies and working conditions that foster mutual respect competence, well-being, and self-esteem in staff members.

I–3 C.2   To create a climate of trust and candor that will enable staff to speak and act in the best interests of children, families, and the field of early childhood education.

I–3 C.3   To strive to secure an equitable compensation for those who work with or on behalf of young children.

Principles:

P–3 C.1 In decisions concerning children and programs, we shall appropriately utilize the training, experience, and expertise of staff members.

P–3 C.2 We shall provide staff members with working conditions that permit them to carry out their responsibilities, timely and non-threatening evaluation procedures, written grievance procedures, constructive feedback, and opportunities for continuing professional development and advancement.

P–3 C.3 We shall develop and maintain comprehensive written personnel policies that define program standards and, when applicable, that specify the extent to which employees are accountable for their conduct outside the work place. These policies shall be given to new staff members and shall be available for review by all staff members.

P–3 C.4 Employees who do not meet program standards shall be informed of areas of concern and, when possible, assisted in improving their performance.

P–3 C.5 Employees who are dismissed shall be informed of the reasons for their termination. When a dismissal is for cause, justification must be based on evidence of inadequate or inappropriate behavior that is accurately documented, current, and available for the employee to review.

P–3 C.6 In making evaluations and recommendations, judgments shall be based on fact and relevant to the interests of children and programs.

P–3 C.7 Hiring and promotion shall be based solely on a person's record of accomplishment and ability to carry out the responsibilities of the position.

P–3 C.8 In hiring, promotion, and provision of training, we shall not participate in any form of discrimination based on race, religion, sex, national origin, handicap, age, or sexual preference. We shall be familiar with and observe laws and regulations that pertain to employment discrimination.

SECTION IV: ETHICAL RESPONSIBILITIES TO COMMUNITY AND SOCIETY

Early childhood programs operate within a context of an immediate community made up of families and other institutions concerned with children's welfare. Our responsibilities to the community are to provide programs that meet its needs and to cooperate with agencies and professions that share responsibility for children. Because the larger society has a measure of responsibility for the welfare and protection of children, and because of our specialized expertise in child development, we acknowledge an obligation to serve as a voice for children everywhere.

Ideals:

I–4.1   To provide the community with high-quality, culturally sensitive education/care programs and services.

I–4.2   To promote cooperation among agencies and professions concerned with the welfare of young children, their families, and their teachers.

I–4.3   To work, through education, research, and advocacy, toward an environmentally safe world in which all children receiv adequate health care, food, shelter are nurtured and live free from violence.

I–4.4   To work, through education, research, and advocacy, toward a society in which all young children have access to quality programs.

I–4.5   To promote knowledge and understanding of young children and their needs. To work toward greater social acknowledgment of children's rights and greater social acceptance of responsibility for their well-being.

I–4.6   To support policies and laws that promote the well-being of children and families. To oppose those that impair their well-being. To cooperate with other individuals and groups in these efforts.

I–4.7   To further the professional development of the field of early childhood education and to strengthen its commitment to realizing its core values as reflected in this Code.

Principles:

P–4.1   We shall communicate openly and truthfully about the nature and extent of services that we provide.

P–4.2   We shall not accept or continue to work in positions for which we are personally unsuited or professional unqualified. We shall not offer services that we do not have the competence, qualifications, or resources to provide.

P–4.3   We shall be objective and accurate in reporting the knowledge upon which we base our program practices.

P–4.4   We shall cooperate with other professionals who work with children and their families.

P–4.5   We shall not hire or recommend for employment any person who is unsuited for a position with respect to competence, qualifications, or character.

P–4.6   We shall report the unethical or incompetent behavior of a colleague to a supervisor when informal resolution is not effective.

P–4.7   We shall be familiar with laws and regulations that serve to protect the children in our programs.

P–4.8   We shall not participate in practices which are in violation of laws and regulations that protect the children in our programs.

P–4.9   When we have evidence that an early childhood program is violating laws or regulations protecting children, we shall report it to persons responsible for the program. If compliance is not accomplished within a reasonable time, we will report the violation to appropriate authorities who can be expected to remedy the situation.

P–4.10   When we have evidence that an agency or a professional charged with providing services to children, families, or teachers is failing to meet its obligations, we acknowledge a collective ethical responsibility to report the problem to appropriate authorities or to the public.

P–4.11   When a program violates or requires its employees to violate this Code, it is permissible, after fair assessment of the evidence, to disclose the identity of that program.

The National Association for the Education of Young Children Statement of Commitment*

As an individual who works with young children, I commit myself to furthering the values of early childhood education as they are reflected in the NAEYC Code of Ethical Conduct.

To the best of my ability I will:

- Ensure that programs for young children are based on current knowledge of child development and early childhood education.
- Respect and support families in their task of nurturing children.
- Respect colleagues in early childhood education and support them in maintaining the NAEYC Code of Ethical Conduct.
- Serve as an advocate for children, their families, and their teachers in community and society.
- Maintain high standards of professional conduct.
- Recognize how personal values, opinions, and biases can affect professional judgment.
- Be open to new ideas and be willing to learn from the suggestions of others.
- Continue to learn, grow, and contribute as a professional.
- Honor the ideals and principles of the NAEYC Code of Ethical Conduct.

*The Statement of Commitment expresses those basic personal commitments that individuals must make in order to align themselves with the profession's responsibilities as set forth in the NAEYC Code of Ethical Conduct.

APPENDIX B

Sample Greeting Letters and Surveys to Children and their Families

SAMPLE INTRODUCTORY LETTERS TO CHILDREN AND THEIR FAMILIES

The following letters were composed by small groups of students in early childhood education classes at Bemidji State University. Many of the groups included experienced teachers. In a few cases the author combined wording from more than one letter. Readers may prefer some letters over others; the samples are intended to provide "starter ideas" for preparing introductory correspondence with families. Some letters were keyed into computers and included computer drawings, such as animals, to give them a friendly appearance. Stickers could also be used for this purpose.

To personalize the letters, the name "Shawn" is used for the child. The name given to the teacher is "Ann Gilbert." The university students recommend that the teacher locate and use the actual name of the parent or caregiver, rather than generic terms like, "Dear Parent(s)," or "To the Parent(s) of_____." In the samples the name of a single parent, "Ms. Reno," appears. The school name, "Central," is used, though the program might be a prekindergarten center as well.

The sample letters are in four types:

1. Greeting letters to children
2. Greeting letters to families
3. Survey letters to help the teacher learn about the child and family
4. Survey letters to obtain information about how parents might be involved.

1. Greeting Letters to Children

These letters are sent together with letters to parents. Usually the correspondence would be mailed a week or two before the start of the program year. A day care program may modify the greeting to send as soon as a child begins attending.

Dear Shawn,

Welcome to our kindergarten class. I am excited about this year and have a lot of fun learning activities planned. I look forward to having you in our classroom and am sure we will have a successful year together.

Your teacher,

Ann Gilbert

(Froggy computer drawing)

Dear Shawn,

Hello, my name is Ann Gilbert. I will be your teacher this fall. I am very pleased to have you in our classroom. We will be doing many fun things this year. On the first day of school we are going to start talking about elephants. When you come to school the first day, I will have a picture of an elephant on my door so you know where to go. Be sure to let your family know they can visit our classroom anytime. See you soon!

Your teacher and friend,

Ann Gilbert

(Elephant computer drawing with the words, "See you at School"!)

Dear Shawn,

I was very happy to hear that you will be coming to my class this year. I know starting school can be a little scary, but you will be meeting new friends and doing many fun things.

Your mother told me she would like to come to our class with you. That is just great. If you like, you are also welcome to bring your favorite toy to play with during play time.

I am really looking forward to seeing you and your mother next week. This year is going to be great fun. I hope you are as excited to come to school as I am. A big welcome, Shawn.

Your teacher,

Ann Gilbert

2. Greeting Letters to Families

Greeting letters to families accompany the letters to children. They should let parents know they are welcome participants in their child's education. Often, the letters invite parents to "greeting meetings," "open house" class days, or introductory conferences—at home or school. Not all parents have an easy time with reading, and teachers need to be alert to this possibility. A transition meeting that includes last year's and this year's teachers or care givers can often provide helpful information about the child and family. **[Note: In some situations, it may not be advisable for teachers to give out their home telephone number, and some teachers may not feel comfortable doing so.]**

Dear Ms. Reno,

Welcome to the world of Central School! I am looking forward to having your child in our classroom this year. I am also very happy to welcome you into our classroom.

Room visits will be all of next week, and I would like to invite you to join us and learn about our "developmentally appropriate" classroom. Parents are always welcome in my class, and if next week is inconvenient, or there is anything you would like to talk with me about, my number at school is _____. At home, you can call me anytime before ten at _____.

Again, I am looking forward to working with you and your child throughout the school year.

Sincerely,

Ann Gilbert

Dear Ms. Reno,

Hi, I will be Shawn's teacher this year. I am pleased that Shawn is going to be in my class.

I would like to set up a time when we could meet sometime soon.

Whatever time is available for you, I'll be happy to set up a meeting. I could come to your home if that would be convenient. I would like to get to know the families before the school year starts. I will be getting in touch with you in the next few days to set up a meeting.

I look forward to getting acquainted with both you and Shawn.

Sincerely,

Ann Gilbert

Dear Ms. Reno,

Hello! It is the start of a new year and I'm excited about having Shawn in our classroom. This fall I have many activities planned, and I would like to invite you to come in and join us. Next week I am going to have two "greeting meetings" for parents to learn about our program. They will be in our classroom on Wednesday and Thursday evenings at 7PM and won't go over an hour. *Feel free to attend either evening.*

At the meetings, we will discuss the activities and projects your child will be doing and also talk about things that you can do to help at home and perhaps at school. I believe that parents are very important in children's education and want parents to feel welcome in our class.

If you cannot make it to either meeting or if there is anything else you would like to talk about, my number at school is _____. At home, you can call me anytime before ten at _____.

Feel free to stop by whenever you have time to visit the classroom.

Thanks,

Ann Gilbert

3. Survey Letters to Help the Teacher Learn about the Child and Family

Survey letters of this type help the teacher to better understand and work with the child and the family. Teachers who use surveys need to be careful not to give the impression of "prying." Instead, they need to convey that the information requested is optional and will help the teacher get acquainted with the child. [**Teachers might wait until after they have met families before asking parents to complete surveys.**] Some teachers prefer not to mail these surveys out at all, but have them completed at orientation meetings or use them to structure the initial parent-teacher conference.

A request for health information is included in some of the letters. This information usually is collected more officially by the school, or program, but sometimes immediate information about health situations can be important.

Dear Shawn and Family,

My name is Ann Gilbert. I am looking forward to this year and what it will bring. I would like to tell you a little about myself. I graduated from Bemidji State University with an Elementary and Early Childhood degree. I have a family of my own, and I am looking forward to sharing things about them with you.

In order for me to get to know you better, will you and someone in your family complete this "open letter"? It will be used to say "hello" to me and your classmates.

If there is anything else you or your family would like to tell me, please feel free to write on the back. You can return it in the addressed envelope.

Your teacher,

Ann Gilbert

Dear Teachers and Friends,

The long official name I was given when I was born is _____.
But my favorite name I like to be called is _____. I am
_____ years old. My birthday is _____.

When I grow up I want to be _____.

My favorite TV show, video, or book is _____.

Some things I like to do are _____.

My favorite food is _____. Something that makes me happy is _____.

Something that makes me sad is _____.

I am excited to see you on the first day of school.

Your Friend,

_____

(Please invite child to write name.
Any way s/he wants to is fine.)

(COMPUTER PICTURE LOGO)
School to Home Family News
Issue Number One, September, 19__/20__

To the family of _____

This first issue of our class newsletter is a survey to help me get to know your child and the rest of your family better. It would be helpful if you fill out the information below and bring it to our first conference (already scheduled on _____). The survey is optional, but it will help me to work with your child and also with a lesson we will be doing on "Ourselves and Our Families." We will be talking about the survey at our conference.

The name your child would like to be called at school

_____

Your child's age _____ Your child's birthdate _____

The people in your family are:

Name _____ Relation to child _____

Name _____ Relation to child _____

Name _____ Relation to child _____

Name _____ Relation to child _____

(If others, write on back.)

Home phone _____ Emergency phone _____

Name and phone of emergency contact person_____

_____

Any allergies or health concerns you want me to know about _____

_____

_____

Your child's:

Favorite toy _____

Favorite TV show, Video or Book _____

Special Pet(s) _____

Favorite story _____

Favorite things to do/play _____

Names and ages of special friends _____
_____

Holidays your family does/does not celebrate _____
_____
_____

Please share any cultural or religious traditions that are important to your family
_____
_____
_____

Please feel free to share anything else about your family that will help me to work with your child _____
_____
_____
_____

4. Surveys about Parent Involvement

Surveys about parent involvement should also be done after the teacher has met the parent. Two ways to distribute the surveys are either at, or by mail after, the greeting meeting. One of the following flyers "Suggestions for Parent Involvement" might be sent with this survey.

Dear Ms. Reno,

Parent involvement is a special part of our program. Here is a menu of ways that parents can be involved, and they are all important. I invite you to participate in as many ways as you can.

I would be willing to:

Read a story to a small group _____ or the class _____

Make materials at home _____

Save materials at home _____

Share about my career with the class _____

Help with special occasions, parties, field trips _____

Share a talent or hobby _____

Share something of our family's cultural background _____

Help with small groups in centers/stations _____

Please comment on the choices you selected _____
_____
_____

_____Right now, I can only help at home
_____I can volunteer in the classroom. The time(s) best for me are _____

Please feel free to visit the class any time you can. You do not need to sign up in advance. I will help you find activities that you are comfortable with. My telephone number at school is _____.

> Thank you,
>
> Ann Gilbert

Dear Ms. Reno,

I enjoyed meeting you and Shawn at the Open House last Tuesday. I am happy to have Shawn in my class and am looking forward to an exciting year for all of us.

Children and parents alike really seem to benefit from working together in their children's education. There are many ways that parents and caregivers can be involved, and they are all important. I invite you to participate in any way you can.

Here are a few things that parents have done in the past. Please check any ways in which you would like to help:

_____Share or read a story

_____Help with small group activities

_____Help with special events (field trips, etc.)

_____Donate materials, such as buttons or milk cartons

_____Talk about my job

_____Bring snacks

_____Other, I can help by _____

I can:

_____come in on a regular basis.

_____come in once in a while.

_____not come in due to my schedule, but can help in other ways.

_____not sure at this time.

Parents are always welcome to come into the classroom to visit or help out. Two great times to come in would be at either 10AM or 2PM when we have learning centers.

Please call me if you have any questions. My school telephone number is _____ .

Just return this letter in the enclosed envelope. I am looking forward to a fulfilling school year for all of us.

> Sincerely,
>
> Ann Gilbert

APPENDIX C

SAMPLE BROCHURE: THE EDUCATION PROGRAM IN OUR CLASS

The following brochure was developed with input from undergraduate and graduate students in early childhood education at Bemidji State University. The brochure needs to be condensed and simplified in order to be used effectively with many parents.

PARENT'S GUIDE: THE EDUCATION PROGRAM IN OUR CLASS

Parents sometimes have questions about our education program. In our class, we use something called **developmentally appropriate practice.** This means that the teaching we do and the materials we use are tailored to the "age, stage, and needs" of each child in the class. Young children learn best when they have active, hands-on experiences that they can personally understand. In our class, we use practices that encourage problem-solving, cooperation with others, and individual expression. Children who become active, confident learners when they are young do better in school when they are older. Our program is designed to help your child learn that he can succeed at school.

This brochure tells about our education program. We go over the brochure during the greeting meeting with parents at the beginning of the school year. If you have questions or concerns, feel free to call me at home or school.

Parents are important in their children's education. You are welcome to visit our classroom and become a part of our education program. You, your child, and I are all on the same team. We share common goals. I look forward to working with you this year.

Why Play Is a Daily Part of Our Program

As a parent you may ask how children learn while they are playing. Through play children learn things that cannot be easily taught. In play children are forced to use their minds. They make decisions and solve problems. They figure out how to make things work and how to put things together. They have experiences from painting to hammering nails to reading books that help them learn how to think. Play helps children to understand symbols—like designs and pictures—that are needed for reading, writing, and arithmetic. Science skills learned through play include observing, guessing what will happen next, gathering information, and testing their guesses. Children use words in their play to share thoughts and feelings, and so their language skills develop.

Through play children master control of their bodies. By playing with dolls or blocks or Legos, children are developing eye-hand coordination. By running and climbing and moving to music, they are developing large muscles and becoming physically fit.

They also learn to get along with others. Children have different ideas when they play. They learn how to listen to others' views, how to lead, and how to follow. They also learn to cope when things don't go the way they planned—for themselves or others. They learn how to solve conflicts with words rather than fists—a very important life skill. They learn to get along with others who have backgrounds different than themselves. Through play, children learn to control and express their emotions.

It is important for children to feel free to learn without fear of making errors. Play allows them to do this. (We have a saying in our class, "Mistakes are OK to make. We just try to learn from them.") Play is more than fun and games. It involves many types of learning and should be a part of every child's life—at school as well as at home.

Why Our Art Is Creative

Teachers in sixth grade would never give a class an essay to copy. They want children to do their own work. It is the same with art in the early years. A teacher who provides a model for children to duplicate encourages copying, and discourages children from thinking for themselves.

Nowadays teachers know more about the importance of art than they did when we were in school. Teachers know that even before children can read and write, they tell stories through their art. Art is the young child's essay, the young child's journal. If we ask a child to tell us about a creative picture, even if it doesn't look like "something" to us, the child often has a story about it. The making and telling of stories through art is important for the development of later skills in reading, writing, and self-expression. But this can only happen if the art is creative, if each child's picture is unique—truly the child's "own work."

Teachers who let children explore freely with materials are using art in a developmentally appropriate way. So are teachers who use spoken words rather than models to motivate children to draw their own pictures. Teachers frequently use themes to encourage creative art. Some popular themes are "what I like to do outdoors in the spring" and "who the people are in my family."

One of the things we now know about art is that children go through stages in their art development. Art that is creative, so that each child's work is accepted, lets each child work at his or her stage of development. Children develop important thinking skills, as well as eye-hand coordination, by doing creative pictures.

Though popular, coloring books and craft projects are *not* developmentally appropriate activities. They do not let young children work at their stage of development. Coloring in lines and copying crafts are easier for children in a later art stage that happens at about age seven. Children who are in earlier stages, such as the scribbling stage or the early picture stage, do not have the skills necessary for coloring in—or cutting out—lines accurately. Such experiences often lead to frustration and feelings that "I'm no good at art." We do not ask a kindergarten child to print like a third grader. For the same reason, we should not ask young children to work at a stage of art development that they have not yet reached. It is better for their development to give them blank paper and encourage creative pictures.

Please appreciate the original art work your child brings home from our class. Save samples and you will see your child's skills progress. Ask your children to tell you about their pictures. Enjoy their responses even if they tell you, "This is not a story to tell; it's a picture to look at." Your enjoyment of their creative art will help them gain ability to express their thoughts and feelings—important skills for school success. Their work will still be charming, and it will be *their own.*

Why We Use the Whole Language Approach

Whole language is an approach to teaching writing and reading. It is based on the idea that children learn language best by using all of its parts together. With whole language, children use all of their communication skills, speaking, listening, singing, art, and beginning writing and reading. In a whole language classroom there is less emphasis on drill of separate skills than in the past.

Here are some important whole language ideas so that you can see what it is all about.

1. Whole language surrounds children with the printed word through story books, labels of objects, lists of words and letters, and opportunities to write. Children learn to read by making sense of the pictures and printed words around them, including their own.
2. Children learn to write by using creative spelling and printing on a daily basis in their journals. With experience they eventually learn how to spell and write correctly, but we do not expect them to when they are young.
3. Writing by children helps them: learn thinking skills, develop their expressive abilities, develop a sense of "authorship," and practice writing mechanics. Important writing mechanics include

sound-letter relationships, sentence structure, and the meanings of words.

4. Reading to and with children acquaints them with printed words, teaches children to love books and reading, and encourages positive attachments between adults and children.

5. Whole language stresses "parents as partners." By encouraging writing and reading in home and school, parents contribute to their children's "literacy development." The whole language team includes the parent, teacher, and child working together.

6. Whole language builds confidence, skill, and self-esteem. It is the "natural approach" to learning to read and write.

Why We Use Real Objects in Our Mathematics Program

Children are very quick at learning to count from 1 to 20 or even 1 to 100. Until they are older in second or third grade, though, they have a difficult time understanding what numbers stand for. They can hold up four or five fingers when you ask them how old they are, but don't really understand what "five years" means. (Ask them how old they think you or other people they know are—and enjoy their responses.) They can count twelve flowers on a worksheet perhaps, but not fully understand what the words "12 flowers" mean.

To help them build a concept of number, children need to sort, compare, match and count **real objects.** The objects provide a "concrete clue" as to what 12 objects really are and later what "12 take away 6" is. Manipulating objects encourages problem-solving and enhances logical thinking. The children will enjoy math and want to experiment more in mathematics.

In our class we begin by using materials that are familiar to the children. (Examples: buttons, keys, rocks, shoes, etc.) One way to get the children excited and involved is to have them bring sets of items from home. These materials will be used for motivation as well as tools for exploring and learning. (I will be talking more about how you can help your child develop a "collection.") When the children are comfortable with the materials in the lessons, they will have an easier time learning basic mathematics concepts. Skills that will aid them in mathematics later include forming sets, matching items, and understanding numeral to number correspondence ($2 = **; 3 = ***$).

We are very excited about our mathematics program. Through manipulating objects, children will have an easier time understanding and enjoying mathematics. (We want to prevent "math anxiety.") We would like to see all components of the education program be positive experiences for the children.

Why We Use a Guidance Approach in Our Classroom

Some forms of discipline may stop classroom problems temporarily, but they tend to have negative side effects. These forms of discipline often lower children's self-esteem, cause children to feel negatively toward school and learning, and lead to behavior or personal problems in the long run. Our class uses a guidance approach to discipline. This is what a teacher does who uses "guidance discipline." She:

1. Provides a developmentally appropriate program that encourages children to be active, involved learners.
2. Teaches children to appreciate themselves and others as worthwhile individuals.
3. Builds a group spirit in which all children know they are important members of the class.
4. Provides children with a few clear guidelines for behavior and a reliable classroom environment so that they can learn from their mistakes.
5. Guides children to use words to settle problems, as much as possible on their own.
6. Addresses problems directly, but respects the individual child by not embarrassing or humiliating.
7. Builds partnerships with parents, so that the teacher and parent can work together to help the child learn and develop.

If you would like more information about our guidance program, please feel free to get in touch. [The teacher may wish to provide other materials such as the position statement, **Developmentally Appropriate Guidance of Young Children,** by the Minnesota Association for the Education of Young Children—Appendix D.]

Why Parents Are Important in Our Program

As you may have figured out from the rest of this brochure, **parents are very important in our education program.** You are the first and foremost educator of your child. We both want the same thing for your child, that he has a successful, productive year in our class—one that will help your child become an effective learner and a happy classmate. To reach this goal, parents and teachers need to work together as a team.

Parents can participate in our program in many ways this year. Each parent's involvement will be a bit different. This pamphlet is to let you know about some of the ways. Remember, you are the first and foremost educator of your child. To whatever extent you can be involved, your child (and our whole class) will benefit.

At Home

1. Appreciate the work your child brings home. Talk with your child about what he is doing in school.
2. Read over the newsletters and notices your child brings home. Note special school events and suggested at-home activities.

3. Read with your child each day. Limit TV viewing and help your child find other activities. Model reading (and writing) in the home.
4. Talk with your child for a few minutes each day about anything he would like to talk about. Be a good listener.
5. Do activities with your child on a regular basis.
6. Save things that we could use in class. We have a need for everything from jars of buttons to items of clothing for "dress-up." Let me know about anything you think we might be able to use. I may ask in the newsletter or by phone or E-mail for special items from time to time.

With the Teacher

7. Feel free to call me. At school my telephone number is _____. Best times to reach me are _____. At home my telephone number is _____. Best times are _____. [Home number optional.]
8. I try to make a home visit to each family during the year. I will be contacting you to discuss whether this would be possible.
9. We have four regularly scheduled parent-teacher conferences during the year. These are very important for us to work as a team. If you can't make a conference, let's talk about another time or place that would be more convenient.
10. On occasion an additional parent-teacher conference may be necessary. I will contact you directly to arrange the conference and will let you know then what the conference would be about.
11. From time to time we have parent meetings, such as the Greeting Meeting. These are optional, but we would love to have you attend.

In the Classroom

12. Because I have an "open classroom" policy, you are welcome to visit any time. We have a special "parents' corner" set up in the room. You are welcome to just observe or to join in. I would be happy to talk with you about things you could do when you visit.
13. Help with special events. We sometimes have class parties, events, and field trips. Parents who can help at these special times are much appreciated.
14. Each week we invite a family to come in and share with the class something that is special to one or more family members. We invite all families to do our "Family Share" sometime during the year. Members can share something of their heritage, a hobby or special interest. I will be talking with you about this.
15. Another way to volunteer is as a Very Important Parent. VIPs come in on a weekly basis for a short period of time and help

with such activities as learning centers or small group reading. We try to accommodate the schedules of anyone who would like to come in on a regular basis, but some times work better than others. Let me know if you would like to become a VIP. We'd love to have you do this.

16. Our program has committees, councils, and an Association. I will be talking about these at the Greeting Meeting. Your participation at this "policy level" will help make our total program run better.

As you can see, there are many ways you can be involved. Please fill out the Parent Survey to sign-up. Your involvement on our team will be much appreciated!

Developmentally Appropriate Guidance of Young Children (Position Statement of the Minnesota Association for the Education of Young Children, 3rd Edition)

This position statement of the Minnesota Association for the Education of Young Children is the third edition of a document first published in 1989. Its intent remains the same: to give direction to the use of developmentally appropriate guidance with young children aged birth to eight.

The importance of guidance techniques that are based on sound child development principles has been well established, made even more so by events of violence in our schools and society since the initial edition. Now in the 21st century, our ability to guide children's development in ways that result in what Piaget called "autonomy" (the ability to make decisions intelligently and ethically) has become a paramount education priority. By responding to classroom conflicts in ways that teach rather than punish and include all in the group, rather than exclude some from the group, teachers of young children are contributing to a more peaceful world.

This document is intended for use by administrators, teachers, and all other caregivers of young children. The term "teacher" is used in a general sense to refer to all adults who care for young children. **Guidance** is defined as an approach to children's development in which conflicts are viewed as teaching and learning opportunities; the adult helps children learn from their mistakes, rather than punishing them for the mistakes they make, assists children to learn to solve their problems, rather than punishing them for having problems they cannot solve.

Teachers who use guidance are sometimes firm but always friendly, protecting self-concept and respecting feelings so that children do not come to label themselves as behavioral failures. MNAEYC holds that teachers of young children should use guidance that is educational in tone and responsive to the child's level of development rather than using punitive discipline.

SUMMARY OF PRINCIPLES FOR DEVELOPMENTALLY APPROPRIATE GUIDANCE

Principle One   The teacher uses guidance in order to teach children democratic life skills.

Principle Two   The teacher regards classroom conflicts as mistaken behavior and uses conflicts as teaching opportunities.

Principle Three   The teacher works to understand the reasons for children's behavior.

Principle Four   The teacher builds and maintains an encouraging class-room in which all children feel welcome as fully participating members.

Principle Five   The teacher uses developmentally appropriate practice to prevent mistaken behavior that is a result of a mismatch between the program and the child.

Principle Six   The teacher functions as a professional rather than a technician.

PRINCIPLE ONE

The Teacher Uses Guidance in Order to Teach Children Democratic Life Skills

A typical purpose of traditional classroom discipline has been to keep children "in line." When teachers make this purpose a priority, they tend to use discipline techniques that rely on "blame and shame" and slide into punishment. Embarrassment-based discipline—singling children out, scolding, using time-out—causes children to feel unwelcome in the group and unworthy. Children may begin to fall into a self-fulfilling prophecy and have more, not fewer, problems in the classroom.

The purpose of guidance is to teach children the **democratic life skills** they need to be healthy individuals and productive citizens.

Democratic life skills include the ability to:

- **see one's self as a worthy individual and a capable member of the group**
- **express strong emotions in non-hurting ways**
- **solve problems ethically and intelligently**
- **be understanding of the feelings and viewpoints of others**
- **work cooperatively in groups, with acceptance of the human differences among members**

Democratic Life Skills Are the Outcomes of Guidance. The attainment of democratic life skills, more than scores on standardized tests and other measures of academic achievement, will keep our society strong, just, and free.

Example Two children first argued then hit and kicked each other over sharing new miniature family figures. The teacher did not take the figures away from the children and give them a time out for fighting. The teacher did separate the children to cool them down and bring them together to resolve the conflict. After discussing the conflict, the children (with the teacher's help) decided that one child would have his two adult figures run "the store." The other child would bring in his rather large family and buy "lots of food and stuff." (This was not the solution the adult anticipated, but the children were satisfied so the adult went with it.) The children agreed that next time it would be better to use their words or get the teacher to help rather than fight.

PRINCIPLE TWO

The Teacher Regards Classroom Conflicts as Mistaken Behavior and Uses Conflicts as Teaching Opportunities

Democratic life skills are a life-long endeavor. Some adults never learn them and most of us have to work hard to use them consistently. Children, with only months of life experience and brain development (a five-year-old is only sixty months), are just beginning to learn these complex skills. In the process of learning, they make mistakes. For this reason, a teacher who uses guidance views the conflicts that children have not as misbehavior, but as **mistaken behavior.** This shift enables the adult to think about what s/he can teach children as a result of the conflict, not what s/he has to do to the children for having it. The shift in attitude empowers the adult to be a mediator and teacher rather than rule "enforcer."

Example Damon didn't make it back from the playground in time and wet his pants. Charissa saw this and with Delray began calling Damon "piss pants Damon." While the class was coming in and finding things to work on, the teacher got Damon dry cloths. She then had a guidance talk with Charissa and Delray. She told them she once wet her pants at school and asked them if they had ever had an accident and wet their pants. Charissa said she did once. Delray said he didn't but his little brother did. The teacher got the children to say how Damon probably felt and then asked them to think of some ways they could help Damon feel better. Later in the day, the teacher smiled when she saw Charissa talking with Damon. She smiled again when she saw Damon and Delray playing together.

PRINCIPLE THREE

The Teacher Works to Understand the Reasons for Children's Behavior

There are always reasons for children's behavior. Working to understand these reasons can assist the adult in helping the child. Although we can never know another person fully, we can increase our understanding and that effort in itself can lead to better relations and progress in learning democratic life skills.

Children Do Things to See What Will Happen.   Children learn from such actions, and others' reactions. Sometimes "experimentation mistaken behavior," if harmless, should be ignored. If the adult decides to intervene, s/he should do so in a way that teaches the child about consequences and alternatives, but also appreciates the child's natural curiosity: the child's need to learn.

Example.   A child marks on a table. "Maria (name change), you can color on paper. Let's get some soapy water and wash the table. Then we'll get some paper to use with those markers."

Children Do Things Because They Have Been Influenced By Others to Do Them, Either at Home or in the Classroom.   With "socially influenced" mistaken behavior, the adult firmly but matter-of-factly reinforces a limit, but also teaches an acceptable alternative for next time.

Example.   Child says, "that damned kid makes me so mad." Teacher (hiding smile) responds: "Peter made you feel upset, and you can tell him or me, but you don't need to call names. We'll get the message."

Children Show Strong Needs (Serious) Mistaken Behavior Because They Have Trouble in Their Lives That Is Beyond Their Ability to Understand and Manage.   Sometimes the trouble can be physical, such as an undetected illness or injury. Other times, the trouble may be caused by a serious situation at home, center, or school. When a child shows rigid or extreme behavior, the adult should be alerted to the need for more information, especially if the behavior continues for more than a day or two. Observing and talking with the child can often add to an adult's understanding. Meeting with other staff can be helpful. A phone call or conference with parents may well be essential to better understanding the problem. Occasionally, consulting with an outside professional can help. When staff fully use their resources for understanding what is going on, a coordinated comprehensive guidance plan is easier to construct.

Example.   A teacher notices that a child shows uncharacteristic irritability especially toward the beginning and end of each week. Talks with a parent determine that the parents have separated and the child is living with the mother during the week and the father on the weekends. The staff works together with the parent to make the transitions more understandable and less traumatic for the child.

Children with serious problems may show them in the classroom because it is the safest place in their lives. These children are asking for help, inappropriately perhaps, but in the only way they can. Often, they are the most difficult to like, but need a positive relationship with a teacher the most. With such children MNAEYC cautions against the use of such labels as "challenging" or "difficult"—even if the terms have intervention programs behind them.

Labels easily cause a teacher to become overly sensitized and to only notice the challenging or difficult behaviors. S/he may miss productive behaviors and admirable qualities in the child and give feedback that is distancing and negative. The child may feel stigmatized, disqualified from group membership, at a time when a sense of belonging is crucial for healthy development. The label a child receives may stick even with future teachers and in future classrooms. Whenever a young child is labeled as a result of having problems, rather than being helped to resolve them, schooling becomes more difficult.

PRINCIPLE FOUR

The Teacher Builds and Maintains an Encouraging Classroom in Which All Children Feel Welcome as Fully Participating Members

Informally defined, an encouraging classroom is a place where children want to be when they are sick as opposed to not wanting to be there when they are well. Trust and acceptance are the foundation of the relationship of an adult and a child. In the encouraging classroom, the teacher is able to build this foundation with every child, even those children who experience frequent conflicts. Except in rare circumstances, which always involve the family and often involve other professionals, the child's status as a member of an encouraging classroom is not up for debate.

In the encouraging classroom, the teacher does not need to love each child—teachers are human and not angelic—but as a professional, the teacher does need to build with each a working environment of trust and acceptance. The reason is that children who gain the understanding that they are valued and belong tend to develop positive self-concepts and have less need to act out against the world. With all children in the encouraging classroom, the teacher's goal is the same, to assist in making progress toward democratic life skills. All of the children are special, just because they are in the class. Some children just need more time and extra help to learn the skills, because life has given them a longer road to go.

Three practices mark the encouraging classroom. **First,** the teacher does not single out children for either praise or criticism. S/he acknowledges individuals privately; then they know the encouragement given is really meant for them. S/he addresses public acknowledgement to the group as a whole. In both cases, the teacher understands that acknowledgement is often more needed by learners as encouragement during the learning process than as praise given after the task is completed.

Example.   The children in my class were making story pictures of thanks to send to the rescue workers in New York after the World Trade Center tragedy. I was really impressed with their efforts and said, "I like how you are all working so hard on your story pictures. Your work shows such thought about all the rescuers did." After I made this comment, I noticed several children smiling as they worked. Some even complimented their neighbors' pictures. One child had made a very detailed picture and was printing "Thk u fr hlg." She said, "But I don't think they could read it." I knelt down and put my arm around her shoulder. I told her I could read it, and did. She said, "Yeah, may be they could," and wrote more words on her picture that I also read back to her.

A second practice of the encouraging classroom is that traditional discipline techniques like time outs and names on the board are replaced by guidance methods like conflict management, guidance talks, class meetings, and comprehensive guidance. We saw an example of conflict management under principle one (the two children fighting over the figures), an example of a guidance talk under principle two (with the two children calling a third a name), and an example of comprehensive guidance under principle three (the child who was experiencing split custody with her parents).

Teachers hold class meetings, even with prekindergarten children, when conflicts in the class become public and affect many members. Instead of traditional punishment of the whole group, the teacher meets with the class to try to resolve the problem together. Guidelines for class meetings typically are that anyone can speak; we need to listen carefully to each other; we tell the truth; we appreciate and respect each other.

Example.   An early childhood class had to walk down the hall of a school to reach the gymnasium. A few teachers complained to the principal that the children were being too loud as they walked down the hall. The teacher held a class meeting to solve the problem. After the children discussed the problem, the teacher asked if anyone had ideas about how they could remember to walk down the hall quietly. One child said, "I know, we can be mommy and daddy elephants who have to tiptoe so we don't wake the babies." To the teacher's amazement, the other children liked the idea. As they walked down the hall the next day, the principal loudly complimented the class. "Ssh," said one of the children, "You'll wake the babies"!

Third, the teacher works with other adults, both teaching team members and parents, to form partnerships that anchor the encouraging classroom. To children, anyone bigger than they are is a teacher. "Official" teachers in encouraging classrooms work hard right from the beginning of the year to build partnerships with other adults. With parents, the teacher might send notes home, make phone calls, do home visits, set up e-mail systems (with some), and generally take the lead to let parents know their involvement and input in the conduct of the class is important.

Orienting all staff (and regular volunteers) to guidance ideas through meetings, workshops, and booklets (like this one) are important. Staff together might make a handout of their own guidance ideas and use this as a basis of discussion with parents. Children who see significant adults in their lives modeling democratic life skills with each other will understand more fully that these skills are important to learn.

Example.   A teaching team consisting of lead teacher, assistant teacher, teacher aide, foster grandparent, and special education teacher met to discuss upcoming parent conferences, to go on this year during the school day. The teacher asked for ideas about how this could happen. The staff agreed on a plan which had these parts. The already established parent corner in the classroom was, with the addition of more comfortable chairs, where the conferences would happen. Each conference would include the lead teacher and one other adult who knew the child well. The other adults would implement a theme planned for the week, which included several independent center activities. The teaching team met with the children to explain what would be happening and that whatever adult was with them was to be their teacher. The children took an active interest in seeing that the plan worked, and the staff felt like a true team, as the conferences were held relatively hitch free.

PRINCIPLE FIVE

The Teacher Uses Developmentally Appropriate Practice to Prevent Mistaken Behavior That Is the Result of a Mismatch Between the Program and the Child.

Much mistaken behavior children do not cause as much as fall into. "Institution-caused" mistaken behavior is often the result of pressures teachers feel to "get children ready for the next level." While we all have a right to expect educational accountability—that children learn productively given their age, development, and experience—as professionals we need to work to reduce the effects of political accountability—the ill informed views of some politicians and administrators that children perform at token high profile levels come whatever. As a veteran kindergarten teacher once said, "My job is not to prepare children for first grade. It is to give them the best possible kindergarten experience they can have."

In the interest of educational accountability—and sometimes to curb the influence of political accountability—teachers monitor and change practices in their classrooms that unintentionally invite mistaken behavior:

- Group activities that require too much sitting and listening.
- Projects and lessons that have prescribed results too easy for some and too difficult for others.
- Schedules that fail to provide balanced routines and efficient transitions.
- Competitive expectations and evaluation techniques that make some children feel like "winners" and some like "losers."

Young children "are wired" for hands-on, active, personally relevant learning experience that fully engage their minds and their bodies. When teachers recognize that children will be more able to perform the tasks of traditional classrooms when they are older—and won't necessarily benefit from "rehearsal"—they understand the connection of developmentally appropriate practice and guidance in the encouraging classroom.

Example. In a kindergarten class of 24 children the teacher had centers set up around the edges of the classroom for reading, "house" and blocks and trucks. The teacher felt pressured to have both a math focus and reading focus right away in the morning "while the children were fresh," and just let the children who were finished use the centers before recess. Gradually, he noted frustration among the children with this arrangement, as the slower workers were not getting time with the centers, some children were rushing their work to have center time, and the children in the centers had to quit soon after they started. Moreover, he noted that the centers seemed too crowded, and some children used the large open center area of the room as a raceway for the trucks. In fact, a couple of the boys referred to this area as "the track."

After attending a workshop on active learning, the teacher added a writing center, art center, music center, science center, and technology center. He spaced the centers around the room to eliminate runways, and clustered them by estimated activity levels. He scheduled an open center time between the academic focus times and asked the children to plan the centers they intended to use and record in journals (with early writing and art) what they did. His morning schedule became more productive, and he began to weave center use into his "focus" times and his periodic themes.

PRINCIPLE SIX

The Teacher Functions as a Professional Rather than a Technician.

Teachers who are technicians react to conflicts in the traditional ways of their classrooms, frequently using discipline that slides into punishment. Rather than seek to understand the mistaken behavior and proactively teach alternatives to it, they react in a knee-jerk manner, enforcing rules to keep children obedient to the authority of the teaching staff. Teachers who are professionals attempt to replace stock reactions to mistaken behavior by using guidance to build and encouraging classroom and teach democratic life skills. As professionals, teachers make decisions about how to respond to behavior based on their judgments of the events at the time.

Still, because they are human, sometimes teachers may jump in too quickly, overreact, show inconsistency, lose their tempers, or otherwise show human frailties. Just as they encourage children to, teachers who are professionals attempt to learn from their mistakes. They know that their job is challenging because young children are just at the beginning of learning democratic life skills. They have accepted the fact that being a caring professional means modeling as well as teaching these skills every day, all the time.

When upset, teachers use methods to diffuse and express their feelings that do not put down the other person. They may pay attention to the "victim" first and talk with the child who did the hurting after they've cooled down. They may use "I messages" to describe their feelings rather than accuse and disparage the "culprits." They may firmly request more information before they make a hasty judgment. They may check themselves before responding to a child who is difficult for them to understand. They may work with others who know a child or family better than they. They monitor their moods and feelings, aware of their impact on teaching effectiveness.

Examples. "Skip, I saw what happened. You need to wait here until I find out if Jenny is all right. We'll talk about it in a few minutes when I've calmed down."

"I am really bothered that the water got spilled out of the aquarium. We need to fill it up quickly and then we'll talk about what happened."

Finally, and most important, teachers recognize that they are learners even as they are teachers, and they continue to learn even as they teach.

Examples
- Teachers and caregivers participate in peer assessment including observation by and of other professionals in order to get feedback and engage in personal review of teaching practices.
- Teachers use collaborations with parents, staff, and outside professionals in order to continue learning about the children they work with.

- Teachers read, attend courses, conferences, and workshops in order to update their store of ideas.
- Teachers use observation and communication skills to learn from the best of all teachers, the children themselves.

RECOMMENDED READINGS

Beane, A. L. (2000). *Bully free classroom.* Minneapolis, MN: Free Spirit Publishing.

Betz, C. (1994). Beyond time-out: Tips from a teacher. *Young Children, 49*(3), 10–14.

Da Ros, D. A., & Kovach, B. A. (1998). Assisting toddlers and caregivers during conflict resolutions: Interactions that promote socialization. *Childhood Education, 75*(1), 25–30.

Elkind, D. (1997, November). The death of child nature: Education in the postmodern world. *Phi Delta Kappan,* 241–245.

Froschl, M., & Sprung, B. (1999). On purpose: Addressing teasing and bullying in early childhood. *Young Children, 54*(2), 70–72.

Gartrell, D. J. (2000). *What the kids said today: Using classroom conversations to become a better teacher.* St. Paul, MN: Redleaf Press.

Gartrell, D. J. (2001). Beyond time-out part one: Using guidance to build an encouraging classroom. *Young Children, 56*(6), 8–16.

Gartrell, D. J. (2002). Beyond time-out part two: Using guidance to maintain an encouraging classroom. *Young Children, 57*(2), 36–42.

Harris, T. T., & Fuqua, J. D. (2000). What goes around comes around: Building a community of learners through circle times. *Young Children, 55*(1), 44–47.

Lawhon, T. (1997). Encouraging friendships among children. *Childhood Education, 73*(4), 228–231.

Logan, T. (1998). Creating a kindergarten community. *Young Children, 53*(2), 22–26.

McClurg, L. G. (1998). Building an ethical community in the classroom: Community meeting. *Young Children, 53*(2), 30–35.

Schreiber, M. E. (1999). Time-outs for toddlers: Is our goal punishment or education. *Young Children, 54*(4), 22–25.

Weber-Schwartz, N. (1987). Patience or understanding? *Young Children, 42*(3), 52–54.

Approved by the MNAEYC Board—November, 2001

Developmentally Appropriate Guidance Committee

Dan Gartrell, Author	Vicki Iverson
Diane McLinn, Chair	Ginny Petty
Roz Anderson	Zoe Ann Wignall
Mary Holub	Katie Williams

Revised by Dan Gartrell and Nancy Johnson—September, 2001

MNAEYC
1821 University Ave.
Suite 296-S
St. Paul, Mn 55104
Dfitzwater-dewey@aeyc-mn.org

INDIVIDUAL GUIDANCE PLAN WORKSHEET

INDIVIDUAL GUIDANCE PLAN WORKSHEET

Child's name_____
Initial Write-Up Date_____

1. Noted Behaviors
Behavior Observed: Thoughts about Behavior:

2. Additional Information
Check procedures used. Then summarize information gained.
__Discussion with child. Date:__   __Discussion with parent. Date:__
__Discussion with other staff. Date:__   __Discussion with other
                                            professionals. Date:__

3. Cooperative Strategy Meeting   **Date:**
Persons attending meeting:

Strategy to be tried:

_____

*An explanation of the Individual Guidance Plan and illustrations for its use were provided in Chapter Eleven. In addition, in both the Instructor's Guide and the **Online Resource/Companion** to this book, a full-length form of the worksheet can be found. Suggested steps for using the IGP accompanies the form in both resources. The worksheet can be used without permission. The author does ask for feedback on its use by e-mail: dgartrell@bemidjistate.edu. Dr. Dan Gartrell, Professional Education Department, Bemidji State University, 1500 Birchmont Ave, Bemidji State University, Bemidji, MN 56601.*

4. Follow-up Meeting or Review   **Date:**

Effort/progress shown by child:

Progress still needed:

Any change in strategy:

5. Summary of Results/Changes as of (Date)_____

6. Summary of Results/Changes as of (Date)_____

7. Summary of Results/Changes as of (Date)_____

GLOSSARY

A

adjustment relational pattern—The level of social relations in which priority is given to showing behaviors expected by significant others.

anti-bias curriculum—An education program designed to prevent the development of bias in relation to racism, sexism, and children with disabilities.

anticipatory set—A feeling of positive anticipation or motivation in children created by the teacher often in a large group setting toward a follow-up activity often done individually or in small groups.

assertive discipline—An organized, "obedience-based" discipline system in which the roles of the student and teacher are clearly defined and the will of the teacher is to prevail.

attachment—A relationship with an adult, when positive, is likely to result in enhanced self-esteem and receptivity to guidance in the child.

authentic assessment—The use of tools such as anecdotal observations, check lists, and samples of children's work to assess children's progress while children are engaged in ongoing activities of the classroom.

autonomy—Piaget's term for the ability to make ethical, intelligent decisions that balance others' viewpoints with one's own. Opposite of *heteronomy*.

B

background violence—Violence that children experience indirectly through media, aggressive play, and witnessing disrespectful interpersonal communications.

being direct—A firm intervention technique with mistaken behavior in which a teacher describes the problem succinctly, directs the child or children to an acceptable alternative behavior, and sometimes expresses the teacher's feelings toward the mistaken behavior.

belonging—A basic need of children codefining Erikson's period in early childhood of initiative versus guilt; failure to meet the need for belonging results in alienation (stigma).

body language—Nonverbal language, such as smiles, eye-contact, and physical proximity used to support children and remind of guidelines.

boisterous activity level—The level of play at learning centers that is very active and often loud.

brevity as quick intervention—A quick, firm but friendly intervention technique in which a teacher uses concise language to reestablish limits.

bucolic activity level—The level of activity at learning centers that is quiet, tranquil.

buffer activity—An activity that uses time productively while waiting.

bullying as violence—Bullying is the assertion of the will of one person upon the other through psychological and physical means. Bullying causes harm to both the victim and the perpetrator and as such is a form of violence.

busy activity level—The level of activity at learning centers that is bustling but not overly active or loud.

C

cardinal principle—The intervention strategy attributed to Ginott in which the teacher addresses mistaken behaviors, firmly if needed, but remains respectful of the personality of the child.

character education—Education for which the outcome is an ability to make decisions that are ethical, intelligent, and socially responsive.

child guidance—Leadership with children that models and teaches democratic life skills.

child negotiation—The process whereby two or more children are able to resolve a conflict peaceably on their own.

child-report—An alternate term for tattling by which children express concerns to teachers about perceived conflicts or emergencies.

children taking charge—The capacity of children in a conflict situation to remove themselves from the immediate site and to negotiate a resolution.

class meeting—A scheduled or unscheduled meeting of the teacher and the class to address business matters and matters of concern to one or more members of the group; other terms sometimes used with specialized meetings include *sharing circles* and *magic circles*.

classroom management—Techniques used with the group to build the encouraging classroom by reducing the need for mistaken behavior in the group.

Code of Ethical Conduct—This position statement of the Minnesota Association for the Education of Young Children "offers guidelines for responsible behavior and sets forth a common basis for resolving the principal ethical dilemmas encountered in early childhood education" (from Preamble of Code).

collaboration—Working in a team with others to solve problems and accomplish tasks that cannot be done on one's own.

commanding choices—Firm direction by the teacher for a child to choose between two alternative appropriate behaviors, one of which may be preferred by the teacher, but either of which is acceptable.

compliment sandwich—An encouragement technique that provides at least two acknowledgments of effort and progress accompanied by one request or suggestion for further progress.

comprehensive guidance—A multifaceted guidance strategy that is used with continuing strong needs mistaken behavior and includes improving the relationship with the child, learning more about the child's situation, nonpunitive crisis intervention, holding one or more meetings with fellow staff and parents, and determination, implementation, and assessment of an Individual Guidance Plan.

conditional acceptance—A classroom atmosphere in which students are aware that they will be accepted or rejected by the teacher on the basis of their performance academically and behaviorally, their backgrounds, or their personalities.

conflict—A disagreement over an action one or more parties has taken, usually involving property, territory, or privilege; a mistaken behavior by a child or children, disagreed with by the teacher.

conflict management—The ability to prevent and resolve disputes in a civil, peaceable manner.

conflict management models—Defined procedures, sometimes involving lessons, verbal steps, and props, that adults and children use to manage conflicts.

conflict resolution—The ability to resolve disputes in a peaceable, civil manner.

constructivist education—The concept that the child constructs knowledge through interaction with the social and physical environment, and the educational strategy that enables this learning process to take place.

contact talk—Conversation between an adult and child for the purpose of sharing time together and becoming better acquainted rather than to accomplish an ulterior purpose.

Continuum of Violence—Represented by Levin's pyramid of violence, the concept explains that the more intensive and ongoing the violence that children experience, the more they are affected by that violence.

conventional discipline—The use of rewards and punishments to keep children under the teacher's control.

cooling-down time—A nonpunitive alternative to the time-out chair in which a teacher removes a child from the group and assists the child to regain control of her or his emotions.

correction by direction—Intervention in which a teacher briefly directs a child to a guideline or appropriate behavior, rather than admonishes about a mistaken behavior.

creative conflict—Disagreement with another that the parties believe can be resolved by negotiation and cooperative problem solving.

crisis intervention—Nonpunitive methods the teacher uses when a conflict has gotten out of hand; a first priority is ceasing a danger of harm or serious disruption.

crisis management techniques—Guidance methods of last resort when a conflict has gotten out of hand such as commanding cooperation, separation, a cool-down time, or physical restraint.

D

day clock—A particular kind of period chart that uses a "one-handed clock" to track routine time blocks in the daily schedule.

democratic life skills—The skills children need to be healthy individuals and productive citizens of a democracy, including the acceptance of self, intelligent and ethical decision-making, cooperative problem solving, and the acceptance of others regardless of human differences.

describe-direct—A brief intervention technique that includes two steps: describing objectively the mistaken behavior; directing children to an alternative acceptable behavior.

describe-express-direct—A brief intervention technique that includes three steps: describing objectively the mistaken behavior; explaining one's feelings about the behavior; directing children to an alternative acceptable behavior.

describe without labeling—An intervention technique in which a teacher "gives words" to a conflict by addressing the situation and avoiding references to a child's teacher.

developmental egocentrism—The inability of young children to understand the complexity of social factors in any situation and to see things from one's own perspective.

developmentally appropriate practice (DAP)—Educational practice that accommodates the development and individual needs of each child in the class.

developmentally inappropriate practice—Educational practice that fails to accommodate the development and individual needs of each child in the class.

diagnosis—Systematic assessment to determine the nature of a difficulty in order to empower the child to overcome it.

diagnosis versus labeling—The difference between a special education diagnosis and a disparaging label that puts a child at risk for stigma.

differentiated staffing—Adults of differing educational and experience backgrounds working together as a teaching team.

direct intervention—A sequence of responses to serious mistaken behavior that involves the teacher's describing what he or she sees, sometimes reporting feelings, and directing to alternative behaviors.

discipline—Derived from the Latin term *disciplina* meaning teaching, instruction. In this progressive sense, synonymous with guidance. In its everyday meaning, the use of rewards and punishments to keep children "in line." As a verb, "to discipline" commonly means to punish in order to bring under the teacher's control.

discussing inclusively—During discussions, the ability to respond in an encouraging fashion to unexpected comments.

disequilibrium—Piaget's term for when the individual experiences contradiction between perceptions and understanding.

displeasure without insult—The use of self-report or *I* messages to explain, without character attack, strong feelings about a mistaken behavior.

E

early childhood—That period of childhood from birth to age eight.

ecological perspective—A comprehensive viewpoint when working with children that encompasses the family's social, cultural, economic, educational, and behavioral dynamics.

educational accountability—The need for educators to validate the effectiveness of the teaching-learning process in order to show that children have achieved educational goals.

emotional intelligence—The capacity to use one's perceptions and understandings of another to work cooperatively with the other in the attainment of mutual goals.

encounterer relational pattern—The most mature level of social relations; behaviors have less to do with expectations of others and more to do with the individual's effort to make meaning out of life.

encouragement—Group or individually focused acknowledgment by an adult that recognizes progress and efforts and supports children's further efforts.

encouraging classroom—A "community" classroom environment in which each child is empowered to feel a sense of belonging, self-worth and a capacity to learn.

engagement—The total involvement of the child in the learning activity.

equilibrium—Piaget's term for when the individual experiences harmony between perceptions and understanding.

experimentation (Level One) mistaken behavior—Mistaken behavior that occurs as a result of involvement in or curiosity about a situation.

extrinsic rewards—Recognition for achievements given by teachers that is outside the intrinsic value of the activity for the child; tends to build dependency rather than autonomy by discouraging personal assessment of the worth of own's efforts.

F

family groups—A grouping system long used in early childhood that includes children of diverse ages and developmental characteristics in the same group, under the supervision of a primary caregiver.

five-finger formula—A strategy for mediating conflicts that includes five steps: cool-down; identify the problem; determine possible solutions; try one; monitor and facilitate the effort.

friendly humor—A quality much appreciated by children that can both prevent and reduce the negative effects of mistaken behavior.

friendly touch—The use of touch to calm and affirm children and to assure them of positive relations with the teacher.

G

grouping patterns—Various social arrangements of learners in an encouraging classroom, based on criteria such as interest and group dynamics rather than inferred ability level, frequently changing during the day.

guidance—A way of teaching that empowers children to make decisions that are ethical, intelligent, and socially responsive. The teaching of democratic life skills.

guidance approach—The use of guidance, distinct from discipline, to reduce the need for and resolve the occurrence of mistaken behavior in ways that are nonpunitive and teach democratic life skills.

guidance talk—A discussion with a child after an incident that helps the child understand how the other felt, what he or she might do to bring about reconciliation, and what acceptable alternative behaviors might be.

guidelines—Agreements often made with the class that identify prosocial behavior; distinct from rules that tend to be stated negatively and lack specific direction to the life skills desired by the teacher.

H

heteronomy—Piaget's term for being influenced in one's judgment by the authority of others—opposite of *autonomy.*

high-level mediation—Intervention by an adult to assist children to resolve a conflict, that calms children, helps them put the conflict into words, and assists them to reach a mutually acceptable solution.

I

I **message**—A communication technique in which one person reports perceptions and feelings to another in a straightforward but respectful manner.

impulse control—The ability to manage one's feelings so as to prevent conflicts with others from escalating, an ability that most young children are just beginning to develop.

inclusion—The educational practice of including learners of diverse abilities and physical and behavioral characteristics in the classroom.

inclusiveness—The ability of teachers to accommodate the expression of ideas by children when those expressions are not what the teacher expected.

Individual Guidance Plan (IGP)—A strategy that is collaborative, systematic, and comprehensive to assist a child showing serious mistaken behavior; involvement of parents in the IGP process is a priority.

industry—A basic need in the middle childhood period defined by Erikson, with inferiority resulting if the child is unable to meet the need.

initiative—A basic need in the early childhood period defined by Erikson, with self-doubt resulting if the child is unable to meet the need.

institution-caused mistaken behavior—Mistaken behavior that results from a mismatch of the educational program and a child's level of development and individual needs, a developmentally inappropriate educational program.

integrated curriculum—Instruction that is interdisciplinary, interrelating separate content areas through thematic instruction.

intentionality—When mistaken behaviors are done on purpose due to an error in judgment.

intervention—Nonpunitive leadership shown by an adult when mistaken behavior occurs.

I to I—A conflict management model that emphasizes three rules: agreement to solve the problem; taking turns in speaking and listening; and respectful, truthful communication.

inviting choices—A friendly suggestion by a teacher that a child might choose to cooperate in a situation.

inviting, requesting, commanding choices—Communication techniques used by a teacher in which she or he uses different degrees of intensity matched to the situation in order to solicit cooperation.

J

joining with parents—The teacher's establishing with parents that they are partners in working for the betterment of the child.

L

labeling—Stereotyping of a child's character as a result of a pattern of mistaken behavior that the child may show.

language arts focus—The time block set aside for integrated language arts instruction, typically including reading, writing, speaking, and listening.

leadership communication—The cluster of communication skills used by a teacher with the group and the individual that encourage life skills and prosocial behavior.

learned behavior—Behavior, including Level Two mistaken behavior, that a child is influenced by significant others to show.

learning centers—Distinct areas within the classroom that provide a variety of related materials for children's use; other similar terms preferred by some professionals include: *learning areas, interest areas, interest centers.*

Level Three day—The kind of day any child or adult can have, when everything goes wrong; a "bad hair day" taken to the extreme.

liberation teaching—The acceptance, support, and empowerment of children who might be singled out negatively from the group for physical, cultural, or behavioral reasons.

listening to life experiences—Contact time that a teacher has with a child, during which the child feels comfortable enough to openly share experiences, thoughts, and feelings.

logical consequences—Responses taken by adults that "fit" a child's mistaken act.

low-level mediation—The level of conflict resolution in which children can calm themselves, define the problem, and reach a solution with minimum support and clarification by the adult.

M

marginal mistaken behaviors—Milder mistaken behaviors that different teachers react to differently and that the same teacher might react differently to on different occasions.

mediation—A conflict management strategy in which a third person, often a teacher, uses high- to low-level intervention to assist others to resolve a conflict.

misbehavior—The conventional term applied to mistaken acts resulting in consequences that often include punishment and the internalization of a negative label, i.e., "naughty," by the child.

mistaken behavior—Errors in judgment and action made in the process of learning life skills. Mistaken behaviors occur at three levels: experimentation, socially influenced, and strong needs.

multicultural education—Curriculum and methods that teach children to respect and learn from points of uniqueness and commonality in various cultures; the celebration of cultural diversity for the commonality of human values that the respectful treatment of cultural differences engenders.

multidimensional classroom—A classroom in which a variety of activities and grouping arrangements occur and the teacher is a manager of the daily program as well as a lead teacher.

multiple intelligences—The theory attributed to Gardner that individuals possess natural intelligence in many dimensions of human behavior, above and beyond the cognitive/analytical abilities usually associated with standardized tests.

N

negative dissonance—A conflict with another that has gone past the point where it can be resolved by negotiation with another, and mediation is necessary if the conflict is to be resolved.

negotiation—A process to resolve conflict used by two or more parties directly involved in a conflict.

negotiation reminders—Statements that direct children to the negotiation process for resolving conflicts.

nonverbal intervention—The use of body language, facial expressions, gestures, or physical proximity to keep learners on-task with a minimum of attention being drawn to the situation.

O

obedience-based discipline—Systems and techniques of discipline the intent of which is to subjugate children to the authority of the teacher.

overfunctioning—The stressful and ultimately exhausting situation that results when teachers feel they must meet unrealistic goals, standards, and responsibilities in the performance of their roles.

P

parent meetings—A vital method of furthering teacher-parent communication and building teacher-parent partnerships, these meetings often involve parents in planning and implementation and may be held at different times to accommodate parents' schedules.

parent-teacher partnerships—The state of relations when parents and teachers have joined together on behalf of the child, partnerships result in involvement in the child's education to the fullest extent possible for the parent.

peace education—The use of curriculum and teaching practice to empower children to learn and advocate peaceful alternatives to violence in daily life and the solving of social and environmental problems.

peaceable classroom—A classroom environment based on self and mutual respect and the practice of preventing and resolving problems using friendly words.

peace props—Objects such as puppets, the talking stick, talk-and-listen chairs, and the peace table that assist children to manage conflicts.

peace table—A child-sized table with peace symbols on it that is reserved for peace education and planned and unplanned conflict management activities.

peer mediation—A system of conflict management in which trained older children in a school mediate conflicts of their peers, frequently used in out-of-classroom situations.

performance assessment—Assessment of children's efforts in selected tasks to determine performance in relation to identified outcomes; measures may include, but are not limited to, pencil and paper tests.

period chart—A visual used to help children understand routine time blocks in the daily schedule.

physical restraint—The passive bear hug that teachers use with children who have totally lost emotional control and an imminent danger of harm exists; the crisis management technique of last resort in the classroom.

play—Self-selected, self-directed activity that is inherently pleasurable and through which the child "learns what cannot be formally taught."

political accountability—Unrealistic expectations of academic performance held by officials and administrators usually for reasons of appearance and often involving single measures of performance, such as scores on standardized tests.

preprimary—Refers in this text to the kindergarten and prekindergarten levels.

preventive guidance—Teaching practices in the encouraging classroom that prevent institution-caused mistaken behavior and reduce the need for mistaken behavior in general.

private encouragement—Recognition of effort and progress directed by a teacher to an individual in such a way as to avoid singling out the individual in relation to the group.

private speech—The talking that young children do with themselves as they engage in learning activities. Vygotsky theorizes that this speech gives the child skills that enable later conceptual acts of cognitive and social-emotional problem solving.

privilege—One of three common causes of mistaken behavior in early childhood classrooms, along with *property* and *territory.*

proactive group management—Positive group management that reduces the need for mistaken behavior by building the encouraging classroom.

problem of the match—Issues that arise when the expectations of teachers about child behavior and academic performance are not in line with the child's development, experience, and immediate needs.

problem puppets—A peace prop involving hand puppets used to instruct and resolve problems; also called *peace puppets* and *power puppets.*

professional teacher—A teacher who does not depend on established routines and practices but takes a positive problem-solving approach responsive to the needs of children and the dynamics of the situation.

property—The most frequent cause of mistaken behavior in the early childhood classroom; two other common causes are *territory* and *privilege.*

protective buffer—Strategies used in liberation teaching to prevent children from being stigmatized by their vulnerabilities and to encourage toward resilience.

public encouragement—Recognition of effort and progress directed by a teacher to the group without the singling out of individual group members.

R

reconciliation—The process of positive resolution of an incident of mistaken behavior that might involve an apology, making amends, and/or reuniting with the group.

reflective listening—A communication technique in which an adult repeats back or supportively acknowledges a remark, action, or implied emotion of a child.

relational patterns—Levels of social relations shown by children; three relational patterns are survival, adjustment, and encountering.

requesting choices—An intervention level of medium intensity in which the teacher communicates a clear expectation that the child will choose from among two or three acceptable options for behavior.

resiliency—The capacity to overcome a vulnerability for stigma by meeting a need for safety, and so being able to engage in learning and personal growth.

routines—Reliable practices happening regularly throughout the day that provide the child with a sense of predictability and order; must be carefully implemented, and occasionally deviated from, in order to sustain the child's full engagement in the program.

S

safeguards—Techniques for managing strong emotions to prevent harm to others, such as monitoring one's feelings, describing conflicts objectively, and expressing feelings nonpunitively (the use of self-report).

scaffolding—The teaching-learning process by which another person aids a learner to move from a comfortable level of performance to a higher level only possible with that assistance.

scheduled class meetings—Meetings that are a part of the daily routine for discussing business, activities, and situations in a mutually respectful manner.

school anxiety—Stress felt by children as a result of routines, activities, or incidents at a school or center that are threatening or harmful.

school readiness—The diverse skills, experiences, and qualities that make initial functioning in the classroom a successful experience for young children.

self-concept—The total collection of thoughts and feelings that an individual has at any point in time about who he or she is.

self-esteem—The feelings one has about one's self at any point in time.

self-fulfilling prophecy—The phenomena that persons who become labeled by others for particular behaviors come to see themselves as they are labeled and show an increase in the behaviors that others have come to expect.

self psychologist—Psychologist who focuses on the developing self as the primary dynamic of human behavior.

self psychology—A branch of psychology that focuses on the developing self as the primary dynamic in human behavior, with mental health being a function of continuing development and mental ill-health the result of obstacles to that development.

self-removal—The arrangement between a child and teacher whereby the child voluntarily leaves a situation in order to prevent a conflict from becoming mistaken behavior.

self-report—The use of *I* messages to express strong feelings to others in a nonpunitive way: "I feel upset when. . . ."

sentence frame—A negotiation reminder in the form of a stock response that individuals use to de-escalate and resolve conflicts.

separation—Helping a child to leave a situation in order to calm down so that a conflict can be resolved.

separation anxiety—The stress that children feel upon leaving the familiar world of the family and entering the unfamiliar world of the classroom.

sharing times—Times set aside during scheduled class meetings when members can express thoughts and feelings about a topic—often a "nonmaterialistic" alternative to show and tell.

socially influenced (Level Two) mistaken behavior—Mistaken behavior that is learned behavior, a result of the intentional or unintentional influence of a significant other.

social knowledge—Mental recognition of arbitrary sets of symbols (the names of "numerals") and behaviors (saying "please" and "thank you") common to a society.

social problem solving—The ability to manage and resolve problems and conflicts in peaceable ways.

socioemotional development—The domain of human development that addresses the social and emotional dimensions together.

starter statements—Statements of encouragement that acknowledge details and effort in children's work, such as "You are really working hard on that story."

stickers and smiley faces—Rewards extrinsic to the effort of the child that tend to build dependence on the teacher rather than autonomy; if used at all, should be to celebrate the efforts of all rather than evaluate individual performance.

stigma—The psychological and social process whereby an individual is negatively separated from the group for cultural, physical, or behavioral reasons.

strong needs (Level Three) mistaken behavior—Mistaken behavior shows itself in extreme, inappropriate behaviors over time and is the acting out of strong unmet physical and/or psychological needs.

superhero syndrome—The identification of a child with a "heroic figure," either real or media-created, the result of which is overly aggressive play.

survival relational pattern—The level of social relations children show when they experience the environment as a dangerous and painful place; behavior patterns are frequently inappropriate and extremely rigid.

T

table talk—The naturally occurring conversing that occurs when individuals are seated around a table working on an activity.

tabula rosa—The view that the mind and soul of the young child is a "blank slate, still to be written upon" by character shaping experiences.

talk-and-listen chairs—A peace prop consisting of two chairs that children use to resolve conflicts; the children take turns in each chair until the problem is resolved.

talking stick—A decorated stick passed from child to child, used to determine speaking order and facilitate the give-and-take necessary to resolve problems.

teacher as professional—When teachers respond to conflict situations by using judgment based on gaining more information and mediating so that all concerned learn democratic life skills, they are functioning as professionals in the classroom.

teaching team—Adults of differing educational levels and experience backgrounds that work together as a team in the classroom.

team-teaching—Two adults of similar educational backgrounds who share duties and tasks.

territory—One of three common causes of disputes in early childhood classrooms, along with *property* and *privilege.*

thematic instruction—Teaching that uses themes as the organizational unit of instruction, rather than the academic subjects taught separately.

three levels of mistaken behavior—Mistaken behavior can be the result of experimentation (Level One), social influence (Level Two), or strong needs (Level Three).

time confusion—The inability to understand time concepts in early childhood due to developmental factors.

time-out—When teachers remove a child from a conflict situation, the common term is to give the child a "time-out." When the purpose is the consequence of an act by the child, with the expectation that the child should "think about" the behavior, the time-out is punishment. When the purpose is to help a child calm down so the conflict can be resolved, the time-out is guidance.

tossed salad approach—An approach to multicultural education in which adults of diverse backgrounds, usually parents, interact informally in the classroom community.

tourist curriculum—The mistaken notion that by studying token facts about a culture, that may or may not be accurate, important instruction about that culture is occurring; for example, "Eskimos live in igloos."

transitions—Events that occur in the process of moving children from one activity to another in the daily program, which the teacher may or may not have planned.

U

unconditional positive regard—Full acceptance of the child as a developing human being and member of the classroom group despite mistaken behaviors that the child may show.

unscheduled class meetings—Meetings of each class called by the teacher (sometimes at the request of a class member) to discuss and find a resolution to problems and conflicts; guidelines for such meetings are that one person speaks at a time, and communication is to be truthful and mutually respectful.

W

webbing—A visual brainstorming activity often done with the group in which content, learning activities, and sometimes teaching methods are generated for thematic instruction.

with-it-ness—The idea that the effective teacher is aware of the important dynamics of behavior in the classroom; that teachers have "eyes in the backs of their heads."

Z

zone of proximal development—The psychological distance at any point of cognitive and social development between what a child can learn on her own and with the assistance of responsive others.

INDEX